J.C.,

Merry Christmas

Love,
Dad & Mom

THE ULTIMATE
SMALL BUSINESS
GUIDE

THE ULTIMATE SMALL BUSINESS GUIDE

A Resource for Startups and Growing Businesses

BASIC

BOOKS

A MEMBER OF THE PERSEUS BOOKS GROUP
NEW YORK

© Bloomsbury Publishing Plc 2004

Cataloging-in-Publication Data is available from the Library of Congress

ISBN-10 0-7382-0913-9
ISBN-13 978-0-7382-0913-5

Basic Books is a member of the Perseus Books Group
Find us on the World Wide Web at www.basicbooks.com

Basic Books publications are available at special discounts for bulk purchases in the
U.S. by corporations, institutions, and other organizations. For more information,
please contact the Special Markets Department at the Perseus Books Group,
11 Cambridge Center, Cambridge, MA 02142, or call (800) 255-1514 or
(617) 252-5298, or e-mail special.markets@perseusbooks.com.

Text design by Fiona Pike, Pike Design, Winchester, U.K.
Typeset by RefineCatch Limited, Bungay, Suffolk, U.K.
Printed in the United States of America

First printing, November 2003

10 9 8 7 6

CONTENTS

Figuring It Out

Marketing Your Idea

DIRECTORY

A Note to the User

The Ultimate Small Business Guide is aimed at anyone thinking of starting or growing a business. Designed for readers to dip into as and when they need practical help on a range of issues, the *Guide* contains advice on:

- planning
- setting up or acquiring a business
- getting to grips with the figures
- finding premises
- marketing your idea
- working with customers
- communicating with customers
- growing your business
- working and selling online
- managing yourself and others
- dignified retreats

All of the above topics are covered in over 130 easy-to-read actionlists, which appear in the following format:

GETTING STARTED—an overview of the main points addressed in the actionlist
FAQS—a series of frequently asked questions on the topic
MAKING IT HAPPEN—fuss-free advice on how to achieve your goal
WHAT TO AVOID—tips on how to avoid common mistakes
RECOMMENDED LINKS—a selection of the very best websites to help you investigate the topic further

This book also contains a **Directory** (pp. 421–497). This section covers over 30 key topics of interest to anyone in business and offers carefully chosen information on the most helpful books, organizations, and a wider selection of Internet sites.

The **Directory** is also available free online to all subscribers to www.ultimatebusiness resource.com. All links are live, so you can click straight through to the site you're interested in. To subscribe, please go to:

www.ultimatebusinessresource.com/register, type in your e-mail address and key in your password: **mybiz**

ACTIONLISTS: PLANNING

Deciding Whether to Start a Business

GETTING STARTED

Starting up your own business can be very rewarding, but there are pressures involved. It's not enough just to have a good, viable idea: you also need to have the right skills and temperament to make the opportunity succeed. Starting your own business is also a risky thing to do, so you need to be aware of what problems to look out for as early as possible. This will help you decide if you are willing and able to take those risks, and will also help you to apply strategies that will reduce them.

Before you go any further, it's important to find out as much as you can about what sort of person you are. Be honest and objective, and discuss the project with friends, colleagues, and relatives. Think about how you have dealt with past challenges, as an indication of your response to difficult new situations. This actionlist will help you to decide whether starting a business is the right thing for you to do.

FAQS

Do I have the right personality to start a business?

While the technical aspects of your business will require specific qualifications, skills, or experience, there are broader demands that are as important. These could include the ability to negotiate with suppliers, mediate between staff, be sociable with customers, be convincing with prospects, think clearly under pressure, take criticism, portray confidence, and use your time effectively.

There is no single type of self-employed person, but experience has shown that there are some characteristics which successful self-employed people often have in common. They tend to be logical, perceptive, organized, and responsible. They are usually extroverted and confident, and able to communicate and get their point across. They are also often sociable, with the ability to lead. Self-employed people are generally single-minded, but able to take advice. They are flexible and adaptable, quick to take opportunities, and ready to take risks. They tend to be tough-skinned, and able to handle failure. They are usually creative and imaginative, always coming up with new ideas for the business, and also hard working, committed, and determined. Finally, they are often individualists, who are not afraid to stand out from the crowd.

Are older people more successful at running a business?

There is no doubt that it helps to have some experience in the workplace, and particularly in the sector in which you want to start a business. Surveys reveal that many successful businesses have been started by people in their 30s who have some management experience. People over the age of 50 (sometimes called "third-age entrepreneurs") are also responsible for many business start-ups, and many think about a change of direction after taking early retirement. Having said that, a wide range of people have established their own businesses successfully and have much to offer. For example, young people have fewer domestic commitments, plenty of energy, new ideas, and the potential to develop and adapt to the challenges of self-employment.

What kinds of skills will I need?

You will almost certainly need technical skills. If you have qualifications relevant to your business activity this will obviously be helpful. Customers, and anyone lending your business money, will be more comfortable if you have the right qualifications. Additionally, certain businesses require exceptional ability, for example design skills, artistic skills, or technical skills.

Business skills are also essential. It is important to understand the principles of business and management, including marketing, strategic planning, accounts, personnel management, and so on. Ideally, you should aim to get some basic training in business administration before you start. If this is not possible (and many people do not have the time or money initially), then read as much as you can to fill the gaps in your knowledge. Leadership skills are important, too. If you expect the business to grow, you will inevitably have to employ people, and the ability to show leadership and to manage people will be critical.

All businesses require an element of selling, and you will need to develop skills in this area if you do not already possess them. Initially it is important to persuade people to support you, and crucial to be able to win over potential customers. It is possible to learn basic selling techniques, but being outgoing and articulate are equally important. Your organizational skills will also be essential to the success of your business. To generate sufficient income, small businesses must be well organized and efficient. It is important that you can organize yourself and others, plan ahead, and manage your time. You also need to have the discipline to set and meet deadlines. Try to think laterally about how many of these skills you have, and don't be put off too easily. Starting a business is challenging, yes, but think about the skills you use in everyday life and how you could apply them to a different context. For example, if you are a woman with a family, or one who has juggled full- or part-time work with family life, think about how you have developed your time management skills, probably without even noticing it.

MAKING IT HAPPEN
Assess Your Abilities and Resources
Starting your own business is a risky thing to do, so you should get to grips with the various risks as early as possible. This will help you decide if you are willing and able to take those risks. It will also help you to apply strategies that will reduce the risk.

You need to ask yourself several questions. Do you have the financial resources, and can you afford to risk these? For example, you might take a secured loan based on the value of your home; what are your plans if the business fails and you are forced to sell your house? Do you have sufficient experience and technical skills to perform the core functions of your new business? Are you familiar enough with the market to be able to assess its needs and adapt to its changes? Do you have the tenacity and discipline to see through hard times when cash will be short and demands will be heavy (from customers, bankers, staff, and, crucially, your family)?

While you might not be able to answer all these questions completely, it really is important to find out as much as you can about what sort of person you are, and to do that you must be honest and objective. Discuss the project with friends, colleagues, and relations. Think about how you have dealt with past challenges, as an indication of your response to difficult new situations.

Look at Your Motives
Why *do* you want to start your own business? There are many good reasons, but there is often the danger of having unrealistic expectations. Here are some reasons that people often give, and some notes of caution:

- **independence.** Yes, it can be irksome working for someone else, but you still need to be disciplined and able to get on with others when you work for yourself.
- **greater job satisfaction.** Self-employment allows you to do the job in your own way, and it is very satisfying when your way is shown to work. You do, of course, also have to take responsibility your way when it *doesn't* work.
- **achievement and success.** There can be some cachet attached to the idea of running your own business, but make sure that you are not trying to prove that you're something you're not. If the venture failed, would you be able to deal with it?
- **more money.** While the thought of being better off financially is naturally attractive, doing it for the money is not usually a good enough motive in itself, and greater wealth

is by no means guaranteed. In particular, beware of starting a business when you have no other choice. In this case, remember the importance of maintaining a positive but pragmatic vision of what you can achieve.

Be Prepared for the Pressures

The pressures of being self-employed are inescapable. You may have to work long hours, and there will be times when things get on top of you. You may well get into debt in order to finance the enterprise. You will need to maintain your faith in your business, often in the face of other people's doubts.

There will be times when you feel lonely and isolated. If you employ people, you will need to be positive and show leadership all the time. There will be times when you need to be tough and prepared to discipline difficult employees, or make difficult demands of your suppliers. You need to be polite and helpful, even when a customer is giving you a hard time.

Many of those who successfully start their own business have the backing of their family. You will be under pressure, working long hours. Your family must be prepared for the impact this can have on family life. Also, you must be sure that your family can accommodate the risks that self-employment can bring, especially in terms of lower income in the initial stages, and maybe even the implications of the business failing. Take time to talk to all members of your family who might be affected by your choice to be your own boss.

WHAT TO AVOID

Assuming That Being your Own Boss is Easy

Everyone at some point has come across a boss who makes his or her life difficult, but don't assume that working for yourself will be all plain sailing. There are many benefits, to be sure, but you have to get used to the idea that the buck stops with you. Make sure you're ready take on that responsibility.

Doing it for the Wrong Reasons

As noted above, don't do it for the money alone. Weigh up the pros and cons of your idea and the impact that starting a business will have on all areas of your life. It will take a lot of effort, but you *can* do it—read on to find out how.

SEE ALSO

Assessing Your Entrepreneurial Profile: Do You Have What It Takes? (p. 5)
Coming Up with a Business Idea (p. 12)
Entrepreneurs (p. 450)
Small and Growing Businesses (p. 422)
Understanding Business Models (p. 44)

Assessing Your Entrepreneurial Profile: Do You Have What It Takes?

GETTING STARTED

Once you've started thinking about starting a business, you need to start thinking about your own role in it. Are you the right type of person to make a success of a new venture? There's a great deal of romance surrounding the notion of being an entrepreneur, but not everyone has the aptitude. And it's important to understand that there's nothing wrong with *not* being an entrepreneur. The world wouldn't function half as well if it were peopled solely with them.

Nevertheless, there are some general personality traits that are key for being an entrepreneur. If the following list seems to fit your personality, you may have what it takes:

- I am persistent, with a great deal of drive and stamina. I see problems as opportunities. I have a good intuitive sense and thrive on new ideas.
- I tend to rebel against authority. I want to be my own boss.
- I am positive, communicate well, and enjoy working with people.
- I have a strong need to succeed, financially and otherwise.
- I'm not afraid to make mistakes, and I learn from them.

FAQS

How can I be sure I've got what it takes?

Before quitting your job and using your savings to start a business, you owe it to yourself to approach your entrepreneurial venture with some practicality. Take a more in-depth personality test and talk to small business advisers—often available at no cost through business associations, community colleges, and organizations such as SCORE (Service Corps of Retired Executives).

How much money will I need?

Whether you want to buy an existing business, purchase a franchise, start your own company, or merely offer services to others from a home office, starting a business depends on first knowing the numbers. People in the same or similar business are a good source of information—use your ingenuity to find out what it cost them to get started and where they got the funds to do so. Other sources include trade associations, franchise organizations, business articles in magazines and newspapers, Internet research, or business consultants.

Besides being an ideas person, what else do I need to be good at?

Success in a new enterprise depends on dedication and the consistent application of good business principles. Some of these principles include: being good with money; being good with people (investors, suppliers, employees, and so on); being a good promoter (marketing, sales, PR); and being good to yourself. Many entrepreneurs burn out before their businesses take hold. In this game, pacing yourself and your business is important.

MAKING IT HAPPEN

Check That You Have the Right Idea

If you've got a great new idea and no competition in sight, you must be sure that the product or service will be of value to customers—at a price at which you can afford to sell it. If your aim is to enter a field with established competitors, you have to know your own strengths and weaknesses, as well as those of your competition. You have to be certain that you can provide a better product or service for a competitive price. Finding out all these things is called "market research," and you'll have to do a thorough job of it to succeed.

Develop a Detailed, Professional Business Plan

This is the key to building a successful

business. Having a well-considered and systematic plan allows you to recognize problems as they arise in time to be able to take corrective action. The plan should be a living document, flexible over time to adapt to changes in the marketplace and your industry. It should include sections on every facet of your business—whether you're a sole proprietor or the executive director of a new manufacturing venture.

Bankroll Your Idea

Take your ideas and business plan to a variety of people, starting with friends and close supporters. Be prepared for critical feedback, and be flexible. Take the inevitable first few comments of "no thanks" as opportunities to fine tune the next presentation. One of the hallmarks of an entrepreneur is the ability to regroup, rethink, and reach a goal in another way.

Seeking publicity for your business is a way not only to notify potential customers but also to get the attention of possible investors. The more people who know about your idea, the better the chances that you'll attract the right investor.

Be willing to share a portion of the company with the right partners, but be wary of finance companies and investors who want full control or the lion's share of the proceeds.

Consider entering a joint venture with another company or position your company to attract start-up funds from federal or state sources.

Practice Your Networking

Being entrepreneurial doesn't mean being a lone ranger. Being successful often depends on your ability to network with potential customers, suppliers, and new investors, and even with those in government who control certain aspects of the business environment.

Plan Your Marketing and PR

An integral part of your business plan involves a marketing plan—how you intend to create the demand for your product or service. While market research tells you the "what" and "where" of your opportunities, the marketing plan outlines the steps by which you will find potential customers and convince them to buy from you. Networking, advertising, and PR (public relations) are all forms of marketing and promotion.

Make Sure You Have the Right Financial and Management Support

Most entrepreneurs are better at ideas than at managing budgets, business operations, and employees. Anticipate that you'll need more capital than you figured at the start, and don't spend beyond the company's means. If you find yourself in a questionable position, make sure you have a network of trusted and experienced advisers to help you see the proper perspective and cover the things you are not naturally good at.

WHAT TO AVOID
Setting up Equal Partnerships

Entrepreneurs often share the start-up responsibilities with a partner or partners. However, sharing 50–50 or by thirds or quarters is a big mistake, because conflicts will inevitably arise and need someone in a controlling position to make a final decision. Choose (or hire) a C.E.O.—someone with the experience and skills needed for success—and give that person a greater decision-making authority and a bigger salary, even if it is only bigger by a small margin.

Having Inadequate People and Planning

Entrepreneurs must become strong managers when the company gets going. Many businesses fail because the people in charge don't have the managerial qualities or strength to cope with the challenges. In addition, stress can put a strain on personal relationships and this can make the challenges harder to deal with. Personality assessments can determine if you're cut out for a managerial position, and managerial training can prepare you for your new role as an executive.

Without proper market research and a solid business plan, a business is more likely to fail. The more advanced preparation that is done, the better the chances for success.

Relying Too Heavily on One or Two Customers

Having too few customers makes your business vulnerable, because it ties your future to the decisions of other organizations. If their business falters, it puts your hard work and dedication at risk—through no fault of your own. The advice of personal financial consultants is appropriate here. Having lots of customers, even though none of them is gigantic, is healthier in the long run.

Causing Cash Flow Troubles through Insufficient Financing

While some people are successful at jump-starting their own enterprise with little or no outside investment, they do so by being fortunate, being modest in their spending, and by plowing profits back into the business.

The majority of businesses, however, don't deliver the projected first-year sales volume. It's better to overestimate your need for capital resources at the beginning and to underestimate your projected sales figures. It's better to be pleasantly surprised at your success than to lose the business and your house because the money isn't there when it's needed.

When contemplating an expansion of your business, be wary of spiraling costs. If you're in a cyclical business or one vulnerable to recession, be sure to be very calculating about your expenses—and develop "Plan B" well before you need to implement it.

Failing to Admit Mistakes

Entrepreneurs are sometimes the last to admit that their idea hasn't the sparkle it once had. Having advisers that you trust is important. Cut your losses and move on if your advisers all agree that you should. Doing so may save the company—if you can move quickly enough to capitalize on your mistakes—or shift the product or service to take advantage of other opportunities.

Underestimating the Competition

Your competition won't stand still for long, once you've demonstrated their weakness in the marketplace with your product or service. Expect them to plug the hole quickly and even try to outflank you in the process. Your business and marketing plans should anticipate how to deal with new initiatives from your competition. If you conduct ongoing research, product and service evaluations, and marketing campaigns, you should always be one step ahead of the competition.

SEE ALSO

Coming Up with a Business Idea (p. 12)
Deciding Whether to Start a Business (p. 2)
Entrepreneurs (p. 450)
Small and Growing Businesses (p. 422)

Making the Decision to Take a Risky Career Move

GETTING STARTED

Everything in business today is risky. There is no such thing as a safe bet. It is certainly risky to leave a familiar job with routines, expectations, and objectives that you're comfortable with to test the limits of your courage and skills in a strange environment, but, as thousands of laid-off employees in global companies can attest, it's not exactly safe holding onto a job that is as dependable as a leaky lifeboat.

Whether you should decide to make that risky career move is entirely up to the nature of the risk and your ability to absorb the possible negative consequences. The risk itself may be made up of any number of factors, such as your ability to move into an unfamiliar job or your ability to move into an unfamiliar organization. Are you jumping from an Old Economy position to a New Economy one? Or are you leaping back into the Old Economy world after trying your luck in a high-tech, high-pressure, go-go New Economy environment? Are you considering leaving a stable, secure position that's limited in its prospects in favor of the white-knuckle environment of a bootstrap start-up? Are you about to move from a solid public organization into a family-owned business? Is the family that owns the business your own?

For some people, the notion of going into a shaky entrepreneurial environment after drawing a steady paycheck for years would be intolerable. For others, depending on only one income source, as opposed to the multiple sources of revenue available to an entrepreneur, may make them feel vulnerable.

The decision you make is entirely yours. The risk you take is entirely yours.

The following points are key questions to ask yourself while considering whether you should take the risk or not:

- Does the benefit outweigh the potential cost of the risk?
- How many people depend utterly on the regular income your current job provides?
- Is there a backup plan in case your gamble fails?
- Is it possible to return to your original position should you decide that your experiment was not as rewarding as you hoped?

FAQS

How can I be sure that I don't regret my ultimate decision?

Give yourself all the time you need to make your choice wisely and calmly. Think it through methodically, and then make the decision. Whatever the outcome, be sure to learn from it in some way.

I'm not comfortable in risky situations. Is there any way I can avoid this problem?

Not if you intend to grow in your career. Indeed, there are no guarantees in today's marketplace, so taking steps to avoid taking a risk might actually be the worst thing you could do.

MAKING IT HAPPEN

Identify What "Acceptable Risk" Means to You

If you are young and single (with no obligations other than to yourself), you can probably afford to take on a few risky career moves. These high profile actions can give you early boosts that could position you for more momentum-driven rewards later in your career.

If you are older, perhaps with a family, you may not be quite as willing to try your luck with a high-risk/high-reward venture, such as a start-up enterprise.

Your capacity to accept risk is entirely a personal one.

Know Your Goals

Make a list of your short- and long-term objectives. Is your current position more or less likely to help you achieve them? If your position is less likely to help you achieve these goals, can you make slight adjustments to your present job in order to position yourself better for achieving your dreams? Or is it necessary to depart from your position entirely, regardless of what you are heading for?

Know What You Value

List your less tangible values. Which opportunity is most likely to help you manifest those values? Your current job or your new possibility? Does one opportunity actually position you to behave in ways that are contrary to those values?

Conduct a Risk/Benefit Analysis

This is the process that will help you determine whether the potential reward outweighs the potential pain. There are several methods for analyzing your potential costs, but the easiest is simply to create two columns. List the potential pain in one column and the potential reward in the other. The column that has the longer list is the one that should receive serious consideration. A variation of this method is to assign points or anticipated dollar values to each item. You can then either compare the grand totals or assess each pain/reward item on its own merit.

Consider the People You Would Be Working With

Who do you have the most in common with? This is not a question of who you would be most comfortable spending an afternoon watching television or playing tennis with. Rather, whose visions and ideals are most compatible with your own?

WHAT TO AVOID
Making the Wrong Choice

As there are no guarantees, there is always a chance that you will make the wrong choice—or at least the choice that feels wrong to you as you begin to experience "buyer's remorse." Have faith in your risk assessment strategy, and carefully watch how that risk plays itself out. There is always something positive to be gained from every adventure.

Making no Choice at All

Making no choice is still making a choice. And this is the one that is almost guaranteed to net you no gain at all.

Modern business is full of risky moves. Those who relish the thrill of the risk, shift, and change will be the ones who will ultimately benefit from the growth and added self-awareness that comes from the adventure of being engaged in contemporary commerce.

Identifying the Purpose of a Business

GETTING STARTED

Whether you're starting up or in business already, it's crucial to be clear about what your business does or will do, so that you can stay focused on the appropriate target market. Prospective lenders or investors in your business will look closely at this purpose when they assess whether you have the strategic direction for future success. You also need to be clear about why you are going into this business in the first place, and what you want out of it. Investors need to understand your motivation and your intentions, so that they can judge whether these match the plans that you set out for the development of the business. This actionlist aims to help you define both your own inspiration and the purpose of your business in order to bring clarity to your direction.

FAQS

Why am I in business and what do I want out of it?

Ask yourself this crucial question first of all, and then consider the other questions that arise in consequence. Will the business supplement your main income or replace it? Are you starting it as an investment, to sell as soon as you can? Is it to provide jobs for family members?

The answers to questions like these will have an impact on the business's aims, development, and strategies. For example, if you are starting a business as an investment opportunity, the focus of your planning will be leading up to your exit—the sale of the business. Your strategies must focus on building the business quickly and maximizing its value to get the best selling price possible. On the other hand, if you are building up a business for a less experienced family member, your plan will focus on a succession strategy. This might mean keeping the business small and easily manageable.

What exactly should my business do?

Be as specific as possible about the kind of business that you are starting. If you are going to open a restaurant, for example, will it be a family restaurant serving good quality, local food at competitive prices in a family-friendly environment? Or will it be more up-market, serving gourmet dishes to discerning customers?

Describe your business in terms of a mission statement that clearly summarizes its purpose and is easily understood by you, your staff, your customers, and your potential investors. If you cannot describe your business in these terms, rethink your business idea; focus on your business's core activities and direction.

What is a business's vision?

A vision reflects what you care about most and represents what your business is trying to achieve. Defining purpose expresses what the business does, while the vision drives the business forward to its long-term aims. Vision is about having challenging but achievable goals within defined time scales. It is simply a statement of your desired competitive position within your best guess of the future environment. Realistic visions can be achieved and will improve staff morale, and once a vision is reached you can further expand your business aims.

A vision is created from the fundamental values of the employees and the purpose and awareness of the current environment of the business.

MAKING IT HAPPEN

Identify Your Customer

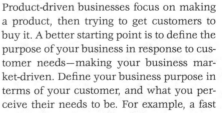

Product-driven businesses focus on making a product, then trying to get customers to buy it. A better starting point is to define the purpose of your business in response to customer needs—making your business market-driven. Define your business purpose in terms of your customer, and what you perceive their needs to be. For example, a fast food restaurant selling healthy food might see its purpose as: "Providing health-conscious eaters with quick, convenient, and tasty take-out meals and snacks all day."

Make Your Purpose Different

To succeed against competitors, your business needs to offer something different. Build this differentiation into your purpose, so that everything you do can be judged in terms of whether it supports the purpose or not. Potential investors want to see your business's unique selling proposition (USP), as this is the basis on which you will compete and on which customers will be attracted.

Write a Mission Statement

At its simplest, your business's mission is a statement of purpose that guides your activities. It is a summary of "what you do." The mission provides the guiding direction for developing strategy, searching out opportunities, and making resource allocation choices. It is built on your core values, so should be easily understood by staff, customers, and financial backers. You can often establish your mission in terms of the question: "What business are we in?"

Decide What You Want Your Business to Be After Two Years

Start by considering what the working environment is going to be like in, say, two years' time. Ask yourself what opportunities and threats there might be, and summarize your vision into a single statement. For example: "Octo aims to be respected as a leading design group working throughout the United States." This business has chosen not to disclose publicly the timescale to

which it is working, but it makes it clear it has a vision.

Try to envisage this so that you can start to move your business towards that point. For instance, you might work towards becoming a market leader, an innovator, specialist, a good employer, a large concern, or a supplier of superior quality.

WHAT TO AVOID

Working Without a Clearly Defined Purpose

If you don't know exactly what the purpose of your business is, it is going to be very difficult to plan for the future, formulate objectives and goals, and design a strategy to achieve them. One of the good reasons for writing a business plan is that it will force you to clarify your purpose; without that clarity, it is difficult to define your markets and your marketing plans.

Taking On Work Outside Your Core Business

It is always a temptation for service-based businesses to take on jobs that are not in their usual line of work. These can often end up taking longer and costing more than anticipated, with poor results for the customer and little likelihood of any repeat business for you. A well-worded business purpose, however, can help keep your mind focused on what your business aims to do and what it is best at doing. One useful book that may help you keep your mind on the job is *The On-Purpose Business: Doing More of What You Do Best More Profitably* by Kevin McCarthy, published in 2002 by Navpress Publishing Group.

SEE ALSO

Entrepreneurs (p. 450)

Coming Up with a Business Idea

GETTING STARTED

You've decided that you want to go into business, but you don't know what that business is going to be. You're looking for a great idea. The best advice is to begin by breaking down the bigger picture into more manageable pieces. First, look at your own skills and knowledge. Consider your present occupation, and whether you could you do your present job working for yourself rather than being employed by someone else. Successful businesses are frequently started by people with practical experience in the type of work that the new venture is entering. They go into business because they decide that they want more independence in their working lives.

It may be that you feel that the skills you have are already oversupplied. If this is the case, it's possible that there is no room in the marketplace for yet another joiner, furniture restorer, or undertaker. Or it may be that you simply do not want to carry on doing the same thing for yourself that you've done for others in the past. You perhaps then need to think of ways in which you could modify the skills and experience that you've acquired while working for somebody else.

Take a careful look at yourself; it could be that your personality or physique suggests a business idea. If you've persistence, charm, and good communication skills, for example, you might be a good salesperson. There are frequent openings for self-employed sales agents to sell other people's products. If you're good at dealing with people, you might be just the person to take up a retail franchise.

FAQS

How do I identify new ideas?

Try brainstorming with friends or relations to see if you can identify any totally new ideas. There are opportunities for entirely new products or services, such as energy conservation, providing better insulation in homes and factories. You may have an idea for a simple device which you think people might use. It might be worth commissioning a search at your local patent office to see if anyone has thought of the idea already.

Can I look at an existing idea in a new way?

Contrary to popular belief, there are few original ideas. Most successful businesses come from modifying, refining, or rethinking an existing business idea. Post-it notes resulted from a glue product that went wrong. Perhaps more important is the fact that it might not have happened if the company had not deliberately set aside time when staff could think about innovative product ideas. Try thinking laterally about existing products or materials you know about.

What goods or services could I provide locally?

Think of the problems and difficulties you've experienced in getting things for your home, garden, or at work, or in your leisure activities. Analyze what the problems were which caused you most inconvenience or cost you the most to put right. Think about times when you've urgently required a service, and then found that it was not available. Alternatively, you might be able to think of parts or products that were hard or impossible to obtain locally. Think about the things that you and your neighbors and friends most frequently complain about. Listen to people talking at the gym or in the supermarket checkout line. Then ask yourself whether there is any way of providing a local service or product for any of these markets, and whether people would actually pay for it.

What goods or services could I provide to local companies?

Do some research among local companies. Find out whether there are any goods or services that they have difficulty in obtaining. A new industrial park, for example, may contain a number of small and medium-sized firms, none of which have their own staff canteen, but all of which need some kind of catering service. Perhaps a sandwich bar could be set up on the grounds. There may be room in the market for a messenger or delivery service linking the industrial park with other industrial centers.

How do I find out about opportunities for tourism or leisure businesses in my area?

The type of tourism business you consider will depend on whether the area is urban or rural, whether it's a popular tourist region, and the demographics of the local population. A business, for example a golf shop, may thrive in an area with a high population of retirees and a high influx of tourists. You may want to consider opening an outdoor activity center in a rural area. Try talking to people working in the local sports center or tourist office. They may have suggestions for market opportunities in the area.

How could I find out about selling goods made by other people?

Many new firms start off by selling goods that somebody else makes. A number of opportunities exist to distribute foreign goods. For example, the United States Department of Commerce publishes a regular magazine listing businesses looking for facilities and distributors (this is available from all U.S. embassies and consulates). Chambers of Commerce have regular listings of businesses seeking partners willing to manufacture under license, or to act as sole distributors.

MAKING IT HAPPEN
Turn Your Hobby into a Business

You may have skills that you acquired as a hobby, but which could form the basis for a business. For example, if you like gardening, you might consider starting a garden design business. If you're good at cooking, you could think about starting a catering service for people entertaining at home.

Work from Home

If you're a parent, and consequently at home a lot of the time, you could think about working from home (if space allows). It might be possible for you to set aside space to sew, knit, or perhaps make soft toys. Another option is to sell products for other people over the phone. There are also an increasing number of opportunities for people to do office work using a computer and modem. This can include anything from word processing letters and keeping accounts up to date, right through to freelance writing and consulting.

Buy an Existing Business

Another option is to consider buying an existing business. However, if you do, make sure you find out why the owner is selling. Even if the seller is retiring, make sure you find out why it wasn't worth his or her while to continue with the business. Make sure you look at the business's accounts, and that you understand them. Businesses for sale are usually advertised in the local paper, and could also be advertised in relevant trade magazines.

WHAT TO AVOID
Not Giving it Enough Time

Don't expect an idea to come to you in a flash; sometimes ideas take time to develop. Also remember that the time you spend on planning will be time well spent when you finally do come up with a great idea.

Not Doing Enough Research

If you fail to do any market research, you'll have far less chance of success. Research will save you time and money in the long run.

RECOMMENDED LINKS

U.S. Chamber of Commerce:
www.uschamber.com

U.S. Small Business Administration:
www.sba.gov

SEE ALSO

Networking and Marketing Yourself

GETTING STARTED

Everyone can always benefit from networking and marketing themselves, but those setting up or running a small business can certainly benefit from getting themselves and their company known. Business is driven by relationships, and networking and marketing yourself require you to build strong and meaningful relationships—many that will be long term. The following are questions to consider as you prepare to network and to market yourself:

- Why are you networking? What is your personal or professional goal?
- What are your strengths that will help you to market yourself?
- What organizations or events will be valuable places for networking?
- How much time do you want to spend on networking, and when will you do it?
- How will you know when you've been successful?

FAQS

Why should I bother to network and to market myself?

Research has shown that people who have a vast network of contacts, who are involved in professional and community activities outside their business, and who look for opportunities to be visible are more successful in their careers.

Isn't networking the same as politicking, and won't it look bad?

Politicking is done for personal gain. Networking is done for the good of your business, rather than for personal gain. If you are a successful networker, people are drawn to you because they know you are well connected and that you have good resources.

When is the best time to network?

Networking should become a way of life, a way of being. You should be networking all the time. As you build professional relationships, be constantly thinking: "What can I offer this person?" "How can I be of help?" The more you try to be of service to others, the more people will want to do things for you, and in the initial stages of a new business this will be a huge help.

MAKING IT HAPPEN

Clarify the Purpose of Your Networking and Why You Are Marketing Yourself

There are many reasons for networking and for marketing oneself. When you are starting up or trying to grow a small business, these reasons may include gaining support for a major project, finding funding, or setting up a partnership with other local businesses. Although it is important to continually build relationships, it is much more effective to know why you are building these relationships and what you hope to accomplish. Everyone has limited time, and this will help you to decide how to prioritize your networking activities.

Make a List of Your Strong Points

It is important to have a sense of who you are and what your strengths are when you are networking and marketing yourself. What are your special skills and abilities? What unique knowledge do you have? What experiences will other people find valuable? What characteristics and beliefs define who you are? Once you have made this list, make copies for your bathroom mirror, for your car dashboard, and for your wallet. Knowing your strengths helps you to remember that other people will value what you have to offer.

Never network from a position of weakness. Always network from a position of strength. Have something of value to offer; otherwise people will see you as an annoyance. And remember to begin networking before you need anything from other people. Join or create a network to build relationships, and do what you can to help others or the organization.

Make a List of Organizations and Events for Networking

Identify professional organizations and events that may be helpful to you in your career or with your project. Look for special interest groups like those for "entrepreneurial women" for example. Get involved. When you are at professional events, make sure that you attend social functions, that you join people for dinner, and that you seek out volunteer opportunities.

Create a Contact List

Keeping in mind your reasons for networking, brainstorm all the people you know who might be of help to you. Prioritize the list according to who is most likely to be helpful. Think about people you have done favors for in the past who might not be of direct help, but who may know someone who can be. After you have spoken to each one, ask him or her, "Who else do you know that can be of help to me?"

Create an Action Plan with a Schedule

Take your list of organizations and events and your contact list, and put together an action plan for making connections. Schedule networking events on your calendar, along with organizational meetings, conferences and so on. Using your contact list, set up a schedule for making a certain number of calls per day or per week.

Meet with People and Attend Events

Before you meet with someone or attend an event, review your list of strengths, and focus on your purpose for networking and marketing yourself. It helps to visualize or picture a successful outcome. Be friendly and professional, but most of all, be yourself. Spend time connecting with people on a personal level before asking for help or sharing your reason for networking. If you are meeting in person with someone on your contact list, always bring a gift— something they can remember you by.

Network on the Net

The Internet is a valuable place to make connections and to learn fruitful information from colleagues. If you have a special interest or a special field, there is sure to be a newsgroup or threaded bulletin board on your topic. If not, start one by setting up a listserve at **www.egroups.com**, **www.topica.com**, or at similar sites. These services are free, and hosting a listserve or a threaded discussion is good for visibility.

Market Yourself

The actions you take depend on why you are marketing yourself, but think of yourself as a brand, "Brand You." When marketers are marketing a product, they look for the "Unique Selling Proposition" (USP). A USP is something relevant and original that can be claimed for a particular product or service. The USP should be able to communicate: "Buy our brand and get this unique benefit." When marketing yourself, you need to define who your "customers" are and what your Unique Selling Proposition is. Your list of strengths above should give you some clues, but the USP needs to be stated in a short phrase. People who are closest to you can often give you suggestions. It might be something like: "I help people to realize their dreams," or "My leadership brings out the best in others," or "I solve problems quickly and simply."

Once you know your USP, brainstorm ways that you can market yourself and your uniqueness. The key is to let people know what you have to offer. Write an article for the company newsletter or a professional newsletter related to your USP. Volunteer to give a talk. Design a project that uses your unique talents and propose it to the right people. Be visible.

Assess Your Progress Toward Networking Goals

You may wish to keep a notebook of your action plans and your progress. It also helps to have someone as a sounding board. That person can be a friend, a partner, or a professional coach. When we feel accountable for our actions to someone we trust, we are much more likely to follow through. It also helps to have someone who is willing to celebrate your successes and accomplishments with you.

Always Say "Thank You"

As you network, many people will offer you information, opportunities, and valuable contacts. In your notebook, keep track of the favors that people have done for you and make sure that you write each one a short and simple thank-you letter. People are always more willing to help someone who has been appreciative in the past.

Be Patient

Networking is a long-term activity. Steven Ginsburg of the *Washington Post* describes networking as "building social capital." You may not see results overnight, and at first should expect to give more than you get. But over time, your network will become one of your most valued assets.

✗ WHAT TO AVOID
Not Wanting to Bother Anyone

Remember that people love to help others. Don't take up too much of their time, and come well prepared. When you ask for someone's time, be specific. Say, "I'd like 30 minutes of your time," and then stick to it. Don't outstay your welcome. Whenever you meet with someone, always be thinking, "Is there something I can do to help this person?" Create a win-win situation.

Coming On Too Strong

Networking is not about selling something to someone who doesn't want it. You are looking for opportunities to create a mutual relationship, where there is give and take. In order for networking to be successful, you have to be interested in developing a long-term relationship. Remind yourself that your focus is on relationship building, not on immediate results.

Not Coming On Strongly Enough

You put yourself in networking situations, but never talk about your needs or interests. This may be because you are not clear enough about why you are networking, or you are networking for reasons that are not particularly important to you. Go back to step one and clarify your purpose.

SEE ALSO
Assessing Your Entrepreneurial Profile: Do You Have What It Takes? (p. 5)

REFINING AND PROTECTING YOUR IDEA

Profiling Your Target Market

GETTING STARTED

Before your business can realistically or effectively begin a marketing campaign, you'll need to be able to answer two vital questions: who is your target market, and what does your target market want or need that your business can provide?

Without detailed and precise answers to these questions you won't be able to define your marketing strategy or implement an effective sales and marketing plan.

It's worth recalling the classic tale of two shoe sales representatives out exploring opportunities in a country in which their company had yet to establish a market. The first sales representative sent back an initial report saying, "everyone goes barefoot in this country, no market here at all." The second sales representative's report, however, was somewhat different: "everyone goes barefoot, massive opportunity for us." Who was right?

This illustrates the necessity for any business to understand accurately the needs of its target customers, in terms of knowing enough about them and gathering sufficient information about what they really want. Without this precise understanding your efforts to market your goods and services won't be effective.

FAQS

How do I identify my target customers?

Your first job when profiling a target market is to be able to identify precisely who your audience is. Can you accurately describe the characteristics of your ideal customers? Which clients currently spend the most with you? Why do they do this? If you don't know the answers, you need to find out.

You'll probably already have a good idea about the groups of people or types of businesses that you think you can sell your service to. For individual customers this might be people of a certain age, gender, socioeconomic status, occupation, or a group with common or special interests such as sports or hobbies. For business customers these might be located in a specific area or in a particular sector, or could have similarities in terms of the customer groups they sell to.

Your aim should be to concentrate your marketing on these groups of people, businesses, or existing customers who are most likely to buy your product or service. Doing this in the most profitable way takes experience, but you may find useful advice in the book *The New Market Leaders: Who's Winning and How to Battle for Customers*, by Fred Wiersema, published by Free Press (2001).

Once you have identified this target group of people or businesses, you'll have completed the first step in profiling your market and now have your list of target prospects— your ideal customers.

Is it about quality or quantity of prospects?

A precision-driven marketing approach— where you have a high-quality list of prospective clients or leads—will, dollar for dollar prove far more productive and profitable than an untargeted blanket approach to generate sales.

Quality of leads, based on your understanding, knowledge, and careful profiling of your customers and their needs, will massively increase your ability to convert them into sales.

MAKING IT HAPPEN

Pinpoint What Your Customers and Prospects Need or Want

Having selected your ideal customer groups you'll now need to be absolutely clear about what they want and need, and exactly what it is that you are going to offer them. This understanding will enable you to develop the specific marketing message and proposition that will most effectively sell the benefits of your product or service to them.

If you get these messages wrong then it's

almost certain that your marketing efforts will fail, as your customers will buy from your competitors instead. Your product, service, or business proposition will have missed the target completely.

Speak to Target Customers Before Developing Your Marketing Strategy

Before you start to develop or choose your marketing strategy it's always worthwhile to speak first to a sample from your target audience. By doing this you'll be able to check that your profile of your intended market has been the right one, and test your assumptions about what you think they want and why they could buy from you.

You could do this by speaking directly to a group of people or you could undertake a survey in the form of a questionnaire which can be posted to a sample of target customers. Alternatively, you could talk to passers-by in a location that is frequented by your ideal customers.

Don't forget that you could also speak to your existing clients or, even better, clients of your competitors, if that is possible.

Double Check that Your Marketing Message Is Right for Your Target Market

Once you have spoken to a sample of your target market and you are satisfied that you have confirmed your assumptions about their needs, you'll be in a position to create or adapt a marketing proposition to sell the benefits of your product or service to that audience. After you have established the basic proposition, consider carefully whether there is anything further that will make your marketing message even more appealing. Will these communications convince them that your service can provide the benefits that meet their exact needs?

Check that Your List of Prospects Is as Precise as Possible

Your prospects list will only be of real use in your marketing campaign if it accurately reflects the profile of the audiences you are targeting. Have the consumers of your product or service been identified in terms of their geographic and demographic profile,

their employment status, profession, special interests, membership of clubs, and so on? Have you compiled a list of your business targets in terms of where they are located, their size, names of the main buyer, repeat purchase rate? Have you identified the best sales channels to enable you to reach these target customers?

Your sales efforts can only be as good as the list of prospects you have selected in your target markets, and that list must reflect the profile of the audience you are developing your marketing proposition to reach.

Insure That You Are Giving Them What They Want

With a thorough understanding of the needs of your ideal customers, you should then strive to create an offering and proposition based on four criteria that will give them a product or service that is:

- exactly what they want from you
- precisely when they need it
- in a way that is convenient for them
- at a price they can afford and are prepared to pay

If you are not convinced that your sales proposition meets all of these criteria, then you'll need to study the profile of your customers again and revise your offering.

WHAT TO AVOID
Failing to Test

The most common mistakes made when targeting products and services towards specific users or customer groups are caused by not testing the assumptions you have made about your audience. You'll waste valuable time and marketing budget if you launch a campaign towards an audience when you have not accurately identified who those customers are, and cannot precisely define what they want and why they could buy from you instead of your competitors.

Lack of Focus

Do not buy into a list of unknown prospects, no matter how attractive it seems to get names of thousands of people you can blanket sell to in the short term.

Find out who they are and where they are located, and test your assumptions about what you believe they want. By testing, you can either confirm that your profiling was right, or you can adjust your offering until you get it right. Being precise will lead to more sales more quickly, and more profit over the longer term. One book you might find helpful when learning to sharpen your focus is *The Discipline of Market Leaders: Choose Your Customers, Narrow your Focus, Dominate Your Market* by Michael Treacy and Fred Wiersma, published by Perseus Books.

SEE ALSO

Coming Up with a Business Idea (p. 12)
Market Research and Competitor Intelligence (p. 469)

Focus On: Competitor Analysis—Turning Data to Insight
Liam Fahey

GETTING STARTED

Competitor analysis (CA) has developed from a simple emphasis on gathering data about competitors, to a much greater indepth analysis of customers' strategies and actions. The most competitive businesses are those that effectively transform data relating to competitors into "decision-relevant" insights. The great advantages of indepth analysis are that it is one means of learning more about the broader competitive environment, and generating insights into customers, distribution channels, suppliers, technology, and competitive dynamics. CA is also used to reflect on and learn about one's own business—its vulnerabilities, limitations, and capabilities relative to current and potential rivals.

When you are analyzing and understanding competitor's marketplace strategy, it is important to consider three central elements:

- What product-markets does the competitor compete in (or want to compete in)?
- How does it compete in those product-markets to attract, win, and retain customers?
- What does it seek to achieve in those product-markets?

This actionlist explains how a greater awareness and understanding of competitors can help you grow your business.

FAQS

What are the main pitfalls when thinking about competitors?

Insight is sometimes flawed or limited in many firms because too much attention is devoted to *current* large market-share competitors, while far too little is given to other types of current and potential competitors. Critical insight into change in customers' buying behaviors often emanates from analysis of smaller rivals or of functional substitute rivals. Sometimes it is especially useful to "invent" a competitor that is not yet in the marketplace. This can be used as a reference point to challenge the firm's existing strategy or potential strategy alternatives.

What are the main sources of competition?

Professor Michael Porter of Harvard Business School has identified five forces affecting competition in an industry, and these provide an interesting lens through which to view current and potential competitors. Porter's five forces are:

- **industry rivalry**—direct competition result-

ing from the activities of companies in the same industry. An example of this is the Cola wars, dominated for much of the 20th century by Pepsi and Coca-Cola.

- **market entry**—new entrants to a market are another source of competition, with firms needing to understand who might enter the market, as well as how and when it will happen. Often the entire product offer provided by the new entrant—including product quality, features and price—could challenge those already in the market.
- **substitutability**—businesses with products or services that may be substituted with alternatives face competition, especially over price. For example, a train operator may face competition from airlines.
- **suppliers**—these businesses wield significant power if the item they provide is scarce or unique, or if there are only a few suppliers. Suppliers have considerable power to damage a competitive position. One response is to build close relations with important suppliers to secure delivery and to control prices.
- **customers**—the power of the customer is

seen as another source of competition. This means considering how dependent the business is on individual customers, the ease with which customers can move to another supplier, the customer's knowledge of the business's competitors and the conditions (price, quality, overall offer) that are prevailing. An example of customer power is provided by the growth of the Internet as a sales channel, which has empowered customers.

What is it about our rivals that we should analyze?

One of the first challenges we face is to decide the focus of competitor analysis. A central question confronts every business: what do we need know about our current and potential rivals? If you view competitor analysis as much more than this, though, and open it out to see it as a source of learning about both the competitive environment and your own business, you'll find that you also need to learn about:

- the competitor's *marketplace strategy*: how it tries to outmaneuver rivals in the marketplace;
- the competitor's *activity/value chain*: how it organized itself to develop and execute its marketplace strategy;
- the competitor's *alliances and networks*: what other businesses it aligns with and how it manages its network of alliances;
- the competitor's *assumptions*: what the competitor assumes about the marketplace and itself;
- the competitor's *assets and capabilities*: what enables the competitor to compete;
- the competitor's *infrastructure and culture*: the nature of the competitor's business.

MAKING IT HAPPEN
Understand the Factors Intensifying Competition

You need to be able to spot when competition may arise or when it is gathering pace. Competition can intensify in several circumstances:

- when the market is expanding or new, as with the computer industry over the last 20 years or the telecoms industry during the last ten years;

- when the stakes are high and there are major profits to be gained or losses to be suffered, notably when there are relatively few businesses in a large market as, for example, with Coca-Cola;
- when the market is set to change, perhaps as a result of developments affecting patents and intellectual property rights (such as when the patent for a clinical drug expires), or as a result of political or legal developments, such as privatization;
- when the market is shrinking or when there is overcapacity in the market chasing fewer customers. This is apparent in major manufacturing industries such as ship-building, steel-making, and car production.

Increase market awareness

Understanding your competitors will be easier if you develop a keen sense of market awareness, including a sense of how your competitors are perceived in your chosen market and why. Think about their:

- pricing policies and product offers
- brand reputation and recognition
- customers' perceptions
- product quality
- service levels
- product portfolio
- promotional campaigns, timing, nature, and channels used
- customer loyalty

Maintaining an awareness of these issues can help in analyzing sources of competitive advantage and disadvantage.

Understand Competitors' Marketplace Strategies

To understand what your competitors are up to, think about:

- **their product and customers,** taking into account the range of products offered, the variety within each product line, the groups of customers reached, and differences across the groups;
- **how the competitor (or competitors) provides value to customers,** taking into account product features, functionality, service, availability, image and reputation, selling and relationships, and price.

All of these issues to take into account are commonly called "indicators."

Assess Competitors' Marketplace Strategies

Analysis only generates real insight when it turns to assessing what change in the competitor's strategy indicates about current, emerging, and potential change in the broader competitive context. You need to work out what such change implies for both the firm's current and potential strategy and decisions.

Assessment begins by evaluating the performance of your rival's strategy. For example, is it resulting in market-share gain? Is it leading to a greater share of individual customers? Is it building a greater brand name and reputation (that in turn could be the basis of further market-share gain)?

Assessment addresses how well the rival's strategy is performing compared to other rivals or to your own firm's strategy. For example, with regard to specific customer segments, or even individual customers:

- is the competitor or our own firm providing greater value along the modes of competition?
- based upon customers' judgments, who is providing superior functionality?
- who is providing more useful services?
- whose image and reputation is more appealing to customers?

It is important to note that these assessments must be based largely on the judgments of the customers themselves.

✗ WHAT TO AVOID
Not Using Data from a Variety of Sources

Think about the wide variety of sources that can provide you with the information on competitors that you need. Start with your own business first—check your IT systems, and ask both your team and your customers. External sources such as analysts, journalists, competitor Web sites, and publications can also be especially useful. Finally, focus on the competitor and always ask, for example, what a change in a competitor's activity indicates about the potential change in a broader competitive context.

Failing to Undertake a Process of Analysis

The basic process in competitor analysis is as follows. First, identify relevant indicators from competitors' behaviors, actions, and words. Second, draw inferences as to what change along those indicators would imply for what the competitor might do in the future (for example, how it might change its strategy), or what it might suggest about developments in the broader marketplace (such as how fast specific products might come to the market or how quickly other products might penetrate particular customer segments).

Competitor analysis is always about detecting change in and around competitors and assessing what change implies for the competitor itself, for the marketplace in general, or for your own business.

Failing to Act

It's vital to use any information gathered to strengthen your own business. Analyzing everything you discover will help you assess and learn about your own company's vulnerabilities, capabilities, and future direction.

Developing and Protecting an Invention

GETTING STARTED

A new invention is often the starting point for a successful business, but the journey from an idea or prototype to a product on a store shelf can be long and difficult. This actionlist looks at the steps involved in this journey, from the protection of the idea, to the financing and marketing of the final product.

FAQS

How can I tell if my invention will sell?

If your invention exists only as a sketch, simple model, or even just an idea, your first step is to express this in concrete form. This could be a complete set of manufacturing drawings or a scale model that can be shown and demonstrated to others while you fully research your idea and evaluate its commercial potential.

To succeed in the market, your product must solve a problem for the purchaser in an original and cost-effective way. Your research and evaluation phase has to achieve four main aims, each of which has spin-off benefits. You must prove that your product is original and demonstrably better than competing products, so that it can be protected with a patent. You must also show that it is marketable, in order to attract venture capital and interest retailers. You must demonstrate that your product can be made, and that the cost and quality of the component parts allow the product to be produced economically. Finally, you must ensure that your product offers a unique selling proposition and that the scope and cost of reaching the target market is affordable.

How do I prove that my product is original?

You have ownership rights to your original creation that allow you to exploit it commercially but, unlike copyright on a book, song, or work of art, these rights are not automatic and must be secured by registration. This means filing a patent claim for your new product. (Remember that it is the actual product that is protected, not the original idea.) You may need the services of a patent lawyer or agent to assist with a search of previous patents and help you register your patent.

How do I show that my product is marketable?

Appropriate market research is essential. You will probably need to carry out qualitative and quantitative research to get an idea of the value and potential of your product in the market. You could try this on your own. Alternatively, if you can afford it, get a market research agency to draw up survey questions from your input.

Qualitative research should show you what people think of your idea or product—its visual appeal, its practicality, and its perceived acceptability. It should also show what people perceive your product as lacking and what improvements they think need to be made. Other questions can be directed at finding suitable names, colors, shape, pack sizes, and an acceptable price range for the product. Remember that the comments and answers you get do not necessarily indicate how well your product will sell; this may depend upon other factors, such as competitive activity or unexpected fashion trends.

Quantitative research evaluates the sales potential of your product: how many people would buy it; how different pricing levels would affect projected sales; whether there would be demand for different versions of the product, and so on.

How do I demonstrate that my product can be made?

This may require the services of a professional designer or engineer to perform a component analysis and to set optimum specifications and quality levels for every part of the product. Other aspects to be determined are the availability and price stability of raw materials, the labor costs and skill required, and the factory or workshop location.

Do I have a unique selling proposition?

The unique selling proposition (USP) is what puts your product ahead of a competitive field, and is a key aspect of your marketing plan. The truly unique feature of your idea can make your product the most desirable in the marketplace, and become the lynchpin of a successful advertising campaign.

Having decided on your product's USP, you should draw up your marketing plan. The plan should include your thoughts on distribution. You need to decide whether the product is a consumer product, or for businesses. Think about whether it will be sold regionally, nationally, or internationally, through direct, retail, or wholesale methods. Also consider whether you will use your own transportation to deliver it or use outside carriers.

Packaging is an important part of your marketing plan. Decide what you will call the product. Consider whether the packaging needs to be suitable for display purposes, whether the produce will be disposable or returnable, and whether packaging regulations might affect your product.

Two other important factors are advertising and promotion. Think about which media will be the most appropriate for advertising: newspapers, magazines, pamphlets, direct mail, the Internet, posters, radio, television, or point-of-sale material. Consider whether you could use exhibitions and trade fairs, and whether you have your own sales force or use agents.

Price is an important consideration, and you need to consider what sales volumes you can expect at different price levels, and how different volumes and prices would affect cash flow. You might need to think about making promotional offers.

Where can I go for more information?

On the Internet, InventNET.com has lots of useful information, including lists of inventors' organizations by state, a directory of patent attorneys, and other useful links.

MAKING IT HAPPEN
Choose the Next Step

Once the research has shown a potential market for your product, you have several options available: you could choose to manufacture and market your invention yourself; you could outsource production, but distribute and market the product yourself; you could merge your production, sales, and marketing with an established partner; or you could license the rights to the invention for others to make and market it.

If you go for any of the first three options, the deciding factor will be your own level of management expertise. If your planned business is small, you will need to decide if you have sufficient skills in manufacturing, marketing, and distribution, and the time to give each area the attention it needs. The last option of licensing to others may well be the preferable one if your real interest is in developing new ideas and innovations.

Develop Your Business Plan

Your invention may have too much scope for you fully to exploit its potential on your own. Or you may feel you do not have the depth of specialized knowledge and skills to develop all the individual aspects of a successful business plan—management, finance, manufacturing, marketing, sales, and distribution—without professional aid, but do not wish to consider a partnership or merger at this stage. Additionally, your potential investors will more easily be persuaded to fund a well-structured business venture that presents an attractive and totally developed plan to them.

Raise Capital

The three main options open to you are private equity, a business loan from a bank, and venture capital.

✗ WHAT TO AVOID

Talking Too Early about Your Invention

Do not describe your invention to anyone before filing a patent application. If you really need to discuss your invention with others before filing, always get them to sign a confidentiality agreement.

Not Considering the Options

Remember the objective is to maximize the revenue from your invention. Consider the option of simply licensing your design to others; this could save you a lot of expense.

SEE ALSO

Applying for a Patent (p. 31)
Coming Up with a Business Idea (p. 12)
Intellectual Property (p. 459)
Registering a Trademark (p. 39)

An Introduction to Intellectual Property

GETTING STARTED

Intellectual property (IP) enables people to own their creativity and innovation in the same way that they can own physical property. The owner of IP can control, and be rewarded for, its use. The four main types of IP are patents for inventions, trademarks for brand identity and copyright for written material and artistic works. This actionlist gives an overview of each of these rights and briefly describes how to obtain them.

FAQS
What do I need to know?

Owners of intellectual property (IP) have the right to benefit from it, sell it, hire it out, or license it out. IP is quite easy for other people to steal or use without permission, so IP law has been developed to define the rights of IP owners and provide them with the ability to protect their rights and defend them through legal action. Some of these rights apply automatically, while others require a registration process to become legally enforceable. It is almost always necessary to register before disclosing your IP concept to others, or your rights will not exist. The U.S. Patent and Trademark Office and the U.S. Copyright Office of the Library of Congress are the government agencies responsible for issuing patents and registering trademarks and copyright.

MAKING IT HAPPEN
Patents

A patent gives an inventor the right, for a limited period, to stop others from making, using, or selling an invention without his or her permission. The term of a new patent is generally 20 years from the date on which the application was filed in the United States. Patent rights are specific to the country they are granted in.

See the actionlist "Applying for a Patent" for full information on how to do what, and when.

There are three types of patents: utility patents, design patents, and plant patents. Utility patents may be granted to any person who "invents or discovers any new and useful process, machine, manufacture, or composition of matter, or any new and useful improvement thereof." "Process" refers primarily to any technical or industrial process; "manufacture" to any manufactured article; and "composition of matter" to chemical compositions, including new chemical compounds. Design patents may be granted to any person who invents a new, original, and ornamental design for any manufactured article. Plant patents are granted to anyone who invents or discovers and asexually reproduces any distinct and new variety of plants.

A patent cannot be granted for an idea—it must be a detailed description of an actual machine, process, article, or matter. The laws of nature, physical phenomena, and abstract ideas are not patentable.

To qualify for a patent, the invention must be new, which means that it cannot have been known or used in the United States, or patented or described in print in the United States or a foreign country, before its invention by the person applying for the patent. It also cannot have been patented or described in print anywhere, or been in public use or for sale in the United States, more than one year before the application for a patent is filed in the United States. In other words, if the inventor describes the invention in a printed publication, he or she must apply for a patent before one year has gone by, or the right to a patent will be lost.

While inventors may prepare their own applications for a patent, most hire a registered patent attorney or agent to prepare the applications and deal with the Patent Office. The U.S. Patent Office publishes a directory of registered patent attorneys and agents, or you may look for one in the Yellow Pages. Although the inventor executes a power of attorney authorizing the patent attorney or agent to act on his or her behalf, the inventor is free to contact the Patent Office about the status of the application and may remove the attorney or agent by revoking power of attorney at any time.

All applications received by the Patent Office are numbered in sequential order, and the applicant will be notified of an application number and filing date by a filing receipt. For more information, you can download a brochure, entitled "General Information Concerning Patents," from the U.S. Patent Office Web site (see address below).

Copyright

Copyright is an automatic right that protects the author of original works, including literary, dramatic, musical, artistic, and certain other intellectual works, both published and unpublished. Copyright gives the creator or first owner of any original work the legal right to control how this material may be used.

Copyright for artistic, dramatic, literary, and musical works originating within the United States is currently set for the author's lifetime plus 70 years. The owner can control how the work is exploited, including copying, adaptation, public performance, broadcasting, and public distribution, and can transfer ownership of copyright to someone else. Some unlicensed use of a copyright work is allowed under a concept known as "fair use." This includes limited photocopying and quotation of extracts for teaching or review purposes.

Copyright comes into effect immediately, as soon as something is created and recorded in some way. Marking your work with the copyright symbol © followed by the date and your name is not legally required in the United States and most other countries but may help should there be any infringement proceedings. Providing evidence that you created the work at a particular time is also a useful precaution. Although it is not necessary to do so, you may register your work with the U.S. Copyright Office.

Trademarks

A trademark is a distinctive word, name, symbol, or device that makes a business's goods and services immediately recognizable. Although registration is not necessary, by registering a trademark your business gets the right to prevent others from using an identical or confusingly similar mark on goods and services that are the same (or similar) to your own.

Anytime you claim a right to a mark, you may use the (TM) (trademark) symbol, whether or not you have filed an application with the U.S. Patent and Trademark Office. However, you may only use the symbol (R) after you have actually registered your trademark with the Patent Office (and not while an application is pending).

To register a trademark, you can use the Trademark Electronic Application System (TEAS) to file your application online, or you may mail or hand deliver a paper application to the U.S. Patent Office. No attorney is necessary, although you may choose to hire one to represent you and file the application. A federally registered trademark can last indefinitely, provided you continue to use the mark and you periodically file affidavits of continued use or applications for renewal. More information can be obtained from a brochure entitled "Basic Facts About Trademarks," available on the U.S. Patent Office Web site (see address below).

WHAT TO AVOID

Not Keeping Records
Mark your products as protected, and keep records of the design and (if applicable) the registration process. This will strengthen any case should registration be challenged or design rights infringed.

Not Taking Out Insurance
It is a good idea to take out insurance against the cost of bringing legal action for infringement of rights.

SEE ALSO
Intellectual Property (p. 459)

Applying for a Patent

GETTING STARTED

Patents are granted by the U.S. Patent and Trademark Office (USPTO) to inventors, giving them the right to prevent exploitation of their inventions by others. The full process of patenting a new invention is time-consuming, expensive, and may require the services of a professional patent attorney or patent agent. You need to be very sure of the commercial viability of your idea before you go ahead with the full process.

The information below is reproduced from the Web site of the USPTO. It is a synopsis of some of the valuable and detailed information on the site, and we suggest strongly that you visit the site to gain a thorough understanding of this complex process.

This actionlist explains the steps to follow to lodge both an initial and a full patent application.

FAQS

What is a patent?

A patent for an invention is the grant of a property right to the inventor, issued by the United States Patent and Trademark Office. Generally, the term of a new patent is 20 years from the date on which the application for the patent was filed in the United States or, in special cases, from the date an earlier related application was filed, subject to the payment of maintenance fees. U.S. patent grants are effective only within the United States, U.S. territories, and U.S. possessions. Under certain circumstances, patent term extensions or adjustments may be available.

The right conferred by the patent grant is, in the language of the statute and of the grant itself, "the right to exclude others from making, using, offering for sale, or selling" the invention in the United States or "importing" the invention into the United States. What is granted is not the right to make, use, offer for sale, sell or import, but the right to exclude others from making, using, offering for sale, selling or importing the invention. Once a patent is issued, the patentee must enforce the patent without the aid of the USPTO.

There are three types of patents:

Utility patents may be granted to anyone who invents or discovers any new and useful process, machine, article of manufacture, or compositions of matters, or any new useful improvement thereof;

Design patents may be granted to anyone who invents a new, original, and ornamental design for an article of manufacture; and

Plant patents may be granted to anyone who invents or discovers and asexually reproduces any distinct and new variety of plants.

Patent Laws

The patent law specifies the subject matter for which a patent may be obtained and the conditions for patentability. The law establishes the United States Patent and Trademark Office to administer the law relating to the granting of patents and contains various other provisions relating to patents.

What rights do I have as the patent holder?

You own your invention. Like any other form of property you own, you may sell it or rent it out. However, patents are territorial rights only. Protection is limited to the countries to which the patent application extends.

What should I do before making an application?

Many inventors attempt to make their own search of the prior patents and publications before applying for a patent. This may be done in the Patent Search Room of the USPTO, and in libraries, located throughout the United States, which have been designated as Patent and Trademark Depository Libraries (PTDLs). An inventor may make a preliminary search through the U.S. patents and publications to discover if the particular invention or one similar to it has been shown in the prior patent. An inventor may also employ patent attorneys or agents to perform the preliminary search. This search may not be as complete as that made by the USPTO during the examination of an application, and only serves, as its name indicates, a preliminary purpose. For this reason, the patent examiner may, and often does, reject claims in an application on the basis of prior patents or publications not found in the preliminary search.

MAKING IT HAPPEN
File an Initial Application
In the United States, there are two types of patent application, non-provisional and provisional.

A non-provisional application for a patent is made to the Commissioner for Patents and includes:
- a written document which comprises a specification (description and claims), and an oath or declaration;
- a drawing in those cases in which a drawing is necessary;
- the filing fee. Applicants must determine that small entity status is appropriate before making an assertion of entitlement to small entity status and paying a small entity fee. Fees change each October. The fee schedule is posted on the USPTO Web site.

Provisional Application for a Patent
Since June 8, 1995, the USPTO has offered inventors the option of filing a provisional application for patent, which was designed to provide a lower cost first patent filing in the United States and to give U.S. applicants parity with foreign applicants. Claims and oath or declaration are NOT required for a provisional application. Provisional application provides the means to establish an early effective filing date in a patent application and permits the term "Patent Pending" to be applied in connection with the invention.

Provisional applications may not be filed for design inventions.

Provisional applications are NOT examined on their merits. A provisional application will become abandoned by the operation of law 12 months from its filing date. The 12-month pendency for a provisional application is not counted toward the 20-year term of a patent granted on a subsequently filed non-provisional application which relies on the filing date of the provisional application.

A surcharge is required for filing the basic filing fee or the cover sheet on a date later than the filing of the provisional application.

A brochure on Provisional Application for Patent is available by calling the USPTO General Information Services at 1–800–786–9199 or 703–308–4357 or by accessing USPTO's Web site at www.uspto.gov.

Steps to Complete the Full Patent Application
The application for patent is not forwarded for examination until all required parts, complying with the rules related thereto, are received. If any application is filed without all the required parts for obtaining a filing date (incomplete or defective), the applicant will be notified of the deficiencies and given a time period to complete the application filing (a surcharge may be required), at which time a filing date as of the date of such a completed submission will be obtained by the applicant. If the omission is not corrected within a specified time period, the application will be returned or otherwise disposed of; the filing fee, if submitted, will be refunded less a handling fee as set forth in the fee schedule.

Patent Marking and Patent Pending
A patentee who makes or sells patented articles, or a person who does so for or under the patentee, is required to mark the articles with the word "Patent" and the number of the patent. The penalty for failure to mark is that the patentee may not recover damages from an infringer unless the infringer was duly notified of the infringement and continued to infringe after the notice.

The marking of an article as patented when it is not in fact patented is against the law and subjects the offender to a penalty. Some persons mark articles sold with the terms "Patent Applied For" or "Patent Pending." These phrases have no legal effect, but only give information that an application for patent has been filed in the USPTO. The protection afforded by a patent does not start until the actual grant of the patent. False use of these phrases or their equivalent is prohibited.

✗ WHAT TO AVOID
Talking Too Early about Your Invention
Don't tell anyone about your invention before filing an application. If you really have to discuss your invention with others before filing, always use confidentiality agreements.

Not Seeking the Right Advice
Basic advice from the U.S. Patent and Trademark Office (USPTO) is freely available from the USPTO Web site (see below), which also provides a searchable directory of patent attorneys/agents by state. Before using the services of any attorney/agent, you should check their qualifications and reputation. If patents are key to your busi-ness, you may wish to make use of a patent watching service. This will report on the patent activities of your competitors, as well as all other activity in your field in foreign countries.

Worrying that the Whole Process Is Taking Too Long
A regular U.S. patent application typically takes three to eight weeks to prepare and file. The U.S. Patent and Trademark Office will then take anywhere from six to 24 months to complete the initial examination of a patent application. After the initial patent examination, the patent examiner and the inventor's patent attorney/agent may enter into discussion to clarify any questions regarding the invention. This may take another six months to a year. If the U.S. patent examiner can be convinced that the claimed invention is able to receive a patent, then a patent commonly takes one to three years to issue after the filing of the original patent application.

SEE ALSO
Developing and Protecting an Invention (p. 26)
Intellectual Property (p. 459)

Using Copyright to Protect Your Work

GETTING STARTED

Copyright is a form of legal protection for the authors of original works, including literature, plays, and other written works; music; choreographed dances; pictorial, graphic, and sculptural works; motion pictures; sound recordings; and architectural works. There are no forms to fill in and no fees to pay: copyright is secured automatically when the work is created on paper or in some other material for the first time. Copyright gives the creator or first owner of any original work the legal right to control how this material may be used.

This actionlist explains the principle of copyright and how you can use it to protect your original material. It also gives guidelines on what to do if you think your copyright is being infringed.

FAQS

What is the purpose of copyright?

Copyright helps creators to gain economic rewards for their efforts and encourages future creativity. It gives rights to creators of certain kinds of material to control the ways in which their material may be used. The rights broadly cover: copying and adapting the work; issuing, renting, and lending copies to the public; performing the work in public; or broadcasting the work. In many cases, the creator will also have the right to be identified on the work. The creator will decide how to exploit the work and how to enforce his or her copyright. He or she can also benefit by selling or agreeing to a transfer of copyright to someone else. Without protection, it could be very easy for others to exploit material without paying the creator.

Who owns copyright?

In the case of a written, dramatic, musical, or other artistic work, the person who created the work is the first owner of the economic rights under copyright. This rule also applies to commissioned works. However, when a work is created during employment, the employer is the first owner of these rights, unless an agreement has been made between the employee and employer indicating otherwise.

Copyright, like physical property, can be bought or sold, inherited, or transferred to another person in another way, for example, as a gift. So some or all of the economic rights may later belong to someone other than the first owner.

What laws enforce copyright?

The first U.S. Copyright Act, which was based on English law, was passed in 1790; subsequent revisions were passed by Congress in 1909 and 1976. The 1976 revision superseded all previous copyright law and took into account recent developments in technology. It also attempted to bring U.S. law in line with international copyright law. The 1976 Act covered: scope and subject matter of works covered, exclusive rights, term of copyright protection, copyright notice and registration, copyright infringement, what constitutes fair use, and defenses and remedies to infringement. For the first time, copyright was extended to unpublished works. In addition, an exception was made to the exclusive rights of owners to make and distribute copies of their works by allowing library photocopying under certain circumstances, for purposes of scholarship, preservation, and interlibrary loan.

The 1976 revision was partly undertaken in anticipation of the United States' decision in 1988 to comply with the Berne Convention, an international accord signed by more than 20 countries that extends copyright protections to authors in all the member countries under each country's national laws. As a result, copyright notice for copyright protection is no longer required in the United States.

In 1998, copyright protection in the United States was extended for the life of the author plus 70 years, under the Copyright Term Extension Act.

What kind of work does copyright protect?

This includes original literary, dramatic, and artistic works, original music, and published editions of works (that is, the style and layout of a publication). Sound recordings on any medium—which can also include recordings of other copyright works, films, and videos—and broadcasts and cable programs are also protected.

How does copyright apply to the Internet?

Under U.S. law, copyrighted material available over the Internet will generally be protected in the same way as material in other media. Generally, it is a good idea to mark each page you put on a Web site with the international © mark, followed by the year of publication and the name of the copyright owner. For example, © 2003 Ann Smith. You could also include information on your Web site about allowing others to use your copyrighted material without permission.

Web sites are accessible from all over the world. If material on your Web site is used without your permission, you would probably need to take action for copyright infringement in the location where the infringement occurs.

MAKING IT HAPPEN
Insure Copyright Protection

Registering a copyright is strictly voluntary, unlike registering a patent or a trademark. You don't actually need to take any action for your copyright to be protected. There are no application forms to fill in or fees to pay. Copyright comes into effect immediately, as soon as something is created and recorded in some way, for example, on paper, on film, as a sound recording, or on the Internet.

It is a good idea, however, to mark your work with the copyright symbol ©, followed by the date and your name, to warn others against copying it. While this is not legally required in the United States and most other countries, marking in this way may help you during infringement proceedings. Take steps to provide evidence that you created the work at a particular time. For example, a copy of your work could be deposited with a bank or an attorney. Alternatively, send yourself a copy by registered mail, leaving the envelope unopened when you receive it.

Although it is not required, registration of copyrighted material is possible and in some cases is recommended. If you wish to sue for infringement of a work, for example, you will need to register it. Registered works may be eligible for statutory damages and attorney's fees in successful litigation. To register a work, you must submit an application along with a copy of your work and a nonrefundable filing fee to the U.S. Copyright Office.

" Fair Use"

One of the exceptions to copyright protection is the concept of "fair use"; this allows some unlicensed copying and other use without infringing copyright. Some copyrighted works may be used (photocopied, for example) to a limited extent, for research and private study, even if for commercial ends (except where the work is a database). Making single copies of short extracts of a work or a single article from a journal may count as fair use. Copying by someone other than a researcher or student is not allowed if copies will be given to more than one person at the same time for the same purpose, for example, for a training session.

The economic impact of the use on the copyright owner is an important factor that the courts consider when deciding whether something is fair use.

Licensing Copyright

As a copyright owner, it is for you to decide whether and how to license use of your work. An exclusive license could be granted, which enables the licensee to use the copyrighted work to the exclusion of all others, including you, the copyright owner. A license can be limited, for example, in duration, or in any other way. It is a contractual agreement between the copyright owner and user.

Enforce Your Rights

Copyright is essentially a private right, so it is up to you to decide how to enforce it. It is sensible to try to resolve the matter with the party you think has infringed your copyright without resorting to official proceedings. If you are unable do this, you might have to go to court. Courts may grant a range of remedies, such as injunctions (to stop the other person making use of the material), damages for infringement, or orders to produce infringing goods. In some cases it may be necessary to demonstrate to the court that you have tried to solve the matter by mediation or arbitration, if you wish the court to consider awarding you the best available remedy, including an award covering your costs. If you decide to go ahead with legal action you must get some professional advice, as this is a particularly complicated area of law.

Deliberate infringement of copyright can be considered a criminal offence. If it is on a large scale, for example, pirate or counterfeit copies of compact discs, then you should inform either an attorney or the police. They can decide whether action, including potential prosecution, is justified. If the police decide not to take any action, you could still consider a private criminal prosecution if you believe there is a criminal offence, and you can still pursue a civil action against the alleged infringer.

Other Ways of Protecting Your Product

Copyright does not protect ideas. Although the work itself may be protected, the idea behind it is not. To protect an original idea, you will need to obtain a patent, which is a fairly complicated procedure. Names, titles, slogans, or phrases are also not protected by copyright; however, these could possibly be registered as a trademark.

Protect Your Material Overseas

There is no such thing as an "international copyright" that automatically protects an author's works throughout the world; however, copyrighted material is protected in most other countries. The United States, the Western European countries, and Russia all belong to at least one of the international conventions, including the Berne Convention for the Protection of Literary and Artistic Works and the Universal Copyright Convention (UCC). Copyrighted material created by U.S. nationals or residents is protected in each member country of the conventions by the national law of that country. For a list of countries that maintain copyright relations with the United States, contact the U.S. Copyright Office.

WHAT TO AVOID
Not Keeping Records
It is essential to keep records showing the date and author of any work produced in which copyright exists.

Not Using the Copyright Symbol
Marking with a copyright symbol ©, followed by the year of publication and the copyright owner's name is not required by U.S. law, but it can deter infringement. It may also be needed for protection overseas.

SEE ALSO
Complying with the Copyright of Others (p. 37)
Intellectual Property (p. 459)

Complying with the Copyright of Others

GETTING STARTED
If your business uses articles, literature, music, or other published work in producing goods or providing services, you may be at risk of contravening the copyright on that work. This actionlist outlines the types of published work that are protected by copyright, and gives guidance on how they may be used in compliance with copyright legislation. All small businesses need to be aware of these issues, as noncompliance can lead to a fine or legal action.

FAQS
What kinds of material do you need permission to use?
Copyright protects various types of works. Any original literary works, for example, books, training materials, computer programs, song lyrics, newspaper articles, and some types of databases, are all protected by copyright. So too are original dramatic works, including dance or mime, and original music. Original artistic works, for example, paintings, engravings, photographs, sculptures, architectural designs, technical drawings, diagrams, maps, and logos are also protected, as are published editions of works (that is, the style and layout of a publication). Sound recordings on any medium, for example, tape or compact disc, are protected, and this can also include recordings of other copyrighted works. Finally, films and videos, and broadcasts and cable programs also come under the protection of copyright. You will need to get permission from the owner of the copyright to use this material or any part of it unless it is subject to a copyright exception (see below).

When do you need permission?
In the majority of cases where you are intending to copy or use copyrighted material, you need to obtain permission from the copyright owner. If you are copying large amounts of material and/or making multiple copies, it is likely that you will need permission.

You must remember that buying or owning an original or a copy of a copyrighted work doesn't grant you permission to use it any way you wish. For example, buying a copy of a book, compact disc, video, or computer program does not necessarily give you the right to make copies (even for private use). Also, you will not necessarily have the right to play or show them in public. Other uses of copyrighted material, such as photocopying, scanning, or downloading from a CD-ROM or online database, all involve copying the work, so permission is generally needed.

However, there are certain exceptions to copyright. "Fair use" is a concept that allows some unlicensed copying and other use without infringing copyright. Some copyrighted works may be copied (photocopied, for example) to a limited extent for research and private study without infringing copyright, even if this is for commercial ends. The exception to this is where the work you are copying is from a database. Making single copies of short extracts of a work or a single article from a journal may count as fair use, too.

Other copyright exceptions exist, for example, where a work is accidentally included in an artistic work, sound recording, film broadcast, or cable program. You can find out more about copyright exceptions by visiting the U.S. Copyright Office's Web site (address given below).

Do I need permission to use material published on the Internet?
If you wish to put copyrighted material on the Internet, or distribute or download material that others have placed on the Internet, you should ensure that you have the permission of the copyright owners.

MAKING IT HAPPEN
Check That Permission is Required

Your first step is to approach the copyright owner to find out whether you need his or her permission to use the work. This can either be done directly, by going straight to the owner, or you can also contact one of the various copyright licensing bodies, if the owner belongs to one of them.

It is more usual to approach the copyright owner directly and ask for permission to cover the use you require. The permissions agreement is a contract between you and the copyright owner, and you can negotiate the terms and conditions, including the way the work is to be used and the permissions fee. There are no rules in copyright law governing what are acceptable terms and conditions; the terms and conditions are solely at the discretion of the copyright owner.

If you need help determining who owns the copyright on a particular work, check with the U.S. Copyright Office, which, for a fee, can conduct a search.

Sometimes copyright owners are members of collective licensing bodies that can be approached for a license. In particular, collective bodies exist for licensing the use of music and sound recordings, printed material, artistic works and characters, broadcast material, films, and television listings. More information about these licensing bodies is given in the next section.

WHAT TO AVOID
Not Checking with the Copyright Owner

It is vital to check with the copyright owner before using copyrighted material. You may be liable for a fine for infringing copyrighted work. The name of the copyright owner should be provided somewhere on the piece of work, but if you are unable to find it, contact the U.S. Copyright Office or relevant licensing body for help.

Not Seeking the Right Advice

The U.S. Copyright Office's Web site (address given below) can provide you with detailed information about copyright and whether you will need to get copyright permission.

SEE ALSO
Intellectual Properety (p. 459)
Using Copyright to Protect Your Work (p. 34)

Registering a Trademark

GETTING STARTED
A trademark is a distinctive word, phrase, symbol, or design that your business can use to make its goods and services immediately recognizable to consumers. It is a good way of differentiating your products and services from those of your competitors, and it implies a consistent level of quality or service. There are several restrictions on what can be registered and protected as a trademark. This actionlist looks at what is involved in successfully registering a trademark, both in the United States and abroad.

FAQS
What is a trademark?
The idea of trademarks was developed in the late 1800s to help established businesses stop competitors stealing their sales and possibly damaging their reputation by imitating their products. A trademark may be a brand name for a specific product or be representative of the business as a whole. Today, a successful brand name or company logo is a valuable asset to its owner.

A trademark is a word, phrase, symbol or design, or a combination of words, phrases, symbols, or designs, that identifies and distinguishes one company's goods from those of other companies. A service mark is the same as a trademark, except that it identifies and distinguishes the source of a service rather than a product. Throughout this article, the terms "trademark" and "mark" refer to both trademarks and service marks.

When is it important to register a trademark?
Registration of a mark is not compulsory, but it does protect the use of the reputation that the mark represents. By registering a trademark, your business gets the right to prevent others from using an identical or confusingly similar mark on goods and services that are the same (or similar) to your own.

If your mark is registered, your business can sue for infringement, with its certificate of registration as evidence of ownership. Without this, you would have to demonstrate that a reputation has been established

with regard to that mark and that its use by others will damage this reputation.

When registering a trademark, you will list the goods and services that your business wants to protect; but the legislation allows you to protect the trademark against confusion with a wider range of goods, including those that may not be similar to your own.

When can the symbols (TM) and (R) be used?
You may use the (TM) (trademark) designation any time you wish to alert the public to your claim to a mark, whether or not you have registered the mark with the U.S. Patent and Trade Office. (The same applies to the SM, or service mark, symbol.) However, you may use the (R) designation only after USPTO has actually registered your mark, and not while the application is pending.

How can I protect a trademark overseas?
Registration within the United States does not give automatic protection overseas; however, certain countries do recognize a U.S. registration as a basis for registering the mark in those countries. In order to register your trademark overseas, you must check the laws of each particular country regarding registration. Note, if you think that you may trade overseas, it is worth investigating existing foreign trademarks before investing in packaging and promotional literature that may have to be changed if a particular trademark is already registered overseas.

What are the requirements for new trademarks?

A new trademark must be distinct from all existing marks (including those of overseas registers that can claim protection in the United States) and from words and symbols that may be in use in the normal course of trade or are customary in the current language.

A mark that arises exclusively from the nature of the goods, gives substantial value to the goods, or is necessary to obtain a technical result cannot be registered. A mark must not be misleading or contrary to public morality, and marks containing representations such as a crown or heraldic symbols are restricted. Registered trademarks should not consist of words or symbols in common usage or which will unnecessarily restrict other traders' activities, because of the monopoly granted to the owner. The exception to this is if it can be shown that the mark has become established as distinguishable through use.

In addition, a trademark must NOT be primarily merely descriptive of the company's goods or services; primarily geographically descriptive; primarily merely a person's last name; primarily ornamental; or primarily descriptive in a deceptive way of the goods and services. For a complete list of the grounds for refusal of a registration mark, see the U.S. Patent and Trademark Office's Web site (address below).

MAKING IT HAPPEN

Before making your application, you should search the trademark register at the U.S. Patent and Trademark Office (USPTO) to see if any existing marks might prevent your mark from being registered. You may conduct a search online at the USPTO Web site, or by visiting the USPTO Trademark Public Search Library at 2900 Crystal Drive, Arlington, VA. You may also search for registered and pending trademarks at a Patent and Trademark Depository Library (PTDL), located in various places throughout the United States. Private trademark

search firms will also conduct a search for a fee.

To make an application, use the Trademark Electronic Application System (TEAS) available at the USPTO Web site to file your application directly over the Internet. If you do not have Internet access, you can access TEAS at any Patent and Trademark Depository Library or any public library with Internet access. Currently the filing fee is $335 per class of goods or services.

Although the USPTO prefers that you file your application electronically, it is possible to mail or hand deliver a paper application. The mailing address is Commissioner for Trademarks, 2900 Crystal Drive, Arlington, VA 22202–3514.

A registered trademark can be maintained indefinitely provided the owner of the registration continues to use it in connection with the same goods or services and continues to file the appropriate applications for renewal.

Domain Names and Trademarks

In recent years, use of the Internet as a trading medium has grown, resulting in a conflict between the allocation of domain names and trademarks. The Internet Corporation for Assigned Names and Numbers (ICANN) has partly resolved these issues through an administrative system for resolving domain name disputes involving trademarks. These measures have led to fewer cases of "cybersquatting" of trademarks in the generic top-level domains. Further steps are now being taken to protect intellectual property at the level of the country code in top-level domains.

WHAT TO AVOID
Not Carrying Out Thorough Research

Before investing in registration, think about why you're doing it. This will help you determine how many classes of goods and services you wish to apply for, and whether you will require protection overseas, now or later. When designing product names and promotional literature, check what your competitors (or businesses in similar fields) have already registered; this will avoid possible complaints later.

Not Being Consistent in the Use of Your Trademark

Always display your trademark in the form in which it was registered. The symbol (R) should be used in conjunction with the trademark in countries in which it is registered, and (TM) where it is not.

Not Enforcing Your Rights

It is possible to subscribe to a professional watching service, so that either the trademark holder or the client can be notified if a third party tries to register a trademark, company name, or domain name which is confusingly similar to that of the client.

SEE ALSO
Intellectual Property (p. 459)

SETTING UP OR ACQUIRING A BUSINESS

Understanding Business Models

GETTING STARTED

There are four main types of legal status available to you when starting a business. These are sole proprietorship, partnership, limited liability company, and corporation. You will need to take into account several considerations when deciding which of these will be best for your new business. For example, you will need to think about taxation and administration implications, the image of the business, legal requirements, financial issues, and so on. This actionlist shows you how to decide which status is most suitable for your business, and raises some of the issues you may need to consider.

FAQS

When is sole proprietorship status suitable?

There are various advantages to operating as a sole proprietor.

The status of sole proprietor is convenient in situations where just one person will own the business and will have final responsibility for its management and development. It is possible to employ other people if you are a sole proprietor, but ultimately the business is the individual, and there is no separate legal status.

There are various advantages to operating as a sole proprietor. You generally do not have to file any special forms or pay any fees to start your business. However, regulations differ by locale, so check with your Secretary of State and city or county clerk's office regarding business licenses, local tax requirements, home/storefront parking, and other local or state regulations. There is less paperwork to deal with regarding legislation and taxation than for a limited liability company or corporation. As the owner, you are entitled to all the profits made by the business.

When is partnership status suitable?

A partnership is a good vehicle to use when your business will involve two or more people owning a business together. Like a sole proprietorship, a partnership has no separate legal identity and does not generally need to be formally registered with a government office. Experts recommend, however, that any partnership be formalized

by a written general partnership agreement (although no law requires one).

There are several advantages to operating as a partnership. The structure of a partnership can be flexible, according to the partnership agreement. There is less paperwork to deal with regarding legislation and taxation than for a limited liability company or corporation. Management responsibilities, risks, and losses are shared. Partners can bring a variety of different skills and experience to the business. More people involved also means that more capital can be raised among them. Partnerships cannot be taken over by other businesses.

There are two other kinds of partnership, a limited partnership and a limited liability partnership (LLP). A limited partnership is a partnership which has at least one partner who is a general partner (that is to say, he or she has management rights and unlimited liability), and at least one limited partner. A limited partner, who may be an individual or a company, contributes a fixed amount (as capital or property) to the partnership, but is only liable for partnership debts or liabilities up to the amount they have contributed. Also, a limited partner may not be personally involved in the management of a company.

A limited liability company (LLC) has the flexibility and tax status of a partnership—business profits or losses are reported on the owners' personal tax returns; the LLC itself does not file taxes—and the benefits of limited liability. The liability of all of the partners is limited to their capital contribution to the LLC, so personal assets cannot be seized to settle debts. LLCs are required to register with their state LLC office.

When is limited liability company status suitable?

A limited liability company (LLC) consists of shareholder/members whose percent of ownership is based on their capital contribution. LLCs are formed when the business requires outside funding for its operations. Managing member(s) hold management responsibility and unlimited liability. Member liability is limited to their percent ownership.

The main advantage of the LLC structure is that its members have limited liability for the debts of the business up to the value of their shareholding. They are not personally liable for company debts. Filing procedures to create an LLC can be complicated and vary by state. Attorney assistance is recommended.

What is a franchise?

If you don't have an original idea for your own business, it may make sense to establish a franchise. A franchise is where a license has been granted by one business (the franchiser) to another (the franchisee), allowing the franchisee to use the trademark and name of the franchiser, as well as its methods for marketing, managing, operations, administration, and so on, within the business.

There are several advantages to franchising. The franchisee, by investing in a proven business format, can become the owner of a business with a well-known brand name, while at the same time overcoming some of the difficulties associated with a new business. The franchisee also receives help in finding and refurbishing premises. Help will be given in obtaining any planning permission and in purchasing stock and equipment, as well as with staff training, marketing, and advertising. The franchisee is therefore able to concentrate on the day-to-day running of the business. The franchiser will be able to provide specialist managerial advice and guidance to help overcome any problems

that a small business is likely to encounter, and the franchisee will benefit from the economies of scale of operating as part of a large organization.

MAKING IT HAPPEN
Start Up As a Sole Proprietor

As a sole proprietor, you can simply start operating your business. Contact your state, county, and city clerk offices to ensure that you have any licenses required. If you have a storefront, make sure you have all of your necessary property and liability insurance coverage in place. If you operate from your home and will have clients visiting your office, find out about parking restrictions and so on.

Start Up As a Partnership

Like a sole proprietorship, when starting a partnership you can simply start operating your business. Partnership agreements with all terms and conditions should be written by an attorney. If you are establishing a limited partnership or limited liability partnership, contact your state office of corporations, Secretary of State, or LLC/LLP office to ensure that you have completed the appropriate paperwork.

Start Up As a Limited Liability Company

A limited company must be registered with your state before trading commences. This requires certain documents, available from the state office of corporations, Secretary of State's office, or LLC/LLP office, to be completed and submitted with a registration fee. An attorney can help you to draw up and submit these documents. A limited liability company must have at least one managing member and corporate officers.

Start Up a Franchise

Before you make a decision, talk to existing franchisees to find out more information about the franchise you are considering purchasing. If you decide to go ahead, and your application is accepted, you will probably find that a first interview with the franchiser is required. This is valuable, as it gives both parties the opportunity to appraise one another. Provided both parties wish to continue, there will be a second interview to begin formalizing the agreement. Take advice from a professional adviser before signing any documents.

Register Your Company

The status of your business venture will determine which specific regulations are applicable to it and who should be contacted. Further advice on all of the information given in this section should be sought from an attorney, an accountant, or a local support organization.

If you are a sole proprietorship, or in a partnership, you are considered self-employed and must apply to the Internal Revenue Service for an Employer Identification Number (EIN), although any income from your business will be reported on your individual income tax return.

If you are a limited liability or an incorporated company, you must register with the appropriate state office by filing articles of organization. While a limited liability company may be taxed as either a sole proprietorship, partnership, or corporation, depending on the circumstances, a corporation pays corporate income taxes.

For sole proprietorships, the name of the business is legally the same as the name of the owner. Likewise for partnerships, the business name is legally the last names of the partners, unless there is a written partnership agreement that specifies some other name. For other types of businesses, including limited partnerships, limited liability companies, and corporations, the legal name of the business is the one registered with the state filing office. If a sole proprietorship or partnership operates under a name other than the legal name—for example, Mary Mullins has a business called Mullins Muffins—many states require that the owner of the business file a DBA ("doing business as") statement.

✖ WHAT TO AVOID
Underestimating your Liability

A sole proprietorship has unlimited liability for the debts of the business, such as bank loans and amounts owing to creditors. This means that if your business fails your personal savings and assets could be at risk. In a general partnership there is unlimited liability, and each partner is personally responsible for the debts of the partnership. As a partner, therefore, your personal assets may be seized to pay off debts. Limited liability companies and corporations must comply with a wide range of complex and detailed legislation that is not applicable to sole proprietorships and partnerships; this can add to the administrative and financial burden.

Mistaking the Protection of a Corporation

Sole proprietors will often decide to establish themselves as a corporation in order to give themselves protection behind the "corporate veil" and protect their personal assets. In fact, the corporate veil provides little or no protection to sole proprietors even if they have established their company as a legal corporation. Thus, before moving from sole proprietorship to corporate standing, speak with your attorney to determine whether you and your business will be given the protection you seek, or if you are just adding unnecessary expenses and paperwork to your operation.

Underestimating the Role of Franchisers

Franchisers exert a fairly high degree of control over the franchise operation, so, although the franchisee is legally independent, he or she will never be completely independent of the franchiser.

The Franchise Proving More Expensive than Originally Thought

Franchises can be expensive investments. After the initial fee, there will be ongoing fees for the continuing support provided by the franchiser. Under the franchise agreement the franchisee may be obliged to buy supplies and equipment from the franchiser which they may have been able to purchase cheaper elsewhere.

Focus On: Working Effectively As a Board Director
Adrian Cadbury

GETTING STARTED
If you have established a limited company, your business will have directors, referred to often as the "board." Boards are in place to direct and not to manage, and they have the task of defining the purpose of their enterprises and of agreeing the strategy for achieving that purpose. In particular, it is important to understand that boards are responsible for:
- appointing chief executives to turn strategic plans that build the long-term value of the business into action;
- supporting and counseling C.E.O.s in how to achieve this;
- providing leadership above all, and it is in this context that the roles of board members need to be considered.

This actionlist explains the workings of a board and how to improve its success.

FAQS
What is the role of the board?
- The role of the board is to direct, not to manage.
- Balance of board membership and choice of individuals are key.
- The chairman (this term refers to both men and women in this role) is responsible for the effectiveness of the board.
- Nonexecutive directors have a particular contribution to make to the work of a board.
- Board committees are important structurally and for the tasks they undertake.
- Executive directors should be appointed solely for the value they can add to the board.
- Board members have different roles; what matters is how they combine to form the board team.

What should be the board's composition?
A single board at the head of a company is the commonest form of board structure and is often called a "unitary board." They are made up of executive and nonexecutive, or outside, directors. ("Two-tier" boards separate these two kinds of director.) Given that both executive and outside directors sit on unitary boards, the first issue is the balance between them. Ten years ago, the ratio for U.K. boards was around two-thirds executive directors and one-third outside directors. This has now moved closer to parity and in future I would expect outside directors to be in the majority. This is already the position in the United States where the chief executive is often the only executive on the board and is usually its chairman as well.

How big should a board be?
There is a clear move to smaller boards in both the United Kingdom and the United States. Some commentators recommend a maximum board size of ten and favor eight or nine, the argument for smaller boards being that they enable all the directors to get to know each other and to contribute effectively in board discussions, thus arriving at a true consensus. The crucial point is that boards are teams and provide collective leadership, so the balance of membership and choice of individuals are key to forming the team.

MAKING IT HAPPEN
Work As a Team

Although board members have different roles, what counts is the way those roles are combined in the board team, and this is why board selection is so fundamental. Directors should only be appointed for the value they can add to the board. All directors should have terms of office to enable renewal to take place, although I am against rigid rules tying retirement to age or length of board service. If you are looking for outside directors, aim to fill gaps in the experience and backgrounds of the existing directors, and involve the board as a whole during the selection process. The chairman, however, has a particular responsibility for the choice of board members, since it is his or her responsibility to turn them into an effective team.

Focus on Priority Issues
This can be accomplished by:
- making sure that the board concentrates on corporate purpose, appropriate strategy, and appointing a chief executive who can turn strategy into action;
- appointing a chairman who is *not* the chief executive, and who will put in place effective measures of the board's performance;
- keeping the board to an absolute maximum of ten members, with a majority of external, nonexecutive directors;
- making sure that nonexecutive directors are independent of management and free from connections that may affect (or be seen to affect) their judgment;
- using the whole board to pick outsiders who can fill gaps in the experience and backgrounds of existing directors;
- training executives in filling their nonmanagerial boardroom role and letting them learn from non-executive posts elsewhere.

Maximize the Contribution of Outside Directors
All directors are equal in that they all carry the same legal responsibilities. Outside or nonexecutive directors are in that sense no different from their executive colleagues. They do, however, have particular contributions to make to their boards by virtue of standing further back from the business. One is in reviewing the performance of the chief executive and the executive team; clearly the outside directors are the only board members in a position to do this objectively.

Another contribution is in relation to potential conflicts of interest, such as those between the interests of the executives and those of the shareholders. Examples are directors' pay, dividends versus re-investment, and whether top appointments should be made from within or outside the company. Decisions on these matters are ultimately the decision of the whole board, but outside directors are well placed to offer direction on where the best interests of the company—to which all directors owe their duty—lie.

Outside directors bring with them their experience in fields which are different from those of the executive directors, and this external experience is of particular value in strategy formulation.

The role of these directors in helping to resolve conflicts of interest does not imply that they have higher standards than their executive colleagues—the difference is simply that they can judge these matters more objectively because their interests are involved less directly.

Clearly Understand the Role of Executive Directors
The duties of executive directors are the same as those of the outside directors. They are as responsible for the monitoring task of the board as the outside directors, who in turn are as responsible for the strategy and leadership of the company as the executives. This means that executive directors have to take their executive hats off upon entering the boardroom and put on their directorial ones. They should only be appointed for the contribution they can make to the board and they are there to further the company's interests—not those of their function or department. It is not an easy transition to make and executive directors can be helped in the adoption of their new non-managerial role through appropriate training or through a non-executive directorship elsewhere.

Manage the Role of Board Committees
As the responsibilities of directors have become more demanding, boards have increasingly formed committees to deal with some of their more detailed work. These committees strengthen the position

of the outside directors, of whom they are made up, and are important for the work they do. The essential point is that they are committees of the board. The board appoints them, sets their terms of reference, and turns their recommendations into decisions.

✗ WHAT TO AVOID
Poor Chairmanship

The chairman is responsible for the effectiveness of the board, and this responsibility rests with that person whatever his or her other duties. It leads to the point that all companies are different and the issues they face are constantly changing. Individual boards have to follow accepted board principles, but in ways which meet their particular circumstances. It is the chairman who has the responsibility of making sure that the make-up of the board is appropriate for the challenges ahead. Similarly, it is the chairman who has the task of welding their directors into an effective team. Effective boards are not brought into being simply by seating competent individuals around a board table—creating effective boards requires effort by their members, but above all coaching and leadership by the chairman, which is an argument for the chairman not also being chief executive.

The chairman is responsible for the running of the board. Responsibilities include the agenda, the provision of adequate and timely information to all directors, and the actual conduct of board meetings. The chairman is also, provided he or she is not chief executive, responsible for putting in place a means by which the board can evaluate their own performance. Where the chairman is also chief executive, his or her duties in relation to the board remain the same, but a deputy or a senior outside director would be responsible for the appraisal of the chief executive and for the review of the board's performance.

Misunderstanding the Role of the Board

Many boards fail to function adequately because their members have differing views, not only about the main challenges faced by the business but even about more fundamental issues, such as the role of the board and its priorities in the short, medium and long-term. One of the first priorities must therefore be to develop a consensus about what needs to be achieved, and how the board will work to do this.

Failing to Work with the Company Secretary

The chairman and board members should be able to look to the company secretary for impartial and professional guidance on their responsibilities, and all directors should have access to the advice and services of a company secretary, who is responsible for ensuring that board procedures are followed. The company secretary must be informed and supportive, working with the chairman to make sure that the board works effectively.

Evaluating an Existing Business

GETTING STARTED

It's often thought that buying a business is simpler than starting your own, but remember that many businesses are sold because they have inherent problems that prevent them from generating sufficient income. If you're buying a business, it's vital that you conduct comprehensive research and analysis in the same way as if you were setting the business up from scratch.

FAQS

What's my first step towards buying a business?

Your first step is to decide on the type of business you're looking for. Think about what size of business you want. Are you, for example, looking for a small local business, or are you aiming for a large national one? Also think about what business sector you're most drawn to—is it manufacturing, retailing, or perhaps services? Consider location too. Are you prepared to change your location and travel, or would you prefer to stay where you are and travel relatively short distances?

What should I be looking for in a business?

Look first and foremost for skills and experience. The most common reason for business failure is people taking on businesses outside their area of expertise, so think long and hard about the skills and knowledge that already exist in the potential business, and whether you can add to those skills. You also need to consider the products and/or services that the business provides. Again, ideally, you should be looking for a business that deals in a product or service that you have some experience of, especially if the operation is particularly complex or technical.

Remember to investigate the level of competition facing the business, especially locally. Make sure you know your competitors' strengths and weaknesses relative to the business you're considering buying, and what their share is of the market. Look at the size of the business, and find out how fast it has grown in the past, and whether

this rate is likely to continue, increase, or decline.

Another important factor to consider is location. Ensure that the business is located appropriately, for example, close to its target market (if location is relevant), and within reach of appropriately skilled employees. You'll also need to judge whether the business needs any major changes requiring a large investment of management time—you may be able to acquire a business at a lower price if this is the case. If the business is already successful, it can probably continue to operate in the same manner, regardless of a change of ownership.

Capital requirements are another issue. Calculate how much money needs to be invested in the venture. This is a crucial factor in determining whether to buy a particular business. Consider whether you'll be able to secure finance for future investment if it's required. Evaluate too the level of profitability of the business. Does it make the amount of profit you're looking for; does it have the potential to expand and grow?

How do I value the business?

It may be useful to employ a business appraiser or financial adviser when valuing the business. The three methods often used are asset value, earnings multiple, and return on capital.

Asset value—To obtain the business's net asset value (that is, what it is worth, in basic terms), the value of the liabilities (that is, a business's financial obligations, such as outstanding debts, loan repayments, outstanding invoices, etc), is subtracted from the value of the assets. The value for the entire business will be the net asset value, plus a value for goodwill, representing the business's reputation and existing customer base.

Earnings multiple—The earnings multiple method requires you to apply a multiple to the earnings from the business. Earnings should take into account interest charges to be paid after purchasing the business, and any loans needed to make improvements. To come up with an a earnings multiple, divide the company's market price by its after-tax earnings over a one year period.

Return on capital—To find the return on capital, you'll need to define a desired rate of return. (Rate of return can be defined as a ratio of the profit made in a financial year as a percentage of the capital employed.) Then the income of the business before interest and tax should be calculated, and this figure should also be given as a percentage of the capital invested. If the figure is less than the desired rate of return, then any purchase should not go ahead.

MAKING IT HAPPEN
Evaluate the Business

You'll need to carry out some research properly to evaluate any business you're considering for potential purchase. You should be able to obtain much of the information you require from the present owner; ask for details, including the business plan, accounts, details of established customers, and so on.

It's a good idea to carry out a SWOT analysis (Strengths, Weaknesses, Opportunities, and Threats) on any potential business purchase. Consider the present position of the business in the market, its past performance, and its potential for growth. Look at its available resources, for example money, assets, manpower, and so on. Investigate the training, experience, and skills available within the business. Check its sources of supply, costs, reliability of material, stock supply, and relations with suppliers.

Find out who the competition is, where it is, and what its strengths and weaknesses are. Research your customers, making sure you know who and where they are, and how loyal they are. You'll need to examine

external factors like industry trends, regulations, and political and economic developments. Consider how much money you'll need for advertising and marketing. The way the business is promoted may have to change. Look at the business's distribution channels, asking yourself how reliable they are and whether they can be maintained once the business changes hands. Calculate the profitability of the business after any initial capital outflow for improvements.

Determine a Price

Obviously, if you become interested in purchasing a business, you'll need to value it and determine a reasonable price in conjunction with the seller. The price of a business may be derived from some of the factors mentioned in the previous section. It will also depend upon an appraisal of the land and buildings. The fair market value of the property is affected by a number of factors. These include the business's location in relation to its customers and suppliers, employees, and competition. The condition of the premises, for example whether improvements are necessary to bring them up to legally acceptable standards, is also an important consideration.

Financial considerations, such as the costs of property maintenance, transfer of title, licenses, leases, property taxes, and so on, need to be taken in to account. There may also be problems over the transfer of a lease on premises. Some leases prohibit assignment.

External factors, such as current interest rates and the state of the property market, influence a property's value. So too will the future outlook, for example whether the property will continue to meet the needs of the business as it grows. There will also need to be a valuation of fixtures and fittings. There may be equipment leases that need to be transferred (for example, the photocopier). Check for any contingent liabilities.

Consider Other Factors

You'll need to negotiate the transfer value of the stock. This should be cost or "net realizable value" (NRV), whichever is lower. For redundant stock the NRV is zero. A recorded valuation and stock count should be carried out by a third party. You'll also need to engage an accountant to evaluate the business's books, bank statements, and tax records to get an accurate picture of the current financial situation and future profitability.

Valuing the goodwill of the business is especially important. Goodwill reflects the cumulative effect of the reputation of the business; its relationship with customers, suppliers, and competition; its market position, and the skills of the staff. You'll need to consider whether the existing staff are suitable for the business, and how they are likely to react to a new owner/manager. Decide what benefits will be offered, for example, maternity benefits, vacation time, and so on. Income tax withholding (both federal and state), FICA tax, pension schemes, and insurance should also be considered.

Make sure that you evaluate the outstanding loans to the business, its relationship with its creditors, and its repayment history. Be realistic about whether you'll be able to obtain financing for the venture, and to repay the loan. Look at pro-forma income statements, balance sheets, and cash budgets. When you estimate how much income the business is likely to generate, it's important to be conservative, especially in the early stages.

WHAT TO AVOID
Rushing Through the Research Stage
If you don't carry out thorough research, you may find you have made the wrong decision. Without enough information, facts and figures, and forecasts, a view of any business's prospects can be easily distorted and misleading.

Not Exercising Due Diligence
You should always exercise due diligence when purchasing a business. You must make sure that what the vendor is saying is correct. Examine all accounts carefully. Ask yourself whether customers are likely to remain loyal once you have taken over the business, and whether suppliers will maintain the same relationship with you. If you don't exercise due diligence, you'll only have yourself to blame for any problems you could have discovered before the purchase.

Not Setting a Price before Bidding
You should have a price band in mind before bidding, otherwise you'll be at a disadvantage. The seller may state an asking price outright, at which time the buyer must be prepared to negotiate. This way you shouldn't spend more than you can afford.

SEE ALSO
Small and Growing Businesses (p. 422)

Setting Up a Business As a Tax-Exempt Organization

GETTING STARTED

A not-for-profit business, or tax-exempt organization, is an organization that does not distribute its profit to its owners. All surpluses are put back into the business or used for other charitable purposes in the community. Sectors including charities, the arts, education, and health care often operate in this way. This actionlist looks at various types of not-for-profit business, how they are established, and how they can obtain financing to fund the business.

FAQS

What is the difference between a nonprofit and a not-for-profit business?

There is no legal difference, but many businesses that want to differentiate themselves from charitable organizations refer to themselves as not-for-profit.

Can any business be tax-exempt?

No. Nonprofit businesses are tax-exempt because they do not pay out profits as dividends to shareholders or as income to owners. All "profits" from the business are immediately reinvested in the organization.

What kinds of tax-exempt businesses are there?

The overall types of organizations that can qualify for tax-exempt status include corporations, community chests, funds, trusts, or foundations. Nonprofit organizations do not have to incorporate, but in many cases it is recommended that the organization do so.

What is a credit union?

A credit union is a cooperative that gives members facilities for saving, borrowing, and other financial services, and is set up, owned, and run by its members. Members save together to create a pool of money from which low-cost loans are made. Credit unions are tax-exempt.

Credit unions can operate to either a state or a federal charter. Member benefits may be affected by the charter to which the credit union operates and, as such, potential members should check out a variety of credit unions in their area.

Credit unions, in most cases, cannot extend business services and loans. Some small businesses use credit unions for their business banking needs. However, credit unions cannot be used for business banking services by legal corporations.

MAKING IT HAPPEN

Establishing a Tax-exempt Business

Usually a nonprofit business will either be an unincorporated association or incorporated as a company without share capital. Once you have decided to form the nonprofit you should contact your Secretary of State or other comparable office in the state in which your organization will operate. That office will provide you with the appropriate application forms and lists of necessary attachments.

Ask for any other materials, whether from your state or from local city or county offices, that explain the rules and regulations governing charitable organizations. You should be provided with guidance regarding charitable solicitations, hiring employees, employer payroll and unemployment tax requirements, registering for sales and income taxes under state and local law, and other matters of interest in managing a nonprofit organization in your state.

If you decide to become a corporation, you will need to provide Articles of Incorporation for your nonprofit organization.

In that case, it is recommended that you work with an attorney to ensure that you have the appropriate paperwork completed at the time of submission.

After you have established your organization as a tax-exempt entity in your state, you will receive an official letter granting nonprofit status. Upon receipt of that letter, contact the Internal Revenue Service for the appropriate forms to file for federal recognition as a tax-exempt organization and to be eligible to receive tax-deductible donations.

Boards of Directors

If your nonprofit organization is incorporated, you will be required to have a Board of Directors or Trustees. Technically the terms "Director" and "Trustee" can be used interchangeably. However, unless your nonprofit is a Trust, the term "Trustee" tends to be used for advisory board members rather than the more formal "Director."

Directors have a fiduciary responsibility for the organization. They are not figureheads nor should they be treated as such. Corporate governance and oversight is of particular importance, which means that you should be particularly careful in selecting and inviting your board members. Once you have your board in place you will be well advised to ask for their counsel and to keep them well informed about the status and direction of the organization. They may also be a good source of funding.

Bylaws

You will also be expected to establish a set of bylaws by which your nonprofit organization works. In many cases, the bylaws are submitted with your application for tax-exempt status to your state.

Bylaws are the operating description of your nonprofit organization. They present your organization's mission and reason for existence along with the constituencies you serve. The structure of the organization, the role of the board, management expectations and requirements, and many day-to-day operating guidelines are included. Ask your attorney, Secretary of State, and local city or

county oversight office for any samples of bylaws that they might recommend for your review. Many samples are also available online as part of various nonprofit organizations' Web sites.

Unincorporated Associations

An unincorporated association does not have a separate legal identity from its owners. The association normally has a constitution that sets out its aims and objectives. It will also have a committee, normally elected during an annual general meeting, at which members are nominated to serve as officers and members. Committee members are all personally liable for debts incurred by the business.

An unincorporated association cannot start legal action, borrow money, or enter into contracts in its own name. This is because it has no legal identity of its own, and in legal terms is only a collection of individuals. It also can't hold property without appointing trustees (usually committee members) to do so on its behalf. There are no formal registration requirements for setting up an unincorporated association.

Audits

Many nonprofit organizations and industries have, as part of their regulations, defined audit requirements during which state or federal auditors review their finances. Find out from your tax advisor or attorney how frequently these audits occur and how best you can prepare.

Sources of Help and Finance for Not-for-profit Businesses

Many nonprofit organizations look for **grant aid** to cover all their costs. Grant aid might come from large companies, grant-giving charitable foundations, or the government. You should remember that there is far more demand for grant aid than can ever be met.

Many charitable, tax-exempt organizations depend upon **donations** to cover their costs. In these cases, a percentage of the donations is allocated as "administrative fees." If your organization is funded by donations, you are advised to keep your administrative fees to a minimum, as many donors make their determinations about which nonprofit organization to support based on the amount that reaches the population to be served.

Sometimes new tax-exempt organizations that are not sure whether they are viable may ask another, more established nonprofit to act as their **fiscal sponsor**. This gives the new organization an opportunity to test the water at a low level of expense and risk and speeds up the process of becoming better established if the organization is a success. If a group is a coalition of several groups working together on a common issue, a fiscal sponsor may be seen as neutral territory for accepting funds. If the group is committed to its mission but just has no interest, or experience, in managing all the administrative functions of a business, a fiscal sponsor could be a good option.

WHAT TO AVOID
Not Getting the Right Advice

Establishing and managing a nonprofit organization is a complex and detailed process. There are personal legal implications for those in charge of the organization if there is any real or perceived malfeasance. As a result, you should make sure that you are working with attorneys and accountants who specialize in nonprofit and not-for-profit organizations.

Not Taking It Seriously

It is important to remember that the management of not-for-profit organizations should be taken just as seriously as the management of for-profit organizations.

SEE ALSO
Small and Growing Businesses (p. 422)
Understanding Business Models (p. 44)

FINDING PREMISES

Renting a Business Property

GETTING STARTED

Many businesses—and most small businesses—occupy premises on a rental basis, covered by a lease or tenancy agreement. This actionlist explains what a lease is, and goes over some of the main issues you need to consider before signing a lease.

FAQS

What is a lease?

A lease is a legal document issued by the landlord of the premises covering the terms of the tenancy. It confers the exclusive right to occupy premises for a fixed term in exchange for the payment of rent.

Check with your attorney that the conditions in the lease serve the purposes of your business and are reasonable.

MAKING IT HAPPEN

The Description of Premises

The description of the premises must be accurate, in order to avoid disputes. Be particularly wary of undefined boundaries, and ask for an accurate plan to be attached to the lease. Your legal rights should be stated in the lease and should include right of access from the nearest public highway. If you are renting part of a building, the right to use common areas leading to your section of the premises should also be included, as should the provision of essential services, for example, gas, electricity, and drainage. The landlord or tenant of adjoining premises is also expected to keep his or her property in good condition. Landlords have rights and obligations under the lease but must allow tenants to occupy the property without interference.

The Term of a Tenancy Agreement

The term means the length of time the agreement is for. Make sure that the occupancy start date corresponds with the date on the lease. It may be difficult to withdraw if the premises are no longer required before the end of the term. Even if premises cease to be in use, you will be liable for payment until the lease lapses. For a small business, a shorter lease or periodic tenancy (from month to month, or quarter to quarter) may be more appropriate.

Some landlords may be prepared to offer a contract called a "tenancy at will," which can be ended at short notice by either side. Such contracts don't offer any security of tenure, however. If extensive alterations or improvements are intended, a short-term tenancy, tenancy at will, is inadequate.

Your Obligations As a Tenant

On signing a lease, the tenant agrees to take responsibility for a number of things. These are explained in more detail below.

Rent

Make sure that the rent and its payment dates are clearly stated. Compare the rents of similar property in the area and, if possible, negotiate a rent-free period, for example, towards the costs of initial repairs or refurbishment. Consider using a real estate agent, experienced in commercial property, to negotiate on your behalf.

Repairs

These may be split into three stages. The first stage is before you occupy the property. It should be in a suitable state of repair, but if it is in poor condition, it will be necessary to prepare a schedule of condition with photographs. The second stage is during the lease. Be aware of your business's responsibility regarding repairs before occupying the premises. The third stage is the end of the lease. The property must be left in an acceptable state of repair. Businesses may be served with a schedule of dilapidation, itemizing repairs that must be carried out. Allowances should be made for everyday wear and tear.

If the entire premises are leased, the landlord may expect the tenant to take full responsibility for all repairs (including structural). In this case, it is advisable to have an inspection performed and to have any defects remedied before signing the lease. It may be possible to negotiate an upper limit to the contributions made toward the cost of repairs or an inclusive rent. Small businesses should go for an internal repairing lease with no liability for structural repairs.

Insurance

The tenant pays for insurance, although the landlord may initially make the payment, reclaiming pro rata from the tenant. Always make sure that insurance is adequate and that policy terms are reasonable.

Service Charge

This applies to a multioccupied building. The landlord will usually pay for common costs, for example, structural repairs, common areas, heating, and building superintendent or security staff. This cost is recharged to the tenants on a proportional basis (normally a ratio of floor areas). It is advisable to ensure that the basis of calculation is stated, that you have the right to see and check the landlord's expenditure, and that you are not paying for any empty areas.

Use

Leases usually contain restrictions on the use of the property. These may relate to a specific type of business, or to a nuisance, for example, noxious fumes and noise. The restrictions normally reflect those imposed by the local zoning board. If the use may change in the future, discuss the possibility with both your landlord and the local authorities. The lease should contain a clause which permits a change of use, subject to the landlord's approval, and stating that he or she must act reasonably.

Assigning and Subletting

Check that the lease allows you to sublet to another business, or better still, to assign the lease. Subletting means that the business

is still liable for the rent, whereas assignment transfers all responsibility to the new tenant.

Alterations

Most standard leases prohibit the tenant from making alterations to the property unless the landlord finds it reasonable to do so. Before signing, consider any potential alterations that may be required, and remember that tenants are normally required to reinstate the property at the end of their lease.

Rent Reviews

Leases normally contain a section stating the schedule for rent increases. Most standard leases only make a provision for rent to increase, but it is a good idea to try to make the landlord agree that rent can also be decreased. If the landlord and tenant cannot agree on a rent, an independent arbitrator can be brought in, providing that this is a term of the lease.

Option to Terminate the Lease

Leases may contain an option to terminate before the end of the lease term on a specific date or dates. This is known as a break clause. One advantage is that if increased or decreased space is required, it is not necessary to wait until the lease ends. If a property is no longer suitable, but the lease term has not expired, it is possible to approach the landlord to see if he will accept a surrender of the lease. This absolves the tenant from all future liability, but the landlord may not agree or may require extra payment.

Guarantor

If the landlord insists that the business act as a personal guarantor, the business will be liable for paying the rent and other costs should it fail. A landlord may request that a third party, for example, an associate company, is obtained to act as guarantor. You may find it difficult to find someone to act on behalf of the business in this capacity. A returnable deposit may be an alternative to this. It is important to avoid giving guarantees.

Improvements

Tenants who carry out improvements beyond repairs at their own expense will not obtain any compensation from the landlord, even if the term is cut short, unless they follow a procedure of giving advance notice. A legal representative should be contacted for more information.

✗ WHAT TO AVOID

Not Holding Your Landlord Accountable

As the tenant, you can make reasonable demands on your landlord—particularly before signing the lease. Determine the dispute resolution acceptable to you. Make sure that the lease terms include your ability to terminate the agreement with no penalty if the landlord does not fulfill his or her repair and maintenance responsibilities or misrepresents service costs, or if the use of the building is interrupted for reasons outside your control.

Not Doing Your Homework

Past or nearby tenants could be contacted for information about the landlord and how he performs his duties. You will need to check that the correct planning permission has been obtained to use the premises for your type of business.

Not Getting the Right Advice

Be wary of one-sided lease agreements and seek professional advice if you are unsure. Avoid committing to a lease that obligates you to make structural repairs should any be needed, particularly if the property is relatively old or is in a state of disrepair, except in circumstances where the tenant commits to such a lease in return for discounted rent or a rent-free period of occupancy.

SEE ALSO

Buying a Business Property (p. 61)
Complying with Fire Safety Regulations (p. 74)
Ergonomics at Work (p. 80)
Establishing and Maintaining Your Home Office (p. 83)
Health (p. 457)
Insurance Coverage for a Business (p. 71)

Buying a Business Property

GETTING STARTED

Buying a property involves greater risks and financial commitment than renting, but sometimes it's the only way to get the right property for your business. Before making the choice, it's a good idea to list all of the factors affecting your decision, ranking them in order of importance. The main factors will be price, location, available finance, and whether the property meets the operational needs of the business. Everyone's needs are different and, as few buildings are perfect, a compromise may be necessary. Once you have found your "ideal" property, you will need to make an offer, raise the finance, and go through the relevant legal procedures.

FAQS

Where can I find out about available property?

There are plenty of places where you can look for the kind of information you're after. Try contacting local authorities, which keep a register of industrial property, real estate agents, or the real estate departments of commercial companies. Check the ads in local newspapers and specialist and trade magazines, and keep an eye out for notices or billboards/signboards posted on interesting looking premises. Don't forget also to spread the word among your personal contacts.

How do I evaluate my requirements when buying a property?

When choosing a building, you need to focus on which attributes are essential for your business to operate effectively. You may also need to decide whether it's preferable to convert an existing building or to buy purpose-built premises. The budget available for the actual purchase and potential renovation/conversion will also need to be taken into account.

MAKING IT HAPPEN

Features to Rank when Evaluating Potential Buildings

You've got a list of properties to look at—there may be a large number of buildings to choose from. The easiest way through the selection process is to list all the important features you require, and then score each property you see against each feature. A major constraint will be the price of the building. Costs can vary significantly. Try evaluating buildings on a "cost per square foot" basis. Check whether the location qualifies for any financial incentives, for example, if it's located in a low-income area.

Location is key. Think about whether the location will be appropriate for your customers, and whether the facilities are appropriate. Does your business need to cater to passing trade? Would it be preferable to be nearer to a key customer or supplier? The location needs to be right for your staff, too. Make sure that the right staff can be recruited locally, and that there is access to reliable public transportation. Staff should feel secure in the area, and have access to facilities such as nearby shops and banks.

Look at the surrounding businesses. Are they growing or declining? Are any of them likely to be a nuisance, for example, through noise or dust caused by the processes? Also, think about where your competitors are sited. Should the business be located near to competitors?

The size of the building will be an issue. There should be a balance between sufficient space, not more than is needed or can be afforded, and enough space to allow for reasonable expansion. If the property is too large, will it be possible to sublet the extra space? The Net Assignable Square Footage (NASF) is the total assignable square footage as measured from the inside wall space of the room. NASF totals do not include areas such as custodial areas, public restrooms, stairways, mechanical rooms, etc. Your architect or interior design engineer will help you determine the appropriate amount of Assignable Square Footage (ASF) for your workspace.

Think about the physical nature of the building. The layout of the site itself should meet all of the operational requirements. Will your building need to be renovated to meet any requirements for the Americans with Disabilities Act (ADA)? Other issues to consider are building density, the number of stories, and the condition of the building, in relation to the amount of money available for repairs. You also need to consider visitor flow, the availability of services, car parking (especially in residential areas), and accessibility (including stairs, elevators, and so on). Other issues to think about are security, storage, and lighting (natural and artificial).

Make an Offer on a Property

Once you've identified a suitable property, an offer should be made to the agent. This offer should be conditional upon planning permission, the building survey, and the Fire Marshal's inspection. It should also be conditional upon raising the finances, the property value, and whether or not the building is vacant before possession, as well as upon certain contract conditions. For example, some new developments have maintenance charges with unregulated annual cost increases.

After your conditional offer is accepted, a building inspector should be employed to undertake a full detailed structural survey. It's advisable to shop around for quotes from building inspectors and to check which details the inspector will evaluate. The survey will usually include a property valuation assessment (PVA) for mortgage purposes.

Obtain Advice on Buying a Property

You will need to consult a number of officials in order to ensure that the building can be used for the intended purposes.

Planning Permission

This is the most important approval required (and the one which the business is most likely to need assistance with). It's

required when building development or change of use occurs. You will need to contact your local planning and zoning commission. It will also be necessary to carry out a business search to find out more about the property. You will need to research the planning commission's zoning area proposals, to ensure that the building will not be affected. You will also need to find out about any restrictions due to historic preservation orders that could hinder development, and additional restrictions on the property because of local by-laws. Finally, make sure you identify the exact use of the building.

Building Regulations

Building codes, standards, and regulations should be verified with the local or state board of Building Regulations and Standards. Building regulations apply to the erection, re-erection, or extension of a building, the material alteration of a building, the material change of use of a building, and the provision, extension, or material change of use of a controlled service or fitting, in or in connection with a building.

Environmental Health Officers

Along with local planners, local authority officers are responsible for the health and physical welfare of the population with regard to dust, noise, odors, and so on.

Fire marshals grant fire certificates and are responsible for confirming that fire precautions are up to standard. Remember to check with your local city or state fire marshal regarding building and fire safety codes.

OSHA makes sure employees have a safe environment in which to work. Check with the Occupational Safety and Health Administration (OSHA) for employee safety requirements.

Legal Aspects When Buying a Property

Before you buy, it's advisable to consult a lawyer or licensed commercial real estate agent experienced in commercial property transactions. They can advise on contracts, planning regulations, financial research, history of building searches, and completion. They should also insure that local and state regulations are met and that there are no outstanding notices or liens on the property.

Your lawyer or real-estate agent will help you determine all closing costs and taxes due on your property.

Financing the Purchase of a Property

Once you have decided on a building, the purchase will need financing. Property is usually financed over 20 or 25 years with the amount advanced as a loan being 60–70% of the property valuation. The lending institution will expect a legal charge on the property for security. Once you have decided on a building, the purchase will need financing.

There are several sources of funding. Check with the Small Business Administration (SBA) to see if you qualify for their loan program. If you want to use a local bank, call around for the best rates of interest. Many will lend on an equity basis, meaning they take stock in the company in return for the capital loaned. You could also look at local business administrations, which may give mortgages for industrial and commercial purchases.

✗ WHAT TO AVOID
Not Considering All the Financial Implications of Buying Freehold

Purchasing a building is a major move, as it ties up a lot of capital in the building rather than in the business. It's essential to ensure that this will not damage the business. Most small businesses do grow, so they should consider carefully before buying a property or building outright. Remember that even

when house prices are rising, commercial property values tend to rise at a lower rate. There is often no real financial advantage in buying instead of renting/leasing. Businesses should make sure that any advantages that do accrue are worth the cost. Also bear in mind that owning a property commits the business to additional expenditure, through obligations to undertake regular checks on electrical supplies and wiring for safety reasons. It's very important to ascertain the rateable value and rates payable on a property, as these can make a huge difference to the overall cost.

Not Seeking the Right Advice

It's advisable to seek advice from commercial real estate agents, local businesses, small business advisers, local authority development officers, and enterprise agencies when making decisions about properties. It's also a good idea to talk to firms in the surrounding area about the property. It may be worthwhile asking why the previous tenant left. It's important to consult your lawyer once a property has been found, and to avoid signing anything immediately.

SEE ALSO
A Guide to Health and Safety at Work (p. 77)
Complying with Fire Safety Regulations (p. 74)
Establishing and Maintaining Your Home Office (p. 83)
Health (p. 457)
Insurance Coverage for a Business (p. 71)
Renting a Business Property (p. 58)

Choosing and Using an Architect

GETTING STARTED

If you are considering doing work of any sort to a building—whether new or existing—you should consult an architect. He or she will not only listen to your ideas, but will also be able to suggest alternative options. It is also part of the architect's service to help with planning permission and building regulations, and to ensure that the plan that is decided upon is strictly followed by the builders.

FAQS

How do I choose an architect?

An obvious but potentially risky way of finding an architect is to select one from the Yellow Pages. Another is to base the choice upon a personal recommendation, or find out who designed projects that are similar to yours that you like. A recommended alternative to these methods is to contact a local chapter of the Institute of American Architects. While the AIA is not a licensing body—the use of the term "architect" generally requires a state license—it does maintain a code of ethical standards and rules of conduct for its member architects and architectural firms. (The AIA Web site address is given below.)

It's important to choose an architect based on the quality of service and product, not solely on the fee. Ask to see a portfolio of the architect's work and visit completed buildings. It's also a good idea to check that your architect has worked on similar projects and has the appropriate design skills.

What is the architect's role?

The architect will discuss your requirements and help you to prepare a brief action plan. He or she will then carry out an evaluation and visit the proposed site before undertaking a feasibility study and investigating any statutory regulations applicable, as well as giving advice regarding other services the project requires. The architect will then prepare a timetable and arrange for planning permission/building regulation applications, as well as developing designs, working drawings, and models; determining the cost of the exercise and the deadline; and preparing structural or engineering plans and construction details.

He or she will also advise on appropriate procurement methods and prepare tender documentation, obtaining bids and analyzing estimates. Once the work has begun they will inspect the site and the progress made. The architect's role includes administering the building contract, submitting financial reports, giving advice on maintenance regimes, and finally providing drawings of the building as built.

MAKING IT HAPPEN

Architects' Fees and Expenses

Architects generally bill in one of two ways: hourly or as a percentage of the construction costs of the project. Architects working by the hour can often provide an estimate of what the total fee will be, based on the number of hours they think they will need to complete your project.

Prepare for Discussions

Once you've appointed your architect, the first stage of the work involves a discussion of the requirements, budget, timetables, and fees. After this discussion and the preparation of a full brief, the architect will draw up a plan of action. In preparation for this discussion, it is a good idea for you to become familiar with ownership rights of the property, for example, rights of way or boundary fences. It is important for you to keep focused on what is to be achieved.

Plan the Construction Project

The second stage is for the architect to visit the site in order to evaluate what might be done. If a site has not been identified, the architect may be able to advise on appropriate locations and accommodation. A sketch proposal may be prepared at this stage as an initial point of discussion and agreement with you.

A feasibility study can then be undertaken by the architect, giving possible alternative options of spatial arrangements and elevational treatment. Restrictions may be imposed on the design by statutory items such as building regulations and fire and means of escape regulations. Health and safety legislation will have to be taken into account, as well as the Americans with Disabilities Act of 1990.

During this design process the architect will advise whether other professionals will need to be consulted, such as a structural engineer or landscape architect.

Preparing the Architect's Designs

Once the plan of action has been agreed upon, the architect will organize meetings and surveys with all the other professionals involved in the project, which will enable cost estimates and outline proposals to be prepared. It's important to be aware that changes to the plans may be necessary as part of this planning process. Decisions on quality of workmanship, materials, and so on are made at this stage, to enable the monitoring of the costs.

Once planning and building regulation approvals have been obtained, the architect will be in a position to prepare detailed design drawings. The number of drawings will be dependent on the size and complexity of the project; they will be used by the contractors at the bidding stage and then on site during construction.

Architects and Building Contractors

The architect can now prepare production information and tender documents. These are then sent to contractors bidding for the work. The architect will provide advice regarding the suitability of bids submitted.

Once the project is underway, the architect can visit the site at regular intervals to inspect the work being carried out. He or she will convene site meetings, to which you may be invited (or will otherwise be given the minutes), and will generally administer the terms of the building contract, give advice on maintenance, and arrange for drawings of the building pinpointing plumbing, heating, and air conditioning systems.

The architect should regularly submit detailed billing statements to keep you fully informed of the costs throughout the various stages of construction.

Architects' Services

In addition to construction projects, many practicing architects can provide a range of additional services. These may include: furniture and interior design, cost estimating and financial advice, and undertaking negotiations with contractors.

WHAT TO AVOID
Choosing Your Architect on a "Fee Basis"

Fees should be negotiated, and, for larger contracts, it is important to meet the architect who will be dealing with the project, as dealings with them could last for a couple of years. This can help in avoiding personality clashes or misunderstandings over requirements. This can be a more important issue than the fee. Decisions should not be made on the basis of fee alone but on the overall value of service.

Not Choosing the Right Architect for the Job

An architect should be selected who can demonstrate an ability to do a job within a specified budget.

SEE ALSO
A Guide to Building Regulations (p. 66)
Health (p. 457)

A Guide to Building Regulations

GETTING STARTED

In the United States, building codes—as well as fire, electrical, and health and safety codes—vary by state; however, there are also federal and local regulations that may apply. The regulations exist to protect anyone in or near a building, and they protect the value of the property itself. They also deal with energy conservation and issues concerning access and facilities for disabled people. For anyone involved in running a small business, it's therefore important to have a working knowledge of what the regulations involve. This actionlist provides a basic guide, but much more detailed information can be found on the Web sites listed at the end.

FAQS

In what instances are businesses affected by building regulations?

There are four main situations where building regulations apply:

1. new construction
2. new addition to an existing building
3. alteration to an existing building
4. demolition

In addition, building regulations may apply in cases where land is being excavated or filled in or where a sign is being installed.

Where can I find out exactly what is involved in and required by building regulations?

Most states have an office that makes and enforces the state's building codes, as well as issuing construction licenses. It may be possible in some instances to access the full text of a particular state's building code online. In other instances it may be necessary to contact the state's housing department or planning board. Building permits may also be downloaded from local government Web sites.

MAKING IT HAPPEN

Comply with Building Regulations

Before you go ahead with making any changes to a building, you need first to have your plans checked and approved. You can do this by filing an application for a building permit with your local building inspector's office or building commission. In addition to the application, you may need to submit a proposal for the work that is to be done, as well as evidence of liability insurance and a copy of your building contractor's license.

Enforcement of the Building Regulations

The approved inspector may make recommendations as work progresses. If the recommended amendments are not made within three months, a final certificate will not be issued and the inspector is obliged to notify the local authority, which in turn may use its powers of enforcement. The local authority can issue a notice insisting on alterations to the work or its complete removal within 28 days.

Other Regulations Relating to Building

- the Construction (Design and Management) Regulations 1994, and 2000 amendment—these concern all owners of commercial property. Under these regulations, owners must appoint an individual as planning supervisor to coordinate the health and safety plan for the project. The regulations apply to all construction, maintenance, and demolition work
- the Construction (Health, Safety, and Welfare) Regulations 1996 (as amended)
- The Fire Precautions Act 1971, as modified by the Fire Precautions (Workplace) Regulations 1997 and 1999 amendments

WHAT TO AVOID

Not Obtaining Planning Permission First

Before getting building regulations approval, it may be necessary to obtain planning permission. Normally, planning permission is applied for first; once approval has been granted, building regulations are then set in motion. If permission is not sought or granted beforehand, the penalties can be severe.

Not Seeking Professional Advice

Building regulations can be complicated, so get professional advice if you feel out of your depth.

SEE ALSO

A Guide to Health and Safety at Work (p. 77)

Choosing and Using an Architect (p. 64)

Complying with Fire Safety Regulations (p. 74)

Health (p. 457)

Insurance Coverage for a Business (p. 71)

Obtaining Zoning and Planning Permission (p. 68)

Obtaining Zoning and Planning Permission

GETTING STARTED

The aim of the zoning and planning system is to balance the need for development with the need to protect the environment. To obtain planning permission, your business will need to apply to its local city and county. Planning Departments should grant permission unless there is a definite planning or environmental reason not to do so.

FAQS

Is planning permission necessary?

Your business will need to check with its local city and county to find out if proposed developments will need planning permission. Fees for the review of planning documents will be payable at the time the documents are submitted.

Internal alterations, external alterations and new developments require planning permission and specific permits. Internal alterations with no affect on the exterior often require simple permits for the work to be done but may still require inspections prior to completion.

Certain buildings are protected for historical purposes. If the building is historically preserved, additional consent and inspection may be required.

Planning permission is not usually required for regular and general maintenance and repairs to building exteriors. However, if street parking will be affected or pedestrian access impacted by scaffolding or other equipment, the city and county planning department should be contacted to determine what, if any, additional permits will be required.

Planning permission is not usually required for the exhibition of a sign that displays the name of the firm or business, and the goods or services supplied. However, the sign must also not exceed the sizes and heights specified by the city and county.

In general, no planning permission will be required for using a domestic residence for business, unless the home will no longer be used mainly as a private residence. You will need to consider other factors too. For example, if the change in use will result in an increase in traffic in the immediate area,

disturb the neighbors, or cause a nuisance, for example, in terms of noise or smells, then permission will be required. Check with the planning department as well as the city or county clerk's office to comply with regulations related to home-based businesses.

You may need to consult the local planning office if you are planning to erect a fence on an existing property, especially if there are dimensional or material restrictions in your area. Building new premises always requires planning permission, and the development plan of the area should be checked to see if proposals are acceptable. Office and shop extensions require planning permission, and so will change of use, unless both the present and the proposed business fall within the same use class and are approved within the same zoning restrictions.

What does the planning department look for?

In considering a planning application, the city and county will take into account the character of the area, road safety and traffic congestion, the need to reserve land for other purposes, and the adequacy of water disposal and sewage. It will also consider the suitability of the site, any development plan policies relevant to the application, archaeological implications, and environmental impacts. The department will also be concerned with building regulations, listed historical building and conservation areas, fire regulations, and even crime prevention and security.

MAKING IT HAPPEN

Apply for Planning Permission

Anyone can apply for planning permission.

You may, however, prefer to appoint an agent to carry out the application on your behalf. The agent could be an attorney or architect, for example. If you, as the applicant, are not the true owner or only have part ownership of the property mentioned in the proposal, then you must inform those who do own or partly own it. Planning permission decisions take weeks, with large and complex applications taking longer.

Your first step is to inform the city or county's planning department of your plans. If necessary, your next step will be to ask to review any development plans or building restriction information for your area in order to assess any possible problems. You should then obtain the application form and find out how many copies to submit. You must then decide on the type of permission you require. You may also want to consult neighbors and people who may be affected by the proposal. Finally, you should submit your application, together with all required documentation and the fee.

Types of Planning Permission

Depending upon your state, county, and city, there are several different types of planning permission that may go by different names. Check with your local Planning Department, an architect, or real estate attorney specializing in planning and development to determine the type and name of permission you require. The following are some typical permission descriptions that may or may not apply to your area.

Outline planning permission simply looks to see whether the development is acceptable in principle. It usually applies when the development involves the erection of a building. Detailed drawings are not normally needed for outline planning permission. Permission, if granted, will be subject to certain conditions, and no construction or other work can begin until necessary approvals based on detailed interior and exterior planning documents are gained.

Full planning permission is required if the business intends to change the use of the property, or to legalize existing works which were built without the necessary permission. To obtain full planning permission, all of the details of the proposal should be submitted.

After the Application for Planning Permission

After you have applied, the application will be acknowledged by the Planning Department. At this point, a discrete reference number will be issued. Since planning permission applications are public domain, your application will also be made available to anyone who wishes to see it. A report will be prepared for the planning committee. Ask your Planning Department approximately how long it will take until you might expect a response. Some communities have required deadline dates by which the Planning Department must respond, including providing detailed information addressing any problems or reasons for refusal. Delays may occur if a site visit or further information is required. If the application is granted, the planned changes must be commenced within the prescribed timeframe dictated by the Planning Department. Should that time expire it will be necessary to reapply. When an application is rejected, the applicant must be told why.

Appeal Against Planning Permission Rejection

It is possible to appeal a rejected planning permission proposal. Before appealing, applicants should make every effort to understand the department's objections and make appropriate corrections either by negotiation or amendment. This back-and-forth process can take weeks. It is also advised that you request one planning officer with whom to coordinate. While time consuming, this is a relatively inexpensive option. You may also be able to request an informal hearing before the Planning Department or the city or county council.

WHAT TO AVOID ✗
Not Getting the Right Advice

Planning permission is a complex area, and it is essential that you get the right advice. It is a good idea, if you are at all unsure, to use an architect, land surveyor, or attorney to assist with the proposal. If in doubt, applicants should consult an expert or the local planning office. If a business proceeds without planning permission, the consequences can be serious.

Not Being Prepared

The more prepared you are the less likely it will be that delays will occur. It will be important to find out when the city or county's planning committee dates are and to ensure that the information submitted meets the committee timetable. It is advisable not only to consult the neighbors about a planning proposal, but also to contact other affected parties, such as the water and sewage company, highway authority, and the Health and Safety Department. It is also important to make sure that the information submitted with the application is complete and easily understood. It will be helpful to ask what additional information, such as photographs, may be required.

Worrying That It Is Taking Too Long

Planning permission is a tedious and stressful process. It's easy to lose your sense of proportion when the process seems to be dragging on for weeks. Remember that planning officers have a difficult job to do and that it pays to be patient and respectful in any dealings with them.

Not Abiding by the Rules

Once the planning permission is obtained, it is essential that you make sure that any work carried out is as described in the approved plans and fulfills all building regulations.

Giving False Information

It is a serious offense to give false information or to withhold information, in order to successfully obtain a lawful development certificate. Penalties can include a fine imprisonment.

SEE ALSO
A Guide to Building Regulations (p. 66)
Health (p. 457)

Insurance Coverage for a Business

GETTING STARTED

Your business needs insurance against risks that might threaten its profitability, such as the theft of equipment, or a work-related injury to staff. Small businesses are more vulnerable to the impact of these incidents, as they often do not have the resources for unexpected expenditure.

This actionlist tells you what insurance your business is legally required to have and describes some optional types of insurance that you could use to protect your business.

FAQS

What insurance is compulsory for businesses?

As soon as you establish your business and before you begin active operations, you should speak with an insurance agent or broker to determine the insurance regulations for your type of business. The agent or broker will be able to tell you the types of insurance that are required, as well as those that are available and may be recommended.

Businesses are required to carry Workers' Compensation insurance immediately upon hiring any employees. Each state has specific business insurance requirements, so you may also want to visit the Web site of your Secretary of State or your state's Department of Commerce to find out more.

If your business is highly complex and can be considered high risk, it may also be in your best interests to talk with an attorney specializing in insurance law to help you determine your coverage options and requirements.

Any injuries or illness relating to motor vehicle accidents that occur while your employees are working for you may be covered separately by your motor vehicle insurance. All vehicles, whether cars, commercial vehicles, or motorcycles, that are used on the road must be insured for minimum third party liability. Insurers normally need to know who will be using the vehicle for business purposes (especially any drivers whose age is lower than 25), what the business use entails, who owns the vehicle, and how it will be used. Make sure you check the licenses of all your drivers. Any serious motor convictions must be advised to your insurer.

What is the difference between insurance agents and brokers?

An insurance agent customarily has an agreement with an insurance carrier, writes policies through that company and can provide cost-effective package deals. An insurance broker shops around with numerous insurance carriers, gets the best coverage for the best price, and can obtain hard to get special coverages.

MAKING IT HAPPEN

Choosing an Insurer

Many new business owners begin by speaking with their personal insurance agent. Find out whether your agent has specific experience in providing business insurance to organizations such as yours or if the company for which they work offers the broad base of coverage your business will need.

After talking with your insurance agent, talk with other business owners, your local Chamber of Commerce members and others to find out with whom they are doing business.

Using the services of a reputable insurance agent or broker will help you find the best product to suit your requirements, at the best value. Agent and broker's services are usually free. If a fee is being added, consider changing agents or brokers.

Different Types of Business Insurance

The types of business insurance available cover a wide variety of needs. The following are just a sample of the types of insurance coverage you should consider. Eventually, as well as looking at the insurance coverage needs for your business, you should ask your agent or broker about the types of health, dental, vision, and other insurance benefit packages you might make available to your employees.

Property

Property insurance, as the name suggests, covers a business for loss or damage to property caused, for example, by fire, flood, theft, or vandalism. Note, however, that damage caused by certain types of natural disasters, such as earthquakes and hurricanes, is often excluded. You should also check to be sure your policy covers computers and phone systems; these may be considered "special property" and require extra, or specialized, equipment coverage. You should cover all your property, including buildings (if you own them), contents, stock, and fixtures. If you rent, ask to see the landlord's insurance policy and check the range of protection that is in place. Property insurance can be important if you manufacture, repair, install, or even retail goods.

Computer Insurance

Computer insurance policies cover you for breakdowns and for loss of information. Check that your insurance covers the computer environment, including the e-mail and Internet access system. Different types of engineering insurance policies are available for machinery. This can cover breakdown and statutory inspection cover.

General Liability

Liability, or casualty, insurance protects your business in case of bodily injury to a person or damage to a person's property that occurs on your premises and/or for which you might be held legally responsible. For example, if a client fell down and injured himself in your office, your liability insurance could cover his heath care costs and expenses. Likewise, if you break something while in a client's home or office, the cost of replacing the item could be covered.

Business Income/Extra Expense

This type of insurance protects your company's income and overheads and compensates you for extra costs incurred and trading profits lost if your business suffers serious disruption, for example, after a fire. You are usually covered for an interruption period of up to 12 months from the date of any loss or damage. If damage to your office would increase the cost of working, you can claim added expense, such as the cost of fitting temporary offices, removal costs and expenses, and increased rent and rates.

Directors and Officers Insurance (D&O)

A director or officer of a company can be sued personally over an increasingly wide range of matters relating to the business. The personal liability of a director is unlimited. Legally, the directors of a company and the company itself are separate entities, and so both may be defendants, separately or jointly, in any legal action or prosecution. To protect the personal assets of individuals and, crucially, to cover the costs of their defense, directors' and officers' insurance is widely used. Directors' and officers' insurance extends to protect the company, rather than leaving it to fund its own defense, acting as a mechanism that also protects the value of a director's personal holding in the company.

Public Liability

Public liability covers you against accidents to members of the public or damage to property that occurs as a result of your business activities. It also covers any related legal costs. This type of insurance is compulsory for certain types of business, for example, health and fitness instructors.

Professional Liability/Errors and Omissions (E&O)

Professional liability insurance, also known as errors and omissions or malpractice insurance, covers you against being sued for giving poor advice or having been in some way negligent. This insurance is obligatory in certain professions such as medicine, law, accounting, and financial services. It is now common in areas such as management and computer consulting, engineering, and design. Coverage usually includes breach of professional duty, breach of copyright, breach of confidentiality, libel and slander, and loss of documents.

Product Liability
Product liability insurance works on the same principle as professional liability insurance, protecting you against claims arising from faulty products that you have sold, manufactured, or installed.

Key Man
Key man cover pays a benefit to the business if a key employee, for example, a business partner, is lost through death or incapacity that would otherwise result in financial hardship for the business.

Disability
Disability, or loss of income, insurance plans cover employees in the event of long-term sickness, paying a percentage of their salaries during the period of incapacity. This relieves your business of the burden of paying for a sick employee. The benefit is paid tax-free after a deferred period that is selected by the policyholder and is paid until retirement, recovery, or death.

This type of insurance is especially important if you work for yourself (a one-person business). Be sure you are covered if your illness or incapacity prevents you from doing the work you currently do, since many policies only cover you if you cannot work at all.

Home Office
A growing number of start-up businesses begin in a person's home. Home office insurance may be needed as ordinary homeowners' insurance policies will not usually cover business liabilities and office equipment.

WHAT TO AVOID
Not Taking Time to Think Clearly
Take time to think clearly about the amount of insurance cover you need. Insure stock for its replacement cost price, without any addition for profit. Plant and machinery should normally be insured on a "replacement as new" basis.

Not Taking Out Sufficient Cover
If you have too little cover, an insurance company can reduce any claim by the percentage to which you are underinsured.

Inappropriate Deductible on Your Insurance Policy
Most insurance policies require you to pay a deductible, covering the first part of any loss. Make sure the deductible on your policy is appropriate. You can often negotiate a reduction in premiums by agreeing to a higher deductible. If most of your claims fall beneath the deductible threshold, you should consider switching to a policy with a lower deductible, but remember, it will cost you more. On the other hand, you may want to avoid making claims just above the deductible, if they would mean increased premiums in subsequent years.

SEE ALSO
A Guide to Building Regulations (p. 66)
A Guide to Health and Safety at Work (p. 77)
Buying a Business Property (p. 61)
Health (p. 457)
Renting a Business Property (p. 58)

Complying with Fire Safety Regulations

GETTING STARTED
As well as endangering life, a fire can be a serious blow to any business. This actionlist will give suggestions on how you can prevent fires breaking out and measures you can take to minimize damage and danger should one occur. Businesses also have legal obligations to protect people in the workplace, and this is also explained.

FAQS
Who can tell me about my legal obligations?
In the United States, fire safety is mainly regulated by each individual state and thus varies across the country. Most states have either public safety offices or a fire marshall's office that oversees and enforces legislation. The Occupational Safety and Health Administration (OSHA) approves and monitors state guidelines on a federal level and has a helpful Web site.

How do I carry out a risk assessment?
You can do this within a general health and safety risk assessment, or as a separate exercise. The risk assessment must consider features of the workplace, such as dimensions and layout, substances used or stored on site, the maximum number of occupants, the activities carried out there, and any other relevant circumstances.

Look for hazards such as combustibles, flammables, and sources of ignition, and consider who will be at risk because of them. Look for places where fire will spread rapidly, or where people might be trapped or injured trying to escape. Use your findings to try to reduce the chances of a fire occurring and to take steps to reduce death, injury, or damage to property, should a fire occur. Draw up an emergency plan, detailing what to do in the event of a fire.

Inform employees of the assessment findings. If the workplace is shared with other employers, inform them of the risks that are found and the action taken (or required) to address them. Cooperation is the key, especially where shared escape routes, fire alarm systems, and so on, are involved.

MAKING IT HAPPEN
Reduce Risks

It is often possible to reduce risks quite cheaply, for example, by removing or reducing the amount of combustible/flammable materials, moving stored materials to a safer location, and removing or reducing the sources of ignition. Materials should not be stored in corridors, stairways, or gangways or obstruct an exit. Waste should not be allowed to build up and should be stored away from the premises until disposed of. Waste and rubbish are major fire hazards. If structural features of the workplace add to the risk, the cost of remedial work may be too high to justify. In such cases, the funds may be better spent on equipment for early detection and/or automatic fire fighting.

Detect and Warn of Fire
Detection of a fire may be rapid and straightforward in an open plan office or rooms that are always occupied. Fires in storage areas and places that are often unoccupied could become serious before they are detected, and you may need to fit fire detection equipment in such areas.

You must have a way of giving warning in case of fire. This need not be a fire alarm system; a shouted warning, hand-bell, or whistle may be sufficient, as long as it is appropriate to the premises. Any warning method should provide audible warning throughout the workplace. The warning method should be tested, and a record kept that this has been done.

Identify Escape Routes
Make sure there are safe means of escape from the premises. The normal ways in and

out will often be sufficient. A building that has recently passed a building inspection (and that has not since been modified) will normally have acceptable means of escape. The distance people have to travel to an escape route should be limited, so they reach safety quickly. A reasonable evacuation time is two and a half minutes. When timing this, consideration should be given to what people must do before leaving, for example, shutting down machines, taking security measures, and checking that areas are clear. If employees know exactly what to do, they will be able to clear the workplace more quickly. If times are too long, rearranging the workplace may cost less than providing extra escape routes.

Doors should ideally open in the direction of escape. They must open in the direction of escape when at the foot of a staircase, or if used by more than 50 people. Fire exits and escape routes must be useable at all times. Doors should be quick and easy to open without the use of a key. Lighting should be adequate: readily available flashlights may be sufficient in a small workplace, but emergency lighting units may be necessary in larger premises.

Exit signs may be required to mark the route. These should have graphic symbols and directional arrows on a green background. Text may also be used. Locate signs where necessary to indicate the route.

Have Means of Fighting Fire
Fire-fighting equipment, such as fire extinguishers, should be available as appropriate and staff should be aware of its location and how to use it. There are several different types of extinguisher—water, foam, dry powder, and carbon dioxide—for different types of fire. They are usually color coded by type for easy identification. A modern extinguisher will be predominantly red with a small area colored to denote the contents, with pictograms to indicate the type of fire it is suited for. Sprinkler systems are triggered off in the event of a fire, and tackle the blaze early on. For certain new buildings under construction, fitting of sprinkler systems is compulsory. Fire blankets can be effective

in putting out a fire but require the right technique in use. The equipment should be visually checked at least monthly, and the check should be recorded. It should be tested annually, usually by outside contractors, and the test recorded.

Train Staff Training on Fire Safety
An employer may nominate someone to help with fire safety measures but still has overall responsibility. Staff must know who the nominee is. That person may need training, including using fire extinguishers. It is increasingly common within the workplace to appoint a Fire Safety Officer. All employees should be familiar with escape routes, how to give the alarm, where the fire extinguishers are, and how to use them. Written instructions should be displayed in the workplace and should also be given to every employee. New employees and anyone else spending some time on site should be taken through the procedure verbally by the person responsible for fire safety. Staff should also be made aware of any particular hazards and how they can ensure their own and other people's safety.

Act in the Event of Fire
A person discovering a fire should raise the alarm at once. Call the fire department or 911; a person may be designated to do this upon hearing the alarm. Attempt to extinguish the fire if practicable, but it must be stressed to everyone that they must not put themselves at risk. Ensure that certain parts of the building have been cleared (a previously designated person may be responsible for this). Implement a system of checking that everyone has left the building, possibly by a designated person taking a roll call at a predetermined fire evacuation location. Don't take risks, use elevators, or return to the building after it has been evacuated.

WHAT TO AVOID
Not Reviewing Risk Assessments
Risk assessments should be reviewed regularly, especially after changes in the workplace, activity, or staffing have occurred.

Not Getting the Right Advice

The Occupational Safety and Health Administration (OSHA) or your state public safety office can give advice related to specific manufacturing processes.

Not Spreading the Word

Draw up a fire preparedness plan, including responsibilities and fire instructions, and ensure that all employees receive a copy.

SEE ALSO

A Guide to Building Regulations (p. 66)
Buying a Business Property (p. 61)
Health (p. 457)
Renting a Business Property (p. 58)

A Guide to Health and Safety at Work

GETTING STARTED

Businesses have a legal responsibility to protect the health and safety of their staff and others on their premises, and there is a range of laws to ensure that they do this. This actionlist explains the main steps you must take to ensure your business complies with health and safety regulations. It contains guidance on policy, ensuring that your fire safety plan is adequate, record keeping, providing personal protective equipment, establishing a first aid procedure, and setting up a safety committee.

FAQS

What are my legal obligations with regard to health and safety?

The Occupational Safety and Health Act of 1970 established legislation to ensure that all workplaces would guarantee that the health and safety of employees be adequately protected by the employer. While this legislation remains in force, individual states have enacted their own legislation to ensure workplace and worker health and safety.

You should become familiar with the federal guidelines as well as those of your state. In some cases the federal guidelines will prevail, but in many cases the state guidelines are the basis for inspection, record keeping and other health and safety related policies, and employer expectations. Your state will be able to inform you of the guidelines with which you must comply.

Where can I go for more information?

There are several organizations that provide advice about health and safety, including The Occupational Safety and Health Administration (OSHA), the National Safety Council, and individual state public health and safety offices. The Web sites addresses for these three are given below.

MAKING IT HAPPEN

Understand Fire Regulations

According to OSHA, your organization should have an emergency action or response plan in case of fire or other emergencies. The action plan should include a site plan for the workplace and a description of the actions employers and employees must take to ensure everyone's safety.

The plan should also include a list of the major workplace fire hazards and their proper handling and storage procedures, potential ignition sources (such as welding, smoking, and others) and their control procedures, and the type of fire protection equipment or systems that can control a fire involving them.

Names or job titles of those personnel responsible for maintenance of equipment and systems installed to prevent or control ignitions or fires should be listed along with the names or job titles of those personnel responsible for control of fuel source hazards.

You should examine whether employees are exposed to risk either because of the work they are doing or by the condition of the premises, plant, equipment, or vehicles. You are also responsible for any risk posed to others, such as contractors and members of the public, which might arise out of the nature of your work or the state of your premises.

To assist your organization in determining the extent of risk and your level of preparedness, you may want to refer to the "Ten Point Checklist for Emergency Preparedness" developed at the University of Tennessee Safety Center and available through the National Safety Council. The checklist comprehensively addresses the categories of Warning Signals, Communication, Evacuation, Utility and Electrical Controls, Fire Suppression, Severe Storm/Tornado Shelter, Management, Housekeeping, Bomb Threats, and Security. After completing the checklist, including comments, you will be able to prioritize the immediate and longer term steps your organization should take to insure the safety of the employees and the property.

Keep Records and Report Accidents

Deaths, major injuries, and dangerous occurrences must be reported immediately, and followed up with a report submitted to the enforcing authority within ten days. An accident which leaves a worker unable to do the full range of their normal duties for more than three days must be reported within ten days. Records must be kept for three years from the date of the incident. The enforcing authority may request to see them.

Record keeping is a crucial component of health and safety compliance. In most cases, organizations with ten or more employees are required to comply with OSHA record keeping regulations.

You must document and report the recordable injuries and illnesses of all employees on your payroll, whether they are labor, executive, hourly, salaried, part-time, seasonal, or migrant workers. You also must document and report the recordable injuries and illnesses that occur to workers who are not on your payroll if you supervise them on a day-to-day basis. If your establishment is organized as a sole proprietorship or partnership, the owner or partners are not considered employees for record keeping purposes.

Self-employed individuals who are working on your premises may not be covered by the OSHA requirements. However, if contract or temporary personnel are working on your site and have an injury or illness, you may be required to provide documentation if you supervise them on a day-to-day basis. You and the contracting or personnel supply service should coordinate your efforts to ensure that each injury or illness is recorded only once.

Provide Protective Equipment

Employers must provide suitable safety equipment (such as hard hats, reinforced footwear, and reflective jackets) for use at work wherever there are risks that cannot be adequately controlled in other ways. You will have to assess what type of equipment is suitable to offer protection against the hazards of the job and to ensure compatibility where more than one item of equipment is needed.

You must make sure that the personal protective equipment is kept clean and in good repair, stored correctly, and replaced when necessary. Your employees must be given adequate information about the equipment and be properly trained to use it.

First Aid

Employers must have facilities to offer first aid to employees if they are injured or become ill at work.

Your first task is to assess the level of first aid likely to be needed. To do this, consider the nature and degree of risk, the number of employees involved, and the location of the business. Extra consideration should be given to employees working in isolated locations, travelling through remote areas, or using potentially dangerous tools and machinery.

The procedures for first aid should be detailed in your health and safety policy, and all staff should be made aware of them. You should also set up a first aid post.

Emergency Response Teams and Training

Emergency response teams are the first lines of defense in emergencies. The National Safety Council recommends that, before assigning team members, employers must ensure that the participating employees are physically capable of performing any assigned duties. The number of teams to be trained will depend upon the size, complexity, and activities of your organization.

Emergency preparedness training should be provided to all management and employees, in addition to the specialized training provided to emergency response team members. The better prepared your workforce is for an emergency, the less likely unnecessary accidents or injuries will occur when an emergency occurs.

At the management level, training should include instruction to managers and supervisors on how to give calm direction and demonstrate their leadership. They must know what to do, what their own responsibilities are, and who is in charge. They should be trained in directing equipment shutdowns and evacuation procedures and in conducting a tally of employees after an evacuation.

Emergency response teams should be thoroughly trained for potential emergencies and their containment. All employees need to know the company's specific emergency procedures, what they are expected to do, from whom they should take direction, and the exact evacuation route from their department.

Employers have an obligation to provide training for new and existing employees as part of the orientation process and ongoing training programs. This needs to cover safety systems used in the workplace, the health and safety policy, and the identity of employees responsible for first aid, fire safety, and the reporting of accidents.

The National Safety Council also recommends that emergency preparedness plans should be tested at least annually with mock drills and facility evacuations.

Secure Premises

Contractors and visitors to your premises are entitled to the same considerations of health and safety as your employees, and they should follow the same safety procedures. The premises should also be secured against unauthorized entry.

WHAT TO AVOID

Not Getting the Right Advice

For more detailed information, as well as practical advice, contact the Occupational Safety and Health Administration (OSHA) or your state public safety office.

Not Keeping Employees Informed

Whether through training programs or posted information throughout the workplace, employees must be kept informed of new regulations, safety procedures, use of safety equipment, security requirements, and so on. The organization should incorporate annual training and review programs to ensure employee safety and to keep employees fully informed of their responsibilities and the actions they need to take.

Not Keeping OSHA or Your State Public Safety Office Informed

Record keeping requirements are legislated for workplace illnesses and injuries. If the organization is not in compliance with the record keeping and reporting requirements, it can lead to expensive fines against the company.

SEE ALSO
A Guide to Building Regulations (p. 66)
Buying a Business Property (p. 61)
Ergonomics at Work (p. 80)
Health (p. 457)
Insurance Coverage for a Business (p. 71)

Ergonomics at Work

GETTING STARTED

Ergonomics concerns the adaptation of equipment, procedures, and surroundings to the people who use them. Its aims involve creating a safe, comfortable, and stress-reduced environment by selecting the right products and systems to customize a workspace for an individual. Ergonomics is normally associated with computer seating and work stations, though it can apply equally to assembly-line work and production, construction, and maintenance.

This actionlist looks at the concept of ergonomics, particularly within the office environment. It then suggests how you might apply the concept to your working surroundings, creating and maintaining a workplace that increases comfort and reduces stress for everyone working in that space.

FAQS

What are the benefits of ergonomics?

Business managers have only recently recognized the benefits ergonomics can bring to their companies. It can improve production and efficiency levels and quality of service, and reduce staff turnover and insurance premiums. Benefits for employees include increased motivation and job satisfaction, less pain and fewer injuries, reduced absenteeism, and general well-being in the workplace.

What can happen if ergonomics are ignored?

If ergonomic practices are not adhered to in the workplace, there may be a number of consequences, ranging from the relatively minor to serious injury. These include general symptoms, such as stress and fatigue, which can build up slowly over a period of time. In some cases, in particular those involving prolonged and repetitive activity, the worker may suffer physical injuries caused by poor posture, applying excessive force, making repetitive movements, and taking too few recovery breaks. Computer-based injuries are commonly known as Repetitive Strain Injury (RSI), Work Related Upper Limb Disorder (WRULD), and Cumulative Trauma Disorder (CTD). RSI includes work-related injuries to the muscles, tendons, and nerves of the limbs; back and wrist injuries are the most common ailments. Workers in construction and maintenance who regularly use vibrating hand tools may suffer hand-arm vibration syndrome (HAVS), the most common of which is "white finger." Employees working with VDUs and computers, or workers doing precise assembly tasks, are prone to blurred vision or unusual eye irritability.

MAKING IT HAPPEN
Ergonomic Awareness

Conduct a diagnostic test of working areas to identify any potential risk factors that may cause discomfort or stress. It is essential to involve all employees in this process, as far as possible, to make them feel they have some control over their working environment. You could start by asking which tasks involve prolonged activity that may lead to physical discomfort, and whether any aspects of the job cause stress. Find out whether particular tasks cause stress or discomfort and which equipment or furniture could improve the working environment.

On the basis of the diagnostic test of the workspace and an awareness of potential problem areas, make the changes necessary. They will help reduce the risk of strain or injury and enhance the working environment. To optimize any ergonomic practices put in place, it is advisable to train employees on the best ways of using the equipment or furniture, as well as on the principles behind it.

Ergonomic Problems in the Workplace

Workplace seating is a common problem and the position and height of chairs and desks are not always suitable. The chair should fit the user, be comfortable, and support the back. No chair is suitable for every worker for every task; therefore adjusting a chair may be essential. Chair backrests and armrests can both help to reduce strain on the back.

Computers and VDUs are another problem area. The glare and/or reflections on monitor screens may make it difficult to read information clearly on the screen. Desks should be positioned perpendicular, rather than parallel, to windows in order to help minimize reflections. Using antiglare filters or screens can also be a useful remedy. Some office lighting, such as unshielded fluorescent strip lighting, is not suitable for use with VDUs. Indirect lighting should be used, such as lamps that direct light upwards or lights with suitable diffusers, which provide glare-free lighting for personal computers. Individual task lighting could be provided for hard-copy work.

The temperature in the office needs to be regulated, as the indoor climate can sometimes be too warm, too cool, or drafty. Furthermore, electrical equipment dries the air, and static buildup around a computer screen attracts dust. A comfortable temperature for office work is between 68 and 75 degrees Fahrenheit.

Selecting Ergonomic Equipment

Once risks have been identified, consideration can be given to the design of the workspace. People vary in height and weight, in physical strength, sensory abilities (vision, hearing, and so on), their ability to handle information and make decisions, and general health. It is therefore essential to take account of these attributes when providing a comfortable and safe workspace and equipment.

Choosing ergonomic office furniture is essential if the working environment is to be improved for employees. The manager should be aware of the performance criteria and standards of various office products, know what they are looking for, and buy from a reputable, knowledgeable manufacturer. Going for the cheapest option may not always result in obtaining the right piece of equipment.

Devising a product check list, like the one below, is a good idea before selecting office furniture. For example:

- Is the item convenient and easy to use?
- Is the item easy to adjust, and does it come with clear instructions?
- Are the materials of the product durable and of good quality?
- Does it offer good fit and comfort?
- Does the item cause any discomfort if used for a prolonged period of time?
- Is the item made by a reputable manufacturer?

A number of manufacturers sell ergonomic office equipment. Using ergonomic office equipment may prevent injury in the first place, avoid an injury recurring, or be useful for workers with disabilities. Examples are an ergonomic mouse to reduce strain on the wrist and lower arm muscles; a keyboard to reduce RSI by using palm rests; and antiglare computer screens to reduce eyestrain.

Best Practice

No amount of ergonomic furniture and equipment in the workplace can compensate for bad practice. It should be ensured that every employee takes a number of preventative measures to reduce the risks of fatigue, stress, and work-related injuries in the workplace. This can be achieved by holding ergonomic awareness training sessions or distributing leaflets with information on good practice.

Highlight the important areas for improvement and point out the benefits, for example, improving posture can result in reduced risk of back and wrist injuries. Suggest other simple measures, such as taking frequent short breaks throughout the working day (which is far better than taking one or two long breaks). This can be combined with doing frequent stretching exercises and breathing exercises to loosen up the muscles and reduce tension.

There are a few ergonomic tips which, if followed by you and your employees, should help reduce the risks of injury and stress. When you lift heavy loads, keep your knees bent and your back straight. Avoid extremes in reaching, twisting, or lifting, and keep any items you use frequently within arm's reach.

Adjust the backrest and armrests of the chair you use to allow you to sit in an upright position without slouching. The backrest should follow the natural 'S' curve of your spine. The height of the chair should be adjusted so that your wrists, hands, and forearms are horizontal with the desk. Your feet should be placed flat on the floor; use a footrest if you need to. Keep your head up and your shoulders relaxed. Your legs and feet should fit comfortably under the desk, so remove any obstacles that prevent this.

Your computer monitor should be at a comfortable distance from the eyes. Make sure there is space on the desk to rest hands and wrists, so that you can keep movement of the wrists to a minimum. Adjust the brightness and color contrast of your computer screen and make sure that all screens are reflection-free and clean. Avoid long periods of repetitive activity; for example, alternate computer-based work with other tasks, such as filing, telephoning, or photocopying.

Relevant Legislation

Although applying ergonomic practices to the workplace is a matter of common sense, it is the business's responsibility to be aware of health and safety legislation in order to create and maintain a safe working environment. In the United States, the Occupational Safety and Health Administration (OSHA) sets the standards, which are outlined in the Occupational and Safety and Health Act of 1970 and various subsequent amendments.

WHAT TO AVOID
Doing Too Little Too Late

Ergonomics should be used in the workplace to help prevent problems. Ergonomic awareness should not just be introduced after a problem becomes apparent, although this is often a common reason for introducing ergonomic practices.

Insufficient Training

Running staff training programs is crucial to raising awareness and gaining commitment to ergonomic practices. Employees should be trained on the best ways to use ergonomic furniture and equipment in their workspace. The reasons for adjusting the equipment to suit their needs should be highlighted.

Not Selecting the Right Equipment

Make sure that the ergonomic equipment you select is suitable for your business and your staff. Carry out a diagnostic test of the workplace before making any decision. An ergonomic consultant could be employed if it is not clear what the best ergonomic practices for the workplace are, or if complicated changes need to be made.

SEE ALSO
A Guide to Health and Safety at Work (p. 77)
Buying a Business Property (p. 61)
Health (p. 457)
Renting a Business Property (p. 58)

Establishing and Maintaining Your Home Office

GETTING STARTED

Many people choose to work from home these days, and most new businesses start off in the home of their owner-managers. If you are thinking about basing your company in your house to begin with, you may need to get used to a new way of working, especially if you've previously been working in a more formal, structured setting. To start, ask yourself the following questions:

- Can I handle the social isolation of a home office on a full-time basis?
- Am I a self-starter?
- How do I rate as a decision-maker, organizer, bookkeeper, and secretary?
- Could I separate business and personal life if both were under the same roof?
- Am I a workaholic and would an office at home worsen that problem?

FAQS

Is working from home as wonderful as it sounds?

Yes and no. For convenience, cost, and comfort, there's nothing quite like a home office. Low overheads, no commute hassles, no office politics, and setting your own hours are a few of the plusses. On the minus side, there's only you—and if you're not disciplined, you'll be spending more time with the kids, the pets, or snacking than working where you belong. It can be a simple formula for failure.

How can I make a home-based business seem professional to customers?

It depends on the type of business, but start with a professional attitude and then buy some good-looking business cards and stationery. Think about adding an attractive logo and using a two-color design on business cards, letterheads, and envelopes. Having a well-produced flyer or brochure that describes your business is also a plus. Quality customer service will do the rest.

E-commerce is relatively easy to conduct from a home office, especially with a Web site that attracts customers. Clients need not know whether you work at home or in a sophisticated office building, so long as you get the job done for them. As with your other materials, the Web site should reflect the personality and professionalism of your business.

What sort of investment is necessary to outfit a home office?

This, too, depends on the type of activity you will be doing—whether it be business or telecommuting, or a personal or family office. But generally, spending between $2,000 and $4,000 should make you well equipped and comfortable. Make a list and a budget beforehand. You don't want to blow your entire savings on setting up the office, then have nothing to spend on attracting business.

MAKING IT HAPPEN
Plan the Layout of Your Office

Planning a home office involves decisions about where to locate the office, how to decorate it, and how to furnish it. You should give lots of thought to this, as it will be the hub of a small business. Some people even make a scale drawing of the room they intend to use, then place to-scale furniture in there to work out the best layout.

Take Account of Tax Considerations

As you're planning to use the office for a small business, most government tax agencies allow you to deduct certain expenses connected to the business. For that reason, the office must be completely dedicated to the business and not merely a spare bedroom with a fold-up desk and your cordless phone. Good record-keeping is very important if you plan to deduct expenses and part of the mortgage interest, utilities, and phone bills for business activity.

Make Sure You're Comfortable and Have the Right Equipment

Office décor is important. Besides getting the right atmosphere (lighting, paint/wallpaper, floor covering), you may need to run more phone and electrical outlets into the room to support the office equipment. Beyond that, having comfortable, functional furniture will allow you to work productively.

Your package of office equipment will depend on your level of activity, but will probably include computer(s) and peripherals, software, phones and phone service for voice, fax, and computer, and maybe even a separate copier and/or scanner. Add a digital camera if you plan to put photos of yourself or your products on your Web site. Consider upgrading connections to the Internet, rather than relying on a computer modem to your Internet provider, especially if you are engaged in e-commerce.

Finally, there are the necessary office supplies and extra storage space for files and records to consider.

Impose Proper Discipline on Yourself

One of the most difficult aspects of the home office is the home itself. How easy it is to tend to house chores, watch TV, sweep the yard, get involved with family things, snack, and otherwise avoid the work that awaits you in your office. Two factors will help avoid the home trap: being excited about your office space and the work—and discipline. Set regular office hours, have a separate business phone, organize your time, and stick to the schedules.

Don't Let Yourself Get Isolated

Being isolated in your home office, you may develop a tendency to cocoon yourself in there or to avoid reaching out, both of which can be unhealthy.

Having a business gives you plenty of opportunity to break away from the office to meet other people socially and professionally. Even if much of your business is conducted by phone and computer, it's still important to network. Invite customers and prospective customers to lunch, if they happen to do business nearby. Join a civic group or professional organization to stay connected and also to generate local interest in your business. Get physical exercise away from the home. Consider taking a class. All these things will help keep you connected, bring in new ideas, and generate lots of personal energy—things you'll value when working alone.

WHAT TO AVOID
Going Halfway with the Office Arrangement

Starting a home office on the dining room table is not a good idea, nor is committing only half-heartedly to making a guestroom into a real office. If you don't treat the office seriously, there's a better than even chance you won't take your work seriously either.

Carve out a separate space and dedicate it as the office. You'll feel better and your work will benefit from that decision.

Succumbing to Workaholic Syndrome

If, while working in an office setting, you've had a tendency to stay there until the work is done, operating from home is a workaholic's dream come true. With the office only a few rooms away, there's a temptation to "get one last thing done" after dinner or on a weekend.

It's important to be professional about your business, but it's also important that you don't let the office become your new home. Set hours, try to manage your workflow into those hours; then shut the door and put up the "closed" sign.

Family Issues

Lots of women see working at home as the answer to two issues—making a living and raising a family. If it were easy to mix kids and work, parents would have been doing it at their business offices long ago.

That said, it isn't entirely impossible either. The trick is balance. You can't afford to be at the beck and call of your children, but you certainly don't want them to feel totally ignored. Racing from the office to untangle toys and do laundry every hour will soon turn your work world upside-down. Closing the door and ignoring the family will have an equally unfortunate effect.

Obviously, day care is an option. Consider it for the days that you might schedule your most critical tasks. On days you set aside for errands, such as paying bills, bookkeeping, research on the Internet, and so forth, you might more easily accommodate the family being around.

Lacking Certain Office Job Skills

When working for other companies, you relied on others with jobs that complemented your own. As your own business-person, at your own business office, you have a lot more duties besides the specific ones that "bring home the bacon." You will be responsible for executive and marketing decisions, financial and administrative details and deadlines, as well as clerical and reception work. Until your business becomes profitable enough to employ other people, you're it.

This is where a business plan makes sense. You need to work out the details of how you'll charge for your products or services. Be careful to figure in the "cost of doing business," which includes the clerical and administrative things, too. Add in a "fudge factor" and some profit. Assuming that you'll work a 40-hour week, set your sights on making a living in 30 hours, then use the other ten hours to take care of the other parts of the business—marketing, promotion, billing, bookkeeping, and business errands.

If you feel you lack the skills to juggle all of these things, or don't have the interest in becoming your own secretary, perhaps you're not cut out for a home business. But if you want to give it a try, you can certainly learn what you need to know about the care and feeding of a small business from books, the Internet, a local chapter of SCORE (Senior Corps of Retired Executives), or a nearby community college.

SEE ALSO
Buying a Business Property (p. 61)
Computers, Information Technology, and E-commerce (p. 440)
Drawing Boundaries: How to Manage Working at Home (p. 86)
Renting a Business Property (p. 58)

Drawing Boundaries: How to Manage Working at Home

GETTING STARTED

Many small businesses are run from the home of the owner-manager. Working from home has become much easier over recent years, especially as technology has become more sophisticated, but for some people (especially those who have been used to working in larger companies) it can take a while to get used to working in a less-structured setting. This actionlist offers some advice on how to get the best from working at home.

FAQS

Will I be able to concentrate on my work when at home? There are so many distractions.

Setting up a suitable work environment and creating boundaries is of vital importance when working from home. It's hopeless trying to balance your laptop on your knee in the kitchen while attempting to avoid intrusions from family or friends; you need to set rules for yourself and others so that everyone can support your efforts rather than sabotage them.

I'm really looking forward to being my own boss, but also enjoy very much the buzz of being in the office. How can I find this level of stimulation?

If you are an extrovert and enjoy the energy of having other people around, it's important to recognize and prepare for this. You could try planning a certain number of days in the office and balance these with quieter, more productive days at home. If you are self-employed, you may need to schedule visits and meetings sufficiently regularly for you to feel involved with and energized by others.

MAKING IT HAPPEN

Plan, Plan, Plan

Once people get used to working from home, they often find it preferable to working in an office. However, to be successful, you need to plan ahead. You will need all the elements of a "real" office: furniture, computer, software, telephone, fax, an e-mail account, and so on. Spend some time setting up your office, because you will probably spend much more time in it than you imagine. Make sure you have a dedicated telephone line so that calls related to work and home don't get confused. Experiment with different office layouts until you feel comfortable with your arrangements.

Create Boundaries

If you have other people at home, make sure you create boundaries around the time you set aside for working. Nonwork interruptions can be frustrating when you're trying to complete a task. Set up boundaries by establishing in advance how you want to manage your time at home, including considerations like the beginning and ending of your working day. It also helps to have a separate room to call your office, with a door you can close so you won't be disturbed. Stick to your guns and people will soon get the message.

If your work requires you to receive visitors, try to find an area where they won't be distracted by your domestic arrangements. Having to ignore the pile of laundry on the kitchen floor is disconcerting when the point of the meeting is anything but domestic. If you are unable to avoid such situations, find a local hotel or restaurant where you can meet for an hour or two. Again, this is about creating boundaries that will enable you to maintain focus and create an impression of professionalism.

Establish a Routine

It is important to differentiate your day between being "at work" and "at home." If your working and resting time becomes confused, it can feel as if you are always on duty, and when you do take a break you may feel guilty that you are not finishing a project. This differentiation comes naturally when you have to travel to and from work. In the absence of this, you need to provide the means of making this shift. It could be signaled by a routine: making a cup of coffee, taking it to your desk, closing your door, and switching on the computer. Once you've done this a few times, this routine creates the boundary within which you can work effectively.

Plan your day so you don't find yourself wasting time. The advantage of working from home is that you have greater control over interruptions. You're no longer a target for passing coworkers to stop and ask you for information or help. A great deal of time is wasted in these "Oh, by the way..." moments, which happen mostly because you are accessible or visible.

Take a Break

Make sure you take breaks throughout the day. It's commonly understood that powers of concentration diminish after about 20 minutes, and continuing to work after this happens can lead to a point where thinking becomes a struggle. Taking a break, perhaps a short walk, can reenergize your thinking capability. Of course breaks need to be balanced by the need to be productive. Try not to get distracted by picking up something else that needs doing. You'll only end up wasting time and lowering your efficiency by spreading your energies too thinly.

Maintain Your Work/Life Balance

Make sure you plan for the end of the day too. It's far too easy to remain sitting in your workspace well into the evening and ignore the private side of your life. Keeping a work/life balance is just as important in your home as it is in an organizational setting.

Find Out about Your Tax Status

If you are self-employed, you will find that having an office at home may allow you to take income tax deductions. Tax relief may be available on your mortgage interest, heating and telephone bills, and the cost of capital equipment and services needed to support your business. The Internal Revenue Service or your accountant will guide you on what tax benefits you qualify for.

WHAT TO AVOID
Losing Your Focus

For those who enjoy dynamic environments and the energy of being in a busy office, working from home may not be enjoyable. It is tempting for such people to create dynamism for themselves by finding activities that distract them from their own company. Flitting around from task to task can create a feeling of being in the flow but may not be very productive. Time spent at the beginning of the day creating a "to do" list can focus your energy and ensure that your day's activities produce a valuable output.

Not Switching Off

It is very easy for people to work beyond the call of duty when the office is located in the home, especially during the hectic first stages of a new business. "I'll just go and answer a few e-mails..." can become a lengthy session in front of the computer that erodes private time. Try to discipline yourself to keep to the rules you've set, and make only occasional exceptions.

Losing Track of Time

If you derive energy from being with people, you may naturally turn to the telephone as a substitute for their presence around you. It's easy to pass much of the day on the telephone and find that the concrete tasks you have to do get pushed into the evening. Again, this is a question of discipline. Give yourself time when you can interact with others, but keep control of it. A large clock on the wall in front of you can be a good reminder of how long you are spending on each activity.

SEE ALSO
Establishing and Maintaining Your Home Office (p. 83)

FIGURING IT OUT

Financing a New Business

GETTING STARTED

New businesses need finance to cover the cost of equipment and expenses before sales generate enough cash to make the operation self-supporting. This actionlist describes the main ways of financing your business. It explains how to work out the amount of finance you need, and what proportion of debt to equity is advisable.

FAQS

What is an angel investor?

An angel investor is an individual who is willing to invest money in a business. The amount available from angels is usually much less than from venture capitalists, but they are often willing to take bigger risks.

What is equity finance?

Equity, or shareholder capital, is the money introduced into a business by the owners. If it is a company, then the equity is introduced in exchange for shares. Investors expect a share of the business's profit. In the case of limited companies, this takes the form of dividends. The person starting a business will normally introduce equity capital, but it can also be raised from external investors, including business angels and venture capitalists. Investors will be looking for an annual dividend, which often can be quite small, and a good return when they sell their shares. Equity is best suited, therefore, to businesses that expect to grow quickly.

What is loan finance?

Loan finance is money that is borrowed from a finance company, such as a bank. Loans are repaid over a period of time, at either fixed or variable rates of interest. The lender will usually require security against a business or personal asset. Terms can vary in length from one year to 25 years, and will usually be determined by the asset that is being financed. The interest rate will reflect the lender's perception of the risk in providing the loan. Loan finance can be provided in different ways.

An overdraft is money that a business can borrow from a bank up to an agreed limit. It provides a business with short-term finance, effectively by running a negative balance on the bank account. This is a particularly good way of funding short-term requirements, such as providing working capital during the course of each month.

Term loans are funds borrowed for a fixed term. Usually, such loans are repayable in equal installments over the term of the loan, although sometimes they can be repaid in a lump sum at the end of the term. Term loans are more attractive than overdrafts for long-term borrowing because repayments are fixed and the cost is usually less. However, lenders are increasingly writing into the small print that term loans are repayable on demand. If the loan has been used to finance capital assets, this could cause problems.

Creditor finance is an excellent way of "borrowing" money, effectively at no cost. Typically, suppliers may give 30 to 60 days' credit for their goods or services before payment is due. If you can sell your product or service and get paid before paying your creditors, then it will generate cash for the business. Your business may have to establish a trading record before credit is given, and it can be withdrawn at any time.

Debtor finance is particularly useful if your business is growing rapidly and is providing credit accounts to its customers. Instead of waiting for your own customers to pay your invoices within a 30- or 60-day period, you can use the services of a third party invoice discounting or factoring firm. Factoring can be an expensive way of speeding up cash flow, but it may reduce administration costs since the factor normally takes on the role of invoice clerk.

Capital asset finance can often be done

through "off-balance-sheet" finance. There are different ways of doing this. Financial leasing allows you to finance the use of an asset rather than owning it. The equipment remains the property of the leasing company; the business has the legal right to use the equipment for the period of the lease, provided that the lease payments are up to date. In a lease purchase arrangement, you have an option to purchase the equipment at the end of the lease period. Through hire purchase, you pay regular installments to a third party, normally a finance house, to purchase ownership of plant and machinery from a supplier. The finance house will own the equipment throughout the period of the agreement, until the last installment has been paid.

MAKING IT HAPPEN
Work Out How Much Capital You Need
The working capital of a business is its current assets (typically stock, cash at the bank, and debtors) minus its current liabilities (typically trade creditors and your bank overdraft). This information is summarized on the balance sheet, although this only gives a snapshot of the working capital requirements at a specific moment in time. Generally, this is the finance required for the short-term running of the business.

The amount of working capital needed will vary during the course of the year and even during the course of a month. You need to allow for the maximum likely working capital requirement. Consideration needs to be given to the variation that can occur within each month. As a rule of thumb, it makes sense to aim for minimum working capital of a month's average sales multiplied by the number of months it takes to collect payment. If you want to be more accurate, then use the following procedure:
1. Determine the average number of weeks that the raw material is in stock.
2. Deduct from this figure the credit period from suppliers, in weeks.
3. Then add the average number of weeks to produce goods or service, the average number of weeks finished goods are in

stock, and the average time customers take to pay.
4. Take the total, and divide it by 52 (the number of weeks in the year). Multiply the result by your estimated sales for the year. The answer will give you a figure for the maximum working capital required.

It would be more accurate to use the cost of sales (direct and fixed), rather than the full selling price, but the above calculation is close enough. If your business is growing, then you need to use the budgeted sales figures, and it is advisable to calculate your working capital needs on a regular basis.

Understand Leverage and Interest Cover
Leverage is the proportion of debt to total capital in the business. The more debt there is relative to equity, the higher the leverage. Introducing more equity, or retaining more of the profits, can reduce the leverage ratio. Most banks look for a leverage of no more than 50%; in other words, your debt should be no more than half of the total capital.

Once you have built up a track record with your bank, you should be able to attract medium-term loans (three- to seven-year loans) to cover the cost of plant and equipment. Established companies may be able to raise long-term debt as a debenture or convertible loan stock, which normally receives a fixed rate of interest and is repayable in full at the end of the term. Long-term debt is usually included with the capital on the balance sheet. The banks will also be more comfortable with a higher leverage, though they still do not like to see it too high. Lease and hire purchase companies will not have as great a concern about leverage as the banks. They will, however, be interested in your cash flow and whether you can afford the repayments.

If you expect to grow quickly and do not have enough of your own money to provide the necessary finance, then you may need to look for equity early on. Banks will be reluctant to keep on providing additional working capital as that simply increases the leverage and increases their risk. Growing too quickly is often known as "over-trading" and is a major cause of business failure. The banks will also want to reassure themselves that you can afford the interest on the loan. So they will look for profits that are at least three or four times the expected interest charge.

WHAT TO AVOID
Not Thinking Ahead
Regularly calculate the total level of funding required for the next year, and split the funding into fixed asset requirements and working capital requirements. Think carefully about the term, the cost, the suitability, the timescale, and any security required. Remember that cost should not be the sole criterion. Keep your lenders informed of your financial position, giving ample warning if you are likely to need to increase your overdraft, for example.

Not Changing with the Times
In times of recession, keep as much of your debt as possible as fixed medium-term loans, and keep your overdraft requirement to the minimum. In times of expansion, when finance is more readily available, it may be more cost effective to use an overdraft.

SEE ALSO
Addressing Cash Flow Problems (p. 114)
Applying for Grants and Funding (p. 99)
Budgeting (p. 435)
Controlling Costs (p. 104)
Drawing Up a Budget (p. 107)
Preparing a Successful Business Plan (p. 96)
Understanding the Role of the Bank (p. 93)
Venture Capital (p. 495)

Understanding the Role of the Bank

GETTING STARTED

Every entrepreneur understands you need a bank account to facilitate payments and receipts, but banks can help your business in other ways too. They provide a range of banking services such as overdrafts, term loans, and equity, as well as financial services like insurance and pensions. This actionlist explains how to choose the best bank for you, and looks at some of the services banks can offer.

FAQS

What is the best way to choose a bank?

Banking is intensely competitive nowadays, so it pays to gather as much information as possible on the services offered. All the major banks have customer charters or codes of practice with full details of their fees, so you should be able to estimate the likely cost to your business. Most banks offer incentives for new customers, for example free banking for the first 12 months; these incentives should only come into play for you as a factor if the decision between banks is marginal. However, most businesses require a loan or overdraft at some point in their development, so ask different banks about this before deciding where to open your business account.

Relationships are critical. You should seek advice and recommendations from professionals and small businesses in the same area, for example, your small business adviser or lawyer, to help find a bank with a good track record. Talk to the bank manager to help you decide whether this is the bank with which you want to work.

How do I open a business bank account?

Opening a business bank account is, like opening any other bank account, pretty straightforward, but be prepared to provide appropriate identification. Bank accounts can generally be opened by depositing a specified amount of money, often as little as $500.00. If you are seeking a loan, banks can often give very fast answers, especially if you need less than $5,000, but expect them to make inquiries about your credit history.

MAKING IT HAPPEN

Borrowing from the Bank

There are two main forms of **loan**; short and long-term. Generally, a short-term loan has a maturity of up to one year. Types of short-term loans include: Working Capital Loans, Accounts Receivable Loans, and other lines of credit. Long-term loans generally have a maturity time of greater than one year but usually less than ten years. Real estate or equipment loans may have a maturity time of 25 years. Long-term loans are used for major business expenses, such as buying a piece of property, construction, furniture, vehicles, etc.

A **loan** is the ideal form of finance to purchase fixed assets. (A fixed asset is a long-term asset of a business, such as a piece of machinery or a building.) The loan term will be geared to the expected working life of the asset being bought. The interest rate may be fixed, which helps accurate budgeting and protects the business's cash flow in times of rising interest rates. Loans with variable rates are also available. The banks can offer insurance to cover disruption to repayments, and loans can be linked to an endowment or pension policy with life and disability coverage also available.

Ask the bank to confirm the loan terms and conditions in writing and analyze them carefully before proceeding. When considering loans, banks normally require a written loan proposal. This should include general information, such as the business name, the names of the principals, the business address, the purpose of the loan, and the exact amount you need. You should also include a business plan, a management profile, a marketing plan, and your financial information.

Few banks will provide an unsecured loan to a business. The bank will normally expect the business to have something to act as security against the loan (property, for example). Alternatively, the bank may ask the directors of your business to provide personal guarantees on the loan.

Banks provide other services, which may be charged for separately on an "as needed" basis, and will be in addition to normal bank charges. Such services can make your banking much more flexible. For example:

- open credit arrangements enable the business to withdraw cash regularly from a branch of the bank other than the branch holding the account;
- your credit cards or debit cards can have facilities for multiple use, and statements can be broken down to show clearly areas of expenditure;
- electronic funds transfer enables funds to be transferred from a business account to another account at another branch or bank on the same day.

Banks can also help with payment issues. For example:

- banker's references are inquiries carried out on behalf of a business into the creditworthiness of its suppliers and customers;
- night safes enable cash or checks to be deposited outside normal banking hours. There is usually a set quarterly charge plus a charge per usage;
- stopped checks are where the bank is instructed not to pay a check that has been issued;
- cashier's checks are similar to regular checks but are drawn on the head office of the business's bank, thus ensuring payment.

Additional Bank Services

Many banks offer a range of international trade services for businesses trading in overseas markets whose suppliers or customers are based abroad. A good number of banks have systems and services in place to offer current, deposit, and loan accounts in dollars and other major currencies. You may also be able to ask for international payment services.

Online banking services are increasingly available, allowing users to deal with the bank via the Internet. This allows instant access to information about their account, saving time and paperwork. It also means users can integrate their internal computerized account system more efficiently with that of the bank. Telephone banking is offered by many banks. As with online banking, this can be used to check accounts, transfer money, pay bills, and so on.

To meet legal requirements and to ensure that the business is covered for unforeseen events, businesses require insurance cover. The banks all have arrangements or partnerships to provide appropriate cover. They can also help with life cover, pensions, and personal savings if required. Linked savings accounts with competitive interest rates can help your business make the most of surplus funds. Reserve accounts allow money to be put aside for taxes and working capital.

Many banks offer free business counseling to new businesses to identify potential difficulties and suggest new facilities and services that may be helpful. Most major banks publish literature on business start up and offer comprehensive information services.

WHAT TO AVOID
Not Giving the Bank Enough Appropriate Information

You expect an efficient and helpful service from your bank; the bank also has expectations of you. Banks do not like surprises, so keep them informed about your business, particularly if you have a loan. If you think that your requirements may change, give the bank good warning. As far as possible, run your accounts and loans in accordance with your agreement with the bank. The bank will then be far more likely to respond positively if you need, for example, to borrow more money. Once your business is up and running, send the bank a copy of your annual accounts each year. If you have a loan, this may be a condition; but even if you haven't, it may help if you think you may need a loan at some point.

Using a Bank Not Covered By the FDIC

The Federal Deposit Insurance Corporation's (FDIC) mission is to maintain the stability of and public confidence in the nation's financial system. To achieve this goal, the FDIC was created to insure deposits and promote safe and sound banking practices. Each depositor is insured up to $100,000. To see if your bank is insured, visit the FDIC Web site (listed below).

Being Unaware of the Bank's Charges

Watch out for hidden charges. People new to business are often surprised by the range of charges imposed on them by the bank in contrast to the free banking personal customers receive, though recently the banks have begun to reduce some of the charges imposed on business customers.

SEE ALSO

Budgeting (p. 435)
Financing a New Business (p. 90)

Preparing a Successful Business Plan

GETTING STARTED

Many new owner-managers write business plans with the sole purpose of convincing a financier to lend them money for starting up. However, a good business plan can help build a stronger foundation for your business. It can help you to clarify your business purpose to yourself and communicate it to your partners and staff; predict future scenarios and address them before they threaten the success of the business; and set targets and objectives so that you can monitor your business performance.

Your plan must be a coherent description of how your business will move from where it is now to where you want it to be. Obviously each business will be different, but the headings below are useful stepping stones to include in your business plan and will make sure that you cover the most important aspects.

FAQS

What should I say about my business?

Be as specific as possible about the kind of business that you are starting. Describe your business in terms of a mission statement or "executive summary" that clearly summarizes its purpose and is easily understood by you, your staff, customers, and potential investors. If you cannot describe your business in these terms, rethink your business idea; focus on the core activities and direction.

What should I use as my starting point?

Try to envision where you might want your business to be in five years' time, so that you can start to move towards that point. For instance, you might work towards becoming a market leader, an innovator, a specialist, a good employer, a large concern, or a supplier of superior quality.

✓ MAKING IT HAPPEN
Make Sure You Cover All the Important Issues in Your Business Plan

As well as being very specific about the type of business you are starting and thinking ahead to where you want to be in five years, there are a number of important elements that you will need to include in your business plan.

Current Market Situation

To earn enough revenue, your business must be able to achieve a share of the markets available. To do this, you'll need to have a thorough understanding of your market environment, including its size and the share that you can realistically achieve. The size of your share will depend on:

- market trends—find out what influences your target market now, and how your product can take advantage of this
- target customers—describe who your target customers are and how many there are; also justify your estimate of the market share you aim to get
- competition—list your competitors and describe their products; also describe how your product will be different.

Current Target Customers

Define the characteristics of the target groups of customers that could buy from your business. Make a list of the features that your products have, and the associated benefits that these features can provide to your customers; then build up a picture of your target customers. For individuals, describe them in terms of characteristics like age, income, location, lifestyle, and marital status. For businesses, consider location, numbers of employees, public or private sector, industry type, and turnover. Carry out some research into how many customers there are in your target group, and how much they spend, and also try to identify trends that tell you whether this group is growing or shrinking.

Competitor Analysis

Competitors may be in the same (direct competition) or similar (indirect competition) business to you. The level and strength of competition in a market indicates how difficult it will be to gain a share of the market. However, it is not simply the number of competitors that you should be concerned about; analyze the following aspects of each competitor's business:

- their products: are their products and services the same as yours? Do your competitors provide something that you don't?
- their customers: are your competitors targeting the same customer segments as your business?
- their share of the market: how large is it, and could you take some of it?
- their strategies: in how they grow, market themselves, and price their products. Can you learn from how they conduct business, or do it better?
- their operations and facilities: what levels of service are customers demanding?

Marketing Strategy

With a clear understanding of your market, you can define your overall strategy. Break this down into objectives and targets relating to the volume and share of the market (or market segments) you hope to achieve, and when you intend to achieve them by. Ask yourself, for example:

- who are your initial marketing targets?
- what products, services or particular deals will you be offering?
- is there a specific volume, value, or share of these markets that you hope to achieve?
- when do you hope to achieve these targets by?
- why are you choosing these markets first?
- who will you target next, in the next six or 12 months?

Marketing Plan

Now that you have a coherent marketing strategy, you need to be clear about how you are going to make it happen. A detailed marketing plan must explain how you go about achieving each of your marketing targets and objectives, either by particular target segment, by type of marketing activity, or both. Such a plan will include some, or all of the following:

- the marketing methods you will use for each segment of the target market
- the specific action you are going to undertake
- a timescale or timetable for each marketing activity
- the people or organizations that are going to carry it out
- the estimated costs to undertake particular marketing activities
- how you will monitor and review progress
- how you will handle the response to your marketing

It will also be important to identify how you will manage the overall marketing plan, in other words ensuring that the entire budget is not spent in the first couple of months, monitoring results, adjusting the plan, and introducing new tactics as you go along.

Sales Targets and Objectives

Your marketing plan, when implemented, needs to be converted into perhaps the most important business goal of all: sales revenues. Set out your forecasts in terms of sales of different product types by volume and value; sales from different customer groups; and sales from different distribution channels.

Operational Requirements

Information about your operational requirements will be required for your financial forecasts, while other information will be needed for your basic operational planning. Outline your plans for premises, equipment, staff, suppliers, and compliance and licensing, and estimate the respective costs involved.

Current Financial Requirements and Financial Forecasts

Your business plan should include a breakdown of your financial requirements, the sources of finance you have available to you, and any additional amount that you may need. This breakdown should include: the cost of starting your business; your personal budget; details of your own personal finance that you intend to invest, as well as of additional finance; a detailed cash flow forecast that will help estimate how much available cash you will have in any particular month; a profit and loss forecast to help estimate when your business will start to make a profit (which will be essential to your medium-term success); and a balance sheet forecast to provide you with a snapshot of the trading position of your business, to identify what your business will owe, what it will own, and how financially strong it will be at a particular point in the future.

Management Processes

Even if you are the only person involved in your business, it is still important to consider your key skills, responsibilities, and management processes. Think about all the following in your plan:

- management team—outline skills and experience;
- key staff and responsibilities—summarize roles and contribution to the business. Be sure to cover these tasks: marketing and sales, finance, recruitment, product development, general management, and administration;
- monitoring and coordination—set out how you plan to monitor performance (against objectives and targets), and to coordinate the key roles in the business.

Business Risks

Your plan should include an honest awareness of the risks involved, as well as how you plan to minimize them. Consider which of the following risks are relevant to your businesses: lack of management experience; no trading history; economic uncertainties; reliance on key staff; reliance on a

few suppliers; reliance on a small customer base; bad customer debts; partnership difficulties; increased competition; security and insurance against burglary and loss; and failure to meet your sales targets. Show that you have thought about all of these issues and that you have contingency plans for coping with them should they occur.

Present Your Plan in a Professional Manner

Once you have researched and drafted all the necessary information, you can compile the plan. Produce a simple but stylish cover for it, not forgetting to include the business name, your address, your phone numbers, e-mail address, and the date. Put an edited, proofed, and double-checked final draft together. Use a transparent plastic cover with a binder, and letter-quality printer and paper. The order should be cover, title page, executive summary, contents page, contents, and appendices.

WHAT TO AVOID

Producing Unrealistic Sales Forecasts
It is a good idea to produce more than one sales forecast, including one for the worst-case scenario, and how you intend to deal with this. If you are over optimistic you may not be able to make the necessary repayments. You must also make sure that any market research is comprehensive enough to give you realistic sales targets.

Not Proof-reading the Plan
You must ensure that the plan is accurate and contains no mistakes. Ensure that at least two people read it thoroughly to check it.

SEE ALSO
Applying for Grants and Funding (p. 99)
Budgeting (p. 435)
Financing a New Business (p. 90)

Applying for Grants and Funding

GETTING STARTED

A grant is financial assistance, usually for a specific project, given to a business by an awarding body. The grant might help you to develop a new product, buy equipment, or run a training program. A grant is usually a one-time payment and will provide funding that covers a percentage of the costs of the project. Unlike loans and venture capital, a grant does not have to be repaid, unless you fail to adhere to the specific terms and conditions of the grant. This actionlist gives information about what grants are available, where to apply for them, and how to make the application.

FAQS

What can I get a grant for?

Grants are available for a variety of projects, but each individual program will offer funding for a specific purpose. Whether or not you qualify for a grant can also depend on other factors such as the kind of business you run, the size of the business, whether the project will create jobs, and where your business is located. The sorts of areas which a grant might cover include consultancy, design, advertising, marketing, and promotion. Grants are also obtainable for business expansion and relocation, improving business premises, and security, and also for businesses going into exporting. They can be awarded for starting up a business, market testing, and capital equipment. Grants are also available for cooperatives and community enterprises, and for environmental improvements. There are grants for information technology (IT) and e-commerce, new technology and innovation, and research and development (R&D), as well as recruitment and training.

Where can I get a grant?

At a local and regionwide level, grants may be available from organizations such as state and city chambers of commerce, state economic development agencies, and state commerce departments.

Nationally, grants are available from various government departments and agencies, such as U.S. Chamber of Commerce, Small Business Administration, U.S. Department of Commerce, U.S. Department of Housing and Urban Development, and U.S. Department of Labor.

How long does a grant application take?

The application process for some grants can take several months (see below), so if your project needs funding immediately it'd be a good idea for you to investigate alternative sources of finance, such as loans. Also bear in mind that businesses are usually required to meet some of the costs of the project (usually at least 50 percent of overall expenditure), so you'll have to be prepared to raise some finance as well.

It's always worth finding out whether your business could attract grant funding, but it may be risky to base any business idea *solely* on the presumption that you'll get it. Most grant funding is conditional and your business will need to meet the specific criteria of the grant programme.

MAKING IT HAPPEN

Before Applying

Contact your local chamber of commerce or state economic development office. Most will have a directory of assistance available locally and nationally. Advisers will be able to put you in touch with the relevant grant-awarding bodies and will be able to help you through the application process.

You will then need to contact the awarding body and check that your project meets the specified criteria of the program. It's important at this stage to find out whether it is actually worth applying, as grant application forms can take a lot of time and effort to complete. If you do decide to proceed, ask them to send you an application form and more detailed information about the grant.

Many programs will require you to supply a project plan or proposal, giving:

- A project description detailing the aim of the project and how the project will benefit your business.
- Details of who will run the project, what experience, knowledge, and skills they have.
- The cost of the project.
- The length of the project and key deadlines.
- The location of the project.
- Why the project needs the support of the grant and what would happen if the support wasn't provided.
- How much money is required.
- How you intend to fund your share of the project's costs.
- How the project complies with the criteria set by the grant provider.
- Details about the business, when it was established, its activities, etc.
- Financial information about the business. This might require the submission of accounts and forecasts.

Make the Application

Read any guidance notes that are supplied with the application. These will give you information on how to complete the form. Application forms will differ widely. The proposal should follow the format required, be clear and concise, and should be tailored to the grant you are applying for.

For national grants, you may have to submit two forms. These will be a short initial form to assess your eligibility for the grant, and then a second form providing detailed information about your business and the project you intend to undertake. It is a good idea to speak to someone involved with administering the grant. They will be able to help you with completing the form. Alternatively, seek the assistance of a business adviser or accountant to help you with your application.

Your business plan will provide a lot of the detail for your grant application. You should make sure that your business plan is up to date and includes information about your experience, future plans, and financial requirements.

After the Application

When you have completed the application, make sure that you check it over thoroughly and that you've supplied all the information required. After you've sent your application, the awarding body may contact you to get more information to help with the assessment. They may also ask you to come to an interview or visit your business themselves.

If your application is successful, you'll probably receive a formal letter offering the grant. This will probably include the agreed program of work, eligible costs, start date, and the time scale. You'll probably have to accept the conditions that apply to the offer within a given period of time. Read the letter carefully, as you will be signing up to a legally binding agreement.

It's likely that you'll have to wait some time before getting a decision on your grant application. This could range from a few weeks (for local grants) to a year (for national grants). Again, bear this in mind and make sure you have some alternative sources to pursue, especially if you need finance quickly.

WHAT TO AVOID ✗
Not Completing the Application Form Properly
If your application is incomplete, it will take longer to process and is more likely to be rejected. Also, if you provide incorrect information, the grant may be reclaimed.

SEE ALSO
Budgeting (p. 435)
Financing a New Business (p. 90)
Preparing a Successful Business Plan (p. 96)

Controlling a Budget

GETTING STARTED

Controlling budgets is a headache for businesses of all size. Many smaller businesses start off on the right foot by putting in place a good bookkeeping system, but then fail to exercise proper financial control and end up in trouble. The only way to make sure that you make a profit is to control the budget efficiently. To do this, you need to estimate your sales income reasonably accurately, estimate your costs precisely, and keep both under control. You also need to charge the right price for your end product in your chosen market(s). It is important systematically to collect all financial documents in a methodical way, and keep all your figures up to date on a daily basis. This actionlist will look at some of the most common problems in controlling a budget, and suggest ways to tackle them.

A book which you might find useful on this subject is *Finance and Accounting for Nonfinancial Managers*, written by William G. Droms. Its 5th edition was published by Perseus in 2003.

FAQS

What is budgeting?

Each year you should prepare a business plan for the business, including your best forecast of sales. A budget is simply that forecast turned into figures. In other words, it is an estimate of sales income together with the costs required to produce those sales.

What is financial control?

Financial control is different from bookkeeping. Bookkeeping is about recording the figures—in other words income and expenditure, receipts and payments, and assets and liabilities. Accurate bookkeeping, of course, is a prerequisite for effective financial control, and computerized accounting packages make accurate bookkeeping very easy.

You then, however, need to use the figures as a basis for effective financial control. It can be difficult to keep the complete picture in your head at all times, so calculating a few simple ratios or using a graph are both good techniques to help you keep up to date.

MAKING IT HAPPEN

Set Targets

Each year set objectives and prepare a business plan. Define your objectives in financial terms, as well as in terms of marketing, quality, and people. If a venture capitalist or business angel has invested in your business, his or her primary concern will often be the rate of return on investment (often referred to in financial documents as "ROI"). If you've invested your own money into the business, you may be expecting smaller returns initially, planning for your business to provide higher returns over a longer period.

Keep the Books

A reliable, easy-to-use accounting system is essential for straightforward effective financial control. Make sure that you keep proper records. The information to record includes: any sales orders received; invoices issued by the business for sales; purchase orders placed by the business; invoices received by the business for purchases; cash receipts, and cash expenditure. Turning this information into graphs, tables, and charts can help to reveal trends, which in turn will help you to revise your forecasts and future planning. A range of accessible computer software, such as Microsoft Excel, will help you to do this.

Conduct a Monthly Check

Bring the account balance up to date and conduct a bank reconciliation every month. The balance represents the business's liquidity; it is the cash immediately available to the business.

Prepare an operating statement by combining the revenue, direct costs, and overhead costs. This records income and expenditure (as does the profit and loss account), not receipts and payments. It ignores some items such as depreciation or bad debts. Each month, you should compare your actual performance with your forecast, both for the month and, ideally, for the year to date. You can then look at some simple ratios and the variances.

Analyze the Available Information

Conduct a ratio analysis. Do this by defining your costs as a percentage of the sales income. This gives you a very quick method of determining whether or not you are on target. If your costs are rising as a percentage of your sales income, then you know that you have a problem to address. Consider your gross profit margin. If the margin is falling, it could be a sign of trouble. Ask yourself the following questions. Has wastage increased? Have costs increased? Monitoring changes closely will help you to react to any problems, preventing them from escalating any further.

Then conduct a variance analysis. A variance is the difference between your target and your actual performance. Variance analysis looks at the differences themselves, rather than comparing different figures, as in ratio analysis. You should review figures for sales, inquiry and order position; material and labor usage; overhead; cash position/cash forecast; stock; and capital expenditure. As you perform the analysis, remember that analyzing variances has to consider more than just differences in cash. There may be major variances even though the overall cash position remains more or less as forecast. Make sure you understand why the figures are changing. There are various possible reasons; for example, is it possible for a reduction in raw material cost to be canceled by increased wastage?

Manage Cash

The operating statement shows the net trading profit but does not show the liquidity (that is, the cash position of your business, and the ability to meet payments). It is important, therefore, that you also prepare a monthly cash flow statement. This reflects when money is received or paid out and includes items such as drawings or taxes which are not regarded as trading expenses. All the figures should be readily available from the account balance.

Remember the importance of actively controlling the budget. Generating the figures is only the first part of the process; you must then take some action. Keep a tight grip on anyone that owes the business money (your debtors). If the level of debtors rises, this could be because your sales are increasing or because your debtors are taking longer to pay. Make sure you define in your terms of trade how quickly you expect debtors to pay, and then ensure that they stick to these guidelines. Put processes in place to deal with late payments or debtors who continually delay their payments.

Similarly, try not to get on the wrong side of your suppliers by taking too long to pay *them*, as they may withdraw your credit facilities. To gain the most benefit, you need to take the maximum amount of credit possible without abusing your agreed terms. Take care to ensure your tax payments are made on time, otherwise you could incur substantial penalties.

Controlling your debtors and creditors carefully will ensure that you're controlling your working capital carefully. If you're building up large sums of cash, do something worthwhile with them, even if only to move it to an account that pays you a better rate of interest. If you expect to need additional working capital, for example, because debtors are rising as your sales increase, then talking to the bank—or your investors—early will reassure them that you really are in control of your business, and they will be more likely to help.

Watch your stock levels carefully. Consider how much stock you have tied up in raw materials, work in progress, and finished goods. If you have too much stock, you may be using excessive storage space and tying up money that could be used in other ways.

WHAT TO AVOID

Setting Too Many Targets

Choose a small number of appropriate targets and focus on a handful of key issues, such as revenue growth, profit, and cash flow. Compiling and analyzing huge amounts of information can be time-consuming and not always of great use if the major points are buried underneath too much detail.

Letting Your Books Get Out of Date

You need up-to-date financial records before you can control your budget properly, so record transactions accurately and promptly.

Losing Track of Cash

The key to making a profit is through the careful control of cash, so that you can pay your debts as they fall due.

SEE ALSO

Budgeting (p. 435)

Controlling Costs

GETTING STARTED

The basis of any successful business is that income should exceed expenses. One way to improve profitability is to increase the sales of your business, but you can also enhance profitability through the reduction of costs. A business that keeps its costs under control will be able to release more resources for growth in the good times, and will be in a better position to survive in recession. This actionlist gives some suggestions on ways to control (and in some cases reduce) the costs of your business.

FAQS

Which costs do I need to control?

In order to be able to control costs, you first need to know about them. Start by identifying each cost clearly, and make sure that you keep records of all bills, receipts, and so on. You will need to review your costs on a regular basis. This will depend on when your accounts are normally completed. It is not enough to calculate whether the business is in profit or loss; you also need to be aware of what normal costs are, so that you can spot anomalies and take action to address them. Some costs will be more important to control than others. It will be important to know what the business's critical costs are, and to concentrate on reducing them.

Who is responsible for controlling costs?

Cost control is the responsibility of everyone working in the business. If you have a team of people working for you, all your employees have countless opportunities to affect costs throughout each day. It is important to be aware that if employees are unhappy at work, they are in a position to do a lot of damage, if only through what they *don't* do. If they are motivated and feel part of the business, they will work economically without supervision. Rising to the challenge of providing this kind of environment for your employees is a test of good management; one approach is to involve employees by asking them to come up with ideas to reduce costs. If you do decide on this approach, though, be careful with the way you phrase this request. Unless the company is in dire straits and you are thinking of

making redundancies, don't give them the impression that their jobs are on the line as part of this cost-cutting measure!

Many people assume that because the volume of expenditure is so much larger than they are used to in home life, any savings they might make are insignificant. Every little does help, though, so let your team know that cutting back on what look like insignificant costs will help the business overall.

MAKING IT HAPPEN

Use Cost Control Measures

One effective cost control measure is to carry out a cost benefit analysis. Cost awareness should be part of the planning process. In meetings, planning sessions, or in personal planning, the overall impact of any decision should be understood in terms of business profitability. In other words, the benefits of a particular course of action should be set against the cost. For example, a person may be assigned to carry out a piece of research that could, in fact, be done quicker by a consultant, or bought off the shelf. Additionally, the work may in fact have an insignificant impact on profitability, and you need to ask whether it is worth doing at all. In such cases, you will need to be quite pragmatic and ruthless.

Another method of cost control is value analysis (VA), which involves a detailed examination of each part of a product, service, or system to determine if there is any way in which its costs could be reduced without affecting quality. Value analysis is usually done in a group and it is therefore a good way to involve employees and increase general awareness of cost control. Each aspect of the product should be brought under the spotlight. The group has to decide, for example, whether the product is necessary; whether it can be made with cheaper materials; whether it is actually cheaper to buy than to make; whether it can be made more quickly; or whether it can be simplified to reduce potential faults. Other aspects to look at might be reducing the material that is used to make it, or reducing wastage. Economizing on the use of raw materials can be a very effective cost-saving measure.

Your company could also examine its purchasing methods. It is a good idea to look for discounts for buying in bulk. You should also be prepared to haggle, and it is important to review the cost of supplies and suppliers on a regular basis. In fact, no bill or invoice that your business receives should be taken for granted. For example, your landlord could be persuaded to reduce rent payments if you think they are unfair. If you feel that rates are too high, your local property valuation service may be able to help you with your property's assessment value. Stock control is another potential area for savings. Accurate control will reduce storage and working capital costs. Providing effective security should reduce the cost of stock lost through theft.

Look at Potential Areas for Cost Savings

Staff costs often contain the greatest scope for savings. Aspects that you might consider include employing fewer people to do the same task. Also ask yourself whether your employees are motivated and monitored appropriately, to ensure that they deliver value for money. Look at their remuneration to check that it is appropriate; too much is costly, too little may lead to a high staff turnover (which is also costly) and may damage performance. Effective management techniques will increase the value you get from staff.

Energy costs could be reduced if your employees are encouraged to use energy responsibly, in the same way as they do at home. Most people today care about the environment and this can motivate them to save energy. It is often overlooked that some of the biggest savings available to businesses lie within some of their most basic costs, for example gas and electricity. It is worth having meters double checked, especially if the business uses a lot of energy. Thermostats should be set correctly. You shouldn't underestimate the impact of proper insulation measures, which can produce long-term savings. Your business may also be eligible for grants to insulate the property. Local utility companies often provide free advice and information on ways of saving energy. Another area for you to consider is changing long-standing suppliers of telecommunications, gas, and electricity. You will need to compare the prices and contract terms offered by the numerous companies now supplying basic utilities and telecommunications.

Telephone calls are another basic company cost offering potential savings. It is necessary for some private calls to be made from work, but you may find that some of your staff are taking advantage. Make sure that you outline a policy for the use of phones for personal calls. This should be agreed and circulated. Staff should also be made aware of any possible disciplinary action that could be taken against them for breach of the policy. It is possible to get itemized bills for each extension, which should discourage misuse of phones. Staff should also be trained in the efficient use of the telephone, to reduce the length of calls.

Photocopiers are easy to use and the expense can soon get out of control if usage is not monitored. Make sure that all copies are logged, allocated to a cost center, and that the initials of the person taking the copy are recorded. Staff should be charged for personal copies and discouraged from making unnecessary copies. Someone should be made responsible for monitoring copying, and usage should be reviewed regularly. Make sure that all staff know exactly how to use all the facilities on the copier. This in itself can reduce costs, for example printing double-sided copies can save time and money.

Some staff may be tempted to take office stationery home for their own use. You could consider keeping the stationery cupboard locked and making someone responsible for issuing materials. Scrap paper can be recycled as stapled writing pads. Used laser printer cartridges can be sent off to be refilled at a discount price. Recycling is good for the environment, and can save a business money. All waste should be considered for potential recycling or resale to recycling companies. For example, there are companies who will buy industrial plastic waste for recycling.

Finally, it is a good idea to have a clear expenses policy. It is possible to reduce misuse of expenses by drawing up guidelines so that everyone understands what is, and is not, acceptable. Expense claims should be cleared by a manager before being paid. Make sure that expenses for individuals are reviewed periodically, and anomalies investigated.

WHAT TO AVOID
Making False Economies
Don't cut back on the wrong things. If you reduce the level of service your customers are used to, you'll probably end up losing the business money. Similarly, if you make working conditions too harsh, for example, by cutting back on pay, benefits, and training, your staff will become demoralized and will not perform—indeed, you run the risk of them leaving.

Ignoring Rising Costs
Confront cost problems immediately rather than put them off and hope they'll go away. It's much better to act sooner and to stop the problem from escalating.

SEE ALSO
Budgeting (p. 435)
Drawing Up a Budget (p. 107)
Financing a New Business (p. 90)

Drawing Up a Budget

GETTING STARTED

Every business needs to plan its spending on the basis of what it expects from sales income; without this tool, you can't be sure that your business will survive. Budgeting is simply the name given to the process of working out what you expect your business to earn and spend in a given period. It also gives you the ability to check how the business is doing from week to week, or month to month; without this check, you can easily overspend. This actionlist explains how you can make use of your budget, and how to draw one up.

FAQS

What can I use a budget for?

It's important that you use your budget as a control mechanism. At the end of each month, you should enter the actual figures for sales and expenses next to the figures that were forecast. If there are substantial differences between the budgeted figures and the actual figures, then you need to do something about it. For instance, if your sales are too low, you may need to reconsider your marketing strategies. If sales, on the other hand, are higher than planned, then you may need to reconsider your staffing levels or raw material supplies, in order to cope with the rising demand. Also, if your expenditure is too high, you'll need to find ways to bring costs down.

How do I estimate sales and expenditure?

The starting point for drawing up a budget is for you to estimate future sales and expenditure. The sales budget can be split into the number of different products your business plans to sell; the number of units of each product that you plan to sell; the price that you plan to sell each unit for; and the place or area where you plan to sell them.

You'll need to split your expenditure budget into production costs or variable costs (such as materials, power, and subcontractors); overhead costs or fixed costs (such as rent and salaries); and capital costs (equipment).

MAKING IT HAPPEN

Budgeting for Sales

If your business is a new one, forecasting sales will be particularly tricky for you, because you don't have actual sales from the past on which you can base your expectations. Instead, you'll have to make sure that your budget is based on good research. It must also be closely tied to a realistic marketing plan that will generate the sales you expect. It's important not just to guess your sales figures. Also, don't start by looking at your planned expenditure and then just deriving a sales forecast to cover the cost.

Make the sales budget as detailed as you can. You need to make it very clear what you plan to sell, and at what price. Set out your expected sales on a monthly or quarterly basis. If your business sells a range of products, make sure that you prepare sales budgets for each of them. If your products are sold in more than one area, then you may find it helpful to have a sales budget for each area.

Budgeting for Expenditure

Now that you have prepared the sales budget, you have the basic foundations for working out what your expenditure will be. For your purposes, the expenditure budget can be split into a production budget and an overheads budget. If you know how many products you'll sell, you can work out the direct costs of producing them. These direct costs will then make up the production budget, and will vary with the level of production. The overhead costs will stay more or less constant.

The Production Budget

The production budget is made up of items like the materials and components that go into the product.

If you have a sales team, you also need to include commission paid to them. (If sales people earn a regular retainer as well, this retainer would normally be regarded as a fixed cost.) Make sure that you include the cost of subcontractors, where people are being paid as independent contractors to perform a certain, defined job.

Discounts are usually shown in the budget as a direct cost.

There are some expenses, such as depreciation, that are usually treated as fixed overheads. However, if you want to be particularly accurate with your production budget, you could include these, especially if you can clearly associate them with specific products.

The Overheads Budget

Once you have prepared the production budget, you'll need to consider the other costs that the business will incur. These will include the salaries for you and your staff, income tax withholding, both federal and state, FICA (Federal Insurance Contributions Act) tax, and pension contributions. You'll also need to include rent and company insurance, and telephone, Internet, and e-mail account costs. Any interest on money that you have borrowed will also need to be included in your overheads.

If your business is in manufacturing, it's likely that the above will represent a relatively small proportion of the total costs. On the other hand, if you have a service sector business, it's likely that overheads will represent a very high proportion of the cost. Include all overhead costs, including interest payments and drawings (how much money you plan to take out of the business). Remember that you are taxed on the total profit (if you are self-employed), so allow for this too. If your business is registered as a

company, and you expect to take high dividends, make sure that you budget for this as well.

Your business may aim to allocate the overheads to each product, or may prefer to retain overheads as a single budget. Whichever path you choose, it's important that you ensure that the price for each product makes a reasonable contribution to the overheads.

Budgeting for the Full Cost of Production

You're now in a position to pull together the production budget and the overheads budget into a single production cost budget. If there is more than one product or service, then there will be a production budget for each. There will also be variable overheads for you to add for each product. There is no need for you to split fixed overheads across products at this point, since the object of this exercise is for you to be able to determine the total costs.

Capital Expenditure Budget

If you expect to buy capital equipment, you'll need to decide how you'll pay for it (whether in cash or through a loan), and make sure that you budget for these payments in the relevant months. This is essential information if an accurate forecast is to be prepared, particularly where the business may have to take out a loan to finance the purchase and will have to meet a repayment schedule that includes interest. The Internal Revenue Service doesn't consider an operating lease to be a purchase, but rather a tax-deductible overhead expense. Lease payments can therefore be deducted from the corporate income.

If the business decides to lease equipment, it's important to make sure that you read all the small print of the lease agreement.

Cash Flow

If you operate your business on a cash basis, in other words taking in cash for your sales and paying cash for your purchases, then it's fairly easy to see if you are living within your means because you'll have cash left over at the end of the month if you're making a profit. Very few businesses, however, operate like this. It's far more likely that you'll be selling goods or services in one month, and not receiving payment until the following month, or the month after that. Similarly, you may be buying raw materials one month, but not paying for them for at least another four weeks. A budget will help you keep track of your cash flow in and out of the business, and keep control.

Once the budgets have been prepared, you can use the data that has been accumulated in order to prepare financial forecasts. This will include a cash flow forecast, but you should also include a forecast of the profit and loss statement, and the balance sheet. The cash flow forecast should set out, on a month-by-month basis, all cash inflows and outflows from the business for the following 12 months; this will help you to determine your working capital needs. The profit and loss forecast will help you to check that your business remains profitable.

WHAT TO AVOID

Not Setting Realistic Targets
If you set realistic targets, you'll be able to tell whether sales and expenditure have gone to plan, and you'll also be able to foresee problems and opportunities in time to take action.

Not Bothering to Prepare a Cash Flow Forecast
It's important to remember that a cash flow forecast is as important as the budget itself. While the budget can tell you if your business is generally profitable, it might not alert you to cash flow problems.

SEE ALSO
Budgeting (p. 435)
Controlling Costs (p. 104)
Financing a New Business (p. 90)

Understanding the Tax System

GETTING STARTED

The United States, arguably, has the most complicated tax system in the world. The American Tax Code alone contains over 7 million words. (In comparison, the Holy Bible contains approximately 700,000.)

In addition to understanding federal taxes, you also need to become familiar with your state and local tax systems. It is advisable that you discuss any concerns with your lawyer, accountant, or tax preparer.

RECOMMENDED LINKS

Internal Revenue Service:
www.irs.gov
1040.com:
Tax Information for Everyone:
www.1040.com

Small Business One Stop Resource
  (sponsored by the IRS):
www.irs.gov/business/small/index.html
State and Local Tax:
Tax and Accounting Sites Directory:
www.taxsites.com/state.html

Managing Creditors and Debtors

GETTING STARTED

All businesses have trading relationships with both suppliers and customers. At any point in time, those suppliers who are extending credit to your business by letting you pay for goods or services after you have received them, are known as your creditors. Customers who owe you money for goods or services that you have supplied are known as your debtors.

The balance between when you need to pay your creditors and when you receive payment from your debtors has a major effect on the cash flow of your business. Getting the balance right is important in determining what cash will be available to your business in the short term, and for identifying the cash needs (often referred to as "working capital") of your business as it grows.

FAQS

Why do I need to manage creditors and debtors?

Knowing how much you owe, how much you are owed, and when payments are due to be made or received, allows you to forecast your cash flow over several months and ensures that you will have enough money in the bank for other regular business payments, such as salaries and rent. This can be particularly important for businesses that are seasonal, or that have a high spend with their suppliers several months before their customers pay them.

How does this affect the working capital required by a business?

When the value of your creditors equals the value of your debtors, there is no effect on the working capital needs of your business, assuming payment terms are the same. However if the value of your debtors increases relative to the value of your creditors, then the working capital used by your business rises. This is a typical situation faced by businesses as they grow. If you are able to increase the value of your creditors while maintaining the value of your debtors then you can reduce the working capital needed by your business.

What are standard payment terms?

There are no firm rules for credit terms, but there are accepted practices that are widely adopted. Normally the credit period is either based on the date of the invoice or on the month of the invoice. The most standard credit term based on the date of invoice is 30 days—that is, the invoice is due for payment 30 days after the date on the invoice. If you are providing several invoices to a customer in any one month, it is normal to use "net monthly terms." This means that all invoices for a particular month are grouped and paid together at the end of the following month. Using net monthly terms greatly simplifies the process for both supplier and customer, reducing the payment process to only once a month, irrespective of the number of invoices issued.

What is debtor finance?

For many businesses the amount owed by their debtors is the largest single element of their balance sheet. If your business is trading in a business-to-business environment, there is the potential to use the services of a third party finance company who will make money available to you, based on the security of your debtor balances. This service is called "factoring" (it may also be called "accounts receivable financing") and can range from the provision of just finance against your debtor list to a full sales ledger and credit control service. The initial advance payment is usually up to 80% of the value of the invoice, with the remaining balance being due either at an agreed maturity date, or when your customer pays the factor. This type of service is especially useful for fast-growing businesses, who can suffer from a shortage of working capital.

What is creditor finance?

This is the term used for "borrowing" money from your creditors to fund your working capital. It is typically used by retail businesses, where you sell your products or services for cash, and yet obtain credit from your suppliers.

Are trade suppliers my only short-term creditors?

Although trade suppliers are usually viewed as being the creditors of your business, you should actually include all of the organizations that you owe money to in the short term. This means that the term "creditors" is more formally split between trade creditors—which will include your trade suppliers to your business—and other creditors, which will include organizations such the IRS, if you are an employer.

MAKING IT HAPPEN

Managing your creditors and debtors is vitally important to the smooth and effective operation of your business. Doing this effectively will save you money, and may even make the difference between your business surviving or failing.

Manage the Relationship with Your Creditors

Suppliers are vital to the operation of your business and the role that they play is often undervalued. For many suppliers, how you manage the payment of their account is a key to a successful long-term relationship. The main issues for a good working relationship with your suppliers are for you to be:

- professional in your handling of their account, by conforming to the agreed credit terms, and not wasting their time through poor administration;
- honest with them if you have cash flow problems and are unable to meet their normal payment terms;
- straightforward in your commercial negotiations—look to negotiate better terms from your suppliers, but base this on the volume of business and how this has grown

over a period of time, and the fact that you manage your account well.

Use a Credit Card to Obtain Credit

In situations where it is difficult to obtain credit from your suppliers, then you should consider using a credit card to make payment for goods. This has the effect of giving the supplier immediate payment, but also giving you 30–50 days' credit. However, when making a payment with a credit card, there may be a surcharge added to the invoice.

Manage the Relationship with Your Debtors

If providing credit to your customers is important to your business, then it is vital to set up effective credit-control procedures.

Get your customers to complete an account application form, giving details about their business and its legal structure, and details of references. Supply them with a copy of your standard terms and conditions of sale, and make sure they are aware of (and acknowledge) your payment terms, and what their credit limit is. Keep records of quotations and delivery notes to ensure that disputes can be quickly resolved by you providing the missing information, if needed, and ensure that you have efficient accounts administration systems that allow you to send invoices promptly and follow up with regular statements and reminders.

Monitor your customers' payments. If you are unhappy with them then speak to the person who places the order as well as the finance department. If they still do not pay, be prepared to halt supplies and to take further action to collect the debt if necessary. You may even decide to withdraw credit facilities if a customer is a persistently poor payer.

You should produce a regular debtors list, preferably in balance order, so that you can easily review how much each business owes to you and how old their debt is. You need to concentrate your efforts on those customers that have the oldest and largest debts to ensure that your time is used most cost effectively.

✗ WHAT TO AVOID
Taking a Narrow Focus

Do not focus all of your efforts on getting better payment terms from your creditors at the expense of not managing your debtors more effectively. If your business regularly struggles to pay its creditors because of slow payment from your debtors, this will be an indication that your business does not have sufficient working capital. You will then need to decide if you can manage your debtors better, and reduce the average credit period given, or whether you will need to get additional finance into the business to increase your available working capital.

SEE ALSO

Addressing Cash Flow Problems (p. 114)
Budgeting (p. 435)
Issuing Invoices and Collecting Debts
   (p. 117)

Addressing Cash Flow Problems

GETTING STARTED

Running out of cash is probably the biggest cause of small businesses failing. There are many reasons behind a cash crisis, so it is crucial that you understand them and know how to prevent a short-term problem leading to business failure. No matter how good your balance sheet may look in terms of physical assets and outstanding debtors, your ability to convert these to actual cash at critical times can make the difference between survival and failure. This actionlist looks at some of the main causes of cash flow problems, and suggests some ways of overcoming such problems.

For more information on cash flow issues, you may find *Keys to Managing Your Cash Flow* by Joel G. Siegel and Jae K. Shim (Barrons, 1992) useful.

FAQS

How does the behavior of my customers affect my cash flow?

Slow payment by your customers is a main cause of cash flow problems. Remember that a sale is only completed when your invoice has been paid in full. Many businesses concentrate on generating new sales, but fail to set up credit control procedures until they actually experience cash flow problems. These procedures should be in place from the start.

If a key customer becomes insolvent this can also cause cash flow problems. If your business is very dependent on a few major customers, you are always exposed to the risk of one of them having their own financial problems, which could result in you not getting paid. This could be disastrous if the income from that client makes up a big chunk of your overall revenue and you are relying on that money to pay your creditors or employees.

How does poor planning affect cash flow?

Poor financial planning can cause huge problems. Your business must plan for certain payments, such as Value Added Tax, Pay As You Earn tax, and personal or business tax bills. You need to build these payments into your cash flow forecasts and then ensure that sufficient funds will be available at those key times. Also make

sure that any purchase of equipment is scheduled for payment when your cash position is stronger, or is structured over a longer period to reduce its impact on your cash flow.

If your business plan focuses on turnover and neglects profit, this can also lead to a cash flow crisis. A business is only able to generate a positive cash flow by generating profits from its trading activities. If you prioritize the turnover of your business, then you may improve sales but this might lead to spending more than you earn (a problem known as negative cash flow). This can be a particular problem if the business has to invest in new equipment and staff as it grows, as these costs are often incurred well in advance of you receiving your additional sales revenue.

Another common reason for cash flow problems is inappropriate planning for stock purchases. It is very tempting to over commit, especially as many suppliers will offer you discount incentives to purchase larger quantities of their goods; on the face of it, this could look very attractive because it holds the promise of making you a larger profit. However, you need to think carefully before committing to large orders of stock, particularly while you are establishing your business. If you order bulk purchases and then the items quickly go out of fashion or have a short shelf life, you can be left with stock that you cannot sell but that you still have to pay for.

How does the rate of growth of my business affect cash flow?

Another common reason for problems with cash flow is insufficient working capital. This means that there is not enough money initially invested in the business to allow it to operate effectively on a day-to-day basis. It can also be a problem when a business grows rapidly and needs to produce more than normal without having the income to fund that growth; this is called over-trading.

MAKING IT HAPPEN
Plan Effectively

Preparing a cash flow forecast and then putting it to good use is the basis for avoiding many cash flow problems. The forecast allows you to anticipate most cash flow problems that could occur during the normal course of running your business. It also allows you to do a sensitivity analysis, in which you can test the effect of lower sales or slower payment on your cash flow.

Develop Good Relationships with Suppliers and Customers

You must adopt tight credit control procedures. Set up procedures for managing the whole process of giving your customers credit. Start with only giving credit to approved customers, check when their accounts are due for payment, and ensure that they pay according to your agreed terms. Also make sure that you have efficient administration procedures for raising your invoices promptly and sending statements to your customers. In this way, you will not add to payment delays.

Offering incentives for early payment is another good way to encourage your customers to pay more quickly. You could do this by offering a discount if they pay either on delivery or within a certain number of days (typically between seven and 14 days) from the invoice date. Typical levels of discount are between 2% and 5%, but the exact level will depend on your profit margins and on how important early payment is to you.

As your business grows, you can look to negotiate better credit terms with your suppliers. Initially, this may be achieved by progressing from paying at the time of purchase, to having a 30-day credit account. If the majority of your customers expect to have 60-day credit accounts, then you should aim to agree 60-day payment terms with your suppliers.

Get Help

Debtor finance is an option for businesses that are growing rapidly. In this case, it is possible to use the services of an invoice discounter or factoring company. These companies enter into an arrangement where they will provide your business with an advance (usually 80%) on the value of your invoices, as soon as these invoices are raised. Interest is then charged on the balance drawn, and there is a service charge. Factoring companies can also take control of collecting payments from your customer directly, which can save you the costs of using your own staff to manage this process.

An agreed overdraft facility with your bank allows you to borrow money as and when required, up to an agreed limit. It is a relatively cheap way to finance working capital if you have large variations in cash flow during the course of a month (or if your business is very seasonal), because you only pay interest on the amount actually borrowed. However, if you are continually relying on your overdraft, it can be expensive; more importantly, it may also highlight that your business needs additional working capital, or a longer-term form of finance. With an overdraft, you are also exposed to "repayment on demand," which means that your lender can ask for full repayment at any time; a "term loan" with fixed monthly installments is safer from your point of view, as the lender can usually only demand full repayment if you default on your installments.

If your business needs to invest in new equipment, but does not have the cash, then you can look to fund this with asset financing, in the form of a term loan, a hire purchase loan, or a leasing deal. This avoids the large cash outflow on the full price of the equipment, and gives you a fixed level of repayment over a set period (usually between two and five years). In situations where the asset is being used as security for the finance, it is likely that you will still need to provide at least a 10% deposit.

WHAT TO AVOID
Not Thinking Ahead
Don't be taken by surprise. Keep a close eye on your bank balance and your debtors' book and look ahead a few weeks at what expenditure you will have to make. Cash flow problems are best caught early, and the more time you can give yourself to respond, the better.

Procrastinating
Don't be fooled into thinking that cash flow problems will resolve themselves; they won't go away! Talk to your bank and your suppliers as soon as you think there might be a problem. This way, you assure them that you are at least doing your homework, even if there are difficult times ahead. If you don't act, you run the risk of affecting your relationship with your bank, suppliers, and customers. Your bank will be far more receptive to dealing with your cash flow problems if you approach it before the problem occurs.

SEE ALSO
Budgeting (p. 435)
Financing a New Business (p. 90)
Managing Creditors and Debtors (p. 111)

Issuing Invoices and Collecting Debts

GETTING STARTED

When your business supplies goods or services to its customers, you need to record these transactions formally with a document called an invoice. This document becomes particularly important when you let your customers defer payment for the transaction, by offering them credit. From the date that the invoice is issued, until it is paid, the value of the invoice is regarded as a debt to the business. This actionlist explains the invoicing procedure and offers advice on how to deal with customers who won't pay up on time.

FAQS

Why do you need to issue invoices?

An invoice is a formal record of trading between two parties. It confirms details of the goods or services supplied, and the prices charged. It is used as the basis for all financial management and accounting processes in a business, and is a key document in business tax records. An invoice that is issued by your business to confirm a sale is then a crucial document for customer, as it acts as proof of purchase.

Are there different types of invoices?

Yes. There are three types of invoice documents that can be issued.

1. Pro-forma invoice—this is issued by a business when it does not have credit facilities set up with its customer, and acts as a request for payment for goods prior to despatch. This insures that payment is received, and is often used when two businesses have not traded before.

2. Standard invoice—a standard document issued to confirm a trading transaction. It is normally classed as a sales invoice by the business that has sold the goods and as a purchase invoice by the buyer.

3. Credit note—this is issued to cancel an original invoice or part of an invoice when goods are returned or a pricing error has been made. If the original invoice has been settled prior to the credit note being issued, then the buyer will be entitled to alternative goods up to the value of the credit note.

What details should be included on an invoice?

All invoices need to convey certain key pieces of information as supporting evidence for taxation and to avoid questions from customers which may lead to delays in payment. These are:

- a unique identifying number
- your business name, address, and its legal status
- a date of issue, which becomes the tax point
- your customer's name (or business name) and address
- a description of the quantity and type of goods or services supplied
- freight or shipping prices
- the payment terms for the invoice

Must an invoice always be issued?

You do not always need to issue an invoice to your customer, but you will need to keep a record of the transaction. Many retail businesses issue sales receipts to their customers rather than fully-detailed invoices. This is acceptable for small one-time transactions that are paid for at the time of purchase. Most business-to-business transactions require an invoice to be issued.

Is there anything that can be done if the customer will not pay the invoice?

You need to establish as soon as possible why your customer will not pay the invoice. If it is a simple issue, such as a genuine pricing or quantity error, then it should be simple to resolve. However, if the reason given is not acceptable and a compromise cannot be reached, you will need to take action to recover the money owed. This can be done in several ways:

- Using a local small claims court. The amount you can recover is generally limited to between $2,000 and $5,000.
- instructing a lawyer to pursue the debt for you. This may just involve him or her sending a letter on your behalf, or managing the whole process of pursuing your claim through the court system.
- engaging the services of a collection agency, who will either manage the process for a fixed fee, or work on a commission of the debt that is collected.

You need to balance the time that it will take for you to pursue your customer for payment against the costs involved with using the services of a lawyer or collection agency.

MAKING IT HAPPEN

If your business only issues a small number of invoices, then you can use a computer and word-processing package, or even manually write out the invoices. You will need to produce two copies, one for your customer and one for your own records. This simple approach can work well, but once you start to offer credit it makes more sense to use an integrated accounts system that manages both invoicing and credit control.

Establish Procedures for Credit Control

If you offer credit to your customers, then the issuing of a sales invoice is just part of the sales process, and the transaction is not completed until the invoice has been fully settled. Many businesses are very successful at selling their goods or services and yet still fail because they are unable to collect the money owed to them. Therefore, it is vital to set up processes that minimize the risk of your customers failing to pay you.

Make sure that credit is only offered to credit-worthy customers, and that you agree payment terms with them in advance. Check the accuracy of invoices before you send them out, and provide customers with monthly statements showing their account balance. When credit terms are exceeded, send reminder letters and follow up with telephone calls, and be prepared to put a customer's account on hold if there is no good reason for non-payment.

Investigate Reasons for Non-payment

Even when you adopt these procedures there are going to be situations that lead to an invoice not being paid on time. You will then have to decide on the best approach to recover your debt, and a lot will depend on the approach of your customer, their size and importance to your business, and the size of the debt. There are several reasons for non-payment.

Habitual slow payer—Sometimes new customers are acquired suddenly, and it is only after you've supplied them for a while that you find out why: their previous supplier had closed their account because of continuing problems with late payment. These types of customers will go through long delaying tactics as a matter of course and can waste a huge amount of your (or your finance department's) time in chasing them. Undertaking credit checks can help to minimize this risk, but often it is only by adopting very tight credit control and setting low credit limits initially that you can limit the problem. If the problems continue, you may then have to decide between charging higher prices to reflect your extra costs, or refusing to give your customer credit.

Disputed invoices—Misunderstandings about the terms of a transaction are quite common, and the easiest way to avoid them is to make sure that each stage of the sales process has been documented. If this information is not complete, you may have to face negotiating a compromise with your customer, which should mean that you get paid for at least part of the invoice. If there is no room for compromise and you believe that your case is strong, then you should look at formal recovery of your debt as the best way forward—although the process can be time consuming and expensive. If the dispute does end up in court, you will need to be able to demonstrate that you have explored all avenues to resolve it, so you should document the process carefully.

Financial difficulty—This is probably the most common reason for non-payment of an invoice, and is often masked by your customer behind lots of other reasons. You need to identify whether this is a short-term cash flow glitch or a major financial problem that is likely to result in your customer becoming insolvent. In situations where a customer faces a short-term difficulty, it may be possible to agree to payments in installments over a specific period. If you do agree to this approach, make sure you confirm it in writing and then monitor the situation carefully to ensure that your customer maintains these special payments.

If a customer's business faces long-term or extreme cash flow problems it is likely to be unable to pay your debt. Knowing the legal status of your customer's business is important under these circumstances, because this will determine how you can pursue the recovery of your debt. Often the best that you can hope for is that you can claim title to the goods that you have supplied, which may still have some value to you. For this reason, you should insure that a retention-of-title clause is used in all of your terms of sale and all invoices which involve the sale of goods.

WHAT TO AVOID
Delaying Sending Out Invoices

Issue invoices promptly after a sale. Taking too much time will lead to delays in you getting paid because payment terms will be based on the invoice date and not the date that you supplied the goods or services.

Being Overly Sympathetic to Customers' Financial Problems

If there's no valid reason for non-payment, don't delay the process of debt collection because you're worried about upsetting your customer. This may just lead to your business being owed more and possibly not getting paid at all if the customer's business ceases trading.

SEE ALSO
Budgeting (p. 435)
Managing Creditors and Debtors (p. 111)

Understanding the Role of Price

GETTING STARTED

The price that you charge for your product or service needs to reflect your costs on the one hand and the strength of the market on the other. Setting a price too high can result in lost sales, while undercharging can eat into your profits and possibly lead to you being unable to deliver on your contracts. This actionlist contains advice on how to go about calculating prices, in a way that will suit both your business and the market. One book on the subject that you might also find useful is *Power Pricing: How Managing Price Transforms the Bottom Line* by Robert J. Dolan and Hermann Simon, published in 1996 by Simon & Schuster.

FAQS

What is the difference between price and cost?

The *cost* of producing your product or service is the total costs for the business, both direct and fixed, divided by the number of products that you sell. The *price* that you charge depends on what the market will stand, that is, on what the customer will pay. The difference between price and cost is profit—or loss!

How do I work out how much I can charge?

You need to research the market carefully in order to determine the price that you can charge. This is most difficult when you are starting up, since you have little information on which to base your pricing decisions, other than reviewing the prices charged by your competitors and your own market research with potential customers. Once you are in business it becomes easier, since you can adjust your prices and review the effects they have on demand.

Will charging less than my competitors win customers?

Many people have difficulty calculating the cost of their products or services and, as a result, let their competitors effectively set the price, thinking that, as long as they undercut that price, then they will succeed. However, cost leadership is a strategy that often fails for small businesses, since they lack the economies of scale necessary to make the price really competitive and end up losing money as a result.

What is gross profit?

The gross profit is the selling price minus the direct costs involved in making the product or delivering the service. Direct costs (sometimes known as variable costs, because they vary with the output) include such items as raw materials, purchased components, and sub-contracting. Fixed costs (sometimes known as overheads—items such as rent, taxes, depreciation, and insurance) are then deducted from the gross profit, resulting in the net profit. So you need to sell enough at your chosen price to cover all the direct and fixed costs, and make a profit as well.

What is the break-even point?

The break-even point is the point where the income from sales exactly equals all the costs incurred by the business. More sales will result in a profit; fewer sales will result in a loss.

Can I change the price once it is set?

The price can always be changed, but there is often customer resistance to the raising of price if the rise is too great, or if you change it too frequently.

MAKING IT HAPPEN
Remember the Two-step Process

There are two steps in setting price: the first step is to determine the costs of delivering a product or service; the second step is to set a price that is high enough to cover the costs, but low enough to be competitive.

Research the Market

You need to start with an idea of what you may be able to sell and the price at which you might be able to sell it. This information comes from your market research. It is necessary to have a sensible estimate of likely sales volumes, otherwise you will not be able to calculate the direct costs. This is less important if you are selling a service where there are very low, if any, direct costs. But it is very important if you are in manufacturing, particularly if the direct costs (like raw materials) are of a high value. Prepare an income and expenditure forecast using different prices. Estimate what effect a price increase will have on your sales. Consider the prices offered by your competitors. If your prices are much higher, are you offering sufficient extra benefit to entice customers to buy from you?

Calculate the Costs

There are a number of different ways of allocating costs to products and services, but the key requirement is to know all the costs—direct and fixed—for an expected level of sales. Don't forget to include depreciation and your deductions if you are self-employed. Once you have the cost, then you have the bare minimum price for a given level of sales.

Provided the costs are less than the price that you set when you did your market research, you will make a profit—assuming, of course, that you also sell the volumes that you predicted.

Conduct a Break-even Analysis

Once you know your costs and estimated selling price, you are in a position to calculate how many products, or hours of your time, you need to sell to break even (that is, to cover all your costs).

One way to calculate the break-even point is to draw a graph that shows sales volume on the horizontal axis and money on the vertical axis. First show the overhead costs. This will be a horizontal line since these costs are, generally, fixed for all volumes of production.

The direct costs can then be added to the overhead costs to give total costs for a given volume of output. A line representing total costs can be plotted. The sales income can then be plotted to show how much income will be generated for a given volume of sales. Remember that sales income starts at zero for zero sales.

The point where the sales income equals the total cost shows the break-even point. A higher price will achieve break-even with fewer sales. A lower price may attract more customers, but will require higher sales to break even. The further above break-even that a business can operate, the greater its margin of safety.

Set Targets

Once you have determined your price and defined the break-even volume that you need to sell, set an annual target, broken down into monthly targets, designed to generate you a reasonable profit.

It can often be helpful to plot the targets for sales and actual sales on a graph to monitor progress regularly. If the business does not achieve its targets you will need to take remedial action.

Review

Review your sales volumes and income regularly. Ensure that you are making a profit; if you are not, you will need to take corrective action, perhaps involving changing the price.

WHAT TO AVOID
Setting the Price Too Low

The greatest danger when setting a price for the first time is to pitch it too low. Raising a price is always more difficult than lowering one, yet there are great temptations to undercut the competition. It is clearly important to compare your prices to your competitors', but it is essential that your price covers all your costs and contributes towards your profit.

Failing to Cost Accurately

Many businesses run into difficulties, and some fail because they do not cost their work accurately. They fail to check the actual costs of a job against the estimated costs. While they cannot turn back history and re-price, they can at least amend their prices for future sales. Not doing this is likely to result in failing to achieve targets for profit and profitability.

Under Utilizing Assets

Many businesses buy expensive equipment and fail to include all the depreciation when they are estimating costs. If you are buying expensive equipment, you need to think carefully about how you will recover the cost.

SEE ALSO
Budgeting (p. 435)
Determining Price Positioning and Flexibility (p. 123)
Pricing (p. 480)

Determining Price Positioning and Flexibility

GETTING STARTED
Setting the price of a product or service is often regarded as a financial issue, but in reality it's also a marketing issue. Of course, the price has to cover all the costs and generate a profit, otherwise the business will not survive, but equally, you won't necessarily want to charge the most that you can manage, because you want customers to think that you offer good value for money, and you want repeat business. This actionlist looks at some of the main issues for you to consider when setting your prices.

FAQS
How do I set the price?
Setting a price is a two-part exercise. First, you need to calculate all of your costs and then divide this figure by the number of products, or days of service, that you expect to sell. This gives a minimum price at which your business can break even but not make a profit. Second, you need to research the market to determine the maximum price that could be achievable for your product or service. You can then set your actual price somewhere between the two.

If my price is lower than my competitors', will I sell more?
Many businesses believe that if they set their price lower than their competitors, then they will win greater market share. This is known as "cost leadership." Small businesses, however, are usually too small to achieve the economies of scale necessary to enable them to fix a really competitive price. If you are in this position, you need to "differentiate" your product or service in order to secure a competitive edge. This could be done on the basis of better quality, better service, or quicker delivery, for example. You may find that quicker delivery is an extra benefit for which your customers might be willing to pay.

What happens if I increase my prices?
Fixing a price is a juggling act between strategy, pricing, and cash flow. If your price is too low, the income may not cover all your costs. If the price is too high, even

with a well-differentiated product, you may have difficulty attracting enough customers. However, maximizing profit does not necessarily mean selling high volumes at low profit. It may be possible to sell low volumes at high profit. The challenge that you face is to find the right balance.

In general, changing the price will cause a change in demand. Small businesses often find that they can put up the price without losing too many customers, thus increasing profitability. But you also need to understand the potential effect that a price change will have on your customers. It's a good idea to warn them that prices are going to rise, and to explain why. A good relationship with your customers can improve their perception of the value you are offering.

How much flexibility do I have?
The amount of flexibility that you have largely depends on the way that your product or service is perceived in the marketplace. A cost leadership strategy gives you almost no flexibility, because you have to respond to the price set by your competitors. A differentiated strategy is based on demonstrating how your product or service is quite different from your competitors; the particular benefits of what you offer give you more flexibility in setting your price.

MAKING IT HAPPEN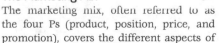
The Marketing Mix
The marketing mix, often referred to as the four Ps (product, position, price, and promotion), covers the different aspects of

marketing. It's the marketing mix that conveys your message to your customers.

Your price needs to reflect the position that you want to adopt in the market place. If you adopt a position of quality, you will want (and will probably need) to charge a premium price. If your product or service is regarded as mass-produced, and therefore of lower quality, then the price should be at the bottom end of the spectrum.

Pricing Strategies

There are a number of possible pricing strategies that you could adopt:

- **Cost-based pricing** is when total costs are calculated and a mark-up is added to give the required profit. The mark-up is usually expressed as a percentage of the cost. Different types of businesses will apply varying mark-ups; for example, the mark-up on jewelry is enormous compared to the mark-up on food products.
- **"Skimming"** is where you initially charge a relatively high price to recover investment costs quickly if the product is new. As your competitors follow your lead and launch their own products to compete and enter the market, you lower the price.
- **Negotiating prices individually** with customers, based on the quantities they are prepared to buy. If you wish to sell to a particular market, then you might sell one product or service more cheaply (as a **loss leader**) to gain market entry. You balance this by selling other products or services at a higher price. This can be risky, as the danger is that everything becomes a loss leader.
- **Expected price** involves finding out what the customer expects to pay. If you are selling a high-quality product, do not underprice. Often the customer expects to pay more (for instance, if the product or service has a certain "snob" value), and you could diminish the premium value of your product or service if you underprice, making it less attractive to the customer.

- **Differential pricing** is where you charge different segments of your market different prices for the same service; for example, you may decide to offer discounts to certain people, such as senior citizens or the unemployed, or charge lower rates for quiet periods.
- **Lifetime pricing** is a technique you can adopt if your product price is higher than your competitors' and you want to encourage customers to look at the cost of ownership over the *lifetime* of the product. This might work well if, for example, your product is likely to last longer, thus reducing depreciation. Also, the cost of maintenance may be lower, reducing the annual cost.

WHAT TO AVOID
Relying on Cost Leadership

Do not simply aim to undercut your competitors; cost leadership is a difficult strategy for small businesses to pursue. Instead, aim to differentiate your product or service.

You Aren't Selling Enough

Ensure that you are selling enough products at your chosen price to cover all of your costs and to generate a profit. Keep a careful eye on your sales and if you are not selling enough at your chosen price, then you need to take remedial action.

Treating Price as a Simple Calculation

It's best to regard price as part of the marketing mix, rather than a straight financial calculation. You need to consider all the parts of the equation carefully. Make sure that you research the market thoroughly, and that you are familiar with your competitors' pricing strategies and your customers' needs.

SEE ALSO
Budgeting (p. 435)
Pricing (p. 480)
Understanding the Role of Price (p. 120)

Focus On: Pricing
Michael de Kare-Silver

GETTING STARTED

In recent years, many companies of all sizes have not found it easy to increase profits. Economic conditions, government policies against inflation, increased competition on pricing (including producers from the less-developed countries), and more sophisticated customers around the world have all put pressure on volume and price in many industries. Not surprisingly, companies have turned to levers more directly in their control—such as reducing costs and better process management—as sources of profit growth. This has led to a focus on what is known as reengineering (a method of changing the processes within a business in order to improve the quality of the products and thereby gain competitive advantage), downsizing, and outsourcing.

However, reengineering can only go so far in boosting profits and there is a growing realization that more opportunity and potential may lie on the top line. Pricing, especially, is an undiscovered weapon. There is significant profit potential for companies in challenging this area, and in "re-engineering" their price position.

How can a company check whether it making full use of its pricing opportunities? Consider the following questions, all of which focus internally on the business:

- What percentage of senior management time is spent on pricing?
- How much senior management time is spent with customers?
- Is competitor pricing tracked in similar detail?
- How frequently is pricing specifically and rigorously reviewed?
- Is the company organized in a way that makes sure that a "balanced" pricing decision is made?
  Also, consider the external issues, that is, those facing the market:
- Do you understand your competitors' future pricing strategies and plans?
- Is there a clear understanding of what the company sees as added value, compared to what the customer sees? Do the two match up?
- Does your company have a clear pricing strategy? Is it differentiated for the differing circumstances and market position of each product group and each customer?
  This actionlist explains how to use pricing to improve profitability.

FAQS

What are the main issues affecting pricing?

- **Economic forces**, including monopoly and the extent of competition. There is an increasing amount of antitrust legislation designed to ensure that prices are fair and do not abuse a market dominant position at consumers' expense. Supply and demand affects pricing, as generally, when supply exceeds demand, prices will fall. The converse is also true: when demand exceeds supply, prices will rise.
- **Market issues** such as customer perceptions and behavior. Successful pricing is based on a clear understanding of the specific needs and nature of the target market. The culture and maturity of the market also affects pricing decisions, so if there is an acceptance of a particular type of pricing structure or approach then strategies will often follow this. Finally, if the market is in decline, then prices may need to be cut, simply to compete for a dwindling number of available customers.
- **Market competitiveness** clearly affects pricing decisions. If there are a large number of direct competitors, pricing can be a valuable tool—or at times it can be a complete irrelevance, as the market knows

the price and will accept no deviation from it. Where few direct competitors exist, then there may often be a greater degree of latitude for pricing decisions.

- **Product issues** such as cost are fundamentally significant when setting prices. It may be desirable for products to be sold at a loss to establish market-share or drive out competitors. Frequently of greatest significance are the product's benefits and the value it provides customers, although this needs to be closely related to other factors such as costs and competition.

MAKING IT HAPPEN
Understand the Routes to Effective Pricing

The more you know about which products make money and which lose, the more you can adopt a better strategic and selective pricing policy. Three main routes can be identified that lead to more effective pricing:

- exploiting market advantages;
- changing the decision-making process on pricing;
- testing whether all the different pricing options are being proactively pursued.

Of course, some companies enjoy market or structural circumstances that make pricing management easier. Have they just fallen by luck into those situations, or have their advantages been "engineered" more deliberately? Some companies have used strategic alliances to create market and structural barriers deliberately—by locking up a vital supply of raw materials, say, and making it hard for others to function.

Select the Best Pricing Strategy

Not only can companies make structural moves that are more easily within their control, there are also as many as 12 different pricing strategies available. They often appear to be underexploited. The challenge is frequently not lack of familiarity with the particular pricing option. It is more about:

- having enough management time to check whether the particular pricing options have been fully considered;
- understanding the significance of pricing

for competitiveness (the market's price sensitivity);
- examining price opportunities and developing insights on an individual product line basis, rather than across a range;
- management's ability to challenge sales-led pricing decisions;
- the effectiveness and rigor with which the pricing strategies are implemented;
- the information systems needed to support, monitor, and refine these activities.

Use Customer Information Management

There are four approaches to consider, the first of which are based on "segmentation." In simple terms, this means dividing up data relevant to your research into appropriate sections.

- **Category segmentation.** You can gain insight into each of your product lines by looking at each one's profitability and pricing.
- **Customer segmentation.** This approach identifies pricing opportunities by using detailed customer information.
- **"Bundling".** As core product/service prices come under pressure, companies add related products and services where pricing is more robust (and which equally reinforce the value proposition of the core product/service).
- **Managing trade terms.** This means managing the level of discounts given to customers to improve overall returns.

Exploit Structural Advantages

Four options are highlighted here:

- **lowest cost/lowest price**: cost advantages allow market invaders to price lower their products or services and thereby grow share rapidly.
- **supply and demand management**: as an illustration, better hotel occupancy systems have enabled leaders to quote more aggressive room tariffs.
- **supplier-customer "balance of power"**: this can be exploited to make sure that suppliers "contribute" to gross margin success. Tough management of the supply price means that you will have greater

flexibility when you come to fix the price for your end-consumer.

- **"open-book" and partnership-pricing**: the open-book approach was pioneered in the automotive industry. Sharing information about costs has enabled better suppliers to justify and push through selective price increases.

Develop an Innovative Pricing Strategy and Lead the Market

Pricing can be used to innovate and establish a leadership position in the market. This is accomplished first with branding. It means developing consistently high levels of branding and advertising, thus enabling the company to maintain a price premium. Next, consider the total value proposition of your product or service and which of the following five strategies are most appropriate:

- **technology-driven**: continuously developing a niche. This works best with technically advanced products that can give really boost your gross margin.
- **first in**: continually focusing on being first to market gives initial pricing advantages, as well as other benefits.
- **best at**: leadership on all features valued by the customer can give price leadership in both "value pricing" of certain products and "premium pricing" for certain others.
- **share leadership**: restructuring the portfolio of products offered so that it focuses only on market share leaders, where you have more control over pricing and other levers.
- **innovative consumer value**: providing a clear mixing of quality, value, and service to lead in the eyes of the customer.

WHAT TO AVOID
Not Consulting Widely on Pricing Issues

Price decisions are too often made by too few people. Only by sharing the responsibility for pricing can managers begin to understand the importance that pricing can have on the success of any business. Ultimately, decisions on pricing must be measured against other critical factors, such as data on customers. In the final analysis, pricing can be an exercise in both innovation and leadership.

Avoiding Short Term Action

Shorttermism in pricing is, as in most other areas, something to avoid. There are, however, at least two short term pricing options to increase profits, without damaging the company's future prospects or room for maneuver:

- price squeeze: at one company that had recently been brought back from the brink of business failure, the new chief executive insisted that each product line price be "squeezed" up 1%. Despite initial internal resistance, this was successfully implemented, and had an immediate impact on the company's net profit.
- price elasticity: have you looked at the way that price and volume relate to each other? Do they balance? For example, products with a low margin (that is, where there isn't a big difference between their production cost and their selling price) can be priced up relatively aggressively so that even if you sell fewer of them (less volume), the impact won't be that bad.

Failing to Understand the Potential Value of Changes in Pricing

How can you tap into significant pricing potential? By removing the roadblocks that typically operate within the organization—such as:

- leaving responsibility for pricing to your sales team (Who has ever seen a salesman who wanted to increase prices?);
- allowing little or no finance team involvement to make sure that decision making is balanced;
- if you're not the owner-manager, accepting senior management's remoteness from the reality of your market—this makes it difficult to challenge sales views;
- a lack of data on the true net profitability of individual services/products to either your company or your customers.

Creating a Balance Sheet

WHAT IT MEASURES

The financial standing, or even the net worth or owners' equity, of a company at a given point in time, typically at the end of a calendar or fiscal year.

WHY IT IS IMPORTANT

The balance sheet shows what is owned (assets), what is owed (liabilities), and what is left (owners' equity). It provides a concise snapshot of a company's financial position.

HOW IT WORKS IN PRACTICE

However they are presented, assets must be in balance with liabilities and shareholders' equity. In other words, assets must equal liabilities and owners' equity.

Assets include cash in hand and cash anticipated (receivables), inventories of supplies and materials, properties, facilities, equipment, and whatever else the company uses to conduct business. Assets also need to reflect depreciation in the value of equipment such as machinery that has a limited expected useful life.

Liabilities include pending payments to suppliers and creditors, outstanding current and long-term debts, taxes, interest payments, and other unpaid expenses that the company has incurred.

Subtracting the value of aggregate liabilities from the value of aggregate assets reveals the value of owners' equity. Ideally, it should be positive. Owners' equity consists of capital invested by owners over the years and profits (net income) or internally generated capital, which is referred to as "retained earnings"; these are funds to be used in future operations.

As an example:

ASSETS $
Current:

Cash	8,200
Securities	5,000
Receivables	4,500
Inventory & supplies	6,300

Fixed:

Land	10,000
Structures	90,000
Equipment (less depreciation)	5,000
Intangibles/other	
TOTAL ASSETS	129,000

LIABILITIES $

Payables	7,000
Taxes	4,000
Misc.	3,000
Bonds & notes	25,000
TOTAL LIABILITIES	39,000
SHAREHOLDERS' EQUITY (stock, par value shares outstanding)	80,000
RETAINED EARNINGS	10,000
TOTAL LIABILITIES AND SHAREHOLDERS' EQUITY	129,000

TRICKS OF THE TRADE

- The balance sheet does not show a company's market worth, nor important intangibles such as the knowledge and talents of individual people, nor other vital business factors such as customers or market share.
- The balance sheet does not express the true value of some fixed assets. A six-year-old manufacturing plant, for example, is listed at its original cost, even though the price of replacing it could be much higher or substantially lower (because of new technology that might be less expensive or vastly more efficient).
- The balance sheet is not an indicator of past or future performance or trends that affect performance. It needs to be studied along with two other key reports: the income statement and the cash flow statement. A published balance sheet needs to include prior period comparatives.

SEE ALSO
Accounting (p. 428)

Reading a Balance Sheet

GETTING STARTED

A balance sheet will tell us something about the financial strength of a business on the day that the balance sheet is drawn up. That situation changes constantly, so you could say it is more like a snapshot than a movie. Although the method of producing a balance sheet is standardized, there can be a certain element of subjectivity in interpreting it. Different elements of the balance sheet can tell you different things about the how the business is doing.

This actionlist gives an overview of a balance sheet and looks at a brief selection of the more interesting figures that help with interpretation. It's important to remember that a lot of these figures do not tell you that much in isolation; it is in trend analysis or comparisons between businesses that they speak more lucidly.

FAQS

What is a balance sheet?

A balance sheet is an accountant's view, the book value of the assets and liabilities of a business at a specific date and on that date alone. The term "balance" means exactly what it says—that those assets and liabilities will be equal. In showing how the balance lies, the balance sheet gives us an idea of the financial health of the business.

What does a balance sheet not do?

A balance sheet is not designed to represent market value of the business. For example, property in the balance sheet may be worth a lot more than its book value. Plant and machinery is shown at cost less depreciation, but that may well be different from market value. Stock may turn out to be worth less than its balance-sheet value, and so on.

Also there may be hidden assets, such as goodwill or valuable brands, that do not appear on the balance sheet at all. These would all enhance the value of the business in a sale situation, yet are invisible on a normal balance sheet.

MAKING IT HAPPEN

Here is a very simple company balance sheet:

Fixed Assets	1,000
Current Assets	700

Less Current Liabilities	400	
Net Current Assets		300
		1,300
Less Long-term Loans		200
Net Assets		1,100
Profit and Loss Account		500
Share Capital		600
Shareholders' Funds		1,100

Define the Individual Elements

- *Fixed Assets*—items that are not traded as part of a company's normal activities but enable it to function, such as property, machinery, or vehicles. These are tangible assets (meaning you can kick them). This heading can also include intangible assets (you cannot kick them). A common example is "goodwill," which can arise upon the acquisition of one business by another.
- *Current Assets*—items that form the trading cycle of the business. The most common examples are stock, debtors, and positive bank balances.
- *Current Liabilities*—also items that form the trading cycle of the business but represent short-term amounts owed to others. Examples will be trade creditors, taxes, and bank overdrafts–broadly, any amount due for payment within the next 12 months from the date of the balance sheet.
- *Net Current Assets*—not a new figure, but simply the difference between current

assets and current liabilities, often shown because it may be a useful piece of information.

- *Long-term Loans*—debt that is repayable more than one year from the date of the balance sheet.
- *Net Assets*—also not a new figure, but the sum of fixed assets plus net current assets less long-term loans. In other words, all of the company assets shown in its books, minus all of its liabilities.
- *Profit and Loss Account*—the total of all the accumulated profits and losses from all the accounting periods since the business started. It increases or decreases each year by the net profit or loss in that period, calculated after providing for all costs including tax and dividends to shareholders.
- *Share Capital*—the number of shares issued, multiplied by their nominal value. The latter is the theoretical figure at which the shares were originally issued and has nothing to do with their market value.
- *Shareholders' Funds*—not a new figure, but the sum of the profit and loss account plus the share capital. It represents the total interest of the shareholders in the company.

Learn to Interpret Them

Note that balance sheets differ between one industry and another in the sense of the range and type of assets and liabilities that exist. For example, a retailer will have little in the way of trade debtors because it sells for cash, or a manufacturer is likely to have a far larger investment in plant than a service business like an advertising agency. So the interpretation must be seen in the light of the actual trade of the business.

Reading a balance sheet can be quite subjective—accountancy is an art, not a science and, although the method of producing a balance sheet is standardized, there may be some items in it that are subjective rather than factual. The way people interpret some of the figures will also vary, depending on what they wish to achieve and how they see certain things as being good or bad.

Look First at the Net Assets/Shareholders' Funds

Positive or negative? Our example, being a healthy business, has net assets of a positive $1,100. Positive is good. If there were 600 shares in issue, it would mean that the net assets per share were $1.83.

If it had negative assets (same thing as net liabilities), this might mean that the business is heading for difficulty unless it is being supported by some party such as a parent company, bank, or other investor. When reading a balance sheet with negative assets, consider where the support will be coming from.

Then Examine Net Current Assets

Positive or negative? Again, our example has net current assets of a positive $300. This means that, theoretically, it should not have any trouble settling short-term liabilities because it has more than enough current assets to do so. Negative net current assets suggest that there possibly could be a problem in settling short-term liabilities.

You can also look at NCA as a ratio of current assets/current liabilities. Here, a figure over one is equivalent to the NCA having a positive absolute figure. The ratio version is more useful in analyzing trends of balance sheets over successive periods or comparing two businesses.

A cut-down version of looking at NCA considers only (debtors + cash)/(creditors), thus excluding stock. The reasoning here is that this looks at the most liquid of the net current asset constituents and again a figure over one is the most desirable. This is also a ratio that is more meaningful in trends or comparisons.

Understand the Significance of Trade Debtor Payments . . .

Within current assets, we have trade debtors. It can be useful to consider how many days' worth of sales are tied up in debtors—given by (debtors × 365)/annual sales. This provides an idea of how long the company is waiting to get paid. Too long, and it might be something requiring investigation. However, this figure can be misleading, where sales do not take place evenly throughout the year. A construction company might be an example of such a business: one big debtor incurred near the year end would skew the ratio.

... and Trade Creditor Payments

Similar to the above, this looks at (trade creditors × 365)/annual purchases, indicating how long the company is taking in general to pay its suppliers. This is not so easy to calculate because the purchases for this purpose include not only goods for resale but all the overheads as well.

Recognize What Debt Means

Important to most businesses, this figure is the total of long and short-term loans. Too much debt might indicate that the company would have trouble, in a downturn, in paying the interest. It's difficult to give an optimum level of debt because there are so many different situations, depending on a huge range of circumstances.

Often, instead of an absolute figure, debt is expressed as a percentage of shareholders' funds and known as "gearing" or "leverage." In a public company, gearing of 100% might be considered pretty high, whereas debt of under 30% may be seen as on the low side.

✘ WHAT TO AVOID
Believing That Balance Sheet Figures Represent Market Value

Don't assume that a balance sheet is a valuation of the business. Its primary purpose is that it forms part of the range of accounting reports used for measuring business performance—along with the other common financial reports like profit and loss accounts and cash flow statements. Management, shareholders, and others such as banks will use the entire range to assess the health of the business.

Forgetting That the Balance Sheet Is Valid Only for the Date at Which It Is Produced

A short while after a balance sheet is produced, things could be quite different. In practice there frequently may not be any radical changes between the date of the balance sheet and the date when it is being read, but it is entirely possible that something could have happened to the business that would not show. For example, a major debtor could have defaulted unexpectedly. So remember that balance sheet figures are valid only as at the date shown, and are not a permanent picture of the business.

Confusion over Whether in Fact All Assets and Liabilities Are Shown in the Balance Sheet

Some businesses may have hidden assets, as suggested above. This could be the value of certain brands or trademarks, for example, for which money may not have ever been paid. Yet these could be worth a great deal. Conversely, there may be some substantial legal action pending which could cost the company a lot, yet is not shown fully in the balance sheet.

SEE ALSO
Accounting (p. 428)
Reading a Cash Flow Statement (p. 139)

Creating a Profit and Loss Account

WHAT IT MEASURES

A company's sales revenues and expenses over a period, providing a calculation of profits or losses during that time.

WHY IT IS IMPORTANT

Reading a P&L is the easiest way to tell if a business has made a profit or a loss during a given month or year. The most important figure it contains is net profit: what is left over after revenues are used to pay expenses and taxes.

Companies typically issue P&L reports monthly. It is customary for the reports to include year-to-date figures, as well as corresponding year-earlier figures to allow for comparisons and analysis.

HOW IT WORKS IN PRACTICE

A P&L adheres to a simple rule of thumb: "revenue minus cost equals profit."

There are two P&L formats, multiple-step and single-step. Both follow a standard set of rules known as Generally Accepted Accounting Principles (GAAP). These rules generally adhere to requirements established by governments to track receipts, expenses, and profits for tax purposes. They also allow the financial reports of two different companies to be compared. Note that in the United Kingdom and several other nations, sales, revenues, and receipts may all be designated as turnover.

The multiple-step format is much more common, because it includes a larger number of details and is thus more useful. It deducts costs from revenues in a series of steps, allowing for closer analysis. Revenues appear first, then expenses, each in as much detail as management desires. Sales may be broken down by product line or location, while expenses such as salaries may be broken down into base salaries and commissions.

Expenses are then subtracted from revenues to show profit (or loss). A basic multiple-step P&L looks like this:

MULTIPLE-STEP PROFIT & LOSS ACCOUNT ($)

NET SALES			750,000
Less: cost of goods sold			450,000
Gross profit			300,000
LESS: OPERATING EXPENSES			
Selling expenses			
Salaries & commissions	54,000		
Advertising	37,500		
Delivery/transportation	12,000		
Depreciation/store equipment	7,500		
Other selling expenses	5,000		
Total selling expenses		116,000	
General & administrative expenses			
Administrative/office salaries	74,000		
Utilities	2,500		
Depreciation/structure	2,400		
Misc. other expenses	3,100		
Total general & admin expenses		82,000	
Total operating expenses			198,000
OPERATING INCOME			102,000

LESS (ADD): NONOPERATING ITEMS		
Interest expenses	11,000	
Interest income earned	(2,800)	8,200
Income before taxes		93,800
Income taxes		32,360
Net Income		**61,440**

P&Ls of public companies may also report income on the basis of earnings per share. For example, if the company issuing this statement had 12,000 shares outstanding, earnings per share would be $5.12, that is, $61,440 divided by 12,000 shares.

TRICKS OF THE TRADE

■ A P&L does not show how a business earned or spent its money.
■ One month's P&L can be misleading, especially if a business generates a majority of its receipts in particular months. A retail establishment, for example, usually generates a large percentage of its sales in the final three months of the year, while a consulting service might generate the lion's share of its revenues in as few as two months, and no revenues at all in some other months.
■ Invariably, figures for both revenues and expenses reflect the judgments of the companies reporting them. Accounting methods can be quite arbitrary when it comes to such factors as depreciation expenses.

SEE ALSO
Accounting (p. 428)

Reading a Profit and Loss Account

GETTING STARTED

A profit and loss account is a statement of the income and expenditure of a business over the period stated, drawn up in order to ascertain how much profit the business made. Put simply, the difference between the income from sales and the associated expenditure is the profit or loss for the period. "Income" and "expenditure" here mean only those amounts directly attributable to earning the profit and thus would exclude capital expenditure, for example.

Importantly, the figures are adjusted to match the income and expenses to the time period in which they were incurred—not necessarily the same as that in which the cash changed hands.

FAQS

What is a profit and loss account?

A profit and loss account is an accountant's view of the figures that show how much profit or loss a business has made over a period. To do this, it is necessary to allocate the various elements of income and expenditure to the time period concerned, not on the basis of when cash was received or spent, but on when the income was earned or the liability to pay a supplier and employees was incurred. While capital expenditures are excluded, depreciation of property and equipment is included as a noncash expense.

Thus if you sell goods on credit, you will be paid later but the sale takes place upon the contract to sell them. Equally, if you buy goods and services on credit, the purchase takes place when you contract to buy them, not when you when you actually settle the invoice.

What does a profit and loss account not show?

Most importantly, a P&L account is not an explanation of the cash coming into and going out of a business.

MAKING IT HAPPEN

Here is a simple example of a profit and loss account for a particular year:

Sales		1,000
Opening Stock	100	
Purchases	520	
	620	

Closing Stock	80	
Cost of Sales		540
Gross Profit		460
Wages	120	
Other Overhead	230	
		350
Net Profit before Tax		110
Tax		22
Net after Tax		88
Dividends		40
Retained Profit		48
Retained Profit Brought Forward		150
Retained Profit Carried Forward		198

Note that the presence of stock and purchases indicates that the business is trading or manufacturing goods of some kind, rather than selling services.

Defining the Individual Elements

- *Sales*—the invoiced value of the sales in the period.
- *Stock*—the value of the actual physical stock held by the business at the opening and closing of the period. It is always valued at cost, or realizable value if that is lower, never at selling price.
- *Purchases and Other Direct Costs*—the goods or raw materials purchased by the business for resale—not capital items used in the business, only items used as part of the direct cost of its sales. In other words, those costs which vary directly with sales, as distinct from overheads (like rent) which do not.

When a business holds stock, the purchases figure has to be adjusted for the opening and closing values in order to reach the right income and expenditure amounts for that period only. Goods for resale bought in the period may not have been used purely for that period but may be lying in stock at the end of it, ready for sale in the next. Similarly, goods used for resale in this period will consist partly of items already held in stock at the beginning of it. So take the amounts purchased, add the opening stock and deduct the closing stock. The resulting adjusted purchase figure is known as "cost of sales."

In some businesses there may be other direct costs apart from purchases included in cost of sales. For example, a manufacturer may include some wages if they are of a direct nature (wages of employees directly involved in the manufacturing process, as distinct from office staff, say). Or a building contractor would include plant hire in direct costs, as well as purchases of materials.

- *Gross Profit*—the difference between sales and cost of sales. This is an important figure as it measures how much was actually made directly from whatever the business is selling, before it starts to pay for overheads.

The figure is often expressed as a percentage ratio, when it is known as the "gross profit margin." In our example the GPM is 460:1,000—or 46%. Ratios are really only useful as comparison tools, either with different periods of the same business or with other businesses.

- *Overheads*—the expenses of the business which do not vary directly with sales. They include a wide range of items such as rent, most wages, advertising, phones, interest paid on loans, audit fees, and so on.
- *Net Profit before Tax*—the result of deducting total overheads from gross profit. This is what the business has made before tax is paid on that profit.
- *Tax*—This will not actually have been paid in the year concerned, but is shown because it is due on the profit for that period. Even then the figure shown may not be the actual amount due, for various reasons,

such as possible overpayments from previous years. Tax can be a very complex matter, being based upon a set of changeable rules.

- *Net Profit after Tax*—the result after deducting the tax liability—the so-called bottom line. This is the amount that the company can do with as it wishes, possibly paying a dividend out of part of it and retaining the rest. It is the company's reward for actually being in business in the first place.
- *Dividends*—a payment to the shareholders as a reward for their investment in the company. Most publicly listed companies of any size pay dividends to shareholders. Private companies may also do so, but this may be more for tax reasons. The dividend in the example shown is paid out of the net profit after tax, but legally it is not permitted to exceed the total available profit. That total available profit is comprised of both the current year's net profit after tax and the retained profit brought forward from previous years.
- *Retained Profit*—the amount kept by the company after paying dividends to shareholders. If there is no dividend, then it is equal to the net profit after tax.
- *Retained Profit Brought Forward*—the total accumulated retained profits for all earlier years of the company's existence.
- *Retained Profit Carried Forward*—the above figure brought forward, plus the current year's retained profit. This new total will form the profit brought forward in the next accounting period.

How to Interpret the Figures

A lot of accounting analysis is valid only when comparing the figures, usually with similar figures for earlier periods, projected future figures, or other companies in the same business.

On its own a P&L account tells you only a limited story, though there are some standalone facts that can be derived from it. What our example does show, even in isolation, is that this business was successful in the period concerned. It made a profit, not a loss, and was able to pay dividends to shareholders out of that profit. Clearly a pretty crucial piece of information.

However, it is in comparisons that such figures start to have real meaning.

The example figures reveal that the gross profit margin was 46%, an important statistic in measuring business performance. The net profit margin before tax was 110:1,000, or 11%. You could take the margin idea further and calculate the net profit after tax ratio to sales as 88:1,000, being 8.8%. Or you could calculate the ratio of any expense to sales. In our example, the wages:sales ratio is 120:1,000 or 12%.

If you then looked at similar margin figures for the preceding accounting period, you would learn something about this business. Say the gross margin was 45% last year compared with 46% this year—there has been some improvement in the profit made before deducting overheads. But then suppose that the net profit margin of 8.8% this year was 9.8% last year. This would tell you that, despite improvement in profit at the gross level, the overheads has increased disproportionately. You could then check on the ratio of each item of the overheads to sales to see where this arose and find out why. Advertising spending could have shot up, for example, or perhaps the company moved to new premises incurring a higher rent. Maybe something could be tightened up.

Another Commonly Used Ratio
Another ratio often used in business analysis is return on capital employed. Here we combine the profit and loss account with the balance sheet by dividing the net profit (either before or after tax as required) by shareholders' funds. This tells you how much the company is making proportionate to money invested in it by the shareholders—a similar idea to how much you might get in interest on a bank deposit account. It's a useful way of comparing different companies in a particular industry, where the more efficient ones are likely to derive a higher return on capital employed.

WHAT TO AVOID
Assuming That the Bottom Line Represents Cash Profit from Trading
It does not! There are a few examples where this is the case: a simple cash trader might buy something for one price, then sell it for more; his profit then equals the increase in cash. But a business that buys and sells on credit, spends money on items that are held for the longer term, such as property or machinery, has tax to pay at a later date, and so on, will make a profit that is not represented by a mere increase in cash balances held. Indeed, the cash balance could quite easily decrease during a period when a profit was made.

SEE ALSO
Accounting (p. 428)
Reading a Cash Flow Statement (p. 139)

Creating a Cash Flow Statement

WHAT IT MEASURES
Cash inflows and cash outflows over a specific period of time, typically a year.

WHY IT IS IMPORTANT
Cash flow is a key indicator of financial health, and it demonstrates to investors, creditors, and other core constituencies a company's ability to meet obligations, finance opportunities, and generally "come up with the cash" as needs arise. Cash flow that is wildly inconsistent with, say, net income, often indicates operating or managerial problems.

HOW IT WORKS IN PRACTICE
In its basic form, a cash flow statement will probably be familiar to anyone who has been a member of a club that collected and spent money. It reports funds on hand at the beginning of a given period, funds received, funds spent, and funds remaining at the end of the period.

That formula still applies to a business today, even if creating a cash flow document is significantly more complex. Cash flows are divided into three categories: cash from operations; cash-investment activities; and cash-financing activities. Companies with holdings in foreign currencies use a fourth classification: effects of changes in currency rates on cash.

A standard direct cash flow statement looks like this:

CRD, Inc.
Statement of Cash Flows
For year ended December 31, 20__

CASH FLOWS FROM OPERATIONS	$
Operating Profit	82,000
Adjustments to net earnings	
Depreciation	17,000
Accounts receivable	(20,000)
Accounts payable	12,000
Inventory	(8,000)
Other adjustments to earnings	4,000
Net cash flow from operations	**87,000**

CASH FLOWS FROM INVESTMENT ACTIVITIES	
Purchases of marketable securities	(58,000)
Receipts from sales of marketable securities	45,000
Loans made to borrowers	(16,000)
Collections on loans	11,000
Purchases of plant and real estate assets	(150,000)
Receipts from sales of plant and real estate assets	47,000
Net cash flow from investment activities:	**(−121,000)**

CASH FLOWS FROM FINANCING ACTIVITIES	
Proceeds from short-term borrowings	51,000
Payments to settle short-term debts	(61,000)
Proceeds from issuing bonds payable	100,000
Proceeds from issuing capital stock	80,000
Dividends paid	(64,000)
Net cash flow from financing activities	**106,000**
Net change in cash during period	72,000
Cash and cash equivalents, beginning of year	27,000
Cash and cash equivalents, end of year	**99,000**

TRICKS OF THE TRADE
- A cash flow statement does *not* measure net income, nor does it measure working capital.
- A cash flow statement does not include outstanding accounts receivable, but it does include the preceding year's accounts receivable (assuming these were collected during the year for which the statement is prepared).

- Add to a cash inflow any amounts charged off for depreciation, depletion, and amortization, since cash was actually spent.
- Cash equivalents are short-term, highly liquid investments, although precise definitions may vary slightly by country. These should be included when recalculating the movement of cash in the period.

- There are alternative ways to present cash flow from operations. Some texts, for example, omit earnings and adjustments, and list instead cash and interest received, cash and interest paid, and taxes received.

SEE ALSO
Accounting (p. 428)

Reading a Cash Flow Statement

GETTING STARTED

In their annual report, most public companies must publish a cash flow statement—together with the profit and loss account and a balance sheet. As the name suggests, the purpose of a cash flow statement is to explain the movement in cash balances or bank overdrafts held by the business from one accounting period to the next.

The balance sheet shows the assets and liabilities at the end of the period, with comparative figures for the start of it. The profit and loss account shows how much profit was generated by the business in the period. The cash flow statement is the third part of the financial picture of the business over the period.

FAQS

What is a cash flow statement?

Over an accounting period, the money held by a business at the bank (or its overdrafts) will have changed. The purpose of the cash flow statement is to show the reasons for this change. If you look at the actionlist on profit and loss (**Reading a Profit and Loss Account (p. 134)**), one of the common mistakes illustrated was the erroneous belief that the profit was equal to the cash generated by a business. It is not, but the cash flow statement is the link between profit and cash balance movements. It takes you down the path from profit to cash. The figures are derived from those published in the annual accounts, and notes will explain how this derivation is arrived at.

What does a cash flow statement not show?

In the same way that a profit and loss account does not show the cash made by the business, a cash flow statement does not show the profit. It is entirely possible for a loss-making business to show an increase in cash, and the other way round too.

MAKING IT HAPPEN

Here is a simple example of a cash flow statement for a particular year:

Net Cash Inflow from Operating Activities		7,020
Returns on Investments and Finance Costs		
Interest Paid	820	
Less Interest Received	90	
Net Cash Outflow from Finance Costs		(730)
Taxation		(1,060)
Capital Expenditure		
Sale of Fixed Assets	760	
Less Purchase of Fixed Assets	4,420	
Net Cash Outflow from Capital Expenditure		(3,660)
Dividends Paid		(1,530)
Net Cash Inflow before Financing		40
Financing		
New Loans	1,000	
Loan Repayments	(300)	
Finance Lease Repayments	(100)	
Net Cash Inflow from Financing		600
Increase in Cash		640

Define the Individual Elements

- *Net Cash Inflow from Operating Activities*—broadly this is the profit of the business, before depreciation plus the change in debtor and creditor balances. There may also be other items included here. In the statutory annual accounts of companies, there will be an explanation to show how this net cash inflow figure is derived from the profit and loss account and balance sheet. Depreciation is excluded because it does not represent a cash cost.

Debtor and creditor balance changes are included here because they represent an inflow or outflow of cash to the business. Thus if customers owe you less or more at the end of a period than at the beginning of it, it follows that there must have been cash flowing in or out of the business as a result. A reduction in debtors means that cash has come in to the business, and the reverse for an increase in debtors. The same applies to the creditor balances of suppliers. An increase here means a cash inflow, with a decrease denoting an outflow.

- *Returns on Investments and Finance Costs*—these figures comprise interest received on cash balances, less interest paid on debt. There could be other forms of investment income here, such as dividends on shares owned.
- *Net Cash Outflow from Finance Costs*—this is not a new figure but the net result of the above items, identified as returns on investments. In our example the result is an outflow of cash. That is, the interest paid on debt exceeded the interest received on cash. It could in some circumstances be the other way around, where for example a business has substantial cash balances earning interest.
- *Taxation*—self explanatory, this is the outflow of cash arising from corporation tax paid by the business. It can on occasion be an inflow, where the company has obtained a repayment of corporation tax for some reason.
- *Capital Expenditure*—this is cash expended on fixed assets bought for the business, less cash received from the sale of assets no longer required by the business.

- *Net Cash Outflow from Capital Expenditure*—this is not a new figure but the net result of the above items, identified as expenditure on new fixed assets less receipts from the sale of disposals of such items. In our example there is a large outflow, which generally would be the norm. It can happen sometimes though that a business realizes more from the sale of fixed assets in a particular period than it expends on items acquired.
- *Dividends Paid*—self explanatory; this is the outflow of cash arising from paying dividends to shareholders.
- *Net Cash Inflow before Financing*—this is not a new figure but a subtotal of the items above. In our example, the figure of $40 shown happens to be an inflow but it could just as easily have been an outflow. There is no typical figure here; it is just as common to see net inflows as outflows.

It is important to understand what this figure represents. It is the net cash result of running the business in the period concerned, after paying tax to the government and dividends to the shareholders. However, as its label indicates, it doesn't include any financing.

- *Financing*—this term includes the raising of new loans, the repayment of old ones and other methods of financing such as issuing new shares. In the example the company borrowed $1,000 in new loans, which creates a cash inflow of that sum, and repaid $300 on old debt plus a further $100 on equipment leases (which are another form of finance), making a net inflow on finance of $400.
- *Increase in Cash* (the bottom line)—adding the net inflow of $600 from finance to the $40 generated by business operations gives us an overall net cash inflow of $640. This is the bottom line. It means that we have $640 more in the bank at the end of the accounting period than at the beginning of it.

Learn to Interpret the Figures

As suggested above, the cash flow statement is the third section of the primary set of accounting documents used to explain and analyze businesses. It is a "derived schedule," meaning that the figures are pulled from the profit and loss account and balance sheet statements, linking the two.

Its purpose is to analyze the reasons why the company's cash position changed over an accounting period. For example, a sharp increase in borrowings could have several explanations—such as a high level of capital expenditure, poor trading, an increase in the time taken by debtors to pay, and so on. The cash flow statement will alert management to the reasons for this, in a way that may not be obvious merely from the profit and loss account and balance sheet alone.

The generally desirable situation is for the net position before financing to be positive. Even the best-run businesses will sometimes have an outflow in a period (for example in a year of high capital expenditure), but positive is usually good. This becomes more apparent when comparing the figures over a period of time. A repeated outflow of funds over several years is usually an indication of trouble. To cover this, the company must raise new financing and/or sell off assets which will tend to compound the problem, in the worst cases leading to failure.

Cash is critical to every business, so the management must understand where its cash is coming from and going to. The cash flow statement gives us this information in an abbreviated form. You could argue that the whole purpose of a business is to start with one sum of money and, by applying some sort of process to it, arrive at another and higher sum, continually repeating this cycle.

WHAT TO AVOID
Confusing "Cash" and "Profit"
As mentioned previously, the most common mistake with cash flow statements is the potential confusion between profit and cash. They are not the same!

Not Understanding the Terminology
It is clearly fundamental to an understanding of cash flow statements that the reader is familiar with terms like "debtors," "creditors," "dividends," and so on. But more than appreciating the meaning of the word "debtors," it is quite easy to misunderstand the concept that, for example, an increase in debtors is a cash outflow, and equally that an increase in creditors represents an inflow of cash to the business.

SEE ALSO
Accounting (p. 428)
Reading a Balance Sheet (p. 129)
Reading a Profit and Loss Account (p. 134)

Calculating Accounts Receivable Turnover

WHAT IT MEASURES
The number of times in each accounting period, typically a year, that a firm converts credit sales into cash.

WHY IT IS IMPORTANT
A high turnover figure is desirable, because it indicates that a company collects revenues effectively, and that its customers pay bills promptly. A high figure also suggests that a firm's credit and collection policies are sound.

In addition, the measurement is a reasonably good indicator of cash flow, and of overall operating efficiency.

HOW IT WORKS IN PRACTICE
The formula for accounts receivable turnover is straightforward. Simply divide the average amount of receivables into annual credit sales:

sales / receivables =

receivables turnover

If, for example, a company's sales are $4.5 million and its average receivables are $375,000, its receivables turnover is:

$$4,500,000 / 375,000 = 12$$

TRICKS OF THE TRADE
- It is important to use the average amount of receivables over the period considered. Otherwise, receivables could be misleading for a company whose products are seasonal or are sold at irregular intervals.
- The measurement is also helpful to a company that is designing or revising credit terms.
- Accounts receivable turnover is among the measures that comprise asset utilization ratios, also called activity ratios.

SEE ALSO
Accounting (p. 428)
Calculating Asset Utilization (p. 149)

Calculating Acid-test Ratio

WHAT IT MEASURES
How quickly a company's assets can be turned into cash, which is why assessment of a company's liquidity also is known as the quick ratio, or simply the acid ratio.

WHY IT IS IMPORTANT
Regardless of how this ratio is labeled, it is considered a highly reliable indicator of a company's financial strength and its ability to meet its short-term obligations. Because inventory can sometimes be difficult to liquidate, the acid-test ratio deducts inventory from current assets before they are compared with current liabilities—which is what distinguishes it from the current ratio.

Potential creditors like to use the acid-test ratio because it reveals how a company would fare if it had to pay off its bills under the worst possible conditions. Indeed, the assumption behind the acid-test ratio is that creditors are howling at the door demanding immediate payment, and that an enterprise has no time to sell off its inventory, or any of its stock.

HOW IT WORKS IN PRACTICE
The acid-test ratio's formula can be expressed in two ways, but both essentially reach the same conclusion. The most common expression is:

**(current assets – inventory) /
current liabilities = acid-test ratio**

If, for example, current assets total $7,700, inventory amounts to $1,200 and current liabilities total $4,500, then:

(7,700 – 1,200) / 4,500 = 1.44

A variation of this formula ignores inventories altogether, distinguishes assets as cash, receivables, and short-term investments, then divides the sum of the three by the total current liabilities, or:

**(cash + accounts receivable +
short-term investments) /
current liabilities = acid-test ratio**

If, for example, cash totals $2,000,

receivables total $3,000, short-term investments total $1,000, and liabilities total $4,800, then:

(2,000 + 3,000 + 1,000) / 4,800 = 1.25

There are two other ways to appraise liquidity, although neither is as commonly used: the cash ratio is the sum of cash and marketable securities divided by current liabilities; net quick assets is determined by adding cash, accounts receivable, and marketable securities, then subtracting current liabilities from that sum.

TRICKS OF THE TRADE
- In general, the quick ratio should be 1:1 or better. It means a company has a unit's worth of easily convertible assets for each unit of its current liabilities. A high quick ratio usually reflects a sound, well-managed organization in no danger of imminent collapse, even in the extreme and unlikely event that its sales ceased immediately. On the other hand, companies with ratios of less than 1 could not pay their current liabilities, and should be looked at with extreme care.
- While a ratio of 1:1 is generally acceptable to most creditors, acceptable quick ratios vary by industry, as do almost all financial ratios. No ratio, in fact, is especially meaningful without knowledge of the business from which it originates. For example, a declining quick ratio with a stable current ratio may indicate that a company has built up too much inventory; but it could also suggest that the company has greatly improved its collection system.
- Some experts regard the acid-test ratio as an extreme version of the working capital ratio because it uses only cash and equivalents, and excludes inventories. An acid-test ratio that is notably lower than the working capital ratio often means that inventories make up a large proportion of current assets. An example would be retail stores.

- Comparing quick ratios over an extended period of time can signal developing trends in a company. While modest declines in the quick ratio do not automatically spell trouble, uncovering the reasons for changes can help find ways to nip potential problems in the bud.
- Like the current ratio, the quick ratio is a snapshot, and a company can manipulate its figures to make it look robust at a given point in time.
- Investors who suddenly become keenly interested in a firm's quick ratio may signal their anticipation of a downturn in the firm's business or in the general economy.

SEE ALSO
Accounting (p. 428)

Calculating Amortization

WHAT IT MEASURES

Amortization is a method of recovering (deducting or writing off) the capital costs of intangible assets over a fixed period of time. Its calculation is virtually identical to the straight-line method of depreciation.

Amortization also refers to the establishment of a schedule for repaying the principal and interest on a loan in equal amounts over a period of time. Because computers have made this a simple calculation, business references to amortization tend to focus more on the term's first definition.

WHY IT IS IMPORTANT

Amortization enables a company to identify its true costs, and thus its net income, more precisely. In the course of their business, most enterprises acquire intangible assets such as a patent for an invention, or a well-known brand or trademark. Since these assets can contribute to the revenue growth of the business, they can be—and are allowed to be—deducted against those future revenues over a period of years, provided the procedure conforms to accepted accounting practices.

For tax purposes, the distinction is not always made between amortization and depreciation, yet amortization remains a viable financial accounting concept in its own right.

HOW IT WORKS IN PRACTICE

Amortization is computed using the straight-line method of depreciation: divide the initial cost of the intangible asset by the estimated useful life of that asset. For example, if it costs $10,000 to acquire a patent and it has an estimated useful life of ten years, the amortized amount per year is $1,000.

$$\$10,000 \ / \ 10 \ = \ \$1,000 \text{ per year}$$

The amount of amortization accumulated since the asset was acquired appears on the organization's balance sheet as a deduction under the amortized asset.

While that formula is straightforward, amortization can also incorporate a variety of noncash charges to net earnings and/or asset values, such as depletion, write-offs, prepaid expenses, and deferred charges. Accordingly, there are many rules to regulate how these charges appear on financial statements. The rules are different in each country, and are occasionally changed, so it is necessary to stay abreast of them and rely on expert advice.

For financial reporting purposes, an intangible asset is amortized over a period of years. The amortizable life—"useful life"—of an intangible asset is the period over which it gives economic benefit. Several factors are considered when determining this useful life; for example, demand and competition, effects of obsolescence, legal or contractual limitations, renewal provisions, and service life expectations.

Intangibles that can be amortized can include:

Copyrights, based on the amount paid either to purchase them or to develop them internally, plus the costs incurred in producing the work (wages or materials, for example). At present, a copyright is granted to a corporation for 75 years, and to an individual for the life of the author plus 70 years. However, the estimated useful life of a copyright is usually far less than its legal life, and it is generally amortized over a fairly short period.

Cost of a franchise, including any fees paid to the franchiser, as well legal costs or expenses incurred in the acquisition. A franchise granted for a limited period should be amortized over its life. If the franchise has an indefinite life, it should be amortized over a reasonable period not to exceed 40 years.

Covenants not to compete: an agreement by the seller of a business not to engage in a competing business in a certain area for a specific period of time. The cost of the not-to-compete covenant should be amortized over the period covered by the covenant unless its estimated economic life is expected to be less.

Easement costs that grant a right of way may be amortized if there is a limited and specified life.

Organization costs incurred when forming a corporation or a partnership, including legal fees, accounting services, incorporation fees, and other related services. Organization costs are usually amortized over 60 months.

Patents, both those developed internally and those purchased. If developed internally, a patent's "amortizable basis" includes legal fees incurred during the application process. Normally, a patent is amortized over its legal life, or over its remaining life if purchased. However, it should be amortized over its legal life or its economic life, whichever is the shorter.

Trademarks, brands, and trade names, which should be written off over a period not to exceed 40 years. However, since the value of these assets depends on the changing tastes of consumers, they are frequently amortized over a shorter period.

Other types of property that may be amortized include certain intangible drilling costs, circulation costs, mine development costs, pollution control facilities, and reforestation expenditures. They can even include intangibles such as the value of a market share or a market's composition: an example is the portion of an acquired business that is attributable to the existence of a given customer base.

TRICKS OF THE TRADE

- Certain intangibles cannot be amortized, but may be depreciated using a straight-line approach if they have a "determinable" useful life. Because the rules are different in each country and are subject to change, it is essential to rely on specialist advice.

- Computer software may be amortized under certain conditions, depending on its purpose. Software that is amortized is generally given a 60-month life, but it may be amortized over a shorter period if it can clearly be established that it will be obsolete or no longer used within a shorter time.

- Under certain conditions, customer lists that were purchased may be amortized if it can be demonstrated that the list has a finite useful life, in that customers on the list are likely to be lost over a period of time.

- While leasehold improvements are depreciated for income tax purposes, they are amortized when it comes to financial reporting—either over the remaining term of the lease or their expected useful life, whichever is shorter.

- Annual payments incurred under a franchise agreement should be expensed when incurred.

- The Internet has many amortization loan calculators that can automatically determine monthly payments figures and the total cost of a loan.

SEE ALSO
Accounting (p. 428)
Calculating Depreciation (p. 157)

Calculating Annual Percentage Rate

WHAT IT MEASURES

Either the rate of interest that invested money earns in one year, or the cost of credit expressed as a yearly rate.

WHY IT IS IMPORTANT

It enables an investor or borrower to compare like with like. When evaluating investment alternatives, naturally it's important to know which one will pay the greatest return. By the same token, borrowers want to know which loan alternative offers the best terms. Determining the annual percentage rate provides a direct comparison.

HOW IT WORKS IN PRACTICE

To calculate the annual percentage rate (APR), apply this formula:

$$APR = [1 + i/m]m - 1.0$$

In the formula, **i** is the interest rate quoted, expressed as decimal, and **m** is the number of compounding periods per year. For example:

If a bank offers a 6% interest rate, paid quarterly, the APR would be calculated this way:

$$
\begin{aligned}
APR &= [1 + i/m]m - 1.0 \\
&= [1 + 0.06/4]4 - 1.0 \\
&= [1 + 0.015]\,4 - 1.0 \\
&= (1.015)\,4 - 1.0 \\
&= 1.0614 - 1.0 \\
&= 0.0614 \\
&= 6.14\% \text{ APR}
\end{aligned}
$$

TRICKS OF THE TRADE

- As a rule of thumb, the annual percentage rate is slightly higher than the quoted rate.
- When using the formula, be sure to express the rate as a decimal, that is, 6% becomes 0.06.
- When expressed as the cost of credit, remember to include other costs of obtaining the credit in addition to interest, such as loan closing costs and financial fees.
- APR provides an excellent basis for comparing mortgage or other loan rates; lenders do not always disclose it, however
- When used in the context of investment APR also can be called the "annual percentage yield," or APY.

SEE ALSO
Accounting (p. 428)

Calculating Asset Turnover

WHAT IT MEASURES
The amount of sales generated for every dollar's worth of assets over a given period.

WHY IT IS IMPORTANT
Asset turnover measures how well a company is leveraging its assets to produce revenue. A well-managed manufacturer, for example, will make its plant and equipment work hard for the business by minimizing idle time for machines.

The higher the number the better—within reason. As a rule of thumb, companies with low profit margins tend to have high asset turnover; those with high profit margins have low asset turnover.

This ratio can also show how capital intensive a business is. Some businesses, software developers, for example, can generate tremendous sales per dollar of assets because their assets are modest. At the other end of the scale, electric utilities, heavy industry manufacturers and even cable TV firms need a huge asset base to generate sales.

Finally, asset turnover serves as a tool to keep managers mindful of the company's balance sheet along with its profit and loss account.

HOW IT WORKS IN PRACTICE
Asset turnover's basic formula is simply sales divided by assets:

sales revenue / total assets

Most experts recommend using average total assets in the formula. To determine this figure, add total assets at the beginning of the year to total assets at the end of the year and divide by two.

If, for instance, annual sales totaled $4.5 million, and total assets were $1.84 million at the beginning of the year and $1.78 million at the year-end, the average total assets would be $1.81 million, and the asset turnover ratio would be:

4,500,000 / 1,810,000 = 2.49

A variation of the formula is:

sales revenue / fixed assets

If average fixed assets were $900,000, then asset turnover would be:

4,500,000 / 900,000 = 5

TRICKS OF THE TRADE
- This ratio is especially useful for growth companies to gauge whether or not they are growing revenue, for example, turnover, in healthy proportion to assets.
- Asset turnover numbers are useful for comparing competitors within industries. Like most ratios, they vary from industry to industry. As with most numbers, the most meaningful comparisons are made over extended periods of time.
- Too high a ratio may suggest overtrading: too much sales revenue with too little investment. Conversely, too low a ratio may suggest undertrading and an inefficient management of resources.
- A declining ratio may be indicative of a company that overinvested in plant, equipment, or other fixed assets, or is not using existing assets effectively.

SEE ALSO
Accounting (p. 428)
Calculating Asset Utilization (p. 149)

Calculating Asset Utilization

WHAT IT MEASURES

How efficiently an organization uses its resources and, in turn, the effectiveness of the organization's managers.

WHY IT IS IMPORTANT

The success of any enterprise is tied to its ability to manage and leverage its assets. Hefty sales and profits can hide any number of inefficiencies. By examining several relationships between sales and assets, asset utilization delivers a reasonably detailed picture of how well a company is being managed and led—certainly enough to call attention both to sources of trouble and to role-model operations.

Moreover, since all the figures used in this analysis are taken from a company's balance sheet or profit and loss statement, the ratios that result can be used to compare a company's performance with individual competitors and with industries as a whole.

Many companies also use this measure not only to evaluate their aggregate success but also to determine compensation for managers.

HOW IT WORKS IN PRACTICE

Asset utilization relies on a family of asset utilization ratios, also called activity ratios. The individual ratios in the family can vary, depending on the practitioner. They include measures that also stand alone, such as accounts receivable turnover and asset turnover. The most commonly used sets of asset utilization ratios include these and the following measures.

Average collection period is also known as days sales outstanding. It links accounts receivable with daily sales and is expressed in number of days; the lower the number, the better the performance. Its formula is:

accounts receivable /
average daily sales =
average collection period

For example, if accounts receivable are $280,000, and average daily sales are 7,000, then:

280,000 / 7,000 = 40

Inventory turnover compares the cost of goods sold (COGS) with inventory; for this measure, expressed in "turns," the higher the number the better. Its formula is:

cost of goods sold / inventory

For example, if COGS is $2 million, and inventory at the end of the period is $500,000, then:

2,000,000 / 500,000 = 4

Some asset utilization repertoires include ratios like debtor days, while others study the relationships listed below.

Depreciation / Assets measures the percentage of assets being depreciated to gauge how quickly product plants are aging and assets are being consumed.

Depreciation / Sales measures the percentage of sales that is tied up covering the wear and tear of the physical plant.

In either instance, a high percentage could be cause for concern.

Income / Assets measures how well management uses its assets to generate net income. It is the same formula as return on assets.

Income / Plant measures how effectively a company uses its investment in fixed assets to generate net income.

In these two instances, high numbers are desirable.

Plant / Assets expresses the percentage of total assets that is tied up in land, buildings, and equipment.

By themselves, of course, the individual numbers are meaningless. Their value lies in how they compare with the corresponding numbers of competitors and industry averages. A company with an inventory turnover of four in an industry whose average is seven, for example, surely has room for improvement, because the comparison indicates it is generating fewer sales per unit of inventory and is therefore less efficient than its rivals.

TRICKS OF THE TRADE

- Asset utilization is particularly useful to companies considering expansion or capital investment: if production can be increased by improving the efficiency of existing resources, there is no need to spend the sums expansion would cost.
- Like all families of ratios, no single number or comparison is necessarily cause for alarm or rejoicing. Asset utilization proves most beneficial over an extended period of time.
- Studying all measures at once can devour a lot of time, although computers have trimmed hours into seconds. Managements in smaller organizations may conduct asset utilization on a continuing basis, tracking particular measures monthly to stay abreast of operating trends.

SEE ALSO

Accounting (p. 428)
Calculating Accounts Receivable
  Turnover (p. 142)
Calculating Asset Turnover (p. 148)

Calculating Contribution Margin

WHAT IT MEASURES
The amounts that individual products or services ultimately contribute to net profit.

WHY IT IS IMPORTANT
Contribution margin helps a business decide how it should direct or redirect its resources.

When managers know the contribution margin—or margins, as is more often the case—they can make better decisions about adding or subtracting product lines, investing in existing products, pricing products or services (particularly in response to competitors' actions), structuring sales commissions and bonuses, where to direct marketing and advertising expenditures, and where to apply individual talents and expertise.

In short, contribution margin is a valuable decision-support tool.

HOW IT WORKS IN PRACTICE
Its calculation is straightforward:

sales price – variable cost = contribution margin

Or, for providers of services:

total revenue – total variable cost = contribution margin

For example, if the sales price of a good is $500 and variable cost is $350, the contribution margin is $150, or 30% of sales.

This means that 30 cents of every sales dollar remain to contribute to fixed costs and to profit, after the costs directly related to the sales are subtracted.

Contribution margin is especially useful to a company comparing different products or services. See the example below.

Obviously, Product C has the highest contribution percentage, even though Product A generates more total profit. The analysis suggests that the company might do well to aim to achieve a sales mix with a higher proportion of Product C. It further suggests that prices for Products A and B may be too low, or that their cost structures need attention. Notably, none of this information appears on a standard income statement.

Contribution margin also can be tracked over a long period of time, using data from several years of income statements. It can also be invaluable in calculating volume discounts for preferred customers, and break-even sales or volume levels.

TRICKS OF THE TRADE
- Contribution margin depends on accurately accounting for all variable costs, including shipping and delivery, or the indirect costs of services. Activity-based cost accounting systems aid this kind of analysis.
- Variable costs include all direct costs (usually labor and materials).
- Contribution margin analysis is only one tool to use. It will not show so-called loss leaders, for example. And it doesn't consider marketing factors like existing penetration levels, opportunities, or mature markets being eroded by emerging markets.

SEE ALSO
Accounting (p. 428)

	Product A $	Product B $	Product C $
Sales	260	220	140
Variable costs	178	148	65
Contribution margin	82	72	75
Contribution margin (%)	31.5	32.7	53.6

Calculating Cost of Goods Sold (COGS)

WHAT IT MEASURES
For a retailer, COGS is the cost of buying and acquiring the goods that it sells to its customers. For a service firm, COGS is the cost of the employee services it supplies. For a manufacturer, COGS is the cost of buying the raw materials and manufacturing its finished products.

WHY IT IS IMPORTANT
Cost of goods sold may help a company determine the prices to charge for its products and services, and the volume of business that it needs to maintain in order to operate profitably.

For retailers especially, the cost of the merchandise sold is typically the largest expense, and thus an absolutely critical business factor. However, understanding COGS is an important success factor for any business because it can reveal opportunities to reduce costs and improve operations.

COGS is also a key figure on an income statement (also called the profit and loss account), and an important consideration in computing income taxes because of its close relationship to inventories, which taxation authorities treat as future income.

HOW IT WORKS IN PRACTICE
Essentially, COGS is equal to a company's opening stock of goods and services, plus the cost of goods bought and direct costs incurred during a particular period, minus the closing stock of goods and services.

A critical consideration is the accounting policy that a company adopts to calculate inventory values, especially if raw materials prices change during the year. This may happen often, particularly when inflation is high. Inventory values under a First In First Out (FIFO) policy reflect original or older prices of materials, while a Last In First Out (LIFO) policy reflects current (and often more expensive) prices. Somebody computing COGS first needs to know which policy is being used, because this will affect inventory values.

COGS for a manufacturer will include a variety of items, such as raw materials and energy used in production, labor, benefits for production workers, the cost of raw materials in inventory, shipping fees, the cost of storing finished products, depreciation on production machinery used, and factory overhead expenses.

For a retail company such as Wal-Mart, COGS is generally less complex: the total amount paid to suppliers for the products being sold on its shelves.

COGS is calculated as follows:

Stocks at beginning of period	$20,000
Purchases during period	+ $60,000
Cost of good available for sale	= $80,000
Less inventory at period end	– $15,000
Cost of goods sold (COGS)	= $65,000

Because the counting of inventory is an exhaustive undertaking for retailers, doing it quarterly or monthly would be open to error. Accordingly, taxation authorities allow them to estimate cost of goods sold during the year.

Determining these estimates requires details of the gross profit margin (retailers typically use the preceding year's figure). This figure is then used to calculate the cost ratio.

Begin by assuming that net sales are 100%, then subtract the gross profit margin, say 40%, to produce a cost ratio of 60%: 100% – 40% = 60%. A monthly COGS calculation then looks like this:

Inventory at beginning of month	$10,000
Purchases during month	+ $25,000
Cost of goods available for sale	= $35,000
Less net sales during month	– $28,000
Cost ratio 100% – 40%	= 60%
Estimated cost of goods sold	= $16,800
	($28,000
	×60%)

There is one sample to review, because calculating COGS for manufacturers requires additional factors:

Inventory at beginning of year		$20,000
Purchases during year	+	$50,000
Cost of direct labor	+	$15,000
Materials and supplies	+	$12,000
Misc. costs	+	$3,000
Total product expenses	=	$100,000
Less inventory at year-end	−	$15,000
Cost of goods sold (COGS)	=	$85,000

TRICKS OF THE TRADE

■ Anyone who wants to determine COGS must maintain inventories and know their value!

■ Because goods returned affect inventory values and, in turn, cost of goods sold, returns of goods must be reflected in COGS calculations.
■ Merchandising firms may use different inventory accounting systems, but the choice has no bearing on the actual costs incurred; it only affects allocation of costs.
■ COGS should not include indirect costs like administration and marketing costs, or other activities that cannot be directly attributed to producing or acquiring the product.

SEE ALSO
Accounting (p. 428)

Calculating Creditor and Debtor Days

WHAT THEY MEASURE

Creditor days is a measure of the number of days on average that a company requires to pay its creditors, while debtor days is a measure of the number of days on average that it takes a company to receive payment for what it sells. It is also called accounts receivable days.

WHY THEY ARE IMPORTANT

Creditor days is an indication of a company's creditworthiness in the eyes of its suppliers and creditors, since it shows how long they are willing to wait for payment. Within reason, the higher the number the better, because all companies want to conserve cash. At the same time, a company that is especially slow to pay its bills (100 or more days, for example) may be a company having trouble generating cash, or one trying to finance its operations with its suppliers' funds. Ultimately, companies whose creditor days soar have trouble obtaining supplies.

Debtor days is an indication of a company's efficiency in collecting monies owed. In this case, obviously, the lower the number the better. An especially high number is a telltale sign of inefficiency or worse. It may indicate bad debts, dubious sales figures, or a company being bullied by large customers out to improve their own cash position at another firm's expense. Customers whose credit terms are abused also risk higher borrowing costs and related charges.

Changes in both measures are easy to spot, and easy to understand.

HOW THEY WORK IN PRACTICE

To determine creditor days, divide the cumulative amount of unpaid suppliers' bills (also called trade creditors) by sales, then multiply by 365. So the formula is:

$$\textbf{(trade creditors / sales)} \times 365 = \textbf{creditor days}$$

For example, if suppliers' bills total $800,000 and sales are $9,000,000, the calculation is:

$$\textbf{(800,000 / 9,000,000)} \times 365 = \textbf{32.44 days}$$

The company takes 32.44 days on average to pay its bills.

To determine debtor days, divide the cumulative amount of accounts receivable by sales, then multiply by 365. For example, if accounts receivable total $600,000 and sales are $9,000,000, the calculation is:

$$\textbf{(600,000 / 9,000,000)} \times 365 = \textbf{24.33 days}$$

The company takes 24.33 days on average to collect its debts.

TRICKS OF THE TRADE

- Cash businesses, including most retailers, should have a much lower debtor days figure than noncash businesses, since they receive payment when they sell the goods. A typical target for noncash businesses is 40–50 days.
- An abnormally high creditor days figure may not only suggest a cash crisis, but also the management's difficulty in maintaining revolving credit agreements.
- An increasing number of debtor days also suggests overly generous credit terms (to bolster sales) or problems with product quality.

SEE ALSO
Accounting (p. 428)

Calculating Current Ratio

WHAT IT MEASURES
A company's liquidity and its ability to meet its short-term debt obligations.

WHY IT IS IMPORTANT
By comparing a company's current assets with its current liabilities, the current ratio reflects its ability to pay its upcoming bills in the unlikely event of all creditors demanding payment at once. It has long been the measurement of choice among financial institutions and lenders.

HOW IT WORKS IN PRACTICE
The current ratio formula is simply:

current assets / current liabilities = current ratio

Current assets are the ones that a company can turn into cash within 12 months during the ordinary course of business. Current liabilities are bills due to be paid within the coming 12 months.

For example, if a company's current assets are $300,000 and its current liabilities are $200,000, its current ratio would be:

300,000 / 200,000 = 1.5

As a rule of thumb, the 1.5 figure means that a company should be able to get hold of $1.50 for every $1.00 it owes.

TRICKS OF THE TRADE
- The higher the ratio, the more liquid the company. Prospective lenders expect a positive current ratio, often of at least 1.5. However, too high a ratio is also cause for alarm, because it indicates declining receivables and/or inventory—signs that portend declining liquidity.
- A current ratio of less than 1 suggests pressing liquidity problems, specifically an inability to generate sufficient cash to meet upcoming demands.
- Managements use current ratio as well as lenders; a low ratio, for example, may indicate the need to refinance a portion of short-term debt with long-term debt to improve a company's liquidity.
- Ratios vary by industry, however, and should be used accordingly. Some sectors, such as supermarket chains and restaurants, perform nicely with low ratios that would keep others awake at night.
- One shortcoming of the current ratio is that it does not differentiate assets, some of which may not be easily converted to cash. As a result, lenders also refer to the quick ratio.
- Another shortcoming of the current ratio is that it reflects conditions at a single point in time, such as when the balance sheet is prepared. It is possible to make this figure look good just for this occasion: lenders should not, therefore, appraise these conditions by the ratio alone.
- A constant current ratio and falling quick ratio signal trouble ahead, because this suggests that a company is amassing assets at the expense of receivables and cash.

SEE ALSO
Accounting (p. 428)

Calculating Days Sales Outstanding

WHAT IT MEASURES

A company's average collection period, or the average number of days it takes a firm to convert its accounts receivable into cash. It is also called the collection ratio.

WHY IT IS IMPORTANT

Knowing how long it takes a company to turn accounts receivable into cash is an important financial indicator. It indicates the efficiency of the company's internal collection, suggests how well a company's customers are accepting its credit terms (net 30 days, for example), and is a figure that is routinely compared with industry averages.

Ideally, DSOs should be decreasing or constant. A low figure means the company collects its outstanding receivables quickly. Typically, DSO is reviewed quarterly or yearly (91 or 365 days).

DSO also helps to expose companies that try to disguise weak sales. Large increases in DSO suggest that a company is trying to force sales either by accepting poor receivable terms or selling products at discount to book more sales for a particular period. An improving DSO suggests that a company is striving to make its operations more efficient.

Any company with a significant change in its DSO merits examination in greater detail.

HOW IT WORKS IN PRACTICE

Regular DSO requires three figures: total accounts receivable, total credit sales for the period analyzed, and the number of days in the period (annual, 365; six months, 182; quarter, 91). The formula is:

(accounts receivable / total credit sales for the period) × number of days in the period = days sales outstanding

For example: if total receivables are $4,500,000, total credit sales in a quarter are $9,000,000, and number of days is 91, then:

(4,500,000 / 9,000,000) × 91 = 45.5

Thus, it takes an average 45.5 days to collect receivables.

TRICKS OF THE TRADE

■ Companies use DSO information with an accounts receivable aging report. This lists four categories of receivables: 0–30 days, 30–60 days, 60–90 days, and over 90 days. The report also shows the percentage of total accounts receivable that each group represents, allowing for an analysis of delinquencies and potential bad debts—a figure that appears on a profit and loss account.

■ A rarely used related calculation, best possible DSO, shows how long it takes a company to collect current receivables:

(current receivables / total credit sales for the period) × the number of days in the period = best possible DSO

So, current receivables of $3,000,000 and total credit sales of $9,000,000 in a 91-day period would result in a best possible DSO of 30.3 days (3,000,000 / 9,000,000 × 91).

■ Only credit sales of merchandise should be used in calculating DSO; cash sales are excluded, as are sales of such items as fixtures, equipment, or real estate.

■ Properly evaluating an acceptable DSO requires a standard for comparison. A rule of thumb is that DSO should not exceed one-third to one-half of selling terms. For instance, if terms are 30 days, an acceptable DSO would be 40 to 45 days.

■ A single DSO is only a snapshot. A fuller picture would require at least quarterly calculations, and some companies review DSO monthly.

■ DSO can vary widely by industry as well as company. For example, clothing wholesalers have to have the goods on retailers' shelves for months before they will be sold and the retailer is able to cover invoices. However, a computer wholesaler with a lengthy DSO suggests trouble, since computers become obsolete quickly.

SEE ALSO
Accounting (p. 428)

Calculating Depreciation

GETTING STARTED

Depreciation is a basic expense of doing business, reducing a company's earnings while increasing its cash flow. It affects three key financial statements: balance sheet; cash flow; and income (or profit and loss). It is based on two key facts: the purchase price of the items or property in question, and their "useful life."

Depreciation values and practices are governed by the tax laws of both national governments and state or provincial governments, which must be monitored continuously for any changes that are made. Accounting bodies, too, have developed standard practices and procedures for conducting depreciation.

Depreciating a single asset is not difficult: the challenge lies in depreciating the many assets possessed by even small companies, and is intensified by the impact that depreciation has on income and cash flow statements and on income tax returns. It is essential to depreciate with care and to rely on experts, ensuring that they fully understand the current government rules and regulations.

FAQS

What is depreciation?

It is an allocation of the cost of an asset over a period of time for accounting and tax purposes. Depreciation is charged against earnings, on the basis that the use of capital assets is a legitimate cost of doing business. Depreciation is also a noncash expense that is added into net income to determine cash flow in a given accounting period.

What is straight-line depreciation?

One of the two principal depreciation methods, it is based on the assumption that an asset loses an equal amount of its value each year of its useful life. Straight-line depreciation deducts an equal amount from a company's earnings throughout the life of the asset.

What is accelerated depreciation?

The other principal method of depreciation is based on the assumption that an asset loses a larger amount of its value in the early years of its useful life. Also known as the "declining-balance" method, it is used by accountants to reduce a company's tax bills as soon as possible, and is calculated on the basis of the same percentage rate each year of an asset's useful life. Accelerated depreciation also better reflects the economic value of the asset being depreciated, which tends to become increasingly less efficient and more costly to maintain as it grows older.

What can be depreciated?

To qualify for depreciation, assets must:
- be used in the business;
- be items that wear out, become obsolete, or lose value over time from natural causes or circumstances;
- have a useful life beyond a single tax year.

Examples include vehicles, machines and equipment, computers and office furnishings, and buildings, plus major additions or improvements to such assets. Some intangible assets also can be included under certain conditions.

What cannot be depreciated?

Land, personal assets, inventory, leased or rented property, and a company's employees.

MAKING IT HAPPEN

In order to determine the annual depreciation cost of assets, it is necessary first to know the initial cost of those assets, how many years they will retain some value for the business, and what value, if any, they will have at the end of their useful life.

For example, a company buys a truck to carry materials and finished goods. The vehicle loses value as soon as it is purchased, and then loses more with each year it is in service, until the cost of repairs exceeds its overall value. Measuring the loss in the value of the truck is depreciation.

Straight-line depreciation is the most straightforward method, and is still quite common. It assumes that the net cost of an asset should be written off in equal amounts over its life. The formula used is:

**(original cost – scrap value) /
useful life (years)**

For example, if the truck cost $30,000 and can be expected to serve the business for seven years, its original cost would be divided by its useful life:

(30,000 – 2,000) / 7 = 4,000 per year

The $4,000 becomes a depreciation expense that is reported on the company's year-end income statement under "operation expenses."

In theory, an asset should be depreciated over the actual number of years that it will be used, according to its actual drop in value each year. At the end of each year, all the depreciation claimed to date is subtracted from its cost in order to arrive at its "book value," which would equal its market value. At the end of its useful business life, any undepreciated portion would represent the salvage value for which it could be sold or scrapped.

For tax purposes, some accountants prefer to use accelerating depreciation to record larger amounts of depreciation in the asset's early years in order to reduce tax bills as soon as possible. In contrast to the straight-line method, the declining-balance method assumes that the asset depreciates more in its earlier years of use. The table below compares the depreciation amounts that would be available, under these two methods, for a $1,000 asset that is expected

to be used for five years and then sold for $100 in scrap.

While the straight-line method results in the same deduction each year, the declining-balance method produces larger deductions in the first years and far smaller deductions in the later years. One result of this system is that, if the equipment is expected to be sold for a higher value at some point in the middle of its life, the declining-balance method can produce a greater taxable gain in that year because the book value of the asset will be relatively lower.

The depreciation method to be used for a particular asset is fixed at the time that the asset is first placed in service. Whatever rules or tables are in effect for that year must be followed as long as the asset is owned.

Depreciation laws and regulations change frequently over the years as a result of government policy changes, so a company owning property over a long period may have to use several different depreciation methods.

TRICKS OF THE TRADE

- With rare exceptions, it is not possible to deduct in one year the entire cost of an asset if that asset has a useful life substantially beyond the tax year.
- To qualify for depreciation, an asset must be put into service. Simply purchasing it is not enough. There are rules that govern how much depreciation can be claimed on items put into service after a year has begun.
- It is common knowledge that if a company claims more depreciation than it is entitled to, it is liable for stiff penalties in a tax audit, just as failure to allow for depreciation causes an overestimation of income.

Straight-line Method		Declining-balance Method	

Year	Annual Depreciation	Year-end Book Value	Annual Depreciation	Year-end Book Value
1	$900 20% = $180	$1,000 – $180 = $820	$1,000 40% = $400	$1,000 – $400 = $600
2	$900 20% = $180	$820 – $180 = $640	$600 40% = $240	$600 – $240 = $360
3	$900 20% = $180	$640 – $180 = $460	$360 40% = $144	$360 – $144 = $216
4	$900 20% = $180	$460 – $180 = $280	$216 40% = $86.40	$216 – $86.40 = $129.60
5	$900 20% = $180	$280 – $180 = $100	$129.60 40% = $51.84	$129.60 – $51.84 = $77.76

What is not commonly known is that if a company does not claim all the depreciation deductions it is entitled to, it will be considered as having claimed them when taxable gains or losses are eventually calculated on the sale or disposal of the asset in question.

- While leased property cannot be depreciated, the cost of making permanent improvements to leased property can be (remodeling a leased office, for example). There are many rules governing leased assets; they should be depreciated with care.

- Another common mistake is to continue depreciating property beyond the end of its recovery period. Cars are common examples of this.

- Conservative companies depreciate many assets as quickly as possible, despite the fact that this practice reduces reported net income. Knowledgeable investors watch carefully for such practices.

SEE ALSO
Accounting (p. 428)
Calculating Amortization (p. 145)

Calculating EBITDA

WHAT IT MEASURES

A company's earnings from ongoing operations, before net income is calculated.

WHY IT IS IMPORTANT

EBITDA's champions contend it gives investors a sense of how much money a young or fast-growing company is generating before it pays interest on debt, tax collections, and accounts for noncash changes. If EBITDA grows over time, champions argue, investors gain at least a sense of long-term profitability and, in turn, the wisdom of their investment.

Business appraisers and investors also may study EBITDA to help gauge a company's fair market value, often as a prelude to its acquisition by another company. It also is frequently applied to companies that have been subject to leveraged buyouts—the strategy being that EBITDA will help cover loan payments needed to finance the transaction.

EBITDA, and EBIT, too, are claimed to be good indicators of cash flow from business operations, since they report earnings before debt payments, taxes, depreciation, and amortization charges are considered. However, that claim is challenged by many—often rather intently.

HOW IT WORKS IN PRACTICE

EBITDA first appeared as leveraged buyouts soared in popularity during the 1980s. It has since become well established as a financial-analysis measure of telecommunications, cable, and major media companies.

Its formula is quite simple. Revenues less the cost of goods sold, general and administrative expenses, and the deductions of items expressed by the acronym, or:

$$\text{revenue} - \text{expenses (excluding tax and interest, depreciation, etc.)} = \text{EBITDA}$$

or:

$$\text{revenue} - \text{expenses (excluding tax and interest)} = \text{EBIT}$$

This formula does not measure true cash flow. A communications company, for example, once reported \$698 million in EBIT but just \$324 million in cash from operations.

TRICKS OF THE TRADE

- A definition of EBITDA isn't as yet enforced by standards-making bodies, so companies can all but create their own. As a result, EBITDA can easily be manipulated by aggressive accounting policies, which may erode its reliability.
- Ignoring capital expenditures could be unrealistic and horribly misleading, because companies in capital-intensive sectors such as manufacturing and transportation must continually make major capital investments to remain competitive. High-technology is another sector that may be capital-intensive, at least initially.
- Critics warn that using EBITDA as a cash flow indicator is a huge mistake, because EBITDA ignores too many factors that have an impact on true cash flow, such as working capital, debt payments, and other fixed expenses. Interest and taxes can and do cost a company cash, they point out, while debt holders have higher claims on a company's liquid assets than investors do.
- Critics further assail EBITDA as the barometer of choice of unprofitable firms because it can present a more optimistic view of a company's future than it has a right to claim. *Forbes* magazine, for instance, once referred to EBITDA as "the device of choice to pep up earnings announcements."
- Even so, EBITDA may be useful in terms of evaluating firms in the same industry with widely different capital structures, tax rates, and depreciation policies.

SEE ALSO

Accounting (p. 428)

Calculating Economic Value Added

WHAT IT MEASURES
A company's financial performance, specifically whether it is earning more or less than the total cost of the capital supporting it.

WHY IT IS IMPORTANT
Economic Value Added measures true economic profit, or the amount by which the earnings of a project, an operation, or a corporation exceed (or fall short of) the total amount of capital that was originally invested by the company's owners.

If a company is earning more it is adding value, and that is good. If it is earning less the company is in fact devouring value, and that is bad, because the company's owners (shareholders, for example) would be better off investing their capital elsewhere.

The concept's champions declare that EVA forces managers to focus on true wealth creation and maximizing shareholder investment. By definition, then, increasing EVA will increase a company's market value.

HOW IT WORKS IN PRACTICE
EVA is conceptually simple and easy to explain: from net operating profit, subtract an appropriate charge for the opportunity cost of all capital invested in an enterprise—the amount that could have been invested elsewhere. It is calculated using this formula:

net operating profit less applicable taxes – cost of capital = EVA

If a company is considering building a new plant, and its total weighted cost over ten years is $80 million, while the expected annual incremental return on the new operation is $10 million, or $100 million over ten years, then the plant's EVA would be positive, in this case $20 million:

$100 million – $80 million = $20 million

An alternative but more complex formula for EVA is:

(% return on invested capital – % cost of capital) × original capital invested = EVA

TRICKS OF THE TRADE
- EVA is a measure of dollar surplus value, not the percentage difference in returns.
- Purists define EVA as "profit the way shareholders define it." They further contend that if shareholders expect a 10% return on their investment, they "make money" only when their share of after-tax operating profits exceeds 10% of equity capital.
- An objective of EVA is to determine which business units best utilize their assets to generate returns and maximize shareholder value; it can be used to assess a company, a business unit, a single plant, office, or even an assembly line. This same technique is equally helpful in evaluating new business opportunities.

SEE ALSO
Accounting (p. 428)

Calculating Elasticity

WHAT IT MEASURES

The percentage change of one variable caused by a percentage change in another variable.

WHY IT IS IMPORTANT

Elasticity is defined as "the measure of the sensitivity of one variable to another." In practical terms, elasticity indicates the degree to which consumers respond to changes in price. It is obviously important for companies to consider such relationships when contemplating changes in price, demand, and supply.

Demand elasticity measures how much the quantity demanded changes when the price of a product or service is increased or lowered. Will demand remain constant? If not, how much will demand change?

Supply elasticity measures the impact on supply when a price is changed. It is assumed that lowering prices will reduce supply, because demand will increase—but by how much?

HOW IT WORKS IN PRACTICE

The general formula for elasticity is:

**elasticity = % change in x /
% change in y**

In theory, x and y can be any variable. However, the most common application measures price and demand. If the price of a product is increased from \$20 to \$25, or 25%, and demand in turn falls from 6,000 to 3,000, elasticity would be calculated as:

– 50% / 25% = – 2

A value greater than 1 means that demand is strongly sensitive to price, while a value of less than 1 means that demand is not price-sensitive.

TRICKS OF THE TRADE

There are five cases of elasticity:

- E = 1, or *unit elasticity*. The proportional change in one variable is equal to the proportional change in another variable: if price rises by 5%, demand falls by 5%.
- E is greater than 1, or just *elastic*. The proportional change in x is greater than the proportional change in y: if price rises by 5%, demand falls by 3%.
- E = infinity, or *perfectly elastic*. This is a special case of elasticity: any change in y will effect no change in x. An example would be prices charged by a hospital's emergency room, where increases in price are unlikely to curb demand.
- E is less than 1, or just *inelastic*. The proportional change in x is less than the proportional change in y: if prices are increased by 3%, demand will fall by 30%.
- E = 0, or *perfectly inelastic*. This is another special case of elasticity: any change in y will have an infinite effect on x.

There are more complex formulae for determining a range of variables, or "arc elasticity."

Elasticity can be used to affirm two rules of thumb:

- demand becomes elastic if consumers have an alternative or adequate substitute for the product or service;
- demand is more elastic if consumers have an incentive to save money.

SEE ALSO
Accounting (p. 428)

Calculating Interest Cover

WHAT IT MEASURES

The amount of earnings available to make interest payments after all operating and non-operating income and expenses—except interest and income taxes—have been accounted for.

WHY IT IS IMPORTANT

Interest cover is regarded as a measure of a company's creditworthiness because it shows how much income there is to cover interest payments on outstanding debt. Banks and financial analysts also rely on this ratio as a rule of thumb to gauge the fundamental strength of a business.

HOW IT WORKS IN PRACTICE

Interest cover is expressed as a ratio, and reflects a company's ability to pay the interest obligations on its debt. It compares the funds available to pay interest—earnings before interest and taxes, or EBIT—with the interest expense. The basic formula is:

$$\textbf{EBIT / interest expense =}$$
$$\textbf{interest coverage ratio}$$

If interest expense for a year is $9 million, and the company's EBIT is $45 million, the interest coverage would be:

$$\textbf{45 million / 9 million = 5:1}$$

The higher the number, the stronger a company is likely to be. Conversely, a low number suggests that a company's fortunes are looking ominous. Variations of this basic formula also exist. For example, there is:

$$\textbf{operating cash flow +}$$
$$\textbf{interest + taxes / interest =}$$
$$\textbf{cash flow interest coverage ratio}$$

This ratio indicates the firm's ability to use its cash flow to satisfy its fixed financing obligations. Finally, there is the fixed-charge coverage ratio, which compares EBIT with fixed charges:

$$\textbf{EBIT + lease expenses / interest +}$$
$$\textbf{lease expense =}$$
$$\textbf{fixed charge coverage ratio}$$

"Fixed charges" can be interpreted in many ways, however. It could mean, for example, the funds that a company is obliged to set aside to retire debt, or dividends on preferred stock.

TRICKS OF THE TRADE

- A ratio of less than 1 indicates that a company is having problems generating enough cash flow to pay its interest expenses, and that either a modest decline in operating profits or a sudden rise in borrowing costs could eliminate profitability entirely.
- Ideally, interest coverage should at least exceed 1.5; in some sectors, 2.0 or higher is desirable.
- Interest coverage is widely considered to be more meaningful than looking at total debt, because what really matters is what an enterprise must pay in a given period, not how much debt it has.
- As is often the case, it may be more meaningful to watch interest cover over several periods in order to detect long-term trends.
- Cash flow will sometimes be substituted for EBIT in the ratio, because EBIT includes not only cash but also accrued sales and other unrealized income.
- Interest cover also is called "times interest earned."

SEE ALSO
Accounting (p. 428)

Calculating Marginal Cost

WHAT IT MEASURES

The additional cost of producing one more unit of product, or providing service to one more customer.

WHY IT IS IMPORTANT

Sometimes called incremental cost, marginal cost shows how much costs increase from making or serving one more, an essential factor when contemplating a production increase, or seeking to serve more customers.

If the price charged is greater than the marginal cost, then the revenue gain will be greater than the added cost. That, in turn, will increase profit, so the expansion in production or service makes economic sense and should proceed. Of course, the reverse is also true: If the price charged is less than the marginal cost, expansion should not go ahead.

HOW IT WORKS IN PRACTICE

The formula for marginal cost is:

change in cost / change in quantity

If it costs a company $260,000 to produce 3,000 items, and $325,000 to produce 3,800 items, the change in cost would be:

$325,000 – $260,000 = $65,000

The change in quantity would be:

3,800 – 3,000 = 800

When the formula to calculate marginal cost is applied, the result is:

$65,000 / 800 = $81.25

If the price of the item in question were $99.95, expansion should proceed.

TRICKS OF THE TRADE

- A marginal cost that is lower than the price shows that it is not always necessary to cut prices to sell more goods and boost profits.
- Using idle capacity to produce lower-margin items can still be beneficial, because these generate revenues that help cover fixed costs.
- Marginal cost studies can become quite complicated, because the basic formula does not always take into account variables that can affect cost and quantity. There are software programs available, many of which are industry-specific.
- At some point, marginal cost invariably begins to rise; typically, labor becomes less productive as a production run increases, while the time required also increases.
- Marginal cost alone may not justify expansion. It is best to determine also average costs, then chart the respective series of figures to find where marginal cost meets average cost, and thus determine optimum cost.
- Relying on marginal cost is not fail-safe; putting more product on a market can drive down prices and thus cut margins. Moreover, committing idle capacity to long-term production may tie up resources that could be directed to a new and more profitable opportunity.
- An important related principle is contribution: the cash gained (or lost) from selling an additional unit.

SEE ALSO
Accounting (p. 428)

Calculating Payback Period

WHAT IT MEASURES
How long it will take to earn back the money invested in a project.

WHY IT IS IMPORTANT
The straight payback period method is the simplest way of determining the investment potential of a major project. Expressed in time, it tells a management how many months or years it will take to recover the original cash cost of the project—always a vital consideration, and especially so for managements evaluating several projects at once.

This evaluation becomes even more important if it includes an examination of what the present value of future revenues will be.

HOW IT WORKS IN PRACTICE
The straight payback period formula is:

cost of project / annual cash revenues = payback period

Thus, if a project cost $100,000 and was expected to generate $28,000 annually, the payback period would be:

100,000 / 28,000 = 3.57 years

If the revenues generated by the project are expected to vary from year to year, add the revenues expected for each succeeding year until you arrive at the total cost of the project.

For example, say the revenues expected to be generated by the $100,000 project are:

	Revenue	Total
Year 1	$19,000	$19,000
Year 2	$25,000	$44,000
Year 3	$30,000	$74,000
Year 4	$30,000	$104,000
Year 5	$30,000	$134,000

Thus, the project would be fully paid for in Year 4, since it is in that year the total revenue reaches the initial cost of $100,000.

The picture becomes complex when the time value of money principle is introduced into the calculations. Some experts insist this is essential to determine the most accurate payback period. Accordingly, present value tables or computers (now the norm) must be used, and the annual revenues have to be discounted by the applicable interest rate, 10% in this example. Doing so produces significantly different results:

	Revenue	Present value	Total
Year 1	$19,000	$17,271	$17,271
Year 2	$25,000	$20,650	$37,921
Year 3	$30,000	$22,530	$60,451
Year 4	$30,000	$20,490	$80,941
Year 5	$30,000	$18,630	$99,571

This method shows that payback would not occur even after five years.

TRICKS OF THE TRADE
- Clearly, a main defect of the straight payback period method is that it ignores the time value of money principle, which, in turn, can produce unrealistic expectations.
- A second drawback is that it ignores any benefits generated after the payback period, and thus a project that would return $1 million after, say, six years, might be ranked lower than a project with a three-year payback that returns only $100,000 thereafter.
- Another alternative to calculating by payback period is to develop an internal rate of return.
- Under most analyses, projects with shorter payback periods rank higher than those with longer paybacks, even if the latter project higher returns. Longer paybacks can be affected by such factors as market changes, changes in interest rates, and economic shifts. Shorter cash paybacks

also enable companies to recoup an investment sooner and put it to work elsewhere.

■ Generally, a payback period of three years or less is desirable; if a project's payback period is less than a year, some contend it should be judged essential.

SEE ALSO
Accounting (p. 428)

Calculating Return on Assets

WHAT IT MEASURES
A company's profitability, expressed as a percentage of its total assets.

WHY IT IS IMPORTANT
Return on assets measures how effectively a company has used the total assets at its disposal to generate earnings. Because the ROA formula reflects total revenue, total cost, and assets deployed, the ratio itself reflects a management's ability to generate income during the course of a given period, usually a year.

Naturally, the higher the return the better the profit performance. ROA is a convenient way of comparing a company's performance with that of its competitors, although the items on which the comparison is based may not always be identical.

HOW IT WORKS IN PRACTICE
To calculate ROA, divide a company's net income by its total assets, then multiply by 100 to express the figure as a percentage:

(net income / total assets) × 100 = ROA

If net income is $30, and total assets are $420, the ROA is:

30 / 420 = 0.0714 × 100 = 7.14%

A variation of this formula can be used to calculate return on net assets (RONA):

$$\text{net income / fixed assets +}$$
$$\text{working capital = RONA}$$

And, on occasion, the formula will separate after-tax interest expense from net income:

$$\text{net income +}$$
$$\text{interest expense /}$$
$$\text{total assets = ROA}$$

It is therefore important to understand what each component of the formula actually represents.

TRICKS OF THE TRADE
- Some experts recommend using the net income value at the end of the given period, and the assets value from beginning of the period or an average value taken over the complete period, rather than an end-of-the-period value; otherwise, the calculation will include assets that have accumulated during the year, which can be misleading.
- While a high ratio indicates a greater return, it must still be balanced against such factors as risk, sustainability, and reinvestment in the business through development costs. Some managements will sacrifice the long-term interests of investors in order to achieve an impressive ROA in the short term.
- A climbing return on assets usually indicates a climbing stock price, because it tells investors that a management is skilled at generating profits from the resources that a business owns.
- Acceptable ROAs vary by sector. In banking, for example, a ROA of 1% or better is a considered to be the standard benchmark of superior performance.
- ROA is an effective way of measuring the efficiency of manufacturers, but can be suspect when measuring service firms or companies whose primary assets are people.
- Other variations of the ROA formula do exist.

SEE ALSO
Accounting (p. 428)

Calculating Return on Investment

WHAT IT MEASURES

In the financial realm, the overall profit or loss on an investment expressed as a percentage of the total amount invested or total funds appearing on a company's balance sheet.

WHY IT IS IMPORTANT

Like return on assets or return on equity, return on investment measures a company's profitability and its management's ability to generate profits from the funds investors have placed at its disposal.

One opinion holds that if a company's operations cannot generate net earnings at a rate that exceeds the cost of borrowing funds from financial markets, the future of that company is grim.

HOW IT WORKS IN PRACTICE

The most basic expression of ROI can be found by dividing a company's net profit (also called net earnings) by the total investment (total debt plus total equity), then multiplying by 100 to arrive at a percentage:

$$\textbf{(net profit / total investment)} \times \textbf{100} = \textbf{ROI}$$

If, say, net profit is $30 and total investment is $250, the ROI is:

$$30 / 250 = 0.12 \times 100 = 12\%$$

A more complex variation of ROI is an equation known as the Du Pont formula:

$$\textbf{(net profit after taxes / total assets)} = \textbf{(net profit after taxes / sales)} \times \textbf{sales / total assets}$$

If, for example, net profit after taxes is $30, total assets are $250, and sales are $500, then:

$$30 / 250 = 30 / 500 \times 500 / 250 = 12\% = 6\% \times 2 = 12\%$$

Champions of this formula, which was developed by the Du Pont Company in the 1920s, say that it helps reveal how a company has both deployed its assets and controlled its costs, and how it can achieve the same percentage return in different ways.

For shareholders, the variation of the basic ROI formula used by investors is:

$$\textbf{net income + (current value – original value) / original value} \times \textbf{100} = \textbf{ROI}$$

If, for example, somebody invests $5,000 in a company and a year later has earned $100 in dividends, while the value of the shares is $5,200, the return on investment would be:

$$100 + (5,200 – 5,000) / 5,000 \times 100 =$$
$$(100 + 200) / 5,000 \times 100 =$$
$$300 / 5,000 = .06 \times 100 = 6\% \text{ ROI}$$

TRICKS OF THE TRADE

- Securities investors can use yet another ROI formula: net income divided by common stock and preferred stock equity plus long-term debt.

- It is vital to understand exactly what a return on investment measures, for example assets, equity, or sales. Without this understanding, comparisons may be misleading or suspect. A search for "return on investment" on the Web, for example, harvests everything from staff training to e-commerce to advertising and promotions!

- Be sure to establish whether the net profit figure used is before or after provision for taxes. This is important for making ROI comparisons accurate.

SEE ALSO
Accounting (p. 428)

Calculating Return on Sales

WHAT IT MEASURES

A company's operating profit or loss as a percentage of total sales for a given period, typically a year.

WHY IT IS IMPORTANT

ROS shows how efficiently management uses the sales dollar, thus reflecting its ability to manage costs and overhead and operate efficiently. It also indicates a firm's ability to withstand adverse conditions such as falling prices, rising costs, or declining sales. The higher the figure, the better a company is able to endure price wars and falling prices.

Return on sales can be useful in assessing the annual performances of cyclical companies that may have no earnings during particular months, and of firms whose business requires a huge capital investment and thus incurs substantial amounts of depreciation.

HOW IT WORKS IN PRACTICE

The calculation is very basic:

(operating profit / total sales) × 100 = percentage return on sales

So, if a company earns $30 on sales of $400, its return on sales is:

30 / 400 = 0.075 × 100 = 7.5%

TRICKS OF THE TRADE

- While easy to grasp, return on sales has its limits, since it sheds no light on the overall cost of sales or the four factors that contribute to it: materials, labor, production overhead, and administrative and selling overhead.
- Some calculations use operating profit before subtracting interest and taxes; others use after-tax income. Either figure is acceptable as long as ROS comparisons are consistent. Obviously, using income before interest and taxes will produce a higher ratio.
- The ratio's operating profit figure may also include special allowances and extraordinary non-recurring items, which, in turn, can inflate the percentage and be misleading.
- The ratio varies widely by industry. The supermarket business, for example, is heavily dependent on volume and usually has a low return on sales.
- Return on sales remains of special importance to retail sales organizations, which can compare their respective ratios with those of competitors and industry norms.

SEE ALSO
Accounting (p. 428)

Calculating Working Capital Productivity

WHAT IT MEASURES

How effectively a company's management is using its working capital.

WHY IT IS IMPORTANT

It is obvious that capital not being put to work properly is being wasted, which is certainly not in investors' best interests.

As an expression of how effectively a company spends its available funds compared with sales or turnover, the working capital productivity figure helps establish a clear relationship between its financial performance and process improvement. The relationship is said to have been first observed by the U.S. management consultant George Stalk while working in Japan.

A seldom-used reciprocal calculation, the working capital turnover or working capital to sales ratio, expresses the same relationship in a different way.

HOW IT WORKS IN PRACTICE

To calculate working capital productivity, first subtract current liabilities from current assets, which is the formula for working capital, then divide this figure into sales for the period.

sales / (current assets –
current liabilities) =
working capital productivity

If sales are $3,250, current assets are $900 and current liabilities are $650, then:

3250 / (900 – 650) = 3250 / 250 = 13

In this case, the higher the number the better. Sales growing faster than the resources required to generate them is a clear sign of efficiency and, by definition, productivity.

The working capital to sales ratio uses the same figures, but in reverse:

(working capital / sales) × 100% =
working capital to sales ratio

Using the same figures in the example above, this ratio would be calculated:

250 / 3250 = 0.077 × 100% = 7.7%

For this ratio, obviously, the lower the number the better.

TRICKS OF THE TRADE

- By itself, a single ratio means little; a series of them, several quarters' worth, for example, indicates a trend, and means a great deal.
- Some experts recommend doing quarterly calculations and averaging them for a given year to arrive at the most reliable number.
- Either ratio also helps a management compare its performance with that of competitors.
- These ratios should also help motivate companies to improve processes, such as eliminating steps in the handling of materials and bill collection, and shortening product design times. Such improvements reduce costs and make working capital available for other tasks.

SEE ALSO
Accounting (p. 428)

Defining Assets

WHAT THEY MEASURE

Collectively, the value of all the resources a company uses to conduct business and generate profits.

Examples of assets are cash, marketable securities, accounts and notes receivable, inventories of merchandise, real estate, machinery and office equipment, natural resources, and intangibles such as patents, legal claims and agreements, and negotiated rights.

WHY THEY ARE IMPORTANT

No business can continue for very long without knowing what assets it has at its disposal, and using them efficiently. Assets are a reflection of organizational strength, and are invariably evaluated by potential investors, banks and creditors, and other stakeholders.

Moreover, the value of assets is also a key figure used to calculate several financial ratios.

HOW THEY WORK IN PRACTICE

Assets are typically broken down into five different categories:

- Current assets. These include cash, cash equivalents, marketable securities, inventories, and prepaid expenses that are expected to be used within one year or a normal operating cycle. All cash items and inventories are reported at historical value. Securities are reported at market value.
- Noncurrent assets, or long-term investments. These are resources that are expected to be held for more than one year. They are reported at the lower of cost and current market value, which means that their values will vary.
- Fixed assets. These include property, plants and facilities, and equipment used to conduct business. These items are reported at their original value, even

though current values might well be much higher.

- Intangible assets. These include legal claims, patents, franchise rights, and accounts receivable. These values can be more difficult to determine. Accounts receivable, for example, reflect the amount a business expects to collect, such as $9,000 of the $10,000 owed by customers.
- Deferred charges. These include prepaid costs and other expenditures that will produce future revenue or benefits.

TRICKS OF THE TRADE

- Assets do not necessarily include everything of value, such as the talents of individuals, an organization's collective expertise, or the value of a customer base.
- Classic definitions of assets also often exclude or undervalue trademarks, even though there is universal agreement that these, for example, the three-point star of Mercedes-Benz or Coca-Cola's red logo, can have enormous value.
- Fixed assets are valued at their original cost, because of the prevailing opinion that they are used for business and are not for sale. Moreover, current market value is essentially a matter of opinion.
- Determining the value of patents can be challenging, because a patent has a finite life span, its value declines each year, and its useful life may be even shorter.
- Some scholars contend that the principal assets of "knowledge-based" businesses such as consulting firms or real estate development companies are, in fact, its people. In turn, their aggregate value should be calculated by subtracting the net value of assets from market value.

SEE ALSO
Accounting (p. 428)

MARKETING YOUR IDEA

Choosing Your Marketing Strategy

GETTING STARTED

Defining and implementing a rock solid marketing strategy is probably the single most important factor that will contribute towards the long-term sustainable success of any business venture, yet most businesses don't have one. Even if businesses do have a strategy, it is often then not followed and implemented 100% from top to bottom. For that reason, small businesses that do have the vision to create a dynamic, customer-focused marketing strategy, and also the determination to implement it, usually have the competitive edge. It is these businesses that will have a real opportunity to do something special. They will create the "buzz" that will set them apart from their competitors.

This actionlist gives more information about how to choose, implement, and maintain a dynamic marketing strategy. A book that you may find useful to read on the subject is *101 Ways to Market Your Business*, written by Andrew Griffiths, and published by Allen & Unwin.

FAQS

What is a marketing strategy?

Having a marketing strategy is different from having a marketing plan. A marketing strategy involves choosing a realistic, measurable, and ambitious goal that you think your business can achieve on a sustainable basis. With a marketing strategy, each marketing tactic you use is 100% focused on reaching and surpassing that overall goal.

What is a marketing plan?

A marketing plan will include all of the tactics and actions that are designed to achieve the overall strategic goal. It will also include a timetable for their implementation. In other words, the plan will detail what you will do to make the strategy happen.

Why don't most businesses have a strategy?

The vast majority of businesses in all sectors market themselves in the same way as their competitors. They use supply-driven marketing messages based on product features; they design unfathomable Web sites; they create bland slogans and statements about what their business does. They do this because it is easy. Businesses also do this because their owners/managers know their products and services better than anyone else; as a result, they promote themselves in terms that they understand, but that their customers do not. They also do it because they look at what their competitors are doing and fall into the trap of doing the same things. Instead, what they should be doing is differentiating themselves by creating a unique proposition that gives them a real competitive edge.

MAKING IT HAPPEN

Set Your Sights

The first thing to do is to decide on your ultimate goal. Every business will have different strategic objectives for its own specific situation. No matter how high you set your sights, your marketing strategy should drive everything that your business does to achieve that objective.

You might aim to double turnover in 12 months; to maximize the value of your business in three years in order to sell it; or to increase your market share threefold in six months. You will only make the most of your chances of achieving or surpassing your goal by following a well thought out, meticulously implemented marketing strategy. With your business's marketing efforts accurately aimed and 100% focused on the needs of the target market, you are far more likely to succeed. If the aim is wrong, and your understanding of the market is wrong, you will achieve mediocrity, or fail altogether.

Choose the Right Marketing Strategy

Your business can achieve competitive advantage if it chooses a marketing strategy that sets your business apart from everyone else. There is no magic formula for doing this. You cannot just import or implant an off-the-shelf strategy into a business. It is up to you to choose and define your marketing strategy in your own business situation.

However, there are a number of key factors that will help you choose the right strategy. You need to know exactly who your customers or target prospects are, and where they are located. You also need to know exactly what these people want and need, why they need it, how they need it, and when they need it. You will have to be confident enough to develop or create a unique selling proposition (USP) that you can offer to completely fulfill your customers' needs. You must then ensure that you test your proposition in your chosen market first. Once the proposition is tested, you will need to analyze the results, and use them to refine the proposition until you are sure it is right.

Implement Your Strategy

You should only attempt to implement your strategy fully when you are absolutely sure that your unique selling proposition is right. Your task then is to get your message across to your market. You need to ensure that your unique selling proposition is articulated in all of your marketing messages, campaigns, and sales channels. It is important that you recognize when your proposition is working so that you can then market it fast, first, and aggressively in your sector. Only in this way will you achieve an unassailable lead over your competitors.

Keep Ahead of the Game

In the 1990s everyone spoke about being "market-led." Today, market conditions change at bewildering speed. Any number of factors can play a part in this, including technology, customers' tastes, fashions, trends, media influences, and so on. If you want your business to survive in the 21st

century, you must make the right choice of target market. You then need to focus everything the business does on providing unique value and benefits to meet the needs of that chosen market, and you need to do this better than your competitors.

Your business and your marketing strategy cannot stand still. What is unique today is widespread tomorrow, and unwanted the day after that. The vital ingredient in a truly dynamic marketing strategy is to strive continually to discover new and better ways to add value for your customers, and keep your proposition unique in your chosen market.

Everytime you put your strategy into action, you will also learn something new about your customers' needs, and whether your proposition is right for them. The implementation of your marketing strategy should be a continuous process of creating a proposition to satisfy your customers; testing it; and learning from it. You can learn from it by recognizing what is right and doing more of it, or changing what is wrong as soon as you realize it isn't working.

WHAT TO AVOID
Missing the Target

The most important aspect of any marketing strategy is making sure that you have chosen the right market at which to aim your products and services. You may have utterly convincing sales messages and advertising copy, and you may be brilliant at selling and articulating the benefits of your service. If you haven't selected the right target audience in the first place, however, or if you haven't understood what that audience needs, you will almost certainly fail. Make sure you select the right market, with the right profile of consumers who have a propensity to buy your products or service. Then you will be able to aim your proposition, and the benefits it brings, directly at them.

Standing Still

To succeed in your market you need to keep up to date with changes in customer preference and buying patterns. You also need to keep up with the seemingly relentless changes in technology and other external forces. If you don't make the effort to move forward constantly, your competitors will steal your market share, your biggest customers, or your intended new market, before you have a chance to do anything about it.

Lack of Focus

The biggest mistake is to stop focusing on your market. You have to ensure that you are continuing to provide the unique value and benefit your customers need and expect from your service. Take your eye off the marketing ball for a second, and your strategy will fall flat on its face.

SEE ALSO
Market Research and Competitor Intelligence (p. 469)
Profiling Your Competitors (p. 186)
Researching the Size of Your Market (p. 177)

Researching the Size of Your Market

GETTING STARTED

It's important to find out what potential your business has to generate revenues and profits in your chosen market sector, and the only way to do this is to carry out thorough market research. The better the data you have about your market, the better equipped you will be to make informed decisions about your business. Good market research will help you establish the most important objective of all—in other words, your sales targets. Your financial backers, business partners, key staff, and other key stake holders will also have a keen, if not vested, interest in your sales potential and the market share you believe you can realistically achieve.

Before you can estimate the share of the market you want to attain, you'll need to have researched the *overall* size of the market. Its size could be calculated in terms of its volume (that is to say, the number of buyers), and its value (in terms of annual total spend), or both. This actionlist will help you to do this. A book which you may find useful on the subject is *Marketing Research Toolbox: A Concise Guide for Beginners*, published by Sage Publications.

FAQS

What do I need to know about my customer group?

Assuming you have already accurately profiled the customer group that you consider to be your ideal market audience, you need to know how many potential buyers the group consists of, and how much they currently spend.

What else do I need to know before I set my sales targets?

Once you have found out how many potential buyers you have, and how much they spend at the moment, you need to find out whether your market is growing or declining. You then need to decide what sales levels you are going to aim for.

MAKING IT HAPPEN

Find Out the Number of Potential Buyers

Your target audience will comprise groups of businesses, groups of individuals, or both. Calculating the size of this overall market, that is to say the number of people who could potentially buy from you, will only be possible once you have considered who they are, their unique characteristics, and where they are located. It may be the case in your business situation that your potential customers live close to you. For example, you may offer a service that people generally will travel only a short distance to

purchase. For some services, people are prepared to travel a reasonable distance, for example, up to an hour, to buy something. In other instances, distance is not an issue, as consumers will purchase by mail order or via the Internet.

You need to ask yourself whether location or proximity to your service is an issue for your target audience. This will help you to scope the potential size of your market when you add this factor into the profile of your customers' buying characteristics. This is important to help you target the number of buyers you think you can reach with your marketing.

Research How Much Buyers Spend in the Market

Establishing how many buyers there are for your service is only part of the equation. You will also need to understand how much these buyers are prepared to spend on a product or service such as yours, in terms of each time they buy, and in terms of how frequently they buy.

Knowing your market size is meaningless unless you can attach a value to the volume of potential buyers you have. That value is also meaningless unless you understand the repeat purchase rate, in other words how many times they buy or use your service in weeks, months, or over a year. This information is vital when forecasting sales revenues for your business plan or forthcoming budget.

Establish if the Market is Expanding or Declining

Having established the number of buyers, the amount they spend, and their frequency of purchase, you will need to understand the market potential. You should ask yourself whether your market will be the same size in six or 12 months' time. Look at the trends, to see if they suggest that your customers will be spending more, the same, or less. Try to predict whether there will be any more buyers seeking your type of product and service.

There may also be other target audiences with similar buying characteristics and needs that you will be able to access through your marketing. It is vital that you do not just settle on the information you have about the size of your market now, and miss opportunities to reach a wider audience in a year's time, without even realizing it. Similarly, a trend showing a decline in the number of buyers, or their purchase rate must be identified and acted on before it is too late.

Analyze What Share of Your Overall Market You Want to Achieve

The target market share you set for your business will help you determine the precise marketing effort, methods, channels, and budget you require to achieve it. However, it is not as simple a matter as just having good data about the volume or value of your market, or the underlying trends. There are also your competitors' activities to take into consideration. You need to ask yourself whether there is likely to be more competition in a year's time. Find out what the trends are. Try to predict whether your competitors will have new, better value, more innovative services than yours. You will need to keep a very close eye on their marketing activities, for example, special promotions, free gifts, guarantees, after sales service, and so on. This might give them the edge over your business, and a chance to steal a greater share of the market

you have targeted or established for yourself.

Find Information about Market Size and Trends

Business and market information is available from a variety of sources. Some is free, but you will probably have to pay for more in-depth statistics, trends, and forecasts. The reference section of your local public library will have a business section carrying published market reports on hundreds of sectors. They will also have government statistics and documents, trade magazines, and national and local business directories. If they do not have the publications themselves, they should have a directory of them, together with details of their costs and where you can obtain them. If you want local population or business information you should contact your local council.

The Internet is also a good place to start, although if you are not an experienced researcher this could be time consuming, or you may end up not finding what you really want. However, employing one of the main search engines and carrying out a search using terms containing the name of the market sector you are in, the type of information you need, a product name, geographic area, and suppliers' or competitors' names, should bring up a good range of relevant Web sites for your business.

You may find the following sites helpful:

- for information on market trends in the United States—FXI Research (**www.fxi-research.com**)
- for information about statistics and trends—Statistical Abstract of the United States (**www.census.gov/statab**)
- for information on potential business buyers—U.S. Venture Exchange (**www.usventureexchange.com**), Yellow Pages Online (**www.yellowpages.com**), or United States Chamber of Commerce (**www.uschamber.com**)
- for information when you are starting up or a newly established business—StartUp Journal: The Wall Street Journal Center for Entrepreneurs (**www.startupjournal.com**)

✘ WHAT TO AVOID
Not Being Up to Date

It is vitally important to ensure that your estimates of the size of your market are based on current data and trends. If you make decisions based on out-of-date information, or fail to spot the trends in your sector, you will either miss the opportunities to obtain a greater share of the overall market, or your competitors will steal your market share.

Taking Your Eye off the Target

Do not make this research a one-off task. If you fail regularly to research what is happening to the size and structure of your market, you will lose touch with your existing audiences and potential new customers.

Failing to Spot the Trends

You must continually try to look at the bigger picture in your sector, and not just one particular aspect of the market, or the statistics relating to it. Look for trends in terms of potential buyers you could reach, the average value of purchase they make, and how often they are buying. Keep an eye out for new entrants in your sector, and the share of the overall market they are taking.

SEE ALSO

Choosing Your Marketing Strategy (p. 174)
Market Research and Competitor Intelligence (p. 469)
Profiling Your Competitors (p. 186)

Focus On: Planning Marketing
Malcolm McDonald

GETTING STARTED

Most managers accept that some kind of procedure for planning a company's marketing helps to sharpen their focus, making the complexity of business operations manageable and adding a dimension of realism to the business's future plans. This procedure is known as marketing planning. It is a managerial process with a logical sequence of activities leading to the setting of marketing objectives and the formulation of plans for achieving them.

As with any plan, it needs to be as clear and simple as possible. This also needs to be reflected in the sales approach, which has to be as straightforward for customers as possible and remove any obstacles to actually making the sale. This actionlist explains how to cope with market uncertainty by:

- developing a *strategic* marketing plan;
- developing a *tactical* marketing plan;
- reviewing current thinking about markets and marketing.

FAQS

Why is it important to plan marketing?

The contribution of marketing planning to the success of a business, whatever its size or area of activity, lies in its commitment to detailed analysis of future opportunities to meet customer needs. It offers a wholly professional approach to selling to well-defined market segments those products or services that deliver the desired benefits. Such commitment and activities shouldn't be mistaken for budgets and forecasts, which have always been a commercial necessity. Marketing planning is a more sophisticated approach concerned with identifying what sales are going to be made in the longer term and to whom, in order to give revenue budgets and sales forecasts a real chance of being achieved.

What are the main features of marketing planning?

Successful marketing planning is the cornerstone of developing strong, durable, and robust businesses. Overcoming an organizational culture that acts as a barrier to effective marketing planning is essential if performance is to be optimized and long-term goals are to be achieved. Given the complexity of the rapidly changing business environment and the high number of variables that influence business performance,

it is necessary for managers or owner-managers to have an effective means of making the situation manageable. Thorough and detailed analysis of how to meet future customer needs provides a sophisticated and reliable method for building long-term success. Marketing planning enables your business's vision to become a reality.

MAKING IT HAPPEN
Review Current Thinking

From an extensive review of the current research into strategic marketing planning, five principal conclusions emerge.

- There is a clear consensus about the benefits of the strategic marketing planning process.
- Strategic marketing planning and the marketing orientation that accompanies it are clearly associated with improved performance across most market situations.
- In unsuccessful companies, the process of strategic marketing planning is poorly adhered to in practice, and is frequently used as a pretext for inadequate budgeting and tactical programs.
- The primary barrier to strategic marketing planning lies in the culture of the company and the values that stem from that culture.
- Although the degree of formality of the process can range from a highly creative,

entrepreneurial approach to the more structured, rational process described here, there is universal consensus among strategic thinkers and planners that some kind of managerial planning process has to be used to manage the link between a business and its environment.

In large, multinational, multiproduct, multicultural businesses, then, it is usual to find a structured process for marketing planning; in smaller businesses with fewer complex products or markets, the management of the process outlined here tends to be much less formal and structured. The process and the steps, however, are the same in all consistently successful companies.

Understand the Level of Marketing Plan

There are two principal kinds of marketing plan.

The strategic marketing plan. A strategic marketing plan is a plan for three or more years. It is a written document outlining how owner-managers or managers perceive their own position in the market relative to their competitors (with the advantage they have over their competitors accurately defined), what objectives they want to achieve, how they intend to achieve them (strategies), what resources are required (budget), and what results are expected. Three years is the most common strategic planning period. Five years is the longest, but is becoming less common because of the speed of technological and environmental change. Strategic marketing-driven plans are not to be confused with scenario planning or the kind of very long-range plans formulated by a number of Japanese companies (which often have planning horizons of between 50 and 200 years!).

The tactical marketing plan. A tactical marketing plan is the detailed scheduling and costing of the actions necessary for achieving the first year of the strategic marketing plan. The tactical plan is thus usually for one year.

Develop the Contents of a Strategic Marketing Plan

The contents of a strategic marketing plan are as follows:

- mission statement, setting out the raison d'être of the business and covering its role, business definition, distinctive competence, and future indications.
- financial summary, summarizing the financial implications over the full planning period.
- market overview, providing a brief picture of the market, including market structure, market trends, key market segments, and (sometimes) gap analysis.
- SWOT analysis, analyzing the strengths and weaknesses of the business compared with competitors against key customer success factors, and considering opportunities and threats, usually for each key product or segment.
- issues to be addressed, derived from a SWOT analysis (of strengths, weaknesses, opportunities, and threats) and usually specific to each product or segment.
- portfolio summary, offering a pictorial summary of the SWOT analysis that makes it easy to see at a glance the relative importance of each of the four elements; it is often a two-dimensional matrix in which the horizontal axis measures the organization's comparative strengths and the vertical axis measures its relative attractiveness.
- assumptions, listing the underlying assumptions critical to the planned marketing objectives and strategies.
- marketing objectives, usually consisting of quantitative statements (in terms of profit, volume, value, and market share) of what the business wishes to achieve; they are usually given by product, by segment, and overall.
- marketing strategies, stating how the objectives are to be achieved; they often involve the four Ps of marketing: product, price, place, and promotion.
- resource requirements and budget, showing the full planning-period budget, giving in detail the revenues and associated costs for each year.

Develop the Contents of a Tactical Marketing Plan

The contents of a tactical marketing plan are very similar, except that they often omit the mission statement, the market overview, and SWOT analysis, and the plan goes into much more detailed quantification by product and segment of marketing objectives and associated strategies. An additional feature is more detailed scheduling and costing of the tactics necessary to achieve the first year's planned goals.

Complete the Process of Marketing Planning

This involves:

- identifying what sales will be made in the longer term and to whom, in order to turn revenue budgets and sales forecasts into reality.
- analyzing your strengths and weaknesses compared with competitors' against key customer success factors, and similarly review the business's opportunities and threats.
- completing the strategic marketing plan before the tactical plan. Write your strategic marketing plan to cover three or more years, defining competitive advantage, objectives, strategies, and budgets.
- building marketing strategies round the four Ps of marketing: product, price, place, promotion.

- writing a tactical marketing plan, detailing schedules and costing for the specific actions necessary to achieve the first year of the strategic plan.

WHAT TO AVOID
Failing to Implement the Marketing Plan Successfully

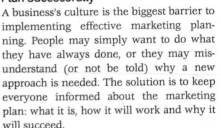

A business's culture is the biggest barrier to implementing effective marketing planning. People may simply want to do what they have always done, or they may misunderstand (or not be told) why a new approach is needed. The solution is to keep everyone informed about the marketing plan: what it is, how it will work and why it will succeed.

Disorganized Planning

The output of the process (the plan) needs to spell out how an business expects to achieve its objectives; however, people may view the planning process as an academic exercise, or they may not have the skills or experience to plan effectively. Also, strategic marketing planning needs to precede tactical marketing planning. The planning process is universal, although how formal its implementation is will vary from business to business.

Focus On: Marketing—The Importance of Being First
Al and Laura Ries

GETTING STARTED

Most managers believe the basic issue in marketing is convincing a prospective customer that you have a better product or service. Not true.

The basic issue in marketing is creating a new category you can be first in.

Marketing is not a battle of products, it is a battle of *perceptions*. To win the battle of perceptions you have to become the leader in a category. Prospects assume the leader must be better because "everybody knows the better product or service will win in the marketplace." How do you become the leader? You launch a new category you can be first in. It doesn't have to be a big technological advance. Sometimes the simple ideas are the easiest to get into the mind. And where do you win the battle? You win the battle inside the mind of the prospect.

This actionlist explains how to dominate your market sector.

FAQS

For a small company, how do the principles of marketing differ from those that apply to a large company?

The principles are exactly the same, only a small company usually manages to stay small by ignoring these principles. The truth is, every large company was once a small company that became big by doing the right things. The biggest mistake a small company can make is thinking of themselves as a small company instead of thinking of themselves as a big company in its gestation period.

How does a market leader achieve its leadership?

Not by introducing a better product or service. Invariably the leader in the category got to be the leader by being the first brand in a new category. Some examples:

- Coca-Cola, the first cola.
- Dell, the first personal computer sold direct.
- Domino's, the first home delivery pizza chain.
- Gatorade, the first sports drink.
- Red Bull, the first energy drink.

What big companies introduced these brands? None. They were all started by small entrepreneurs like Tom Monaghan (Domino's Pizza) and Dietrich Mateschitz (Red Bull). Most of these companies started small, then grew up over an extended period of time.

Some consultants have called this leadership phenomenon, "the first mover advantage," but that is not so. It's an advantage, but it's not the reason that most leader brands were first in their categories. It's the "first minder" advantage. That is, the brand that gets into the mind first is the winner, not the brand that was first in the category. Du Mont made the first television set; Hurley, the first washing machine; and Red Rock, the first cola; the MITS Altair 8800 was the first personal computer, but these and many other brands failed to get into the minds of their prospects. You don't win in the marketplace. You win in the mind.

If you weren't first in your category and you can't win by being better, what can you do?

The answer is obvious: start a new category you can be first in. Marketing is more a battle of categories than it is a battle of products. Winning companies think category first and product second. They try to categorize what they do, not in terms of being better, but in terms of being different.

When Procter & Gamble introduced Tide many years ago, they could have called the product a "new, improved soap." Tide was a soap then, and Tide is a soap today, in the sense that soap is a "cleansing agent." But Tide was made from synthetic materials rather than the fats and lye found in traditional cleaning products like Ivory, Oxydol, and Rinso. Tide could have been called a synthetic soap, but that would have nailed the brand to the soap category. So Procter & Gamble called Tide the "first detergent," a totally new category, and even today Tide is the leading brand of detergent in the United States.

MAKING IT HAPPEN
Create a New Category You Can Be First In

When Michael Dell set up the Dell Computer Corporation, he could have sold his "better" products through conventional computer stores, but he didn't. Instead he launched the first brand of personal computer sold direct by phone. Today Dell is the world's largest selling brand of personal computer and still doesn't sell any computers through conventional computer stores.

Get the Launch Right

Before you launch (or relaunch) a new product or service, ask yourself:

- What is the name of the category? Not a name that you might like, but a name the industry gives the category.
- What is the brand name of the leader in the category? Not necessarily the sales leader, but the brand that customers perceive to be the leader.

If there is no dominant brand, or at least not a dominant brand in the mind of most prospects, jump right in with your product or service and try to quickly establish your leadership. Cut prices, cut deals, hire sales people, launch massive publicity campaigns, do everything you can to seize the leadership position before someone else does.

Promote your brand as the leading brand.

"It's so easy to use," says AOL, "no wonder it's number one." Leave no piece of marketing material or Web site or TV advertisement or radio commercial without mentioning your leadership. Leadership is the most important aspect of any marketing campaign. Why? Prospects assume the better product or service will win in the marketplace. Therefore, if you are the leader, you must have the better product.

If there is a dominant brand, then move on and set up a new category you can be first in. But make sure you have a new name to match the new category. You can get in serious trouble if you try to use an existing name.

You can't dictate the category name. Only the industry and the media can do that. Therefore, you have to launch your new brand with publicity and get the media to establish the category name for you.

Avoid Falling into the "Better Product" Trap

Odd as it might seem, a small company is more likely to make the "better product" mistake mentioned above than a large company. Cynical marketing people who don't really care about "building a better product" often populate large companies. Their focus is on marketing, distribution, packaging, display, and other sophisticated ways to hype sales. It's the small company entrepreneur who believes deeply in the superiority of his or her product that is most likely to bet the ranch on this strategy.

However, unless you are already the leader in some aspects of what you do, these programs are bound to fail. People just naturally assume that the leader must have the better product or service.

WHAT TO AVOID
Failing to Establish a New Category or Product Sector

There's almost always a way to set up a new category. Unfortunately, most companies refuse to even consider the possibility of a new category because "there's no market." Of course, there's no market. If there were, it wouldn't be a new category. That's the most difficult thing to overcome. You have to have faith that you can succeed in getting acceptance for a new category. Furthermore, a new category doesn't necessarily represent a big, technological advance. Soapsoft, the first liquid soap, was a big commercial success. How difficult is it to take a tub of soap and liquefy it?

Using an Existing Name for the New Product Sector

How difficult is it to take regular beer and add water? Miller Lite, the first light beer, was a big success, but ultimately paid a big penalty for it. Instead of creating a new brand to match the new category, the company used a line extension name which just about killed their regular beer brand (Miller High Life) and caused them to lose their light beer leadership to the competition. A new category needs a new name.

SEE ALSO
Raising Awareness of Your Brand (p. 247)

Profiling Your Competitors

GETTING STARTED

Competitor information helps you protect and grow your business. You need to build a detailed profile of your direct competitors, their strengths, weaknesses, and relationships with customers, as well as thinking more widely about competition for your customers and their spending. To help you do this, compare the performance of your business with that of your main competitors by measuring factors that are important to quality of service and use the comparison as the basis for a program of performance improvement.

Whether you sell yourself or you have a sales team, competitor information can be obtained from many different sources. Publications, the press, and the Internet have information readily available that can help you compile intelligence on competitors, and corporate brochures and annual reports are also excellent sources of published information. Maintain a file of press cuttings on your competitors' activities, using their trade publications as a source.

Published industry surveys can provide a useful insight into purchasing patterns and competitors' Web sites can provide valuable information on their resources, plans, and capabilities.

FAQS

Why is competitor intelligence so important?

Competitive activity can have a significant impact on your own plans. If you are about to run a marketing campaign or new product launch, competitive activity could limit its effectiveness—so you need to know about it. You may also identify growing threats to important accounts. Unless you monitor activity and take appropriate action, your business faces an unknown risk.

Who are my competitors?

Many small companies already know their main, direct competitors. Often they have worked with them or encountered them at trade events or heard of them through customers. It is dangerous, however, to assume you know all the competitors.

It is often useful to think laterally about who might be in competition for your customers. Many products and services could be classed as nonessential and so customers may be choosing to spend their discretionary budget between two very different market sectors. In addition, as a specialist, you could find yourself in competition with a larger company who give away a competing service as a promotional device.

Should competitor research be carried out internally or by an independent research company?

You can carry out the research internally, provided you have the resources. Much of the source material is in the public domain, so you should be able to obtain it yourself and you must never ignore the wealth of information you already have in your company or can gain through your own contacts. However, if you wish to research customer attitudes (to compare your company to the competition), you may need to use an independent research organization. Customers may not be completely honest with your own representatives.

How reliable is published competitor information?

You have to make assumptions about the accuracy and quality of any published information that is used for research. Much of the material will be published to provide information for customers, so it is unlikely to be misleading. However, realistically, you can only use the latest and best information that is reasonably available.

MAKING IT HAPPEN
Identify the Competitive Threat

Competitor information helps you to

identify how you can protect your most important business and, more positively, how you can strengthen your position with customers in situations in which your competitors are currently holding a larger share of the business than you. These are the main questions:

- How many competitors do you have? Are they direct or indirect?
- Who are your major competitors—those that threaten your most important customers?
- How much of your business do they threaten? Quantifying the threat helps you prioritize.
- Where are your main competitors located? How do they compare in size? Are they growing? Map them and track them.
- How do your products compare with competitive offerings? What about price? Distribution? Image and reputation? Service quality?
- What are customers' attitudes towards your competitors and towards your own company?
- Which customers might switch to competitors and why?
- How strong are competitors' relationships with key customers or key decision makers? How long have competitors been dealing with them?
- Have you got the skills and resources to overcome the competitive threat?
- Are any competitors making inroads into businesses in which you are currently the dominant supplier?
- Who are your competitors' main customers?
- Have your competitors invested in links with customers that would make it difficult for other suppliers to make inroads?
- Can you (or your customers) identify weaknesses in your competitors?
- Which of your competitors' customers do you want to win?

Compare Key Competitive Factors

Listed below are a number of factors that are important to meeting customer needs. You can score these factors (0–10, where 10 is the best in the market) to see how your business and your main competitors compare. The results should be used as the basis for a program of performance improvement. As far as possible you should give priority to the things that matter *to your customers* rather than your own opinion:

- evidence of an excellent service culture, for example, problems quickly resolved by frontline staff rather than reference to higher managers
- high levels of after-sales service and support offered
- product adapted readily to meet customer specifications
- evidence of commitment to quality measurements such as ISO 9002, or similar industry schemes
- promises made to customers, for example in sales literature offering money-back guarantees or precise delivery schedules
- evidence of feedback encouraged, for example comment forms or toll free telephone numbers made widely available
- flexible approach to pricing such as the use of price incentives or finance schemes to appeal to different types of customer. Willingness to negotiate prices for important customers
- staff knowledgeable about the product and willing to share this knowledge and give advice to customers
- good reputation with agents, distributors, or other intermediaries
- overall reputation. For example, how do your staff or customers rate the company?

Use the Sales Force

If you have one, the sales force can obtain competitor information from many different sources. By talking to customers, salespeople can find out about competitors' direct sales calls, marketing campaigns, special offers, and new developments. They can also obtain similar information from retailers or distributors. Crucially, they can get a feel for the customers' awareness and attitude towards your competitors..

Analyze Published Information

Information is readily available from publications, the press, and the Internet that can help you compile intelligence on different aspects of competitors' business, including:

- main markets
- customers
- resources and financial performance
- product range
- new products
- plans for growth

Obtain Competitor Literature

Corporate brochures and annual reports are available for some companies. You can sometimes obtain copies from exhibitions and customers or as downloads from competitors' Web sites. Often just visiting your competitors offices you can pick up brochures and leaflets.

Monitor the Press

Maintain a file of press cuttings on your competitors' activities, using their trade publications as a source, or depending on your budget, you might consider using a press cuttings agency to gather material for you. Smaller companies can give a member of staff (for example, a sales person) responsibility for gathering and keeping data on a particular competitor.

Analyze Industry Reports

Published industry surveys can provide a useful insight into purchasing patterns in different market sectors. You can sometimes obtain information on competitors, market share, and industry trends.

Check the Internet

Competitor Web sites can provide valuable information on their resources, plans, and capabilities. As well as checking the company information and product pages, you should read any customer case studies on the site and monitor the news section to find out about new developments. Trade publications are increasingly available in electronic editions, making it easier for you to monitor the press.

Visit Exhibitions

Competitors' exhibition stands can be valuable sources of information. Most organizations only participate in exhibitions that are important to their current or future business plans.

Monitor Competitors' Promotional Activities

Analyzing competitors' promotional activities will help you to respond to their activities. By monitoring their advertising, promotions, exhibition presence, press activities, and Internet information, you can assess possible strategies. These are some of the possible scenarios:

- heavy advertising expenditure could indicate a competitor trying to win greater share or attempting to remedy losses in that market;
- price promotions may indicate that your competitors want to be perceived as value-for-money suppliers or it may be an emergency response to declining sales;
- press announcements about new production facilities could indicate that your competitors are trying to increase their business significantly. They may become more cost-effective and able to offer lower prices, or may be taking on additional overheads that they must finance;
- announcements about new branch or dealership openings could mean that competitors are expanding into new territories;
- recruitment drives may signal a change in direction, a growth strategy or a sudden loss of staff.

All of these can mean that your competitor is spending more money and you might compare this with published accounts (available through credit reference agencies) to gain an indication of their financial health.

Marketing and trade publications can be useful sources of information on competitor marketing activity.

Appoint a Research Company

If you do not have the internal resources to monitor competitive activity, you can use an independent research company to carry out all the tasks outlined above. You can also ask them to explore customer attitudes to competitors. Customers may be more willing to provide this information to an independent organization.

Consider Benchmarking

Benchmarking compares your performance with that of other, similar companies. Competently done, it will give you a baseline assessment of your company's efficiency and some insight into where competitors may be gaining competitive advantage over you.

WHAT TO AVOID
Overlooking the Obvious Sources

Some competitor intelligence is freely available from the Internet, the press, and other published sources and, most of all, from your staff, your customers, and your competitors themselves. Information from these sources can provide a valuable starting point for developing detailed competitor profiles.

Ignoring Competitor Information

Competitor information is only valuable if you use it to refine your own strategies or take defensive action to protect your business. Simply gathering information without analysis or action is wasteful.

Acting on Incomplete Information

Be cautious about acting on competitor intelligence. Published sources can only provide a partial picture, and more strategic information is likely to be confidential. This means that you may make incorrect assumptions in planning your response to competitor action.

Using Out-of-date Information

Records should be carefully checked and maintained. Using poor quality data can ruin the best campaigns.

SEE ALSO
Choosing Your Marketing Strategy (p. 174)
Researching the Size of Your Market (p. 177)

WORKING WITH CUSTOMERS

Conducting Market Research

GETTING STARTED

Businesses of all sizes need to keep on top of changes or developments in their chosen markets so that they can make sure that the product or service they offer fits the bill. This actionlist gives you some ideas on how to carry out different types of market research.

Telephone interviews are a quick and cost-effective way to obtain opinions from a sample of customers. This type of research can be used to assess your customers' reaction to a change in the product or service, or to measure awareness of a company or product. One of the downsides of this approach, however, is that can be difficult to reassure people that you are carrying out legitimate research—most people will think you're trying to sell them something!

Mail surveys are ideal for customer satisfaction surveys or detailed surveys that take time to complete. However, it can be difficult to obtain a worthwhile rate of response, and you, as the researcher, have little control over the process. Incentives may be needed to improve response and there is a risk of incomplete responses.

Group discussions or focus groups are ideal for identifying issues of concern to customers and assessing customer reactions to potential changes. This type of research is open-ended and can highlight important customer issues that the researcher may not be aware of. However, group discussions are not representative and can be influenced by a dominant member of the group.

The personal interview is ideal for obtaining detailed information on attitudes to products and services or getting feedback from specific individuals. Personal interviews allow in-depth discussion of complex topics and give you greater control over the response.

An omnibus survey is a cost-effective method of researching several topics at the same time. The same survey is used to carry out regular research on a number of different products by telephone or personal interview. You should check that the other topics in the survey are compatible with your own products.

FAQS

Can we carry out market research ourselves, or should we use a consultancy?

Market research is a professional discipline and depending on your industry and what you need to find out, you may get more meaningful results by using a consultancy. They are trained to detect possible errors in research results, and their independence is reassuring to people who are being interviewed. The main problem for small businesses is, naturally, the expense. Review your budget and see if you can afford outside help.

You can carry out a limited amount of research yourself, developing and mailing questionnaires or carrying out limited telephone interviews. Again, there is a risk that people may feel that your research is a thinly disguised sales pitch.

How do I carry out quick and effective research?

Without incurring great costs, you often have the opportunity to research your own customers. Every time you or a member of your staff meet a customer you can discover important information. Record this information and create opportunities to share it.

More formal research may include a space on delivery notes or invoices, enclosures with products, or follow-up phone calls to ask customers' opinions. Be cautious about asking for too much (or too personal) information..

How reliable are the results from focus groups?

The results are as reliable as the quality of the participants and the people who run the sessions. It is easy for individual participants to dominate a group and influence the course of discussions. If the person running the discussion asks the wrong questions, the resulting discussion may prove worthless. Make sure those in charge are well briefed.

We have limited resources for research. Should we participate in an omnibus survey so that we can make the best use of our budget?

An omnibus survey is an ideal way to share expensive research resources and reach a large audience. However, you must be sure that the audience is relevant to your company's business. Ask for a profile of the research audience and check the names of other organizations which have used the survey. If there is a reasonable match to your own business, it could be a cost-effective solution.

MAKING IT HAPPEN
Interview Customers by Telephone

Telephone interviews are a quick and cost-effective way to obtain opinions from a sample of customers. They can be used to assess customer reaction to a change in the product or service, or to gauge satisfaction ratings compared to competitors. The makeup of the sample is crucial; it is more important to know the views of valuable customers.

Speed Up Research

The main benefit of telephone research is speed. A large number of interviews can be conducted in a short space of time, and data can be gathered and processed quickly. Telephone interviews also cost considerably less than personal interviews. As long as they are brief and to the point they are non-intrusive and easy to arrange. A customer may be too busy for a personal interview, but willing to spend a short time on the phone.

Be careful about a senior decision-maker being contacted by a junior member of staff or an independent researcher, though, and always bear in mind the effect on the customer's relationship with you.

Don't Confuse Telephone Research with Selling

Telephone interviews have limited scope because people may not be prepared to spend a long period of time on the telephone. It can also be difficult to get across complex concepts by telephone.

Follow industry guidelines:
- define the target audience;
- draft a questionnaire and test it with colleagues;
- make the calls at times likely to be convenient for the target audience, but check when you call that it is convenient; if not, offer to call back ;
- identify the purpose of the call and give an indication of the likely duration;
- use faxes, if necessary, to send more detailed information for discussion.

Use Mail Surveys or Questionnaires

Questionnaires are very difficult to compile well. Mail surveys are delivered directly to customers and they can be a quick and relatively inexpensive method of obtaining information. They are ideal for customer satisfaction surveys or detailed surveys that take time to complete. However, it can be difficult to obtain a reasonable rate of response and you cannot assume that the responses will be representative of all customers.

Assess the Value of Mail Surveys

Mail surveys are relatively inexpensive. The costs include outward and return postage and stationery. They are precise and can be targeted at specific customers or prospects. They are also voluntary, because there is no pressure on the customer. The main problem, however, is the low response rates; incentives may be needed to improve it. There is also a risk of questionnaires and survey forms returned incomplete or incorrectly completed. You may face a slow response because there is no time pressure on the customer so you must take this into account in your planning.

Improve the Response from Mail Surveys

Response rates can be influenced by many different factors. For many consumer goods markets less than 5% would be normal and 15% or more would be extremely high. For highly involved customers in some sectors you might anticipate much more. If you need to improve response think about:

- offering an incentive, such as entry into a prize draw, for returned questionnaires;
- simplifying the questionnaire;
- reassuring the customer that information will be kept confidential;
- enclosing a stamped addressed or business reply envelope.

Hold a Group Discussion

In group discussions, or focus groups, customers and prospective customers are invited to discuss a particular topic, usually under the guidance of a researcher. They are ideal for exploring and, possibly, identifying issues or problems which concern customers, and assessing customer reactions to potential changes.

There is no limit placed on what the group can discuss, and this format can highlight important customer issues that the researcher may not be aware of. Many customers welcome the opportunity to discuss products and services with their colleagues and have an opportunity to contribute to change. The disadvantages are that group discussions are not representative, and they can be biased or influenced by a dominant member of the group. It is also difficult to quantify results.

You need to be cautious in planning group discussions. By and large they should not be used to identify only what is wrong with a product or service and it may cause problems to have several important customers in the same room. Groups composed entirely of customers with grievances will also have limited value.

To set up a group discussion:

- invite eight to ten customers—this number is controllable, but with fewer people it may be difficult to maintain discussion;
- thank customers for participating and put them at their ease;
- record the discussion if possible, using a tape recorder;
- advise people that their comments are being recorded and that all material will be treated in confidence;
- if conducting a group amongst consumers (not your customers) you might consider providing participants with a gift for taking part;
- consider using more than one group to gather a range of views.

You could also consider using an independent researcher to run the discussion.

Conduct Personal Interviews

In a personal interview, a customer and an interviewer work through a series of predetermined questions. The personal interview is ideal for key customers and for obtaining detailed information on attitudes to products and services, or initiating the process of getting feedback. The interview can take place in a customer's home or office, or in a public place. It can be prearranged by telephone, mail, or personal contact.

Personal interviews allow in-depth discussion of complex topics and give you more control over the response. They offer greater accuracy, and results are easy to analyze. Meeting people in a working environment can give an indication of their real purchasing intentions. The main disadvantages are the time and cost of recruiting interviewers and conducting interviews and the risk of interviewer bias.

Before you carry out personal interviews, you should identify the groups or individuals you wish to contact. You should advise the customer about the length of time the interview is likely to take and respect the confidence of the customer.

Use an Omnibus Survey

An omnibus survey is a cost-effective method of researching several topics at the same time. The same survey is used to carry out regular research on different products by telephone or personal interview. They are appropriate for measuring attitudes and behavior toward different types of products and services or monitoring changes in attitude among groups of consumers.

Before participating in the survey, you should check that the other topics in the survey are compatible with your own products and that the overall length of the survey is not excessive. It may reduce costs, but the audience may not give enough attention to all topics.

✘ WHAT TO AVOID
Asking Obvious Questions
Be aware that you may already know much about your customers and their attitudes and behavior. In a business-to-business market, you may know more than your customer. Before undertaking research, be sure it is necessary.

Assuming Formal Market Research Is Necessary
For many smaller companies, and some quite large ones, expensive research does not meet their needs. Companies with just a handful of very important customers would do better to concentrate on their relationship with these key accounts. For example, local retailers will often know their own area well and may simply need to engage their regular customers in conversation.

Not Planning Properly
Market research may generate considerable amounts of data and you will need to have the time and resources to analyze and turn it into useful information. Alternatively, if you set out without a thorough plan you may find that you have missed a crucial piece of information and face the embarrassment of having to revisit customers.

Choosing the Wrong Research Technique
Each research technique has different applications, benefits, and disadvantages. You have to decide whether you need depth of information, speedy results, or cost-effective research. A market research consultancy may be able to provide advice on an appropriate approach but you need to have a very clear picture of your needs, and how the information will be used.

Relying on Limited Results
For reasons of cost or time, some research programs may provide limited results. It is important to put the research findings in context and take account of the limited findings when you are making important decisions. Market research consultancies use proven techniques to evaluate results and should advise you to use their findings with caution.

Using Research to Sell
Too many companies contact customers and prospects claiming to be carrying out market research. During the course of the research, the company then attempts to sell a product or service on the basis that the respondent has expressed an interest. This is a betrayal of trust and can prove damaging to valid research.

SEE ALSO
Getting More Feedback from Customers (p. 196)

Getting More Feedback from Customers

GETTING STARTED

Customer feedback is essential for improving products and services and for identifying and correcting any problems at an early stage. Offer customers a choice of feedback methods to encourage them to respond, but make sure that all methods are as easy to use as possible. For high-value goods, a structured follow-up mechanism encourages customer comments on purchases.

FAQS

What is the best feedback mechanism?

For customers, the choice of feedback mechanism is probably a matter of personal preference. Some may prefer the anonymity of a postal questionnaire or response through a Web site. Others may wish to discuss their concerns and get an immediate response over the telephone. To insure that you get as much feedback as possible, give customers a choice.

Do we need to use incentives to encourage feedback?

Customers may provide feedback if they feel strongly enough about an issue. Someone who has a serious complaint is likely to let you know. However, customers who have less pressing comments may not bother, feeling that their feedback is unimportant. Incentives may encourage them, but only if the incentives are appropriate.

Should we use an independent research organization to obtain feedback?

Using an independent research organization demonstrates to customers that you take their feedback seriously and provides an objective, independent channel for comments. You may also find that customers are willing to talk to a research organization about issues that they might be reluctant to discuss with your company directly. You must, however, be sure that the costs of employing a market research company are justified in the light of what you may discover. You and your own staff (if you have any)—especially field staff and sales people—may already know a great deal about customer opinion.

MAKING IT HAPPEN
Find Out What Customers Think

It is essential to find out what your customers think about your products, your service, and your company. This information can be vital for identifying problems before they become serious. It can also provide valuable input into the product development process. You can use the feedback to:

- improve products
- tailor products and services to the needs of individual customers
- identify new product opportunities
- highlight potential problems
- develop focused marketing and customer service plans
- strengthen customer relationships
- reduce customer losses

You can also use the feedback as part of your promotional message.

Ask Customers before You Develop a New Product

By explaining your plans and involving customers in product development, you can strengthen relationships and provide a service that is mutually beneficial. Questions could include:

- How can we improve the current product?
- What problems need to be overcome?
- What new features would customers welcome?
- Do the plans represent an improvement?
- Would customers make more use of a product that included the features they have highlighted?

Ask about Purchasing Experience

When a customer buys a product, include a brief questionnaire with it, asking about the customer's buying experience. Questions could include:

- Where did you buy the product? How often do you buy it?
- Why did you choose the product?
- What other (competing or complementary) products do you buy, and how often?
- Why did you choose the retail outlet?
- Where did you hear about the product and retail outlet?
- How did you find the service offered by the retailer?
- Would you visit the retailer again?
- Do you have any specific comments about the product or retailer?

The questionnaire could take the form of a business reply card and should be brief.

Follow Up a Product Sale

If the product is a reasonably high-value one, you could set up a follow-up mechanism to find out about the customer's experience in using the product. Typical intervals would be a week after purchase, a month after purchase, and six months after purchase. The first follow-up would check that the customer had no initial problems, while the subsequent follow-ups would ask about the customer's experience in using the product. Having a scale such as 1–5 (where 1 is "very poor" and 5 is "very good") enables comparisons to show improvement over time.

Follow Up Servicing and Maintenance

The standard of after-sales service can be critical in determining overall customer satisfaction with your company. After every service or maintenance visit, contact customers to insure that they were satisfied with the standard of service they received. Questions could cover:

- convenience of scheduling a service
- punctuality and response time
- standard of service
- attitude of employees
- availability of spare parts

It is a good idea to use scales as described above to enable comparisons over time. This kind of follow-up can be handled by business reply questionnaire or telephone call.

Set Up a Customer Satisfaction Program

Customer satisfaction has become one of the most important issues facing businesses in every market. Customer satisfaction programs are known by many different names, such as customer service, customer satisfaction, and customer focus. Their common theme is meeting the customers' requirements and insuring that all aspects of the business contribute to customer satisfaction. The intention is to build repeat business. If customers are satisfied with the product and the standards of service they receive, they will return to the business or the retail outlet again and again for both major and minor purchases.

Measure Satisfaction Regularly

A customer satisfaction index takes the results from a number of satisfaction surveys and assigns a numerical value to key customer satisfaction indicators. A local outlet is then given an overall index of performance which can be compared with other outlets and measured on a year-on-year basis. The survey questionnaire asks customers to respond to questions with a scale of satisfaction: fully satisfied, very satisfied, satisfied, not satisfied, very dissatisfied. Alternatively, customers can be asked to respond on a numerical scale, where, for example, 1 is very dissatisfied, 10 is very satisfied. They can also provide written comments on aspects of the service and, in some cases, ask for specific actions, such as an explanation from a departmental manager.

Set Up a Customer Hotline

As well as formal mechanisms, you should also set up facilities to encourage customers to provide feedback at any time. A telephone hotline allows customers to call with queries or complaints about any aspect of your products or service. Calls to the hotline should be free, and the telephone number should be included in all your customer communications. The hotline should be staffed by people trained in customer handling techniques, and it should be continuously monitored to insure that customers receive a suitable response. All calls should be recorded so that the call patterns can be analyzed to identify any recurring problems.

Include a Feedback Mechanism on Your Web Site

You should include a simple feedback mechanism on your Web site. This provides a similar function to the telephone hotline and provides customers with an alternative, easy-to-use channel for complaints, queries, and other issues. Users should have to complete only minimal personal details, such as name and e-mail address, before submitting their comments. Alternatively, you can allow users to submit their comments anonymously.

Use Incentives to Encourage Feedback

You will increase response if you offer an incentive such as a free gift. You could also set up a regular prize draw for visitors who submit comments.

Establish a User Group

You can encourage feedback and build a sense of community by setting up a user group. The user group would operate as a forum for discussing all issues of concern to customers, such as quality, performance, standards, and future developments. The group would include representatives from your own company and from a cross-section of your customers. The comments from the user group provide valuable feedback on current performance, and help to identify needs that can be met through new product development.

Respond to Feedback

Let visitors know that you have received their comments, and thank them for their feedback. When you have taken corrective action, tell them what you have done so they see that their effort is not wasted. This can encourage further feedback. If a visitor highlights a serious problem, keep them informed on progress.

WHAT TO AVOID

Failing to Act on Feedback

The most important way to encourage feedback is to demonstrate that you can respond. The point of gathering feedback is to identify concerns and problems before they become serious; however, unless you act on that feedback, the exercise will be wasted. Industry experience indicates that customers who have a problem resolved are far more likely to remain customers than those who receive no response. If you act on customer input during the product development process, it indicates a high level of partnership and helps to strengthen customer relationships.

Making It Difficult to Provide Feedback

If you want to encourage feedback, make it easy for your visitors. Calls to telephone hotlines should be free. Mail surveys and questionnaires should also have the return postage paid. Any questionnaires should be brief and should not ask for much personal information. You should also provide facilities on your Web site for customers to provide feedback or submit a response to a survey using an electronic form.

Poor Complaints Management

If you do not record and analyze complaints and other feedback, you may not spot emerging trends. A series of complaints on the same issue indicates a recurring problem that could be dangerous to your company if it is not resolved quickly. Establish a formal mechanism for recording all feedback.

SEE ALSO

Conducting Market Research (p. 192)
**Involving Customers in Product or
    Service Development (p. 199)**

Involving Customers in Product or Service Development

GETTING STARTED

For some people "new product development" means inventing something wonderfully new. In reality, though, the vast majority of new products are modifications of existing ideas. In some cases, "new product development" can also mean adding an element of service onto a (physical) product.

The power of new product development is that your business may be able meet a customer's need more closely than the competition. Involving customers creates the possibility of your product or service being tailor-made for them, thereby encouraging loyalty.

FAQS

Is there a risk in letting customers evaluate new products before launch?

There are two risks. First, the customer may be extremely disappointed with the product if quality is poor. Second, there is a risk that competitors could find out about your plans indirectly. The quality issue is one that you should deal with: if a product is not right, it should not be given to customers in any form—it is not enough simply to promise future improvements. The security risk of a leak to competitors can be minimized through disclosure and confidentiality agreements, although these provide no real guarantee. However, the advantages of involving customers outweigh the risks, so evaluation is worthwhile.

How practical is it for customers and suppliers to collaborate on product development?

There are different levels of collaboration. Some may involve regular meetings to provide input and review progress. These meetings can be held on site or remotely, using videoconference links. In some cases, customer staff may work alongside the supplier team for all or part of the project. Secondment like this can provide other benefits for the customer by improving the technical knowledge of their staff.

Does preannouncement put new product launches at risk?

Some companies, particularly in the IT sector, have put themselves under unnecessary pressure by trying to meet a series of preannounced release dates. The schedule may not allow proper time for development, resulting in failure to meet the date, or the release of a product that is not ready. Both are potentially damaging.

MAKING IT HAPPEN

Ask Customers before You Launch Your Product

If you are planning a new product or re-developing an existing one, ask your customers for their views on the existing product and what they would like to see in a new one. By explaining your plans and involving customers in product development, you can strengthen relationships and provide a service that is mutually beneficial. Questions could include:

- How is the product used?
- How can we improve the current product?
- What problems have been encountered?
- What new features would customers welcome?
- Do the plans represent an improvement?
- Would customers make greater use of a product that included the features they have highlighted?

Set Up a User Group

You can encourage feedback and build a sense of community by setting up a user group, which can be online and may allow customers to share experiences or solve one another's problems. The user group can operate as a forum for discussing issues of mutual concern to customers, such as quality, performance, standards, future developments, and customer concerns. The group would include representatives from your own company and from a cross-section of your customers. Comments from the user group provide valuable feedback on current performance and help to identify needs that can be met through new product development.

Ask Customers to Evaluate New Products

Customer evaluation, or beta testing, is well established in the software industry. Customers test new products or upgraded versions before they are released to the market. They identify any problems in using the software, thus providing valuable feedback on product performance.

Issue New Product Announcements

Another valuable practice from the IT industry is to preannounce new products. For example, a company will set a number of release dates during the coming year when it will release new versions of products. The company outlines the new products and gives customers the opportunity to provide input to the development process. The major benefit for customers is that they can align their own business development plans to the release dates.

Work in Partnership with Customers

Product development can be a joint initiative where you work closely with specific customers to develop products that meet their specific needs. This approach is a valuable one where:

- your customers have developed partnership sourcing to take advantage of your technology;
- your customers have technology and technical skills that complement your own, and a joint project can produce more effective results;
- you want to strengthen relationships with key customers by working in partnership on joint development projects.

Understand Your Customers' Markets

The new products you develop could enable your customers to improve their competitive performance, so it is important to understand their markets. Tell customers about your product plans and ask them for input to your development process. By building a detailed picture of their markets, you can align your own plans with them, and develop products that are tailored to their needs.

- What are their main markets?
- What is their position in the marketplace?
- Who are their main competitors?
- How are their products regarded in the marketplace?
- What are the key success factors in the market?
- What are the long-term product trends?
- What new technical developments will be needed to succeed?
- Could innovation by you help your customers to succeed?
- Are your customers considering entry into new markets?
- Do you have product development plans that are relevant to the new market?

Understand Customer Strategies

It is equally important to understand your customers' business strategies: their corporate direction and key objectives, and how they aim to succeed. By aligning your product development objectives with theirs, and showing how your products or services can help them to achieve their strategic business objectives, you can improve the chances of your new products being successful.

There are two possible approaches to customer-focused product development. Where your customers want to become market leaders through innovation, your new product programs can help them develop the right level of innovation without investment in their own skills. Where they want to succeed through competitive pricing, you can help them reduce overall costs by developing cost-effective products.

Assess the Value of Your Products and Services

Products that help your customers to meet their strategic business objectives can increase the chances of new product success. The more your customers depend on your new product, the more demanding they will be. If you can keep up with their demands, try to anticipate and meet them and you'll not only help yourself but also create barriers for your competitors.

For example, if your customer must develop new products quickly in order to retain and protect market share, your own new products can be critical to their product development program.

Analyze Your Customers' Technical Requirements

In assessing new product development opportunities, you should analyze how your products can help your customers. They can use your skills in a number of ways:

- improving the performance of their own products and services by using your design and development skills. They may gain privileged access to your technical skills to improve their own competitive performance;
- using your technical expertise to enhance the skills of their own technical staff, enabling them to make a more effective contribution to their own product development process;
- using your technical resources to handle product development on a subcontract basis. This provides your partners with access to specialist resources or to additional research and development capacity to improve the performance of their product development programs;
- using your technical expertise to develop new products that they could not achieve themselves. This provides your customers with new technology, and allows them to diversify in line with your specialist skills;
- using your design skills to improve through life costs (the total cost of owning and using a product, including purchase price, maintenance, and any other related costs). By carrying out value engineering studies on your customers' products, you may be able to reduce overall costs and improve reliability by designing components that are easier to assemble and maintain.

WHAT TO AVOID
Not Involving Your Customers Sufficiently

Product development should be focused on customer needs. Although most companies carry out research before development, the research may not provide the detailed input that is essential. Product development may also be driven by technology, with no clear market focus. The more your customer depends on your product, the more likely it is to succeed, so involving customers can pay real dividends.

Ignoring User Groups

There are many examples of companies who have set up user groups in response to a crisis and then failed to use them. This can be frustrating for customers and wasteful for the companies. User groups provide a valuable perspective on products and services, and their feedback can provide real benefits for the product development process.

Failing to Understand Customer Strategies

Where the supplier/customer relationship is that of a partnership, products are developed and customized to help customers meet their business objectives. It is essential, therefore, to understand customers' markets and business strategies so that your product plans can be integrated with theirs.

SEE ALSO
Getting More Feedback from Customers (p. 196)
Retaining Existing Customers (p. 205)

Converting Leads into Sales

GETTING STARTED

If you are trying to grow your business, finding leads (that is, potential new customers), is just the beginning. Before they can benefit you in any way, you need to turn the leads into sales. This actionlist offers a systematic approach to doing this and to making sure that the leads are of the right kind in the first place, which will cut down on wasted time and resources.

FAQS

How far can services such as telemarketing take over from the sales force?

These services can be used to handle many of the sales teams' routine functions: carrying out initial research, qualifying prospective customers, making appointments, and maintaining regular contact. They should not be used as a substitute for face-to-face selling if that is important to your customer relationships. In addition, remember that some people may have placed their names on "do not call" lists and that contacting them by making unsolicited phone calls may lead to significant fines. Make sure you are contacting the right people from the outset.

What is the best way to measure lead conversion?

Measuring sales as a percentage of initial leads is too simplistic an approach; it is more effective to measure at each stage of the process. For example, only 50% of initial leads may turn out to be suitable prospective customers. If the leads have been well qualified, the sales team may be able to convert 20% of the final prospect list. Measuring results at each stage helps you focus the right level of resources and plan future lead generation programs.

Should we try to get as many leads as possible?

The quality of the leads is as important as the number. Following up a large number of unsuitable leads is a waste of resources, but getting as many good leads as possible is important to any company that wants to expand its business.

MAKING IT HAPPEN

Qualify Your Leads

Your lead generation program may have given you large numbers of leads, but not all of them will convert to sales. Some may be poor prospects, while others may simply be gathering information rather than planning a purchase. Good prospects have the following characteristics:

- the financial resources to purchase your product;
- the authority to make a purchase decision;
- a genuine need for your product or service;
- the desire to learn more about your product;
- plans to make a purchase in the near future.

Telemarketing can be used to qualify the leads. Call the contact and ask for more details of their inquiry so that you can send information tailored to their needs. Just sending a brochure, with no accompanying letter and no understanding of the prospective customer's needs, is a waste of money.

Qualifying questions can include:

- Are you the person who makes the purchasing decision? If not, who does?
- Is your company currently buying this product?
- What quantities do you buy, or how much do you spend on the service?
- When are you likely to make your next purchase?
- What information do you need on our product and company?

Choose a One-step or Two-step Process

In the case of some products and services, the lead generation and sales conversion processes can be combined. These are known as one-step programs, and are equivalent to direct selling operations. They are suitable for:

- inexpensive products
- information services such as newsletter or magazine subscriptions
- office supplies
- software
- low-value financial offers

In a two-step program, the prospective customer (prospect) requests initial information. You send the information and then continue following up until the prospect is ready to buy. Two-step programs are suitable for:

- expensive offers
- complex technical products
- professional services
- high-value financial services

Plan the Conversion Process

Lead conversion can be a long-term continuous process, the duration of which depends on the complexity of the product and of the decision making process. For example, how many people are involved or how important is the product to the customer (or the customer's business)?

For a complex product, the process could be:

- identifying key decision makers;
- sending information to key decision makers;
- arranging meetings with decision makers;
- providing sample products for evaluation by the customer;
- bidding for a contract against competition;
- final negotiations;
- purchase;
- after-sales service and support.

You must decide how you will handle each stage of the process, who will be involved in the sales team, and how you will manage communications with the prospect.

Another example could be where the product and the purchasing process are simpler, but the prospect is reluctant to change suppliers. The conversion process could take a long time, so you must plan a program to maintain contact and move the prospect away from the existing supplier. Actions could include:

- personalized direct mail with product information;
- regular updates on new developments in the company;
- targeted special offers to encourage the customer to try the product.

Allocate Responsibility

Normally, the marketing department generates leads and the sales department follows up. It is important for the two departments to work together to integrate their activities and make sure that the company focuses on the kind of high-quality prospects it really needs. Sales departments frequently complain about the quantity and quality of leads. They want as many leads as possible so that the final number of new sales is high; however, they may also complain if too many of the leads are of poor quality and do not meet the right criteria. Collecting a large number of high-quality leads can be a difficult balancing act. Some sales teams prefer to do their own qualifying, while others prefer to leave that to others so that they can concentrate on face-to-face meetings with prospects.

Back the Sales Team with Telemarketing

Telemarketing can be used to enhance the performance and productivity of the sales force. The telemarketing team can be responsible for following up sales leads, qualifying prospects, setting up appointments, and maintaining contact with longer-term prospects. This frees the sales force for increasing the number of face-to-face meetings and for concentrating on the most likely prospects. The integration of telemarketing with the sales force can play an important part in reducing overall sales costs. The cost of keeping a sales team on the road continues to soar, and it may not always represent the most cost-effective way of reaching the right people.

Maintain a Contact Diary

A contact diary can help you plan the conversion process and make sure that the sales team does not miss any important contact opportunities. It also makes sure that the sales backup team integrates its follow-up activities with the field sales force. Computer software is available which allows sales teams to operate a sales diary and record details of meetings and other follow-up activities. The same software can be used by the management team to monitor progress and make sure that no important contacts are overlooked. Contact diaries can include details on the customer, the customer's likes and dislikes, availability for meetings or telephone calls, their buying limits/authorization, and even personal information that helps maintain a relationship with them.

Track Progress

It is essential to track progress at each stage of the conversion process. If the prospect is important, you may wish to allocate additional resources to win the business. If a prospect is of only minor importance but is taking time and resources, you may want to refocus the efforts of the sales force. The progress from initial lead to customer goes through a number of stages:

- raw lead: an initial inquiry from any source;
- suspect: an inquiry that has been qualified and has the potential to become a paying customer;
- prospect: a lead that has been qualified in more detail;
- inactive lead: a prospect who will not buy now but has future potential;
- dead lead: a prospect who has little potential to become a customer;
- customer.

You might also include lapsed customers in this process as a source of qualified leads.

Choose the Right Contact Frequency

A single mailing, telephone call, or direct response advertisement may produce results, but a series of quality contacts will have greater impact and make sure you meet your response targets. Multiple direct marketing activities raise levels of awareness with each contact, follow up contacts who have not responded, and move individual respondents further along the decision making process.

Use Personalized Contact

Personalized one-to-one mailings are an ideal form of communication for companies with detailed information on their prospects. The letter reflects the individual prospect's main interests and concerns, and the offer can be tailored to the prospect's needs. Subsequent mailings can build an individual relationship with the prospect.

WHAT TO AVOID
Focusing on the Wrong Prospects

Sales teams have a natural tendency to deal with friendly prospects and avoid the difficult ones. From a business perspective, however, they may be dealing with the wrong people. The qualifying process should be used to identify the most important prospects in order to improve the targeting of the sales force.

Poor Management

Lead conversion can be a long, complicated process, so it is essential to monitor progress and manage the program carefully. Lead conversion can use a lot of sales force and telemarketing resources, and careful planning can make sure that it is carried out effectively.

Putting All the Burden on the Sales Force

In some organizations, the sales force is given total responsibility for generating leads, qualifying them, and converting them into sales. This may not represent the best use of sales force resources. Telemarketing or other tools can be used to supplement the sales force and take over routine tasks.

SEE ALSO
Handling Customer Inquiries (p. 213)

Retaining Existing Customers

GETTING STARTED

Just about every business will depend to a certain extent on repeat sales from customers that have already bought from them. In fact in some cases, repeat sales from existing customers will be the biggest revenue-generating source. However, many business owners do not realize or understand that establishing a long-term relationship with a loyal customer base is as important, if not more important, than getting sales from new customers in the first place.

If your business is one of those where customers are likely to come back and buy the same product or more products from you over again, then it will be vital that you do everything you can to keep them satisfied and loyal to your business for as long as possible. This actionlist contains some ideas on how to ensure that this is the case. One book on the subject you may also find useful is *The Loyalty Effect: The Hidden Force Behind Growth, Profits and Lasting Value* by Fredrick Reichheld, published by Harvard Business School Press in 1996.

FAQS

Why do I need to bother with customers when they've already bought from me?

Having profiled and targeted your ideal market audience and made those all important first sales, your business will only really outstrip those of your competitors in the long term when you truly understand why those customers have bought from you. Only by recognizing this will you have a unique opportunity to persuade them to buy from you again and again.

How can I gain the edge over my competitors?

Even if you are lucky enough to be the first into a new market it won't be long before someone else follows suit. What can you do to ensure customers stay loyal to you as long as they are in the market for your service? Can you create a unique selling proposition (USP) that will lock them into your business and not that of your competition? The vast majority of businesses concentrate on achieving a profit from first time or single sales and fail to appreciate that meeting the needs of their customers over the longer term will reap far greater benefits.

MAKING IT HAPPEN

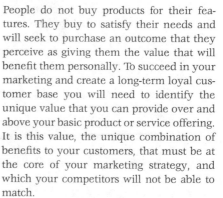

Identify What Unique Benefits You Can Offer

People do not buy products for their features. They buy to satisfy their needs and will seek to purchase an outcome that they perceive as giving them the value that will benefit them personally. To succeed in your marketing and create a long-term loyal customer base you will need to identify the unique value that you can provide over and above your basic product or service offering. It is this value, the unique combination of benefits to your customers, that must be at the core of your marketing strategy, and which your competitors will not be able to match.

Offer Value that Will Make Customers Loyal to You

The key to this is not to think about individual features of your service, but to concentrate on how the benefit within that product or service impacts on your customers' long-term personal needs. These needs often fall into the following categories.

- **A feeling of belonging.** People like people, and they like to do what other people like themselves are doing—for example, being in associations, or in membership schemes. They like being part of a cause and surrounding themselves with people they consider to be their peers. Can you offer something to your customers to satisfy their sense of belonging? Is there something that they can join as part of their purchase of your service? Could you set up a user group? Can you publish a top sellers' list for your products?

- **Self improvement and self esteem.** Just as with belonging, people will often choose to purchase something that makes them feel better, fitter, healthier, or just more important. Do you recognize something in your customer's requirements where your product or service can help them satisfy this need? Can you include this in your USP and marketing message?

- **Being reminded that they have made a good choice.** For customers in many situations the purchase decision is fraught with fear of making the wrong choice. Look for ways you can remind or reward your customers for making the right purchase by buying from you. Can you think of ways to make it a risk free, 100% secure experience for the buyer, for example through extended warranties, money back guarantees, or free after-sales support for long periods? Can you make this better than what your competitors are offering?

- **A sense of achievement.** Is there a way that you can make your customers feel that, by buying from you now and in the future, they are going to put themselves in a much better situation or position than they were in before? Can you create something unique in your after sales service? Is it possible to offer some form of loyalty points scheme, future discounts, or reward scheme that delivers more benefits the longer they remain as your customer?

- **Being educated about your service.** Do you go out of your way to tell customers regularly and in detail about the wise decision they have made in buying from you? Do you let them know how they can get even more benefits by buying again, or can access special offers in the future only available to loyal customers of your business? Publishing a customer newsletter with informative, interesting, and relevant information about how they can make best use of and get more value from your service, is a very popular method of achieving this.

- **Getting a personal and relevant service, exactly when they need it.** More than anything else your purchasers will place the greatest long-term value on your business and your product if they feel they will continue to receive personal attention and care from you whenever they need it. They must be made to feel that they are your most important customer every time they deal with you. Are there ways you can make the sales experience with your firm more fun, more exciting, more rewarding, more personal, and more relevant than it is at the moment? More importantly, can you make this a better experience than is being offered by your competition?

Insure that Your USP Aims to Keep Them Loyal

Gaining loyalty and the trust of your customers can only be achieved if they feel you are fulfilling their exact needs, and that they will continue to receive value from you that meets their needs in the future. Your USP needs to communicate the loyalty building value that your service will provide and that your competitors cannot match. Every time your customer wants to re-purchase your type of product or service, your marketing proposition must make it as difficult as possible for them to say no to you. Does your USP express this value strongly enough? Think of the services that you repeatedly buy from other suppliers yourself. Why do you remain loyal to them? What is it that makes you want to keep on purchasing from them? If you can recognize what this is, you should aim to replicate the same value in the service you provide to your own customers.

WHAT TO AVOID
Letting Customers Forget
You have done all the hard work and built up a solid customer base, but a fatal error will

be to let them forget why they bought from you or the extra value they can receive by continuing to buy from you in the future. Your loyalty building strategy should look for continual ways to communicate with and educate your customers about the benefits of your service, competitions, special offers, new product lines, open days, and so on. A newsletter, especially by e-mail, is a very popular and cost-effective way of doing this. If you let them forget you are there, or what you can offer them, they will eventually buy from someone else instead.

Failing to Make Them Feel Appreciated

Each customer must feel as if he or she is the most important one you have. Failing to recognize this is an opportunity for them to try a different service, and you may lose their loyalty in favor of your competitors. If you have the names and addresses of your customers, aim to write to them and thank them for their patronage on a regular basis. When they first buy from you, ask them if they would like to receive advance details of special offers or new products in the future. If they agree, ask for their telephone number, e-mail, or other contact details and ensure you communicate with them regularly.

Whenever possible, reward them with loyalty building discounts and offers for repeat purchases, or ask them individually—as one of your most valued customers—for their views and opinions about how they use your service and how you can improve it for them. If they feel appreciated, their loyalty and their trust in you and your service will almost certainly follow.

SEE ALSO

Communicating Customer Service (p. 211)
Corporate Hospitality (p. 222)
Involving Customers in Product or Service Development (p. 199)
Public Relations (p. 485)
Selling and Salesmanship (p. 490)

Extending a Product with Service

GETTING STARTED

Service is frequently relegated to maintenance and problem solving. However, done properly, service can be a key differentiator between you and the competition. Meeting customer requirements in the most appropriate and efficient way adds enormously to the perceived value of your product and can sometimes increase the profitability of your relationship.

FAQS

My product is a market leader. Why would services be important?

Services can add further value to a product, providing incremental income and increasing customer loyalty. Services provide you with an opportunity to continue dealing with a customer long after the initial sale and raise barriers around your customers.

I already offer free installation and maintenance with my products. Does that add value?

Yes. But whilst some customers may expect this, others may not or may not value this service. Many companies have recognized the importance of service to certain customers, and have changed their service strategy accordingly. Instead of offering free service to everyone, they have upgraded the services, increased the range of services offered, and therefore, in some cases, started charging customers. Although customers may initially object to being charged for something that seemed to be free, they may see the value of a service that now more closely meets their needs.

I don't have the skills or resources to deliver services. How can I offer my customers a service?

You can either build your own service team through recruitment and training or work in partnership with a specialist organization which will deliver service on your behalf.

My customers have their own internal service people. Why should they want to use my services?

Many companies have internal service departments. They can be expensive to maintain, however, and are sometimes lacking in essential skills, for example, they may not be trained in the latest software. By demonstrating the potential savings and benefits of outsourcing a service, you can persuade them to switch to you.

MAKING IT HAPPEN
Differentiate Your Product with Service

Service is proving to be a key differentiator in many market sectors. In many companies, however, the role of the service department should be more than simply maintenance and problem solving. For example, a company supplying industrial dishwashers to the restaurant trade must ensure that they can respond quickly to breakdowns—replacing the machine if necessary rather than simply scheduling a repair visit. So, to take full advantage of the service opportunity, it is important to explain the benefits of effective service to customers, and present your service operations as convenient, cost-effective, and strategically important.

Meet Key Service Attributes

These are some of the key features that customers may be looking for in a service offer:

- one contact point, simplifying contact and service administration;
- direct contact with a technical specialist, providing an immediate response to problems or queries wherever the customer is located;
- quality support to a standard such as ISO 9000, giving independent reassurance that service standards are high;

- support round the clock means that it is available when the customer needs it, and minimizes interruption of their business;
- service options give a choice of service levels, which can be aligned to customers' needs;
- investment in support means long-term commitment to the customer.

Provide One Contact Point for Service Resources

Whether your customers have a technical query, a service request, or a product inquiry, or need advice, guidance, or information, they should be able to call one number for direct access to all your support resources. Ideally, you'll have specialists on the spot to deal with their requests. If they can't answer the query straightaway, make sure that the right person calls the customer back.

Offer Direct Contact with Technical Specialists

Your customers may have a technical query, and want to talk to an experienced specialist straight away. When they call the technical help desk, they should be talking to a highly skilled person with extensive technical support and field experience. It may mean locating support staff in accessible locations to be able to make visits quickly and efficiently.

Provide Good Quality Support

When your customers have a service request, they should be able to contact a central service point where a service coordinator ensures that the right specialist help is available. Service coordinators should make sure that customers get the fastest and most effective response to their requests. In some cases, service points can deal with requests directly but, if not, they can assign an engineer to visit the customer site within agreed times. All service processes should be assessed to ISO 9000. If customers have any queries, there should be an "escalation procedure" to move a customer complaint up to a more senior

team member if the person dealing with the complaint initially cannot resolve it. This should ensure a prompt resolution of any problems.

Offer Flexible Service Options

You can provide your customers with a choice of flexible service options to suit their operational needs and to increase their loyalty. If your customers have inhouse support, you can support their team with an efficient spares delivery service, or manage their spares for them. You can also offer to enhance the skills of your customer's in-house team with training, advice and guidance, technical support, and access to specialists. You may go as far as offering consultancy on a fee basis, utilizing your specialist knowledge to help your customer.

Invest in Support

High quality service for your market may require a significant investment in the service infrastructure; the right premises, efficient service communications, and a sophisticated service management system to enable you to enhance your response and performance even further. It may require you to appoint one person with specific responsibility for customer service or, perhaps, develop a dedicated support Web site.

Add Value to a Product

Improving your customer service may add value and help to differentiate your products and services from the competition. By analyzing the products and services in your range (and those of your competitors), you can add relevant value and improve a customer's perception of your business. Some examples are

- business services that free up customer staff to do more important tasks, or help managers perform their jobs better. Training, for example, can insure that staff make more effective use of the products the company buys;
- complementary services to make a consumer product more attractive, such as film processing offered with a camera;

■ convenience services added to a basic service to enhance it. Insurance companies, for example, might add a helpline or list of approved repairers to help their customers recover more quickly from an accident.

Develop Product/Service Packages

To add value to products and to increase customer loyalty, put together "bundles" of products and services that reflect customer needs. The list below shows examples of this.

"Adding-in" Services

■ Specialist package tours, including flights, hotel, and guides.
■ A building company includes plans and planning application services.

"Leaving-out" Services

■ "Fastfit" car repair centers, without non-essential services.
■ Specialized conveyancing services without using solicitors.

Added Value Services

■ Home delivery of fast food or videos.
■ Support and advice through helplines.

Changing Distribution Channels

■ Direct sales, bypassing retailers, such as organic vegetable "box schemes."

■ Electronic delivery, such as delivery of technical drawings and specifications.

WHAT TO AVOID
Offering Only Basic Services

Basic services such as installation, maintenance, and upgrades are available from many different service organizations. They do not differentiate you and they do not add value. Higher-value services, requiring skill, knowledge, or experience, are the keys to success.

Failing to Invest in a Service Infrastructure

Customers expect a quality service. That means you have to invest in people and infrastructure. Ideally, your services should conform to recognized industry standards. If you fail to deliver the right standard of service, you could damage customer relationships.

Missing Service Opportunities

Customers require many different services during the time they own a product. Their requirements could include advice, consultancy, and design before the sale; installation, and training; followed by maintenance, upgrading, and other after sales services. Each of these represents an opportunity to earn incremental income and maintain contact with the customer.

Communicating Customer Service

GETTING STARTED

Your business won't survive without customers, and you need to get across how much you value them. To communicate well externally, you need to have in place a clear, consistent, internal communications strategy too. If you have a team of people working with you, let them know how they each contribute to your business's success, and the way they interact with your customers is a key part of this.

FAQS

Who is responsible for customer service?

Everyone in a business, contributes to overall customer satisfaction, even if their jobs do not involve direct customer contact. Broken delivery promises, inaccurate invoices, or poor telephone handling can cancel out the benefits of a good product or service.

Why are award programs important to the success of customer service?

Customer service staff are in the front line, facing difficult customers and frequent problems. Award programs can help to maintain motivation and demonstrate that their contribution is important.

Isn't customer service the same as marketing?

Certain aspects of customer service—understanding customer needs, delivering a service, tailoring the offer to meet customer requirements—are the same, but the scope of marketing is much broader.

Is customer service just a set of personal skills?

Personal skills are important, but a company can put in place processes and programs that improve the customer's experience and make it easier and more convenient for the customer to do business.

MAKING IT HAPPEN

Communicate Clearly

When a company changes its focus towards customer service, it is essential that everyone is involved. Change creates an atmosphere of uncertainty, so it is vital that everyone understands the important issues and feels that they can contribute to the success of the change. In an atmosphere of uncertainty, customer service levels can be adversely affected.

Build Understanding

Organizational changes can have a significant impact on employees, suppliers, and distributors—so it is vital that they are thoroughly briefed. Change can be a powerful positive factor rather than a cause for concern, and change can demonstrate that a business is committed to improvement and progress.

Encourage Commitment

Implementing a customer service policy requires commitment and involvement from all employees. Before implementing a program, it is sensible to find what the level of commitment is and to include staff in discussion. The most important part of the process is the follow-up. Too many employees believe views will be ignored.

Encourage Improvement

As far as possible, training should be offered to all staff to help them understand the importance of customer care. A customer satisfaction guide could be issued, describing the most important elements of customer service and the standards which apply.

Maintain Motivation

Motivation and award programs can help to maintain high levels of interest in the customer service program and build a high level of commitment to the program's success. Award programs that reward continued improvement in levels of customer satisfaction maintain momentum and give customer service programs a high profile. They are therefore valuable in building team spirit and a commitment to excellence.

Provide a Vision

Clear visions and strong, motivating language focus attention on the importance of customer service programs. It is also essential that the program is led from the top. A key figure should be involved personally in every aspect of the program—talking to groups of employees and using every public relations opportunity to raise the profile of the program.

Develop Champions

The leader cannot achieve all the objectives alone, so it is essential that other people with influence can take on the role of supporting the message throughout the business. Management commentators often call these people "champions." Their task is to build commitment and enthusiasm for change. They may be the very people who could undermine change if left out of the process, though.

✘ WHAT TO AVOID
Treating Customer Service As a Departmental Function

Customer service is often thought of as something relevant only to those staff who are directly involved with customers. This is too limited a view, because customer service is relegated to a sales or complaints handling process.

Managing Customer Service at Departmental Level

If customer service is treated as a line management function, staff will not appreciate its critical importance to the success of the business. Customer service must be led from the top, with the direct involvement of a senior manager.

Failure to Develop Customer Service Skills

It's a common misconception that customer service quality depends solely on personal skills. Customer service standards can be improved through training and through the introduction of customer service programs.

Low Recognition

Customer service has long suffered from low recognition. Motivation and reward programs, together with leadership from the top, can help to redress the balance.

SEE ALSO
Corporate Hospitality (p. 222)
Handling Customer Inquiries (p. 213)
Handling Customer Problems (p. 216)
Retaining Existing Customers (p. 205)

Handling Customer Inquiries

GETTING STARTED

Businesses need mechanisms to cope with inquiries or requests for help from both existing and potential customers. This actionlist offers some information on the different options open to you.

Helplines are essential for delivering support, service, advice, and information to customers and add value to a business. To provide the best service, use staff with extensive, up-to-date product knowledge and train them in customer service techniques to ensure they can deal effectively with different types of query or problem. To maximize the benefit to users of the service, deal with queries immediately where possible, or arrange to call the customer back on more complex queries, and ensure that the customer is satisfied with the response at the end of the conversation.

FAQS

Should helpline services be offered free to customers?

Helpline services fall into a number of categories: support, help with problems, advice, and useful information. The support categories should be free because they are essential for customer satisfaction. The information services also can be seen as a customer service, something that adds value to the original purchase. You may feel it strengthens customer relationships to continue offering them free. Information services offered to the general public are valuable services that can be charged, usually through a premium rate number.

Which staff should work on the helplines?

Trained customer service staff can help customers report a problem effectively and may be able to offer advice or help up to a certain level. When the query goes beyond their level of knowledge, you should have a two-stage process in which the customer service representative takes the initial call and arranges for a specialist to call the customer back within an agreed time.

Can a helpline service be handled by an external organization?

Provided the external organization's team undergoes thorough training, there is no reason why the helpline cannot be out-sourced. The practice is common in the computer industry.

MAKING IT HAPPEN
Establish a Helpline

The most important thing about a helpline is that it really needs to *help*, so there are a number of rules to remember when creating one.

- Make it convenient: offer customers an 800 number facility to encourage contact, and set opening times to suit customer calling patterns.
- Get the right staff: use staff with extensive, up-to-date product knowledge, and make sure that they are trained in customer service techniques so that they can deal effectively with different types of query or problem.
- Provide the right backup: helpline staff need to have access to any existing product, technical, or service databases, as well as guidelines on the actions they can take to deal with different types of complaint. Make sure they also have lists of contacts for authorization of different types of action and information.
- Make the service fast and reliable: deal with queries immediately or arrange to call the customer back on more complex queries, and operate an "escalation procedure" (see below for more information) to deal with complaints that cannot be resolved within agreed time scales.
- Check and double check: follow up to make

sure that, if a customer was promised a return call within an agreed time scale, it did happen and that he or she is satisfied with the response.

Plan Helpline Staffing Levels

There's nothing worse that getting to a helpline but then being kept on hold for a long time. It really is crucial to get your staffing levels right, so ask your telephone supplier to provide a report on the number of calls to the helpline number, as well as the average waiting time, and then analyze the pattern of calls during the day/week/month/year, identifying the peaks and troughs. This will help you to determine the current and planned level of calls per day; the ratio of staff to calls, and therefore how many helpline staff you need.

If you have very marked peak and off-peak periods, decide whether you can meet demand using current staff resources, or whether it might be beneficial to use technologies such as voicemail to handle some of the incoming calls. If you can afford it, you could also consider using an external call handling service to manage overload or peak traffic.

Identify Helpline Skills

Make sure that your staff meet a checklist of appropriate helpline skills. These might include product knowledge, telephone technique, and technical, product service, administrative, and customer service skills.

Develop Helpline Skills

Regardless of how good your staff are, there are always ways in which you can help them improve and develop their skills. Assess the skills required for different types of helpline service, compare these with the current skills of your helpline staff, and identify the areas that need to be improved. Implement training and monitor performance improvements, ensure that staff know how to use any new technology, and obtain customer feedback to evaluate performance.

Provide Customer Information for Helpline Staff

Your staff will be able to provide a prompt response and personal service if they've been given enough customer information. Make available the information you already have, such as existing customer records, data generated by responses to advertisements or promotional activities, and so on, and make sure it is checked and updated. Take the opportunity to capture customer information each time a customer calls, and add further information that is appropriate to the helpline service, such as service records. Use a simple code to access information quickly, for example, name, account number, and Zip code, and include prompts to contact customers with details of new products and services.

Establish Helpline Escalation Procedures

There are always some calls that cannot be dealt with immediately, so you need to have an escalation procedure in place to make sure they don't slip through the net. Identify critical types of helpline requests, including technical support, complaints, and breakdowns, and set target response times for such queries. Appoint a supervisor to monitor conformance to target response times; escalate any queries that exceed target times to a designated manager, and monitor the responses to escalated queries.

Record Helpline Usage

In order to make sure you are meeting demand properly, you need to record helpline usage. How many calls does your helpline receive: per day; per week; per month; per year? What types of call does it receive and what is the volume of each type of call? Which customers are the most regular helpline users? Which media generate most inquiries to the helpline? What is the impact of promotional campaigns on helpline activity? Which products receive most/least: complaints, queries, or requests for support? What are the most frequent complaints, queries, and requests for support? Which type of request uses most resources? What is the average call time for different types of request?

Promote the Helpline Service

Above all, make sure customers know what help is available to them. Include the helpline number in advertisements, publications, Web site pages, and other promotional material, as well as on invoices, delivery notes, instructions, user guides, and other product documentation.

✗ WHAT TO AVOID
Putting the Wrong People on the Helpline

The people who run the helpline should have good customer handling skills and a level of product and technical knowledge that enables them to provide the right answer or put the customer in contact with the right specialist.

Inadequate Resources on the Helpline

When customers call a helpline, they are looking for a quick response. Phones that go unanswered for long periods of time show poor customer service. Putting a customer in a queue of other callers is satisfactory only for a short period of time.

Failing to Call the Customer Back

If you cannot deal with queries immediately, let the customer know when someone will get back to him or her, and then check that the return call has been made.

SEE ALSO
Communicating Customer Service (p. 211)
Converting Leads into Sales (p. 202)
Handling Customer Problems (p. 216)

Handling Customer Problems

GETTING STARTED

Even the most professional service companies will inevitably face a problem with a customer that, if left unresolved, may lead to a loss of business. Customers who know that their problems are taken care of are more likely to be fully satisfied with the services that are available. A key factor in resolving customers' problems is the ability to reassure them that help is on the way. Having in place a process to respond quickly and effectively to a problem enables a company to deliver the highest standards of customer care at a time when the customer most needs it.

This process, sometimes called incident management, is particularly suitable for larger companies or if the customer is likely to suffer a great deal of inconvenience because of the incident. However, the principles can be applied to any business, however small.

- The incident management approach is to appoint one person, trained in customer service skills, to deal with a customer throughout an incident.
- The role of the personal incident manager is to take responsibility for the provision of appropriate services.
- An incident management program has two main elements: the infrastructure to deliver the service and the personal skills to provide the right level of customer care.
- Skilled staff members are essential to the effective delivery of the service, and training may be necessary.
- Many equipment manufacturers use incident management techniques to support their customers after a disaster.

FAQS

Should incident management form part of all service offerings?

It depends on the type of service that is offered. If the service is critical to the customer's business process—telecommunications or computing, for example—incident management would be important. Disruption to those services could damage the customer's business.

Why is a personal incident manager necessary?

During an incident, effective coordination of support services and regular communication with the customer are essential. By appointing a single person to take responsibility for coordination and communication, you can guarantee continuity and reassure the customer by giving them a single point of contact.

Is it possible to plan for future incidents?

It isn't just possible; it is essential. Industry research indicates that a high proportion of companies who did not have a documented plan failed to recover lost business. Planning is just as important as quality support services.

MAKING IT HAPPEN
Deal with Customer Incidents

Customers who know that their problems are taken care of are more likely to be fully satisfied with the services that are available and will be happier to deal with the same company in the future. Quality experts found that a key factor in delivering time-guaranteed services was the ability to reassure customers that help was on the way. Customers would then be prepared to wait until help or support arrived, even if there was a long gap between reporting the incident and having it resolved. Other research has shown that customers whose complaints are satisfactorily dealt with are likely to be more loyal than those who had no complaint in the first place.

Identify Opportunities for Incident Management

A number of scenarios can be used to identify situations where support like this could be valuable.

- The customer could suffer a great deal of inconvenience and stress as a result of the incident. Reducing the stress and inconvenience would help to demonstrate high levels of care and increase customer satisfaction.
- The incident could threaten the efficiency of the company business, and measures must be taken to limit the damage.
- The customer does not have the skills and resources to resolve the problems on the spot and is dependent on external forms of support.
- The customer has paid for a support package and has agreed to a certain level of response. The company must respond within the agreed levels.
- The speed of response is seen as a competitive differentiation and is positioned as an integral part of the service package.
- Failure to deal with the incident quickly could have a critical effect on the customer's business or personal activities.
- The incident could have legal implications, and the customer needs high levels of advice and guidance.

Set Objectives for Incident Management

In developing a response and support strategy, you should set a wide range of business objectives:

- to provide the highest levels of quality response and customer support throughout an incident;
- to minimize inconvenience for the customer;
- to make sure that incidents are resolved promptly within agreed time scales;
- to make sure that support resources are deployed effectively to maximize customer satisfaction.

Introduce Incident Management

The incident management approach is to appoint one person, trained in customer service skills, to deal with a customer throughout an incident.

Incident management can be applied to any service led organization where the customer needs to be kept informed, for example, maintenance and support services for vital equipment or disaster recovery services where the customer faces difficult and unfamiliar decisions and needs support.

Appoint a Personal Incident Manager

The role of the personal incident manager is to take responsibility for the provision of appropriate services and to reassure the customer that help and support are on the way. In the smaller company, this may be a senior manager, even the managing director, but whoever takes the role must have the authority to take appropriate action. The personal incident manager:

- takes the incoming calls from the customer, establishes the location, and identifies the form of support needed;
- provides individual guidance to the customer on action to be taken with an indication of the support that will be provided;
- deals with the customer's immediate queries;
- makes detailed arrangements to put support services into operation;
- monitors the progress of support services and keeps the customer up to date if possible.

Offer Disaster Recovery Services

Many equipment manufacturers use incident management techniques to support their customers after a disaster such as fire, accident, or system breakdown. If the customer loses essential equipment such as computers or telephones for an extended period, this could seriously threaten the future of their business. Industry research shows that only a minority of companies dependent on the computer have a formal disaster recovery strategy and points out that loss of a system for more than a few days could put them out of business.

Plan and Implement Disaster Recovery

A disaster recovery program has a number of stages:

- helping the customer identify critical activities that should be covered in the event of a disaster;
- training staff members and managers to prepare for a disaster by simulating the conditions of an emergency;
- preparing a contingency plan;
- providing replacement equipment and services in the event of an incident;
- providing support and project management resources during an incident;
- providing full support to restore normal service.

Throughout a disaster, the customer would have access to an incident manager who would coordinate the rescue and recovery activities, and provide advice, guidance, and support. The principle is similar to that of the personal incident manager, where customers are given re-assurance that incidents will be resolved and that they can be sure of the highest standards of support throughout the incident.

Create the Infrastructure for Incident Management

The program has two main elements: the infrastructure to deliver the service and the personal skills to provide the right level of customer care. The infrastructure requires a significant investment to make sure that the service can be delivered rapidly and efficiently throughout the country. Depending on the complexity of the project, it might include:

- communications to provide a rapid response to customer questions, and put the service into operation;
- a trained support team to deliver the service;
- quality-controlled suppliers to support the direct response team;
- a control center to manage the operations and coordinate the response;
- a network of contacts and suppliers to

provide the specialist services that form part of the response.

Develop the Right Skills

Skilled staff members are essential to the effective delivery of the service. The skills requirements would include:

- incident management skills, to deal with customers who may be in stressful situations;
- project management skills, to coordinate and implement a response;
- technical skills, to deliver the service;
- communications skills, to coordinate the elements of the program.

WHAT TO AVOID
Failing to Communicate with the Customer during an Incident
Research shows that customers who receive regular progress updates feel reassured that they are getting the right level of support. Anxiety levels are high during an incident, but regular communication helps customers deal with the incident and contributes to overall customer satisfaction.

Having No Escalation Procedure
A company should have a formal escalation procedure for dealing with customer incidents. If support staff cannot resolve an incident within an agreed time scale, the incident should be reported to a more senior manager, who would then commit more resources. If there is no escalation procedure, the incident can get out of hand and damage customer relationships.

Failure to Train Staff in Customer Care
An incident creates high levels of stress in an organization, and support staff must be trained to deal with this.

SEE ALSO
Communicating Customer Service (p. 211)
Handling Customer Inquiries (p. 213)

Increasing Customer Lifetime Value

GETTING STARTED

"Customer lifetime value" (CLV or LTV) is a way of measuring how much your customers are worth over the time they are your customers. Increases in customer retention can increase sales and profits significantly. It is important to retain customers, but not at the cost of other essential marketing activities.

Putting customers into key categories helps clarify analysis and acts as the basis for marketing activities designed to improve customer lifetime value.

FAQS

What's the difference between customer lifetime value and customer loyalty programs?

Customer loyalty programs are designed to retain as many customers as possible, regardless of their real value. The customer lifetime value calculation indicates the contribution individual customers make to profitability.

Why are lapsed customers important?

If they can be "revived," they tend to behave like new customers and become regular buyers once again, with good potential lifetime value.

Is customer retention more important than acquisition?

Acquisition should never be neglected, because existing business may decline for reasons outside your control. Industry experience indicates, however, that existing customers make a comparatively greater contribution when marketing costs are taken into consideration.

Do we want to retain all our customers?

Not necessarily. Some customers may not be profitable. Using customer lifetime value, you can calculate the cost and contribution of each customer.

MAKING IT HAPPEN

Apply the Customer Lifetime Value Concept

Customer lifetime value is a way of measuring how much your customers are worth to you, over the length of time that they remain your customers.

The lifetime for customers will vary from industry to industry, and from brand to brand. The lifetime of customers should come to an end when their contribution ceases to be profitable unless steps are taken to revitalize them.

Benefits from Customer Lifetime Value

Industry experience indicates that a number of benefits apply.

- A 5% increase in customer retention can create a 125% increase in profits.
- A 10% increase in retailer retention can translate to a 20% increase in sales.
- Extending customer lifecycles by three years can triple profits per customer.

Identify Categories of Customer

Before calculating customer lifetime value, it is possible to analyze your customers according to four key attributes. This can help to clarify analysis and act as the basis for marketing activities to improve customer lifetime value.

- Frequency—how often they purchase (regular customers are more likely to purchase in the future)
- Recency—how much time has elapsed since the last purchase (recent customers are more likely to purchase again)
- Amount—how much they spend (higher spending customers are likely to be more committed)
- Category—what sort of product they buy (some products will be more profitable than others and some may be one-off purchases)

Year	Annual Customer Expenditure	Annual Marketing Costs	Annual Net Contribution
0	$12,000	$15,000	$-3,000
1	$10,000	$6,000	$4,000
2	$8,000	$6,000	$2,000
3	$7,000	$6,000	$1,000
4	$6,000	$4,000	$2,000
5	$5,000	$4,000	$1,000
Totals	**$48,000**	**$41,000**	**$7,000**

Calculate Lifetime Value

In a consumer business, customer lifetime value is calculated, in practice, by analyzing the behavior of a group of customers who:
- have the same recruitment date
- are recruited from the same source
- bought the same types of product

In a business-to-business environment, a similar approach can be used.
- Isolate particular customers, and examine them individually.
- Analyze the behavior of different groups, segmenting your customer database by factors such as industry, annual turnover, or staff numbers.

The basic calculation has three stages.
- Identify a discrete group of customers for tracking.
- Record (or estimate) each revenue and cost for this group of customers, by campaign or season.
- Calculate the contribution, by campaign or season.

Refine the Calculation

Other factors can be introduced to make the calculation more relevant. In a business-to-business environment, for example, it may be the sales representatives who generate sales. In this case, the calculation should include the representative's "running costs" and the cost of any centrally produced sales support material.

Evaluate a Campaign

The table shows the calculations for a group of customers who were recruited through a direct response advertising campaign that ran in the spring of year 1. The table tracks their expenditure over a five-year period.

Divide the total contribution by the number of customers in the group. Say there are one thousand customers: the average lifetime value per customer is $7. But this compares favorably with a short term analysis which, in the first year, would show a loss of $3 per customer recruited.

Analyze the Results

A company may offer different products or brands which are marketed under different cost centers. If a customer is a customer of more than one cost/profit center, there is a choice of approaches:
- examine customers of each brand and ignore multipurchases;
- build a more detailed model that combines and allocates the cumulative costs as well as the cumulative profit in the appropriate proportions.

Use Customer Lifetime Values to Improve Marketing Performance

There are four important applications:
- setting target customer acquisition costs
- allocating acquisition funds
- selecting acquisition offers
- supporting customer retention activities

In the example above the decision was taken in Year 4 to reduce marketing costs on this group of customers. Equally valid may be an increase in expenditure aimed at reactivating customers—this is a classic retention activity.

Set Target Customer Acquisition Costs

If a customer is expected to generate more than one sale, the allowable cost can be greater than the cost allowed for the first sale—the classic loss-leader approach to customer acquisition, illustrated in the example table above. However, overspending on customer acquisition can also be ruinous. A reasonable calculation is to recruit only from those sources that yield new customers at less than half the estimated lifetime value. On that basis, the worst sources will have a cost per customer close to a lifetime value, while the average cost per customer should be far lower.

Allocate Acquisition Funds

Different recruitment sources will provide customers with different lifetime values. After identifying those values, spend more on the best sources.

Select Acquisition Offers

The lifetime value of a customer may depend on the type and value of their initial purchase. In turn, this can lead to decisions about which products and offers to use when advertising externally, or when considering how to upgrade existing customers.

Support Customer Retention Activities

Once the typical lifetime value of a group of customers is known, companies can decide how hard to work at retaining them. It is not a foregone conclusion that all customers are worth having. Activities should be tailored to the customers who are most valuable.

Increase Value with New Offers

A financial services company can increase customer lifetime value by cross selling a range of different products and services.

WHAT TO AVOID
Trying to Retain the Wrong Customers

Customer retention costs money in terms of sales and marketing funds. However, customer lifetime value analysis indicates that not all customers are worth retaining. You should carefully select the customers who are likely to yield the highest returns over a period of time and prioritize the allocation of marketing resources to these.

Offering Customers a Limited Range of Products

When you have identified the most valuable customers, you need to have a wide range of products or services to offer them. Cross-selling and upselling are the best ways to increase customer lifetime value, but this can be difficult with a limited product range. Customers are your company's most valuable asset; think about "share of customer wallet" rather than just share of market.

Spending Too Much on Acquiring New Customers

Customer lifetime value analysis reinforces a traditional marketing rule of thumb, that it costs less to retain existing customers than to acquire new ones. Overemphasis on new business development could be a bad move since existing customers are easier to sell to.

Corporate Hospitality

GETTING STARTED

Corporate hospitality (or entertainment) is widely used by businesses of all sizes as a means of forging and strengthening relationships with people who are important to the success of the business. It can be aimed at internal audiences (staff) through motivational events, or at external audiences (existing clients, potential clients, and even members of the local community) as part of a careful sales and marketing strategy. It provides an opportunity to get to know staff or customers, and to allow them to get to know the manager, business, and product better.

FAQS

What are the advantages and disadvantages of internal corporate hospitality?

Corporate hospitality may be used to improve staff morale, perhaps by motivating a sales team, raising customer awareness, building team working skills, celebrating a special occasion, or increasing business profits. Advantages can include improved communications and understanding, an improved organizational spirit, and a reduction in staff turnover through improved loyalty and greater motivation.

You do, however, need to be aware of some of the disadvantages to this approach. If you're holding a social event, make sure that all employees have an equal opportunity to attend. Give as much notice as you can so that people can make arrangements, such as finding a babysitter if they have children. Also think very carefully about whom you wish to reward. For example, a gift given to one individual may be regarded as favoritism. It's important to exercise discretion and to be aware of the potential risks of damaging staff morale.

Also think long and hard about running a corporate event for employees because you think staff morale is low. There may be more practical reasons for staff discontent, for example salary or promotion problems, or lack of equipment, and team building activities are unlikely to rectify such problems—they could even compound them. Get to the root of the problem first and then decide whether a corporate event is the best way of solving it.

What are the advantages and disadvantages of external corporate hospitality?

External corporate hospitality promotes your business to existing or potential clients, providing an environment to meet clients socially, and using the informality of a social event to find out more about the client's needs. The expectation is that it will help you to develop business contacts, and the business to sell more products and services.

Corporate hospitality can help to increase customer loyalty, differentiate your business from the competition, target the best prospects (your existing customers), increase word of mouth recommendations, raise and maintain the profile of your business, and build positive relationships. The main disadvantages are that external clients may not be able to accept this hospitality, and that there may also be considerable costs involved, but check with your accountant to see if any expenses could be considered tax-deductible or are within range of your budget.

MAKING IT HAPPEN
Types of Corporate Hospitality Event

There are many events and activities on offer to choose from. Make sure the activity is appropriate for your purpose, and put the emphasis on having fun!

Spectator Events

A small business is unlikely to have the budget required to entertain clients and/or staff at lavish major spectator events such as the Super Bowl or the World Series. However, you could think about inviting clients and/or staff to popular events such as golf, horse racing, opera, a music concert, or the theater.

Social Events

You may want to invite existing clients to a lunch, dinner, or party. Social events for staff are more likely to be linked to a special occasion, such as Christmas, New Year, or for hitting a specific sales target.

Participation Events

Common examples of this type of event include multi-activity days, rock climbing, skiing, and sailing. Don't force employees into taking part in physical activities if they don't want to, however—that really will damage morale. It's essential that you obtain adequate insurance cover so that your business is covered in the event of accidents. Unless the client is a personal friend, it's unlikely that a participation event would involve clients—it might be embarrassing if a client was defeated at a sporting event! However, a business meeting could be arranged to take place with a round of golf.

Family Occasions

You might also consider showing your appreciation for an employee on a special occasion, for example a wedding or the birth of a child, by offering a gift. Alternatively, you may decide to run a informal family fun day in the form of a small local gathering with side-shows and attractions for the children, such as a bouncy castle or an arts-and-crafts section. Celebrating a family occasion with a client is unlikely as it's usually considered a private affair, outside of the business relationship.

Team-building Events

These are a common form of corporate incentive for staff. The traditional outward-bound day may not be suitable, as it places physical rather than mental demands on the participants, and therefore may not favor everyone. Work-related simulation activities, for example running a fictional business, may be more appropriate. The key to the success of such an activity is that the purpose is clearly communicated to all those involved, so explain to everyone why they are doing the activity, and that they are not just having a fun day out. The greatest benefits can be derived from such events when they are followed through and when the lessons learned from the activity are applied to the workplace. While team building is thought of as an employee activity, some companies/suppliers may have a long history of trading with the business so that their employees could also be invited to join in team building events.

Using Event Organizers

You might enjoy organizing small-scale events personally, such as the staff Christmas party or a business lunch, or you might ask another employee to do so. Alternatively, you may decide to engage the services of an event organizer to carry out the planning and staging of larger events. There is stiff competition in this field, with a wide range of event organizers, suppliers, and venues to choose from. The Sodexho Alliance, for example, provides a number of services for customers in the business, education, and health industries, "including food services, housekeeping, groundskeeping, plant operations and maintenance, and integrated facilities management." (See Web site link at bottom of this article.) Event organizers work in close collaboration with outside suppliers, including hotels, tent and marquee hire companies, audio and visual equipment hire companies, and so on. They use a wide variety of venues, ranging from large stately homes to small hotels.

Event organizers usually offer a package tailored to your needs and objectives, timetable, budget, and guest profile. The price depends on the number of people being entertained, the type/number of activities chosen, the duration of the event, and whether catering and accommodation are included. Choose an organizer who offers an inclusive event price and be aware of hidden costs, such as staff accommodation and meals. Ask to see the organizer's terms and conditions so that you know what is in the small print; for example, what happens if an event is cancelled due to bad weather (you can take out insurance to cover this). In addition, check that the event organizer has adequate public liability insurance.

Costs of Corporate Hospitality
Budget carefully for the cost of providing corporate hospitality and set aside money in your marketing budget at the beginning of the financial year, rather than using surplus money that may be left over at the end. You may need to cut out corporate hospitality altogether if there is a downturn in business. All instances where a client/member of staff has been entertained are a legitimate business expense and should be included in the corporate hospitality budget. These include all business lunches with existing and potential clients, and the staff Christmas party.

Corporate Gifts
Corporate gifts can be used as part of your marketing strategy, targeted either at an individual or a group of people. They can be also used to offer a goodwill gesture or to serve as a reminder to customers. Gifts may be given as a staff incentive too, or as a special award. Corporate gifts should be appropriate to the event and reflect something about your business. Typical examples may be a Christmas card bearing your company logo, or a fun item such as a pen or small notebook. It's also often a good idea to leave a reminder of your business name with a client. The gift need not be expensive but should be of appropriate quality. More expensive items may give the impression that the client is valued

more highly. However, be aware that local authorities and some private companies do not allow their employees to accept gifts at all, as an extravagant gift may be seen as an attempt to bribe an official or influence a contract. Offering a corporate gift to an employee may be seen by the tax authorities as payment in lieu of wages, or as a bonus.

WHAT TO AVOID
Poor Planning
Arrange events well in advance, and choose a suitable time, activity, and location. Don't leave it to the last minute, as this will prove stressful and also mean that not everyone you'd like to attend can come along.

Not Arranging Insurance
The importance of the employer's duty of care towards their employees cannot be overstated. Make sure you take out public liability insurance.

Not Evaluating Events
Evaluate each event properly once it's over. For example, you could measure events for your customers for quantifiable results, such as increased sales.

Not Taking Allowable Expenses into Account
Contact the Internal Revenue Service to find out what are considered to be allowable business expenses.

SEE ALSO
Communicating Customer Service (p. 211)
Managing Key Accounts (p. 225)
Retaining Existing Customers (p. 205)
Selling and Salesmanship (p. 490)

Managing Key Accounts

GETTING STARTED

It's said that 80% of the average business's income will come from just 20% of its customers, so it makes sense to dedicate time and resources to keeping those key accounts satisfied. More than this, you also need to ask yourself how you could better serve the needs of these key accounts, to build loyalty and more business with them.

Your business needs both a commitment and a strategy to manage its key accounts. The first step is to understand and appreciate the need to allocate resources. Research in the United States suggests that larger businesses have been consciously reducing their number of suppliers. The positive side of this is that, if you as a supplier successfully meet your key customers' needs, you're likely to progressively capture more of their business. One of the results is that customers come to rely on your special insight into their needs, and the cost (to them) of changing suppliers then grows.

Your strategy then needs to outline what you want to achieve with your key accounts, and how you plan to achieve this. Make sure that there is a particular person (preferably a senior manager or supervisor) in your business who has the final responsibility of ensuring that each key customer is happy with your service. If you have a formal customer relationship management (CRM) system, this should support your key account strategy by recording the date and nature of all contact with the clients. One book you may find useful for more ideas is *Key Account Management and Planning: The Comprehensive Handbook for Managing Your Company's Most Important Strategic Asset* by Noel Capon, published in 2001 by Free Press.

FAQS

Why is key account management necessary?

The loyalty of your big customers is too important to leave unmanaged. Consider what would happen if the salesperson dealing with a big customer were to resign suddenly and leave certain important duties undone; this could undermine years of trust and cooperation. On a more day-to-day level, your important customers need to know that they can turn to someone senior in your business if there are problems in the business relationship.

How do you identify a key account?

This will obviously depend on how many customers you have, and whether they are evenly spread in terms of the amount that each of them spends with you. As a rule of thumb, you could view any customer who brings in substantially more business than average as a key account. Your challenge will be to see how many of these customers

you can treat in a preferential way, given the limits of your time and resources.

Do you need key account managers?

Many small businesses will not have the capacity to appoint a large number of people to work exclusively as key account managers. In reality, you'll probably want to build the job of account manager into jobs that already exist in your business. For instance, as the owner of your business, you'll most likely have an important role to play in managing key accounts; but you'll do this in addition to the various other responsibilities that you have. In the same way, you could get certain senior staff to take on responsibility for other customers, in addition to their core responsibilities.

MAKING IT HAPPEN
Implement a System

To manage your key accounts successfully, you need to build your contact with them into an on-going process, so that:

- someone senior is allocated responsibility for looking after each key account;
- regular contact is maintained with—and feedback requested from—each key customer;
- targets are set for the revenue expected from each key account;
- the health of the relationship with each key customer is monitored regularly.

Develop and Empower Senior Staff

Your big customers want to feel that they have the ear of a decision maker in your business. They need to know that if they are dealing with your business through your key account manager, that person must be experienced and authorized to make decisions so that problems are quickly resolved. From your point of view, this requires an on-going effort to develop the management and people skills of your employees. Especially as your business grows, you'll need to delegate these import-ant responsibilities and rely on others to retain your customers' loyalty.

Consider a Customer Relationship Management (CRM) System

As communications technology allows businesses and the individuals within them to become more efficient, you might find it difficult to keep track of each contact with a customer. If you're prioritizing the management of key accounts, you may want to build this into a formal CRM system. This is generally provided as a computer program, and can hold contact details of all your customers, as well as details of their orders and communications with your business. The value of these systems is that they allow important information to be shared among different people in your organization, so there is no duplication of contact with the client and everyone within your business is fully up to date. It's particu-larly useful when a problem arises and the history of an order needs to be tracked, or when the relevant person is out of the office and someone else needs the latest informa-tion on a transaction.

Keep it Personal

One of the main advantages of making individuals responsible for managing key accounts is that trust and co-operation can be built up on a personal basis. Even in our high-tech world, it's still true that people prefer to do business with people they like and trust. Being systematic about this rela-tionship need not detract from the person-to-person value.

WHAT TO AVOID
Waiting for Complaints

Be proactive in finding out what your key customers feel about your service. Contact them regularly for feedback; do not wait for them to come to you with a complaint. This also creates an opportunity to talk to them about their own activities, and to get early warning of any future work that your business might be able to gain from them.

Becoming Complacent

The danger of having a regular customer for a long time is that you can easily take their business for granted, and get complacent about your attitude to them. Make sure that everyone in your business from the recep-tionist to the bookkeeper is aware of who the key accounts are, so that they are particularly well received whenever they interact with the business.

Putting All Your Eggs in One Basket

By concentrating your efforts on your key accounts, you run the risk of paying insuffi-cient attention to your other customers; indeed, it may even detract from your efforts to find and nurture new customers. This makes you over-reliant on just a few customers, where the effect of losing their business could be disastrous.

SEE ALSO
Corporate Hospitality (p. 222)
Perfecting Your Pitch: Delivering Presentations (p. 231)
Selling and Salesmanship (p. 490)

COMMUNICATING WITH YOUR CUSTOMERS

Perfecting Your Pitch: Preparing Presentations

GETTING STARTED

Being able to cope with presentations is a very valuable skill for the owner-manager of a small business. Presentations are useful in many situations, such as pitching for business, putting a case for funding, and addressing staff meetings. Few people like speaking formally to an audience, but there are many real benefits and, as you gain experience in giving presentations, you'll probably find that it becomes less of a worry, and even enjoyable. This actionlist will give you some suggestions for preparing the content of your presentation, looking at the objectives for your presentation, the audience you'll be addressing it to, and the best way to get your points across.

FAQS

What objectives should I set?

The starting point for any presentation is to set clear objectives. Ask yourself why you're giving the talk and what you want your audience to get out of it. Also consider whether using speech alone is the best way of communicating your message, and whether your presentation would benefit from using visual aids and slides to further illustrate its main points. When you're planning and giving the presentation, keep your objectives in mind at all times—they'll focus your thoughts. Having an objective for giving the presentation will ensure that you're not wasting anyone's time, either your audience's or your own.

What do you need to know about the audience?

Before you plan your presentation try as best you can to find out who is going to be in your audience, and their expectations. For example, the tone and content of a presentation to the managing director of another firm will be very different from one addressed to potential users of a product. It's important that you know the extent of the audience's knowledge about the topic you'll be discussing. Their familiarity with the subject will determine the level at which you pitch the talk. Try to appeal to what will motivate and interest these people.

MAKING IT HAPPEN

Write Your Speech

When it comes to presentations, there is no substitute for detailed preparation and planning. While everyone prepares in different ways, all of which develop with experience, here are a few key points to bear in mind while you're preparing.

Start by breaking up the task of preparing your speech into manageable units. Once you know the length of the presentation—say 15 minutes, for example—break the time up into smaller units and allocate sections of your speech to each unit. Then note down all the points you want to make, and order them logically. This will help you develop the framework and emphasis of the presentation.

Keep your presentation short and simple, if you possibly can, as it will be easier for you to manage and remember. If you need to provide more detail, you can supply a written handout to be given out at the end. A shorter presentation is usually more effective from the audience's point of view, too, as most people dislike long presentations, and will not necessarily remember any more from them.

Avoid packing your talk with facts and figures; you could instead use graphs and charts to illustrate these where they are essential. Aim to identify two or three key points, and concentrate on getting these over in a creative fashion.

Visual Aids and Equipment

With any presentation, you'll need to consider whether to use visual aids, such as transparencies for an overhead projector (OHP), or a computer presentation package, such as PowerPoint. Remember that visual aids should only be used as signposts during the presentation, to help the audience focus on the main point. It's important not to cram too much information onto one visual aid as you'll probably find that you lose the attention of your audience while they try to read everything on it. Make sure the audience can see the information by using big, bold lettering, and bear in mind that images are often far more effective than words.

At its most basic, a personal computer can be used to develop and produce a series of slides which can be printed onto acetates for use on an overhead projector. A more common usage is to link up the PC with a projector in order to show the information on a large screen.

If you're going to use slides, you should try to standardize them to make them look more professional. Use templates where possible to make sure that they don't blend together, and again try not to put too much information onto a single slide, or it will become difficult to read. A sensible guideline is to include no more than six points per slide and to keep the number of words you use for each point to the absolute minimum. Think of what you're writing as the prompts for what you want to say.

The most common presentation packages are Microsoft PowerPoint and Corel Presentations. These will allow you to develop a presentation using slide templates. You can make full use of charts, graphics, or even photographs to bring your information alive. Packages such as PhotoShop or Paint Shop Pro will allow you to scan in or manipulate photographs, or you could also use some of the available animations for transitions between slides.

You should pay particular attention to the layout and text on the slides and remain consistent throughout. Select a background that contrasts well with the text, and colors that are strong and provide contrast. It may also be a good idea to include the business's logo on all of the slides. It's important, always, to proofread your slides and transparencies. There is nothing more noticeable, or more unprofessional, than a typo or grammatical error projected to ten times its size on a screen!

Practice as many times as you can to make sure that you're very familiar with your speech—allow plenty of time for rehearsal before the event. Once you're confident that your presentation is right, resist the temptation to change it. Remember, *you* may have heard the speech many times, but the audience will be hearing it for the first time. It's also a good idea to practice your speech using the equipment you intend to use; slide projectors and video machines should be tested in advance to make sure you know how to operate them. Make sure you have a contingency plan to cope with any unforeseen mishaps. During your rehearsals, it will also be important to time your speech to ensure it's not too long or too short. Remember that you'll probably need to allow time at the end for a question-and-answer session. Resist the temptation to bring your script into the presentation and instead write the main points on numbered cards, known as cue cards, to provide reminders.

Prepare the Venue

Make sure that an appropriately-sized room has been organized for your presentation; take into account the number of people you're expecting; and ensure there is enough seating, lighting, ventilation, and heating. It's a good idea to provide some refreshments for participants such as tea, coffee, and water.

You also need to make sure there will be no interruptions, for example by phone calls, fire drills, or people accidentally entering the room. Whether you're presenting at your own office or elsewhere, you must make sure that any equipment or props you need are available and set up properly before the presentation starts. If you're presenting away from your office, for example, at a conference or a client's premises, it's a good idea to visit the site beforehand to make sure it provides the necessary facilities.

✖ WHAT TO AVOID
Not Researching Your Audience
A good knowledge of the audience is absolutely crucial in finding the correct pitch. It's no good blinding your audience with technical jargon if they only have a basic grasp of the subject. Similarly, a very knowledgeable audience will soon switch off if you spend the first few minutes going over the basics.

Long Presentations
If your presentation absolutely has to be longer than 20 minutes, it may be a good idea to insert some breaks so that your audience remains fresh and interested.

Not Checking the Room and Equipment
This can be disastrous! Imagine, for example, arriving and finding that there is no facility for delivering PowerPoint presentations, and you have no other method of showing slides. Make sure you're familiar with the environment in which you'll be presenting.

RECOMMENDED LINKS
Public Speaking and Speech Writing:
www.speechtips.com
Toastmasters International:
www.toastmasters.org

SEE ALSO
Perfecting Your Pitch: Delivering Presentations (p. 231)
Presentation/Speaking (p. 478)

Perfecting Your Pitch: Delivering Presentations

GETTING STARTED

A presentation is an ideal environment for you to promote your business and its products or services. You have a captive audience, are able to provide them with relevant information, and can answer any questions they may have on the spot. For a presentation to be a success you must be able to hold the attention of the audience and leave them wanting to know more.

Giving presentations does not suit everyone, but practice does help. To give a successful presentation you will need to be able to command your audience's attention and speak in an articulate, fluent fashion. Some people are natural presenters, while others find it more difficult, but practice and feedback from previous audiences will help you develop your presentation skills. This actionlist will give you some ideas for structuring, preparing, and delivering your presentation.

FAQS

How should I structure my presentation?

Structure is essential for any presentation. There should be an introduction, a main body, and a conclusion. You can be witty, controversial, or even outrageous if the mood of the presentation allows but, whatever approach you try, your chief aim is to arouse the audience's curiosity, and to get your message across.

What is the best way to introduce my presentation?

The introduction to your presentation needs to attract your audience's interest and attention. A good opening is also for your own confidence, because if you start well, the rest should follow easily. Plan your opening words carefully for maximum impact: they should be short, sharp, and to the point. Let your audience know how long your presentation will take, as this will prepare them to focus for the period of time you expect to speak. Summarize the contents of your presentation, so that your audience can work out how much information they will need to absorb. Explaining the key points in the first few sentences will also help your mind to focus on the task at hand and refresh your memory on the major points of your presentation. It sometimes helps to get started if you can learn your first few sentences by heart. Let your

audience know if you are happy to interact with them throughout the presentation. Alternatively, inform them that you will be holding a question and answer session at the end.

What should I do in the main body of the presentation?

The main body of the presentation will be dictated by the points that you want to make. Use short, sharp, and simple language to keep your audience's attention, and to ensure that your message is being understood. Include only one idea per sentence and pause after each one, so as to make a mental full stop. Use precise language to convey your message, but make sure that your presentation sounds spontaneous—it shouldn't sound like a chapter from a textbook. You need to convey your message clearly, without masking the salient points with drivel. Stick to your original plan for your presentation, and don't go off at a tangent on a particular point and miss the thread of your presentation. Why not try using metaphors and images to illustrate points? This will give impact to what you say, and help your audience to remember what you have said.

How should I conclude my presentation?

You should close by summing up the key points of what you have covered. The closing seconds of your presentation are as crucial as the opening sentence. Consider what action you would like your audience to take after the presentation is over and attempt to inspire them to do it.

MAKING IT HAPPEN
Posture and Delivery
There are certain techniques to do with your posture, and the way that you deliver your presentation, that can be used to improve its impact. Maintain eye contact and address your audience directly throughout your presentation. Try to be aware of your stance, posture, and gestures without being too self-conscious. Don't slouch, as you'll look unprofessional. The best way of avoiding this is by always standing when you are doing a presentation. Don't fiddle, for example with a pencil or a piece of paper, try to keep still, and avoid moving around excessively. All these things are distracting for an audience, and will mean that they are missing important points in your presentation.

Remember that your audience has come to learn something. Try to sound authoritative, sincere, and enthusiastic. If you don't sound as if you believe in yourself, this will come across to the audience. Think about the way in which you are speaking. Most people need to articulate their words more clearly when addressing an audience. There is usually no opportunity for the audience to ask you to repeat a word you have missed. Aim to sound the vowels and consonants of words clearly. Be aware, also, of your vocal expression. Try to vary volume, pitch, and speed of delivery to underline your meaning, and to maintain the interest of your audience. Try not to use too many acronyms that are specific to your business or industry, as you can't be 100% sure that everyone in the audience will know what they mean. If you do need to use them, introduce them and explain them early in your presentation so that everyone can keep up.

Cue Cards, Visual Aids, and Equipment
It's tempting (and, if you're a nervous presenter, comforting) to have the full version of your speech in front of you, but it's best to avoid this and use cue cards instead. These will have a few headings referring to the main subject areas of your speech, and a few key points. In this way you can remember the key points you want to convey, but you have the freedom to talk naturally about them, rather than speaking from an over-rehearsed script, and this will make you seem more spontaneous. You may, however, wish to write the introduction out in full on your first card.

Be careful when using visual aids and equipment in the presentation as these can also be distracting for an audience. Use a pen to point out details on the overhead projector itself, rather than the screen, as this is much clearer. Flipcharts should be written on quickly in long hand, but try not to turn your back on the audience as you write. Commonly available presentation packages often have a facility to enable you to link to specific slides. Additionally, if a specific topic needs further explanation, you could have a built-in series of links so that you can move to some extra slides to explain a particular point. If you intend to use sophisticated technology, then have a technician on hand to help out. It is important to have a contingency plan in case your technology crashes. Make sure you have either a back-up disk, or an alternative presentational medium, or both.

Close Your Presentation
If you are answering questions at the end of your presentation and you don't know the answer to a question, tell the person you will find the answer and get back to them later. This will save time, and also prevent you from giving an incorrect answer. If the question is a general discussion point, you could always try throwing the question open to the floor; you may be able to get an interesting discussion going between the members of your audience. If you plan to use handouts to add to your presentation's content, make sure that you give these out at the end. Otherwise the audience will be flicking through your handout instead of listening to you.

✘ WHAT TO AVOID
Lack of Enthusiasm

If you don't have any interest or excitement in your own speech, then don't expect your audience to have any. Listening to a single voice for 20 minutes or more can be difficult for an audience. You must try to inject enthusiasm into what you are saying. You could consider planning some kind of inter-action with your audience, too, in the form of activities or discussion.

Speaking Too Quickly

Don't rush your presentation; it is important to take your time. The audience will find it difficult to understand you, or to keep up, if you talk too fast. Make sure you summarize your main points every five minutes or so, or as you reach the end of a section. This will help to clarify the most important issues for your audience, and it is then more likely that they will remember the central issues long after you have finished your presentation.

Not Checking Equipment

There is nothing more irritating for an audience, who have all made an effort to turn up on time, than to have to sit around and wait while you struggle to get your laptop to work, or sort your slides out. Make sure everything is exactly in place well before your audience begins to arrive. A technician should be on hand if you are planning to use sophisticated technology.

Not Interacting with the Audience

Be careful not to look at the floor during your presentation, or to direct your speech at one person. Try and draw your whole audience into the presentation by glancing at everyone's faces, in a relaxed and unhurried way, as you make your points. Keeping in tune with your audience in this way will also help you judge if people are becoming bored. If you do detect this, you could try to change the tempo of your presentation to refocus their attention.

SEE ALSO
Managing Key Accounts (p. 225)
Perfecting Your Pitch: Preparing Presentations (p. 228)
Presentation/Speaking (p. 478)

Writing a Sales Letter

GETTING STARTED

Most small businesses need to sell by mail in some shape or form. A sales letter is a low-cost selling tool that can be adapted and modified according to circumstances. A good letter by itself can be enough to get the message across, but in most cases sales letters are used in conjunction with other promotional materials such as brochures, samples, and reply envelopes. Some mailings allow for an instant response, often in the form of an order. Others may set the scene for follow-up telephone calls and personal visits in the hope of establishing a longer-term relationship. As the first contact with a client, it's essential that the sales letter sets the right tone and this actionlist explains how to do this.

FAQS

How can I use sales letters?

A sales letter can be used in a variety of ways. It could be the first step in preparing the customer for a phone call or visit, perhaps raising questions that will be answered later.

It may aim just to raise general awareness about the product or service as part of an overall promotional effort. In this case, it doesn't need to contain all of the information the client requires, which can be supplied through other media. However, if the letter has vague objectives, it will be difficult to measure results. If your business sells to a select group, this type of letter won't appeal and will be a waste of time. Letters to a select group are different from letters to a wider audience. If contacts represent good sales potential, each letter should be written with their particular needs in mind. Letters can also be adapted for a variety of different groups that you might approach at different times.

If you are targeting customers repeatedly, for example, to inform them about new products, new offers, tax-related offers, and seasonal offers, the sales letter should take each offer into account, reinforcing the basic promotional message while providing enough variety so as not to bore the reader or make them feel pestered. Sometimes, a sales letter is used to accompany responses to requests for information, and this presents an ideal opportunity to sell.

MAKING IT HAPPEN
Planning a Sales Letter

You need to set down on paper exactly what you want the letter to do. List your points under three headings: Inform, Sell, and Encourage Action.

It's easy to miss out basic information in a letter in an effort to sell the benefits, so remember to include the product name, the price, the business name and address, and order details. If necessary, include more detailed information about the product as well as brochures, other inserts, an envelope, and some sort of reply device.

In order to sell your product, you have to be persuasive and get customers to view it favorably. Remember, there are limits to what a letter can achieve, and the recipient may need a number of opportunities to decide, so think about making your letter part of a sales drive, including offers, telesales, and so on.

Encourage the customer to take further action towards a sale, for example, by reading enclosures, sending or phoning for more information, or placing an order. Follow up requests for further information with further mailings or telesales and make sure arrangements are in place before the next letter is sent.

Contents of a Sales Letter

Position key information at the beginning of your letter, and expand on it later. If you have a special offer running, mention it in the first paragraph to attract the reader's attention and make them read on. Make sure you describe how the product works and what it is meant to do in a way that enables the potential customer to visualize it. If you want to draw attention to certain features, why not highlight them with bullet points? You can always expand and give more detailed product information in brochures.

Describe your product's benefits clearly and simply, and try to think of the product from the customer's viewpoint. For example, if the photocopier you offer allows your customer to print documents direct from his or her personal computer so that there's no need to invest in a printer as well, tell them how much money they could save. Don't be afraid to spell out the benefits.

Avoid making exaggerated claims and remember that the customer does not have a chance to ask questions as he/she would in personal selling. If you do make claims, back them up with examples, such as endorsements from current users and case histories. If your business has large or well-known customers, enclose a testimonial from them, but make sure that they are sincere, specific to the product, and signed by the user.

Encourage immediate action wherever possible. Ask for a response, and keep asking for it throughout the letter. Make it easy for the reader to take the next step, by enclosing partly filled-out forms, postage-paid envelopes, and 800 numbers. Give incentives if you can and reward prompt action, for example, with a time-limited discount. Give the reader the option to send for more information, perhaps with samples or a demonstration, and record the details of customers who go to the trouble of doing this, for future sales efforts.

At the end of the letter, reinforce your message by repeating the offer, the guaran-tee, the cost, and the value of the product or service.

Presentation of a Sales Letter

Direct mail is a popular method of promotion, and prospective customers are often inundated with it. You must distinguish your business from the others so that its material stands a chance of being read and not put straight in the recycling bin. Materials of an unusual size or color should stand out. Keep samples of the competitors' mailing materials on file.

Avoid "Dear Sir/Madam" if possible, and try to find out the recipient's name, taking care to spell it correctly. Alternatively, appropriate titles should be used, for example, if ski equipment is being sold, then "Dear Skier" could be used. Don't ever use "Dear Friend," and avoid sexist titles. The top and the bottom of the letter are key attention areas, so a postscript can be useful for announcing or reinforcing a special gift or offer.

A headline will grab initial attention and can be used to state a major benefit of the product or service; it also helps the reader to decide at a glance if the letter is of interest. Break the letter up into short paragraphs with subheadings, which gives the reader an overview of the contents at a glance. The reader can then read the sections that most interest him or her.

Keep the tone of the letter natural, conversational, warm, and easy to read. Use short words and sentences, and avoid jargon and complicated grammar or vocabulary. Use "you" rather than "I" or "we." Remember that you are addressing an individual person, not a crowd.

Choosing an appropriate typeface will have a big impact on how easy the letter is to read. Black on white is easier to read than the reverse. Avoid using uppercase too much and remember that very small type makes reading difficult. Important words can be emphasized by underlining, italics, bold, and capitals, but take care not to vary the typeface too much or the reader will be distracted by the look rather than the content of the page.

A Sample Sales Letter

Mr. F. Giles
Beacon Hill Country Store
Boston, MA 02116

ASHBURY COUNTRY PRESERVES—A TASTE OF SUMMER

Send for our discount sample pack now!

Dear Mr Giles

For a limited period only, Ashbury Country Preserves is providing country stores in New England with an opportunity to test our exclusive range of pure fruit preserves at discount prices.

An Exclusive Product
Made with fresh fruit harvested from our own farm set in the rolling Pennsylvania country-side, Ashbury Country Preserves are made to an original recipe. Our preserves provide the traditional real fruit taste that discerning shoppers are looking for. A growing number of outlets now stock Ashbury Country Preserves. Exclusive food shops in both city and country find this high-quality food product is a reliable seller and an attractive addition to their stock range.

An Attractive Offer
Packed in distinctive octagonal 1lb jars, with attractive floral labels and lid covers, our preserves contain only fresh fruit and sugar. Each jar (strawberry, raspberry, and blackcurrant) retails at $2. We supply at $1 per jar, but discounts are available for long-term purchasing commitments. Our introductory pack represents a price of 50 cents per jar. Supplies are delivered in packs of 36. We will also supply a distinctively painted wooden display stand to regular customers by agreement. Our brochure and order form are enclosed.

An Elite Market
Ashbury Country Preserves are ideal for the high-quality food retailer. We supply a select group of retail outlets in the Philadelphia area. Established customers include Liberty Hall Visitors' Shop, the First National Deli chain, and the famous Franklin's department store.

I hope you will be able to take advantage of our offer, which lasts until March. I will be telephoning you shortly to discuss our products, but if you have any questions in the meantime please do not hesitate to call.

Yours sincerely

Jenny Jumper
Sales Executive

✘ WHAT TO AVOID
Not Treating the Mailing Package as a Whole

Refer frequently to the other parts of your mailing package, to encourage the reader to read the letter several times. It might be a good idea to test a draft letter out on some established customers, and ask for their feedback.

Not Making the Most of Previous Mailings

If your business does a lot of direct-mail selling, invest in a personal computer and a laser printer if you haven't got one already. This makes it easier to customize the basic letter for a variety of purposes. You can also keep a mailing database and carry out mail merges so that letters can be personally addressed. Microsoft Word gives helpful advice on creating mail merge documents and once you get the hang of it, you'll find they don't take long at all.

SEE ALSO
Creating Impressive Direct Mail Material (p. 254)
Direct Marketing (p. 443)
Improving the Response to Direct Mail (p. 258)

Selling by Mail Order

GETTING STARTED

Mail-order selling has developed as businesses have recognized it as a good way of getting customers without the overheads of retail premises. Small, specialist catalogs have performed well by using this strategy, particularly in selling niche items like hand made shirts, kitchen equipment, and luxury and organic foods. This actionlist looks at the advantages and disadvantages of mail-order selling, and also explains some of the legal implications.

FAQS

What are the advantages of selling by mail order?

Selling by mail order is good for cash flow because payment is in advance for goods that the business may not even need to stock, and payment terms are of 30 or 60 days for purchases. Costs can be kept down because there is no need to rent main commercial area premises, and little or no need for holding stock. Flexible working hours can be introduced, bringing in staff at busy times. If the business is a specialist retail or manufacturing outfit, setting up mail order is a good way of extending your catchment area. Also, mail order can be used with all customer income levels.

What are the disadvantages of selling by mail order?

People may be reluctant to send money to an unknown firm at a distant address. You will need to send frequent direct mail brochures or catalogs with offers to attract more sales. Mail order also imposes limitations on what product(s) can be sold.

MAKING IT HAPPEN
Choose the Product

You need to consider whether there is a market for the item you have chosen; customers should see the advertised product and need it enough to send for it. Try to choose a product that is not generally available and that doesn't require demonstration. You will also need enough of the product to fulfill orders. It should be reasonably cheap, even with postage, and must be straightforward to pack and send. If possible, choose a group or set of products. This encourages

people to keep coming back, especially if there is money off future items.

Promote It

Unlike a shop, which will attract passersby, people need to be told what your mail-order business offers, and how and why they should buy it. There are various ways to get your message across. Direct mail is one. You can rent lists of names and addresses from a list brokerage service until you have built up your own. Data can be broken down specifically, so that tiny sections of the population who are very likely to buy can be targeted.

If you are offering several items, or your product is complicated, then using leaflets or catalogs will be the best means of promotion. Production costs for such materials can be high, so consider charging for catalogs. That way only serious potential customers will request a copy; you can offer to refund the cost if the customer then orders.

Small advertisements are another way to sell. Place advertisements in special-interest media to narrow down the target market. Some national papers and magazines have specific sections for small mail-order businesses. To increase the response rate, make sure your timing is right, and don't squeeze too much information into a tiny space. Use a good headline and a few words, with a drawing rather than a photo. Coupons have a good response rate. Respondents fill in a coupon and you send them a more comprehensive leaflet or catalog.

Give a guarantee; you are expecting customers to buy having seen only a few words and a drawing, so they should be able to send the product back at the business's expense. Don't use box numbers. These have a low response rate and can give the impression that your firm is being evasive. Keep price and postage separate and give a delivery time.

Web sites can be used to promote your business and generate orders. It may also be worth investigating taking payment through the site.

Track Responses

It is important to be able to assess the success of targeting. Make sure that all your coupons are coded with an identifying letter or symbol, to show their origin. If there is not room for this, then a slightly different name or address could be used for each media source.

Keep a record of where each response comes from (media, personal recommendation, direct mailing, and so on), and whether the response becomes a sale. This allows you to determine which advertisements lead to sales, as opposed to just responses, and to target advertising even more effectively in the future.

Aim to break even on the cost of mailing with your first set of orders. Then convert the requests into regular, loyal customers. This conversion rate should be significantly higher than the initial response rate. If brochures and leaflets are sent out and there is little or no response, some respondents could be telephoned and asked why. However, before making any calls make sure that the customer has given you prior permission so that your company is not in violation of the national Do Not Call regulations for telemarketers.

Get Paid

The traditional system of offering cheap credit through agents is declining in popularity; most people want to buy only for themselves. Most small mail-order firms ask for payment with order. It's a good idea to wait for a check to be cleared before the goods are sent.

If possible, credit cards should be accepted. Customers prefer this as it is convenient and offers protection.

Web sites offer secure payment by credit cards using systems such as PayPal. Many of these providers offer a broader range of merchant bank services, which may include some of the payment options listed above. It would be well worthwhile to determine whether your business would be best served using a single source as its merchant bank, as many of these banks reduce their individual transaction rates when there are more services being purchased.

Package and Deliver

Managing the delivery process efficiently is the core element of customer service for mail-order businesses. Test different packaging in U.S. Mail conditions by sending items to and from the business. A separate packaging area should be set up with materials to hand. The importance of secure, efficient packaging should be emphasized to staff.

Think about how your business will deliver. Possible offers include free delivery, or free delivery for orders over a specified amount; and guaranteed next day delivery, or a surcharge for guaranteed delivery within 48 hours. Your business needs to decide whether such guarantees can be met, and whether the expense is worth the corresponding increase in customers and customer loyalty. Arrangements with shippers such as Federal Express, UPS, and others that offer discount rates can increase customer satisfaction and loyalty.

Direct Marketing and Direct Selling Support

Organizations such as the Direct Marketing Association (DMA), Association for Interactive Marketing (AIM) and Internet Alliance (IA) provide assistance, guidance, and political lobby support to direct mail providers.

The Direct Selling Association provides assistance to manufacturers who sell direct to the customer. If your mail order business is for your own manufactured goods, it would be worthwhile to subscribe to the DSA code of ethics and show that commitment on your marketing materials.

Supplier Relations

If you do not manufacture the goods you are selling, make arrangements as quickly as possible with your suppliers so that they can support your organization's needs. The holiday season or particular celebration days such as Valentine's or Mother's Day may require more products, more quickly. Others may be slower. Ask your supplier about setting up a just-in-time (JIT) inventory system so that they can respond as and when you need without you having to carry excess inventory. Also find out whether they have electronic direct order entry systems that would make the order process more efficient and effective for you both.

WHAT TO AVOID
Not Being Prepared

Make sure that you have the resources to set up this type of business. It may look like an easy way of selling, but you need to be certain that you have the right product and that you have pinpointed the right market for it.

Worrying about Lack of Response

Your business may only get a few replies initially, but if these lead to high-price, high-margin sales, then it can be worth it.

SEE ALSO
Direct Marketing (p. 443)

Telemarketing

GETTING STARTED

Telemarketing is a marketing strategy that uses telecommunications and computers, or a manual contact system, to make sales calls and build leads for the sale of your product or service. This actionlist looks at the best ways to structure your own telemarketing operation and considers the use of an independent telemarketing agency.

FAQS

How do I set up an in-house telemarketing operation?

Office design can significantly affect performance, so if your budget allows, use a consultant experienced in call center design. The office should be arranged so that individuals can make or answer calls in private yet still feel part of a team. Good sound insulation is essential. Workstations should be comfortable, and equipment should include lightweight headsets and antiglare computer screens.

Think carefully about recognition and remuneration. In the case of outgoing calls, you could consider a results-based plan. For staff handling incoming calls, you could offer bonus payments for hitting cross-selling (selling customers different products within your range) or up-selling (selling customers a higher-priced version of a product they have bought previously) targets. You could run a pilot program to evaluate variable factors such as lists, people, markets, equipment, and management, before embarking on a full program.

How do I introduce a telemarketing program?

A telemarketing operation won't reach its full potential in isolation, and needs to work with other parts of the business—cooperation is the key to success. Everyone involved in marketing, sales, and production needs to understand the reasons for its introduction, what benefits it will bring, and the impact it will have. Sales people may feel threatened by telemarketing, so you must explain how telemarketing will complement their activities.

The first step is to do an overview of the business operations and then to identify the telemarketing objectives. Then carry out a cost-benefit analysis and draw up a detailed step-by-step plan for implementing and running the operation.

MAKING IT HAPPEN
Implement a Telemarketing Program ✔

First you need to target your telemarketing program. The targets should be identified for outgoing calls. You can do this by analyzing existing customer life cycles, looking at how recently a customer bought something, how frequently he or she buys, and of what value the purchases are. Prospects can also be identified by geographical location, from lapsed customers, and from bought lists of names. Incoming calls are usually generated through advertising, which must itself be targeted. Ideally, rank target groups by potential return on investment.

Second, you must test your telemarketing program. There are specific methods for calculating how big a sample to try, but for a campaign of any real size it is advisable to work on 500 to 1,000. After determining the sample size, you can work out the level of human and telephone resources needed for the trial period. The trial gives your business a chance to monitor results and modify the details of the program.

Third, you need to implement your program, depending, of course, on the test results. Budgets must be set for the program, and you will need to consider the investment required, operating costs, the cost-saving benefits of the program, and the extra revenue likely to be produced through additional orders.

Fourth, you should evaluate the program.

You will need to work out costs, and productivity levels in terms of rates of response and conversion (contacts into sales). Telemarketing should produce quantifiable results. With accurate figures, it is possible to establish future activity budgets and be able to compare the cost-effectiveness of telemarketing against alternative sales and marketing methods, or as a support to the existing methods.

Use Databases for Telemarketing

You will need to purchase or develop a database to store information on customers and prospects. Databases range from simple systems (like a computerized card index system) to relational databases that allow data to be analyzed in various ways. Consider what categories of information the database should hold, data entry methods (for example, directly during the customer's telephone call, or later by transfer from paper records), how the information will be accessed, how reports will be generated, and quality standards and procedures (to keep data accurate and up-to-date).

The ideal source of telephone contacts is your business's own database. However, you may wish to buy contact lists from a specialist agency. It is a good idea to shop around: list-provision is a competitive business. Similar lists may be available through several brokers at different prices. Be aware that lists go out of date very quickly. The quickest way to check the accuracy of a list is by phone.

Call Management

Call management affects the service provided to callers and the cost-effectiveness of your telemarketing operation. There are two main methods of managing incoming calls.

1. A Special Automatic Caller Distributor (ACD) transfers incoming calls to the first available person, or plays a message indicating that calls are being taken in the order in which they are received. ACDs also produce useful call-management information.

2. Call Sequencers answer calls with a message saying that the call will be taken as soon as possible, or giving the caller an option to leave voicemail for a return call.

ACDs and Call Sequencers can be located on the premises and are available from a number of companies. Additionally, caller-controlled systems let callers select the person or department with whom they wish to speak by pressing buttons on their telephone, or through voice recognition.

Recruitment and Training for the Telemarketing Operation

The performance of a telemarketing operation depends on the people on the phones. They must be skilled in creating rapport, overcoming objections, responding to criticisms, and directing conversations. Make an initial evaluation of candidates over the phone. Assess whether they come across as genuine, interested individuals who enjoy contact with people; whether they are clear communicators; and whether they listen well, taking in all the information they are given. You will need to consider whether candidates would work well in a demanding atmosphere without becoming discouraged. This is particularly important, as rejection is part of the job. Training is vital; appropriate courses for telemarketing managers and staff are widely available.

Leading and Motivating Staff in a Telemarketing Operation

All telemarketing teams need a leader, someone with excellent interpersonal skills and the ability to motivate staff. Team leaders should start and finish each day with upbeat team briefings. Before making calls, it is important that everyone knows his or her target for the day. At the end of the day, results can be discussed and the day should be closed on a positive note. The team leader should be located near the team, and team members should be encouraged to swap information and call attention to problems. Calls should be monitored unobtrusively to see who needs help in developing their style and skills.

Using Scripts in Telemarketing

Telemarketing staff need to direct every conversation in a planned and controlled yet natural way. You will need to develop a script or structured call plan covering all stages of the conversation, from greeting callers and answering questions to taking orders and signing off. Many telemarketing departments provide their agents with computer-based scripts. These often have built-in intelligence; for example, when an answer is filled in by an operator, the computer provides the most appropriate question to ask next. Information from callers can be typed directly onto a form onscreen.

Writing a multi-option telemarketing script is a specialized skill; a professional may be hired to do it. Staff should be allowed to spend time role-playing first. It is useful to tape trial conversations and check that they sound natural. Well-prepared scripts should control the message being delivered and ensure that customers receive correct information. They also ensure that the right information is collected and make it easier to analyze results. However, there can also be drawbacks; in the hands of the inexperienced, scripts can sound false and contrived, and they can diminish initiative in more experienced staff.

Using an Outside Telemarketing Agency

Some telemarketing agencies specialize in inbound telemarketing, others in outbound, but many operate in both fields. Make sure you know exactly what services *your* business requires and try to visit each agency in person, seeing how it works and talking to the staff. Check the agency's client list, and ask permission to contact several clients for references, and also find out about the agency's database system and what management information it can provide. Ask for a written response to your questions, with a detailed calculation of costs. Don't forget to confirm that the agency has the capacity to handle full implementation if the trial goes well.

Monitoring performance is essential, so arrange for regular reports on all key activities, including lost calls, response rates, and data quality. You could also make some test calls and check that everything is operating within specified timescales. If people are declining an offer, try to find out why—changing the script might help. Finally, reward outstanding results and thank staff personally to keep their motivation high.

WHAT TO AVOID

Not Researching Thoroughly

It's a good idea to look at the marketing procedures used by the business's competitors, especially telemarketing programs.

Not Getting an 800 Number

It is worth considering getting an 800 telephone number; 800 calls are charged to the business. They are available from several telecommunications companies and are popular in telemarketing.

SEE ALSO
Direct Marketing (p. 443)

Understanding the Uses of a Database

GETTING STARTED

Many small businesses use a personal computer (PC) for administrative tasks like accounts, word processing, and so on. Some form of database package is often run on the same machine. Databases are useful where a lot of information needs to be held in a standardized format. Most commonly, databases are used to keep a record of existing and potential customers, enabling orders to be processed and direct mail promotions to be carried out. Information is obtained (for example, on an order or inquiry form) and then keyed into the database. Basic databases might be mailing lists, categorized according to a variety of criteria (such as, location, past customer, or potential customer). At the other extreme, databases can be used to store large quantities of information for reference purposes.

FAQS

What is a database?

A database is in many ways like a traditional card index, but can contain a large number of records in a fraction of the space. A card index is only easily accessible in the order in which it was filed, but database records can be sorted into any order and individual records can be found, viewed, and amended in moments. Databases allow users to carry out statistical analysis to print out sets of records. The information can be carried on computers and transferred to other locations via the Internet.

Most databases have structures based on records and fields. A record is an entry within the database (for example, the details of a single inquiry or individual customer). A field is an item of information within a record (such as an inquiry date, a name, or a postcode). A database can be ordered by a particular field (for example, alphabetically, numerically, or chronologically), and sets of records can be extracted from the main database according to chosen criteria (for example, all current customers who have not placed an order for over three months).

What can a database do?

A database allows you to manipulate and exploit large sets of records far more efficiently than by using manual methods. A database can provide:

■ **searching and updating**—individual records can be found quickly, even when the details given are incomplete. They can then be updated as required.

■ **grouping and targeting**—sets of records can be selected according to different criteria. This is very useful for targeting groups with different products or different promotions.

■ **printing and mail merge**—lists, address labels, personalized letters, and many other customized documents can be generated for selected groups.

■ **statistical analysis**—data can be analyzed and presented in a form which aids management decision making, such as monthly sales figures, or customer profiles.

Other uses include keeping track of products sold or purchased; stock control systems linked into bar code readers; and databases designed to store and analyze the data from questionnaires. Some databases can be used to make the data available to an Internet or intranet Web site.

MAKING IT HAPPEN
Decide What You Need from a Database

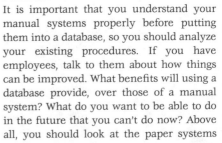

It is important that you understand your manual systems properly before putting them into a database, so you should analyze your existing procedures. If you have employees, talk to them about how things can be improved. What benefits will using a database provide, over those of a manual system? What do you want to be able to do in the future that you can't do now? Above all, you should look at the paper systems and procedures that will be required to keep the database up to date. You might find that you will need to devote more staff time to data processing than before, though there should be time or cost savings in being able to access and use the data more rapidly.

When the costs of running the system have been evaluated, you should make sure that the benefits of acquiring a database are sufficient. How often will mailshots be done? How many inquiries will be processed daily? How often will reports be required? You should have very specific ideas of the benefits which a database will bring to your business before even starting to look at the technical requirements. It's important to concentrate on the benefits rather than features. If the business runs a network of computers, think about whether the database is a resource that several people may want to share.

Construct a Database System

There are a number of essential steps that you will have to take when constructing a database system, all of which will have to be taken into account when working out how long it will be before the business starts to reap the benefits.

Planning and Resourcing

Computerizing your business's records can fundamentally change work procedures. It is important to plan for the introduction of the new system. Transferring data into a database is time consuming if it is being converted from a paper-based system, so maybe you could consider using temporary staff for the task. Computerized and paper systems could be run in parallel until it is certain that the new system is reliable and everyone is using it correctly.

Designing Input Systems and Screens

It is important to decide exactly what data needs to be stored in the database records, as there is a great temptation to keep more than will be needed. Just remember that the more data you store, the more that has to be

gathered, inputted, and maintained—and there are real costs attached. You should think carefully about what information you really need, and what you will use it for. Input screens should show information in a logical and readable fashion, and the layout should match any paper forms used for data collection.

Data Entry and Retrieval

Accurate and consistent data input is vital. Standards for data entry should be drawn up before anyone starts to input information—for instance, you need to decide how the system will handle business names (the standard solution is to record a firm's name as it appears on its letterhead). It is also advisable to have consistent rules on spacing between letters and words (otherwise W H Smith could be W. H. Smith, WH Smith or W.H.Smith) —they mean the same to a person, but to a computer they are very different. If a database was searched for an exact match, the entry may be missed if the data entry person was inconsistent (though some databases offer an option to search for the closest matching entry, which should find the record). If codes are to be used to categorize records, it is important to standardize the coding and notify data entry staff in advance. It is usually possible to set the system to reject entries that do not match valid code lists.

Administration

You should have systems in place for keeping data up to date, which may simply involve giving someone responsibility for making changes to the database as they are required. Addresses and contact names should be checked on a regular basis to ensure they are accurate, and defunct records should be deleted regularly so that the system only contains useful information. Employees should be fully trained in the use of the system, and you must make sure that working conditions comply with OSHA regulations. It is also essential to make regular backup copies of data in case the system breaks down. In addition, procedures should be in place to ensure that the only people to access the data are authorized to do so—particularly if information is held on individuals. The Federal Trade Commission offers information on privacy initiatives on its Web site (the address is given below).

✘ WHAT TO AVOID
Introducing a Database without Weighing Up the Costs and Benefits

The business must be committed to computerizing the records system and budget accordingly, as new IT systems often involve considerable expense. Computerization should be seen as an investment which allows the business to do more with the information. The necessary staffing and administrative backup must be in place to ensure the database works properly: there is no point introducing a system which isn't really going to provide major benefits to the business.

Introducing a Database System Before It Is Ready

Using a database before it's fully ready can cause many problems, so be sure to plan carefully before implementing a database system to replace any of your manual systems. Also make sure that you have a period when both systems run alongside each other so that you can iron out any problems with the database before abandoning your old system altogether.

SEE ALSO
Direct Marketing (p. 443)

Raising Awareness of Your Brand

GETTING STARTED

Brand awareness is an important factor in customer purchasing decisions. Brand values relate to many areas, from product attributes to less tangible aspects of a company's reputation. By identifying the key values of your brand you can establish how your products, your services, and your company are perceived by different types of customer.

FAQS

Can a small company use branding?

Absolutely. You have to understand your own brand, since you will have a brand or corporate image in your market whether you like it or not! Smaller companies increasingly compete with large, well-known brands—sometimes globally—so the aim of branding is to differentiate your company or product and to convey its unique attributes.

How important are brand values?

Branding is frequently perceived as a consumer marketing discipline. However, industry experience indicates that business-to-business purchasing is a complex process influenced by intangible perceptions as much as by hard facts on product performance.

MAKING IT HAPPEN

Identify the Most Important Elements of a Brand

The key attributes of a business brand may include:

- fitness for purpose—is it the best at what it does?
- value for money—if not offered at always the lowest price, does it represent a good deal compared to the competition, even if it isn't better?
- quality—is it simply better built or better managed?
- extendability—does the brand work in many related markets?
- company reliability—does the brand come from a good "stable?"
- proven products—is the brand associated with established successes?

- investment in product development—is innovation significant?

Find Out What Is Important to Your Customers

Although these brand values can be applied to business products in general terms, it's vital to understand how individual customers rank the values. This can be determined in several ways, described below.

Talk to Customers

This is the simplest way to find out what they value, but take care not to talk exclusively about the physical benefits of a product. There will almost certainly be aspects of service that are as important. You should also ask "open" questions about the competition, for example:

- Who else have you looked at?
- What do you think of them?
- What is their biggest strength or weakness?
- What do other people think of them?

Conduct Customer Surveys

To find out what your customers consider important, conduct a survey; if your budget runs to it, this should be done through a market research company so that respondents feel the survey is independent. It should ask respondents how they rank the different brand values and how they believe your company and a number of competitors compare across these values.

Run a Focus Group

A focus group can be used to cover the same ground as the customer survey, but it enables you to cover the subject in greater depth and to raise issues that you may not anticipate or that would normally be outside the scope of a survey. Focus groups are ideal for identifying branding issues that concern customers, assessing customer reactions to potential changes, or identifying any problems customers are experiencing.

Review Industry Trends

Industry associations and publishers produce regular surveys into buying behavior in their industry sector. These surveys can highlight issues that concern the whole market.

Find Out about Customer Purchasing Requirements

An increasing number of business customers use formal criteria to evaluate potential suppliers and monitor their performance. These purchasing criteria indicate the factors that your customers believe are important and can help to identify the key messages you should include in your own brand communications.

Communicate through All Channels

Advertising and marketing communications are the most important media for raising awareness. However, there are several other direct and indirect channels, including:

- products—the design and brand symbolism can convey significant brand values
- services—the way you deal with customers can demonstrate your commitment to their needs
- packaging—can carry messages regarding your brand
- distribution facilities—can give an impression of your approach and values
- Web sites—must be consistent with your key brand values
- customer service facilities—must deliver the promise of the brand

Assess Your Product Branding

Do your products communicate your key brand values? The most important values are listed above but include every aspect of your company that your customer may experience.

If customer research shows that you are perceived as poor in any of these areas, or, if customers are not aware of your strengths, you must look closely at your product development program. Also review your customer communications to see how customers build their image of your brand.

Brand Your Services

Service capability can also help to differentiate a company.

Many companies have underestimated the importance of service to their customers and have therefore not adequately communicated their service capabilities. Raising awareness of service capability is therefore an important aspect of brand communication. You can increase awareness through product advertising, product literature, direct marketing, and product public relations, as well as through service communications.

Communicate Brand Values through Packaging

Packaging raises awareness of brand values by the way in which it reflects the corporate identity. The right packaging can visually support your brand through the use of your logo, slogans, promises, and company values.

Don't Forget to Include Your Branding Distribution Facilities

Your distribution facilities can affect awareness of your brand. Again, if your budget allows, vehicles, uniforms, and premises should carry the same logo and key messages as other mediums of communication.

Distribution is an area that is frequently overlooked in branding programs, but it can make an important contribution to customer perceptions of your company. For example, the cleanliness of a delivery van shows a level of professionalism.

Build Brand Values through Your Web Site

An effective e-commerce Web site is one in which the various technical and design components all work together to generate customer interest, build trust, communicate product value, and support convenient profitable transactions. Even if you don't sell directly from your Web site, the key is that your customer must feel they have gained something from the visit that exceeds the "cost" (even if only in time) of visiting.

Brand through Customer Service Facilities

Your customer service facilities have a major impact on the way your customers perceive your company. Customer contact takes place both before and after a sale, and these contacts can prove critical in shaping customer attitudes. When your customer service team handles inquiries, orders, or complaints effectively, it creates awareness of positive brand values.

Monitor Levels of Brand Awareness

Customer perceptions change over a period of time. Continuous research should be carried out to monitor customer attitudes. This type of research is known as tracking research, and it helps to measure the effectiveness of brand communications programs.

✘ WHAT TO AVOID

Failing to Monitor Customer Perceptions

Regular research is critical. You must know how you are perceived by your customers so that you can plan the way your brand is represented in the future.

Overlooking Individual Customer Preferences

Industry research may give you a broad view of the brand values that are important to customers. However, it's more important to understand how individual customers—particularly your most important customers—rank individual values. This can be achieved only by continuous detailed research into individual customer needs.

Ignoring Important Communication Channels

Brand values are communicated through many different channels, not just advertising and marketing media. Customers' attitudes and perceptions are shaped by packaging, customer service, distribution, and products as well as by other factors. Make sure every aspect of your business reflects the brand values that are important to your customers.

SEE ALSO

Planning a Cost-effective Direct Marketing Campaign (p. 250)
Planning an Advertising Campaign (p. 268)
Producing Press Material (p. 261)

Planning a Cost-effective Direct Marketing Campaign

GETTING STARTED

Direct marketing works most effectively when it is aimed at a precise audience that cannot be easily reached by any other medium. A campaign should be carefully planned in accordance with the target market and the product or service concerned. Short-term results can be measured accurately and directly by the level of response, so the effectiveness of a campaign can be assessed quickly. There are, however, many different factors that can affect the outcome, such as product price or the quality of the campaign material. As with any direct approach, it is essential to make it as easy as possible for customers to respond.

FAQS

Is direct marketing the same as direct mail?

No. Direct marketing (DM) is any marketing activity that depends on a direct and measurable response. Conventional advertising can be "direct," as can telephone, fax, e-mail and, of course, the Internet. Direct mail is direct marketing communication sent by post and therefore often has a poor reputation because of the amount of unsolicited mail that people regularly receive.

Can direct marketing be used to sell products?

There are many situations in which you can use direct marketing to build direct sales. You may not have a sales force or a retail network, so customers can only buy direct from you. If you want to sell to niche markets, or if your customers are widely spread or even global, direct marketing may be the only cost-effective way of reaching them. If you decide to sell direct, you must insure that the products themselves are suitable for selling through direct marketing—that is, that they do not have to be demonstrated, or inspected by the customer.

How does direct marketing build relationships with customers?

The stronger your relationship with your customers, the more opportunities you have to influence the future direction and success of your business. If your company depends on a few key customers for most of its business, you can use direct marketing to improve customer loyalty by building long-term relationships with them. You may also need to use it if your customers want to rationalize the number of suppliers, and you want to remain on the approved list.

Is direct marketing only effective for reaching a small audience?

There are numerous examples of successful large-scale mailings. However, the key to direct marketing success is reaching the right people in a cost-effective way. Large-scale mailings based on poorly researched mailing lists may yield results, but there will also be a high level of wastage. The more precise your mailing, the more likely you are to succeed.

MAKING IT HAPPEN

The key stages of a direct marketing campaign are described below.

Set Campaign Objectives

Direct marketing objectives can be initially expressed in general terms.

- Encouraging prospects to buy directly in response to a direct marketing campaign.
- Generating leads for the sales force or retail network.
- Supporting sales force activity.
- Improving the effectiveness of other forms of communication.
- Raising awareness of a company, product, or service among clearly identified customers and prospects.

- Maintaining effective contact with customers and prospects.
- Building relationships with customers and prospects.

However, these general objectives should be translated into precise, measurable objectives, for example:

- Raising awareness of your product range among 35% of technical directors in the mechanical engineering sector.
- Insuring that purchasing managers of your ten top corporate customers are contacted at least once every two weeks.
- Increasing direct sales of supplies by 15%.

Define the Target Market

Do you want to reach all customers and prospects, or are you targeting specific groups? Direct marketing is a precise medium, so your campaign could be aimed at just a few key decision makers or thousands of potential users. To plan your direct marketing campaign, you should ask questions such as:

- Who buys your type of product?
- Who influences the purchasing decision?
- How many prospective customers (prospects) do you want to reach with the direct marketing campaign?
- How many prospects can you normally convert to customers, and how long does it take?
- How do they currently get information about your products?
- Is direct marketing the best (or only) way of reaching the target audience?

The more information you have about your target audience, the more precise you can make your campaign. In an ideal world, direct marketing would allow you to communicate one to one with every prospect, but, in practical terms, you are more likely to be communicating with groups that share certain characteristics. For example, you could reasonably expect that "all fleet managers in the northeast of California managing more than thirty vehicles" would have similar needs in respect to their day to day job.

Plan Campaign Timing

A direct marketing campaign can run at any time, so you do not have to consider advertisement publication dates. However, timing may be dictated by other factors—lead times for producing mailing material, seasonal purchasing patterns, product availability, or tender dates. These are some of the factors to consider in planning the timing of your campaign:

- When is your customer likely to be making the buying decision?
- How long is the selling or buying process? How many stages are involved? Who is involved?
- Does your direct marketing campaign have to tie-in with the timing of any other marketing activity, such as an exhibition, advertising campaign, or sales force visit?
- If you are launching a new product, when will the product be available?
- How long will it take to produce the material that is to be mailed?
- When will you be able to follow up the campaign?
- What will you do if you get fewer responses than you need *or* more than you can handle?

Decide On Your Contact Strategy

A single mailing, telephone call or direct response advertisement may produce results, but a series of appropriate contacts will have greater impact and insure you meet your objectives. There are several benefits from repeated contracts:

- raising levels of awareness with each contact;
- educating potential clients about your product/service;
- following up those who have not responded;
- moving individual respondents further along the decision making process;
- maintaining contact during extended decision making processes.

There is no hard-and-fast rule about the frequency of individual campaigns; a company trying to get a prospect to make a decision may make contact several times a week, while a company aiming to maintain long-term customer loyalty may need to contact customers only monthly or quarterly.

Develop a Response Mechanism

Action is a vital ingredient of any direct marketing campaign, and it is essential that you make it easy for your prospects to respond. First, decide if your prospects are to place an order, request a sales visit, or ask for further information. Then decide which of the five basic types of response mechanism is the most appropriate: mail, telephone, fax, e-mail, or Web site address.

Keep Track of the Campaign

You must be prepared to keep records of every aspect of your campaign. You will have to set up the systems to capture data before your campaign (or test) campaign starts. Aim to know at the very least:

- what was sent (the offer, the pack/letter, and so on) and to whom (the lists used and reason for selection)
- the anticipated response (for example, percentage initial response and percentage purchase)
- the actual response
- the costs and the return—in other words, did your campaign make a profit?

Test the Campaign

Part of the flexibility of direct marketing is that you can test your approach before committing resources to the full campaign. There are several variables that can be tested:

- the target audience—the most important element
- the offer—what exactly you are offering for sale (including any incentive)
- the creative approach—the look and feel of the communications
- the response mechanism—how easy it is to respond, for example, using an 800 number or Business Reply
- frequency and timing—including the way you follow up inquiries

The test campaign can be carried out in a number of ways:

- on a sample of the target market;
- in a defined sales or geographical territory;
- in a particular sector of the target market.

The most effective test campaign is the one that achieves the highest response levels and committed DM organizations test continuously to drive down their costs and drive up response rates. Indeed, every campaign should be considered a "test" to improve on previous campaigns. Each best-performing campaign then becomes the "control" against which others can be evaluated.

Plan Split Campaigns

Testing your campaign may reveal that different approaches work more effectively in different market sectors. If budget allows, you can develop a series of campaigns that vary the offer, the creative approach, frequency, timing, or other factors, but insure you keep track of these variables so that you can use the best-performing campaign format next time.

Set Target Response Levels

In the long term, a campaign may increase awareness, improve customer relations, or cut the cost of sales. However, the simplest and most immediate measure of a direct marketing campaign is the response level it generates. In setting your target response levels, you should aim for a realistic figure that is within budget. Note that:

- response levels as low as 1 or 2% are regarded as the industry norm for large companies sending mail to "cold" lists ;
- response rates in the region of 5% are therefore regarded as high;
- response rates in the region of 10–20% have been reported by companies who have integrated other forms of marketing communications;
- far higher response rates can be experienced by specialist companies communicating vital information to a very committed list of supporters.

Many different factors can affect the level of response, including price, quality of the mailing list, the promotional offer, and quality of copy and design. A test is very often the only way to set an initial target response rate for future campaigns.

✗ WHAT TO AVOID
Using DM Unnecessarily

While the principles of direct marketing can help any company in its communications and selling, sometimes direct *mail* is used when the existing channels are preferable. Customers who are used to a personal visit and face-to-face negotiations may feel aggrieved if you try and deal with them at a distance.

Failing to Set Measurable Targets

The results of a direct marketing campaign can be measured precisely by the number of responses. This makes it a particularly accountable medium. It is therefore important to set realistic, measurable objectives. If your target is to generate leads from 2% of the target audience, this will determine how many people you mail, the type of offer you make, and the response mechanism you provide. It will also tell you very quickly if your budget balances—how many of those leads need to convert into customers to cover your costs?

Poor Audience Selection

With direct marketing you can communicate with a single prospect or with 50,000. However, there may be more cost-effective ways of communicating with 50,000 prospects. Direct marketing works most effectively when it is aimed at a precise audience that cannot be easily reached by any other medium and, crucially, when you want a response. For example, you may find there is a specialist magazine or newsletter that precisely covers your target market.

No Integration with Other Communications

If your marketing budget is split between different communications activities such as advertising, sales promotion, and press and public relations, it is essential that each activity works as effectively as possible. You can use direct marketing in conjunction with other methods of communication. If you place advertisements in publications that only reach a general audience, you can reinforce the advertisements with personalized communications to selected prospects. If your advertisements include a response mechanism, keeping to direct marketing principles will insure effective follow-up. You can also tailor your product and corporate literature to the information needs of different market sectors by including direct marketing material.

SEE ALSO
Raising Awareness of Your Brand (p. 247)

Creating Impressive Direct Mail Material

GETTING STARTED

When you are marketing your product or service, you may find you need an effective and precise marketing tool that you can personalize in order to more accurately reflect the needs of customers and prospective customers. If so, direct mail may be what you need. It can be eye-catching and creative, and allows you to include different types of enclosure to provide additional details on the product or service being offered.

Another benefit of direct mail is that its easy to measure its results precisely, so that you can assess how you've done with a particular campaign or approach. As part of this process, you need to include an easy response mechanism for the customer, such as a business reply envelope, or contact details such as an e-mail address, so that your customers can give you feedback.

FAQS

Don't customers just throw direct mail in the bin?

No, but attitudes vary enormously. According to research (DMIS Sector Intelligence Surveys and DMIS Business to Business Direct Mail Trends Survey 2000) consumers opened and read over 80% of direct mail items relating to travel, but only 16% of those about home insurance. Business managers opened more than 70% of their direct mail but, on average, filed only 13%.

Is it possible to create effective direct mail?

Like any other marketing activity, work must be directed towards an objective. The more information you have, the more focused the work. Direct mail is a very precise medium, so it is possible to create highly customized and attractive mailings that meet the information needs of your chosen prospective customers (prospects).

How far can personalization go in direct mail?

Of course, mailings to a small number of customers can easily be personalized, and should be. Provided you have the budget, larger mailings can be personalized down to individual level (one-to-one marketing). As an example, you could write individual letters to each of your prospects, or include an incentive tailored to their individual preferences. Practical financial constraints usually prevent this degree of personalization, so most companies concentrate on limited customization, addressing specific sector concerns or tailoring special offers to different types of business.

Can the quality of direct mail creative work be measured?

Direct mail is an extremely accountable medium, and the results can be measured precisely, making it possible to judge whether or not a particular creative approach has worked. However, creative work is only one of the factors that influence campaign success, so many companies test different creative approaches to try to identify how they affect results. Remember, though, that the offer's recipient is more important than the presentation of the offer itself, so targeting should be your priority.

MAKING IT HAPPEN
Create Good Quality Mailing Material

Direct mail is the most precise marketing medium, but campaigns will be effective only if they combine precise targeting with good creative work.

In theory anything can be sent by post, but most mailings consist primarily of printed material—letters, leaflets, and brochures. Three-dimensional objects can be mailed and can stimulate interest, but they must be relevant and cost-effective. A striking envelope design can also add impact to a mailing.

Use Direct Mail Letters Effectively

Letters are a universal communication medium and an integral element of any direct mail campaign. They can be used on their own as a personalized form of communication, and can also be used to support and personalize other standard mailing items. Letters can be customized easily and cost-effectively to meet different sector marketing requirements.

Personalize Letters

Personalized one-to-one mailings are an ideal form of communication for companies with detailed information on their prospects. The letter should reflect the individual's main interests and concerns, and the offer can be tailored to the individual prospect. Subsequent mailings can build an individual relationship with the prospect.

The key features of this type of letter are:

- it is personalized to the individual reader;
- it offers direct and valuable benefits;
- it builds future relationships with the customer by promising regular offers.

Letters can also be customized by market sector, offering specific benefits to groups of customers.

Use Letters to Support Other Mailing Material

Direct mail letters can also be used to accompany other material—a product brochure, management guide, or even an invoice, for example. The letter can customize the mailing by including information specific to the individual prospect or market sector, or by making a further offer to the prospect.

Include Enclosures

Enclosures can include:

- catalogs
- sales leaflets or brochures
- price lists
- management reports or surveys
- information on special offers
- samples, free gifts, or incentives

There are a number of criteria for selecting enclosures:

- they should be relevant to the prospect's needs;
- they should not make the mailing impractical or costly because of size or weight;
- they should improve response, size of order, or frequency of order—if they do not they are an unnecessary cost.

Treat Envelopes Creatively

Postal authorities specify a number of preferred envelope sizes which help them to handle mail more efficiently. Companies that wish to use specific postal response services must use the preferred layouts indicated in the authority's design specification. However, using non-standard envelope sizes can add greater impact to a mailing. Envelopes can be designed in a number of ways to achieve greater impact:

- they can include advertising messages ;
- addresses can be handwritten to add a personal touch ;
- they can incorporate corporate design elements such as logos or company colors.

But be aware of occasions when a clearly, but wrongly identified envelope may depress response, such as if the item looks like a routine statement.

Create Three-dimensional Enclosures

Three-dimensional enclosures can add impact and novelty value to a mailing. They can be used to send product samples by mail, to send promotional items, or to improve response by creating interest. However, it is important that they be relevant to the prospect's needs, that they do not make the mailing too expensive, and that they do not contravene mail regulations.

Include a Response Mechanism

If your mailing is designed to stimulate action, it should include an easy-to-use response mechanism such as a business reply card or envelope, or contact details such as a toll-free telephone number, e-mail address, or Web site address.

Use Professional Creative and Production Services

Quality and impact are essential to the success of a direct mail campaign. Creating an effective direct mail item requires professional skills, and is best handled by suitably experienced people. Although many of the direct mail processes are straightforward, your company may not have the skills or resources to achieve the best possible results. External specialists provide a range of direct mail services, including copywriting and design, printing letters, and producing three-dimensional enclosures.

Specialists include:

- direct mail agencies
- advertising agencies
- marketing communication consultancies
- design consultancies
- creative consultancies
- printers

However, there may be occasions when you decide to create simple direct mail items yourself.

Write Persuasive Copy

Use a powerful headline to get the attention of the reader. Words such as "free," "new," and "improved" attract attention, while price benefits such as "sale" and "reduced" are also useful. Keep your writing style simple, with short sentences and paragraphs; in longer mailing items, use headings and subheadings to make sure that the reader picks up key messages without having to read the complete text. Tell your prospects what they need to know in order to make a decision about your product or service. Your message should deal with your customers' most important concerns and requirements. Describe benefits to the prospect, not features of the product: for example, a power drill that features extremely high operating speeds may be technically interesting, but the benefits to a builder are greater productivity and the opportunity to finish a job quickly. Offer the prospect a clear, powerful proposition. Your copy should encourage the prospect to take action—contact the company for more information, ask for a demonstration,

or order immediately to qualify for a promotional offer. Describe your biggest benefit first, then remember that everything that follows should be designed to make the potential customer move on to the next stage.

Create a Well Designed Layout

Design quality is also important in getting a message to prospects clearly and effectively.

- Keep the layout simple to insure immediate comprehension.
- Use photographs, diagrams, or illustrations if they help to clarify a point or create impact.
- Use the most legible type faces and sizes to make text easy to read.
- Use bold headings or a larger type size for the headline or to emphasize important statements.

WHAT TO AVOID

Using Mailing Unnecessarily

When customers already know your company and do business with you, it can be off putting for them to be treated as "prospects." Always check that your mailing is an effective means of communicating.

Producing Standard Mailing Material

Direct mail is a precise medium. You can use that precision to talk to specific customer groups or individual prospects with tailored messages and offers. Too many mailings fail to address prospects' individual needs and concerns. Research will help you to identify the key messages for different prospects, and to build them into your mailing.

Failing to Plan

All mailing activity must be planned with sufficient time and resources. Rushing a mailing can lead to embarrassing and costly mistakes. Not anticipating response can lead to disappointed customers.

Failing to Measure

Direct mail campaigns are measured on their results: they should deliver inquiries or sales. If they do not deliver results, even the most creative campaigns should be considered failures. Make sure that you set realistic targets for your campaign. If you do not reach the targets, change the targeting, the offer, the format, or timing until you find one that delivers the results you want.

Making Mailings Too Complex

Some mailings contain so much material they can be daunting to deal with, so the prospect may lose interest.

SEE ALSO
Improving the Response to Direct Mail (p. 258)
Writing a Sales Letter (p. 234)

Improving the Response to Direct Mail

GETTING STARTED

The simplest and most immediate measure of a direct marketing campaign is the response level it achieves. Many different factors can affect response rates; it is important to test the variables before committing all your resources to a particular approach, and you should aim for a realistic figure that is within your budget.

Define your target market precisely. The more precisely you target, the better your response rates will be. Make it easy for your prospects to respond, and test your approach before committing resources to the full campaign.

FAQS

Why are direct mail responses so low?

The figures quoted are industry averages. They can vary upward or downward depending on the industry and the type of mailing. Remember that a small percentage of a mass mailing can provide you with a reasonable level of new prospects. To put the response rates into perspective, compare the response and the cost of response with an equivalent amount of spending on advertising.

Should direct mailing always be tested?

If it is practical, test direct mail on a small proportion of the market. Although direct mail is a precise medium, testing can refine the process even further. With so many variables in a mailing campaign, you can test different elements individually and plan your full campaign on the basis of the best response rate.

Should direct mail effectiveness be measured by response or by sales?

The ultimate test of any marketing campaign is an increase in profitable sales. However, direct mail, on its own, cannot deliver sales. Sales depend on pricing, the quality of your products, sales representatives, customer service, competitive activity, and many other factors. Direct mail should be given a specific role and measured by how it fulfills that role.

MAKING IT HAPPEN
Set Target Response Levels

- Response levels as low as 1 or 2% are regarded as the industry norm.

- Response rates in the region of 5% are regarded as high.
- Response rates in the region of 10–20% have been reported by companies who have integrated other forms of marketing communications.

Define Your Target Market Precisely

Do you want to reach all customers and prospects, or are you targeting specific groups? Direct marketing is a precise medium, so your campaign could be aimed at one key decision maker or thousands of potential users. The more precisely you target, the better your response rates will be.

Integrate the Campaign with Other Marketing Activities

Direct marketing campaigns can run at any time. However, performance can be improved by integrating the campaign with other marketing activities such as an exhibition, advertising campaigns, or sales force calls. With integrated campaigns, overall awareness levels among customers and prospects will be much higher. Your direct marketing offer will have a much higher chance of success.

Choose the Right Campaign Frequency

A mass mailing, telephone call, or direct response advertisement may produce results, but a series of quality contacts will have greater impact and insure you meet your response targets. Multiple direct marketing activities provide a number of benefits:

- they raise levels of awareness with each contact;
- they follow up contacts who have not responded;
- they move individual respondents further along the decision making process.

Make It Easy for Prospects to Respond

If you want to improve response rates, it is essential that you make it easy for your prospects to respond. Web site or e-mail addresses, postage-paid envelopes, and 800 numbers provide easy-to-use response mechanisms that can boost response. You should monitor the response levels from different sources to see which is the most effective.

Test Your Campaign

To guarantee the success of your campaign, you should test your approach before committing resources to the full campaign. There are a number of variables that can be tested:

- the offer
- the creative approach
- the target audience
- the response mechanism
- frequency and timing
- integration with other communications programs

Use Split Campaigns

If budget allows, you can develop a series of campaigns that vary by offer, creative approach, response mechanism, frequency, and timing.

Improve Your Mailing Lists

Getting the mailing list right is vital. Basic mailing lists simply include names, addresses, job titles, and telephone numbers of customers and prospects. The basic list can be refined by adding information about buying patterns, lifestyle, and many other factors—providing a comprehensive picture of customers and prospects.

Check All Internal Sources of Information

Your customer records are probably your most valuable asset, as they invariably generate the highest response rates when they are mailed with relevant information. The most important sources are:

- customer records
- customer correspondence, including records of complaints
- warranty records
- service records
- sales prospect files
- sales force reports
- records of lapsed customers
  Simple segmentation of your internal lists might give you categories such as:
- customers who have bought in the last six months
- lapsed customers
- customers who spend over $X a year

Add External Sources of Information

Your internal lists are likely to yield high response rates. However, if you are moving into new market sectors, internal lists may not provide the information you need. External lists are available from a number of different sources, including list brokers, magazine publishers, directory publishers, trade associations or professional institutes, commercial organizations, and retailers. To achieve a high response rate, check how closely the list matches your customer profile.

Commission a Special List

Standard lists may not give you the degree of match you need. The successful preparation of a tailored list is directly related to the quality of the brief, and you should provide the supplier with a detailed description of your target audience.

Keep Refining Your Lists

- Make sure that the list is kept up to date with new customer and prospect data.
- Include coupons and other reply mechanisms with every form of communication, and add the responses to your lists.
- Encourage the sales force to provide up-to-date customer and prospect information.
- Maintain an active search program in appropriate Web sites, magazines, and

newspapers to identify new prospects for your list.

Check the Accuracy of Lists

To improve response and reduce waste in your mailing campaigns, it is important that your lists are regularly checked for accuracy. The two main problems are:

- duplication, where the same individual appears several times on the same list, possibly in different guises, for example as Ron Smith, R. T. Smith, and Mr. Smith;
- out-of-date information, where the original recipient has moved, or, for business mailings, changed jobs.

Use Personalized Letters

Personalized one-to-one mailings are an ideal form of communication for companies with detailed information about their prospects.

If the database or mailing list holds complete names and other information, direct mail letters can be personalized in a number of ways, such as including the name in the address and greeting and throughout the text

Use Telemarketing

Direct mail response levels can increase significantly when telemarketing is used. It offers a range of benefits:

- selective: contact can be initiated and maintained with all or selected groups of customers and prospects;
- precise: the calls can be targeted;

- flexible: the offer and the message can be varied;
- fast: calls can be made immediately;
- responsive: because telemarketing is interactive, it encourages response;
- measurable: the effectiveness of a telemarketing campaign can be measured precisely.

WHAT TO AVOID

Setting Unrealistic Response Rates

Direct mail is a precise medium. However, it is easy to set unrealistic targets for response. Figures such as 5% or 6% would be seen as extremely high in many industries.

Failing to Integrate Direct Mail with Other Marketing Activities

Direct mail works most effectively when it is part of an integrated marketing campaign. Advertising can be used to raise the company profile; direct mail would be used to reach specific prospects with a targeted offer, and telemarketing could be used to back up the mailing with follow-up calls.

Poor Mailing Lists

Good response rates depend on high quality mailing lists. If your lists contain duplicate addresses, out-of-date information, or incorrect data, response will be poor.

SEE ALSO

Creating Impressive Direct Mail Material (p. 254)
Writing a Sales Letter (p. 234)

Producing Press Material

GETTING STARTED

Newspaper, television, trade press, and radio journalists are always looking for stories. Supply information in the form of press releases, feature articles, or advertorials—in the right format and to the right person—and you can gain great publicity for your organization.

FAQS

Will the press be interested in us?

Journalists are always looking for stories and they work under great pressure, so a well-written, informative, and current press release is always welcome. They won't, however, be interested in you unless you have a story to tell. Like customers, editors will want to know what makes your company different from others. Local media will be interested in how you fit in with the community; and the trade press will be more interested in new products and ideas.

It is worth developing a relationship with editors in order to understand how you can help them. By concentrating on the kind of news and story they want you can save yourself time and increase the chances of your story being published.

Should we produce our own press material or use the services of an external agency?

An external agency can take a more objective view of your press material and may have experience of writing for the publications on your distribution list. That means they can tailor material for individual publications and make sure that it is printed. They may, however, lack product knowledge and require considerable training to achieve the right results. If your company produces complex technical products, you may split the task, keeping technical press releases in-house, and using an external agency to produce company or business material.

Can we use the same press release for all the publications on our distribution list?

You can issue a single release, but you will increase the chances of getting into print if you tailor information to the needs of individual publications. By talking to journalist, reading previous issues, and studying publishers' readership data, you can identify the type of material that is likely to be printed or broadcast.

What should we do if an editor does not publish the information in a press release?

There could be a number of reasons for nonpublication that are outside your control, such as lack of space, the release missing the copy date, or another story coinciding with your release. Your story may appear in the next issue, if space allows. However, the editor may have decided that your information was wrong for the publication or not newsworthy. A quick call to the editor may help you find out the reason. If your material was unsuitable, you may be able to provide something more relevant for future issues.

MAKING IT HAPPEN
Plan Your Press Release

A press release is a piece of information distributed to newspaper, television, or radio journalists which is published or broadcast as a piece of news. It can cover a variety of topics, including:

- information on new products or services
- information on developments in a company
- news of new appointments or promotions

An effective press release should contain news rather than thinly disguised advertising, and it should reflect readers' interests.

The release may be used without modification if it is newsworthy, timely, and if space permits. The press release may be cut to fit available space without any further reference to you. In some cases, a journalist or editor may contact you for further information and rewrite the item in the style of the publication. It is often a good idea to provide additional background information to help journalists in this task. Information such as product specifications, contact details, or alternative photographs are useful. Some companies offer such information specifically for journalists on a section of their Web site. Sometimes the information may not be used, because it is not newsworthy or not relevant to the readership. Alternatively, although the main press release may not be used, an accompanying photograph may be used with a caption.

Produce Your Press Release

The following guidelines will help you produce an effective press release:

- Press releases should be typed double-spaced.
- The source of the release should be clearly identified.
- A contact name for further information should be provided.
- Any limitations on use or timing of publication should be clearly highlighted, for example, "not for publication before..."
- The most important information should be included in the early paragraphs. If an editor is short of space, the press release will be cut as simply and quickly as possible, probably from the bottom upward.
- Quotes are useful and are frequently used by editors.
- Photographs or diagrams add value to the release and may help to insure publication.
- The style of writing, even the length of sentences and paragraphs, should match the targeted publication as far as possible.

Distribute Your Press Release

Press releases can be delivered by hand or by mail, depending on quantity. They can also be sent by e-mail or placed on a Web site so that they can be picked up by visiting journalists. Wherever possible, they should be sent to a named individual. Information on editorial contacts, with details of their special interests, is available in publications

like *Public Relations Quarterly*, which is updated regularly. If you do not want the information published before a certain date for reasons of commercial security, include an embargo—"not for publication before. . .."

Time Your Press Release

Check the publication dates of magazines or newspapers on your distribution list. This information is available in publications such as *Public Relations Quarterly*. An editorial copy date will be indicated. Make sure that your release reaches the editor by that date at the latest.

Plan Feature Articles

A feature article, which could be 500–2,000 words in length, is published in a magazine and credited to an organization. The article may be on technical or business developments in an industry, or on other subjects that provide practical or topical information for readers. The article may form part of an industry survey. This type of feature provides an opportunity for organizations to demonstrate their expertise and professionalism.

Feature articles can cover a variety of topics, including surveys of new industry or technical developments, practical "how to" articles, or reviews of research projects.

If it is reasonably well written, the article may be used without modification; it will be published when space permits, or may be used as part of a special survey. In some cases, a journalist or editor may contact you for further information and rewrite the item in the style of the publication.

Produce Feature Articles

An effective feature article should reflect readers' interests and contain information that is useful to them. It should also bring them up to date with recent developments.

The following guidelines should help you prepare a feature article.

- Feature articles should be typed double-spaced.
- Length should be discussed with the editor, but is likely to be between 500 and 2,000 words, with 1,000 words as the average.

- A contact name for further information should be provided.
- Photographs or diagrams, with a caption for every item, add value to the article.

Distribute Feature Articles

Feature articles should only be sent to one publication at a time, although they can be modified for use in other markets. Wherever possible, they should be sent to a named individual. In some cases, the initiative may come from the publication and the editor will provide you with details of requirements.

Time Feature Articles

Check the publication dates of magazines or newspapers on your distribution list. An editorial copy date will be indicated. Make sure that your release reaches the editor by that date at the latest. You should also ask the editor for a list of special editorial features. The article may be suitable for inclusion in a survey.

Produce Advertorials

An advertorial is a special category of feature article, combining advertising and editorial, which is used to promote products and services. These are the key characteristics of an advertorial. It:

- may include a reader offer, such as a chance to participate in a competition;
- should be identified as an "advertisement feature";
- is produced in the form of an editorial rather than in a conventional advertisement format, even though the space is paid for.

The writing guidelines are similar to those for press releases and feature articles but you are paying for the space and you have considerably more control over what is published. Newspapers and journals will often help with the layout.

WHAT TO AVOID
Writing Information That Is Not Suitable for a Publication

It is important to study the publications that are on your distribution list. Editors know very quickly what is relevant or interesting to their readers. If your material is not suitable, it will not be used. Study the editorial content and check the readership figures, which are usually available from the publication.

Providing News Stories That Are Out of Date

"Old news is no news" and that means a story could be wasted. It's easy to get the timing right with a daily or weekly publication, but it can be tricky to decide on the right date to send a news story to a monthly publication. The publication can provide you with the dates when your copy will be required, but you have to make sure that those dates tie in with your own schedules. If you have to release a sensitive news story early to catch a publication date, you can protect your interests by putting an embargo clause on the release, saying "not for publication before. . .."

Confusing Editorial with Advertorial

A press release or feature article should provide factual, newsworthy information. It should not be a blatant advertisement for the company. Editors are not keen on items that are thinly disguised advertisements.

SEE ALSO
Raising Awareness of Your Brand (p. 247)

Setting Advertising Objectives

GETTING STARTED

Clear objectives for a communication campaign are essential, whether it is intended to generate leads or encourage brand switching. These objectives should be in place well before a campaign begins, so that each campaign has a specific task. In addition, the desired results should be measurable so that you can be sure the campaign is worth the investment.

FAQS

What can communications achieve?

Communications are about influencing the customer or potential customer in the way they make decisions. No matter how good your communications, they cannot overcome the problems caused by poor products, inefficient service or distribution, or uncompetitive pricing.

Should advertising be judged on sales results?

Advertising should certainly be measured, but there may not be a direct correlation between advertising and sales. Advertising may generate a large number of leads, but the sales force may not be able to convert those leads to sales.

Should advertising agencies be judged solely on the results they deliver?

There has been a trend towards judging agencies on measurable results. This has been driven partly by the increasing importance of direct marketing agencies who claim to be driven by results, and partly by the desire of marketing executives to increase accountability. Some agencies have gone so far as to base their fees on results, rather than traditional agency payment. The problem is that results are dependent on so many other aspects of marketing. An agency could claim that it has no control over the performance of the sales force or the quality of the product. It is essential therefore that you agree on a definition of success.

Is it possible to set a number of different objectives for the same advertising campaign, particularly when budgets are limited?

It *is* possible, but it may not be a good idea. An effective campaign has a single focus with a specific, measurable result. By mixing objectives, you may achieve only part of the outcome you want.

MAKING IT HAPPEN
Set the Right Objective

You must have clear objectives for your campaign. There are many different advertising objectives, so identify a specific task for a specific campaign. This might be:

- raising awareness of a company, product, or service within a clearly identified target market;
- communicating the benefits of a product or service;
- generating leads for the sales force or retail network;
- encouraging prospects to buy directly through a direct response campaign;
- persuading prospects to switch brands;
- supporting a special marketing event such as a sale or an exhibition;
- making sure that customers know where to obtain the product;
- building confidence in an organization.

Whatever your general objectives, you should be clear how much of that is dependent on the communications and how much dependent on other aspects of your marketing effort, such as the sales force (if you have one).

Make the Objectives Measurable

To insure you design a cost-effective campaign that delivers results, advertising objectives should be translated into precise, measurable targets, as in the following examples.

Consumer Product

- Target market: 500,000 ABC1 prospects in a given region.
- Marketing objective: achieve high level of product understanding .
- Advertising objective: persuade 15% of targeted prospects to request a free sample.

Business Product

- Target market: 5,000 specialist machinery designers in (specified) industrial processes.
- Marketing objective: increase market share to 20% (that is, recruit 1,000 new clients).
- Advertising objective: persuade 40% of prospects to request product fact file.

Raise Awareness

This objective is usually the starting point for advertisers and is especially important if your company is entering new markets where you do not have an established reputation, or you are trying to influence important decision makers who may not be aware of your company. Awareness advertising can also be used if you are launching new products which appeal to specific sectors of your market, or if research shows that customers and prospects are not aware of the full extent of your products and services.

This type of objective would be important for a company launching a new range of products. For example, to raise awareness of its new range, one company planned to advertise in a group of special interest consumer magazines designed for its target audience. The advertisements included the telephone number of an information line, that generated a large number of inquiries. Editorial articles in the same group of publications backed up the advertising by providing more detailed information for consumers. You should, however, be wary of specifying awareness targets. Awareness on its own will not sell products and, if this is your aim, you will have to integrate your campaign carefully with other elements of your marketing to meet your targets.

Likewise awareness amongst the general public is very different from awareness in a very small, specialized market, so you should be clear about who you are trying to reach

Communicate Benefits

Product advertising should lead on benefits. This type of advertising is important when research shows low awareness of product benefits. It should also be used if your products have recently been improved, or if you need to counter competitors who have introduced products with similar or better benefits.

For example, if research shows that your company's products are perceived as old-fashioned or poor value for money, you need to take action to correct this impression and communicate the real benefits of your products.

Generate Sales Leads

Advertising's role is to provide leads that can be followed up by a field sales force or tele-marketing team. Lead generation is important if marketing success depends on the performance of the sales force. Sometimes, customers or prospects have a complex decision making structure and you cannot identify some of the decision makers. Advertising that generates inquiries can identify the right people and open the door for the sales team. It can also be used to identify prospects when you are entering new market sectors where you do not have an established customer base. The final use for this type of campaign is to generate leads for agents, distributors, or retailers who handle your local marketing.

Sell through Direct Response

Direct response advertising is the most measurable form of advertising. The advertising budget provides a direct return in terms of incremental sales. This objective can be important if customers can only buy direct from you. In an increasing number of markets, customers prefer the convenience of buying direct, and you have to decide whether to bypass your existing distribution channels. If you are targeting niche markets which are not covered by retail outlets, direct response can be used to complement your distribution channels. Selling direct is not always a practical proposition. Where product inspection or demonstration is important, direct response may not be appropriate.

In the personal computer market, for example, manufacturers found that businesses and individuals were willing to buy personal computers "off the page" or via the Internet. The products were regarded as commodities and the resulting price competition put pressure on margins. The result was a considerable growth in the level of direct sales, with manufacturers using large format advertisements or inserts in computer and business publications. Direct selling meant that the manufacturers could reduce prices by avoiding the cost of selling through retail outlets.

Encourage Brand Switching
Brand switching advertising plays an important role in winning new customers as the first stage in a customer relationship program. It helps you to increase market share or maintain share against competitive actions, and is also important if you are introducing new products that offer greater benefits than competitive products.

Support a Marketing Event
This objective can be important in a number of situations, for example, taking part in an exhibition where an important new product will be launched, or holding a sale, or promoting a seminar or other customer event at which you wish to insure customer participation. Advertising helps to build traffic for your event and insures that the event attracts the right prospects. A company that sponsors senior executive seminars as a way of building its credibility could run advertisements in the business press to promote a seminar.

Help Customers Obtain the Product
Advertising can help to drive business to retail outlets or distributors, or improve the performance of your distribution network by showing the range of services available from the outlets. It can also counter competitive action, if, for example customers are using other distributors to obtain spare parts and service. To win back this important business, advertising could show locations of retail outlets and explain why the authorized distributor should be the first choice for customers.

Build Customer Confidence
Capability advertising or corporate advertising is sometimes dismissed because it is difficult to measure, but is important when a company has been undergoing significant change, or is entering new markets where it's not established. It also provides support when a company is trying to win key account business, or if competitors are threatening important business.

WHAT TO AVOID
Setting Objectives That Cannot Be Measured
Advertising objectives should be measurable for two important reasons. First, to make sure that advertising represents an adequate return on investment. Second, to measure the effectiveness of the campaign itself so that future advertising can be improved or modified to deliver better results.

Setting Objectives That Are Too General
A general objective, such as raising awareness, is important, but often is seen as the only objective. Advertising objectives should be closely linked to marketing objectives so that advertising is used to perform specific tasks within an overall marketing framework. You should be sure that what you want to achieve is possible with communications and acknowledge the importance of other elements of your marketing, crucially the product itself or your pricing strategy.

Failing to Integrate Communications Objectives with Other Marketing Objectives
It is important that some advertising objectives, such as generating more leads, should

be integrated with the other activities that will increase sales. It may be necessary to increase sales force training to improve the team's ability to convert leads into sales. Advertising alone cannot be expected to deliver sales.

SEE ALSO
Planning an Advertising Campaign (p. 268)
Preparing an Advertising Brief (p. 275)
Selecting and Working with an Advertising Agency (p. 271)

Planning an Advertising Campaign

GETTING STARTED

Any communications campaign needs to have clear, measurable objectives, whether it is designed to communicate product benefits or to support an event. In order to achieve these objectives, it must also be planned carefully. There are eight main stages to consider, from defining the target market to setting a budget.

FAQS

Do I need an advertising campaign?

Often the term advertising campaign is used when the more holistic term "communications campaign" would be more appropriate. Advertising strictly only refers to paid-for space or time in media such as newspapers or radio. On the other hand, direct mail, sales promotions, exhibitions, or any of a range of communication tools can be used in a campaign to support your marketing. To decide if you need a communications campaign, you should be fairly sure that the problem you want to address can be solved best by communications. For example, finding new customers or prospective customers is often best accomplished by advertising or direct mail, but converting inquirers into customers may be better dealt with by you or your sales team (if you have one) in person.

Who is responsible for campaign planning—the client or the advertising agency?

Both parties contribute. The client sets the overall marketing objectives and the specific communications campaign objectives. The agency develops an advertising strategy based on those, but may seek to modify the campaign objectives. Timings will be determined by the client's product and marketing plans, together with practical considerations such as publication dates and lead times.

Why is it necessary to plan a campaign in so much detail?

To be effective, advertising and communications must meet specific measurable objectives. The objectives affect choice of media, creative strategy, overall budget, and lead times. Overlooking any of those details could weaken the effectiveness of the campaign.

Should planning be applied to the creative process?

There is an assumption that creative work takes place in a vacuum. Like any other marketing activity, it must be directed toward an objective. The more information a creative team has, the more focused its work.

MAKING IT HAPPEN
Set Campaign Objectives

It is important to set clear objectives for an advertising campaign. It is essential to identify a specific task for a specific campaign. This might be:

- raising awareness of a company, product, or service within a clearly identified target market;
- communicating the benefits of a product or service;
- generating leads for the sales force or retail network.

To insure you design a cost effective campaign that delivers results, advertising objectives should be translated into precise, measurable targets.

Identify Key Planning Activities

There are eight main stages in planning an advertising campaign:

1. Define the Target Market

Who is your campaign aimed at?

An understanding of your audience will influence the media you select and the creative treatment of your advertisement.

To define your target market, you should ask questions like these:

- Who buys your type of product?
- Who influences the purchasing decision?
- In business buying, who are the important decision makers?
- Do you need to communicate with the actual buyers or those who influence the purchasing decision?
- How many potential buyers are there?
- How many users are currently buying your product and what is your share of the market?
- Which prospects do you want to reach with the campaign and where are they located?
- What are the characteristics of these people (for example, age, sex, income, job title), and what are their most important considerations in choosing a brand or a supplier?
- What does research tell you about their attitudes toward your company and your products?
- How do they currently receive information about your products?
- What is the role of advertising in reaching the target audience?

2. Select Media

There are four important factors to consider in selecting campaign media:

- how closely the audience profile of the medium matches your target audience;
- the comparative costs of reaching the target audience through different media;
- whether the frequency of the medium matches the timing of your campaign;
- the creative opportunities of the medium for the communication of your message.

3. Plan Campaign Timing

When should your campaign run? You have to consider a number of factors first in relation to the purchasing pattern of your products:

- When are your customers making their buying decisions?
- Do you know when your customers hold product/purchasing review meetings?
- If you are launching a new product, when will the product be available?

- Does your advertising campaign have to tie in with the timing of any other marketing activity, for example, an exhibition, direct marketing campaign, or sales force call?
- How quickly will you be able to follow up the campaign?

You also have to take into account production and media lead times:

- What is the next available publication or broadcasting date?
- When does the media owner require your advertisement?
- How long will it take to produce the advertisement?

4. Decide Campaign Frequency

Campaigns raise levels of awareness with each appearance and increase the number of opportunities to see the advertisement. They also move individual respondents further along the decision making process and maintain contact during an extended process. Campaigns reinforce the impact of the message by repetition and provide an opportunity to communicate multiple or complex messages about the company or the product range.

Frequency is determined by a number of factors:

- frequency of publication, that is, how often the publication appears;
- frequency of broadcast: radio or television commercials can be broadcast many times during the same day, if the budget allows;
- your budget, although a number of appearances in the same medium will earn a discount that makes the entire budget go further;
- the behavior of consumers or buyers: if a buying decision is made only annually then timing may be more crucial than frequency.

5. Plan Creative Treatment

To achieve good results, you must develop a comprehensive creative brief. These are the main elements:

- campaign objectives;
- description of the target audience;
- the main concerns of the target audience: why they buy; what they consider; how they view different products and suppliers;

- the main benefits of the product or service: why the product is different from competitive offerings; what is new; why the benefits are important;
- the core message or proposition—what the prospect is being offered: the opportunity to sample or buy; further information; a sales visit; an incentive; or a discount;
- the planned response: should the prospect contact the company, send off an order, wait for a phone call, or simply absorb the information?
- the media—size and mechanical details;
- the supporting activities—telemarketing, advertising, sales follow-up, tie-in promotions.

6. Develop a Response Mechanism

Action is a vital ingredient of any advertising campaign and it is essential that you make it easy for your prospects to respond. First, decide which action your prospects are to take:

- place an order
- arrange a sales meeting
- request further information
- visit a retail outlet
- try the product

Review the cost, convenience, and practicality of response options, including telephone, mail, fax, e-mail, and Web site.

7. Set a Budget

A campaign budget will include direct, indirect, and variable costs. Direct costs include the production costs of advertisements, including design, writing and production, and media costs. Indirect costs include the cost of setting up response handling, either by internal resources or an external supplier, and the management costs of planning and controlling the campaign. Variable costs include the cost of handling the campaign response, for example, 800 number costs and telephone resources, or costs of postage-paid services; the cost of meeting the response—supplying

and distributing the material that is requested; and the cost of servicing the response—sales or telemarketing costs in dealing with the potential volume of new business.

8. Set Schedules

To set a campaign schedule, work back from the launch date and work out how long each individual activity will take.

WHAT TO AVOID

X

Poor Targeting
Without a clear picture of your target, market advertising can be wasteful. You should always aim for the best match between the audience and your ideal customers—subject, of course, to your budget.

Failing to Integrate Advertising Plans with Other Marketing Activities
Advertising must be integrated with other related marketing tasks. Poor sales force performance, for example, could waste the contribution of a highly successful advertising campaign that provided a large number of sales leads.

Trying to Take Shortcuts on Lead Times
Advertising lead times are influenced by a number of factors including publication dates, production lead times, and product availability.

Trying to Achieve Advertising Objectives with Inadequate Resources
If companies try to achieve targets without committing the right budget, it will mean either that advertisements do not appear frequently enough to have impact, or that production quality is sacrificed.

SEE ALSO
Preparing an Advertising Brief (p. 275)
Selecting and Working with an
Advertising Agency (p. 271)
Setting Advertising Objectives (p. 264)

Selecting and Working with an Advertising Agency

GETTING STARTED

If your budget will stretch and you are able to engage an advertising agency to help you spread the word about your product or service, you need to choose an agency that can provide the right selection of services. These can include consulting, strategy, creative work, media, and integration with other communications activities. Important factors in selecting an agency include its approach, reputation, and financial stability. Careful selection can avoid problems that cause breakdowns in the agency/client relationship.

FAQS

Do I need an advertising agency?

Many small to medium-sized companies don't. However, the skills offered by agencies are just as specialized as those offered by your accountant. Many agencies will be able to offer services other than advertising, including direct marketing, sales promotion, and public relations. Indeed they may not call themselves an "advertising" agency at all. Agencies that offer a wide range of skills are often called "full-service" agencies. If you know what you want to achieve, but are not sure if advertising is the best course, discuss the issues with a number of different agencies.

I want to work with a specific agency, but they already handle the account of a competitor. Should I work with that agency?

This problem occurs frequently, particularly when agency mergers occur, and the new group finds that its client lists include conflicting accounts. The decision to continue handling conflicting accounts is sometimes taken by the agency, and sometimes by the clients. It can be particularly difficult if the agency is seen as an industry specialist, with considerable expertise in a particular market. Sometimes the problem can be resolved by handling the conflicting accounts through separate agency teams.

How do I know that an agency can maintain its standards in day-to-day business, once they have won the initial pitch?

Sometimes agencies field a special senior team to win new business, and then hand the day-to-day account to a completely different team. Since a good relationship between agency and client is so important, you should insist on meeting the team who will actually work on the business.

Is it essential to appoint an agency to handle advertising campaigns?

A full-service agency may not be essential, particularly if you have the resources to handle part of the task internally. Creative consultancies, media specialists, or integrated agencies can take on specialist tasks.

MAKING IT HAPPEN
Choose the Right Type of Agency

Depending on the type of agency, you can use a comprehensive service or specific services including:

- initial consulting;
- development of an advertising strategy;
- creative proposals, copywriting, design, and production of advertisements;
- media planning, negotiation, buying, and administration;
- integration of advertising with other communications activities.

Whatever you decide, ask to see examples of previous campaigns and for an honest appraisal of their effectiveness.

Work with a Full-service Advertising Agency

Full-service agencies handle all aspects of an advertising program. You should select a full-service agency if you do not have any internal skills or resources for handling advertising, or if extensive advertising is important to the achievement of your marketing objectives.

Use a Media Independent

A media independent handles only media planning and buying and so is likely to be interested only if you are spending a considerable amount on buying space in newspapers and magazines or airtime on TV or radio. By concentrating on media, the independents can often negotiate better deals with them than full-service agencies. Many smaller advertising agencies use media independents to handle their media buying. If you can handle campaign planning and creative work in other ways but do not have any internal skills or resources for media planning and buying, then you should use a media independent.

A media independent could prove useful if you spend a large amount of your budget on media and you want to take advantage of specialist buying skills to get better positions or lower rates. You may find that certain media will not deal with you, because you are an advertiser. In that case, a media agency can provide valuable support.

Choose Creative Independents

Creative independents handle only creative work such as copywriting and design. By specializing in this way, the independents can often achieve more effective advertising than full-service agencies. You would have to handle campaign planning and media in other ways. There are three types of creative independent:
- freelance staff, either combined writer/art director teams, or individuals;

- design consulting companies offering advertising as part of a communications service;
- specialist creative independents: small agencies that either have their own creative teams, or manage freelance teams.

You should consider using a creative independent if you can handle campaign planning and media in other ways but do not have any internal skills or resources for creative work. If advertising is a small part of your marketing activity, you could develop effective campaigns by taking advantage of specialist creative services.

Work with an Integrated Agency

Integrated agencies handle all aspects of an advertising program and integrate advertising with other media. Agencies offer integrated services in two forms:
- as a single integrated agency, in which all campaigns are handled by the same team;
- as an agency group, in which non-advertising campaigns are handled by specialist companies within the group.

An integrated agency may be suitable if other tools, such as direct marketing, publications, and sales promotion are as important as advertising, and you want all of the activities integrated and handled professionally. Any extra cost incurred will be well worth it.

Use the Media's Own Expertise

One alternative to using an agency is to ask the newspaper, magazine, or radio station to help. Often they will offer basic design or writing services free of charge. However they are rarely as skilled as specialists and you may find it difficult to make your advertising stand out or to maintain consistency over time.

Evaluate Advertising Agencies

There are a number of important factors in selecting an agency.
- Approach: what is the agency's philosophy, and how does it work in practical terms?
- Track record: what campaigns has the agency produced, and how effective have they been?

- Reputation: does the agency have an established reputation in your market? Are you able to approach other clients to give their assessment of the agency?
- Accountability: how does the agency measure the performance of its campaigns?
- Client relationships: what is the current client list, and how many of these clients are enjoying long-term relationships? What is the average length of account tenure?
- Disciplines: does the agency offer all disciplines from within its own resources, and can it offer the full range of services?
- Staff: does the agency have the staff to handle complex, large-scale programs? What is the consultancy's recruitment and personal development policy?
- Financial stability: what is the agency's recent performance? Does it have the stability and resources to sustain an effective level of service over the long term?

Check Agency Performance

According to research conducted by the U.K.-based Henley Centre, clients believe the ten most important questions regarding agency performance are:

- Does it take the trouble to understand your business?
- Can it use creativity effectively to sell your products?
- Does it have real creative flair?
- Does it get work done on time?
- Does it have a good understanding of your consumers?
- Does it believe in defining advertising objectives beforehand?
- Does it keep costs within budget?
- Does it use research to aid its creative work?
- Is it strong on media buying?
- Is it thorough and hard working?

Obtain Information about Advertising Agencies

There are a number of useful sources of information about agencies:

- the American Association of Advertising Agencies publishes information about agencies;

- individual agencies provide videos of their agency credentials;
- specialist magazines publish regular news about agencies and their clients and your own trade publications may mention agencies which specialize in your market.
- Talk to friends and colleagues, even if in different businesses, to find out which agencies are reliable.

Avoid Problems in Client/Agency Relationships

Reports in the trade press highlight a number of factors that create conditions for a breakdown:

- The client believes that the advertising has not delivered results, or not had the planned effect on the marketplace.
- The agency feels that poor results are caused by marketing, product, or management problems on the client side.
- The client does not like the advertisements for subjective reasons.
- The agency fails to understand the client's business.
- A failure of communication means that the agency cannot respond to the client's real needs.
- Frequent changes in the agency team or client team make continuity difficult.
- Poor agency administration can let down good creative work.
- Relationships can become stale.

WHAT TO AVOID
Choosing the Wrong Size of Agency
A large agency may have the resources and scale to support national or international campaigns, but if your account is small, you may get poor service from a junior team. It may be more appropriate to work with a smaller agency, where you will get personal service from the senior people.

Choosing the Wrong Type of Agency
Agencies, like any other business, develop specialties. Their expertise may not coincide with your needs. The most important division is between a consumer and a business-to-business agency but, beyond that, agencies develop expertise in certain

industries or markets. Look carefully at the agency's client list to find the right match.

Relying on a Creative Pitch

Agency selection is frequently made on the basis of a pitch—a presentation that shows how an agency would tackle a specific project. Although the presentation gives an insight into the agency's working methods, it is an artificial guide to potential performance.

Not sharing information with the agency

Clients often expect a lot from a new agency, but can be disappointed when the agency does not know something "obvious" about the client's business. The agency can only know what you know *if you tell them*. If you are concerned about confidentiality, discuss this and get a signed agreement from the agency management.

Not Discussing the Budget in Enough Detail

Agencies work for a fee and, like you, will want to make a profit. You will only get good service when they feel your business is worthwhile for them. From the outset discuss how much you plan to spend and what you want to achieve—competent agencies will tell you from the outset what is possible.

SEE ALSO

Planning an Advertising Campaign (p. 268)
Preparing an Advertising Brief (p. 275)
Setting Advertising Objectives (p. 264)

Preparing an Advertising Brief

GETTING STARTED

To get the most from working with an advertising agency, you need to make a start by putting together a comprehensive creative brief. This must cover all aspects of the project: background, objectives, research, competitors, product information, and the target audience. It's worth spending time on making the briefing information as complete as you can, as otherwise you run the risk of wasting time and money on a campaign that has little impact.

FAQS

Why is a detailed brief important?

It will start the campaign on exactly the right foot. An imprecise and undetailed brief may mean that the work is aimed at the wrong audience. Provide the agency or consultancy with as much information as possible so that they can produce a campaign that achieves results.

Who should be involved in preparing a creative brief?

The people who evaluate a creative brief should also be involved in preparing or approving the brief. It can be difficult to deal with objections and criticism from someone who does not understand the brief. On the client side, the briefing team is likely to include the marketing executive, sales executive, and any relevant marketing specialists such as promotions or direct mail executives. The person who has the final say—whether it is you yourself or your business partner—must be involved in defining the brief. The team should also include product or research specialists to provide detailed information on the product and prospective customers. The agency team should also be involved in preparing the brief, although this does not always happen in practice.

Should an agency brief always have measurable objectives?

The more specific the brief, the easier it is to assess the results of the creative work. It is not always possible to set a measurable objective, but this should be the goal. Agencies may argue that results depend on factors outside their control, but it should be possible to isolate the communications objectives and identify a way of measuring them. A direct response campaign, for example, can be measured by the number of responses, while a corporate campaign could be assessed through attitude surveys conducted before and after the campaign.

MAKING IT HAPPEN

Plan the Campaign Approach

How will you present your message? Most publications and commercial broadcast media carry high volumes of advertising. Your advertisement must achieve immediate impact to succeed. There are three essential checks that can be applied to creative work in any media:

- it must have immediate impact;
- it must meet the needs of the reader or viewer;
- it must stimulate a response.

Provide Background Information

Your briefing of the agency or consultancy should begin with the background to the project:

- What is the overall aim of the project?
- What threats and opportunities does the business face?
- Why is the project being produced?
- How does the project fit into the overall marketing program?
- Why is it necessary to advertise and what is it intended to achieve?

The background material should include any research that you have carried out or used. You should ensure that the project works in the context of other marketing activities of yours and of competitors.

Produce a Comprehensive Brief

To achieve good creative results, you must develop a comprehensive creative brief. These are the main elements:

- campaign objectives;
- description of the target audience;
- the main concerns of the target audience: why they buy; what factors they consider; how they view different products and suppliers;
- the main benefits of the product or service: why the product is different from competitive offerings; what is new; why the benefits are important;
- the core message or proposition: what the prospect is being offered—the opportunity to sample or buy, further information, a sales visit, an incentive or discount;
- the planned response: should the prospect contact the company, send an order, wait for a phone call, or simply absorb the information offered?
- the media: scope and practical details;
- the supporting activities: telemarketing, advertising, sales follow-up, tie-in promotions.

Information of this kind would enable writers and designers to approach the creative process in a disciplined, logical way. Great creative ideas may occur in a vacuum, but they are more likely to be a response to a clearly defined problem.

The creative brief is important whether you are using external suppliers or carrying out the creative work internally.

Set Out Objectives

The brief should set out a number of objectives, including the overall corporate objective and the marketing objective. State the communications objectives and how they contribute to the wider marketing objectives. For example you may want to make potential customers in a new region aware of your product in order that sales staff can work more effectively.

The campaign objectives should be detailed and specific. Examples could include:

- Generate 3,000 prospects and convert 3% of them.

- Make sure that key decision makers understand the product's business benefits.
- Raise awareness among 20% of the target audience.

Provide Access to Any Research Information

The creative team should be aware of any relevant research information, including:

- customer surveys, interviews, or analysis
- industry surveys
- competitor analysis
- product reviews
- press comment on the product or company
- feedback from focus groups
- results of previous campaigns

Include Information on Competitors

The brief should include detailed information on these questions:

- Which competitors provide a similar product or service?
- How does the competitive offering compare?
- What are the product's key benefits against the competition?
- How are competitors perceived by customers?

This information can help creative teams identify some of the key benefits that will differentiate the product from competitors' offerings. It will also show how other companies have tackled the problem of describing the product.

Provide Comprehensive Product Information

The product or service should be described in detail:

- What is it?
- What is it used for?
- How does it operate?
- What are the main benefits for the customer?
- What are the advantages over competitor products?

If the team can use or experience for themselves your product or service in the same way as a customer, then this will greatly enhance their understanding.

Describe the Target Audience

Describing the target audience helps the creative team to focus on the key decision makers:

- What types of company buy the product?
- Which business sectors are they in?
- How big are these companies?
- Who are the main decision makers?
- What is their role in the decision making process?
- What are their business concerns?
- What is their perception of your company and its products?

Establish Target Perceptions

The creative team should be aware of any key messages that are important to the target audience. The task of the creative team is not to invent these messages; it is to communicate them as effectively as possible. The brief should therefore set out the perceptions that the target audience have now and those they should hold once the campaign is finished.

Get Approval of the Brief

The brief should be circulated to all members of the group involved in briefing and approving the project. No creative work should begin until the brief has been signed off by everyone involved. Once the brief has been approved, members should not be able to change it without good reason.

Be Clear about Payment Terms

Some agencies will present their ideas without expecting payment, but most would rather not. If you cannot pay for initial ideas, make this clear before expecting anything of value from the team. If, however, you *can* pay, agree the amount and establish who will own the ideas once the initial presentation is finished.

Describe the Review Process

Let the creative team know how their work will be reviewed and evaluated. This can take place at a number of levels:

- review by the agency and client teams
- evaluation in focus groups
- pilot campaigns in test markets

WHAT TO AVOID
Making the Brief Too Specific

It is possible to make a brief too specific, thereby ruling out creative approaches that may achieve outstanding results. For example, setting out the creative approach in the brief before the creative team has had an opportunity to consider it will produce very limited results. The creative team needs information to focus their attention on the problem, not suggestions on how the problem should be solved.

Not integrating Creative Work

Although the brief should allow the agency creative team complete freedom, it is equally important that creative work across different media should be integrated. If advertising is the dominant medium, and a team is working on direct marketing, they should relate their approach to the advertising theme. Repetition of the same creative theme across different media reinforces the key messages and can improve overall awareness.

Concentrating Too Hard on Creativity, and Not Enough on Results

Creative work should be accountable. The agency may have a brilliant, award-winning creative idea, but if it fails to produce the intended results it may be a waste of money. The creative team should therefore be aware of the specific objectives of the campaign; it is not enough just to get attention.

SEE ALSO
Selecting and Working with an Advertising Agency (p. 271)
Setting Advertising Objectives (p. 264)

Working with Your Local Community

GETTING STARTED

Corporate social responsibility (CSR) started as little more than corporate philanthropy and involvement in the community. However, CSR is about far more than that. It's about taking a responsible approach to every aspect of your business. It covers almost any activity of a business, so there is a good chance that you may be doing something already. Every business has an impact on society through what it produces, how it employs and develops its staff, how it purchases supplies and sells its products or services, how it affects the environment, and how it acts in the community. Social responsibility can help any business to succeed. It can build sales, develop the workforce, encourage enthusiasm, and increase trust in the business as a whole. Businesses are stronger and work better when they have the support and respect of all their stakeholders; their customers, suppliers, staff, and communities.

This actionlist aims to introduce you to some of the ideas behind corporate social responsibility, and to suggest some ways in which you could take your business forward in this respect.

FAQS

Is corporate social responsibility relevant to small businesses?

Corporate social responsibility is not just for large corporations—it's essential for all businesses to think about their role in the community and their responsibilities to all of their stakeholders. Corporate social responsibility is about business behaviors that not only deliver commercial objectives, but that also have a positive social impact. It is for their own long-term good, as well as for reasons of principle, that businesses should aim to be responsible in all their activities, and to embrace the principles of sustainable development in their widest sense.

What are the key principles of social responsibility?

Businesses can help to improve the lives of their customers, suppliers, staff, and shareholders by enabling them to share in the wealth the business creates. They should deal honestly with their suppliers and competitors, and act as good citizens in their local communities. Sincerity, truthfulness, and keeping promises not only contribute to credibility, but also to the effectiveness of business transactions. Businesses clearly have to respect the rule of law, but in many cases it makes good economic sense to do rather more than the legal minimum.

Why is corporate social responsibility important?

Customers, suppliers, and employees are all becoming more interested in the way that businesses behave. A good reputation can open doors, win loyalty, and create staff enthusiasm. Social responsibility is about getting business benefits from being a good corporate citizen. It is not random philanthropy. Done well, it raises your profile in the most positive way. Responsible businesses do not just gain respect; they can gain real business benefits too.

Can small businesses afford a social responsibility program?

Businesses can choose to support community initiatives with money, but in most cases being responsible is simply about ensuring the right behavior. There may be a cost associated with this, in the sense that behaving irresponsibly is cheaper, but in the long run behaving responsibly will enhance your reputation and do more to help you retain customers and staff.

How do you get the best value for social responsibility?

As with every other aspect of your business, you need to review carefully your activities and ensure that you are getting a return, whether it is in terms of staff feeling more motivated, lower staff turnover, a better reputation locally, or higher sales.

MAKING IT HAPPEN
Reflect Stakeholder Needs

Businesses need to provide customers with the highest quality products and services consistent with their specified needs. You need to treat customers fairly, ensure health and safety, and respect human dignity. You can also engage with customers in social projects. This is often called "cause-related marketing" and can increase customer appreciation of a product while simultaneously delivering a social benefit.

Every business has an interest in being an employer of choice. In a competitive job market, this can be a real advantage. This means paying staff fairly, providing a good working environment, communicating openly and honestly, respecting staff suggestions, avoiding discrimination, and promoting personal development and continuous learning. It increasingly means ensuring that staff can balance their work and the rest of their life, with appropriate flexibility in working patterns.

Businesses have a responsibility to manage assets effectively to provide investors with a fair and competitive return. Different businesses will take different views about what constitutes the most appropriate level of social engagement; but the importance of sustainable behavior is now being reflected in legal requirements.

Businesses have a responsibility to deal fairly with suppliers. The relationship should be free from coercion and should aim to foster stability in return for value, quality, and reliability. Some businesses, for example, prefer suppliers whose values reflect their own. This can mean avoiding sub-contractors who have poor labor practices. Small businesses often think that this does not apply to them, but you may find yourself caught up by human rights requirements if you supply larger organizations. One obligation that applies to every business is to pay suppliers on agreed terms.

Businesses, of whatever size, see involvement in the local community as part of being a good corporate citizen. It is no longer enough to argue that businesses contribute to society simply by creating jobs and wealth. Enlightened self-interest plays a part; businesses understand they need an educated and healthy workforce to work for them, a healthy business sector to provide suppliers and customers, and a "license to operate."

Community investment is more than just giving money. While that is important, benefits also accrue, for example, from giving away old equipment, or getting staff involved with community organizations. There may be merit in reflecting your business's core competences in the ways in which you become involved in the community. You may want to look for mutually beneficial arrangements, so that you get some return, perhaps in terms of publicity and reputation.

Some Basic Steps to Take

The first thing to do is to look at your own practices systematically. If you don't yet have a statement of business principles, you may like to think about creating one. Ideally, it should insist on honesty, integrity, and fairness in all aspects of your business. You could consider committing the business to an external code or set of business principles that provide a framework for you and your stakeholders to measure your progress on environmental, social, and community issues. You might also consider using some of your marketing budget to associate your business with a social cause.

Consider how your stakeholders feel about the business. Identify your most important stakeholders and their concerns, and relate them to your business interests. Think about ways in which you could be more socially responsible in your relationships with your stakeholders. You could set out to seek mutually beneficial relationships with contractors, suppliers, and customers, as well as with other stakeholders, such as communities and local government. Make sure that you pursue ethical supply chain management. Remember to promote your business principles at all times.

Review your business's current policies and processes. One good area to think about is waste recycling and the use of renewable sources of energy and materials. Consider whether there are any ways to avoid materials that are known to be toxic or to damage the environment. Introduce a social and environmental strategy, and set targets for your business. You could, perhaps, establish an environmental management system (EMS) with objectives and procedures for evaluating progress.

It is important to measure how well you perform and to make it clear to your staff that you care about this. Any success should be celebrated; remember that people feel good about getting social responsibility right. Make sure that you communicate what you are doing. You could include a passage on this area in your annual review, mention it in newsletters, or even produce a special report. Let people know what you are doing, because it will affect their view of your business.

In order to be socially responsible, you must respect the rights of yourself and your staff. You can do this by providing good and safe working conditions, and introducing health and safety policies. Ensure that all your staff understand these and adhere to them. It is important to develop and make the best use of the talent of your staff. You should provide training opportunities and mentoring, so that promotion from within the organization is maximized. Encourage your staff to be involved in the planning and direction of your company. Your commercial success depends on their commitment and talent. Show staff that you are open to job-sharing, flextime, and other family-friendly policies.

Encourage staff volunteering in the community, as well as supporting the community with financial contributions and help in kind. Look for opportunities to make surplus product and redundant equipment available to local schools, charities, and community organizations. You can also help your local community by buying from local suppliers.

WHAT TO AVOID
Treating Social Responsibility as an Isolated Activity

The most common mistake is seeing social responsibility as an add-on, rather than as an integral part of your business strategy. It is important to regard social responsibility as one of the ways in which you can build the reputation of your business. In other words, you should treat it as seriously as you treat all the other aspects of running your business.

SEE ALSO
Small and Growing Businesses (p. 422)

GROWING YOUR BUSINESS

Analyzing Your Business's Strengths, Weaknesses, Opportunities, and Threats

GETTING STARTED

SWOT analysis (Strengths, Weaknesses, Opportunities, and Threats) is a method for assessing a business, its resources, and its environment. The analysis is often completed as a part of business and marketing plans to understand a business and its markets, and to show potential investors that all options have been thoroughly considered.

The essence of the SWOT analysis is to discover what you do well; how you could improve; whether you are making the most of the opportunities around you; and whether there are any changes in your market—such as technological developments, mergers of businesses, or unreliability of suppliers—that may require corresponding changes in your business. This actionlist will introduce you to the ideas behind the SWOT analysis, and give suggestions as to how you might carry out one of your own. For further information, you might be interested in looking at *Planning to Succeed in Business*, written by David Irwin, and published by Pitman in 1995.

FAQS

What is the SWOT process?

The SWOT process will focus on the internal strengths and weaknesses of you, your staff, your products, and your business. At the same time, it will look at the external opportunities and threats that impact on your business, such as market and consumer trends, changes in technology, legislation, and financial issues.

What is the best way to complete the analysis?

The traditional approach to completing SWOT is to produce a blank grid and then list relevant factors in the appropriate boxes. You may find that some factors appear in more than one box. A factor that appears to be a threat could also represent a potential opportunity. A rush of competitors into your area could easily represent a major threat to your business. However, competitors could boost customer numbers in your area, some of whom may well visit your business.

What is the point of completing a SWOT analysis?

By completing a SWOT analysis, you will be able to pinpoint your core activities and identify what you do well, and why. It will also point you towards where your greatest opportunities lie, and highlight areas where changes need to be made to make the most of your business.

MAKING IT HAPPEN
Know Your Strengths

Take some time to consider what you believe are the strengths of your business. These could be seen in terms of your staff, products, customer loyalty, processes, or location. Evaluate what your business does well; it could be your marketing expertise, your environmentally-friendly packaging, or your excellent customer service. It is important to try to evaluate your strengths in terms of how they compare to those of your competitors. If you and your competitors provide the same prompt delivery time, then this cannot be listed as a strength. However, if your delivery staff is extremely polite and helpful, and your competitor's staff has very few customer-friendly attributes, then you should consider listing your delivery staff's attitude as a strength. It is very important to be totally honest and realistic. Try to include some personal strengths and characteristics of your staff as individuals and the management team as individuals.

Recognize Your Weaknesses

Try to take an objective look at every aspect of your business. Ask yourself whether your products and services could be improved. Think about how reliable your customer service is, or whether your supplier always delivers exactly what you want, when you want it. Try to identify any area of expertise that is lacking in the business. You may find, on consideration, that you need some more sales staff, or financial help and guidance. Don't forget to include location as an aspect to consider. Think about whether your location is right for your type of business, whether there is enough parking, or sufficient opportunity to catch passing trade.

Your main objective during this exercise is to be as honest as you can in listing weaknesses. Don't just make a list of mistakes that have been made, such as an occasion when a customer was not called back promptly. Try to see the broader picture. The weakness might be that your systems or processes do not ensure that customers are contacted exactly when they need to be.

It is a good idea to get an outside viewpoint on what your weaknesses are. You may strongly believe that your years of experience in a sector reflect your business's thorough grounding and knowledge of all of your customers' needs. A customer, however, may view this wealth of experience as portraying an old-fashioned approach, and an unwillingness to change and work with new ideas.

Spot the Opportunities

The next step is to analyze your opportunities, and this can be tackled in several ways. External opportunities can include the misfortune of competitors who are not performing well, providing you with the opportunity to do better. There may be technological developments, such as broadband arriving in your area, or a new process enhancing your products. There may be some legislative changes affecting your customers, offering you an opportunity to provide advice, support, or added services. Changes in market trends and consumer buying habits may provide the development of a niche market, of which you could take advantage before your competitors, if you are quick enough to take action.

Another good idea is to consider your weaknesses more carefully and work out ways of addressing the problems, turning them around in order to create an opportunity. For example, a supplier who continually lets you down could be turned into an opportunity by sourcing another supplier who is more reliable. A member of staff who leaves could provide the opportunity for a re-evaluation of duties in a more efficient way, or the appointment of a new member of staff who brings additional experience with them.

Watch Out for Threats

Analyzing the threats to your business requires some guesswork, and this is where the analysis can be overly subjective. Some threats are tangible, such as a new competitor moving into your area. Other threats may only be intuitive guesses that result in nothing. However, being vigilant will mean that if a potential threat becomes real, you can react much quicker, having already considered your options and perhaps put some contingency planning into place.

Think about the worst things that could realistically happen, such as losing your customers to your major competitor, or the development of a new product far superior to your own. Listing your threats in your SWOT analysis will provide ways for you to plan to deal with the threats, if they ever actually start to affect your business.

Use Your Analysis

After completing your SWOT analysis, it is vital that you learn from the information you have gathered. You should now plan to build on your strengths, using them to their full potential. You can also plan to reduce your weaknesses, either by minimizing the risk they represent, or making changes to overcome them. Now that you understand where your opportunities lie, make the most of them and ensure you capitalize on every opportunity in front of you. Try to turn threats into opportunities. Try to be proactive and put plans into place to counter any threats as they arise.

To help you in planning ahead, you could combine some of the areas you have highlighted in the boxes; for example, if you see an external opportunity of a new market growing, you will be able to check whether your internal strengths will be able to make the most of the opportunity. Do you have enough trained staff in place, and can your phone system cope with extra customer orders? If you have a weakness that undermines an opportunity, it provides a good insight as to how you might develop your internal strengths and weaknesses to maximize your opportunities and minimize your threats.

The SWOT process is to fill in the four boxes, but the real benefit is to take an overview of everything in each box, in relation to all the other boxes. This comparative analysis will then provide an evaluation that links external and internal forces to help your business prosper.

WHAT TO AVOID
Focusing Just on a Few Issues
Don't just focus on the large, obvious issues, such as a major competitor encroaching on your business. You need to consider all issues carefully, such as whether your Internet system provides everything you need.

Completing Your SWOT Analysis on Your Own
It is important to encourage other people's contributions to help you complete your SWOT analysis; don't try and do it alone. Other people's perspectives can be very useful, particularly as they may not be as close to the business as you are.

Using Your Analysis for the Next Ten Years
Don't do a SWOT analysis once and then never repeat the exercise. Your business environment will be constantly changing, so use SWOT as an ongoing business analysis practice.

Relying on SWOT to Provide All the Answers
Use SWOT as part of an overall strategy to analyze your business and its potential. It is a useful guide, not a major decision-making tool.

SEE ALSO
Identifying Opportunities for Your Business (p. 285)
Small and Growing Businesses (p. 422)

Identifying Opportunities for Your Business

GETTING STARTED

The business world today is fast moving, and the pace of change can at times seem bewildering. The environment in which your business operates is changing all the time, and there are many different factors that influence it. There are continual changes in your market, your customers' needs and preferences, the technology you use, your sales channels, and the way you can deliver your products or services. These changes can bring threats to your business, but they will also, undoubtedly, bring opportunities.

It is important that you periodically take a step back and try to analyze the way in which your business currently operates. Think about the factors that may promote change. Try to identify threats, and make sure you are prepared for them. It is also important, however, that you spot the many opportunities that arise. This actionlist will give some advice on how to spot opportunities, and make the best of them.

FAQS

What am I successful at so far?

Ask yourself what your current business success is based upon. If you can explain how you became successful in the first place, you have more chance of being able to repeat that success again. Carry out an analysis of your current strengths and weaknesses, and try to establish how these are contributing to your current success, or lack of it.

What opportunities can I identify?

Write down a list of the opportunities you think you can exploit. These opportunities might be a natural extension of what you are doing already, or an adaptation of what you currently do. Alternatively, they could involve branching out into something completely different.

Which opportunity can I exploit most quickly, and most profitably?

Most businesses will be able to say that there are many new opportunities for them. It is more difficult to identify those opportunities that have realistic potential. Before you plunge headlong into pursuing every opening that arises, try to identify the one prospect that provides the most immediate, long term, profit-making potential for you. Try to be honest with yourself; decide if the opportunity you are selecting is really the one that will have the greatest impact on your business future. You may find some useful advice in the book, *Targeting Profitable Customers: How to Do It, How to Profit from It* by Malcolm McDonald and Ian Dunbar, published by Palgrave Macmillan.

How can I prepare my business for change?

The needs of the market change continually. Trends can be influenced by technology, fashion, lifestyle, and the economy as a whole. No small business can avoid these effects. Try to identify the trends that are affecting your business now, and over the next 12 months. Try to spot the opportunities those trends will create, as well as the threats they may pose. You need to think about how to prepare your business to adapt its products, prices, marketing methods, sales channels, or overall customer experience in order to make the most of these opportunities.

MAKING IT HAPPEN
Attracting New Customers

Look at the way you acquired your existing customers. Make sure that you understand why they buy from you. It may be that you have used different methods to attract customers, so try to identify which is your most productive method of generating business. By doing this, it may be possible to repeat this success. Speak to your existing customers to find out why they buy from you. If you have customers who have bought from you in the past, it may be possible to ask them why they have stopped buying from you now. Try to find out what you need to do to encourage them to buy from you again.

Retaining Existing Customers
Work out your current client retention rate. Think about ways in which you could improve it. It may be that you already have an existing, loyal customer base, where there is a high degree of trust in the service you provide. However, there may still be potential to offer add-ons to your current service. Look out for opportunities to generate or improve repeat levels of sales. You might consider offering new products, or adaptations of products, or upgrades of your existing service to your customers.

Find out your average sales value per customer, and think about ways in which you can improve it. Try to encourage feedback from your customers and ask if there is anything they need that you currently do not supply. You may be able to build some of these things into your service. It may also be worth carrying out a formal piece of research with a sample of your customers, to help identify opportunities for new services or products.

Expanding Your Customer Base
Think about whether there are customer groups that you do not sell to at present, but who you believe would benefit from your services. Write a list of specific businesses or business types you do not currently sell to, then identify reasons why they might buy from you. If you sell to individual consumers, make a list of specific groups of individuals who could benefit from your service. Write down the characteristics that made this group distinctive, for example, their age, gender, race, occupation, income, hobbies, membership of clubs and associations, and so on. Write down a list of the benefits that your existing products and services can provide to these groups of people.

Unique Selling Propositions
A key question to ask yourself when assessing whether you can exploit the opportunities you are facing, is how you can make yourself different from your competitors. There must be something about your business, products, or the way that you market your service that sets you apart. You will not be able to exploit your opportunities if you provide the same products and services at the same prices and in the same way that your competitors do.

Identify your unique selling proposition (USP). Make a list of all your main competitors; it may be helpful to do this in the form of a grid. Write down areas where you can do something more, better, cheaper, faster, or just differently than them. Identify any specific locations where your competitors don't operate. Find out if they supply to any customer groups that you currently don't. From your list, try to identify two or three key areas where you can position your service or product as being different, or better, than your rivals.

The way you differentiate products, prices, customer service levels, marketing messages, money-back guarantees, upgrade offers, or overall company image will ultimately determine whether you will succeed in capitalizing on new market opportunities.

Partnerships with Other Businesses
It is unlikely that any small business on its own will be able to meet all of the opportunities that it is facing and exploit their full potential. It can often prove really worthwhile to identify other businesses that offer complementary services to your own, which are aimed at the same, or similar, customer groups. By doing this you can open the doors to opportunities for your business that you would otherwise be unable to develop. There are several ways in which you could work in partnership with another business. For example, you could

access their products to sell to your existing customers. You could develop a new product or service based on a combination of your own and another business's product. Both businesses could share costs in joint marketing campaigns, for example at trade fairs, in catalogues, or in brochures. Alternatively, another business might be able to sell your product to a customer group that you currently do not reach. These "piggyback" marketing relationships are increasingly popular, and can help small businesses to develop opportunities very quickly.

WHAT TO AVOID

Spreading Yourself Too Thinly

You must try to avoid a scattergun approach to pursuing the opportunities you are facing. Don't spread your ideas so thinly, that you end up being ineffective in everything you try to achieve.

Being Unrealistic

If you are not selective enough, and have not sufficiently considered the full impact on your ability to develop or deliver a new product or service, or carry out a marketing campaign to a new target audience, you will not make the most of the opportunities that exist. If you do not honestly assess what you have done right and wrong in the past, there is a real danger of repeating mistakes, and failing to achieve your potential.

SEE ALSO

Analyzing Your Business's Strengths, Weaknesses, Opportunities, and Threats (p. 282)
Small and Growing Businesses (p. 422)
Understanding the Effects of Growth (p. 288)
Understanding the Role of Partnerships for Small Business (p. 291)

Understanding the Effects of Growth

GETTING STARTED

All businesses need to plan strategies for growth or run the risk of declining, often suddenly. The most successful approach to growth is an integrated one, in which the business's owner or management team look at how all aspects of the business can work together to reap the benefits of growth. For example, a successful new sales promotion strategy put together by the marketing department has brought in many new customers. In principle, this is fantastic news, but what will happen if the customer services department hasn't taken on enough new staff to deal with new accounts, or if the shipping department cannot cope with the increased demand in orders? All that effort will be wasted, so put plenty of time into planning and look at the whole picture so that you understand exactly what growth means for your business.

FAQS

How do I keep control of a growing business?

Many businesses that start small get by without a proper plan of exactly whom they will serve, how they will focus their resources, and what they aim to achieve. However, as a company grows, it becomes more difficult to operate effectively without a solid and detailed plan. It's a good idea to prepare a business plan (or adapt the one you have already written in the past) to plot the future direction of your company and to address the demands of growth. Consult a business adviser for help with this important task.

How do I make sure that the growth is sustainable?

If your business has tended to grow without specific marketing efforts, you may need to find out more about your market before you can be confident the growth will continue. If you're not sure where the increased customer demand is coming from, you cannot be certain if it will last.

As a start, find out where your most ready markets are and get a better picture of what they want. Look carefully at how your customer base is evolving as it grows; there may be segmentation occurring which requires you to push your product in the direction of new markets.

What are the legal implications of growth?

If your business started life on a "sole proprietorship" basis (or even as a partnership), you may, after a period of growth, have to consider whether incorporation as a limited company would be more beneficial. This change would involve more paperwork and compliance requirements, but would limit your personal financial liability. This is important to consider as turnover grows and your business's financial requirements and risks begin to dwarf your personal resources.

Issues of contractual liability also become more pressing as the size and number of your transactions increase. In time there will be more at stake, and you need to protect yourself and your business with good contracts and terms—both with your suppliers and your customers.

It's very important that you do your research properly and get good professional advice, preferably from your accountant and a solicitor experienced in commercial law, before you make any major decisions. Discuss your options well in advance of any big change.

MAKING IT HAPPEN
Find Finance for Growth

Growing a business without the necessary working capital or investment is difficult at best, and at worst could endanger the whole enterprise. Supplying larger orders or providing a service to more customers invariably means investing in productive capacity long before you get a return on that investment. Sources of finance to help you do this will depend on how much you need and what exactly you need it for.

Bank loans are a common form of finance for growing businesses. Getting substantial amounts of investment finance may require you to relinquish part of your ownership—for instance, selling shares in your company or taking in another partner—and could involve venture capitalists or angel investors.

Hire New Employees

Moving from operating as a sole trader to a partnership or an employer can be a difficult step to take, as it represents many changes for the owner-manager. However, if the business is to grow, it may be an essential progression.

Entrepreneurs have to learn to delegate tasks and relinquish control of some business operations in order to create the capacity for growth. The recruitment of appropriately skilled individuals who are trustworthy, reliable, and dedicated to the job is important. Success depends on the efforts of others, not just the entrepreneur's motivation.

Taking on employees involves substantial costs. When considering cash flow, you will need to take into account the costs of recruitment, training, pension contribution, employee liability, FICA, taxes, health and safety regulations, and personal records, as well as the cost of a salary.

Be selective about who you employ, as it is important to ensure that they will fit in with you or your other employees. Employee dissatisfaction results in low quality products, an unpleasant atmosphere, and general disruption to the flow of business.

An alternative to taking on more employees may be to bring in a partner. Before establishing a partnership, you will need to decide exactly how responsibilities will be split and how soon the partner will have full business control. It is particularly important that you completely trust and feel able to work with the new partner.

Consider subcontracting some work if you are reluctant to employ people directly, though do make sure you assess the firms to whom you intend to subcontract work carefully; an irresponsible company will damage your reputation. Subcontracting may also be a way to increase your customer base, especially if the subcontracted firm offers parallel goods or services to your own.

Consider Relocation

Many small firms are initially run from small, low cost premises—often the home of the owner-manager. As the business expands, so will the work area needed. For some idea of what to expect, consider how expensive it is to move house. For a firm to open additional branches, considerable strategic planning is needed to ensure success. You should be concerned not only with site selection, financing, and staffing, but also with the degree of independence each site will have and the adequacy of information and accounting systems.

Increase Efficiency

To deal with the challenges of growth it is essential to run a well-designed operation. If you need to increase capacity, make sure you allow plenty of time to test out new systems and products and ensure that they work properly. It is all too easy for costs to get out of control. Ensure you invest in suitable cost control systems as you increase capacity—you may need help to do this. Are you working to optimum efficiency? There is no point expanding inefficient systems into bigger ones.

Telecommute

Telecommuting may be an appropriate way to deal with growth. Having employees working from home reduces the pressure on space, decreases overheads, and keeps the office size to a minimum.

✗ WHAT TO AVOID
Not Being Fully Committed to Growth
Decide once and for all if you really are committed to further business growth. There is little point in expanding the business if you decide that you prefer working in a small operation. Are you prepared to deal with the challenges of increased responsibility? Don't fall into the grass is greener trap and think that growing the business won't take up that much of your time and energy. It will, and you need to be sure you have the right people and places in place to help you do it (see below).

Not Having the Capabilities to Run a Larger Team of Employees
Expanding the business will mean that you'll have to learn how to develop and manage a larger working team or employ a manager to help you do that. Be brutally honest with yourself and conduct a "time audit," that is, a detailed breakdown of how you spend your day. Be realistic about how much time you have to spare from the day-to-day running of the business to manage growth. If you think that you can't do it all yourself, think about what new systems and how many new staff you'll need to make sure you can all cope. If you think you can incorporate the extra responsibilities into your day, you might want to undertake a professional management qualification yourself or attend some courses on managing staff.

Not Having Enough Funds to Generate Growth
You must make sure that you fund all your plans to increase capacity. Again, be realistic and be prepared to limit your objectives or delay growth plans until you can commit safely to the levels of funding they require.

SEE ALSO
Identifying Opportunities for Your
Business (p. 285)
Small and Growing Businesses (p. 422)

Understanding the Role of Partnerships for Small Business

GETTING STARTED

Small businesses can enter into partnerships with other businesses working towards a mutually agreed objective. They can be long-term partnerships (for example, developing a new product), or short-term (for entering a new market). Partnerships are especially useful if you are seeking to exploit the new opportunities and challenges created by today's global marketplace. By teaming up with another business possessing complementary skills, you can achieve the strengths needed to exploit new opportunities and undertake new challenges. Inevitably there are risks involved; however, many of the potential problems can be anticipated and avoided by taking sensible steps in advance.

FAQS

What are the benefits of partnerships?

Clearly the overriding benefit of developing partnerships is obtaining access to the extra resources brought by the other partner, and achieving goals which would not be possible alone. When the partner business is operating in another country from your own, there can be additional benefits of access to international markets or new products to import. There are other important advantages too.

- Businesses who would otherwise only be able to reach a new market by over-committing themselves can do so without risking the rest of the business.
- By pooling resources, smaller businesses have more chance of winning a large contract, as they will be seen as being more secure and reliable.
- Partnerships allow small businesses access to technology, know-how, and customers that they could not have reached on their own.
- Partnerships can increase your databases of customers and contacts.

MAKING IT HAPPEN

There are several steps you will need to take before choosing a partner to work with.

Decide What You Want from a Partner

What are the general aims of the partnership? Are you aiming to access a new market, develop a new product, or raise its profile in a certain area? Although details can be worked out at a later date, you need to decide if your partner will be expected to input money, technological know-how, publicity, and so on.

For many reasons, joint ventures based on equal partnerships work best, and by teaming up with another small business, each party is able to contribute without either feeling they are working for the other. However, it is important to resist the urge to approach a business which is very similar to yours. It is better to team up with one that offers complementary skills and services so that you can both contribute without being in direct competition. There will also be less disagreement over which business has most to gain from the partnership.

Investigate Possible Partners

Once a likely candidate has been found and a positive response received, you need to make certain checks. Doing this before you finalize your commitment will make sure that a partner can be trusted. Check that there are no court judgments against them, whether they pay suppliers on time, and what their customer service record is like. If you are working with another business, some of its reputation may rub off onto your business; so it is important that it is good.

Assess Whether You Can Work Together

Many partnerships, especially between small businesses, break up because of personality clashes. A good working relationship must be developed if the partnership is going to work. In many ways working with someone who has a different business style can be helpful, for example, one partner may be less cautious, and the other more so. However, it is important that the business ethos of the two firms is similar; for example, if one partner regards employees as his or her greatest asset, whereas the other considers employees just to represent a huge wage bill every month, it may be very difficult to work well together.

Form the Partnership

The aim of the partnership should be clear from the outset, and put into writing. You should seek legal advice when drafting the formal agreement. The written plan should not only cover goals, financial contributions (such as profit sharing, purchasing, and expenses), and any joint training, but also factors such as any time limit on the partnership and how to end it if necessary. You should make provision for any intellectual property issues which may occur; joint product development, especially technological development, could leave both parties in joint ownership of a patent or copyright. This could cause problems if the partnership dissolves on a negative footing.

Trust is essential; if partners are continually checking up on each other, there is not much hope for the strength of the venture. You are not obligated to reveal everything about the business to the other party if it is not relevant to the project in hand. However, you should decide on how much information the other business can have access to, for example, will it have access to your existing customer base? It is important not to give away unnecessary information and to think carefully before revealing anything that is confidential.

Work Together, Not As Rivals

It is important that you maintain an open working relationship with your partner and avoid treating them like a rival. As with any project, ample time should be given to strategy, planning, promotion, implementation, and back up such as after-sales care.

You should also ensure that employees are given adequate time to get to know the counterparts they will be working with in the partner business, and if possible joint training should be given to both sets of employees to inform them of the goals of the project. Good communication is also essential—so make sure you keep employees informed of progress.

WHAT TO AVOID
Not Doing Enough Research into Your Potential Partner

You really need to find out as much as you can about any potential business partners. If you're not fully aware of the way the other business works and what their objectives are, disputes can arise. For example:

- personality clashes develop with other managers—these can be especially invasive in smaller businesses, where the owner of the firm is likely to have imprinted his or her style on the business, working methods, and staff
- one party feels it is contributing more and effectively carrying the other
- one side takes a disproportionate share of the profits
- there is a mismatch between the two parties in terms of goals
- disputes arise over legal issues such as ownership of copyright material or other intellectual property which has been produced/developed by the partnership

Not Putting the Agreement into Writing

It is easy for different businesses to enter a partnership with differing ideas and goals. Similarly, it is surprising how often two parties will come away from the same meeting with different ideas of what was agreed. Although each may have slightly different aims to achieve, the overall aim of the project should not be in doubt and the best way to achieve this is to have a written agreement signed by both parties.

SEE ALSO
Identifying Opportunities for Your Business (p. 285)
Small and Growing Businesses (p. 422)

Timing the Decision to Export

GETTING STARTED

The lure of foreign markets can be tempting for a small business looking for new customers, especially when your national market is becoming saturated. Such an expansion, however, needs to be thoroughly researched and carefully considered to ensure that the timing is right, both for the business and the market being considered. For a start, your business needs to have proved the success of its products or services closer to home, where the risks and costs of entry are generally going to be lower. This should be reflected not just in customer satisfaction but also in the commercial success of your business over a number of years; it is essential to proceed from a strong financial position if you want to develop markets abroad.

You will need to establish the commitment of your management team, based on in-depth knowledge of exactly what will be involved in the export effort. This support will be important in getting over the many (and unexpected) hurdles of entering a market for the first time. Be prepared to hold back on pursuing your ideas until everyone is "on board." Once this commitment is solid, you can develop the plans, capacity, and systems for your business to launch an export program confidently.

Thorough analysis and understanding of the market you want to enter is vital. Your research and PEST (political, economic, social, and technological) analysis should provide you with a reliable insight into your new market to assess whether this is the right time to enter an export market. Sometimes this acronym is rearranged to read "STEP" analysis.

FAQS

How long does the planning take?

It is possible to fast-track the export planning and development process so that you can be winning your first export orders within six months. On the other hand, the circumstances of your business might require a year or two before you feel comfortable to start exporting. As a practical guideline, you could aim at achieving some progress within a year, but be aware that unexpected problems might force you to take longer.

Is it important to pioneer new markets?

There is obvious merit to being among the first to exploit a new export market, but the risk of being a pioneer may outweigh the possible benefits. It is usually businesses with deep pockets which venture into uncharted territory, and other businesses following will learn by the earlier mistakes. When considering the timing of a new market entry, be aware of all the unknown factors that could cost you dearly. Start with small orders, for instance, and make sure all agreements are in writing and signed by both parties.

MAKING IT HAPPEN

Conduct a PEST Analysis

A PEST analysis—standing for political, economic, socio-cultural, and technological—of the market you plan to enter will ensure that you appreciate all the important factors that impact on your work there.

- **Political factors.** The political arena influences the regulation of businesses and the spending power of consumers and other businesses. Consider issues like: How stable is the political environment? What is the government's overall economic policy? Is the government likely to change tax regulations soon? What is the government's position on marketing ethics? Does the government have a view on culture and religion? Is the government involved in regional trade agreements?

- **Economic factors.** Consider the state of the economy you are planning to enter. This is especially important when planning for international marketing. You need to look at issues like interest rates, the level of inflation, the employment level per capita, long-term prospects for the economy, and gross domestic product.

- **Social factors.** The social and cultural influences on business vary from country to country, so you should consider questions like: What is the dominant religion? What are the attitudes to foreign products and services? Does language affect which products make it into the market? How much time do consumers have for leisure? What are the respective roles of men and women within society? What is the average life span? Are the older generations wealthy? Does the population have a strong opinion on green issues?

- **Technological factors.** Technology is vital for your competitive advantage, so consider these questions: Will technology help reduce the cost and quality of products and services? Do the technologies offer consumers and businesses more innovative products and services such as Internet banking and new generation mobile telephones? How is distribution changed by new technologies? Does technology offer businesses a new way to communicate with consumers?

Set Time-bound Objectives

Within the constraints of your particular business and sector, set some time frames that you can work towards. You need to take into account the level of funding available to implement your plans; the revenue that you expect from your capital outlay; the extent to which your export business will strengthen its position, and the extent to which exports further the overall mission of your business.

Test and Modify Your Product First

In your export development plan, give yourself time to test your product in the market and to make any modifications that might be necessary. Do this before launching a full-scale marketing campaign so that you can deliver, from the start of proper trading, a final product closer to local requirements.

Build Up Skills and Capacity

From your market research, you will develop sales forecasts to use in developing production and supply plans. When timing your export launch, make sure you give yourself enough time to employ and train the necessary people, and to install the systems you will need to meet the demand you expect. You will be working hard to get these new export customers, but you will not be able to keep them if you have not developed the capacity to deliver on new order levels.

Choose the Moment

There may be factors peculiar to your new market that you need to consider when timing your entry. If certain trade barriers or customs duties are being changed or removed, this could present a good opportunity to start trading with a lead on competitors. There may also be certain times of year that see more trade in your sector, particularly if it is seasonal. You would need to consider the conditions on the supply side (for instance, if you are exporting fruit when it is in season at home) and the demand side (where you would want to enter the new market at a time when those fruits are in short supply).

WHAT TO AVOID
Rushing In

The size of a market is no guarantee of its willingness to let in new entrants. Indeed, large markets are often those most heavily contested by big and small players, owing to the high stakes. Take your time in doing your research and in finding the best point of entry.

Unrealistic Expectations of Quick Returns

Most small businesses will be constrained in their export efforts by their limited funds and resources, so your export plan will be tailored to take account of your individual situation. With this in mind, be careful not to expect miracles from a new market. If you are working through an agent or distributor, they might give an overly optimistic forecast of what they might sell; you need to know enough about the market to make a realistic assessment of these forecasts, so that you do not expect too much, too soon. This can be particularly dangerous if your export effort is drawing on cash or resources that are vital to your core, local market.

SEE ALSO
Exporting for the First Time (p. 299)
Small and Growing Businesses (p. 422)

Exporting—Methods of Market Entry

GETTING STARTED

Many first-time exporters feel unsure about the best way to approach their export market and how to manage a complex marketing and distribution process from a distance. This actionlist explains the various ways to approach market entry and also suggests how to choose a sensible market entry method for your business.

FAQS

What do the terms "direct" or "indirect" exporting mean?

Direct exporting means actively developing your venture into overseas markets. This approach requires a great deal of preparation and considerable investment of time. You could employ someone to take charge of part of the process or to act as a representative in the chosen market. Alternatively, you may choose to manage the whole process yourself. Examples of direct exporting include joint ventures, using agents, or selling through trade fairs.

Indirect exporting usually means exporting through customers in the United States, which may eliminate the need for traveling abroad and dealing with complex export processes. However, it still requires considerable commitment. It can be a useful route into selling abroad for small-to-medium enterprises (SMEs), and provides a means of testing product viability in new markets.

Where can I go for advice and information on exporting?

The U.S. Government Export Portal (see address below) offers a range of market information and assistance for exporters, as well as links to other trade resources. The U.S. Commercial Service also offers valuable assistance to help businesses export goods and services to markets worldwide.

Trade associations often have links with international groups or lists of contacts in export markets. Some have well-developed export services and can arrange joint ventures and trade fair visits, as well as provide general advice. All the major banks have international divisions that should be able to

provide useful contacts and give general advice on the financial implications of particular export options.

Many attorneys have special expertise in contract law abroad and should be consulted when signing up an agent or distributor. Freight forwarders are an important part of the distribution process and can also provide advice on terms and paperwork. It may also be helpful to consult the national and trade press of the proposed export market and any international export journals. Often export representatives seeking customers will advertise in these publications.

MAKING IT HAPPEN
Choose an Exporting Method

Look carefully at your proposed market and customers. Clarify the existing channels of distribution for your business's particular type of product. A trade visit will provide a good opportunity to study the local business structure. Are there any legislative issues which will affect sales, such as restrictions on choice of representatives? How do existing customers prefer to do business? For example, many large organizations do not like unsolicited approaches but channel all their buying through an agent.

In many cases, the nature of the product or service being exported will determine the selection of entry method. Make a list of any factors that may affect the way the product should be sold, using experience of the U.S. market where applicable. For example, what level of technical backup and promotional investment will be required? Think about your available resources, such as staff time, language skills, technical and marketing resources, as well as finance. How will domestic business be affected if technical staff are busy dealing with problems abroad?

Investigate Methods of Entry

Commission agents seek orders on behalf of a client in return for an agreed commission on each order. The agent is briefed on appropriate prices and terms and then approaches businesses within a designated area. Agents legally bind the business they represent to any contracts they sign for product orders. They generally seek sole agency rights for a country or region. Agents do not deal with shipping or payment, which must be arranged separately from the United States. An agent will accept no credit risk on stock unless they are a "del credere" agent, charging a higher commission to compensate for the credit risk involved.

Distributors hold stocks of products from which they fulfill local orders. Unlike agents, they usually take legal title to the goods, buying from a business and selling on their own account at prices that they fix themselves. They usually also oversee the export process. It is normal to grant the distributor an agreed area of operation and to take orders from that area through them only.

Sell Direct Using the Business's Own Resources

It is possible to sell direct to individual customers or outlets abroad. This may be appropriate where the customer base is narrow or limited, for example, luxury goods stocked by a small number of exclusive outlets, and when there is little need for servicing or after sales care. However, selling direct will involve considerable resources of time and money.

Attend Trade Fairs

Fairs and exhibitions are held worldwide, attracting customers and suppliers involved in various trades. If your business is considering exhibiting, contact the relevant trade association. Even if your business doesn't exhibit, there will be opportunities to make contacts, research the market, find agents or wholesalers, and develop sales leads.

Consider Franchising

Franchising involves selling a business as a ready-made package to local operators in return for fees and other income, for example a percentage of annual profits. Franchising is a means of expanding rapidly while limiting management responsibility. The operation must be unique in some way to be a viable franchise. The franchisee contributes towards capital and resources, as well as paying a license fee, while the business is expected to provide a range of support, including training and technical services.

Consider License Agreements

A business can grant another firm the right to use its product names, technical specifications, processes, or patents by drawing up a license agreement. A fee (which may or may not include royalties) is charged for the licensed rights. Licensing may depend on the business securing protection for intellectual property rights in the country concerned and may also require government approval.

Consider Joint Ventures

There are many types of joint venture. It may be possible to identify a suitable U.S. firm that is willing to enter into a partnership to begin exporting. This provides an opportunity to pool resources and expertise, but it is important to find a firm with strengths that balance your existing weaknesses. Export clubs can be a good means of locating potential partners.

You could make an arrangement with a compatible business abroad. You might, for example, agree to manage each other's export trade, or combine in a joint operation to enter a specific market or markets. This often involves joint investment. Another option is to work with an international firm. Large international companies, whether U.S. based or in the export market, often seek new products for their sales portfolio. If initial research indicates that a product could work well within a particular business's range, this "piggy back" method is worth exploring.

Investigate Export Houses

Export houses are firms with a detailed knowledge of international sales, who specialize in financing and servicing exports. The price paid for the product on offer will reflect their costs, but in some cases the importer pays the export house fees.

Export consultancies are generally small consultancies specializing in particular markets and services. They usually accept responsibility for all aspects of export administration or will offer particular services and support.

Export merchants buy products outright from the manufacturer and sell them abroad. They usually take delivery and make payment in the United States, and often specialize in certain products. When dealing with a new product, they will require an agreement to protect their investment in building overseas sales, and they may also request product or packaging changes to meet their market requirements.

Confirming houses place orders with manufacturers and suppliers on behalf of overseas organizations and attend to all transportation arrangements. They can also act as agents for U.S. manufacturers and seek orders from their overseas contacts.

Buying Houses

Large overseas businesses, for example, grocery or retail chains, often have buying houses in the United States. These have huge purchasing budgets, and, although businesses usually still have to deal with the physical process of exporting, they are guaranteed fairly large-scale sales.

WHAT TO AVOID
Not Researching Thoroughly

Different markets and countries operate in different ways. In many countries, particularly those in the Middle East and Africa, government regulations may dictate the choice of representation (usually an approved agent), and may stipulate the level of commission. It is important to remember that the best method in one market may not work in another. Many businesses which export to a number of markets deal directly in some areas, while using intermediaries to sell to other territories.

SEE ALSO
Exporting (p. 453)

Exporting for the First Time

GETTING STARTED
Exporting can be a rewarding way for a small firm to develop and grow. At the same time, it presents challenges and risks that are different from those in the domestic market. This actionlist will help you identify potential problems and plan for them.

FAQS
Why should I export?
There are many reasons why small firms seek to export. These might relate to the personal aims of the owner or manager (new challenges, credibility, added wealth, and so on). They might also relate to the commercial needs of the business (increased turnover and profits, reduced reliance on the home market, and so on).

When is the right time to begin exporting?
Exporting should be seen in the wider context of the strategic business plan. The potential rewards are massive, but a substantial investment is required to achieve them. Beware of overstretching your resources. Often, additional financing and evidence to show that the investment will pay off may be required.

Before you commit your business to the additional costs of export activity, carry out a business "fitness check," to assess whether it is in a condition to sustain the additional effort required (or, indeed, to maintain current levels of activity properly). Five areas that should be of particular concern are: your knowledge of the market; your production, distribution, and sales capacity; your flexibility to meet market needs; the financial resources available to you; and management, staffing, and skills resources.

MAKING IT HAPPEN
Know the Key Factors for Success
Successful exporters demonstrate management commitment to exporting and will have carried out thorough research and planning. They will have conducted market visits and research validation and will have developed contacts and relationships. They will have a feel for foreign cultures and languages and an eye for detail in export documentation and procedures. They will also have put the emphasis on quality.

Avoid Potential Problem Areas
A number of problems can arise that may not appear to be directly related to exporting. The added challenge of exporting, whether successful or not, can show up the flaws in a business. Growing firms can find it hard to recruit staff with the right knowledge and experience. Recognize your limitations and be prepared to use appropriate external advisers. They can provide strategic guidance, commission research, and act as a sounding board for problems.

The cost of breaking into foreign markets is frequently underestimated. The venture should be seen as an investment, covering the initial costs of research, developing contacts, and the losses incurred before sales begin to cover the extra cost. It may be necessary to explore separate financial arrangements in order to support any exporting ventures. Pricing is another potential problem area. Having established the market potential for the product or service, the price the market will bear is crucial in determining how profitable the returns will be.

Accepting substantial new business without thinking through all the implications can be risky and may cause operational problems. Cash flow problems destroy many promising firms, and payment can take longer for exports. Stock control is a particular issue in terms of capital and prompt delivery. The administration of orders, insufficient production capacity, and extensive transit times may produce delays unacceptable to the customer.

All investment of management and staff time, money, and costs must be taken into account. It will be necessary to consider factory costs, export packing, inland transportation and handling costs, export transportation costs, insurance costs, overseas handling and transportation costs. There are also taxes: any customs duties payable overseas; freight forwarders' charges, inclusive of documentation; any direct office costs, including any salesperson's commission; overseas agents' charges; advertising; costs of money and credit; and cost of insurance coverage against exchange rate risk when applicable.

Work with Other Organizations

A lot of advice, information, and support is available to exporters through business support organizations, much of it free. The U.S. Government Export Portal (see address below) is an excellent source of information and provides a number of helpful services and links.

There are also organizations that can provide the necessary expertise to help a business to develop an export market. For example, the Manufacturing Extension Partnership (MEP) is a nationwide network of over 400 not-for-profit centers that work directly with U.S. manufacturers on a wide range of issues, from process improvements and worker training to business practices and applications of information technology.

Transportation and Distribution

There are many unfamiliar issues involved in the exporting of goods, including aspects of transportation and distribution that may have not been a problem in the past. The following paragraphs cover some of these issues.

Freight forwarders offer comprehensive documentation and transportation services, not necessarily using their own vehicles. They undertake door-to-door services for shipments. An efficient freight forwarder will take advantage of the keen competition between transportation operators to secure the best prices. You might also consider

using a freight forwarder to deal with documentation. Simple typing errors can lead to long and costly delays at overseas customs. Freight forwarders can be found in most metropolitan areas and are usually listed in the Yellow Pages under "freight" or "transportation." In addition, the National Customs Brokers and Forwarders Association of America can provide exporters with information about their members (see address below).

Suitable packaging should be used to ensure that goods reach their destination undamaged at the most economical cost. For export, packaging may have to be tougher and/or meet specific legal standards. Particular attention should be paid to any printed descriptions on the packaging. Another issue is the terms of delivery. The point at which the business's responsibility for the goods ends and that of the overseas buyer begins is determined by the contract terms. As there is a wide range of options available, it is essential that the business is fully aware of its responsibilities regarding insurance and contractual obligations.

Manage the Risks

If you explore foreign markets directly, reduce the initial financial investment and risk by focusing on one, or fewer, markets. In exporting it is even more important that delivery promises are kept and products are acceptable and reliable. The administration and documentation and the physical distribution of products can be handled efficiently by external specialist companies. Marketing, including overseas visits, can be contracted out to self-employed export marketing specialists.

There are various types of risks to consider when exporting. Insurance will cover straightforward commercial risks such as those encountered during transportation. More critical is the risk that an overseas buyer may refuse to accept delivery of goods ordered or may take delivery, refuse to pay, and disappear. It is therefore essential to put all of the terms (Incoterms) of the contract in writing, and select a secure method of getting paid (normally through a bank) which is appropriate to the risk involved.

Political risks can vary from political instability (military coups) to the sudden imposition of restrictions by a government on payments for importers. Currencies may fluctuate wildly or cease to be convertible into other currencies, making them effectively valueless. Current assessments of political and economic risks can be obtained through the U.S. State Department, the Office of the U.S. Trade Representative, or U.S. embassies and consulates abroad.

Interest rate risks can be especially important in the case of high-value capital ventures where there is a long period of time between the initial planning work and final payment for the product. In such cases, calculations of cost should take account of the charge for the money required. There is also a risk that the rate of exchange between the U.S. dollar and the buyer's currency will change between the agreeing of terms and the completion of the deal. Hedging mechanisms are available that enable exporters to protect themselves from exchange rate changes, and banks can provide further details.

WHAT TO AVOID
Exporting When Your Business is Unfit
Exporting can put pressure on a business. It is essential that your business is running efficiently before taking on the added complications of exporting.

Not Getting the Right Advice
Take full advantage of the free advice and information available. Some of the government agencies listed below can assist with finding partners who can give the right type of support for your business's own particular products and markets.

Providing Inadequate Training
Training on exporting, for both management and employees, is essential. Training will enable your business to make an informed decision about which foreign markets to investigate, and how to go about exporting to them.

SEE ALSO
Export Documentation (p. 302)
Exporting (p. 453)
Timing the Decision to Export (p. 293)

Export Documentation

GETTING STARTED

To the small business exporter, the required documentation can seem daunting, but it is worth getting documentation right. Having the correct information and knowing where, when, and to whom to send it, speeds up the processing of individual transactions and inspires confidence in the business. Indeed, where letters of credit are involved, correct documentation is essential to receive payment. Export documentation is subject to frequent change and amendment, and requirements vary from country to country.

FAQS

Why would I need to use export documentation?

Documentation is used to reduce delayed shipment and delivery, to describe cargo, for customs clearance, to indicate the ownership of goods for collection purposes or in the event of dispute, and to obtain payment.

What are Incoterms?

Incoterms are the standard trade definitions most commonly used in international sales contracts, that help traders in different countries to understand one another. Export documentation requirements often depend on the Incoterm used. Incoterms are standardized and internationally recognized abbreviations.

Who can I ask for assistance with export documentation?

Information on export documentation is available through the International Chamber of Commerce, International Trade Association, the Trade Information Center, Export Assistance Centers, and foreign government embassies and consulates located throughout the United States.

Freight forwarders also offer a range of services covering the physical transportation of goods for export, usually including packing and documentation. Export management and documentation services are also an option.

✓ MAKING IT HAPPEN

Review Your Situation

The best way to understand and employ export documentation is to review the

diverse forms that could apply to your specific export situation. Perhaps the best place to start is with Electronic Data Interchange, a form of export documentation that is growing in use.

Electronic Data Interchange (EDI)

Electronic Data Interchange is increasingly important to the international exchange of commercial information. It greatly reduces the time required for document exchange and increases accuracy by eliminating transcription errors. EDI systems use conventions and standards of formatting for correct data delivery. International standards have been devised so that various documents, for example invoices and orders, can be exchanged between companies. Their precise layout makes them simpler to use for trading partners in different countries without a common language.

EDI involves a computer with a modem and communications software (to provide data translation) at either end of a telephone line. The Internet can also be used as a means of sending documentation. Benefits include speed, accuracy (supported by database files), and the ability to send to a large number of recipients using one system. Disadvantages include problems of providing adequate security and dealing with global orders without knowing the integrity of the person doing the ordering.

Beyond EDI

Beyond EDI, there are many other types of export documentation. These types are handily listed, and explained, on the United States Government Export Portal. The following listing comes mainly from that source:

Documentation required for export shipments varies widely according to the country of destination and the type of product being shipped. Determining what additional documentation is necessary can be a frustrating process.

Exporters may want to consider having a reputable freight forwarder handle the formidable amount of documentation that exporting requires as forwarders are specialists in this process.

The following documents are commonly used in exporting, but which of them are necessary in a particular transaction depends on the requirements of the U.S. government and the government of the importing country.

The **Shipper's Export Declaration** (SED or form 7525-V) is available through the Government Printing Office and a number of other commercial outlets. It can be electronically filed.

A **Commercial Invoice** is a bill for the goods from the seller to the buyer. These invoices are often used by governments to determine the true value of goods when assessing customs duties. Governments that use the commercial invoice to control imports will often specify its form, content, number of copies, language to be used, and other characteristics.

A **Certificate of Origin** is only required by some countries. In many cases, a statement of origin printed on company letterhead will suffice. Special certificates are needed for countries with which the United States has special trade agreements, such as Mexico, Canada, and Israel.

A **NAFTA Certificate of Origin** is needed for shipments to Mexico and Canada.

CE Mark requirements must be met in order to market goods in the European Union (EU). Once a manufacturer has earned a CE Mark for its product, it may affix the CE Mark to the product, and then the product may be marketed throughout the EU with-out having to undergo further modifications in each EU member country.

A **Bill of Lading** is a contract between the owner of the goods and the carrier (as with domestic shipments). For vessels, there are two types: a straight Bill of Lading that is non-negotiable, and a negotiable or shipper's order Bill of Lading. The latter can be bought, sold, or traded while the goods are in transit. The customer usually needs an original as proof of ownership to take possession of the goods.

An **Insurance Certificate** is used to assure the consignee that insurance will cover the loss of or damage to the cargo during transit. This certificate can be obtained from your freight forwarder.

An **Export Packing List** is considerably more detailed and informative than a standard domestic packing list. It itemizes the material in each individual package and indicates the type of package, such as a box, crate, drum, or carton. Both commercial stationers and freight forwarders carry packing list forms.

Import Licenses are the responsibility of the importer. Including a copy with the rest of your documentation, however, can sometimes help avoid problems with customs in the destination country.

A **Consular Invoice** is a document that is required in some countries. It describes the shipment of goods and shows information such as the consignor, consignee, and value of the shipment. If required, copies are available from the destination country's embassy or consulate in the United States.

Air freight shipments are handled by **Air Waybills**, which can never be made in negotiable form.

Inspection Certification is required by some purchasers and countries in order to attest to the specifications of the goods shipped. This is usually performed by a third party and often obtained from independent testing organizations.

A **Dock Receipt** and a **Warehouse Receipt** are used to transfer accountability when the export item is moved by the domestic carrier to the port of embarkation and left with the ship line for export.

A **Destination Control Statement** appears on the Commercial Invoice, and Ocean or Air Waybill of lading to notify the carrier and all foreign parties that the item can be exported only to certain destinations.

An **Export License** is a U.S. Government document required for "dual use" exports (commercial items which could have military applications) or exports to embargoed countries. Most export transactions do not require specific approval from the U.S. Government. Before shipping your product, make sure you understand the concept of dual use and the basic export control regulations.

The source for the above listing, which we gratefully acknowledge, is the U.S. Government Export Portal.

WHAT TO AVOID

Not Getting it Right First Time
Make sure your documentation is correctly completed first time; delays caused by missing or incorrect paperwork can seriously affect cash flow. Mistakes can also lead to customs fines or increased duty.

Not Getting the Right Advice
Take as much advice as possible when dealing with paperwork. Talk to an export counselor, the International Chamber of Commerce, the agent or distributor, and so on to insure that you are fully prepared.

SEE ALSO
Exporting (p. 453)
Exporting for the First Time (p. 299)

Importing for the First Time

GETTING STARTED

Importing is the process of bringing goods from one country into another. The main reasons for importing are either to obtain goods or materials from a source which is the cheapest available or of the highest quality for a given price, or to obtain raw materials, components, or finished goods that are not available in this country.

This actionlist explains why you might consider importing, how to go about it, and some of the common pitfalls you should be aware of. If your business is unfamiliar with import procedures, it is a good idea to employ a clearing agent who will deal with procedures on the business's behalf.

FAQS

How might I find sources of supply?

One way is to respond to advertisements placed by would-be suppliers, for example in the trade press or on the Internet. If a supplier is required for particular items, advertise in the appropriate overseas publications and through your business's Web site. Research possible sources thoroughly, and make a personal visit to each supplier on your shortlist.

There are numerous directories of products and services, of which the best known is *Kompass*. Available in book form or on CD-ROM in almost 70 countries, including all the main trading nations, this publication can be found in most main libraries. If direct access to information on suppliers in a particular country proves problematic, the country's embassy in the United States may be able to help. There may also be a joint Chamber of Commerce that encourages trade between the United States and the country of interest.

Sometimes, an individual or organization overseas can be appointed to act as an agent and manage deals with suppliers on your behalf. However, payment of a fee or commission will usually be required, unless the individual or organization works on an export program run by the foreign government.

MAKING IT HAPPEN

Arranging to Import

The simplest way to import is to do it indirectly, which means that someone else handles the importation process, and goods are simply purchased from them. These importers can be wholesalers or import merchants; commission agents or distributors working for the overseas manufacturer; or a U.S. subsidiary of the overseas business. Indirect importing can be less risky as it usually involves buying from a U.S.-registered business covered by U.S. law, and payment is usually in U.S. dollars. It usually costs more than direct importing, however.

Direct importing is when the business is in personal contact with the overseas suppliers. It gives the business more control over the process, and may even prove to be more profitable. However, it will be necessary to find the right overseas suppliers and to handle negotiations, regulations, and paperwork personally.

Potential Pitfalls of Importing

An importer often holds the linguistic advantage over a buyer, and language can be a significant barrier. Specify that any correspondence, particularly quotations and contracts, must be in English. Making initial contact overseas will be easier if the manager or an employee of the business can speak the other language.

The physical distance in moving goods increases the risk of delays and means that client-customer servicing is more expensive. These risks need to be built into planning, especially if the business is run on a Just-in-Time basis. The total cost of the goods bought has the potential to be much higher than the price agreed on for the actual items. Additional costs may include packing, transport, insurance, and customs duty. The business will therefore need to ensure that allowances have been made for such costs in budget calculations, or that they are included in the total contract price that will be paid.

It is essential to consider which currency is to be used in the transaction. A foreign supplier is often much more comfortable dealing in their own currency and may be able to quote a more competitive price. However, you will need to pay for the exchange, and money may be lost if the exchange rate fluctuates between placing the order and making the payment. If the transaction is in U.S. dollars it will be easier to ascertain how much will be paid, but the supplier may ask a higher price for the privilege. The further into the future the transaction is, the greater the uncertainty, and the more it is likely to cost. If orders are likely to be large and frequent, then buying in the foreign currency may be preferable, hedging any risk by agreeing to a forward exchange contract with a bank.

Import Quotations and Orders

State your requirements clearly and consistently when requesting quotations, so that responses can be easily compared. Ensure that you specify the quantity, expected order date, and expected payment terms (for example, form of payment, currency, and payment date). Be clear about details such as specific packaging, labeling, and transportation requirements (including terms of, and responsibility for, arranging delivery). State your requirements for goods to meet specific quality, technical, or safety standards, and the requirements that are related to the business's legal obligations (these will be of particular importance). It is important to agree under which country's legislation any trading contract is made.

The more professional the request looks, the more willing a company will be to do business. The name and title of the person to whom responses should be sent, and also the business's full address, with phone and fax numbers and e-mail addresses, should be provided.

Agreeing to payment terms can be difficult until business creditworthiness has been proven. Signify good intentions by giving the supplier the name of the business's bank and inviting them to ask for a reference (the bank must be informed about this first). There are a number of ways to pay, ranging from cash in advance to cash on delivery. Two of the safest methods for the business and the supplier are letters of credit and bills of exchange. The bank will be able to give advice regarding the details.

Once a supplier has been chosen, the order placed should include the same details as the quotation, with any agreed amendments. It is also important to specify any conditions of purchase. To avoid contract disputes, the supplier must agree to all of the terms of the order, in writing.

Import Controls

Import sanctions, quotas, and other controls can be imposed in the United States or alternatively may be put in place by the export regulations of the supplier's country. Importers should check with the supplier to find out if an export license from the supplier's country will be required. The range of goods subject to controls is extensive, and your business should check with its regulatory body.

Customs and Border Protection, part of the new U.S. Department of Homeland Security, collects duties and can also provide details of what is expected regarding an importer's responsibilities. For example, the Harmonized System is an internationally recognized way of coding imports so they can be recognized in trade statistics, and for the charging of duty. The full code number should be agreed on and quoted on all documents by both importer and supplier.

Transport and Delivery when Importing

Terms of delivery may be encountered in abbreviation form and come from an internationally recognized list, known as "Incoterms." In some cases the definitions of the terms may vary by country, so you should seek advice from the International Chamber of Commerce.

The terms of delivery should always be agreed on in quotations and orders. They determine what the price includes, where delivery of the goods takes place, and where possession passes from the exporter to the importer. These points are important because they will affect decisions such as final cost and insurance responsibility. The choice of transportation used will depend upon the type of goods, and the quantity, urgency, and cost. The route options of air, sea, road, or rail all have advantages and disadvantages. For some goods it may also be possible to use postal services.

In many cases, when importing for the first time it is a good idea to use the services of a freight forwarding company. They usually have agents overseas and can therefore arrange most aspects of overseas transportation and insurance.

✘ WHAT TO AVOID

Not Understanding the Business from an Exporter's Point of View

As an importer, your business may be requested by its overseas contacts to trace goods or services in the United States and then export them. A willingness to fulfill such reciprocal requests will help to build a good working relationship and will also result in an improved knowledge of the supplier.

Not Taking all Costs into Account

If price is a factor, businesses should carefully consider whether importing works out cheaper, especially in cases where payment of duty, transportation costs, agent's commission, and so on, are required. Other factors, such as reliability of supply, may also be an issue.

Not Inspecting Goods that are Received

It is essential that any goods received are inspected promptly, in case it is necessary to reject them or make an insurance claim.

SEE ALSO

Exporting (p. 453)

WORKING ONLINE

Creating a Basic Web Site

GETTING STARTED

A Web site is a way of informing customers and other groups such as suppliers, journalists, or employees about your company. A basic Web site involves delivering essential information that is easy to read and well laid out. In Web site design, simplicity is always best. A Web site must also be actively promoted to make people aware of its existence. When approaching Web site design, ask yourself the following important questions:

- Who are the people that I want to communicate with (your target market)?
- How am I going to structure my information so it is easy to navigate and read?
- How am I going to let people know that my Web site exists?
- How am I going to keep my Web site updated and keep people informed of new content?

FAQS

How much information should I include on a Web site?

Provide the information that your visitors are likely to read. Don't fill your Web site with irrelevant and/or repetitive information as it will clutter your site and make the important information hard to find.

How often should I change content?

You should change your content whenever you have something new and important to say, and whenever content already on the site is out of date. Ideally you should try to publish fresh content every week.

Can I transfer printed copy to the Web site?

Printed copy can be used as a starting point for Web copy, but the structure and length would probably be unsuitable. People like to read short, punchy copy on the Web, so snappy headings and summaries are important. For a Web site to be truly effective, you must also use links (known as "hypertext") so that people can click through for further information.

MAKING IT HAPPEN

Know Who You Want to Reach

Before you do anything, decide who you want to reach. Prioritize your information for your most important audiences. Ask yourself:

- Do I want to reach new customers? In new markets?
- What can I say on my Web site that will turn a potential customer into an actual one?
- Do I want to offer support for existing customers?
- Do I want to provide information to attract new staff?

Keep It Simple

Web site design is about the design and delivery of information, not about graphic design. Only a small proportion of Internet users have access to broadband, so it is best to avoid fancy graphics and moving images. They slow down a site and frustrate visitors looking for information. Good Web site design has simple layout and rich content that is well organized. The best, most successful Web sites in the world don't employ fancy gimmicks; neither should you. Keep it simple. Maximize the content and minimize the presentation.

Structure Your Information Well

When people come to your Web site, they want to find information quickly. They have come for a purpose and they are probably impatient and skeptical. It is therefore essential to make your Web site as accessible and easy to navigate as possible.

A well-structured Web site needs good links that allow the visitor to navigate to other sections of the site. Without these links, a page becomes a dead end.

Include Important Web Site Sections and Links

You should have at least some of the following sections on your Web site. Links to these sections should be provided in a set of essential links placed prominently on every page of the Web site.

Home page

The home page is the first page on your Web site and the most important, as it is usually the first page visitors see. From a linking point of view, the home page is referred to as "Home." It should always be the first link in your set of essential links. The home page itself should be full of punchy, attention-grabbing headings and summaries that quickly inform the visitor of, for example, what you do, what you have to sell, or what special offers you have. The Microsoft home page (www.microsoft.com) is a great example of using a home page well.

What's New

This section contains information on important news, events, and press releases. Always keep this section updated, and make sure that you date each entry. You should plan to add an entry for this section at least once a week, but remember to remove old items too.

About

This section should contain essential information about your business or organization. If the section contains a lot of information it should be broken down into manageable subsections. "About" information includes the following:

- mission: a short description of the organization and what it seeks to achieve;
- key strengths: key products, market position, manufacturing, skills, distribution;
- company background;
- management team: pictures and short biographies of key members of the management team;
- financial information: annual results, reserves, financial management, investment information;

- contact and location details: this should link to the Contact section on your Web site.

Products

This is the core part of your Web site, containing the things you have to sell. It should contain a brief overview of products and services and links to detailed information on specific products or services, containing:

- product/services description;
- product applications;
- business case and ROI (return on investment): how using your product can make and/or save money;
- specifications;
- purchase and delivery details;
- frequently asked questions (FAQs);
- pricing (be sure to specify currency);
- product reviews;
- where you sell to (specify the countries or regions you do or do not sell to).

Purchase

This is an essential link if you have a facility that allows people to buy direct from your Web site. Ideally you should also create a small graphic to be displayed prominently, particularly on the home page, informing customers that they can purchase your products online.

Customers

People want to know who your customers are. Include a list of your key customers and a selection of quotes and case studies

Partners

If you have a number of partners and joint ventures, you should have a section describing them, explaining how they allow you to deliver a better service.

Contact

This section should contain all your essential contact information including:

- e-mail address;
- physical address and map of location;
- telephone and fax.

Search

If your Web site has more than 50 pages, you need a search facility to enable visitors to find information. Aim to search box on every single page of your Web site, preferably near the top.

Offer an E-mail Newsletter

Every Web site should offer an e-mail newsletter. If visitors give their e-mail address on their first visit, you can send them a regular weekly or monthly e-mail newsletter to tell them what's new.

Use Metadata

Every Web page should have a title. Where appropriate, you should create "metadata" for your content. This is a method of describing your content and it should include: classification (type of information), page title and headings, summary, date of publication, author name, and keywords that appear in the text. Search engines use this metadata to index your Web site properly, so that visitors can find quickly what they are looking for.

Make Sure You Have the Proper Footer Information

The bottom of every page should have footer information containing:
- a list of the essential links for the Web site;
- essential contact details: main address, telephone and fax, e-mail;
- the copyright notice;
- your privacy policy.

Remember to Promote Your Web Site

A Web site needs promotion. Promotional strategies include:
- registering with the major search engines (Alta Vista, Google, Yahoo), as well as search engines specific to your industry or sector;
- making sure that your Web site and e-mail address are on all your promotional literature.

Do It Yourself or Get a Design Company

If you are a competent computer user, you may well be able to do most of the work yourself, using packages such as Microsoft FrontPage or Macromedia's Dreamweaver, but you may require a graphic designer to help you with design issues.

WHAT TO AVOID

Being Too Clever

Some sites try too hard to entertain without providing hard information. Animation, multimedia, video clips, and other tricks can obscure important data.

Poor Classification, Navigation, and Search

Good classification, navigation, and search are essential for a successful Web site. Customers expect easy access to the information they want. If they can't find it easily on your site, they will go somewhere else.

Content That Is Difficult to Read

Many Web sites try to impress by using lots of color, but the easiest text to read is black on a white background. Keep paragraphs, line lengths, and documents short.

SEE ALSO
Computers, Information Technology, and E-commerce (p. 440)
Coping with Computer Viruses (p. 318)
Writing Well for the Web (p. 326)

Outsourcing Your Web Site

GETTING STARTED

As your business grows, you may become dependent on a larger and more sophisticated Web site. Running a large Web site is a complex operation that requires substantial IT architecture and support. This can take the focus of your business away from its core business of selling, marketing, and supporting your products and services. It will also tie up any technical staff on your team. Outsourcing involves hiring third party professionals to manage and run your Web site's operations for an ongoing fee.

When approaching outsourcing, remember to:
- ensure that a comprehensive contract is in place, and that there are proper metrics and management structures;
- make sure that you choose a stable, well-funded outsourcing vendor with a good track record for service and support.

FAQS

What are the key factors that drive outsourcing?
- The need to focus on core business activities rather than on building up a large IT function.
- Lack of sufficiently skilled staff to run complex Web operations.
- Flexibility: a quality outsource vendor can respond more quickly to rapid changes in customer demand.

MAKING IT HAPPEN

Develop an Outsourcing Strategy

When considering the outsourcing of Web functions, think about exactly why you want to outsource. Is it:

Do you want to outsource:
- to reduce costs?
- to give greater flexibility?
- because you can't find the right personnel with the right IT skills?
- to guarantee a more reliable service?
- to focus better on your core business?
- to keep your IT department as small as possible?
- to reduce staffing levels?

Be Prepared

Deciding on an outsourcer is a complex and time-consuming process, so think about what you want to achieve and why. When developing your strategy, it is best not to be too open with outsourcing vendors. They will naturally want to sell you what they have, and may try to shape your thinking. It is better initially to go to a quality independent consultant who will help you think through all the issues and develop the comprehensive request for proposals (RFP).

When you finally engage with your shortlist of outsourcing vendors, they will have many detailed questions on how your operations are currently run. If you cannot answer these questions you will slow the whole process down, and will encourage the vendor to put forward a less fully and clearly defined contract than if it had had all the required information.

Choose a Stable, Well-funded Outsourcer

Choose a company that has a good reputation, is well funded, and has a good track record. When choosing an outsourcing partner, ask the following questions:
- How stable and well funded is it?
- Does it have a satisfied customer base?
- Has it successfully dealt before with the same needs as mine?

Make Certain That You Receive the Right Service and Support

The more you outsource, the more dependent you become on your outsourcer, so it is vital that your chosen vendor delivers comprehensive service and support.

Remember That Choosing an Outsourcing Vendor Takes Time

Outsourcing is a major strategic move involving much research and negotiation, so do not impose tight deadlines on yourself.

Ensure That a Comprehensive Contract Is in Place

An outsourcing contract should describe exactly what is to be delivered. It should state penalties for nondelivery. Legal expertise should be brought in early in the process, ideally when the RFP is being developed, so that everyone understands the legal implications of everything required and promised. However, the IT environment is constantly changing, and the contract must recognize this. Quality contracts are designed to facilitate later change and renegotiation.

Avoid long-term contracts. Vendors will argue that, because they have to bear a high up-front cost, you should sign a five to ten year contract with them. This does not make sense in a rapidly changing IT and e-commerce world; a two-year contract is a more reasonable option.

Determine How This Relationship Will Be Managed and Measured

You must develop a set of metrics to measure how the outsourcer is meeting the objectives set by the contract. By doing this regularly, and addressing issues as they arise, major disputes, which benefit neither party, can be avoided.

Outsourcing is as much about managing the day-to-day relationship between you and the outsource vendor as it is about managing the technology. While a contract is important, prevention, by management that keeps a regular track of what is expected and what has been delivered, is better than cure.

Have a Corporate Technology Strategy

You are outsourcing your technology, not your technology strategy, and will always need skilled in-house resources to help you plan your direction from a technological point of view. Your outsourcer cannot do

this; if they do, their recommendations will reflect their own strategy rather than yours.

Remember That Outsourcing Is Outsourcing

You cannot have the same level of control over the day-to-day running of your IT infrastructure after you outsource it, but some businesses forget that and try to achieve such control. This is counterproductive. You chose your outsourcer because they do the job better and more efficiently than you do.

Consider the Security Issues

Outsourcing creates an increased security risk. You must establish that the outsource vendor will adhere to your security policy, and that all work done integrates proper security procedures. Specific questions to ask are:

- What is the outsourcer's security policy?
- What are its data backup and disaster recovery procedures?
- How is your data safeguarded from its other customers?
- How is your data safeguarded from its own employees?
- How is it insured in relation to security breaches?

WHAT TO AVOID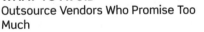
Outsource Vendors Who Promise Too Much

Outsource vendors have been known to over-promise and under-deliver.

Getting Rid Entirely of the Internal IT Web Operation

Some internal IT resource is necessary to take a more strategic view of the Web operation in order to plan its future evolution.

Going for the Lowest Price

Going for the lowest price rarely works out well. Service and support are critical elements in outsourcing, and the outsourcer that offers the lowest price is also, generally speaking, the one who will offer the least support. It is also the one most likely to go out of business.

Not Being Able to Deliver the Right Information

To deliver an outsourcing service, the vendor requires very detailed information on your current IT and Web setup. If you can't provide this information, you slow the whole process down, giving imperfect solutions.

Badly Framed Contracts

Long-term contracts are too often developed on the basis of short-term financial goals, such as cost cutting. Thus, the contract is unsuitable and renegotiation is required.

SEE ALSO

Computers, Information Technology, and E-commerce (p. 440)

Managing E-mail

GETTING STARTED

E-mail is a powerful communications tool. Used properly, it can allow a business to work more efficiently and to communicate more actively with customers. E-mail is fast and cost-effective; however, it is too often treated in a casual manner. Like every other business tool, the use of e-mail needs to be managed and this can seem overwhelming if you don't have that much experience of the online world. This actionlist sets out to give you some pointers, though, so bear in mind the following:

- because e-mail is such an easy form of communication it is often misused, thus leading to e-mail overload;
- if your business has a Web site, it's important to implement and monitor a policy for responding to e-mails so that you can keep on top of them all;
- writing good e-mails is a skill that is too often absent in e-mail communication, but it can be learned.

MAKING IT HAPPEN

Manage E-mail Overload

E-mail has revolutionized the way business is done today, but so many e-mails are sent that there is a danger that important messages may be swamped. It is estimated that by 2005 there will be 36 billion e-mails sent every day. To prevent your business from succumbing to e-mail overload, you need to establish standards on how e-mail is sent and replied to. Training may well be required in order to ensure that you (and your staff, if you have any) understand and implement best practice in e-mail management.

E-mail Management on a Web Site

If you have a Web site, show contact details prominently. A key part of such contact is e-mail. You must decide how many e-mail addresses you will have: will each department have its own special e-mail address, for example, sales@mycompany.com; support@mycompany.com? If you have staff to help you deal with e-mails, decide who e-mails should go to. What happens if the addressee is unavailable? Should managers be cc'd on all incoming e-mails? How will e-mail communication be tracked?

You also need to think about setting some standards for replying to messages. Standards for replying to e-mail must be established. Studies indicate that many businesses are unprofessional at responding to e-mail communications, and those that would never dream of leaving a phone to ring unanswered behave in a lackadaisical manner when it comes to replying to e-mail, so work out a time limit for replying to received messages, stick to it, and monitor it. You may also decide to have an automatic reply message for all your addresses; this will inform the sender that the e-mail has been received, and that a response will be given within X hours.

Write and Reply to E-mails

When you're writing or replying to an e-mail, bear the following points in mind:

- respond quickly, but only respond—or write in the first place—when you have something worthwhile to say;
- make the subject line interesting, if it's not interesting, then the chances of your e-mail being opened are diminished;
- if you are replying to an e-mail, change the subject line as appropriate;
- although the writing style for e-mails is—in general—casual, it should not be over-casual. Don't try to be too friendly. Always strive to be polite. It is good manners to address the person you are communicating with, and to sign/type your name at the end;

- check your spelling; e-mails that are filled with spelling or grammatical errors reflect poorly on the sender;
- keep e-mails short. Get to the point. Long e-mails put people off;
- avoid attachments, unless they are essential. A general rule is never to send an attachment to someone who is not expecting it;
- don't reply in anger. It is very easy to respond to an e-mail that makes you angry. Don't. Count to at least 10 before replying. Remember, e-mail is a rather distant medium of communication, and it is very easy for misunderstandings to occur;
- be careful what you write. Write nothing in an e-mail that you can't defend in a court of law.

SEE ALSO

Computers, Information Technology, and E-commerce (p. 440)
Coping with Computer Viruses (p. 318)
Using E-mail Marketing Effectively (p. 329)

Coping with Computer Viruses

GETTING STARTED

Computer viruses are a growing threat on the Internet, and if your business operates online they are something you need to bear in mind as they cost companies billions of pounds globally every year. By September 2001, it was estimated that one in every 300 e-mails contained a virus, up from one in every 700 in October 2000. In addition, it is now possible to get a computer virus by visiting a Web site or simply by opening an e-mail. To combat computer viruses:

- ensure that you have the very latest antivirus software and that you scan your entire computer regularly;
- ensure that you have the very latest software security patches for your computer;
- immediately delete suspicious e-mails and be very careful when opening unexpected attachments;
- don't download anything from the Internet except from reputable Web sites;
- back up your data regularly.

MAKING IT HAPPEN
Understand Computer Viruses, Trojan Horses, and Worms

In its simplest form, a computer virus attaches itself to computer files, and then seeks to replicate itself. Viruses can infect all sorts of files, from program and system files to Word documents and HTML files. The Internet enables viruses to spread with extraordinary speed.

What is known as a "Trojan horse" pretends to serve a useful function, such as a screen saver. However, as soon as it is run, it carries out its true purpose, which can be anything from using the computer as a host to infect other computers, to wiping the entire hard disk of the computer. Never download software over the Internet unless you are sure of its authenticity.

A computer worm does not try to damage the files it infects. Its objective is rather to replicate itself as quickly and as often as possible. Computer worms are a major drain on the Internet because they clog up bandwidth.

Remember That Prevention Is Much Better Than Cure

Viruses can be extremely difficult to get rid of. You may think you have cleaned them out with your antivirus software, but they may well have inserted hidden code in your operating system that is almost impossible to detect. It is, therefore, essential to stop viruses from getting into your computer in the first place. You do this by:

- making sure that you have the very latest antivirus software; popular antivirus software types include McAfee and Norton;
- joining an e-mail list that will inform you of new virus attacks. As soon as you hear of them, check your vendor for the latest updates;
- scanning your entire computer for viruses at least once a week;
- always making sure that you have the very latest security patches for your computer software. Viruses are always at their most potent in the first hours and days after their release, so it is vital to implement software patches as soon as they become available;
- if you use recent releases of Microsoft Windows, regularly checking www.microsoft.com/security/ for news and updates. Microsoft also has a service that will check your computer for security weaknesses. It can be found at: www.microsoft.com/technet/mpsa/start.asp;
- only downloading software from reputable Web sites;
- deleting suspicious e-mails.

Act Immediately If You Become Infected

Deal with the threat immediately. Never wait, as the longer the virus is on your computer the more files it can infect. Some viruses, such as Code Red, open up your computer system to potential hacking. There is no guaranteed way to know that your system does not contain some malicious code that will be used at a future date, even when the offending virus has been deleted. If a virus such as Code Red has indeed infected your system, and if you want to be absolutely safe, reformat your hard disk and reinstall all your software again.

Cope with Virus Hoaxes

The Internet is full of virus hoaxes that waste time. If you get an e-mail about a new virus, go to the Web site of your anti-virus software provider, and check if the warning is real. In order to judge whether it's a hoax, ask yourself the following questions:

- does the message come from a reputable source?
- does it ask you to e-mail it on to anyone you know? If it does, it's probably a hoax.
- does it have a reputable link for more information?

SEE ALSO

Computers, Information Technology, and E-commerce (p. 440)
Creating a Basic Web Site (p. 299)
Making Your Web Site Secure (p. 350)
Managing E-mail (p. 316)

Understanding the Key Principles of Internet Marketing

GETTING STARTED

If you work online, you need to think about Internet marketing and what it can do for your business. Internet marketing is about giving, rather than getting, attention. An adjunct to traditional marketing, it supports and enhances the overall marketing message by providing comprehensive information that answers consumers' questions about a particular product or service. Internet marketing also exploits the networking capabilities of the Web by leveraging online community activities, linking, affiliate marketing, viral marketing, e-mail marketing, and loyalty programs. When approaching Internet marketing, keep the following in mind:

- when visitors come to a Web site they are already aware of the brand. They want information;
- use Internet technology to understand the needs of your customers, so that you can offer them just the right information and products;
- remember that the Internet empowers the consumer. A dissatisfied consumer can use the networking capabilities of the Internet to undermine your brand.

FAQS

What sort of products and services is Internet marketing best suited to?

Internet marketing is best suited to:

- products and services that require a lot of information to sell. Travel is a very information-intensive product. People want times, prices, and information about the destination. When buying books, they are strongly influenced by reviews, opinions of other readers, tables of contents, and sample chapters;
- products and services that people feel strongly about, such as books, music, and movies. Fans network with other fans in online communities to discuss their favorite artists;
- products and services that are bought by the Internet demographic. Although the Internet demographic has broadened, it is still generally the domain of the well educated and better off. Those working in technology and academia are very well represented.

What about online advertising? Does it work?

As a pure branding tool, online advertising does not have the same impact as television or glossy media, because of bandwidth restrictions. Studies indicate that most consumers avoid interactive ads because they simply take too much time to download.

However, the real power of online advertising is not from a mass marketing point of view but, rather, its ability to reach niche markets and target just the right consumer with just the right product. Advertising success is claimed by opt-in e-mail-based marketing, where consumers request information on a particular product or service. In online advertising, the scattershot approach is out and laser point focus is in.

MAKING IT HAPPEN
Recognize That Internet Marketing is Part of the Overall Package

The objective of Internet marketing should be to integrate it into the overall marketing strategy, where it supports and is supported by offline marketing activities. However, that is not to say Internet marketing doesn't have its own unique characteristics. Internet marketing is not about a big idea, some compelling graphics, and a killer catchphrase. Offline marketing brings consumers to the Web site with such approaches. Their interest has been aroused. They have questions. Internet marketing answers those questions by having comprehensive information on offer. Remember, people are not coming to the Web site to read the brochure again.

Understand the Consumer Better

Effective Internet marketing focuses on getting to know the consumer better. The objective here is to understand consumers' exact needs so that exactly the right products and services can be offered to them at exactly the right time and in exactly the right way. The strength of the Internet is also its weakness, though. While people want information, they also suffer from massive information overload. The Internet marketer who can cut through the overload and bring to time-starved consumers the information they need is much more likely to succeed. Find Web sites and e-mail databases that attract the exact type of consumer you wish to target. Analyze statistics generated as a result of consumers visiting your Web site and react appropriately to key trends that these statistics throw up. With more sophisticated Web sites, you can customize consumers' experiences through personalization systems, whereby a unique and finely targeted set of information and products is presented to each individual visitor.

Back It Up with E-mail Marketing

Since the Web was launched, perceptive marketers have been stressing that every Web site should have an e-mail marketing strategy. Consider that consumers must actively decide to go to a Web site, but with e-mail they join a database in which they can be regularly informed of products, services, and offers that the organization has. The key to e-mail marketing success is getting people who want the information to join a database in which they will receive regular e-mail alerts and newsletters. Of course, the information they receive needs to be of a type and quality that they signed up to get.

Tap into the Networking Ability of the Internet

The Internet is a community and it offers a tremendously powerful means for people and organizations to network. Linking is one of the simplest yet most effective Internet marketing devices there is. It underpins affiliate marketing efforts by Web sites such as Amazon.com. Linking is like embedded word of mouth. If another Web site links to you, it is essentially recommending you to its own visitors. Viral marketing is a network effect, whereby groups of consumers create a buzz about a product or service by e-mailing friends and/or creating their own Web sites. Consumers gain a power through Internet networking that they traditionally did not have. There are hundreds if not thousands of Web sites and activist groups set up by disgruntled consumers with the objective of attacking particular organizations.

Make Advertising and Promotion Highly Focused

A Web site, because it is not a physical store, faces a constant challenge to achieve and maintain awareness among its target market. Traditional offline marketing, such as press advertising or direct mail, plays a key role here, but so too do specific online marketing strategies. Registration with a commercial search engine is an obvious one. This is not some simple, one-off task but an ongoing activity because the rules by which search engines classify sites are constantly changing. Banner ads can be effective, if properly targeted. Banner ad design needs to apply the unique characteristics of the medium, and not simply apply traditional advertising principles. A specialist agency can advise on suitable creative approaches. Getting other Web sites to link can be very effective, but this is a slow process, the rewards of which are delivered over time. E-mail signature files can promote a Web site effectively.

Remember that Affiliate Marketing and Loyalty Programs Can Deliver

The best example of the success of affiliate marketing is that of Amazon.com. Literally hundreds of thousands of Web sites offer books and other products to their visitors using Amazon's affiliate program. It's a win-win situation. The Web site in question offers an extra service that is easy to establish and delivers a certain amount of revenue. The affiliate sponsor opens up a new channel every time another Web site hooks into them.

However, like all marketing techniques, it's not some magic formula. It needs to be thought through properly and applied professionally.

Loyalty programs can work on the Internet, though they have been overhyped. Key elements in the management of loyalty programs are the use of customer databases and the tracking of customer purchasing behavior. The Internet facilitates such activities, and can thus be a medium through which loyalty programs can be run. Getting the incentive structure right is critical to the success of loyalty programs.

Use Online Communities to Build Loyalty
Using chat, discussion boards, and e-mail mailing lists to bring people together to discuss issues of interest can enhance brand loyalty. It can also be a source of unique and cost-effective content. However, it doesn't work in all situations, and online communities that are not properly managed can quickly lose momentum.

Remember that Some Old Marketing Tricks Still Apply
Discounts, competitions, and free offers work as well online as they do offline. While perhaps too much has been offered free on the Internet in order to build business, properly used, these traditional marketing techniques can be effective on Web sites.

✗ WHAT TO AVOID
Being Flashy
Although the Internet has been around since 1996, it is amazing how many marketers still think it's TV on a computer screen. On the Web, visitors don't really care about the graphics; they just want the information. Splash screens, audio, video and Macromedia Flash animations should be kept to an absolute minimum.

Not Building and Leveraging a Customer Database
Bringing people to a Web site without strongly encouraging them to join some sort of a database is a serious mistake. Many consumers will visit a Web site once, rarely if ever to return. It's vital to get them into a database so that ongoing communication can be set up.

Focusing on Volume of Visitors Rather than Quality Targeting
In the early years of the Web there was a frantic rush to build visitor traffic to a Web site, without any real focus on issues such as revenue per visitor, numbers who joined databases. Acquisition costs for visitors were high, and as the large number of visitors did not translate into valuable customers, many business models collapsed.

Focusing Purely on Purchase Activity
There is a need to understand how a Web site contributes to the overall purchasing process. For example, a great many people visit car Web sites before they make a purchase, but very few will actually make the purchase online. The key is to forget about measuring by crude visitor volume numbers and focus on the quality of the targeting, along with the influence that the Web site and e-mail communications have on purchase behavior.

SEE ALSO
Applying a Viral Marketing Approach on the Internet (p. 332)
Computers, Information Technology, and E-commerce (p. 440)
Delivering the Benefits of Affiliate Marketing on the Web (p. 334)
Promoting Your Web Site Effectively (p. 323)

Promoting Your Web Site Effectively

GETTING STARTED
Launching a Web site is like opening up a store in the middle of Antarctica or the Sahara Desert. Nobody will know that you are there unless you promote yourself! Web site promotion is not some one-time event that occurs at launch. It is an ongoing activity that demands a keen understanding of promotional techniques that are unique to the Web. It also requires full integration into offline marketing and promotional activities. When approaching Web site promotion, consider:
- it requires a range of promotional strategies, both online and offline;
- it's an ongoing activity;
- it should be fully integrated into the overall promotional and marketing strategy.

FAQS
Why is Web site promotion of such importance?
In business people talk about "location, location, location." Well, a Web site doesn't really have a location. It's not on a main street where thousands of people walk by every day. Without such physical visibility, a Web site has a major problem attracting consumers. That is one reason why a clicks-and-mortar strategy (combining physical stores with an Internet presence) is deemed so essential for the success of a Web site. In a physical store, and in its marketing and promotional activity, consumers can be exposed to the benefits of the Web site constantly.

What is banner advertising and does it promote a Web site well?
Banner advertising is the use of rectangular advertisements or logos across the width of page on an Internet site. Businesses often place advertisements of this type on a third party's site to attract users to visit their own.

The jury is still out on the effectiveness of banner advertising. However, prices for banner advertising have dropped significantly in recent years and there is certainly value to be had. It's really down to the target market you are after and whether that accurately matches the profile of visitors coming to a particular Web site. Online advertising systems allow for a level of targeting and measurement that is impossible in much offline media. So, if you can get to the right target market at the right price, then the equation makes sense.

Does online advertising and promotion have to cost a lot of money?
No. Online ads have dropped significantly in price and, with proper investigation, very good value can be had. Online promotion requires dedication, but a few hours spent every week can deliver real results.

MAKING IT HAPPEN
Get Linked
Linking is one of the most powerful means of promoting a Web site. A link from another Web site is essentially embedded word of mouth, a recommendation from that site to its visitors also to visit you. The Web is huge, with millions of Web sites, many of them of poor quality. People who use the Internet have become very skeptical and conservative in their behavior. Building credibility is critical. There is no better way to build such credibility than to have hundreds—ideally thousands—of other Web sites linking to you.

Google, perhaps the Web's most popular search engine, achieved popularity because its search results were seen as more relevant than those of other search engines. The way it achieved better results was by analyzing a Web site and seeing how many external Web sites had linked to it. The more links the Web site had, the higher in the results Google placed it. Thus, if you want your Web site to feature prominently with Google, the more links you can get the better.

But linking is not simply about getting placed higher in search engine results. Think of each link as another "road" to your Web site; another way that the visitor can get to you. Getting links is not easy. It involves finding Web sites that attract your target market and convincing them to include a link to you. Usually, they will not do this unless you have valuable content that could be of interest to their customers. Another approach is to pay for a link, either through monthly fees or through what is called "click through payments"—you pay for every visit that results from a particular link.

Get Registered with Search Engines

Because so many people use commercial search engines, it's extremely important that your Web site is properly registered. Keep the following in mind:

- there are hundreds of search engines and directories but only a handful that really matter. These include: Yahoo, Google, Alta Vista, Microsoft Network, Excite, Lycos, Go, HotBot, All The Web, Direct Hit, Look Smart, and Northern Light;
- there may well be specialist search engines and directories for your particular industry. You should register with them;
- all search engines used to be free to register with, but this is no longer the case for an increasing number. You need to consider if the fee is worth it;
- an increasing number of search engines sell special placements in their search results. You can choose a keyword and when that keyword is input by a searcher, a short promotion for your Web site will appear;
- search engines need to be monitored regularly, as they can change the rules by which search results are presented. A set of keywords needs to be drawn up and the search engine regularly searched using these keywords. If you find your Web site is dropping down the results page, you may need to reregister. Also, if you launch a new product or service, you should consider registering that;

- don't register popular keywords with a Web site just for the sake of increased visitors. It achieves very little, and some search engines will remove Web sites that continuously abuse search registration processes.

Use Banner and Other Online Advertising

As stated above, banner advertising doesn't work for everyone, but it may work for your business. It's particularly useful where a new Web site, product, or service, is being launched. Banner ads can be paid for either on a cost-per-thousand (CPM) basis or per click through, where the seller gets paid wherever a visitors clicks on an ad. Online ads should be a call to action, with the key objective being to get the person to click on the ad. There are a variety of online advertising options:

- banner advertisements. These ads can go across the top or bottom of the page or down the side, like wallpaper;
- interstitials. These are ads that appear before the actual Web page loads. They certainly get the visitors' attention but can be very frustrating;
- pop-under ads. These ads launch in a separate browser window and have been controversial.

Consider E-mail as a Form of Advertising

E-mail can be a very effective form of advertising, particularly when the advertiser is reaching a targeted list that has opted in to receive information on particular products or services. But beware of spam: mass distributed unsolicited e-mail. People are increasingly annoyed by spam, and anti-spam legislation has been enacted or is pending in many states and countries. It's not simply about whether spam is legal or not—but it is certainly unethical, and no reputable organization should use such an approach.

Remember E-mail Signature Files

An e-mail signature is the text at the bottom of an e-mail that contains information about the sender. It is also possible to place a short, two-line ad there (e-mail signatures should not be longer than five lines). E-mail signature promotion was used very effectively when Andersen Consulting changed its name to Accenture. For a period after the name change, every time one of Accenture's 60,000 employees sent an e-mail, there was a short e-mail signature ad notifying the receiver of the change of name.

Integrate with Offline Marketing

Every single piece of offline literature should contain the Web site address and, where appropriate, an e-mail address. This includes: all stationery (letterheads, business cards, compliment slips, receipts, invoices); all product packaging; training and support manuals; all ads that are placed in print, radio, or television. If the organization has physical stores, then promotional material should be placed prominently within these stores informing visitors of the Web site. When planning new offline promotional and marketing activities, you should seek ways to get consumers to go to the Web site. For example, entering a competition through the Web site.

Include Competitions and Giveaways

Consumers are as likely to react positively to quality Web-based competitions and special promotions as they do to such tactics in the offline world. Competitions and special offers give the Web site a sense of vibrancy. A key objective of such promotions should be to get consumers to join databases, used in the future to inform people of other special offers and relevant information.

Use Your Home Page

A key objective of a home page is to promote important content, products, and services situated deeper in the Web site. That's the job of sharp, punchy headings and summaries, supported on occasion by small graphics. The Microsoft Web site (www.microsoft.com) is a perfect example of how to use a home page to promote,

special offers, product launches, upgrades, and so on.

WHAT TO AVOID
Seeking Quantity of Visitors over Quality

In the early days of the Web there was a mad rush—fueled by venture capital—to drive as many visitors as possible to Web sites. A stream of new brands emerged, each one seeking to outdo the next with ad spend. There is still a tendency to consider quantity over quality when it comes to building visitor numbers to a Web site. This is a serious and expensive mistake.

Focusing Purely on Search Engines

Search engines are important, but they should still be only a part of an online promotional strategy. Also, abuse of search engines by bombarding them with popular keywords and other visitor-generating techniques merely serves to bulk up visitor figures. It does little or nothing for the bottom line.

Lack of Integration with Offline Marketing

Organizations miss vital and cost-effective ways of promoting their Web sites through offline resources.

Lack of Ongoing Commitment

Too many Web sites have been launched enthusiastically, only to be left to wither in the wilderness of cyberspace. To be successful, promotion must be an ongoing activity.

SEE ALSO
Applying a Viral Marketing Approach on the Internet (p. 332)
Computers, Information Technology, and E-commerce (p. 440)
Delivering the Benefits of Affiliate Marketing on the Web (p. 334)
Understanding the Key Principles of Internet Marketing (p. 320)
Using E-mail Marketing Effectively (p. 329)

Writing Well for the Web

GETTING STARTED

People read differently on the Web, so you need to write differently for the Web. Surprisingly, very few Web sites take the time to lay out their content in a way that will maximize its readability. Don't forget that it is more difficult to read on a screen than from paper so you must write and lay out your content in a more simple, straightforward manner than you would in print. If you want to ensure that your content has the best chance of being read, focus on:

- shorter sentences, shorter paragraphs, and shorter documents;
- plentiful use of short, punchy, and descriptive headings and summaries;
- larger font sizes and sans serif fonts, because they are easier to read;
- straightforward, factual prose.

FAQS

In what way do people read differently on the Web?

They scan, moving quickly across text, always looking in a hurry for the content they need. They are very fact-oriented. People don't read on the Web for pleasure—they read to do business, to be educated, to find out something—so they like to read content that gets to the point quickly.

People like reading short documents with links to more detailed information as appropriate. If a document is long, and people really have no choice but to read it, a significant number of them will print it out. In general, however, long documents tend to go unread.

Why do so many people regard Web content as poor quality?

People don't trust the content they read on the Web because they come across so many Web sites with poor publishing standards. The Web gives everyone access to the tools of publishing, but giving someone a word processor does not make them a good writer.

Too many Web sites lack proper editing standards. They also translate documents that were prepared for print directly to the Web; this may save money in the short term, but if people don't read the content, it is pointless. Some Web sites deliberately try to mislead people with their content. All this gives a poor impression to people who use the Web.

Is writing for the Web a difficult skill to learn?

It is not easy to write well, no matter what the medium is. However, writing for the Web is about concentrating on the facts. You don't need flowery prose; you must be able to communicate the really important information in as few words as possible. This is not an easy thing to do, but with practice most people can master the basics.

MAKING IT HAPPEN
Recognize That If You're Not Read, You're Dead

The connection between writing and reading is one that is not always considered: a surprising number of organizations create vast quantities of content without asking some obvious questions:

- Is anyone interested in reading this content?
- Is it written in a way that is accessible?
- How are we going to let people know that we have just published this content?

Realize That Less Really Is More

Writing is rarely about quantity, but it should always be about quality. It is easier to write 5,000 words of waffle than 500 words that are succinct, but 500 words is what is needed on the Web; less is definitely more.

Editing Is Essential

One of the primary functions of editing is to get a long draft into shape. As George Orwell said: "If it is possible to cut a word, always cut it." We all have pet phrases that we love to put into sentences whenever we can. They may sound good to the writer, but very often add nothing to the meaning of what is being communicated. The Web is about functional writing. Get to the point.

Keep It Short

When writing for the Web:

- documents should rarely be longer than 1,000 words: 500 to 700 is a good length to aim for;
- paragraphs should be between 40 and 50 words;
- try not to let your sentences go over 20 words.

Write for the Reader, Not Your Ego

When writing, always keep in mind who it is you are writing for. Will they understand what you are writing about? Don't write to please yourself—write to please your reader and be clear and precise.

Focus on the Headings

Headings are important on the Web for two central reasons. First, people scan, so the first thing they often do is to look for headings; if the heading doesn't attract their attention, then they probably won't read any further. Second, people use search engines a lot, and the most prominent things in a page of search results are the headings. The heading really has to sell the Web page and convince the person to click for more information.

Writing headings well is an art, but here are a few rules that will help you get the basics right:

- keep them short. A heading should not be longer than five to eight words;
- make your point clear. For example, "Nasdaq crashes to record low" is more informative than "Apocalypse now for investors!";
- use strong, direct language. Don't be sensational, but at the same time don't be vague, and don't hedge;
- don't deceive the reader, for example by using "Microsoft" in a heading just because you think people will then be more likely

to read it. The job of the heading is to tell the reader succinctly what is in the document.

Use Subheadings

In longer documents it is always a good idea to use subheadings, as they break up the text into the more readable chunks that readers like. Subheadings should be used every 5 to 7 paragraphs.

Summarize the Who, What, Where, and When

Next to the heading, the summary is the most important piece of text. It should be descriptive, not wandering or indirect. Tell the reader what the document is about, and who, where, and when the information relates to.

Get Down to Write

"No man but a blockhead ever wrote. . . except for money," according to Samuel Johnson. Sound advice. Writing is not easy but someone has to do it. The first rule of writing is reading: if you are asked to write a technical paper, read how other people write them. Read how they are written on your own Web site, on competitors' Web sites, in industry journals. Find a style that works well and copy it; use its techniques and approach to structure. Don't plagiarize, but never feel ashamed of finding good quality writing and learning from it.

Learn How to Edit

Even if you have an editor, you still want to send him or her a well written draft. Here are a few steps to follow:

- Get a first draft written and don't throw it away.
- Leave it for a while then print it out, or make the font size larger so that the text stands out more.
- Read it as if someone else wrote it. Is it written in a way that the reader can easily understand? What is the writer trying to say? Is this sentence or paragraph necessary? Has the writer covered all the essential facts?

- First drafts are often too long. When preparing the second draft, cut ruthlessly, maybe by as much as half.
- Use your word count carefully. When you are asked to write something, always ask how many words are required. If you are not given a word count then decide on one yourself. Keep it as low as possible.

Explore Collaborative Writing

Computers and the Internet make collaborative writing far easier, and as a result it is becoming an increasingly popular approach to writing content. Collaborative writing works well if:

- the writers spend time working through the objectives of the writing exercise, and reach agreement on such necessary matters as the style, tone, and length of the piece;
- there is a lot of content to be written that can benefit from the input of multiple disciplines;
- people can be given defined segments of content to write, and/or the different skills of different people can be used, for example when one person understands the subject well, while another is a good writer;
- there are professional processes in place to facilitate collaboration;
- the writers know and respect each other.

✗ WHAT TO AVOID
Not Focusing on the Needs of the Reader

A surprising number of Web sites fail to consider who their reader is, simply adding content for its own sake. If you ignore the needs of your reader, then your reader will ignore you.

Putting Non-Web Formats onto the Web

Translating a 40-page Word document into HTML is a simple task; persuading someone to read it is another job entirely. Have you ever tried reading an Adobe PDF file on a screen? It's a painful experience. How many of your customers have read that PowerPoint presentation you translated into HTML?

Putting Every Piece of Content You Can Find on the Web

The Web is not a dumping ground for content. You might have 50,000 documents, with only 5,000 suitable for your Web site. Publishing the other 45,000 simply wastes your readers' time—not something you want to do.

Poor Editing

It is almost impossible to create quality content without sending it through a professional editorial process. No matter how good the writer, his or her content will always benefit by being checked over by an editor.

Long, Rambling Documents

If, after reading the heading and summary, the average Web reader hasn't understood what exactly you are trying to communicate to them, then chances are they will click the Back button. Readers on the Web have become ruthless about their time.

SEE ALSO
Computers, Information Technology, and E-commerce (p. 440)
Creating a Basic Web Site (p. 310)

Using E-mail Marketing Effectively

GETTING STARTED

E-mail should be an essential part of any Internet marketing strategy. If you have someone's e-mail address, you can send them information directly. But with e-mail it is important that the recipient wants the information you are sending. Keep the following in mind:

- e-mail is a relatively cheap, but powerful communications tool—you can send thousands of e-mail newsletters in a simple, cost-effective way;
- e-mail allows you to keep in regular contact with customers and to build up a rapport with them;
- never send unsolicited e-mails (spam). E-mail should only deliver worthwhile information.

FAQS

How often should you contact customers by e-mail?

E-mail is a fast, simple, and cost-effective form of communication, so it is tempting to use it at every opportunity. However, unless the information is valuable, this can become annoying for customers. As a general rule, you should not send e-mail to people more than once a week, unless there is a specific and defined need. People are overloaded and if they see too many e-mails from you they will turn off. Make sure that you stick to your schedule, as people will be expecting it.

Should newsletters be free or chargeable?

It depends on the focus of your business. If you are publishing information, then it is hard to see how a business model can be developed that is advertising only. However, if you are using the information you send to help sell some other product or service, it is highly unlikely that anyone will be willing to pay for it.

What is spam?

Spam is mass distributed, unsolicited e-mail. Spam is a major problem on the Internet today in that it is easy to buy a database of millions of e-mail addresses and send out unsolicited e-mails to them. If you want to be seen as a reputable business, you should avoid sending spam.

What do the terms "opt-in" and "double opt-in" mean?

An opt-in approach is where someone actively decides to give you their e-mail address so that you can send them e-mail. However, the emerging convention is double opt-in. What happens here is that when a person receives a request to subscribe to an e-mail address, they reply to that address for verification that the request did in fact come from there. This ensures that the e-mail address was not maliciously set up by a third party.

Is it better to buy software or can it be rented?

Very often it is better to rent. There are a number of organizations that offer professional e-mail management services. To get a list of such companies, go to a search engine such as Google.

MAKING IT HAPPEN
Isolate the Information Need

The first step in any e-mail strategy is to isolate the information need of your target market. What sort of information would they find useful? Would they like information on new products and special offers? Would they like information on trends within your industry? What sort of information would make them want to give you their e-mail address?

Define Your Publication Scope and Schedule

Once you have defined an information need, you must make clear what the scope of your e-mail publication is. What exactly will the person get if they subscribe? Unless you are delivering very time-sensitive information, a weekly publication is usually sufficient.

Make the Subscription Process Prominent on Your Web Site

Getting people to subscribe is vital to the success of your e-mail strategy. There should therefore be a prominent subscription box on your Web site encouraging people to subscribe. Also, include subscription details in every mailing that you send out. Don't ask too many questions in the subscription process.

Many successful e-mail newsletter providers only ask for the e-mail address of the subscriber. That makes it a very easy and quick process for the potential subscriber. You can always ask for more information later on, when you have established a stronger relationship with the subscriber. As a rule, the more valuable the information is to the potential subscriber, the more information you can ask of them.

Make the Unsubscription Process as Easy as Possible

It is equally important to ensure that the unsubscription process is easy to use. People can get frustrated and angry if they find it difficult to unsubscribe from a service, and some might think you have started spamming them.

If You're Offering a Paid-for Subscription Service, Offer a Free "Teaser" Subscription

If you plan to offer a commercial service where you charge people to subscribe, then it is a good idea to offer a free e-mail that contains brief summaries of what is included in the commercial offering. It may also be an idea to offer a free trial period, so that the subscriber can get an understanding of what you have to offer.

Decide Whether You Want a Plain Text or HTML Version of Your E-mail

There are two basic options for the format you can use when delivering an e-mail to your subscriber base: plain text and HTML. Plain text is just like a normal e-mail, and is the simplest and easiest to produce. HTML is like sending a web page in an e-mail. It will deliver a lot more impact and color, but it is more expensive to produce, and a number of older e-mail systems find it hard to read HTML. If you do decide to use an HTML e-mail approach, it's a good idea to offer a plain text version as well or a significant number of people may be unable to subscribe to your service.

For plain text e-mail layout keep the line length of text between 65 and 70 characters to avoid breaking lines, which make the layout look very ugly, and keep paragraphs nice and short—five to six lines is optimum. Use capitals for headings. Because plain text e-mails do not allow the use of bold or font sizing, capitalizing is the only way to give emphasis. Use a nonproportional font such as Courier, because it remains constant regardless of the e-mail package being used.

Keep the E-mail Short and Punchy

Think of what you are doing as delivering a publication. You're trying to get people to read something that will make them want to act—to buy your product or use your service, for example. The scarcest commodity today is people's time. Nobody will read an e-mail that goes on and on, so focus on having punchy headings and short summaries. Avoid having articles that are longer than 500–600 words. The entire e-mail should not contain more than 1,500 words, unless you have a dedicated audience that you know is willing to read longer pieces. So keep things short, and always have some sort of call to action.

Have a Strong Subject Line

The subject line is what subscribers see first when they download their e-mail. Because people are so busy they often scan the subject line and, if it's not interesting, delete the e-mail. However, if you are sending out a regular publication you may wish to include the title of the publication and date in the subject line. In the body of the e-mail itself, it's a good idea to have a table of contents near the top that lets the reader know what to expect from the rest of the e-mail.

Use Hypertext and E-mail Addresses

It's a good idea to use a hypertext to link back to your Web site, in order to encourage the subscriber to get more information, purchase your product, and so on. However, when writing out a hyperlink (URL) always use the full URL. For example, don't use "www.mycompany.com"; instead, use "http://www.mycompany.com." The reason is that some older e-mail packages will not automatically turn the URL into a link unless you include the full URL. Also, if you have a URL that is more than 65 characters long, put it in angle brackets (< >). Otherwise, a number of e-mail packages will break the URL onto two lines and make it unusable. If you are including an e-mail address, put in a "mailto": before the e-mail address, as this will turn it into a link to the subscriber's e-mail package. For example: "mailto:tom@mycompany.com."

Include the Essential Things Every E-mail Mailing Should Have

Every e-mail you send out should contain the subject line (title) and date, subscription and unsubscription information, copyright and privacy policies (or links to these on the Web site), e-mail contact details (telephone and address may also be included), links back to the Web site, and brief information on the publication schedule and scope.

WHAT TO AVOID
Using a "Bait and Switch" Approach

Be very clear to the potential subscriber about what exactly they are subscribing to. If you specialize in special offers, e-mail and tell them so. Don't pretend that you're going to send valuable updates on a particular industry, and then just send special offers.

Not Meeting a Real Information Need

Ask yourself the question: why would anyone want to read this? Too many e-mail mailings are full of useless, repetitive, or out-of-date information.

Not Keeping to a Publication Schedule

If you say you will deliver an e-mail every Wednesday, do it. Being late risks losing credibility and subscribers.

Not Managing the Subscription and Unsubscription Process Professionally

Make it difficult for someone to subscribe and they just won't bother. By the same token, if you make it difficult for people to unsubscribe they'll become irate, and with good reason.

Spamming People

Never subscribe people against their will or without them knowing. Sending unsolicited e-mail is a "get rich quick" strategy. It will damage your reputation.

SEE ALSO

Applying a Viral Marketing Approach on the Internet

GETTING STARTED

Viral marketing is really another name for word of mouth in the Internet environment. Viral marketing can work in mysterious ways, but what is clear is that the Internet is a medium that offers significant potential for such strategy. Yahoo did little or no advertising in its early years—people told other people that it was a great resource. News about music-swapping services such as Napster, and the independent movie *The Blair Witch Project*, grew like wildfire within universities. Viral marketing works well when:

- the product is new and genuinely different, and is something opinion leaders want to be associated with;
- the benefits are real—people are telling their friends; they are putting their reputations on the line;
- the product is relevant to a large number of people, and it is relatively easy to communicate the benefits.

MAKING IT HAPPEN
Consider Incentives

Some viral marketing campaigns use an incentive-based approach. This involves rewarding people if they inform their friends and a percentage of these friends purchase the product or fill out a questionnaire, for example. It is important to have a cap on the number of people that the first person is asked to inform. For example, ask him or her to tell no more than five people. If the process is open-ended then it's very easy for spam to occur, where someone sends out thousands of e-mails to people they don't know in order to increase their rewards.

Create Useful Information That Will Be Quoted and Passed On

People see the Internet as an information resource. A powerful way of building a brand is to publish information that you allow people to quote and redistribute. There is no better way to enhance your reputation than for someone to pass your newsletter on to a friend, recommending that they should read it. The objective is that you be seen as an expert on a particular subject that is directly related to a product or service you offer. To facilitate such a process, create an "e-mail-to-a-friend" function on your Web site, which allows someone easily to e-mail information on something they have just read.

Recognize That Linking Is Viral Marketing

Linking is another form of word-of-mouth. It's one thing for someone to send an e-mail praising your product or information, but the effect is much better and longer-lasting if that person publishes a positive review on their Web site and links back to you.

Remember That Viral Marketing Works Well When There Is Something Free

People love to tell their friends when there is some great new service that is free. The Hotmail free e-mail service and the Geocities free Web site service grew quickly with little or no marketing spend. The appeal of what is free may be losing some of its luster as the Internet matures, but it is still a powerful driver of behavior.

Emulate the Hotmail Approach

Hotmail was a pioneer of viral marketing. Its success was not simply based on the fact that it was a free service. It embedded viral marketing into the product itself. Every time someone using Hotmail sent an e-mail, at the bottom of the e-mail was the compelling message: "Get your private, free e-mail at http://www.hotmail.com." With Hotmail and other communications services such as ICQ, the very use of the product became a vehicle for marketing and promotion.

Be Wary of Inappropriate Viral Marketing

Done inappropriately, viral marketing can be seen as pyramid selling, chain-letter selling, and/or spam. Every e-mail sent needs to make clear that the business is not involved in spamming or other unethical practices or you'll become tarred with the same brush. If you do attract adverse attention from an irate recipient, remain calm and respond to the complainant in a professional manner.

Some viral marketing campaigns involve people sending e-mail addresses to the business, which then carries out the actual communication. It's important that these e-mail addresses are only used for a one-off mailing, and that they are not added to a database for ongoing communication. Also, when sending out the e-mail, state clearly who referred the recipient to you. Remember that a referral does *not* mean that someone has agreed to receive ongoing communication from you.

SEE ALSO

Computers, Information Technology, and E-commerce (p. 440)
Delivering the Benefits of Affiliate Marketing on the Web (p. 334)
Promoting Your Web Site Effectively (p. 323)
Understanding the Key Principles of Internet Marketing (p. 320)
Using E-mail Marketing Effectively (p. 329)

Delivering the Benefits of Affiliate Marketing on the Web

GETTING STARTED

Affiliate marketing is about paying for performance. In short, it is a type of marketing in which one company induces others to place banners and buttons on their Web sites in return for a commission on purchases made by their customers. Amazon.com is the pioneer of affiliate marketing. It allows other Web sites to publish information of their own choice of books. When people click through to Amazon and buy these books, the Web site in question gets a commission. Affiliate marketing can open up new channels to market for the affiliate sponsor, and be a source of extra revenue for the affiliate Web site. When investigating affiliate marketing, remember that:

- affiliate marketing is more suited to products than services;
- you'll need to work hard with your affiliates if you want it all to work;
- a well-designed compensation package will be critical to success.

MAKING IT HAPPEN

Figure Out If Your Business Is Suited To Affiliate Marketing

- There needs to be a substantial number of Web sites that are attracting your target market. These Web sites need to show a willingness to join an affiliate program. You might be selling medical supplies but that doesn't mean that hospital Web sites will become affiliates.
- Affiliate marketing is better suited to products than to services. It is much harder to track whether another Web site sent you visitors who, after prolonged negotiation, decide to pay you for your services.
- Is the market already saturated with affiliate programs? It would be difficult to set up an affiliate program today that offered commission on book sales.

Have a Strong Value Proposition

As with all good ideas, there are a huge number of companies offering affiliate programs. How is your program going to attract new members? The level of compensation/commission you will offer will be important. However, on its own it will rarely be enough. You will need to work hard with your members by organizing regular competitions, special offers, and other incentives that make for an attractive value proposition both for your affiliate members and the end customer.

Keep in Regular Touch with Your Affiliates

Keeping in regular communication with your affiliates is essential in order to build their enthusiasm and trust. You should plan for an e-mail affiliate newsletter. Your affiliate members are your partners, and unless you treat them as such by working closely with them, they will drift away.

Agree a Compensation Approach

Critical to the success of your program will be how the affiliate is compensated. There are various compensation approaches:

- you might pay commission only; for smaller-price items such as books and music, commission is a popular option;
- for more expensive items such as cars, compensation may be based on paying for qualified leads;
- if brand building is also an important objective, then you might also offer compensation every time a visitor clicks through from an affiliate.

When making payments you will need to decide how often you do it. A problem you may face with partners is that some of them will have achieved very little revenue for a particular period, and it will not be cost-effective to send them a check. So you need to inform partners that there is a certain threshold before payment is made, and that commission earned in one period, if below the threshold, will be added to the commission for the next period. You will need an affiliate agreement that will cover these and other relevant issues.

Innovate, Analyze, Test, and Adapt

There is a need to innovate constantly so as to find the best approach. Affiliate software delivers substantial data and this needs to be carefully analyzed. New initiatives need to be properly tested and you need to be willing to keep adapting and refining your offer until you find something that works for both you and your affiliates.

Decide Whether to Outsource or Buy Software

Organizations can have the choice of outsourcing much of the running of the affiliate program or purchasing software and designing it in-house. It is better to outsource, as it allows you to focus on what you do best—selling and marketing your products and services.

SEE ALSO

Applying a Viral Marketing Approach on the Internet (p. 332)

Computers, Information Technology, and E-commerce (p. 440)

Promoting Your Web Site Effectively (p. 323)

Understanding the Key Principles of Internet Marketing (p. 320)

Getting the Best from E-marketplaces

GETTING STARTED

An e-marketplace is an Internet-based environment that brings together business-to-business buyers and sellers so that they can trade together more efficiently. Used properly, e-marketplaces can make for more efficient purchasing processes, saving time and money for everyone involved. Keep the following in mind:

- An e-marketplace gives the smaller company access to many more sales opportunities and allows it to compete on equal terms with larger companies.
- The technology is still relatively new, as are many of the companies involved. Caution is necessary.
- Which e-marketplace is right for you?
- E-marketplaces should not simply focus on getting the lowest price. Collaboration and the supply of quality information are key benefits they can deliver.

FAQS

What are the key benefits of becoming involved in an e-marketplace?

Reduced sales costs, greater flexibility, saved time, better information, and better collaboration.

What are the key drawbacks of e-marketplaces?

Inertia and resistance to change among key players, costs in changing procurement processes, the cost of applications and setup, the cost of integration with internal systems, and transaction/subscription fees.

What types of e-marketplaces are there?

There are three distinct types of e-marketplace:

Independent: These are public e-marketplace environments that seek to attract buyers and sellers to trade together. Many simply didn't attract a critical mass of buyers and sellers and folded quickly. Such marketplaces have found most success in commodity-based industries, where there are a large number of buyers and sellers.

Consortium-based: These are set up on an industry-wide basis, typically when a number of key buyers in a particular industry get together. They often drive an industry-wide move to achieve common standards for the transfer of information.

Private: These are established by a particular organization to manage its purchasing alone. The organization retains full control, though technology costs can be significant.

MAKING IT HAPPEN

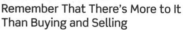

Remember That There's More to It Than Buying and Selling

The early e-marketplaces were little more than auction environments. However, as they've evolved, they have sought to help businesses trade more efficiently with partners. This has involved optimizing communication and collaboration; improved time to market as information flows more quickly between parties involved in the product development process; and better inventory control, through better market feedback.

Consider Joining an Independent E-marketplace

The advantages of joining an independent e-marketplace are:

- you can find new trading partners that you might otherwise not have been aware of;
- it's useful if you need to reduce inventory;
- it can work well when marketing commodity products;
- independents should embrace open infrastructure standards, making them easier to plug into than private e-marketplaces, which may use more proprietary technology.

The disadvantages are:

- a volatile environment, with many independents going out of business;
- they are not really suitable for developing long-term trading relationships;
- confidentiality and security can be an issue;
- many suppliers see such marketplaces as a way to drive down prices and are wary about getting involved. This limits the buying options.

Consider Joining a Consortium-Based E-marketplace

The advantages are:

- less expensive than establishing a private e-marketplace. Charges are usually in the form of subscription fees and/or commission;
- more choice of buyers and sellers;
- cheaper prices, though this isn't always the case;
- enhanced ability to work on industry-wide issues such as achieving common data standards.

The disadvantages are:

- you are setting up a trading environment with your competitors;
- less control than with a private e-marketplace;
- it won't generally integrate as well into backend technology and processes as a private e-marketplace;
- it's more open and thus more generic. If buying/selling relationships are key to your competitive edge, then a consortium-based e-marketplace will not be a huge benefit;
- governments may view such e-marketplaces as cartels or monopolies, depending on the members and their power within the overall marketplace.

Bear in Mind That You Don't Have to Stick with One Type of E-marketplace

You may decide to use a number of e-marketplaces. For example, a consortium-based one for most of your needs, and an independent to give yourself greater choice. A trading partner from an independent e-marketplace may end up migrating into your private e-marketplace.

Recognize That Confidentiality Is Key

One of the major worries regarding involvement in either independent or consortium-based e-marketplace is confidentiality. Over time, a picture will be built up of how an organization trades; this is important information, which could be very valuable to competitors. It's essential that proper security procedures are in place.

Consider Content Management

Content management is an important part of an e-marketplace environment. The system will need to deal with requests for proposals (RFPs), quotations, product diagrams and specifications, pricing, and delivery information. It will need to be able to archive everything in an accessible way, and to deal with version control to give users up-to-date information.

Train and Educate Your Staff

E-marketplaces invariably introduce new ways of doing things. There may be resistance within the business and this will require ongoing education and evangelism. Training will be required for the staff who are expected to operate the e-marketplace.

Sellers Beware

Sellers have been very cautious about getting involved in e-marketplaces because of their initial tendency to focus primarily on price. However, the right e-marketplace can have benefits for a seller, opening up new markets and customers, and providing a way of reducing excess stock.

Consider General Issues

- What is the procedure if you want to develop a one-to-one relationship with a trading partner you meet within an e-marketplace?
- Will the e-marketplace have any role to play in shipping and logistics?
- What is expected of you as a participant? How, for example, do you deliver content and updates?

- What integration work is involved? If it doesn't integrate, what are the costs involved in new processes?
- How are payments to be made?
- How are the request for proposal (RFP) and quotation processes handled? Does the e-marketplace offer software that makes these processes more efficient?
- Is there a certification process in place to ensure that you are dealing with reputable entities?

WHAT TO AVOID
Forgetting About Corporate Inertia

The expectation by e-marketplace providers that businesses would suddenly change their buying and selling habits upon the arrival of new technology was a serious mistake. Relationships and habits build up over years, and change only slowly in most situations.

Ignoring the Fact That There's More to Buying and Selling Than Price

Product quality, support, and personal relationships are still key in business-to-business situations. E-marketplaces that simply focused on pitting seller against seller found that that approach simply didn't work.

Delays in Getting the E-marketplace Up and Running

E-marketplaces are complex. The more partners involved, the more difficult it is to synchronize the information and business processes between each entity. Delays in making some of the best-known e-marketplaces fully functional have hurt the image of the industry.

Failing to Provide a Robust Payments Process

Many e-marketplaces lack a process whereby the participants can immediately settle the whole transaction. The fact that some of the trade must then be completed offline means that both offline and online processes need to be maintained, reducing efficiencies and cost savings.

SEE ALSO
Computers, Information Technology, and E-commerce (p. 440)

Getting the Best from Loyalty Programs on the Web

GETTING STARTED

Loyalty programs reward customers who spend more and/or stay longer with a business. Like much else about the Web, loyalty programs were a gigantic trend that crashed pretty severely. However, much of what went wrong does not reflect an inherent fault in the loyalty model itself, but rather in the vastly overhyped expectations of what loyalty programs can deliver. When considering using loyalty programs on the Web, keep the following in mind:

- you should implement loyalty programs on the Web only after you have your e-commerce fundamentals solidly in place;
- loyalty programs are long-term projects: it can be disastrous to start a loyalty program and then stop it within six months;
- getting the level of incentive right is critical to success—too much and your profits will be hurt; too little and you won't attract members.

MAKING IT HAPPEN
Make Sure Your E-commerce Fundamentals Are in Place First

Top of the list for consumers are service, comprehensive information, appropriate returns policies, and good support. Unless these fundamentals are fully addressed, consumers will see loyalty points only as gimmicks.

Remember That Loyalty Programs Are Long-term Projects

A critical issue with regard to loyalty programs is that, by their very nature, they have to be there for the long term. Loyalty programs ask two key things of consumers: to collect points that will be redeemed at some future date; and to give their loyalty. There is no better way to antagonize a consumer than to start a loyalty program and then six months later—as the member has collected half the points required for that coveted flight—to stop the program. Don't start a loyalty program unless you're in it for the long haul.

Find Out What Makes Your Customer Loyal

If you don't know what makes your customers loyal then you cannot develop a program that will enhance their loyalty. It

is also critical to focus on making your most profitable customers more loyal.

Choose the Right Type of Loyalty Program

The following is a selection of approaches:
- points systems—a very popular approach that gives points to customers based on what they purchase;
- premium customer programs—customers who spend certain amounts of money and are repeat purchasers of a product or service gain special status. This may involve them receiving special service offers, discounts, exclusive offers, gifts, and so on. The important thing here is to make the customers feel special—make them feel that they are getting things that those who are not part of the program don't get;
- buyers' clubs—when a certain number of consumers get together to buy a particular product, they will be offered a special volume discount.

Get the Switching Cost Right

If you offer too much in your loyalty program then your margins will be squeezed, and you will be running to stand still from a profitability point of view. If your incentives are too low then the switching cost for your customer will remain low, and the very purpose of the loyalty program will have been negated. It would seem that the problem with a lot of loyalty programs on the Web was that—fueled by venture capital—major incentives were offered in the hope of attracting huge numbers of members.

Create a Loyalty Path for the Customer

Customers can take loyalty programs very seriously. Some customers see it as an important achievement that they have a "Gold Card," or are seen as a "Premium Customer." There needs to be a clear loyalty path to tap into this sort of loyalty psychology. The customers need to see that the more they spend and the longer they stay with you, the more rewards and better treatment they get.

Keep the Customer Informed

Customers need to be able to check up on their status easily—to see, for example, how many points they have currently accumulated. Keep in touch. Send loyalty club members a regular bulletin that creates a continuing buzz about the loyalty program, announcing competition winners, new competitions, special offers, and so on.

SEE ALSO
Building Loyalty Through Online Communities (p. 341)
Computers, Information Technology, and E-commerce (p. 440)

Building Loyalty Through Online Communities

GETTING STARTED

Online communities allow consumers to engage with one another and with your business through use of interactive tools such as e-mail, discussion boards, and chat software. (Broader and more social online communities are not the topic of this actionlist.) They are a means by which you can take the pulse of consumers to find out what they are thinking, and to generate unique content. As a standalone business, online communities have been found to be weak: they work best when they are supporting the need for the business to get ongoing feedback. Online communities:

- allow the consumer an ongoing voice, thus facilitating greater feedback;
- require moderation and care if they are not to fizzle out, or turn negative;
- offer different options for interaction that reflect the varying ways in which people like to communicate.

MAKING IT HAPPEN

Keep It Moderated

Online communities rarely work if you simply install some discussion board software on a Web site and walk away. The discussion will either quickly dry up, or else drift off to topics that have nothing to do with the company and may well be libelous or otherwise illegal. Thus, to make a success of an online community, quality moderation is essential. Moderators need to combine editorial and chairperson-type skills. They need to be knowledgeable about the subjects being discussed, be enthusiastic, and encourage debate and quality discussion. They require an understanding of legal (particularly libel and copyright) issues, and should have the ability to deal with negative situations where members become overly virulent. Most of all, they need to care and want to make the community work for everybody involved.

Set Up E-mail Mailing Lists

E-mail mailing lists are an excellent way to discuss complex topics over a longer period of time. Members can be drawn from anywhere in the world and come together to share information and experience on a particular theme or subject area. The success of an e-mail mailing list is down to the quality of the contributions and moderation. Done right, it is a powerful way of transferring knowledge. An e-mail mailing list works as follows:

- a moderator establishes a list with mailing list software (this can be bought or rented; renting is usually the best option);
- the theme and focus of the list is published, and people join up, using a Web site form and/or e-mail address;
- the moderator invites contributions and these are duly published by e-mail;
- subscribers react to the initial publication with their opinions and feedback; a selection of these reactions then gets published in the next e-mail sent out;
- if successful, a feedback and opinion loop is created, with new topics of discussion being introduced as older topics have received sufficient discussion.

Set Up Discussion Boards

Discussion boards (also known as newsgroups, discussion groups, or bulletin boards) are areas on a Web site that allow people to contribute opinions, ideas, and announcements. They tend to be more general in nature than e-mail mailing lists, and are more suited to casual, one-off interactions. People require less commitment to participate in such boards. They can generally review a discussion topic without subscribing, although they do have to subscribe if they want to contribute something themselves. Moderation is not as essential here, although it is important to watch out for the emergence of "off-topic" subjects—contributions that are unnecessarily negative and perhaps libelous—and copyright infringement.

A prime example of the success of the discussion board approach is how Amazon.com uses it to allow consumers to publish book reviews. Discussion board software is relatively cheap and easy to install.

Set Up Online Chat

Online chat is real-time, text-based communication. Online chat can be effective when:

- there is a specific event occurring that is of interest to people;
- an expert can be made available to talk about a subject or product.

To be productive, online chat needs to be well moderated. It is really only suited to small groups of people (2 to 20) at any one time. Online chat software is relatively cheap and easy to install.

SEE ALSO
Computers, Information Technology, and E-commerce (p. 440)
Getting the Best from Loyalty Programs on the Web (p. 339)

SELLING ONLINE

Establishing an Enterprise Portal

GETTING STARTED

If your business has grown and you employ a number of staff, you may want to investigate enterprise portals. Put very simply, these are Web sites that assemble a wide range of content and services for staff. Some of this content is published by the organization itself, and some will be acquired from third-party publishers. The principle is to bring together all the key information that staff require to do a better job. When considering developing an enterprise portal, keep the following in mind:

- the word "portal" means different things to different people: to some, it's a souped-up intranet, to others it's a nascent e-marketplace: others will see it as part of a customer relationship management strategy;
- enterprise portals, while great in theory, are complex to develop and expensive to manage;
- an enterprise portal can easily fall into the trap of trying to provide all the information staff could possibly need and providing none of it very well.

MAKING IT HAPPEN
Exploit the Extra Potential

In many ways, an enterprise portal (sometimes referred to as an enterprise information portal) is a fancy name for an intranet. The key difference is that an enterprise portal manages not just internal content, but also external content that may be useful to staff. Such external information could include, for example, specialized news feeds, or access to industry research reports.

Learn from the Public Portals

On the Web everyone is a publisher, but that doesn't mean that everyone is a good publisher or that people will want to read what they publish. Very few public portals have survived, because they have not been able to build a viable business case.

Another portal sector that has seen great change is the much-vaunted "vortal." A vortal, or vertical portal, provides information that is organized around a vertical market sector, such as pharmaceuticals or plastics. Vortals and e-marketplaces have a lot in common, and in many markets may be one and the same thing. Most of these vortals, if they haven't evolved into e-marketplaces, are probably no longer in business.

The lessons that need to be learned from public portals and industry vortals include:

- people are very conservative in the way they consume content. The majority of people go to a few trusted brands;
- running portals is expensive; many have not survived because they did not have a proper business model.

Don't Get Complacent about Having a Captive Audience

The enterprise portal would seem to have a captive audience—employees. But it's not as simple as that. Staff who use an enterprise portal demand high publishing standards. High publishing standards are expensive to maintain, and many enterprise portals are dying because they don't have enough quality content, the content is not being kept up to date, and the whole environment is not properly organized and structured. What many organizations are discovering, to their cost, is that providing all this related information is wonderful in theory, but expensive and difficult to manage in practice.

Know Your Employees' Content Needs

Ask the following questions:

- How are employees' information needs being met at present?
- Are any of these needs not being satisfied properly?
- Can I fill this gap cost-effectively?

- Will my staff trust me to fill this gap?
- Where's the return on investment?

Related information is all well and good, but the key question must be: where is the return on investment? If a member of staff can just as easily get this related information somewhere else, why duplicate the effort? Unfortunately, organizations rarely take the time to examine which content drives the business forward, and which has little effect. But having a Web site is being a publisher, and if you don't understand the impact of your content, you don't understand publishing.

SEE ALSO
Computers, Information Technology, and E-commerce (p. 440)

Managing Payments Online

GETTING STARTED

If your business sells its products or services online, it's absolutely essential you're your online payment system works well, and works safely. The system must be easy to use, as consumers dislike having to go through long, cumbersome processes to purchase products, but it must also be as secure as possible; it's estimated that fraud costs an online business three times as much as an offline one. Remember that:

- consumers may be wary of giving credit card details and other personal information online. Your first step must be to gain their trust;
- fraud and chargebacks are critical issues that can seriously affect an online business;
- there is a wide range of online payment services available, so shop around.

FAQS

What is the most common form of payment on the Internet?

For consumer commerce it is the credit card. In the United States it is claimed that over 90% of all online payments are made by credit card. In Europe, the figure is estimated at 70%. For most business-to-business transactions, payment is usually made offline. New forms of payment are emerging, such as prepaid accounts and payments via cell phone.

What are the key issues facing online payments?

- Fraud is a critical concern that must be addressed comprehensively.
- There is no cross-border integration of payment systems.
- People develop payment habits, and are reluctant to change them.
- Can traditional payment methods adapt to the new environment, or is a brand new system required?
- There is still no comprehensive hard data on how people pay online.

What is a payment culture?

Within any particular country, and sometimes within states or regions of a country, there are distinct approaches to payment, depending on:

- the range of payment options available locally;
- local payment habits;
- local/national payment regulations.

MAKING IT HAPPEN

Understand Your Marketplace

Depending on the country, or the region/ state within a country, people pay for things in different ways. Different countries also have different payment processing approaches and legal obligations.

Understand the Types of Payment Options Available

It is important to understand the range of payment options available before choosing a particular payment method. The options available include the following:

- credit or debit card payment
- credit transfer
- electronic checks
- direct debit
- smart cards
- prepaid schemes
- loyalty plan points-based approaches
- person-to-person payments
- cell phone plans

The approach you choose will depend on your target market. For example, when a Web site targets young people, who often have no credit cards, a prepaid plan can work well. A particular Web site may use a variety of payment approaches, depending on its needs, but the ability to process all the major credit and debit cards is almost always essential.

Check the Characteristics of an Online Payment System

An online payment system should have these key characteristics:

- efficiency and ease of use: a central advantage of doing business online is that it saves time and cuts costs;
- stability and reliability: because payment is such a critical function, it is essential that a payment system is fully reliable. Payment systems cannot afford to be down for any length of time;
- authentication: much online fraud is caused by the absence of proper authentication;
- integration: a payment system must be able to integrate properly with relevant internal information systems, so that, for example, a record of the payment can be added to the account details;
- insurance: facilities such as escrow services must be available to ensure that the seller gets the money and the buyer gets the goods.

Select an Online Payment Service
The most suitable type of online payment service will depend on the volume of business you intend to do and the margins you make on each sale. There is a wide choice of payment services, so it is important to shop around to find the best one. However, whatever service you choose must be able to verify the credit card, process the transaction, and deposit the money in your account.

Key factors you must consider are setup fees, ongoing charges, and software and hardware expenses. Most banks offer some form of online payment service, and can be a good choice. When looking beyond banks, make sure you are dealing with reputable organizations. Those that advertise extremely low charges usually have expensive hidden extras.

Offer a Choice of Credit Card Payment Methods
There are two distinct methods by which credit or debit card payments are made for Internet purchases: payment directly online, and payment by phoning or faxing credit card details. The first method is by far the most popular (88%), but it is advisable to offer both options to potential consumers.

When implementing an online credit card system, a comprehensive security system using a secure server with encryption technology is essential. It is equally important to have comprehensive security procedures for the storage of the information. A database containing confidential information on thousands of individuals is more attractive to a criminal than acquiring a credit card number as it is passed between consumer and seller.

Keep the Process Simple and Fast
Whatever the payment system you choose, make sure to keep the process as simple and fast as possible. Studies have indicated that many consumers abandon the online purchase process, often because it is too long and difficult to understand. Streamlining the purchasing process is extremely important where repeat business is concerned. Amazon.com, for example, has implemented a patented "1-Click" purchase process for repeat customers, avoiding a lot of form filling.

Consider Business-to-business (B2B) Payment Options
While there is a wide range of effective business-to-consumer online payment options, payment for B2B transactions is generally made offline. One reason for this is that the amounts of money involved are usually large. However, one of the key reasons businesses embrace online B2B and join e-marketplaces is to reduce costs and to make transactions more efficient. Being unable to complete the payment online adds cost and inconvenience.

Think about Offering Online Escrow Services
Online escrow services offer to hold payments while the buyer examines the products purchased. If the buyer is satisfied with the products, they then authorize the payment. An online escrow service incurs extra cost because a fee is charged, but it may be worthwhile if it is essential to give the buyer as much confidence as possible.

The system operates by giving the escrow service a tracking number for the delivery. You must agree on the time period allowed to the buyer for examination of the merchandise; you must also establish who pays the shipping fees if the product is returned.

Remember That Fraud and Chargebacks Are Major Issues

Some studies estimate that e-tailers are losing as much as 5% of their margin to fraud—a rate three times higher than for businesses operating offline. For e-tailers on small margins this is a very serious issue. There are many different types of fraud, but a particularly common online form is identity theft, where fraudsters acquire confidential information on an individual and use it to purchase products. Clearly, e-tailers must take great care in this area, otherwise their profits will be eaten away. Fraud detection software is available and should be used.

Chargebacks (disputed payments) are also a major concern. MasterCard claims that, while online purchases represent 4% of total retail transactions, they account for 40% of all chargebacks. Credit card companies have initiated chargeback limits for e-tailers, and penalties are imposed for those who exceed them.

Understand How Payment Systems Work

This is how the process works:
- customers visit your site anytime, during or outside normal business hours;
- they view products and brief descriptions;
- they select products and put them into an electronic shopping cart;
- customers are offered payment options, ideally in their own currency;
- online payment is handled securely, probably by a specialist payment processor;
- payment is approved and confirmed to you and the customer;
- purchases are delivered to the customer.

Choose the Right System

An effective payment system allows your customers to buy online and allows you to manage the process efficiently. A complete payment system includes all the facilities to display products, accept payments, and manage your business. You can also choose systems that can be integrated with existing product display and business management systems. The system should allow you to:
- display products that customers can buy from your Web site;
- calculate any taxes due;
- calculate shipping or delivery charges;
- provide a quick, simple ordering mechanism;
- provide a secure customer payment mechanism;
- accept payment by credit card, debit card, and check;
- handle transactions from customers with approved accounts;
- handle payment for small and large purchases;
- accept payment in local currencies from all the countries where you have customers;
- accept payments in multiple currencies;
- protect your customers and your business against fraud;
- handle customer refunds;
- receive settlement from the payment processor;
- automate stock control;
- simplify administration and accounting;
- expand in line with growth of business;
- minimize the cost of handling transactions.

Select a Payment Processor

You can set up your own payment processing facilities, but if you only handle a small number of transactions or if your transaction requirements are complex this may not be practical. Payment processors can provide you with an established proven system that can grow in line with your business and services of this type are offered by banks and independent specialists.

Using an external provider offers you a number of advantages: there is no need for capital investment from you; there are no hardware, software, and support requirements; high levels of security for your business and your customers are provided; there is a reliable operation, round the clock; and services can expand in line with your business.

Apply for a Payment Account

Many businesses, particularly smaller and medium size operations, can be put off by the complexity of the application process but bear in mind that some suppliers have simpler processes than others. For commercial and security reasons, no company can cut out initial checks but some suppliers have gone out of their way to make the application process as simple as possible. The process varies in a number of areas:

- some independents can make their own internal risk assessment without referring to banks;
- you may or may not have to provide a detailed trading history;
- the proportion of successful applications varies by supplier—independents generally accept a higher proportion of applicants than banks.

Make sure you complete the application forms fully and return all essential documentation, including a customer agreement, direct debit mandate, bank details, and balance sheet.

Offer a clear payment page

Simplifying payment is an important part of the online shopping experience. A clear, easy-to-use order form allows customers to place their orders quickly. The form should include:

- customer details
- delivery requirements
- product details
- quantity
- price
- delivery charges
- total cost

- payment options
- account details, if appropriate
- mechanism to submit the order
- acknowledgment of the order and payment approval

Check the operation of the payment page and insure that any changes to the page layout reflect customer experience and feedback. Also make sure that the page is easy to navigate and simple to complete.

WHAT TO AVOID
Not Understanding Payment Cultures
While credit cards may be very common in the United States, they are not as widely used in Europe. Different countries have different payment habits and payment legislation. Not understanding these is a serious obstacle to online business.

Not Securing Peace of Mind for the Consumer
Consumers are very concerned that their credit card numbers will be stolen on the Internet. They are equally concerned that confidential information that they give to a Web site will not be properly protected. Web sites that fail to show clearly the steps taken to protect customer information are likely to lose potential business.

Underestimating Fraud
Fraud is a pressing issue on the Internet, and can have a serious impact on profit margins.

SEE ALSO
Computers, Information Technology, and E-commerce (p. 440)
Making Your Web Site Secure (p. 350)
Understanding Legal Issues in E-commerce (p. 356)

Making Your Web Site Secure

GETTING STARTED

Internet security is a critically important issue. The Internet is a network, and is thus vulnerable to attack. A poor Internet security policy can result in a substantial loss of productivity and a drop in consumer confidence. Keep the following in mind:

- be continuously vigilant: the perfect Internet security system will be out of date the next day;
- combine software and human expertise: security software can only do so much; it must be combined with human expertise and experience;
- secure internally as well as externally; many security breaches come from inside the business.

FAQS

What are examples of best practice in Internet security?

- Have an Internet security policy.
- If your system has been compromised, seek immediate independent expert help.
- For complete safety after an attack, the best course of action is to reformat the hard disk.
- Strip your computer system down to its bare essentials. The more features, options, and software your system has, the more open it is to attack. This is particularly true for Internet-related software and functions.
- For personal computers, be very careful about always-on connections provided by many broadband suppliers. An always-on connection to the Internet is always open to probing and attack by a hacker.
- Do not download software from the Internet unless you are totally confident about the source.

Are cookies a security threat?

Cookies collect information on how you browse the Web, and are a relatively low security risk. However, cookies can encourage lazy security practices, since they remember user-names and passwords.

Can you get a virus by opening an e-mail?

Yes. It used to be impossible to be infected by a computer virus transmitted by e-mail unless you opened the e-mail attachment. However, more recent viruses such as Nimda simply required the opening of the e-mail itself. Be very careful about unexpected e-mails from unfamiliar sources. If in doubt, delete without opening.

MAKING IT HAPPEN

Develop an Internet Security Policy

Keep the following in mind when developing your Internet security policy:

- many security breaches are internal. The fewer people with access to the inner workings of the system, therefore, the better. Those who are allowed access must be recorded and given specific access rights. Immediately delete revoked and inactive users, or users who have left the business;
- put in place a rigorous procedure for granting and revoking rights of access;
- streamline hardware and software: a complex system is more open to attack. In your server software, for example, strip away as many of the optional features as possible;
- have a password policy. Do not allow simple or obvious passwords and change them regularly;
- have procedures for data backup and disaster recovery;
- have procedures for responding to security breaches;
- be vigilant. The Internet security threat is constantly changing, and constant vigilance is the best security;
- have your security policy audited by an external professional organization, and

have them on call should a major breach occur.

Consider the Benefits of Firewalls

A firewall is software that polices the space between your computer system and the outside world. The design and management of firewalls has become more complex since the advent of the Web because of the vast increase in activity between computers and the Internet. If the firewall is too stringent, it slows everything down and prevents people from carrying out certain legitimate activities; if too lax, the computer is open to attack.

Deal with Viruses

Computer viruses are becoming more sophisticated and widespread. It is essential to have antivirus software and to keep it up to date. It is equally vital to upgrade your computer with the latest software security patches. For Microsoft software, more information on such patches is available at www.microsoft.com/security.

Deal with Hackers

The main objective of a hacker is to gain unauthorized access to another computer, by probing for vulnerabilities on the computer, perhaps the result of flaws in the computer software and/or poor security procedures. Many hackers now focus on Web-based applications, which are still relatively new and have not developed reliable security measures. Security breaches can range from the hacker changing the pricing in a shopping cart to the theft of credit card numbers. The only way to deal with hackers is to implement rigorous security procedures and to monitor activity on the network constantly.

React Rapidly to a Security Breach

After a security breach there are two basic objectives. First, find out what happened so that you can stop it from happening again. Second, find out who did it so that you can prosecute or otherwise deal with them. It is very difficult to prosecute a security breach without hard evidence, and very easy to destroy such evidence. In dealing with security breaches, make sure that:

- you get professional advice, particularly if it is the first time your security has been breached;
- you protect all tracking activity on the system;
- the information collected is technically accurate;
- information is collected from various sources to develop an overall picture of what happened;
- no information is tampered with or modified.

In monitoring for security breaches:

- check access and error log files for suspicious activity;
- be alert for unusual system commands;
- be alert for repeated attempts to enter a password.

Guard against Denial of Service Attacks

Denial of service attacks do not seek to break into a computer system, but rather to crash a Web site by deluging it with phony traffic. Firewalls can be designed to block repeated and unusual traffic from a particular source. Distributed denial of service attacks, where the hacker takes over perhaps hundreds of other computers to carry out the attack, makes the job of the firewall more difficult. Firewalls can, however, be designed to guard against your computer becoming an unwitting host for such attacks on another computer.

Insure you have a Secure Web Server

A Web server is potentially an open door into your network: if someone can break into your server, they are closer to breaking into your entire computer system. Before you set up a Web server you must ensure that you understand and deal effectively with the various security issues. By definition, Web servers interface with the Web and its potential hazards. They are large, complex software programs that embrace open architecture and that have often been developed at great speed.

From an e-commerce perspective, a secure server is a prerequisite. A secure server uses encryption when transferring or receiving data from the Web, turning it into special code that will then be decrypted only when it is safely within the server environment.

Equally important is what happens to the confidential information once it has reached the server environment. Once the information has been acted on, it should be stored in encrypted form. In the case of sensitive information, such as credit card details, it should be deleted.

Restrict Access to Your Web Site

You can restrict access to part or all of your Web site in a number of ways. The most common is by implementing a user-name and password system. However, you can also restrict access by IP (Internet) address, so that only people connecting from a certain address or domain can access information. Perhaps the most powerful approach is to use public key cryptography, whereby only the person with the assigned cryptography key can request and read the information.

Consider the Security Implications of Outsourcing

Outsourcing creates an increased security risk. You must establish that the outsource vendor will adhere to your security policy, and that all work done adheres to proper security procedures. Ask your vendor:

- What is its security policy?
- What are its data backup and disaster-recovery procedures?
- How is your data safeguarded from that of other customers?
- How is your data safeguarded from the vendor's own employees?

- How is it insured with regard to security breaches?

WHAT TO AVOID

Not Being Eternally Vigilant

There is no such thing as a perfect security system. Without constant vigilance, computer systems become an open invitation for hackers and viruses. An essential part of such vigilance is having the very latest security patches and antivirus software installed.

Thinking That You Won't Get a Virus

Viruses are becoming increasingly common. If you haven't had one so far, either you are tremendously lucky or you have excellent antivirus procedures.

Thinking That You Are Anonymous on the Internet

In general, you are not. When you visit a Web site, you will provide some or all of the following information:

- IP address
- time of access
- user-name (if a user-name and password are used)
- the URL requested
- the URL you have just visited
- the amount of data you downloaded
- the browser and operating system you are using
- your e-mail address

SEE ALSO
Computers, Information Technology, and E-commerce (p. 440)
Coping with Computer Viruses (p. 318)
Managing Payments Online (p. 346)

Collecting Consumer Data on the Internet

GETTING STARTED

If your business has a Web site, you'll find that Internet technologies offer a wealth of ways in which information on consumers can be gathered. Such information can either be collected directly as a result of consumers providing details, or indirectly by analyzing consumers' behavior while on a Web site. If you decide to gather information on consumers this way, keep the following in mind:

- privacy is a central concern of people who use the Internet, and they are becoming increasingly wary of Web sites that seek personal information;
- the benefit to the consumer needs to be made clear. Consumers are much more willing to offer personal information when a clear benefit to them can be articulated;
- it is one thing to gather information on consumers but another to analyze it and put it to productive use.

FAQS

Why has privacy become such a burning issue on the Internet?

The Internet has lacked a common and comprehensive legal infrastructure and this has led to an unfortunate situation in which basic consumer rights have been exploited. Web sites have gathered information on visitors in a surreptitious manner. Personal data has been sold on to third parties without making the consumer aware. This behavior has resulted in a consumer backlash. Study after study indicates that privacy is a key issue for those who use the Internet.

What are the key benefits of collecting consumer data?

Getting to know consumers better results in offering them products and services that are more in tune with their needs. This is a key competitive advantage in an information-driven economy. With more and more products becoming increasingly similar in their physical makeup, competitive advantage is achieved through finding out exactly what the consumer wants and meeting those needs precisely. The benefits to consumers are that they receive information and products that more accurately reflect their lifestyles and needs.

Why is it so important to collect information on how a Web site is performing?

A Web site is not like a bricks-and-mortar store in which a manager can walk around and observe what is happening. If there are always long lines at the checkout, and people are leaving the store because of these lines, this should quickly become obvious. However, people may be dropping out in the middle of a purchase process on a Web site, but unless proper data are coming through and being analyzed, no one will know. The number of people visiting the Web site may be dropping off. How will this be known without proper data? Web sites, like offline stores, need to monitor their performance continuously and adapt where appropriate. Without proper data and thorough data analysis this cannot be done.

MAKING IT HAPPEN
Use Web Site Logs to Analyze Consumer Behavior

Web site logs (server logs) track activity on a Web site. Log software is simple to install and can be purchased fairly cheaply, though for larger Web sites it is more complex and expensive. Using log software delivers vital information on Web site performance.

Unless the Web site is hooked into a

personalization system, Web site logs are not able to identify who exactly has visited the Web site. Instead, such logs collect general Web site activity information, including:

- total number of visits to the Web site during a defined period of time.
- visitor frequency. Information on the number of people who visited only once during the period (unique visitors), and those who have visited more than once.
- page impressions/views. Information on the total numbers of complete Web pages visited during the period. This is a key measure for advertisers.
- hits. A totally unreliable measure of Web site visitor activity. Every Web page is made up of a number of components—graphics, text, programming elements. Some pages may have anything from 10 to 20 components. Each of these components is counted as a "hit." Therefore, the total number of hits is generally very high and bears little or no relation to the actual visitor activity.
- most frequently visited pages.

Web site logs can deliver a mind-numbing array of data. This will seem very exciting when you first install the software but can become tedious to wade through every day. Isolate what are the key measures required to deliver a better picture of how the site is performing.

Use Cookie Software to Track Consumers

Cookies are small files that are sent to reside in consumers' browsers in order to track those consumers the next time they visit the Web site. Cookies are an important component in personalization. A typical example of the use of cookies can be seen when people have subscribed to a service on a Web site. Cookies allow the Web site to remember the username and password information, so that they don't have to keep filling it out every time they revisit. This is clearly a benefit for most people. However, cookies have been abused, collecting information on people without their knowledge. When using cookies, clearly explain to people why they are being used and how they benefit them.

Be Cautious about Using Web Bugs that Track Web Site Usage

An alternative technology to cookies is what has become known as Web bugs. Web bugs are not detectable by standard browsers, although there is software that can be downloaded to detect them. Web bugs have been controversial. Their design reflects a desire not to let the person know that they are being tracked. Web bugs are adding fuel to the belief that people's privacy rights are being constantly abused on the Internet.

Collect Information through the Use of Web Site Forms

Web site forms are used to collect information from a consumer in a structured manner. The following are guidelines to follow when designing a form:

- keep the forms as short as possible. If you make the form too long, consumers will simply not fill it out, or will skip over large sections of it.
- if forms have to be long, break them up. Inform the person clearly of how many sections there are.
- clearly mark mandatory fields. In every form there will be fields, such as e-mail addresses, that must be filled out. The convention is to mark the text associated with these fields in red and/or to place a red asterisk beside the field. At the top of the form, a clear statement needs to be made relating to the mandatory fields.
- don't mandate information a consumer can't give. Offer an alternative, for example: "If you don't have a ZIP code, please write 'None.'"
- ask opinion-type questions first. People tend to be more open to giving opinion rather than personal information.
- isolate errors that are made. Never say, "There's an error in your form. Go back and fill it out correctly." Rather say, "It seems you have not filled out your e-mail address. Please fill it out here."
- make sure the fields are of sufficient size. Don't, for example, give people a tiny field when you want their street address, which may be quite long.

- make sure it's accessible to all. Offer an alternative approach for people with disabilities to complete the information requested. Minimum accessibility standards are increasingly required by law.
- test regularly. It's not simply a good idea to test forms to see how user-friendly they are before they are launched. Forms break. As part of Web site maintenance, forms should be tested regularly with sample data.

Follow Best Practice in Consumer Data Collection

People have become rightly uneasy about the abuse of personal information on the Web. To assuage fears and create a win-win situation, put into practice the following:

- clearly inform people why the information is being collected and what purposes it will be used for;
- never use this information in a way that was not originally intended;
- allow the consumer to find out what information has been collected on them;
- allow them to delete any or all of this information;
- publish a comprehensive privacy statement in a prominent position on the Web site.

Protect Consumer Data

Hackers—people who break into computer systems—love to target consumer databases. The reason is that these databases may contain credit card information (it is not advisable to store credit card numbers on a Web site). More usually, hackers know that publicizing the theft of consumer databases will be hugely damaging and embarrassing

to the organization. It is therefore vital that any consumer data collected is properly protected and backed up.

Take Care When Collecting Consumer Data on Children

The rules for collecting consumer data on children are quite naturally a lot stricter than for adults. While the law is evolving, numerous companies have been fined for collecting too much information on children who visit their Web sites. It's not enough simply to check your national legislation on this issue. The Web is international and your Web sites should adhere to international standards when it comes to children's privacy rights.

WHAT TO AVOID ✘
Surreptitiously Collecting Data

People have become very wary about their privacy on the Internet. Too many Web sites have collected data on consumers without them knowing. This may produce short-term benefit but has led to an inevitable backlash.

Collecting Too Much Data

Software today can deliver seas of data, and Web sites with large numbers of visitors can easily get flooded. Not focusing on what is the really important data to collect is a common problem. It's important to remember that analyzing data takes time, and that if tangible benefits are not delivered then it will be wasted time.

SEE ALSO
Computers, Information Technology, and E-commerce (p. 440)

Understanding Legal Issues in E-commerce

GETTING STARTED

In any e-business strategy, it is important to address comprehensively the key legal issues. At a basic level, these are matters such as copyright and libel; at a more advanced level, such things as unique restrictions pertaining to the sale of your product within particular jurisdictions need to be dealt with.

When addressing legal issues on the Web, keep the following in mind:

- prevention is better than cure. Establishing a sound legal structure early on is much easier than trying to firefight legal problems as they occur.
- legal systems are getting a grip on the Internet. More and more laws are being passed that deal with doing business online.
- while you can't deal with the unique legal aspects of every jurisdiction, you still need to isolate the key jurisdictions for your online business and make sure you adhere to their relevant laws.

FAQS

Why should you address legal issues from the start?

Because it's important to guard against unpleasant consequences if you get legal things wrong, or just ignore them. Some early e-commerce businesses adopted the latter approach, believing that cyberspace was a kind of laissez-faire utopia beyond the reach of terrestrial governments. They were wrong, and paid the penalty in many cases.

Is it not the case that many laws do not apply online?

Nobody believes that fallacy any more. Which is fortunate, because courts and governments around the world have shown no hesitation about claiming jurisdiction over online activity—in some cases, even when the Web site in question is hosted on another continent. They have applied civil sanctions (such as injunctions and damages) and criminal penalties (fines and even imprisonment) in certain instances.

Is there a pragmatic approach to dealing with legal issues online?

Yes. The practical approach is to get legal advice on three specific types of territory for your Web site. They are as follows:

- the country (or countries) in which your Web operations are principally based, which will often, but not always, be where the site is hosted;
- the countries that are the primary target market of the Web site;
- any other countries which may claim authority over the Web site, and the breach of whose laws might cause unpleasant consequences. The United States is by far the best example of this: its legal regime has a dauntingly long reach.

MAKING IT HAPPEN

Understand the Different Kinds of Web Sites

While there are many different types of Web sites, they can broadly be divided into those with the following attributes:

- shop window Web sites, which provide information about a company and its products, but without encouraging any significant visitor interaction—rather like an online company brochure;
- contributed content Web sites, which allow visitors to contribute content, such as information about their identity, or postings on message boards;
- full e-commerce Web sites, through which visitors can purchase goods or services, either physical products which are delivered offline, or digitized material which is available for download.

Recognize Shop Window Web Site Issues

Even shop window Web sites have legal issues to address. They comprise various types of digitized content, such as graphics, text, images, music and coding, that raise issues which apply to all forms of Web site.

Web site owners must assume that all such content is protected: either by copyright—which, in effect, disallows its inclusion in another Web site without the copyright owner's permission; or, in some cases, by moral rights—which require the author to be attributed, and that the work should not be significantly modified without the owner's permission.

These clearances can take the form of a license or an assignment of copyright from the relevant rights holder, which might be a third-party Web site designer, photographer, journalist, or (in the more difficult case of music) two or more rights-holding organizations.

In addition, you must ensure that content on your Web site satisfies other requirements, including:

- Using the registered trade marks of a third party as part of your Web site's metadata will generally constitute trade mark infringement. Even a straightforward reference on a Web site to a third party's trade mark can constitute an infringement.
- Hypertext linking, particularly by means of deep linking or framing, to third-party Web sites without the consent of those Web sites should be avoided.
- Misleading price indications, for example where online prices have not been updated, can incur penalties.
- Incorrect product descriptions, where inaccurate statements are made as to the quantity, size, fitness for purpose or performance of goods, can also cause repercussions.
- Unfair comparative advertising, such as comparisons between goods or services that are not intended for the same purpose, must be avoided.

As well as guarding against infringement of third parties' rights, it is important for owners to include wording in the terms and conditions of their Web sites which protects their own copyright and other rights. Usually this is done by means of terms which appear directly on the home page or, more commonly, are linked to/from the home page, as well as at the bottom of every other page on the Web site.

Appreciate Contributed Content Web Site Issues

Web sites that encourage visitors to interact are exposed to several additional forms of legal risk. One of the most basic means of facilitating visitor interaction is a discussion board or chat room. Such environments can pose legal problems, as they are often unchecked and allow visitors to post information without any apparent restriction. You need to recognize that you can find yourself liable, either as a civil matter (where a third party's rights have been infringed) or, more extremely, under the criminal law, unless steps are taken to control material which appears on your Web site.

Some of the most obvious problems here include:

- defamatory statements;
- infringement of copyright material;
- obscene, blasphemous, threatening, racially discriminatory, and other legally objectionable material.

To avoid liability for such material, you need to establish one or more of the following safeguards:

- proactive moderation of material before it appears on the Web site;
- a documented "notice and take down" procedure, under which infringing content is removed from the Web site as soon as it has been notified;
- regular reviewing of material which has been posted, and removal of any which appears problematic.

These issues all need to be addressed in your Web site's terms and conditions, so that visitors (and potential third-party complainants) are aware of the steps taken to prevent infringement. Many prudent owners also require visitors to register with the Web site before they can post messages. This allows the owner to contact the visitor if a problematic posting is made by the visitor, and, in certain circumstances, to provide that visitor's personal and contact information to a wronged third party, or to a law enforcement authority.

Account for Full E-commerce Web Site Issues

Clearly, there is a wide variety of goods and services which are capable of being traded through a Web site. Further, the seller can be either the Web site owner or a third party trading through the Web site, as in an online auction service.

It is impossible to cover here all the issues which the various kinds of products can raise. Many have specific regulations which have been imposed by governments for social, ethical, and fiscal reasons. Examples of these include:

- sale of alcohol
- sale of medicines, particularly prescription-only medicines
- financial services
- betting, gaming and lotteries
- auctions, particularly in various European countries

Depending on the jurisdiction and type of product being sold, a Web site may need to adhere to regulations such as:

- provision of clear information to consumers before the conclusion of a contract, including: the identity of the supplier; the main characteristics of what's being sold; payment and delivery arrangements; and the principal terms and conditions of the contract between seller and purchaser;
- a minimum period during which a consumer may withdraw from the contract for any reason, and reject whatever has been purchased.

Whatever you sell through your e-commerce Web site, it is important that you form a legally binding contract with the purchaser. For example, you might ensure that such a contract is formed by requiring the visitor to scroll through your terms and conditions and click on an "I accept" button.

WHAT TO AVOID
Doing Nothing Because You Think It's Just Too Complicated

It is certainly true that there is a dizzying array of legal issues to ponder when trading over the Web. However, that's not an excuse for doing nothing. There is a basic minimum that can and should be addressed. The key is to understand the legal issues that, if not addressed properly, can have a major impact on your business.

Assuming That the Long Arm of the Law Does Not Reach Online

This is a false assumption. Yes, it is often more difficult successfully to prosecute an organization that is trading over the Web. However, that does not mean that governments and legal systems are ignoring those who they feel are breaking their laws, just because they happen to be on the Web.

Failing to Deal with Copyright and Libel Issues Quickly

If a third party accuses you of libel or copyright infringement, it is imperative that you deal with it urgently. In many courts of law, the longer the libel remains published on the Web site, the greater the penalties.

SEE ALSO
Computers, Information Technology, and E-commerce (p. 440)
Managing Payments Online (p. 346)

MANAGING YOURSELF
AND OTHERS

Managing Your Time

GETTING STARTED

Time is a human concept. Animals do not understand the idea. They live *in* time; they are in the moment; the present is all that counts. Remembering this can be useful in the business world: being able to focus on the present is often an effective way of getting through laborious tasks and not worrying about the past or future.

In business, time is money. Paradoxically, as technology proliferates (with the promise that it will increase productivity), it makes managers' responsibilities more complex—at the same time that there are fewer staff to perform the work. The only realistic solution is to make better use of time.

FAQS

How can I be a better time manager?

The *desire* to be good at time management is half the battle, but you need to be aware of the choices you have to make. These relate to your overall life balance and the values you hold.

As a first step, look at what you need to do and why. If some requests are outside your area of responsibility or expertise, work with your partner(s) and team (if you have one to clarify the boundaries. Delegate as much as you can. Although this might seem difficult in a small business environment, it's a really useful skill to develop and it will benefit the business as whole—things will get done rather than sit on your desk.

You'll also need to be more realistic about your strengths and capabilities. Set realistic deadlines and build in some slack in the schedule to give yourself the best possible chance of meeting deadlines.

I run a very efficient team. One of my team members seems incredibly disorganized. What can I do?

A good team leader often needs to work with individual team members to help them understand what is expected. Set realistic goals and give them adequate time and resources to complete the work. Additionally, if possible, ask them to examine their performance objectively and identify patterns of behavior that contribute to being disorganized. Often time management requires a change in habitual behavior. This can only be achieved by building awareness, charting a clear route, and rewarding success.

I've recently invested in a computerized scheduler but find I am still using my old appointment book as well. How can I get away from using redundant systems?

Plan the time it will take to learn the new technology and transfer your information. Ask for a tutorial from someone who has made the leap already. Then, over a period of a month, wean yourself off the dual system by omitting the appointment book. You'll probably be converted to the versatility and convenience of the computerized scheduler long before the month is out.

MAKING IT HAPPEN
Conduct a Time Audit

You may find it useful to conduct a time audit on your life. What is the balance between the demands placed on you at work and those that define your private life? Does this balance satisfy you, or do you find yourself sacrificing one element for another? One key to good time management is being aware of the wider world in which you live and the interrelationships between its constituent parts. Another key is prioritizing—if in fact there isn't enough time to satisfy all the competing demands—and then choosing how you apportion your time.

Take a large sheet of paper and write your name in the center. Write all the demands of your life around it. Include work hours, commuting, socializing, eating, sleeping, household responsibilities, and family commitments. Remember that taking time for family and friends, exercise, hobbies, vacations, and just plain fun is important. Mark the number of hours you devote to each of these areas on an average day, month, or year. This chart graphically represents your life in terms of the choices and tradeoffs you actually make in areas that are important to you.

Ask yourself whether this is how you want to live your life. You may decide to sacrifice some important areas in the short term, but be aware of what might happen when a particular phase of your life comes to an end. For example, how will you manage if you get married or divorced; when children are grown and leave home; if your business takes off and starts to demand much more of your time; if you have an accident or long-term illness; when you retire?

Decide What Action Needs to Be Taken
Take a highlighter and mark those areas on your chart that need attention. If, for instance, you're spending too much time at work, you need to review your professional objectives and decide how to achieve a better balance.

Life is all about choices. You may find that you can recapture more time by telecommuting, if your employer will permit it and your family will respect the necessary home-work boundaries.

You can probably find other ways to prune wasted hours. For instance, if you like sports or fitness activities, consider finding a club near work where you can go early in the morning instead of having to fit exercise into your evenings.

Look for patterns in the way you use your time. You may find that you are constantly in meetings that run late or that you pick up a lot of work that is not really profitable, or not what you really want to do because you aren't assertive enough in saying no. If you don't have enough time and your own behavior is contributing to the shortage, change your patterns of behavior.

Learn to Use the Right Tools
Time management tools and techniques are only as useful as the time you invest in using them. Common ones include:
- handheld organizers, also known as personal digital assistants (PDAs)
- organizers, both computer-based programs and paper appointment books or schedulers
- "to do" lists
- prioritizing work according to its importance and focusing only on what's essential

If you're a person who tends to concentrate on what's in your in-box or on today's schedule, you may find it useful to stand back and look at the big picture. Your activities don't happen in a succession of unrelated present moments; they mesh into a continuum of past and future. Develop and keep some perspective on how this broader context affects your choices in deciding how you spend your time.

Some Dos and Don'ts of Time Management
If too much work is the issue, look at your workload, prioritize, and refer back to how it

Do	Don't
Conduct a time-management assessment on yourself	Spend time on unnecessary activities or those that don't serve your purpose
Be honest about how long things take	Take on more than you can handle
Build in time for reflecting and learning	Blame others for your own disorganization
Build in time for yourself	Get hung up on process
Delegate wherever you can	Make commitments you can't meet
Anticipate the pressure of commitments you make	Expect others to make up for what you can't do
Communicate with others when you have time conflicts	Give up
Plan ahead	

fits your job description. Decide, perhaps in consultation with partners, which of your tasks add value to the business and its potential, and which would be better delegated to others.

X
WHAT TO AVOID
Buying a New Gadget but Still Relying On Old Time Management Tools

If you're going to buy a new device to help you plan your time better, you need to plan the time to learn to use it competently! Don't buy something and try to pick it up as you go along as this will make you very frustrated *and* inefficient.

Expecting Too Much of Yourself and Becoming Discouraged

Change is difficult and often requires a new set of skills. The principles of time management sound completely logical and straightforward, but in fact we lead extremely complex lives, and these simple principles are hard to put into practice. Don't overwhelm yourself by trying to change everything at once. Instead, estab-lish a series of small, clear goals, and achieve them one by one.

Having Trouble Breaking out of Old Patterns

Old habits do die hard, and one of the hardest to break is the way we structure and use our time. Everyone knows people who are always late or always early, who jump right onto tasks or are terrible pro-crastinators, who are stressed-out work-aholics or who always seem miraculously refreshed and relaxed. The choices we make in managing our time are connected to the way we view ourselves and the world: making different choices affects our sense of identity and our relationships. Take it slowly, look to family, friends, and co-workers for support in making these changes, and don't discount the value of taking workshops or seeking out a con-sultant to help you.

SEE ALSO
Delegating (p. 369)
Managing Stress (p. 363)

Managing Stress

GETTING STARTED

Stress is increasingly a way of life for managers and executives, and when you are running or growing a small business, you may feel as if you have to soak up the stress that in larger businesses would be shared among a larger team. This actionlist sets out to help you to identify different types of pressure and find ways to cope with them.

FAQS

My business partner thrives on stress and expects me to do the same, but I work more effectively in a less intense environment. How can we work well together?

This is a common problem. If you can find a way to work together, however, your differing styles can actually complement each other. Try to broach this issue with your partner, and put together a plan of action.

I work well under pressure and have no problem with it, but it sometimes affects my relationships with others who don't. What do I do?

Although pressure often gives us the boost we need to get a job done well and on time, it can, however, become so habitual that we fail to recognize its constant presence in our workplace. While people can become very focused in such an environment, they may also begin to neglect other parts of their lives such as their relationships with friends and family, or even their health. In the long term stress isn't a healthy permanent fixture in anyone's life.

How do I maximize the benefits and minimize the downside of stress?

Stress can improve our performance, but sometimes to the detriment of relationships and other important parts of your life. Under pressure people often become highly task-oriented and focus solely on immediate or short-term concerns. Observe your own behavior, seek feedback, and decide whether or not stress is affecting you. The earlier you recognize the symptoms, the easier it is to take action to remove or reduce the sources of stress.

MAKING IT HAPPEN

Try to Achieve a Work/Life Balance

Managing stress is about achieving some balance in the elements of your life. Many of us are most susceptible to stress at work, but family and social environments can also exert significant stress in our lives. And in any of these areas, when we're under extreme pressure we sometimes do or say things that, on reflection, we wish we hadn't. Try not to let work be the central focus of your life. For example, take advantage of your vacation and personal days, exercise regularly, and maintain your relationships with friends and family. Having hobbies and interests that help you switch off can also help. If you feel it would be helpful, raise your concerns with your boss.

Recognize the Symptoms of Stress

Symptoms of stress fall into four main categories:

- **physical**—headaches, sweats, panic attacks, raised blood pressure, nausea, sleeplessness, heart palpitations
- **physiological**—overproduction of adrenalin, leading to tension, aggression, feelings of stress in the fight-or-flight syndrome
- **emotional**—depression, feelings of inadequacy, loss of confidence, detachment, denial
- **behavioral**—tunnel vision, short temper, dismissive behavior, self-centeredness, irritability, impatience

Know the Causes and Types of Stress

There are numerous causes of stress in the workplace today, many of which are linked. Some of the most obvious are:

- insufficient resources—not enough time, money, or staff to do the job right

- insufficient *appropriate* resources—skills gaps in certain areas
- unreasonable demands—customers expecting you constantly to be at their beck and call
- inappropriate staffing or staff direction—failure to understand what different people are capable of
- insufficient training
- poor planning
- unrealistic commitments to produce too much, too fast

There are also many *types* of stress. The most common is time pressure—too much to do and too little time to do it in. A number of simple strategies can help you better manage your time. For example:

- Anticipate where time pressures are likely to come from.
- Plan and resource what needs to be delivered and when.
- Prioritize actions to make certain that things are done efficiently.
- Communicate progress to other stakeholders in the task and manage expectations. For example, if a task will take longer to complete than you originally thought it would, be upfront. The sooner you alert people to potential problems, the sooner you can work together to plan for contingencies.
- Understand how others respond to time pressure and work with them.

None of these measures will actually extend any deadlines, but they can allow you to feel more in control.

If time pressure continues to be an issue, it may indicate that you need to reevaluate your role and its demands and resources. Are you delegating enough? Have you prioritized your actions? Are you promising to do too much too quickly?

Find a Solution

Solutions fall into two areas:

- organizational—structure, planning
- personal—intellectual, behavioral, physical

Organizational Solutions

Stress may simply be in the nature of the job, or it may derive from how the job fits in with the rest of the business. In the small company environment, responsibilities may not be as clearly defined as in a larger concern. The boundaries of your role or job may need to be renegotiated. Clearer lines of responsibility, better delegation, and prioritization can help reduce stress.

Better planning and analysis of likely pressure points can help you deliver appropriate resources to the right place at the right time. Sometimes stress is unavoidable, but it's usually possible to minimize its duration and effects.

Personal Solutions

On a personal level, we sometimes unwittingly put ourselves under stress by losing sight of our own abilities. Self-awareness and understanding of our real skills are important. Building and nurturing our own self-confidence is essential.

Be aware of how you respond to stress. Some symptoms you display may be positive and motivating; most are not. Understand your own balance and know how others respond to various behaviors you exhibit. At the same time be aware of stress in others. No two people respond to stress in the same way.

Paying attention to your body and your environment can help manage stress. Exercise is, of course, generally good for your health, but it's also a good way to get rid of stress and frustration. Even stretching in your chair, going for a quick walk, or talking to a friend or confidante can help alleviate stress. Schedule breaks in your work routine through regular short vacations.

It's important to tackle the underlying causes of pressure if you can and not just deal with the symptoms. Obviously this is easier said than done, especially when you're overwhelmed by circumstances such as needing to care for a family member, suffering the breakdown of a close relationship, or negotiating an illness. Above all, remember that you're not alone. Don't hesitate to confide in a friend or coworker or seek counseling if you need help.

WHAT TO AVOID

Thinking Think You Can Do It All Alone

People sometimes take on too much, thinking that they can manage without additional support. Perhaps you think you are saving your business money by covering a number of responsibilities—but in reality you might be wasting money in missed opportunities or inefficiency. Often, under pressure, the one thing we become incapable of doing well is delegating work appropriately. Managing resources better, prioritizing your work load, building in downtime, anticipating pressure points, and monitoring progress are all important ways to help you deal with stress.

Never Saying No

Perhaps you're one of those people who are capable of sustaining high levels of activity over a long period of time, and others think it's natural to expect you always to perform at that pitch. The solution is being assertive and saying no when the pressure gets to be too much. You can't go flat out indefinitely without taking time to recharge.

Succumbing to Long Hours

Sometimes people assume that the longer they work, the better, and that longer hours equals greater productivity. It's just not true. When you are your own boss, there'll be times when you've so much to do you think you should stay up all night to finish the tasks at hand, but try not to do this if you can. Anything you do when you're half asleep you'll just have to do again when you've had some sleep. Shift your focus from the hours that you work and concentrate instead on the achievement of your tasks.

Taking It Out on Others

Stress is no respecter of boundaries. Stress in one area of your life will eventually affect all other elements of your life, too. Be aware of how these pressures may affect your work performance. Try not to transfer them to people who are not part of the problem. Work on the causes and not the symptoms.

SEE ALSO

Delegating (p. 369)
Managing Your Time (p. 360)

Focus On: Managing Projects
Robert Buttrick

GETTING STARTED

The progress of companies has always relied on the management of projects. New plants, new methods, new ventures all require dedicated teams working to strict timetables and separate budgets. However today, managers may spend as much time in interdisciplinary, cross-functional project teams as they do in their normal posts— project management has now become a core competence for all managers. This applies not only to projects undertaken for customers (external projects), but also to those undertaken for the development of the business itself (internal projects).

All businesses, regardless of size, have problems and opportunities they need to address. These may be related to introducing new technology, developing people, or introducing new products, processes, and systems; there is always something, somewhere that needs to be created or improved.

Project management is the key tool for tackling change, and is well suited to meet the needs of modern businesses, big or small. Unfortunately it's too often thought of as something "for techies," rather than the powerful business tool it is. In addition, it's often said it is "too much of an overhead for small businesses." Nothing could be further from the truth. Project management may be as formal or informal as you want— that is your choice. But underlying both formal and informal approaches are the same set of principles, which, if you apply them correctly, will give you the results you need.

In small businesses, project management does not need sophisticated tools and systems—often a big wall, paper, and Post-it stickers are all you need for planning and control. This actionlist outlines techniques for effective project management.

FAQS

What exactly is involved?

Understanding the scope and complexity of project management is an essential first step to achieving success. Project management involves the following key elements:

- making sure your projects are driven by your strategy
- using a staged approach to manage your projects
- placing high emphasis on the early stages
- engaging your "stakeholders" (that is, everyone potentially involved or affected by a project, such as staff, customers, and suppliers)
- encouraging teamwork and commitment
- ensuring success by planning for it
- monitoring against the plan
- formally closing the project

How can I make sure that a project runs smoothly?

Your project will run much more smoothly if you focus on a few basics.

- Set clear boundaries: define strategies clearly so that you are better able to eliminate low-leverage, low-value projects.
- Plan through progressive stages: proposal, initial investigation, detailed investigation, development and testing, trial, operation, and closure.
- Make a good start: concentrate on the early stages of the project, when the decisions taken have a far-reaching effect on the outcome.
- Analyze the project, determine which are the intrinsically risky parts, and act to reduce, avoid, or, in some cases, insure against the risks.
- To make projects succeed, tip the balance

of power towards the project and away from your company's normal management structures.

- Focus progress monitoring more on the future than on completion of activities, which doesn't predict that future milestones will be met.

✓ MAKING IT HAPPEN
Make Sure Your Projects Are Driven by Your Business Vision

Don't waste time on unnecessary projects. Be clear about your company's "vision" (that is, what you want to achieve, how, and when) or you'll risk wasting precious resources on ideas that are ultimately worthless and which will risk the business's overall performance.

Use a Staged Approach to Manage Your Projects

It's very rare to be able to plan a project completely to its conclusion when you've just started work on it. However, it's usually possible to at least plan the next steps in detail and prepare a rough plan for the remainder. As you progress through the project, you gather more information, risk is reduced, and confidence in delivery increases. These progressive steps are called "stages." Companies have their own names for these, but typically they are:

- **Proposal:** identifying the idea or need.
- **Initial investigation:** having a quick look at the possible requirements and solutions.
- **Detailed investigation:** undertaking a feasibility study of the options, choosing a solution and defining it.
- **Develop and test:** building the solutions.
- **Trial:** piloting the solution.
- **Release:** putting it into practice and closing the project.

You should use the same generic stage names **for all your projects**. This makes the use and understanding of the process very much easier, avoiding confusion and the need to learn different terms for various types of project. What differs is the content of each project, the extent to which each stage is used, the level of activity, the nature of the activity, the

resources required, the stakeholders and decision makers needed.

As a minimum you should have two stages (Plan it and Do it!). The five stage model would be for more complex projects. The "stages" are the periods of time during which the work is done. The "gates" are entry points to each stage and are key check points for revalidating a project and committing resources and funding.

Concentrate on the Early Stages of the Project

Decisions taken during the early stages of a project have a far-reaching effect on the outcome, setting the tone for the rest of the project. Creative thinking and solutions can cut delivery times in half and reduce costs dramatically. On the other hand, once development is under way, it's seldom possible to make savings of anything but a few percent whilst introducing changes later can be very costly. The early stages of a project are therefore fundamental to success. Up to 50% of the project life can be usefully spent on the investigative stages before any final deliverable is physically built. Sound investigative work means objectives are clearer and plans more robust; work spent on this is rarely wasted effort.

Engage Your Stakeholders and Understand Their Current and Future Needs

As mentioned above, a stakeholder is any person involved in or impacted by a project. The involvement of stakeholders, such as staff, customers, and suppliers, adds considerable value at all stages of the process. Viewed from a stakeholder perspective, a particular project may be just one more problem they have to cope with as well as fulfilling their usual duties; it may appear irrelevant to them, or even regressive. If their consent is required to make things happen, you ignore them at your peril!

Encourage Team Work and Commitment

If you have a team of people working with or for you, involve everyone so that they all work together. This approach really will deliver the best results. If you are managing the project, be as open as you can with your team and they'll appreciate it.

Smaller business often have an advantage over larger organizations in this area as larger businesses have to draw on people in more (and necessarily separate) departments to collaborate on projects, and this can cause all manner of internal problems. As there are fewer line managers in small businesses, the projects are "business-led" not manager-led, leading to effective delivery. In time, this will also lead to effective change which can be managed as the business grows and matures.

Delegating

GETTING STARTED

If you have a team working with you, delegation is a key skill to acquire or develop. Delegation is not just about giving tasks to others—it's about getting staff to take full responsibility for certain key functions or tasks. In order for a business to grow (and for employees to find new paths of development) new people must be employed to take over established functions, allowing others to develop different aspects of the business.

Owner-managers tend to like being in control of everything. They find it difficult to let go of things that they have created and nurtured, yet this is exactly what they must do if the operation is to grow and develop.

FAQS

Why do people find it difficult to delegate?

There are many reasons why you may find it difficult to delegate. Often, it seems quicker to perform the task yourself rather than bother to explain it to somebody else and then correct his or her mistakes. You might worry that the person will make a bit of a hash of it and it'll take a long time to put right the mistakes they make. On the other hand, you may feel threatened by the competence of an employee who is quick on the uptake and does well. There is a fear that the employee may take over the role of being the person the rest of the staff goes to with their problems. They may even find something wrong with the way *you* do things.

If you lack confidence, you may find it hard to give instructions and you'll put off delegating. If you do delegate, and problems arise because the employee fails to do what you've asked him or her to do, you may doubt your own ability to confront the person about his or her actions. If staff have been given increased responsibilities and have done well, you may not be confident of being able to reward them sufficiently. Conversely, you might be reluctant to delegate tasks that you think are too tedious.

Finally, you may realize that delegation is necessary, but you don't know where to start, or how to go about it. You need some kind of method to follow. The following paragraphs will help put you on the right track.

How can delegation help me?

Delegation offers many benefits. Done well, it will allow you to concentrate on the things you do best and also give you the time and space to tackle more interesting and challenging tasks in the future. You'll be less likely to put off making key decisions and you'll be much more effective. Your staff will benefit too; everyone needs new challenges, and by delegating to them, you'll be able to test their ability in a range of areas and increase their contribution to the business. Staff can take quick decisions themselves and they'll develop a better understanding of the details concerned. Done well, delegation should improve the overall productivity of employees.

It's all too tempting to withdraw into "essential" tasks and not develop relations with your team. The bottom line is that it is wasteful for senior staff to be given high-level compensation for doing low-value work, and passing tasks down the line is essential if the business is to grow. Not knowing how to do this is recognized as one of the biggest obstacles to small business growth. By delegating, you'll have much more time to think strategically about business growth.

Delegation doesn't make things easier (there will always be other challenges), but it does make things more efficient and effective. Essentially, it represents a more interactive way of working with a team of people, and it involves instruction, training, and development. The results will be well worth the time and effort you invest in doing it properly.

When should I delegate?

Delegation is fundamental to successful management—look for opportunities to do it. If you have too much work to do to complete all the tasks at hand, or if you don't have enough time to devote to important tasks, delegate. When it's clear that certain staff need to develop, particularly new employees, or when an employee clearly has the skills needed to perform a specific task, delegate.

What tasks should I delegate?

Begin with any routine administrative tasks that take up too much of your time. There are likely to be many small everyday tasks which you have always done—you may even enjoy doing them (for example, sending faxes)—but they're not a good use of your time. Review these small jobs and delegate as many of them as you can. Being your company's point of contact for a particular person or organization, which is important but can be time consuming, is also an excellent task to delegate.

On a larger scale, delegate projects that it makes sense for one person to handle; this will be a good test of how the person manages and coordinates the project. Give the person something he or she has every chance of completing successfully, rather than an impossible task at which others have failed and which may well prove a negative experience for the person concerned. Tasks for which a particular employee has a special aptitude should be delegated.

Who should I delegate to?

Make sure you understand the person you are delegating to. He or she must have the skills and ability, or at least the potential, to develop into the role and must be someone you can trust. It's a good idea to test out the employee with small tasks that will help show what he or she can do. Also make sure that the employee is available for the assignment—beware of overburdening your

effective workers. Delegation should be spread out among as many employees as possible, so think about the possibility of assigning a task to two or more people.

MAKING IT HAPPEN
Be Positive

Think positively: you have the right to delegate, and you must delegate. You won't get it 100% right the first time, but you'll improve with experience. Be as decisive as you can and if you need to improve your assertiveness skills, consider attending a course or reading one of the many books on the subject. A positive approach will also give your employees confidence in themselves, and they need to feel that you believe in them.

If you expect efficiency from the person you delegate to, organize yourself first. If there's no overall plan of what is going on, it will be hard to identify, schedule, and evaluate the work being delegated. Prepare before seeing the person (but don't use this as a ploy to delay!). Assess the task and decide how much responsibility the person will have. Assess the person's progress regularly and take notes.

Discuss the Task to Be Delegated

When you meet the employee or employees you are delegating to, discuss the tasks and the problems in depth, and explain fully what is expected of them. It is crucial to give people precise objectives, but encourage them to seek these out themselves by letting them ask you questions and participate in setting the parameters. They need to understand why they are doing the task, and where it fits into the scheme of things. Ask them how they will go about the task, discuss their plan and the support they might need.

Set Targets and Offer Support If Necessary

Targets should be set and deadlines scheduled into daily planners. Summarize what has been agreed, and take notes about what the employee is required to do so everyone is clear. If the person is given a lot of creative scope and is being tested out, you may decide to be deliberately vague, but if the task is urgent and critical, you must be specific.

How much support you offer and give will very much depend on the person and your relationship with them. In the early stages you might want to work with the person and to share certain tasks, but you'll be able to back off more as your understanding of the person's abilities increases. Encourage your staff to come back to you if they have any problems—while it is important to have time alone, you should be accessible if anyone has a problem or the situation changes. If an employee needs to check something with you, try to get it back to him or her quickly. Don't interfere or criticize if things are going according to plan.

Monitoring progress is vital—it's very easy to forget all about the task until the completion date, but in the meantime, all sorts of things could have gone wrong. When planning, time should be built in to review progress. If more problems were expected to arise and nothing has been heard, check with the employee that all is well. Schedule routine meetings with the person and be flexible enough to changes in deadlines and objectives as the situation changes.

How Did It Go?

When a task is complete, give praise and review how things went. If an employee's responsibilities are increased, make sure he or she receives fair rewards for it. On the other hand, there may be limits to what can be offered, so don't offer rewards you can't deliver. Also bear in mind that development can carry its own rewards. Such career development issues can be discussed with the employee in periodic reviews, and the results of delegated tasks noted for this purpose. If the person has failed to deliver, discuss it with them, find out what went wrong, and make it a goal to resolve problems in the future.

WHAT TO AVOID 𝗫
Expecting Employees to Do Things Like You Do

Managers often criticize the way things are done because it isn't the way they would have done it themselves. Remember that people prefer working in different ways and concentrate on the results rather than the methods used to obtain them.

Not Giving People a Chance

If you are giving a person something new to do, you must be patient. It will take time for employees to develop new skills, but it is time that will pay off in the end. Have faith in the people around you.

Delegating Responsibility without Authority

It's unfair to expect results from someone with one hand tied behind his or her back. If you are going to delegate responsibilities, make sure that those involved know this, and confer the necessary authority upon the person you are delegating to.

SEE ALSO
Developing Leadership Skills (p. 393)
Managing Stress (p. 363)
Managing Your Time (p. 360)
Small and Growing Businesses (p. 422)

Staff Planning

GETTING STARTED

As your business grows, it will naturally require more people to carry out the work and new skills will be required to handle a wider range of business activities and developing technology. You'll need to have new employees in place in good time to meet increased demand, and you should provide opportunities to develop, train, and promote existing staff. Future salary and training costs need to be built into the cash flow forecast and financial plan. It is important to foresee these requirements and to plan accordingly.

This actionlist looks at the main issues that a small business needs to address as it plans for its staffing requirements.

FAQS

What is the best way to approach staff planning?

A number of statistical methods have been developed to help businesses to analyze, predict, and plan future staffing requirements. Each business is different, so there is no single answer to how best to plan. In basic terms, though, you'll need to forecast sales and plan future production levels, estimate the amount and type of work that will be required, identify who can do this work and how training and recruitment can fill the gaps, and then implement the plan and review its success.

Link staff planning to the wider strategic planning process. Your staffing plan should develop from the long-term forecast for the development of sales and the required increase in working capacity that this represents. The various types of work must be identified and quantified. Costs may then be attached, enabling budgets and financing to be planned. You will need to plan for the long term (for example, five years), the year ahead (relating to the annual budget), and possibly month by month to show how change may be phased in during the year ahead (coinciding with the cash flow forecast). All this should feed back into your main strategic plan for business development.

MAKING IT HAPPEN
Estimate Future Work Requirements

In addition to estimates for future levels of output, you need information about how work is done, who does it, and what the options are for making changes.

The first step is to analyze jobs by clarifying the main job elements and determining how much work is required to carry them out. Don't make too many assumptions about what people do and how they do it. Your staff are more in touch than you are with how things are really done. A minor task may take much longer than you think. Another task may be so boring that it seriously threatens effectiveness and job satisfaction. While a scientific "work study" can be useful, informal discussion and team meetings are a much more diplomatic way to look at how work is done.

You then need to estimate how workloads will increase. From sales forecasts you can work out the required level of production from month to month. These estimates then need to be shown in terms of staffing levels. The number of workers required will often increase in proportion to the volume of work, for example, double the work (usually) requires double the workers. In some cases the workload might be helped by further training or the introduction of different working methods. Nevertheless, it is often helpful to create estimates based on the amount of work required to produce one unit of production (sometimes known as the Workload Method). The work required to produce one unit is split into its constituent parts. Each part is given a time value. These can then be multiplied by the number of units required, giving the total amount of work of each type. For example:

Types of work	Time/unit	@180/month	@200/month
Assembly	1.0	180hrs (24 days)	200hrs (26.6 days)
Testing	0.4	72hrs (9.6 days)	80hrs (10.6 days)
Packaging	0.2	36hrs (4.8 days)	40hrs (5.3 days)

Fluctuations in demand are important in many industries. In some cases you may need to employ some people on a casual basis in order to meet peak demand. Some industries work to annualized hours whereby an employee will work a set number of hours per year but with a staggered working pattern. This may mean that the majority of their hours are in the summer months (for example) but their wages are evenly spread throughout the year. This removes problems of overtime payments for the business and removes the need to be continually training casual workers. It may also help to switch resources or to build up stock in order to even out these fluctuations. On the whole, most organizations will not want extra stock on the premises because of storage costs, fire risks, and so on.

Analyze the Workforce

It can be helpful to profile the people you employ by summarizing and collating information about individuals into a single quick-reference document. For example, you could look at what each person does, areas of competence, qualifications, and development options. If these can be presented on a single sheet it can help you identify the various options for development. Include also basic information, such as salary and length of service.

You can also profile your workforce as a whole, by identifying some key measures for the way it has been developing. For example, you could look at staff turnover (number leaving divided by total workforce) and growth (number of staff year after year). Other measures might include supervision (number of staff per supervisor/manager) and promotion (number of managers from the workforce compared to the number of managers recruited from outside). You could also consider the annual recruitment cost (include the time required to interview and coach new staff), annual training costs, and

productivity (turnover divided by number of staff). Also consider the average time that employees stay with the company, and staff stability (this can be measured by a staff stability index, which looks at staff with long service and provides an indication of their tendency to stay with the organization).

Staff planning is not an exact science. Comparative information may be available through your trade association. Key measures are mainly useful to help you understand the present situation, to set targets, and to measure success. There may be limits to what can be achieved (for example, in your competitive environment, promotion opportunities may be limited or salary increases may be very difficult).

Relate Tasks to Individuals

Adjusting individual work roles can become very complicated. Where a large team is working on a variety of projects, changing one factor can have an impact upon everyone else. You need a simple way to look at who does what, and then to look at what happens if you change who does what, and how this will develop over a period of time. A computer spreadsheet is especially useful for this, enabling you to reconsider values without having to recalculate totals every time.

One approach is to create a matrix that sets individuals against specific work areas. For example, calculating on an average of 18 working days (allowing for sickness and vacation) per full-time employee per month, the diagram (opposite) shows how work (shown in days) is split between a number of employees, for an estimated level of activity in each area.

An overview chart for the year ahead is a useful budgeting tool. A month-by-month chart showing fluctuations in production requirements will help you to plan for change in good time to meet your future commitments.

Types of work	Amount	Ali	Jim	Aisha	Helen	Justin	Omar
Sales and Admin	18	3	12	3			
Research	47		4	15	16	6	6
Edit/Proofing	28		2		2	12	12
DTP	15	15					
Total Days	108	18	18	18	18	18	18

Consider Staff Development Issues

Staff planning provides an opportunity to put into action your plans for developing individuals. Your personnel policy document should be a useful framework to help you take decisions that will affect individual employees.

Job design and job satisfaction are two important areas to consider. As the business and the individuals change and develop, new jobs need to be defined. Roles and job descriptions must be clear cut. If you can, build variety into the jobs. Look for activities that complement each other and suit the skills and experience of the people concerned.

When it comes to management development, be open minded about what people can achieve. Do not assume that certain individuals can't take on new responsibilities. To provide scope for staff to develop, aim to take new people on at the most junior level, promoting existing staff into new positions of responsibility when more senior vacancies arise.

If you are facing new skills requirements, think whether existing staff could be trained to meet them. The cost of training should be offset against the benefits of being able to use someone familiar with the business and who (unlike a new recruit) is not an unknown quantity. Training is a benefit to staff and is also a motivator.

Some kind of plan for pay increases should be considered. If pay is increased ad hoc, you may risk not being able to provide competitive long-term benefits across the board. A clear pay structure will also help long-term financial planning. Seek to compete with similar rates in the industry if you wish to retain your experienced staff.

Lower pay may keep your prices competitive, but you will not be able to hold onto the best staff available. Seek information about standard rates of pay, and create salary levels related to skill and responsibility.

Consider Recruitment Lead Times

It is important to make adequate provision for the time it takes for new people to settle in. Even the most competent people take time to learn about the job and to gain the trust of their colleagues. If you do need to recruit, the lead times for advertising, selection, notice periods, training, and induction can be long. You may need to start the whole process as much as six months in advance of the time when the person's full workload will be required. Recruitment is also a significant workload for managers, and this should also be accounted for in your forward planning.

WHAT TO AVOID
Making It Complicated

Use simple analysis and planning methods for the best results.

Not Thinking about Your Own Staff First

Remember to talk to your staff first about how jobs, individuals, and teams can be developed and improved. Aim to develop and retain your existing workforce before thinking of recruitment from outside.

SEE ALSO
Conducting Interviews and Making Job Offers (p. 378)
Employee Benefits/Compensation (p. 445)
Handling Resignations (p. 403)

Focus On: Finding and Keeping Top Talent
Philip Sadler

GETTING STARTED

Just as businesses have changed dramatically in nature over the last 20 years, so have people's attitudes to their employers—and the attitudes of the most talented people are no exception. Furthermore, knowledge is more important than ever before and a major source of competitive advantage. Attracting, finding, and retaining talented people is therefore vital for success. Not only are people the most decisive and expensive resource, they also determine the success of every activity within the business.

This actionlist explains how to find and keep the best people—a challenge that involves:

- understanding the characteristics of talent-intensive businesses.
- choosing the best ways to attract, recruit and retain the most talented people.
- building the right work environment and culture.

FAQS
What are the characteristics of talent-intensive businesses?

Businesses that are rich in talent can be spotted in the following ways.

- Their principal assets (that is, their talented people) do not appear on the balance sheet (although they are, or should be, the main determinants of the company's market valuation).
- These key assets are mobile. They can, despite contracts of service, simply walk away.
- Talent-intensive businesses rely particularly on creativity and imagination.
- The success criteria for talent-intensive organizations stretch far beyond the accountants' bottom line. For example, winning an award for innovation may weigh far more than profit or cash-flow.

MAKING IT HAPPEN
Find the Best People

Don't assume that finding top talent will be expensive or lengthy: it need not be, even for the most senior appointments. If you have a vacancy, first of all ask your current team to see if they know anyone who might be a good candidate. Because they understand you, the role, and the business, they are best placed to find a good

candidate. There may be other people in your company's network that could also suggest a candidate: shareholders, suppliers, customers, and professional advisers may all be able to recommend good people.

Make sure you allow enough time to make the right appointment, and to insure that others meet the preferred candidate. Time pressures and isolation are two key factors that can lead managers to make appointments that are flawed.

Choose the Best Way to Recruit

The recruitment activity itself can be separated into two quite distinct processes. The first is attracting people whose talent has already been established and recognized elsewhere. This can be called the "transplanting" type of recruiting, equivalent to digging up and repositioning a mature tree or shrub in the quest for an instant garden.

The second process is the "seed bed" or "nursery" approach, recruiting young people straight from school or university, nurturing or developing their emerging talents and bringing them to fruition. This is clearly a longer-term approach and can be a bit risky. For example, you may give too much weight to academic qualifications. Less risky, however, is the process of finding talent among existing employees. Assuming they've been in employment for some time, a well-designed appraisal and development procedure can be a good way of finding promising candidates.

Keep the Best People

Remember that keeping top talent is as much about the people, the job, and the business as it is about the specific individual. Ask yourself at regular intervals the following key questions:

- who are my key people?
- what makes them exceptional?
- how are they feeling? Positive (for example, stimulated, challenged, valued) or negative (under pressure, concerned, struggling to perform at their best)?
- are their working environment and terms and conditions of employment competitive?
- do they know how much I value them?
- what are their aspirations and are they realistic? If so, what am I doing to support them? Do they know I'm doing this?

Finally, it is worth remembering that whether you are trying to find or to keep someone, pay remains important for most people, if not for its own sake, then for the sense of recognition that it brings to the individual.

Build a Culture That Retains Talent

As mentioned above, when it comes to retaining talent within your business, the need for an adequate rewards package goes without saying. What makes the real difference in keeping talented employees loyal, however, is the extent to which the company provides them with a working environment favorable to creativity, self-expression, and the exercise of initiative. Small business have an advantage over larger organizations here, as bigger companies are hierarchical, bureaucratic, and conformist in order to achieve efficiency and uniformity, yet it is just these characteristics that turn off highly creative people.

The chief characteristics of a culture that nurtures talent are:

- effective teams
- authority residing in expertise and competence rather than rank or status
- talented people respecting and recognizing the contribution of the colleagues who support them
- respected leadership—talented people are critical people who do not follow blindly, and know when the emperor has no clothes
- freedom, autonomy, space, and flexibility
- openness and trust
- encouragement of risk-taking

WHAT TO AVOID
Thinking That Money Is Everything

Companies often make the mistake of assuming that cash is the most important factor in attracting or retaining someone, which often puts small businesses at a disadvantage. An outstanding performer in any field is unlikely to move from one business to another if it involves a drop in pay, but there are other factors to consider. In the case of highly talented people, for example, a key influence on the decision whether or not to move jobs is the reputation the recruiting business has in its particular field. Is it at the leading edge? Does it set the pace for its industry? Does the individual feel flattered by being approached? Reputation building, therefore, is a key element in recruiting strategy.

Not Distinguishing Between Recruiting and Finding Talent

The distinction between recruiting talent and finding it is important; sometimes a business looks outside for new talent when the potential for outstanding performance already exists unnoticed among the existing team.

SEE ALSO
Assessing Your Entrepreneurial Profile: Do You Have What It Takes? (p. 5)

Finding Advice on Employment Law

GETTING STARTED
When your business employs people, it must comply with a number of legal requirements, many of which are in place to protect the rights of your employees.

FAQS

Why do I need advice on employment law?
Employment legislation is changing all the time, but it is important that you keep up to date with what is going on in the field of employment law—this will insure that your employees are treated fairly and that you avoid potentially costly employment lawsuits.

Where can I get advice on employment law?
As the law is so complicated, there are a good number of places you can turn to for help. It is very important that you check with a good lawyer if you have any troublesome queries, but we list here some Web sites that may be able to help with common problems:

- Americans with Disabilities Act Homepage: **www.ada.gov**
- Bureau of International Labor Affairs: **www.dol.gov/ilab**
- Bureau of Labor Statistics: **www.bls.gov**
- DisabilityInfo.gov: **www.disabilityinfo.gov**
- Occupational Safety and Health Administration: **www.osha.gov**
- State Labor Offices: **www.dol.gov/esa/contacts/state_of.htm**
- United States National Labor Relations Board: **www.nlrb.gov**
- U.S. Department of Labor Homepage: **www.dol.gov**
- U.S. Equal Employment Opportunities Commission: **www.eeoc.gov**
- Veterans' Employment and Training Service: **www.dol.gov/vets**

WHAT TO AVOID
Assuming You Know Everything about Employment Law
If you are not aware of changes in employment law you cannot comply with them. If you fail to comply, you are at risk of being taken to court by a disgruntled employee and could be liable for large fines if you are found in breach of the law.

Conducting Interviews and Making Job Offers

GETTING STARTED
There are two main purposes to any job interview: the first is to find out whether the candidate is qualified for the job and the second is to provide the candidate with information about the job and the business. It's very important that the interviewer gives every candidate the same opportunities to give the best presentation of him or herself. The candidate should be free to demonstrate his or her qualifications and to ask questions about the business and the job. It is also important that the interviewer knows exactly what he or she is looking for in the candidate, and has prepared questions to elicit information that will help in the final selection process. This actionlist gives advice on preparation for the interview, interview technique, and what to do after the interview is over.

FAQS

What information should be provided before the interview?
Before the interview, give the prospective interviewees clear instructions on how to get to your place of work and also tell them who they should ask for when they arrive. Also tell them what they should bring with them (such as pens, paper, or a calculator), roughly how long the interview is likely to last, and whether they will be reimbursed for travel expenses. If you are going to give them a test (for example, a short proofreading test if you are hoping to recruit an editor), it's polite to let the candidates know first.

Who should carry out the interview?
As a small business owner, you may be the only manager and therefore the sole interviewer. If you do work with others, though, you might like to ask a colleague to join you so that you get another opinion on each candidate. If the interviewee will be working for someone other than you, involve the candidate's prospective manager or supervisor as much as possible. If possible, you might also want to involve someone in the business who has specialist technical knowledge related to the job vacancy.

How long should the interview take?
There are no hard and fast rules, but generally interviews last between 30 and 60 minutes, including time for the candidate to ask questions of the interviewer. Schedule a break of about 20 minutes between interviews to give you time to make notes on the last interview and briefly prepare for the next. Interviewing is a tiring process, so don't schedule more than four or five interviews in a day.

MAKING IT HAPPEN
Prepare for the Interview
Decide what questions you are going to ask, and base these on the selection criteria for the job. Include general questions on the candidate's experience and skills, as well as questions that probe more directly into how well they are suited to the job description. You should also prepare questions specific to each candidate, such as queries about gaps in their résumé, or any issues that are not clear on their application forms. Take the time to read over their applications thoroughly.

As well as preparing questions, you also need to give some thought to where the interviews are to be conducted. Find a place where there will be no interruptions and make sure that you've made any adjustments needed to accommodate an interviewee who has indicated a disability.

Conduct the Interview
The first thing to do is welcome the candidate and introduce yourself, and any other

interviewers who may be present. Follow this by giving a brief outline of how the interview will be structured, and also some background about the organization and the job.

Start the interview with easy "getting to know you" questions, which will help put the candidate at his or her ease. These questions can also be used to build up to more probing, in-depth questions. Ask about the candidate's skills and experience first. When you have covered these, move on to why the candidate thinks they are qualified for the job, and what his or her ambitions and expectations are.

While you are conducting the interview, observe the candidate's behavior. This is often a good indication of his or her general level of confidence, as nonverbal communication is usually a subconscious use of the body to telegraph meaning. It goes without saying that you shouldn't jump to conclusions and make snap judgments, but watch the interviewees' reactions to a range of questions and see how they react under pressure.

Towards the end of the interview, ask the candidate whether they have any questions. It is a good way to find out how much homework about the business the candidate has done, and whether he or she is really interested in the job. Also ask them if they can briefly summarize for you what *they* understand the job to be—this will help you to check that they have grasped the outline you've given them and that you have explained it unambiguously. Finally, remember to thank the candidate for coming to meet you and explain to them what the likely next steps are (for example, if there are likely to be second interviews) and when they should expect to hear from you.

Questioning Techniques

Try to ask open-ended questions that can't be answered by just saying "yes" or "no." When you want more information, make sure you probe for specific answers. If a candidate seems to be avoiding a topic, use follow-up questions to try to fill in the blanks. Encourage candidates to expand on descriptions of their skills, and to demonstrate how they relate to the requirements of the job. Use questions that will encourage the candidate to sell him or herself to you. For example, you could ask questions such as "Why should I hire you?" and "Why do you want to work here?"

It is often a good idea to ask situational questions. These involve the interviewer describing a situation or case related to the business; the interviewee then has to propose a solution to handle the situation. This is a useful way to test problem-solving and reasoning ability. For example, you might ask the interviewee, "Your boss tells you to do a certain task. Shortly afterwards a coworker says they need your help for a high-priority project. What do you do?"

Remember to keep your tone mild and non-judgmental, particularly when asking difficult questions. Keep to a logical sequence of questions so that the candidate does not become confused. Make sure that you allow pauses in the conversation, to give the candidate time to think. It might be difficult, especially if a candidate is struggling with a particularly tricky question, but try not to interrupt—give each candidate the opportunity to get his or her point across.

Assess the Interviewee

It's essential that you give yourself time after the interview to make notes on anything said that is directly relevant to your decision. Do this as soon as you can so that the conversation is still fresh in your mind. If you've prepared properly before the interview, you'll already have decided on key selection criteria; the final decision should be based on how closely each candidate matched the person specification for that particular job. You may find that a marking system, which gives a score to each candidate for each of the areas highlighted in the job specification, makes it easier for you to make your decision.

After the Interview

Once you've selected the person you want to recruit, let them know as soon as possible, preferably by telephone as there is always the possibility that they will have other interviews to attend. Discuss salary (or other benefits) with them at this point and address any queries the successful candidate has thought of since they saw you.

Follow up your conversation with a letter formally confirming the job offer and containing details of start dates and basic terms and conditions. If the selection has been narrowed down to two or three people, they can then be asked to come back for a second interview. Finally, write to unsuccessful candidates informing them of the outcome of the interview as soon as the decision has been made. Some candidates may request feedback on their interview, so be prepared to answer their queries (you might like to arrange another time to telephone them so that you have your notes in front of you).

Draw Up an Employment Contract

You may want to add extra weight to the confirmation letter mentioned above by drawing up an employment contract—understandably, employees want some protection from being dismissed at will, and without an employment contract, they may feel that they're at the whim of employers who don't need legal, concrete reasons for terminating them. From an employer's point of view, without a contract of employment, those you hire aren't necessarily bound to allegiance or secrecy, and could defect to a competitor company without you having any legal recourse. Having a contract might also discourage less than honorable people from applying, knowing that your recruitment and hiring practices would probably turn up something about their past and the baggage they bring with them.

If you are putting together a contract for the first time, here is a list of key elements to include. If you are thinking of overhauling your recruitment procedure and are thinking of rewriting contracts for future employees, the list may include things that have been missing in the past, or that might help avoid future conflicts:

- name of employee and the company
- name of the job and job description

- dates (starting and ending if the contract is for a limited duration)
- conditions of employment (for example, probationary period) and place(s) of work
- the salary or rate of pay, plus details about its calculation and when paid
- company benefits (health and medical, vacation entitlements, sick leave, bonuses, retirement, and so on)
- terms and conditions of employment—place, hours, flextime, and so on
- options for termination and notices required
- process for filing a grievance and recourse for appealing disciplinary action
- confidentiality, non-disclosure, and non-compete clauses (so that essential information cannot be taken to any new jobs that the employee takes up in the future)
- ownership rights to property and product (intellectual and real) developed while employed

WHAT TO AVOID
Asking Discriminatory Questions

Legally, there are many questions that you must not ask because they are considered to be discriminatory. Three of the more obvious ways in which your questions could be seen in this light are described below:

- **Sex discrimination.** Obviously everyone should avoid making sexists comments, but you must also avoid questions such as "Are you planning to start a family?". If you refuse to employ someone because they say that they are, you are being discriminatory, and the candidate can lodge a complaint against you.
- **Racial discrimination.** Similarly, you must not discriminate on grounds of race. This covers both ethnic background and country of origin. Do not ask candidates if they have any religious affiliations.
- **Disability discrimination.** If the candidate discloses a disability, you cannot use it as a reason not to employ him or her unless it is justified. For example, somebody who is visually impaired would not be able to take up employment as a driver, but he or she could take up a variety of roles in an office setting with the right equipment. If

it will only take small adjustments for a disabled person to do a job and that person is the best-qualified candidate, then you have to make the adjustments. Any questions relating to disability have to be carefully worded and must center on how you can enable the candidate to do the job with the disability, rather than on why the disability would exclude the candidate.

Making Unjustified Assumptions

It's very easy for stereotyped assumptions to creep into the interview process. In particular, you should beware of rejecting candidates on the grounds of a "gut feeling," or the idea that they would not "fit in." Employment review boards are increasingly suspicious of such comments, as they are seen to be based on discriminatory assumptions, and may lead to complaints and legal challenges.

Causing the Candidate to Believe They Have Been Offered the Job

It's very important that you avoid making statements during the interview that could be alleged to create a contract of employment. It's easy to find yourself saying "you" when you are describing what the successful candidate would be doing in his or her job (for example, "You would be liaising with partners on a variety of projects."). Try to avoid this as much as you can, and use more general terms such as "the post-holder." You should also avoid making excessive assurances about job security. Courts have, on occasion, held that promises made during interviews created contracts of employment.

SEE ALSO
Employee Benefits/Compensation (p. 445)
Staff Planning (p. 372)

Running a Payroll System

GETTING STARTED

As soon as your business starts to employ people (including company directors), you will need to set up and manage a payroll system. This will allow you to make the correct deductions from staff wages or salaries, make the necessary payments to the Internal Revenue Service on time, and maintain an orderly system of pay-related records.

This actionlist explains the requirements for administering staff wages, including the deduction of federal and state income tax, FICA (social security and medicare payments), and health insurance and retirement plan contributions. At first glance, the process might look rather complicated, but actually it is quite simple, if a little time consuming.

FAQS

What must I deduct from employees' pay?

You are responsible for ensuring that all federal and state taxes are deducted from your employees' paychecks. In addition, benefits that are part of the employee compensation program such as medical, dental, vision, and other co-payment benefits should be deducted. Any 401k, other retirement or stock purchase deductions should also be reflected in the employees' pay.

How often should my employees be paid?

You determine the frequency of employee pay based on the cash flow needs of your business, the cost of the payroll system per pay period, the type of business you are in, and how frequently your competitors pay their comparable employees. You can change how frequently you pay; but if the change is going to be made, it is better that the payments are more frequent rather than less.

Who isn't on my payroll?

Independent contractors who are performing work for your organization are not on your payroll. Independent contractors are responsible for their own tax payments. Also, if your organization uses temporary personnel hired through a service, you pay the contracted fee per employee. The personnel service, not your organization, generates a paycheck to the employee with the appropriate deductions.

MAKING IT HAPPEN

Choose the Payment System Your Company Needs

There are three typical forms of employee payment. They are paper checks, direct deposit, and payroll debit cards. Paper checks are the oldest, and most expensive, form of employee payment. In that case, a separate check is generated for each employee, usually on specially prepared and costly paper, delivered to the Human Resources department whether from your internal payroll department or an outsourcing provider, and then distributed to each employee.

Direct deposit allows employees to have money deposited directly into their bank account. The employee is provided with a "paystub" or statement that shows the gross pay as well as all deductions. One of the benefits for employees of direct deposit is that the money is in their account more quickly than if they were to deposit a check. Many companies offer a choice of check or direct deposit to their employees.

The third, and newest, form of payment is the payroll debit card. This system was devised because many employees either don't have bank accounts or choose to cash their paychecks at check cashing services at a high fee. Payroll debit cards are plastic cards, which are either designed to be used like an ATM card only or carry the VISA© or Mastercard© logo, in which case they can also be used like a credit card. Employee pay is deposited into each employee's "account" and the monies are immediately available by using the card. As with direct deposit, employees are provided with a paystub or statement to show the gross pay and deductions.

Pay and Benefits Statements and Reports

At each pay period, employees should receive a paystub or statement that shows their gross pay for the period along with all withdrawals made. This is a very important document for all employees but particularly for those who work overtime. It is their best way to track whether all their hours are reflected in the pay system. The information on the statement should also reflect year-to-date numbers and any accrued vacation available to the employee.

You may decide to provide your employees with a quarterly, biannual, or annual report itemizing their gross pay, deductions, and payroll-related benefits. By providing employees with that information, you can make sure that you have the correct information for each; including their address, phone number, number of exemptions, selected benefits program and carriers, 401k or other pension or stock option withdrawals and matching payments; show their contribution toward taxes, and also show the contributions made by the company whether to taxes or toward their benefits.

In-house or Outsourced Payroll Systems

The decision to keep payroll in-house or to outsource it to one of the many payroll system suppliers will be based on the size of your company and the complexity of your payroll system. For many start-ups and very small businesses, it is not cost-effective to have a payroll service generate paychecks. However, due to the tax regulations and complexity of the process, you may want to have your accountant take care of that function.

However, the earlier you find out about outsourced payroll services, the better served you, your company, and your employees will be. Many services provide special packages for small businesses that

can reduce your costs and the headaches involved in keeping the payroll accounts up-to-date.

Find out if your payroll service will pay any tax penalties if they make mistakes in the tax filing process. Also find out if they will do the tax filing for you.

Payroll Systems and Employee Satisfaction

Payroll systems are the first and best way for employees to see the company's commitment to them. If payroll systems are designed to be on-time and correct, even with the diverse and complex deductions involved, the employees know that you are paying attention to their best interests. While payroll systems are not usually thought of as a method to increase morale, they have that immediate impact on the organization and are well worth your time to analyze and ensure that the best service to your employees is being given each pay period.

Payroll Systems and Human Resource Management

One of the best ways to track how your company is using its personnel is to analyze the payroll system. Many employees are working on a variety of projects that may cross department lines. As a result, they are being paid from a variety of budgets coming from different departments and projects. Your payroll system should provide the specific information you and your management team need to track and analyze how your human resources are being utilized, what the impact is on the various projects your company is pursuing, how much expense is overhead and how much goes directly toward profits and more. By using your payroll system in that way you will be better able to plan and budget both by your fiscal calendar and by project.

WHAT TO AVOID
Not Doing Your Homework

There are always regulatory changes being made that impact your payroll systems.

Whether it is new laws on overtime payment by compensatory time or changes to the percentages of mandated tax deductions, make sure you or your payroll service have the most up-to-date information available.

Not Getting the Right Advice

Beyond your internal or outsourced payroll service, consult a CPA or other outside source that specializes in payroll issues. You may want to set up a regular audit or review of your payroll systems to ensure that you are in compliance with federal and state regulations, have adequate payroll insurance coverage, are working with the appropriate provider and more.

Not Paying Your Employment Taxes

Your business will have regular employment tax payments due to the state and federal government. These must be paid on time and in the correct amount, otherwise your business could be fined and you might face time in jail.

SEE ALSO
Employee Benefits/Compensation (p. 445)

Complying with the Minimum Wage Laws

GETTING STARTED

All businesses in the United States must comply with the Federal Fair Labor Standards Act (FLSA) minimum wage laws, which require them to pay workers at least the national minimum wage. This actionlist gives the current national minimum wage rate, explains who it applies to, and lists the exceptions. It also describes which elements of workers' pay are included in the minimum wage, and stresses the importance of keeping relevant records.

FAQS

How much is the national minimum wage?

The minimum hourly rate for adult workers aged 20 or over is $5.15 before deductions. For workers under the age of 20, the minimum hourly rate is $4.25 per hour during the first 90 consecutive days of employment. The minimum wage increases periodically.

Do states have different minimum wage rates?

Individual states often have minimum wage rates that exceed the national minimum wage. In such cases, if the business is located in a state that requires a higher level of payment, the state level must be paid. In addition, businesses must comply with state regulations regarding overtime, tipping, and other specific requirements.

Who does the minimum wage apply to?

There are two types of coverage to which the minimum wage applies. The first type of coverage is called enterprise coverage. This applies when your business has a minimum of two employees and makes over $500,000 per year. The other application of enterprise coverage is if your business is a hospital or a business providing nursing care for residents, schools, pre-schools, or government agencies.

The second type of coverage is individual coverage. This applies to employees who are involved in any form of interstate commerce, including but not limited to working for an organization that manufactures or sends products to another state, makes calls between states, or if your employees pro-

vide janitorial services in a building which is used for interstate commerce.

Domestic service workers, such as housekeepers, full-time babysitters, cooks, and others are also included in the individual coverage and must be paid the minimum wage.

Who is exempt from the minimum wage?

Not all workers qualify for the minimum wage. For example, employees who receive tips directly from customers can be paid as low as $2.13 per hour if their total tips received are at least $30.00 per month and their total compensation, including tips, reaches the minimum wage requirement for their state.

If your employees include full-time students, you can apply for a certificate from the Secretary of Labor entitling you to pay not less than 85% of minimum wage. The certificate also limits the number of hours the students can work.

For student learners who are at least 16 years old and are participating in vocational programs, a certificate can be obtained from the Department of Labor entitling you to pay not less than 75% of minimum wage.

A certificate can also be obtained exempting you from paying the minimum wage to disabled workers whose earning or productive capacity is impaired by physical or mental injury or other reasons. In such cases, application must be made to the Secretary of Labor for a certificate of exemption.

How many hours must a person work to qualify?

There is no minimum period that a person must work before they qualify. The minimum wage is payable for the time when a worker is required to be at work or available for work. This includes time spent training and traveling for the purposes of the job (this does not include commuting to and from work).

As an employer, you must pay an average hourly rate of no less than the minimum wage appropriate to the worker.

When does the minimum wage apply?

You must pay the minimum wage for all the time an employee is required to be on premises, on duty, or at a prescribed workplace. An employee's workday, or that time for which the minimum wage must be paid, is generally defined as the time period between when an employee commences and ceases his or her principal activities.

However, minimum wage payment may be required in other circumstances. The FLSA provides detailed information about additional applications of the minimum wage, including but not limited to the following:

- Waiting time: when an employee is engaged to wait by the employer, for example, a firefighter waiting for an alarm.
- On-call Time: time that an employee is required to remain on call on the premises; this may or may not apply to on-call time that the employee performs at home or some other location not on premises.
- Rest and meal breaks: rest periods of 20 minutes or less are covered, meal periods generally are not covered; you must, however, pay for meal periods if the employee remains at his or her desk doing work.
- Sleeping time: this applies to those who work on a 24-hour duty roster.
- Lectures, meetings, and training: time spent by employees at your direction or with your approval in any of these venues.
- Travel time: there are a variety of categories of travel time ranging from "home to work" (which may or may not be covered) to "home to work travel on a special one-day assignment" (which would be covered);

you should review the FLSA requirements before assigning employees any travel and ensure that their pay reflects the appropriate travel time due them.

MAKING IT HAPPEN
Keep Good Records

As an employer, you must keep records to prove that your workers have received at least the minimum wage. No particular format is required; however, there are certain data you must obtain and keep about each employee, the hours he or she worked, and the wages earned.

According to the Department of Labor Web site, these include the employee's full name and social security number, their address including zip code, birth date (if they are younger than 19), the employee's gender and occupation, time and day when the employee's workweek begins, the hours worked each day and total hours worked each workweek, the basis on which the employee's wages are paid (by hour, week, piecework, or other), their regular hourly rate, total daily or weekly straight-time earnings, overtime earnings for each workweek, additions to or deductions from the employee's wages, total wages paid each pay period, and the date of payment and pay period covered by each payment.

If any queries arise about minimum wage payments, it is up to the employer to prove they have paid the minimum. It is not the employee's responsibility to prove that he or she has not been paid it. Records must be kept for a minimum of three years after the relevant pay reference period.

Understand Employee Rights Concerning the Minimum Wage

Your business must conform to the Federal Fair Labor Standards Act in both pay levels and record keeping requirements. Remember that many states have different minimum wage levels that exceed those of the federal government. Check with the Secretary of State, Commerce, or Labor in your state or with the U. S. Department of Labor to determine the amount you must pay your employees.

Enforcing the Minimum Wage

The Wage and Hour Division of the Department of Labor enforces the minimum wage laws. This Division has programs that provide education to employers and employees as well as oversight of employers' activities to ensure that the law is being applied correctly and employees are paid their appropriate wage.

✗ WHAT TO AVOID
Not Keeping Employees Informed

You should display details of the minimum wage prominently in your workplace so that your employees know their rights. The Department of Labor provides signs with the necessary and appropriate information for employers at no charge.

Refusing or Neglecting to Pay

Refusing or wilfully neglecting to pay the federal or state minimum wage is a criminal offense. Your records will be crucial to making your case regarding alleged inappropriate pay levels. Make sure you keep complete records and have appropriate certifications in case of exemptions.

Not Getting the Right Advice

Talk with your employment attorney and accountant to ensure that your employees are being paid the right wages. Make sure, if you have any exempt employees or special circumstances, that you have the appropriate documentation to support your pay schedules.

SEE ALSO
Employee Benefits/Compensation
  (p. 445)
Employment Law (p. 447)

Setting Up Job Shares

GETTING STARTED

Job sharing, also known as Shared Work programs, is an arrangement in which two employees share the responsibility of one full-time position with the salary, paid leave, pension rights, and fringe benefits divided between them, according to the time each works. This actionlist looks at some of the advantages and disadvantages of job sharing, and provides a brief guide to setting up a job-share program.

FAQS

What are the advantages of job sharing?

Job sharing enables employees to retain the responsibility and status of full-time work while being able to work shorter, and often more flexible, hours. Job sharers are usually better paid, more highly skilled, and have better prospects for promotion than most part-time workers.

Job sharing benefits the employer too. Job sharing programs can help you to retain skilled and experienced staff who are unable or don't want to work full-time but do not wish to leave their present job. It can also help to reduce absenteeism, as each job sharer has a greater amount of free time to organize other commitments and domestic responsibilities. As job sharers work fewer hours, there may also be less time taken off for stress-related disorders.

Job sharing can insure greater continuity of work. When one job-share partner is sick or on vacation, at least one half of the job is still being done, and it may be possible to organize the job-share agreement so that both partners can be present at peak times. The job may also be performed with greater effort and motivation. Job sharing also enables employers to utilize the skills and experience of two people for the price of one. Job sharers can organize their workload to take advantage of respective strengths and weaknesses, so that their capabilities are used to the full.

What are the disadvantages of job sharing?

Job sharing usually increases administrative costs. However, recruitment will often be for one worker to make up the job share (as you'll normally have one person on your team

already), and if two workers are employed at once, costs such as advertising, orientation, and so on, can be combined for the two.

Poor communication can be a problem, and it may be difficult to call meetings. Address this by making sure that both job sharers are kept properly informed of all developments, and, if possible, incorporate an overlap period, even if it's just a few hours a week, so that sharers can discuss their work. Ask both sharers to keep good records of what they do, have done, and are expecting to do so that everyone is clear and work isn't duplicated.

The job share may make extra work for managers in terms of allocating work, coordinating the work of the sharers, and communicating requirements. This will vary with the type of job and organizational structure. The division of responsibilities of the post will also need careful consideration.

MAKING IT HAPPEN
Start a Program

Before you implement a job-share program, make sure that everyone in your business understands, approves of, and accepts the principles of job sharing, especially those who will have contact with the job sharers. Be aware of prejudices against part-time workers, who may be regarded as less committed to the company. Other considerations that you need to bear in mind are discussed in more detail below.

Create a Job Description

A detailed job description, clearly defining the duties and responsibilities of the job, will make it easier to divide responsibilities according to requirements. Many clerical posts can be split by hours, providing continuous coverage. Management and professional jobs can be split by client, referral, project, and areas of expertise. Some jobs may have quite autonomous responsibilities, for example, different client caseloads, whereas others may require both job-share partners to contribute to the same project. In that case, if the job involves making important decisions, it will be necessary to decide if one partner's decisions must be upheld by the other.

Working Hours

Job shares can be split in a variety of ways. Common patterns of work include split days, with one employee working in the morning and one in the afternoon; split weeks, where one employee works one half of the week and one the other; alternate weeks; or no fixed schedule, which is a less formal arrangement. Work out which pattern will suit the requirements of the job and the employees involved. Jobs may not always be split equally; one sharer may want to work fewer hours than the other. Bear in mind, however, that if one sharer only has very few hours, it may be difficult to replace that person if he or she leaves.

Overlap Periods

Most job shares incorporate an overlap period for sharers to discuss developments and communicate problems. The length and frequency of the overlap periods will depend on the pattern of hours worked and the splitting of responsibilities; job sharers in a secretarial post may only need five minutes a day to discuss unfinished work, whereas partners who share a job as environmental consultants will obviously need more time to discuss clients and workloads.

Workspace

Job sharers will often share the same working area. However, if there are significant periods of overlap, it may be necessary to provide extra accommodation.

Training and Orientation

If possible, job sharers should attend orientation training together. This will help to develop a working relationship and ensure that both receive the same training. Further training can either be undertaken individually, according to areas of expertise and interest, or together, in areas of shared training needs.

Management and supervision

Job-share posts will require more management time, with an emphasis on good verbal and written communication. Meetings could be alternated between job sharers, and every third meeting could be with both in attendance.

Promotion

It is usual to allow job sharing "units" to apply for promotion on equal terms with full-time employees. Some organizations only consider the sharers together, and promote either both of them or neither of them; others will consider them individually as well as together, and promote the best person for the job.

Vacations

Job sharers usually receive the same amount of vacation as full-time workers, but they are paid in proportion to the number of hours worked. For example, where a job-share partner works the equivalent of half a full-time job, working five half-days a week, he or she may be allowed to take 15 days of vacation, the same as other employees, but only 7.5 of those will be paid vacation. Public holidays may cause some difficulties, as they usually fall on a Monday and therefore mostly within one job-share partner's working period. Public holidays are usually split into hours and divided between partners, with the time taken elsewhere by one partner.

Pension Plans

Pensions are usually paid pro rata, depending on the number of hours worked by each individual.

Recruiting Job Sharers

Decide which jobs will be open to job sharing and how they will be advertised. In many cases these will be internal applications, and it will be important to decide whether or not those wishing to job share must identify a partner before applying. Consider whether separate application forms are required from each partner, whether they have to justify why they want to job share and demonstrate how they are compatible to do so on the application form, and whether they will be interviewed together, or separately, or both. Decide how applications from job sharers without a partner should be treated. Careful selection is necessary when recruiting two people for a job share. Their qualifications, experience, and skills should be compatible, and they should appear capable of forming a close working relationship. You must also consider whether you will make the position a full-time job, if you are only able to recruit one partner.

Employment Rights

Job shares usually consist of two people sharing the workload normally assigned to one person. This usually involves a weekly workload spread over between 15 and 20 hours. The workers have the same rights as full-time employees.

What to Do if One Partner Leaves

If one job-share partner leaves, the procedure adopted by many organizations is to offer the job on a full-time basis to the remaining partner. If he or she does not accept the offer of full-time employment, the next step is to advertise the position as a job share, detailing the number of hours available. If no suitable replacement is found within a reasonable length of time (this time period varies considerably between organizations but is usually between three and six months), the remaining partner may be offered a part-time position or be redeployed elsewhere, if possible.

WHAT TO AVOID
Not Keeping People Informed

An employer should inform all employees and management about the principles behind job sharing, and how it differs from part-time work, before a job-share program is implemented.

Not Getting the Right Partners

How well a job share works depends on the people involved, so extra care will need to be taken with recruitment and selection procedures. It is important that both partners are able to communicate and interact well with each other, as well as with other employees, managers, and outside contacts.

SEE ALSO
Employment Law (p. 447)

Employing People with Disabilities

GETTING STARTED

As an employer, you have a general duty not to discriminate against any employee. The Americans with Disabilities Act (ADA), which was enacted in 1990, prohibits discrimination and ensures equal opportunity for people with disabilities in employment, state and local government services and programs, public accommodations, commercial facilities, and transportation. It also mandates the establishment of TDD/telephone relay services for the hearing impaired.

This actionlist explains what is expected of employers when they interview and employ a disabled person. It describes the legal requirements and also suggests ways to improve the employment environment to accommodate disabled staff.

FAQS

What is a disability?

The ADA defines a person with a disability as someone who has a physical or mental impairment that substantially limits one or more major life activities, that is, activities that an average person can perform with little or no difficulty, such as walking, breathing, seeing, hearing, speaking, learning, and working.

What are my legal obligations?

The ADA requires employers to consider the ability of the person and to make reasonable adjustments in working arrangements or to the physical features of the premises. You need to take steps to prevent these arrangements or features from placing the disabled person at a disadvantage. You will need to consider how effective the adjustments will be in helping the disabled person, whether they are practical to implement, how much they will cost, and whether you can afford them. An employer is not expected to make adjustments that would pose undue hardship on the operation of the business. Undue hardship means significant difficulty or expense when considered in relation to factors such as the business's size, financial resources, and the nature and structure of its operations. An employer is not required to lower production standards to make an accommodation.

During the interview process, an employer may not ask job applicants about the existence, nature, or severity of a disability; however, applicants may be asked about their ability to perform job functions. A job offer may be conditional depending on the results of a medical examination, but only if such an examination is required of all new employees in the same job category. An employer is generally not required to provide personal items such as eyeglasses or hearing aids.

MAKING IT HAPPEN

Prevent Discrimination When Recruiting

If you're using advertisements to recruit new staff, it's good practice to welcome applications from people with disabilities. Provide information about the job in an accessible format such as large print (which people with learning disabilities or sight difficulties will find easier to read) or with illustrations.

Some people with learning disabilities can fill in an application form themselves; others will need help. Consider allowing candidates to submit an application in different formats, such as by telephone, audiotape, or e-mail. It's good practice to include a question on the application form to ask applicants if they would have any special requirements at an interview.

Make Your Workplace Friendlier to Disabled Staff

If any physical feature of your premises, or any arrangements made by you, causes a substantial disadvantage to a disabled person compared with nondisabled people, you have to take reasonable steps to address this. Physical features include things like a building's design or construction, access to a building, fixtures, fittings, furnishings, equipment, or materials. For example, the design of a workplace may make it difficult for someone with a hearing impairment to hear.

The ADA gives a number of examples of steps that you may have to take. You may have to make adjustments to premises, such as providing a wheelchair ramp, or allocate some of the disabled person's duties to another employee. Another step might be to transfer the person to fill an existing vacancy, or to assign the person to a different place of work. Other examples include altering the person's working hours, or allowing him or her to be absent during working hours for rehabilitation, assessment, or treatment. You may be required to arrange for training for the person, to acquire or modify equipment, or to provide a reader, interpreter, or extra supervision.

Avoid Discrimination against Disabled People

Take care that your actions, or lack of them, do not lead to what is known as "constructive dismissal," a situation in which a disabled employee's job is made too difficult for them to continue. Your employee can then take legal action if you did not make reasonable adjustments to enable them to do their job.

If an employee complains of, or shows signs of, physical pain, such as back pain caused by lifting, or stress related to work, it's best to talk to him or her about it and see if anything can be done to remedy the situation. Record all interviews of this kind, even if the employee says that it's not a problem.

Adopting good practice can help minimize or avoid the risk of costly litigation. Good practice is about looking beyond the disability to what the person can actually do, sometimes with a bit of adjustment to the workplace or working practices.

WHAT TO AVOID
Not Getting the Right Advice

The ADA Web site (address given below) is a useful first stop in a search for information on best practice. Remember at all times that ignorance is not an excuse for not complying with the law, however, and seek professional advice if you are at all unsure of how to proceed.

Not Demonstrating Your Commitment to Equal Opportunities

Show that you have a commitment to equal opportunities. Mention disability explicitly in any equal opportunities policy and reassure any disabled applicants that their needs will be met. Make sure all your staff implement such policies.

SEE ALSO
Employment Law (p. 447)

Developing Leadership Skills

GETTING STARTED

There are many myths about leaders—starting with "leaders are born and not made." Owner-managers of small businesses might not necessarily have been in a leadership role before they started their company, and while some people are naturally better suited to leadership roles than others, the good news is that the necessary skills *can* be learned.

FAQS

Now that my business is growing I've taken leadership workshops and understand the theory of being a good leader. How do I put this into practice?

Being an owner-manager will give you plenty of opportunities to put your new skills to the test, but remember that leadership capability does not emerge overnight; it takes time and practice, so don't expect too much of yourself too soon. Why not make a start, though, by leading a new project, where you can test out the skills you've acquired? Make sure you plan carefully for resources and support. Taking this first step will give you the opportunity to test out your responses to this new situation. In turn, you'll then be able to evaluate what has worked and what hasn't, and help you plan what to do or avoid doing next time.

I seem to command an audience easily when I make presentations, but will I make a good leader?

Commanding an audience is a great skill and many leaders have it, but it's not the sole requirement. Leaders also need to be problem-solvers and have originality and flair, confidence and self-knowledge, strong interpersonal skills, the ability to listen, visioning capability, good organizational skills, and so on. Your ability as a speaker suggests that you're articulate and self-confident. If you possess the other qualities too, you are well on the way to being the leader your business needs.

MAKING IT HAPPEN

Understand the Various Facets of Leadership

There are different types of leadership styles. Think of three shepherds. The first opens the gate and walks through, allowing the flock to follow—this shepherd **leads from the front**. Another stands behind the sheep and pushes or guides them through, demonstrating a **supportive leadership style**. The third moves from front to back and sometimes to the middle of the flock, demonstrating an **interactive leadership style**. For leaders to exist there must be followers, and the needs of followers change depending on the context. Knowing how to apply different leadership styles can help you respond equally effectively in many different kinds of situations.

Another school of thought recognizes four leadership styles: directive, process, creative, and facilitative, each one related to a personality type. Being relaxed, for example, doesn't necessarily mean you can't be a leader. It does mean that you have natural tendencies for a certain style of leadership. And you may be able to learn other styles—more dominant, intuitive, or structured—as you become more confident and practiced in leadership. Try to work with your preferred style until you are comfortable enough to branch out.

Specific leadership styles work best in particular situations. A structured leader, for example, is likely to succeed in a situation where process is important, for example, in running an operation. The relaxed or facilitative leader is especially well suited to managing a group of professionals.

Dominant leaders may be needed in businesses focused on creating change.

Get Some Training

If your budget permits, a leadership course will help you gain a fuller understanding of what leadership is, and, by extension, how it will work for your business. Courses usually range from business theory to developing strategy to and understanding business risk.

Build Self-awareness

Your leadership style is the means by which you communicate. The more self-aware you are, the more effectively it will work for you. This means knowing:

- what you're like as a person
- what your preferences are
- what your goals are
- how other people perceive you and your objectives
- how you are motivated to achieve them

Numerous tests and questionnaires can be used to help you explore your personality and preferences; they are widely available from books, the Web, consultants, and other sources. Surveys are also useful. Business schools have valuable data on expected leadership behaviors. You can combine information from all these sources to establish a benchmark for yourself.

Apply Leadership Skills

Leadership opportunities are often thrust upon us unexpectedly, but in a small business environment you'll come across them more frequently. As in most situations, your best bet is to start with an analysis of the situation. Decide what is needed and how you can best achieve it.

Some leadership positions require you to set the objectives for others to follow. In these situations scheduling, consultation, and team building are essential to success. Leaders often need to work as intermediaries between two groups—those wanting the results (boards, investors, etc.) and those who will deliver the results. In this case you need to establish good communication channels with both parties. Try to pick teams that have a good balance between competent managers and energetic, loyal team members. Teams need consistent, positive energy levels to sustain momentum, and a thoughtful mix of talent—not choices based on friendships or politics—is the best guarantor of success.

If you are trying out new systems or approaches, make sure you surround yourself with the right people, create a framework for support, and document the process so you can later evaluate how well you did.

WHAT TO AVOID
Mirroring Other Leaders Too Closely

People new to leadership roles may try to copy a leader they respect, because the person provides a ready-made model. This can create a false impression of what you're really like, or, worse, make you look foolish for trying to mimic a style incompatible with your own personality. Leadership behaviors come from within. Identify what it is you respect in the other leader and think about how you can best display that attribute. If it doesn't work, don't be afraid to try a new approach.

Not Working at It

Many people hope that they have natural leadership skills and accept leadership positions without getting training or making mental adjustments. This sink-or-swim approach works sometimes, but you shouldn't count on it. Building up leadership skills, increasing awareness of yourself, and evaluating what you do have much more potential for success.

SEE ALSO
Delegating (p. 369)

Focus On: Win–win Performance Appraisals
Patrick Forsyth

GETTING STARTED

As your business grows and you recruit employees, you or your office manager will need to conduct performance appraisals. These face-to-face discussions (ideally undertaken annually) are an opportunity for an employee's work to be discussed and reviewed, and should aim to improve motivation and performance during the coming year. Unfortunately, many managers dislike conducting appraisals and worse, many employees rate their appraisals as worthless—or something even less flattering. In reality, appraisals are a major opportunity for both managers and staff.

This actionlist will review:

- why appraisals are necessary and will examine the benefits to managers and staff. Primarily, they insure and improve future performance.
- how effective appraisals should be planned and undertaken to maximize their positive impact while avoiding negative pitfalls.
- the impact of appraisals on the long-term success of the business. Appraisals provide considerable opportunity for improving ongoing operations, effective management, and catalyzing change.

FAQS

What are the reasons for performance appraisals?

There are many positive reasons why appraisals are necessary. They give managers an opportunity to review individuals' past performance, plan their future work and role, and set and agree specific individual goals for the future. Making time to hold a meeting with the person to be appraised also allows for on-the-spot coaching which in turn can identify development needs and set up development activity.

In addition, appraisals can:

- allow the exchange of feedback;
- reinforce or extend the reporting relationship;
- act as a catalyst for delegating work;
- focus on longer-term career progression;
- underpin or increase motivation.

Often a negative reason is the close relationship between appraisals and employment legislation (for example, lack of appraisal may make it impossible to terminate someone's employment). This is also a factor to keep in mind.

Overall the underlying intention is to improve future performance. The good appraisal presupposes that even the best performance can be improved, and seeks to increase the likelihood of future plans being brought to fruition.

How should the appraisal be organized?

For a well organized appraisal, you need to:

- allow enough time. You need to do the job and also to reflect the importance of the occasion. Few appraisals will be accomplished properly in less than an hour; some may last two or three hours or more—and will still be time usefully spent.
- allow no disturbances. Pausing to take even one telephone call sends out the wrong signals.
- create a suitable environment. Appraisals should be held somewhere private, comfortable, perhaps less formal than across a desk, yet suitably business-like.
- put the individual at ease. Remember that, even with good communication beforehand, appraisals may be viewed as somewhat traumatic. Anything that can be done to counter this is useful.

MAKING IT HAPPEN
Prepare Throughout the Year

Unsurprisingly, the key to effective appraisals is preparation by both parties. The manager must:

- spend sufficient time with staff during the year.
- communicate clearly and thoroughly the purpose and form of the appraisal so that people know what to expect. Employees should understand the need for appraisal, its importance, the specific objectives it addresses, and how both parties can get the best from it.
- prepare throughout the year, keeping clear records. Keeping an appraisal collection file means you don't have to rely on memory. In this, you should note matters that can usefully be raised at appraisals, making notes and filing copies of documents that will assist the process.

The appraisee (or team member) should keep running records and plan in detail the kind of meeting he or she intends to have.

Successful appraisal is the culmination of a year's worth of thinking. Recalling every detail of an employee's working year is difficult, but you can only appraise properly by being informed.

Relevant background information needs checking: for example, the appraisee's job description (which may need amendment after the appraisal), specific past objectives, possible changes to the job, its responsibilities, or circumstances, and the records of any previous appraisals.

Prepare Carefully and Plan

- Prepare written notification. As well as confirming mutually convenient timing, this should recap the purpose of the appraisal and highlight background information. Distribute copies of any documents or forms you intend to use or refer to during the meeting.
- Study the appraisee's file, making sure that you have all the information you need about what was supposed to happen during the year and what actually did happen. Make notes of points needing discussion and ensure that you can navigate the

documents easily as the meeting progresses.

- Review agreed standards and identify any that are no longer relevant or that need to be changed.
- Draft a provisional assessment. Brief notes can provide a starting point, prompt the agenda, and link to the system. Don't prejudge the discussion or make decisions prematurely.
- Assess your initial thoughts. Check your rationale, asking yourself a why question about anything noted at this stage. If no clear answer comes, more research may be necessary.
- Consider specific areas of the appraisal. It may be clear that some training is necessary, for example. Again without prejudging, it may be useful to check out what might suit and formulate a suggestion before the meeting.
- Think ahead. Remember that the most important part of the discussion will be about the future. You may need to plan particular projects and tasks, taking both development and operational considerations into account.
- Consult with others. Speak to those who work or deal with the appraisee to get a complete picture.
- Be clear about the link with a pay review. Many managers feel this should be kept for a separate occasion. Otherwise it can be difficult to stop appraisees from thinking all that matters is the potential increase.

Handle the Appraisal Effectively

Before you go any further, make completely sure that everybody being appraised understands the need for appraisal, its importance, its objectives, and its mutual benefits. When the appraisal starts:

- explain the agenda and how things will be handled. Remember to ask what the appraisee's priorities are.
- act to direct the proceedings. Do not, however, ride roughshod over the appraisee.
- ask questions. Open questions prompt and focus discussion.
- listen. The meeting is primarily an opportunity for the appraisee to communicate. In

a well-conducted appraisal, the appraisee should do most of the talking; the manager's job is to make that happen.

- keep primarily to agreed performance factors. Don't indulge in amateur psychology or attempt to measure personality factors. Also, keep primarily to performance factors, getting the appraisee to do most of the talking—while you listen hard.
- use the system. Use systems and appraisal forms to guide the meeting; working through the form systematically will ensure most of what needs to happen does.
- encourage discussion. Consider the appraisee's personal strengths and weaknesses, successes and failures, and their implications for the future. Concentrate the appraisal process on future performance, and don't confuse it with discussion of remuneration.
- set out action plans. Describe those that can be decided there and then (who will do what, when); note those needing more deliberation in terms of when and how action will be taken. Deal with each factor separately, for example, by devoting time to development action.
- conclude on a positive note. Always thank the appraisee for the role he or she has played and for the past year's work. Link this to any subsequent documentation.
- follow up appraisals promptly, sending all necessary written material to the appraisee and flagging any opportunity for further discussion.

WHAT TO AVOID
Treating Appraisals As an End, Rather Than a Means to an End
Appraisals achieve most when placed in a long-term context and linked to ongoing operations. Bear in mind:

- the ongoing management relationship: an effective appraisal should make all management processes through the year easier.
- the link with training and development: consultation, counseling, mentoring, and informal discussions are all just as important extensions of appraisal as formal training.
- motivation: appraisals must themselves be motivational, and what stems from them must assist ongoing motivational activity.

Dwelling Too Much on the Past
This should not really account for more than 60% of the discussion at most; you also need to discuss future activities, priorities, development needs. and objectives.

Being Too Directive, Highly Critical, or Being Perceived as Being Critical
Successful appraisals are dynamic, positive discussions, not a witch-hunt or a chance to heap blame and ignominy on someone. (If you do need to tackle a problem, do it when the problem arises, and don't just store it up for the appraisal!)

Giving Comments and Feedback Poorly
The appraiser must be clear, honest, and open in his or her comments. The more you hedge, the more chance there is that misunderstandings will creep in.

Failing to Follow Up after the Meeting
There is one key action here: to complete all documentation and confirmations that are necessary promptly after the meeting. Send copies to the appraisee, flagging any opportunity for further discussion. If your business is big enough to have a personnel department, send a copy there too.

Focus On: Mentoring
Max Landsberg

GETTING STARTED

Mentoring suits smaller organizations especially well. It can build productively on the small-world environment in which "everybody knows everybody else" to enhance professional skills and relationships. It can also make up for a potential lack of advanced HR systems—systems the smaller firm might be unable to afford.

- Mentoring is crucial to developing employees and retaining them.
- Mentors give advice on a spectrum of topics, ranging from specific skills to broader issues of career direction.
- Mentees gain advice, access to established networks, and broader personal and professional perspectives.
- Though mentoring happens naturally to some degree, it can be boosted by programs which match seasoned employees to colleagues who are new either to the business or to their role. These programs are designed to have a measurable impact.

This actionlist offers advice on how to get the best from a mentoring relationship, whether you're a mentor hoping to keep a valued member of staff, or a mentee aiming to build your role in a small business.

FAQS

What is mentoring?

Mentoring is the process by which wisdom and experience is shared between two people, one of whom (the mentor) is typically senior to the other (the mentee). The advice that the mentor conveys to the mentee supports development of the mentee's skills, career, and networks.

Most of us have probably acquired our mentors more by luck than through planning, but with the erosion of traditional career ladders and the increasingly organic and unstructured composition of the modern firm (especially small firms), individuals and companies alike are seeing ever greater merits to this once informal relationship.

What is the scope of a mentoring relationship?

In a business setting a mentoring relationship focuses on skills, career, and personal development. At the start of their relationship, neither the mentor nor the mentee can anticipate all the issues that they'll end up discussing. Nevertheless, both parties should be aware of the topics that they might usefully discuss, or which might emerge anyway. These topics fall into two broad categories: helping the mentee to achieve learning and career goals, and building the mentee's confidence and self-awareness.

Career issues typically include:
- whether the mentee's career vision and goals seem relevant and viable;
- how to "decode" the business's feedback to the mentee, for example, from an annual performance review or from a promotion received or missed;
- what experience and expertise to acquire in the short and long term;
- where to find role models with whom the mentee can identify;
- how the mentee should best interact with his or her manager;
- whether to accept an internal (or external) job offer;
- how best to promote an initiative within the business that the mentee has conceived;
- how to react to unacceptable behavior experienced by the mentee, for example, apparent bias, favoritism, or harassment;
- how to deal with the effects of a personal or family problem.

Issues of **confidence and self-awareness** may include:

- how the mentee can make a frank review of his or her own strengths and weaknesses;
- whether feedback received by the mentee about his or her personal style is accurate or not;
- how to overcome apparent career set-backs, or feelings of isolation or depression.

Despite this great breadth of role, mentoring relationships do have limits. If you are a mentor, remember to:

- focus on advice rather than "rescue";
- *not* build a nepotistic relationship in which you try to exert undue influence in favor of your mentee;
- direct the mentee to a professional counselor if needed.

MAKING IT HAPPEN
Understand Different Types of Mentoring

There are four main types of mentoring which an individual may seek, or which a business may wish to promote. Note that these four models are not mutually exclusive, and also that most people have more than one mentor, each of whom may play complementary roles.

Informal or **"natural"** mentoring happens when a more experienced person decides to take a less experienced person under his or her wing, often to give career advice. Such relationships form spontaneously and are usually based on a similarity of interests, expertise, or personal history. These relationships tend to grow and flourish and often continue after one or both the people leave the business.

Situational mentoring is the providing of advice for a specific circumstance, such as when the mentee has to implement a new computer system, or set up a new office. Although these relationships are often short-term, they can develop into a longer term mentoring connection.

Positional mentoring occurs when the mentor is the manager of the mentee. All good managers mentor their team members to some extent, but there are natural constraints to the effectiveness of this approach. Firstly, the mentee may find it difficult to raise issues of switching jobs or

roles. Secondly, the mentor will not provide an impartial view of their relationship as superior and junior. Thirdly, the manager may be accused of favoritism, if one of his or her mentees advances more rapidly than others.

Formal mentoring programs emerged during the 1990s in an attempt to gain the advantages of natural mentoring while recognizing the limitations of positional mentoring. They are discussed in more detail below.

Understand the Benefits for All Parties

Mentees are the most obvious beneficiaries of mentoring—they receive advice, guidance, access to contacts and networks, reassurance, and a broader perspective on their careers. Mentors also benefit, however. They typically strengthen their interpersonal skills, find insights into the workings of their business and teams, and have the satisfaction of seeing others grow. Finally, businesses benefit through better recruitment, orientation, and retention of staff; better communication across all areas of the business, faster learning within the company, and a stronger overall culture.

Excel As a Mentor

As a mentor, you will sometimes need to be a coach, sometimes a motivator, or guide, counselor, role model, or provider of contacts. To excel in these roles, you will need to:

- help the mentee to focus his or her efforts, and to clarify goals;
- prompt the mentee to develop effective strategies, and act as devil's advocate to challenge them;
- help the mentee to identify appropriate resources, contacts, and role models;
- share knowledge and wisdom based on your own experiences;
- act personally as a source of inspiration and motivation, while maintaining confidentiality.

To accomplish this, ask penetrating questions that help the mentee distinguish "real" issues from apparent ones; accept the mentee unconditionally, asking "how" or "what" rather than "why"; listen actively to the mentee's feelings as well as to the words; and volunteer your observations where appropriate. Having said that, don't aim to become a personal "fixer" of your mentee's problems. Instead, help your mentee learn how to develop problem-solving skills that will feed into his or her overall development.

Excel As a Mentee

If you are being mentored by someone else, be open, take initiatives, and show your consideration for your mentor's time.

In terms of openness, be open about your objectives and aspirations, but also be open to feedback or other observations made by your mentor. If your mentor finds that any frank comments are met with defensiveness, the relationship will soon wither.

In taking initiative, be proactive in meeting with your mentor, and in relating to him or her: arrive at your meetings fully prepared and with clear objectives, and take the lead in suggesting new ways of viewing your issues. Actively follow up on any ideas generated in the meetings, and let your mentor know of progress you make.

Finally, show consideration for the mentor's investment of time. This involves: identifying what the mentor wants to derive from the relationship; accommodating the mentor's schedule when arranging meetings; and providing feedback, praise, and thanks in an appropriate way.

Getting the Best from Mentoring Programs

Larger businesses increasingly use formal programs to encourage mentoring and to reap its benefits. Compared with natural mentoring (see above), formal mentoring tends to be based on more specific objectives. It also aims at more measurable impact (e.g., employee retention); runs for a more limited period; typically involves discussions of more prescribed structure; and is based on pairing that is balanced more in favor of the mentee.

Such programs require focus, and typically aim to support employees who are new to the business, new to a role, or who are part of a group that is in some way specialized or disadvantaged. Efforts to provide mentoring for *all* employees in a business rarely succeed, if those efforts are based purely on formal programs. The broader objective of "mentoring for all" is best tackled as part of a wider program of cultural change, which should also examine how the company's day-to-day business is conducted.

WHAT TO AVOID
Not Building the Right Program for Your Business

It's important to tailor any mentoring program to your own business's needs—what might work somewhere else won't necessarily work for you. Here are some key elements to consider.

- decide whether to adopt a formal program, or one that includes some element of natural mentoring;
- have simple criteria for people's eligibility to be mentees and mentors, and for the maximum number of mentees per mentor;
- agree whether mentees choose mentors (recommended), or vice versa; establish a matching process that is seen as fair by everyone;
- explain the ground rules clearly, for example, a commitment to a duration of one year, the ability to terminate the relationship at any time with no blame, and complete confidentiality;
- provide training for mentors and mentees, and set out the expected benefits;
- plan how you will check whether the program is working. Monitor it periodically. Reward, praise, or thank the mentors;
- do not over-design the program: make it clear to potential mentees that the quality of mentoring they receive will in large measure depend on their own ability to attract mentors.

Focus On: Building Great Teams
Meredith Belbin

GETTING STARTED

The problem about the word "teamwork" is that it has become too popular and has therefore lost its meaning. A person thought to be good at teamwork is all too often someone who fits into a group and keeps out of trouble. Complying with majority decisions and being willing to do anything that's required is seen as being ideal behavior, but if everyone behaved like that, a team just wouldn't work effectively—a flock of sheep may hang together well, but their only accomplishment is to eat grass.

Teams and team-based working has developed into the normal way of structuring organizations of all sizes and undertaking tasks, yet it is a difficult aspect of leadership and is usually developed through experience. In the context of a small business, you as the owner or owner-manager, are likely to be the leader of your team. Every leader has his or her own style, and when developing a high performing team this needs to combine with an understanding of:

- the benefits of team-building—what it can achieve and what the leader should be striving for;
- team roles and dynamics—how teams work and achieve their greatest success;
- the key stages of team development—what they are and how to support the team in each stage;
- the features of a successful team and team leader;
- how to avoid potential problems and pitfalls.

FAQS

What makes a good team leader?

Leadership, in broad strokes, is the capacity to establish direction and motivate others toward working for a common aim. Successful teamwork depends on the team leader's ability to make sure all team members know their common aim and what they each need to do to achieve it.

Naturally, all teams are different and have their own dynamic and all leaders develop their own style for forming, developing, and leading them, but there are some general characteristics of a good team leader. For a team to work, it's essential that all members are committed, so leaders must be supportive, enthusiastic, and motivating people to work with. They must organize and communicate well in order to coordinate team efforts both *within* the team and with others *outside* the team. During difficult or stressful times, team leaders need to be approachable, good listeners who can offer feedback and advice.

What are the features of a good team?

It goes without saying that successful teams are ones in which people do not waste time trying to achieve success at the expense of others. Instead, they work at understanding each other, and communicate honestly and openly. They are committed to the team's success and are respectful and supportive of each other by sharing information and experience.

Conflict is unavoidable in most work situations, but a good team will work through it and reach an understanding by generating new ideas. A good team also acknowledges the role of the leader and understands when he or she needs to act and make a decision (i.e. in an emergency or if there is a major problem or disagreement).

MAKING IT HAPPEN
Focus on the Work

For anyone interested in productive teamwork, it's often better to start with the work rather than the team. First of all, think about whether the job in hand really does need a team to tackle it. Some types of work, such as repetitive or unskilled tasks and, at the other extreme, specialist activities, are best performed by loners. Rounding up such people and making them members of a team risks producing a double disadvantage: their personal productivity falls and their privacy is invaded. While it's currently popular to strive for such an "all inclusive" approach in the workplace and some people argue that isolated workers need a social dimension to their work, there are often few benefits to forcing this set-up on someone. Introverts need work suitable for introverts, while extroverts need work appropriate to extraverts.

Enable the Team to Succeed

The team approach for organizing work depends on empowerment, that is, making sure that each person is allowed to perform to the best of his or her abilities. This relies on trust, the confidence that a manager places on the qualities and caliber of the employees. It also depends on how well members of a group have developed an understanding of each other's strengths and weaknesses. That's why, if your budget allows, training in teamwork is so important and why it helps to understand the language of team roles.

Reward Teams at the Right Time

All teams need to be assessed, but how should it be done so that it is positive and constructive? One way is to set objectives for teams and judge how well these have been met. This view is popular in the "top-down" school of management, where, as the name would suggest, senior managers make all the decisions and these are then passed down through the ranks to employees. In larger organizations, this approach is given added impetus by performance-related bonuses.

The argument put forward is that teams need fixed incentives to perform well, an assumption linked with the converse view that without such an incentive the team will not perform satisfactorily. I believe this approach is likely to backfire. Success in meeting given criteria depends partly on circumstances and contingencies, and may not be commensurate with effort or skill. Objectives may be too easy to reach or too difficult. In the end, people may focus more on the shortcomings of the incentive than

on the sense and purpose of their work. Retrospective awards for good team performance (that is, given once the project is complete) are better received than prospective rewards for teams given set targets.

Stick to the Essentials of Effective Teamworking

Again, start with the work and think about whether it really calls for a team at all. If you do decide that a team is the best way to tackle a task, work out who will be doing what; also, decide which remaining responsibilities can be assigned to individuals, and make them subject to personal accountability.

If possible, train your team so that it plays to the best strengths of its individual players. Make sure each person is allowed to develop ownership, pride, and maximum commitment to the team's responsibilities. One way you can do this as team leader is by delegating effectively Finally, understand what motivates the team—what gives it its momentum?

WHAT TO AVOID

Misunderstanding People

While it's obviously crucial that you understand the nature of the work being undertaken, you also need to be aware of the skills, experience, and approach of those doing the work. Taking account of people's strengths and motivations can certainly help to build or break teams.

Misunderstanding Teams and What They Need to Succeed

Don't become too glib about the terminology— "team" and "teamwork" too easily become glib terms, so check their meaning. Remember to spend time on evaluating whether you really need a team to complete a given task before you embark on a team exercise, and if you do go ahead bear in mind that not everyone flourishes in a team—some people will need more support than others.

If you are the team leader, remember that you have to allow team members the freedom to do what their role entails—empower them. Give them all the information they need and set boundaries to make sure that things happen.

Handling Resignations

GETTING STARTED

Although it is disappointing to lose key people, especially in a small business environment where some of your employees will have been with you from the start, resignations give companies a chance to plan ahead and recruit people who can contribute to the organization's growth. Personnel shifts can be a catalyst for taking a fresh look at what's working and what isn't, and deciding what kinds of changes would be most productive.

From the employees' standpoint, resignations allow people to move on in their careers, learn new skills, and take on new responsibilities. An individual leaving a company is not necessarily withdrawing his or her loyalty or influence over its future direction. Indeed, past employees may well be instrumental in instigating joint projects or ventures that will change the fortunes of the business where they once worked.

FAQS

My second in command has just resigned. How can I convey this information to the rest of the team without risking a drop in morale?

Convene the team, along with the person who has resigned, to discuss the resignation and its implications. Showing your concern about their feelings and asking for input invites team members' involvement and gives them a sense of control. It will also give you an opportunity to discuss any structural or resource issues arising from the departure.

I run a team of specialists who are hard to replace, and as soon as one left the others started to follow. What can I do to prevent talent from hemorrhaging out of the company?

Take your team's exodus as an opportunity to identify and resolve problems. Are terms of employment better elsewhere? Have conditions in your business deteriorated without your being fully aware of the slippage? Conducting exit interviews should help you identify your weak points and structure improvements. Invite remaining staff to participate in the planning. This might be a good time to review your company's medium- and long-range strategic plans. Would reorganizing or consolidating departments help reverse the disaffection? Are there others you can promote into these vacancies? Or will your company need to make changes in order to attract new talent?

A member of my team has asked to leave full-time employment and become a contractor to the business on a project basis. Is this a good idea?

Businesses are increasingly turning to contract employees to give them more flexibility and cut direct payroll costs. In many instances, contract employees are responsible for the cost of their own office space off-premises as well as funding their own benefits such as health insurance, vacations, pensions, and so on. However, contract employees will often charge more for their services than they received in salary. The key issues are costs and benefits. Another part of the equation is how you manage the situation with other team members to make sure there's no ambiguity about how work is to be done and who has responsibility.

I was handed a resignation by someone whom I was happy to see leave. However, he's changed his mind and asked to stay on the job. How do I handle this?

If you feel strongly that your business would be better off without this person, you're within your rights as the supervisor to deny his request. If you think the person might be suited for a job elsewhere in your company, you might advise him to discuss his prospects with the human resources department.

✓ **MAKING IT HAPPEN**
Be Prepared
Most small and growing businesses value a stable work force. Inevitably, however, a certain percentage of your employees will leave every year, taking their skills and experience with them. Handling every one of these departures well is very much in the company's interest: every former employee is a public witness to the character and culture of your company.

Acknowledge the Employee's Intention to Leave
Verbal notice may be acceptable, but it's usual for a resignation to be submitted in writing so the process of removing the employee from the payroll and preparing a final account of benefits begins promptly.

Confirm the Leaving Date
Notice periods vary according to the position and the seniority level of the departing employee. If the person who is leaving wants to negotiate an early departure, you need to consider your existing resources and the volume of work pending. If work priorities allow, you may be willing to go along with the request.

Transition
Depending upon the nature of the work that the departing employee was engaged in, you need to plan for a smooth transition of projects and responsibilities. This might range from a simple plan developed jointly by the employee and his or her manager to negotiations involving a broader group of people who will be affected by the resignation.

A transition program may be quite involved. It takes times to brief coworkers, tie up administrative loose ends, and perhaps instigate some training in areas where special skills are required. If the organization is reducing its work force by natural attrition and the employee isn't going to be replaced, the person's responsibilities need to be reallocated.

If the person who is leaving has built a network of relationships important to the organization, you need to plan for continuity. If he or she has developed personal relationships with clients or suppliers, these are likely to continue. Personal loyalties may leave your organization vulnerable to loss of business, especially if the former employee becomes your competitor in the marketplace. Having clients or suppliers meet with the employee's replacement, perhaps with the departing employee present, can help maintain continuity in key relationships.

Conduct an Exit Interview
It's good policy to schedule exit interviews, usually conducted by a member of the human resources team. Invite departing employees to discuss their job, their reasons for leaving, and any other subjects of concern to them.

The exit interview should be a positive experience, even when the employee uses it to air grievances. Listen carefully to what each employee tells you; you may get new information or confirm previous reports of dissatisfaction with company policies or practices. Let exit interviews be learning experiences that clue you in on making the organization a better place to work.

Remember Other Considerations
It is sometimes appropriate to ask an employee who resigns to leave the premises immediately—for example, when the employee has access to confidential information and is leaving to join a competitor, there is risk of disruption or sabotage, or the work has dried up. In these cases it's usual to pay the individual a severance allowance based on two weeks' notice or some other negotiated criterion.

Leaving a job—even under the best of circumstances—is not always comfortable; handling someone's departure sensitively makes the experience easier. In most instances, it's customary to host a farewell event of some kind and give a gift to show appreciation for the employee's work.

✗ WHAT TO AVOID

Taking It Personally

Taking a resignation personally can lead to distress on both the employee's and employer's side. People leave their jobs for a wide variety of reasons; resigning isn't necessarily an act of betrayal. Try and be open to hearing the reasons behind the decision and exploring the options, if there are any.

Ignoring the Implications of the Resignation

Ignoring the reality of someone's departure can leave you vulnerable. Everyone involved needs to pitch in to make sure that the leaving causes as little disruption as possible, so try bringing those affected by the move together to create a smooth transition.

Showing That You're Pleased the Person Is Going

No matter how unlikable, annoying, disruptive, or incompetent the employee has been, try not to show your delight that he or she is leaving: it's disrespectful to the departing employee and demoralizing for those who remain. Behave with professionalism from the moment you receive the resignation throughout the exit process, and leave your ego to one side.

SEE ALSO
Staff Planning (p. 372)

DIGNIFIED RETREATS

Deciding Whether to Sell Your Business

GETTING STARTED

The reasons behind selling your business will determine how you approach the task, and will also affect your expectations of the transaction. If you are selling so that you can retire, for instance, you could sell at any time over a number of years to get the best offer available. Selling due to ill health may require a quicker sale, but if the business is in a good state it need not be immediate. If the business is in financial crisis, a low selling price may be necessary for a quick sale before you lose too much money. A forced sale may also be due to changed market circumstances or technological changes. As well as business-related reasons for sale (such as diversification, receivership, or bankruptcy), you may also have personal reasons for wanting to sell up, such as a death in the family, or the breakdown of a partnership.

FAQS

When is the best time to sell?

Ideally, you should sell your business after a number of consecutive profit-making years, so that prospective buyers can be sure that the business is a viable concern and that they can make realistic estimates of future earnings. The selling value of your business will tend to be based largely on what the purchaser expects to earn in the few years immediately after acquiring the business. Depending on the sector you are in, and the expectations of investors in that sector, the purchaser will want to be sure that the business delivers a minimum rate of return so that they can recover the purchase price within a number of years.

If the business is not yet profitable, or has been through an unprofitable patch, consider building it up for a few years before putting it on the market. This is often the only way of retrieving some value from your business for all the investment you have made in product development, market recognition, customer loyalty, and sweat equity. Without some hard evidence of profit-making history or potential, you could find it difficult to put a realistic sale value on your business.

What are the alternatives to selling?

If you are selling because of financial problems, consider whether the prospects for the business really are so bad. Have you considered the options? For example, could a manager or partner be taken on to help you cope, or to address the main problems? Could particularly troublesome aspects of the operation be minimized?

It is important to compare realistically the costs of selling up with the costs of keeping going. What is the most likely outcome from the sale, for instance, and will this be a financial solution? Look at alternatives like:

- selling assets (such as land and machinery) and then leasing them back to the business to improve cash flow;
- taking on a partner who will contribute capital and take on some responsibilities;
- scaling down operations to focus on the most profitable work.

Should I sell all or part of the business?

Raising cash is often the motivation behind the sale of a business. But selling your whole business is a big step, and will often prevent you from building on your experience in that sector (you will usually be required to sign a "restraint of trade" agreement preventing you from competing with your old business for a number of years). This may undermine your own position, and make it difficult to develop your career the way that you would like. One way around this is to sell only part of your business to raise some capital, and use this to strengthen the portion that you keep.

MAKING IT HAPPEN

Prepare the Business for Sale

There are a few aspects of the business that you can usefully focus on in preparation for a sale—the most important of which are listed below.

■ **Reduce discretionary expenditure.** This is expenditure not necessary to keep the business going. You don't necessarily have to eliminate discretionary expenditure, just highlight it to potential buyers. Common areas of discretionary expenditure include travel and entertainment, and running expensive company cars.

■ **Reduce costs.** Other expenditure can also be reduced, but it is important not to cut back in vital areas. Buyers will often look for consistent expenditure trends. A sudden reduction in expenditure will be very noticeable and potentially negate the positive effects you were hoping it would have on potential buyers.

■ **Maintain your property and assets well.** If you have leased property, contracts and rent reviews should be obtained. Keep machinery in good condition, using maintenance contracts if necessary.

■ **Improve your working capital position.** For instance, reduce excess stock levels and make better use of creditors.

■ **Keep employees informed.** Most businesses hinge on the skill and experience of certain key workers. The sale may unsettle them, so keep them informed and secure their loyalty (it might be necessary to consider incentives).

■ **Make sure you have the loyalty of key customers and suppliers.** This can often be done with long-term contracts, as buyers will be keen to ensure continuity of supply. If the business operates under license, it is important that you ensure the license is transferable to potential buyers.

Determine a Price

Valuing a small business can be difficult, as there is no public trading share price that can be simply multiplied by the number of shares issued. Determining the value will involve the hard figures such as assets, liabilities, historical earnings, and cash flow, as well as more subjective figures such as projected earnings, know-how, quality of management, and goodwill. External factors also need to be considered, such as current market conditions and industry popularity. Ultimately, however, what a business is worth comes down to what both parties agree it is worth. Get some expert help to make sure that you get the best price possible.

Check the Legal Status

The legal status of the business for sale is very important to bear in mind, mainly because it defines exactly who owns the various assets to be sold. If you operate as a sole trader, you own all the assets of the business and it is up to you if, and how, they are sold. Similarly, partners will own their share of the assets, and any sale must be agreed according to the provisions of the partnership agreement. A limited company is a separate legal entity from its owners. In this case, selling the business may simply be a matter of selling shares in the business, or the shares might be retained while the equipment, premises, and goodwill are sold.

WHAT TO AVOID
Waiting Too Long

Perhaps the worst time to sell a business is once it is deep in debt. If you are forced into a sale, the chances are that you will not get a reasonable price—even if your business is still potentially profitable. By taking on debts, and perhaps even a loss-making enterprise, a purchaser is also taking on the substantial financial risk that the business will not respond to remedial action. The purchaser will therefore want to reduce this risk by paying a lower purchase price and keeping cash in reserve to fund possible future losses. For your part, you need to plan as far ahead as possible to anticipate what trading conditions might be like at the time you wish you sell. It is easier to demand a premium price when business is growing; that way, a purchaser is more likely to acknowledge some "blue-sky" value and pay for it.

Setting an Unrealistic Asking Price

When determining your asking price, do not get carried away by the theoretical prospects of your business. While there may well be potential for a new investor to exploit, this must be weighed against the hard realities of what is possible within your business and within your particular market. The financial history of your business will be the foundation on which valuations are based, so build your arguments on that.

Protracted Negotiations

Keep your negotiations about selling as short as possible. If you can, set yourself some deadlines for certain key decisions about who to sell to, under what terms, and at what price. This will avoid the danger of letting the selling process drag on for too long. There is inevitably going to be a feel-ing of insecurity among staff and customers, so it is best for all parties to conclude a deal as quickly as possible. Bear in mind that a successful sale might not be agreed, in which case everyone is expected to return to business as usual; this is often difficult after months of uncertainty.

SEE ALSO
Bankruptcy and Business Failure (p. 432)
Finding Potential Buyers for Your Business (p. 414)
Management Buyouts (p. 462)
Understanding the Legal Ramifications of Winding Up a Business (p. 419)
Venture Capital (p. 495)

Knowing the Value of Your Business

GETTING STARTED

Knowing the value of your business is very important if you are considering selling it or looking for external investment into your venture. Ultimately, the value of a business comes down to what both parties agree it is worth. A company which has shares listed on the stock exchange has a clear value in the number of shares in the company, multiplied by their value set by the exchange. The share value in a small business, however, is harder to calculate and must take into account such elements as assets, liabilities, profitability, customer base, goodwill, and trading history.

This actionlist provides some general "rules of thumb" on how to value your business, or how to check that it has been properly valued by someone else.

FAQS

Who should value the business?

If you're using a business broker, it will be down to them to value your business. However, it would still be wise to value the business yourself so that you can relate to the price that the broker has specified. For whatever price they place on your business, you should establish how they arrived at this figure so that you can agree that the price is fair.

Likewise, if you use an accountant to value your business, you should still value the business yourself so that you can satisfy yourself that they have given a reasonable and fair value. After all, who knows your business better than you do?

It may be that you decide to value the business alone, without the assistance of professionals; however, their input could add valuable credibility to your arguments when it comes to negotiating a final price and terms with prospective buyers.

How is a business valued?

Valuation is not an exact science. It is difficult to set the value of a business at a single figure, as so many factors should be taken into account. Hard figures such as assets, liabilities, historical earnings, and cash flow must be accounted for, but more subjective figures such as projected earnings, know-how, quality of management, and goodwill should also be used. External factors should be considered, such as current market conditions and industry popularity. What you consider to be the value of your business and its final selling price may differ considerably depending on the circumstances surrounding the sale or investment into the business. Is the buyer eager to buy quickly? Is there more than one investor/buyer interested? What form will the payment or investment take? What is the level of risk involved for the buyer or investor? How urgently do you want to sell?

Do you need to compare your business with similar businesses?

Before proceeding with the valuation, you should compare the financial results of your business with those of similar organizations within the same industry. This will help you determine whether there should be a premium added or discount given over the value of comparable businesses. Financial comparisons should be made using several measures, including: sales growth; gross margin; earnings before tax as a percentage of sales; return on assets; current ratio, and debt-to-net-worth ratio. What is the growth rate of the business compared to the industry as a whole? Is the business gaining or losing market share?

MAKING IT HAPPEN
Value the Business

The final valuation figure will depend on the technique adopted. There are effectively three methods of valuing a business—net assets, multiple of earnings, and standard formulas.

Calculate Net Assets

Valuing a business by calculating its net assets is the most easily understood method, and the one most commonly used for small businesses. The net assets (the net worth of the business) are shown on the balance sheet. If everything was sold at the value recorded on the balance sheet, the amount of money realized would be equal to the net assets. Sometimes buyers are reluctant to pay much more than net asset value, as it is very difficult to make a suitable allowance for intangible assets such as goodwill. The value of other intangibles can also be considered, such as ownership of patents, trademarks, and copyrights; the value of long-term contracts, license agreements, and so on.

The net-assets figure may need to be adjusted to reflect the true worth of the assets. Buildings, for example, may be worth more than shown on the balance sheet. Equipment, especially computers, may be worth far less. You may need to enter into negotiations about how assets will be valued, but take into account replacement value and realizable value.

Calculate the Earnings Multiple

The earnings multiple calculation for valuing a business is based on the price/earnings ratio (P/E ratio). The P/E ratio is the price of one share to the earnings (that is, the net profit after tax) attributable to that share. The P/E ratio gives an indication of how much investors are prepared to pay to buy the shares.

If, for example, a company has earnings per share (EPS) of 18.5 cents and one share costs $5 then it has a P/E ratio of 27 (500 divided by 18.5). You can apply this to any business. Take the net profit, apply a suitable multiplier, and that gives you the value of the business. Try selecting a suitable multiplier by looking at the P/E ratios for quoted companies, usually printed in the financial sections of newspapers. However, you will need to apply a discount to take account of the smaller size, the greater risk, and the difficulty for investors wishing to sell shares in private limited companies.

Typically, you should apply a discount of 30–40%, though if your profit is less than $1 million, the discount should probably be at least 50%.

For example, you have achieved earnings of $100,000 per annum over a number of years and can show that this trend is likely to continue. If, in your business sector, the average P/E ratio is 12, you then need to apply a discount of 50%, which then gives a multiplier of 6. This implies that the business is worth $600,000. You should remember to exclude nonrecurring expenditure (such as onetime purchases) when you calculate the earnings for a particular year.

Understand Standard Formulas

Standard methods of valuing a business have become established in some industry sectors. For example, the valuation of a local courier service depends on the average daily delivery; and insurance agents often multiply their gross commission one to two times to work out the value of their business. There may be an accepted formula applied in your business sector, and it may be worth investigating this further before committing yourself to any valuation process.

Divide the Shares

Valuing the business only gives you a starting point. If you are looking for an external investor, you then have to negotiate the proportion of shares that might be exchanged for a certain amount of finance. The owners of a business will have invested their own finance—though this should, in effect, be reflected in the valuation. They will also have invested considerable time and effort to build up the business to the point where they are seeking additional equity. This, too, should be recognized and rewarded.

One way of doing this is to add a notional amount to the net asset valuation to represent the "sweat equity"—that is, the hard work and effort already applied to build the business up to its current position but which is not reflected in the valuation of the business. If, for example, a business has a net asset valuation of $50,000, a further $50,000 might be added as sweat equity. An investor providing an additional $50,000 would then receive 33% of the shares.

The Buyer's Valuation

The value that you place on your business, whichever method you choose, is very unlikely to be the price that you receive: it merely forms the starting point for negotiations. You should therefore add a little to the price, say 5–10%, as you can always expect the buyer to try and negotiate a lower price, even if they feel they have found a bargain.

The buyer will not value the business until they have seen the business inside and out. After this, they will probably involve their accountant or agent to help reach a realistic value for your business. It's likely that they will use a different valuation method to the one you have used, as quite often buyers will find a value that compensates for the expected return they hope to receive by investing in the business.

Buyers will always have a keen eye on the future performance and profitability of your business. You should therefore prepare to be offered an amount that reflects how profitable your business is expected to be in the future.

In basic terms, you have to acknowledge one important rule of valuation: a business is only worth what someone is willing to pay for it.

WHAT TO AVOID
Having Unrealistic Valuations
You are aiming for an achievable valuation— one on which both parties can agree—so you need to be realistic. If you're using the P/E ratio as the basis of your valuation, make sure you select a realistic ratio and discount it by an amount which is appropriate for the size of your business.

Getting the Wrong Advice
The first common mistake is hiring the wrong adviser. For example, many sellers decide to hire an attorney but will often be attracted to the first contact they find and consequently overlook the more qualified and experienced people. This leads to the wrong decisions and advice being made at crucial moments in the selling process. The same scenario can be applied to business agents and accountants.

SEE ALSO
Bankruptcy and Business Failure (p. 432)
Management Buyouts (p. 462)
Venture Capital (p. 495)

Finding Potential Buyers for Your Business

GETTING STARTED

If you've decided to sell your business, potential buyers could come from a number of sources including competitors, suppliers, customers, and new market entrants. While you might want to reach as many potential buyers as possible, you will probably want to keep your dealings confidential until you decide to inform employees, suppliers, and customers.

For many small businesses, networking is one of the most effective ways of communicating with parties who may be interested in buying you out. However, if you need to be more proactive about the process, and do not have the time to pursue it yourself, you could employ the services of a business broker (see below for more information). A broker will actively seek out interested parties, either directly or through networking with other business brokers. Your broker could also advise and support you through the negotiation and sale of your business. To advertise your business yourself, the most effective media are newspapers, magazines (both in your sector and specialist publications advertising businesses for sale), and the Internet. The Internet is fast becoming one of the most popular ways to advertise a business for sale, its main advantage being that it can reach a wide and global audience quickly. Although not the best source of advertisements for all businesses (for example, those with a very defined, local appeal), it's highly recommended for small businesses with a wider appeal.

FAQS

What is a sales memorandum and why use one?

A sales memorandum is a detailed description of your business that you can provide to prospective purchasers. It outlines the history, products and services, assets, and market and financial performance of your business. It needs to include your reason for selling and your asking price. The memorandum should also include a detailed business plan for the next few years, and the likely outcomes of that plan. The aim of the memorandum is to inspire interest from prospective buyers, as well as to anticipate some of the questions that they may want answered.

What could a business broker do for me?

A business broker will research the market for prospective purchasers of your business. She or he will work with you to establish a list of businesses or individuals who might be interested in finding out more about your business. Your broker will arrange the signing of confidentiality agreements, and hold preliminary discussions with some or all of the interested parties. He or she will then process the responses and advise you

on which options are worth pursuing, leaving you with more time to get on with running the business.

How do I keep the process confidential?

When you advertise your business in a newspaper or magazine, or on the Internet, do not mention your business name. Simply describe the sector you are in, your turnover and your asking price, as well as your regional location (but do not give the exact town or city). Give the interested parties a P. O. Box or an e-mail address to reply to. Before you provide any information to an interested party, get a confidentiality letter or agreement signed by the interested party (this usually only relates to information that is not publicly available). You can then release a sales memorandum with a request for a response on a given date.

What is a qualifying buyer?

When you consider the replies to your advertisements, you need to sort out those serious inquiries from those that will only waste your time. Draw up a list of qualifying buyers, and limit your distribution of sales memoranda to this group only.

MAKING IT HAPPEN
Spend Time Preparing the Business for the Sale

Spending some time preparing the business for sale can enhance the price. Issues to consider include: reducing discretionary expenditure (for example travel and entertainment); reducing business costs without cutting back on vital areas (buyers will look for consistent spending patterns and sales figures); making sure that any property and equipment is well maintained; and reducing excess stock levels to improve the level of working capital.

Decide What Type of Buyer You Want

If you want cash from a deal, it may rule out buyers below a certain size. If you're looking for a friendly purchaser who will safeguard future employment of staff and management, there is little point talking to known "asset strippers," that is, those who set out to acquire a company and sell its assets for a profit without regard for the acquired company's future business success.

In conjunction with your professional advisers, you should put together a list of possible buyers. You may well hold market information about prospective trade buyers, but do not rule out prospective new entrants to the sector. Non-executive directors, or specialist professional advisers, should have the ability to identify "non-trade" buyers who may be prepared to pay a premium to enter your market.

Keep your target list to manageable proportions. If you have to advertise, the time drags on and you end up sending out the wrong signals to the industry as well as receiving time-wasters.

Prepare a Sales Memorandum

It is advisable to prepare your sales memorandum with an adviser or accountant, or with the business broker who is helping you sell your business. You could consider preparing a summary of the main points of interest as well as a more comprehensive document. The former can be sent out to all parties that express an interest in your business. The latter should only be sent to those parties who then request more information.

Select Qualifying Buyers

Look for buyers who want to add to their own business profiles; these are generally the most likely to put in a serious offer. They will often be players already in your sector, so they will understand how your business would contribute to their own. They will also have a good idea of the financial benefits they could derive. It is important that you try to establish whether the interested party has the finance necessary to purchase your business. Otherwise, this might become a problem as your negotiations proceed.

Send Out Confidentiality Letters

Once you have identified those parties that you believe to be serious about buying your business, you need to send confidentiality letters to them. Make sure that the letters are professionally drafted. They will need to be signed and returned before you send out the sales memoranda. It is a good idea to give a deadline of about two weeks. This will also help you establish which parties are prepared to give priority to the matter.

Send Out Sales Memoranda

This can be done in two phases. The first phase involves sending out a summary. Distribution of the full sales memoranda should then be limited to those parties who have read the summary and have requested a full document. This indicates that they are genuinely interested in finding out more.

WHAT TO AVOID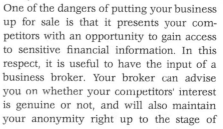
Releasing Too Much Information to Competitors

One of the dangers of putting your business up for sale is that it presents your competitors with an opportunity to gain access to sensitive financial information. In this respect, it is useful to have the input of a business broker. Your broker can advise you on whether your competitors' interest is genuine or not, and will also maintain your anonymity right up to the stage of narrowing down to a few genuinely interested parties. You will need carefully to balance the need for interested parties to see your financial history, with the possible commercial advantage that a competitor could gain from this information.

Spending Too Much Time with Time-wasters

There are bound to be a number of responses to your advertisements which simply do not warrant following up. It is important that you identify these as early as possible, as you will probably need to spend a considerable amount of time with each of the interested parties in the near future. You should only pursue expressions of interest from parties that look like serious businesses with enough finance to make a reasonable offer. Carrying out a credit check, or sourcing a company report, can provide useful insights into your potential buyers.

SEE ALSO
Bankruptcy and Business Failure (p. 432)
Deciding Whether to Sell Your Business (p. 408)
Management Buyouts (p. 462)
Venture Capital (p. 495)

Selling Shares

GETTING STARTED

People sell shares in their companies for a variety of reasons. They may be hoping to raise additional finance, or alternatively could be hoping to dispose of the company by selling all or most of the shares. Shares can be sold to angel investors, venture capitalists, individuals, and other businesses—the motive for buying shares may well be different depending on who buys them, and purchasers' expectations of dividends and exit routes will also differ.

This actionlist provides a rough guide to the main points you need to take into account when considering whether to sell shares.

FAQS

What are shares?

Shares in a company represent a proportion of the ownership of that company. Initially, shares are exchanged for cash and that cash is then available to the business. This pot of cash is known as the "equity capital" or as the "share capital." Shares can be sold by the owner of a company, though in a small, unquoted business, there are regulations governing the way in which the shares can be sold.

Can a company sell shares at any time?

Companies set an authorized amount of share capital in their Memorandum of Association (MOA), that is, the total number of shares that the company is permitted to sell. The authorized share capital can be raised at any time by the shareholders, and the company can then sell the additional shares. Unquoted companies normally include a "pre-emption" clause in their Articles of Association (AOA) requiring that any additional shares are first offered to existing shareholders before being offered to other potential new investors.

Are there different types of shares?

Companies can create different classes of shares. The main, voting shares are known as "ordinary shares" or common stock. Companies also often create "preference shares" or "preferred stock" in order to raise equity capital. In the event of a company being wound up, the preference shares are considered for repayment before the ordinary shares.

Preference shares usually attract a fixed dividend (provided, of course, there is enough profit to cover the dividend). Sometimes these shares are cumulative—if the dividend is missed one year, it is carried forward until such time as there is sufficient profit to pay it. Dividends on ordinary shares cannot be paid until the dividend on the preference shares is paid. Preference shares are usually redeemable, meaning that the company can buy them back and cancel them, if it so desires. Usually they are repaid at par (that is, for the amount for which they were bought), but the repayment amount can be varied. The values for redemption are normally set out in the company's AOA.

What is internal rate of return?

You may have heard talk of equity investors expecting high levels of return—typically 35–40% internal rate of return. That return does not come solely from dividends, but includes the return achieved when the shares are eventually sold. The total rate of return, from income and capital growth, on an annualized basis, is known as the internal rate of return.

What is private equity?

Private equity is simply the term used for finance from venture capitalists, seed funds, and angel investors in exchange for a share of the business.

What is an exit route?

The term "exit route" is used to describe the way that an angel investor or venture capitalist exits from an investment. In general, there are just three routes: flotation of the company; a buy back from the founders of the business; or a trade sale. In practice, early investors may also exit by selling shares to a bigger investor. For example, an angel investor might exit when a venture capitalist decides to invest and provides an exit route for the angel investor by buying his or her shares.

What is an IPO?

An initial public offering (IPO) is the term used if you sell shares to the public through a stock exchange, such as New York Stock Exchange (NYSE) or the American Stock Exchange (AMEX).

✔ MAKING IT HAPPEN
Sell a Business

In order to sell your business you will need to make sure that you have up-to-date accounts, and be willing to spend time talking to prospective purchasers. If your objective is to sell your business, say, because you want to retire, or want the money to start a new venture, then in most cases your best bet will be to use a business transfer agent, who will help you advertise the business and seek prospective buyers. It is worthwhile, though, to mention local accountants and business support organizations your intention to sell your business, as they may well have clients who would be interested in buying.

You may want to stay in the business, or buyers may wish you to stay, at least for a period, so think about whether this is of interest. Some buyers may want to structure a deal over two or even three financial years; this improves their cash flow and maintains a period of stability and continuity in the business, but may also help your tax position. Some buyers may want an earnout, whereby at least part of the price is dependent on future profit levels—so it is important to be realistic about future prospects.

Raise Equity for Investment

If your objective is to raise money to reinvest in the business, then you need to do much more work. You need to consider what makes the business attractive to an equity investor—do you have proprietary intellectual capital; do you have the potential for high returns; is there an attractive exit route; and, perhaps most important of all, do you have the management team in place to make it all happen? If the answer to these questions is yes, then you need to prepare a detailed business plan setting out the business's prospects for the next three to five years. You need to demonstrate, too, that you have the determination and commitment to succeed.

Find an Investor

The hardest part is finding potential investors. The best starting point is to talk to your local business support organization. The advisers there will be able to help you prepare your business plan, but will also be able to give advice on approaching angel investors and venture capitalists.

WHAT TO AVOID
Exaggerating the Figures

Be realistic in valuing your business—but also make an allowance for the sweat equity that you have put into your business.

Not Spending Enough Time on Your Proposals

Venture capitalists receive hundreds of plans for every one in which they invest—so you need to work hard to capture their attention and persuade them that your business should be the one to receive their money. Regard this as a marketing exercise. You need to grab their attention—and then you need to build on that by making a solid case for investment.

SEE ALSO
Bankruptcy and Business Failure (p. 432)
Management Buyouts (p. 462)

Understanding the Legal Ramifications of Winding Up a Business

GETTING STARTED

Winding up or liquidation is the process of gathering in the assets of a business, to settle the corporate debts. Once this process is completed, the business is then dissolved. It is important to take advice about whether this is the best route for your business. If it is insolvent with serious debts, there may be no choice—creditors can petition for its liquidation. Where the operation is solvent, however, or you as the owner confidently expect to be able to pay off debts, then the potential options for voluntary dissolution should be explored.

FAQS

How is a partnership wound up?

As a partnership has no separate legal identity, it may be dissolved by an agreement between the partners, or by notice of dissolution given by one partner to the others. The partnership agreement may provide for dissolution after a specified period of time, or on other set terms.

Once an agreement has been reached, dissolution may proceed in the normal way—usually handled by the partners themselves. Partnership accounts are prepared and the dissolution will be advertised. All clients must be given notice that the business has been wound up—issuing of this notice represents the end of the partners' authority to agree to contracts and transactions with clients.

How is a private limited company wound up?

Liquidation is a legal process resulting in a company ceasing to exist. Liquidation involves distributing a company's assets to pay off its creditors' debts. Following liquidation, the company is wound up. A company may be wound up either voluntarily by its shareholders, or through the courts by creditor petitioning.

MAKING IT HAPPEN

Be Aware of the Legal Implications when a Partnership Is Wound Up

Where a business is insolvent and partners cannot pay its debts, it may be treated as an unregistered company, to be wound up

(usually in the State Bankcruptcy Court) under the terms of the Federal Bankcruptcy Code. Under the principle of unlimited liability, however, once partnership assets have been exhausted in the payment of creditors, each partner can be made bankrupt and creditors may lodge petitions against the partners' individual estates. Wealthier partners may find that partnership creditors will pursue their assets before those of their co-partners.

When joint bankruptcy orders are made against partners, an official receiver immediately becomes trustee of the partners' separate estates and trustee of the partnership. The partnership is then wound up—that is, assets will be gathered in and used to settle business debts, and the partnership dissolved.

Appraise the Assets of the Partnership

Unlike sole traders, whose personal and business assets are counted together for the purposes of creditors in bankruptcy, in a partnership, separate accounts must be kept of the joint (partnership) estate, and of each partner's individual estate. Once a partnership is dissolved, separate statements of affairs for joint and individual estates must be lodged with the court.

It is an offense to knowingly dispose of valuable assets before the bankruptcy, either by giving them away or selling them cheaply to relatives or friends, unless it can be proved that the disposal was an innocent transaction.

Pay Creditors

Through unlimited liability, a situation may arise where two sets of creditors are chasing payment of debts from partners—creditors owed money by the business, and personal creditors of individual partners. In this case the partnership assets pay off partnership debts, and partners' individual estates are used to pay off their personal debts. Any surplus in the joint estate then goes to the partners' estates in proportion to their share in the partnership, while any surplus from partners' estates goes to the joint estate to pay off partnership debts.

Certain "secured creditors" may have direct claims on specific assets which will be satisfied first of all. Other creditors may be designated "preferred," "ordinary," or "deferred," being paid according to their status.

A shortfall in the partnership estate may be "proved for" (claimed) in the individual estate equally with the individual creditors' claims.

Consider Voluntary Liquidation

If a company is facing serious financial trouble, its members/directors may decide that liquidation is the only option for the business. To guarantee that you are taking the right steps to improve your company's situation, check with appropriate legal counsels and see what options are available to you.

Consider Compulsory Liquidation

Compulsory liquidation occurs when a court orders a company into liquidation. This normally happens following a winding-up petition from a creditor, or group of creditors. However, the company itself or its directors may also file a winding-up petition. Following a court order, an official receiver will be appointed as liquidator by the court to handle the winding up of the company and investigate the possible causes of the liquidation.

Remember Employees' Rights when a Business Is Wound Up

An employer may owe debts to employees for wages, salary, or accrued holiday pay. If it is solvent when it ceases trading, employees may also be entitled to workers compensations. Where insolvency leads to winding up, "preferential" debts can be designated and must be settled. The remainder is designated as ordinary debts.

WHAT TO AVOID
Not Drawing Up a Deed of Partnership when Setting Up

When forming a partnership, a deed of partnership should be drawn up. It should specify arrangements to be followed in insolvency. Otherwise the partnership is subject to the relevant provisions of the Partnership Act 1890, which may not best suit the needs of the business.

Providing the Wrong Information

The court and any insolvency practitioners should be provided with all the information they require—omissions or false statements can result in criminal proceedings.

SEE ALSO
Bankruptcy and Business Failure (p. 432)
Deciding Whether to Sell Your Business (p. 408)
Management Buyouts (p. 462)
Venture Capital (p. 495)

DIRECTORY

Small and Growing Businesses

BOOKS AND DIRECTORIES

101 Best Businesses to Start 3rd ed.
Philip Lief Group, Russell D. Roberts,
Sharon Kahn
New York: Random House, Inc., 2000
720pp ISBN: 0767906594
This popular book offers helpful, practical
advice on where to start if you are looking
for a new business opportunity. Each of
the businesses listed is described fully
and entries include: profit projections;
information on costs; strategies for success;
and assistance on planning staff
requirements.

Beating the Odds in Small Business
Tom Culley
New York: Fireside/Simon & Schuster, 1998
320pp ISBN: 0684841835
This book is a survival manual for new
businesses, and systematically explains and
analyzes every key "survival priority" upon
which the sustainability of a new business
is dependent in the critical first years. The
author shows how the odds can be turned
in your favor by avoiding the distractions
of chasing easy success in order to get
rich quick, and instead focusing only
on the harsh realities of the business
jungle.

Business Development: A Guide to Small Business Strategy
David Butler
Woburn, Massachusetts: Butterworth-Heinemann, 2001
192pp ISBN: 0750652470
This book aims to help owner-managers of
small businesses draw up a plan for the
long-term future. The subjects covered
include: reviewing performance, resource
implications, sales and marketing strategy,
market expansion, staffing, and financial
performance. The standards for business
development established by the Small Firms
Enterprise Development Institute (SFEDI)
are appended.

Business Planning: A Guide to Business Start-Up
David Butler
Woburn, Massachusetts: Butterworth-Heinemann, 2000
276pp ISBN: 075064706X
This book contains all the factual
information required to produce a
successful business plan for presentation to
a potential source of finance or for use in an
NVQ portfolio. It is in line with the major
syllabuses for business start-up and can be
used as a course guide for anyone
completing a formal NVQ level 3
qualification in this area.

The Business Valuation Book: Proven Strategies for Measuring a Company's Value
Scott Gabehart and Richard Brinkley
New York: AMACOM, 2002
350pp ISBN: 0814406424
Accurately valuing a business can be a
daunting task for many businesspeople, but
this book illustrates how the basic principles
of business valuation are straightforward.
Following the ARM (Adjusted cash flow,
Rules of thumb, Market comparables)
approach, the reader is led through the
principles of: establishing an asking price
and selling terms; planning and settling tax
issues; obtaining financing; establishing risk
management levels; and implementing an
Employee Stock Ownership Plan (ESOP).
The pack contains a CD-ROM full of
practical tools.

Capitalizing on Success
Neil Coade
Stanford, Connecticut: International Thomson Business Press, 2000
195pp (Smart Strategies Series)
ISBN: 1861527659
This book takes a practical approach to the
process of business development. After
discussing the stages of business growth, it
considers the challenges that face emerging

businesses and may prevent them from reaching their potential. As a means of meeting those challenges, it stresses the importance of effective leadership, good management practice, and creative people able to move the business forward.

Effective Small Business Management 6th ed.
Richard M. Hodgetts, Donald F. Kuratko
Stanford, Connecticut: International Thomson Publishing, 1997
700pp (Dryden Press Series in Entrepreneurship)
ISBN: 0030247578
Intended for students and lecturers as well as owner-managers, this book provides an introduction to the world of small business and the fundamentals of effective small business management. Its contents include: opportunities for getting into small business; start up concerns; managing operations; marketing goods; finances and inventory control; and current issues in small business.

The E-Myth Revisited: Why Most Small Businesses Still Don't Work and What You Can Do About Yours Rev. ed.
Michael E. Gerber
New York: HarperCollins, 1995
268pp ISBN: 0887307280
First published in 1986, this best-selling book provides information and guidance on starting and maintaining a small business or franchise. "E-myth" stands for "entrepreneurial myth" and refers to Gerber's belief that entrepreneurs do not necessarily make good business people. The book shows the reader how to simplify the systems involved in running a business, and instead create an incredibly organized and regimented plan, so that the systems can more or less run themselves, freeing the entrepreneur's mind to focus on long-term strategy.

Entrepreneur's Ultimate Start-up Directory
James Stephenson
Irvine, CA: Entrepreneur Media, Inc., 2001
428pp ISBN: 1891984330

This book offers an extensive listing of business ideas, covering more than 1,300 potential start-ups across over 30 industries. It covers new and traditional business areas, including working from home and working via the Internet. Each entry is rated according to the following criteria: ease of start-up; estimated cost and potential income; possibility of exploiting the idea online; skills required; whether the start-up could be run part-time; and licensing/franchising opportunities.

Fast Track Business Growth: Smart Strategies to Grow without Getting Derailed
Andrew J. Sherman
Washington, D.C.: Kiplinger, 2002
630pp ISBN: 0938721887
An aggressive business-growth strategy may lead your business into uncharted territory. This A-Z manual assists the formulation and implementation of the right growth strategies.

Finding Your Perfect Work: The New Career Guide for Making a Living, Creating a Life
Paul Edwards, Sarah Edwards
New York: Penguin Putnam, Inc., 2003
480pp ISBN: 1585422169
This book is aimed at those in the crucial first phase of setting up a business: assessing yourself. Considering what you really want to do and get from your own business is explored in depth here, and the book contains worksheets to help the reader pinpoint their own strengths, weaknesses, and goals.

Go It Alone: The Streetwise Secrets of Success
Geoff Burch
Oxford: Capstone, 2003
336pp ISBN: 1841124702
An easy-to-read, practical guide to those thinking of starting their own business, packed with anecdotal advice. The author's very original and humorous approach helps get across his wealth of experience in entrepreneurship and sales.

Growing Business Handbook: Strategies for Planning, Funding, and Managing Business Growth 5th ed.

Richard Willsher, Adam Jolly, eds.
Dover, New Hampshire: Kogan Page, 2002
320pp ISBN: 0749424753
Designed to help businesses with an established market position, this handbook presents a range of practical strategies for managing growth. The contributors, who come from a variety of backgrounds, provide advice in areas including funding options, competition, managing the risks, making the most of IT, external relations, and competitive purchasing.

Growing Your Own Business: Growth Strategies for Meeting New Challenges and Maximizing Success

Gregory F. Kishel and Patricia Gunter Kishel
Lincoln, Nebraska: iUniverse, 2000
256pp ISBN: 0595147925
Focusing on the key decisions needed for creating and maintaining your business from start-up to maturity, this book offers information and guidance in areas such as planning, financing, team building, marketing, expansion, taxation, and transition.

Grow Your Business

Mark Henricks
Waterloo, Ontario: Entrepreneur Press, 2001
450pp ISBN: 1891984209
Author Mark Henricks guides the reader through a wide portfolio of issues that include: assessing a business's strengths, setting targets, managing risks, negotiating bureaucracy, and handling the competition. Focused on the contemporary business climate, which has witnessed a growing number of new businesses, Henricks takes the fledgling business from infancy and helps it to maturity.

How to Grow Your Business Without Driving Yourself Crazy: Tools to Tackle Barriers to Growth, Profitability and Ease

Mike Van Horn
San Rafael, California: The Business Group, 2002

304pp ISBN: 0971411425
Aimed at small business owners and entrepreneurs, this book provides the tools and information in order to avoid the common pitfalls faced by small business owners. The style is chatty, and the book contains charts, tips, and tables.

ISO 9001 2000 for Small Businesses 2nd ed.

Ray Tricker
Woburn, Massachusetts: Butterworth-Heinemann, 2001
460pp ISBN: 0750648821
This book explains the requirements of the new ISO 9000 2000 standard and looks at how smaller companies can benefit from it and set up their own quality management systems. Background information on ISO 9000 and the importance of quality control and quality assurance is provided.

Kick Start Your Dream Business: Getting It Started and Keeping You Going

Romanus Wolter
Berkeley, California: Ten Speed Press, 2001
304pp ISBN: 1580082513
This book contains practical advice for anyone thinking about starting a small business as well as supportive real-life examples of successful entrepreneurship.

The Loyalty Effect: The Hidden Force Behind Growth, Profits, and Lasting Value

Frederick F. Reichheld
Boston, Massachusetts: Harvard Business School Press, 1996
352pp ISBN: 1578516870
Loyalty is not dead, and this book explains why, demonstrating the power of loyalty-based management as a profitable alternative to a constant flux of employees, investors and customers.

New Venture Adventure: Succeed with Professional Business Planning

Ueli Looser, Bruno Schlapfer, eds.
New York: Texere Publishing, 2001
217pp ISBN: 1587990032

This manual, written by consultants from McKinsey, offers professional advice on starting up a business. The book opens with an overview of the stages a typical start-up company will go through and a consideration of what constitutes on attractive business idea. The main focus is on the preparation of a professional business plan and an example of a business plan is provided. The book also covers the questions of how to value a start-up business and how to raise equity.

The Next Level: Essential Strategies for Achieving Breakthrough Growth
James B. Wood
Cambridge, Massachusetts: Perseus, 2000
224pp ISBN: 0738201596
An accessible guide to planning and managing the stages of company growth, *The Next Level* centers around the use of a powerful, field-tested diagnostic tool, the Inc. Growth Strategy Analysis. James Wood carefully shows entrepreneurs and established business leaders alike how to analyze their organization's growth potential, identify the key constraints to future growth, and put into practice the strategies that will enable them to arrive at new levels of expansion and profit generation.

The On-Purpose Business: Doing More of What You Do Best More Profitably
Kevin W. McCarthy
Colorado Springs, Colorado: Navpress Publishing Group, 2002
192pp ISBN: 1576833216
Written in a story format and with a spiritual backdrop, this book examines the principles of management and introduces the "On-Purpose" model, which focuses on all areas where each individual joins, belongs, and contributes to an organization.

Outsmarting Goliath: How to Achieve Equal Footing with Companies That Are Bigger, Richer, Older and Better Known
Debra Koontz Traverso
Dover, New Hampshire: Kogan Page, 2000
215pp ISBN: 0 7494 3298 5

The author presents practical advice on how to help small business present a professional image, produce high quality marketing materials, and win contracts that may seem out of reach for a small company. The book also outlines innovative ways to enhance company profile.

Setting Up and Running a Limited Company: A Comprehensive Guide to Forming and Operating a Company as a Director and Shareholder 4th ed.
Robert Browning
Oxford: How To Books, 2003
189pp ISBN: 1857038665
This guide is aimed at anyone thinking of establishing a limited company and addresses statutory requirements as well as advising on best practice. The book includes information on: the responsibilities of shareholders and directors; setting up your business; preparing financial records; sourcing venture capital; and retreating gracefully if things don't go to plan.

Small Business Marketing Management
Ian Chaston, Terry Mangles
New York: Palgrave, 2002
275pp ISBN: 0 333 98075 1
This book is designed to give undergraduate and postgraduate students an understanding of the small business marketing process, including positioning, competitive advantage, product management, pricing, and distribution. The impact of e-commerce and the Internet, the marketing of services and international marketing are also covered. The text is supported by real-life case studies and published research findings.

Small Time Operator: How to Start Your Own Business, Keep Your Books, Pay Your Taxes, and Stay Out of Trouble 25th ed.
Bernard B. Kamoroff
Willits, California. Bell Springs Publishing, 2000
200pp ISBN: 0917510186
Kamoroff presents the reader with the essentials of building a business, from obtaining initial permits and licenses, to

seeking financing, locating the right business area, establishing an accounts and bookkeeping system, and taking on new staff. Continually updated, Kamoroff is conscious of reflecting the very latest thinking in tax and business management.

Spare Room Tycoon: Succeeding Independently—The 70 Lessons of Sane Self-Employment

James Chan

London: Nicholas Brealey Publishing, 2000
224pp ISBN: 1857882474

Written by a entrepreneur with over 20 years' experience of working from home, this book is aimed at anyone thinking of setting up a home-based business. It offers support and tips on how to avoid isolation and to spread the word about your business. The book focuses on "soft" skills, such as work/life balance, building confidence, and coping with the emotional demands of being your own boss and offers reassuring anecdotal advice.

Start Up: An Entrepreneur's Guide to Launching and Managing a New Business 5th ed.

William J. Stolze

Franklin Lakes, New Jersey: Career Press, 1999
288pp ISBN: 1564144231

This book is aimed at those setting up or expanding a business and is a practical guide to launching and managing a new enterprise. It includes various case studies and sample business plans.

The Startup Garden

Tom Ehrenfeld

New York: McGraw-Hill, 2001
288pp ISBN: 0071368248

Ehrenfeld identifies a current trend towards entrepreneurship, and in this book he shows his readers how they can construct their own perfect job. *The Startup Garden* takes the reader through the processes involved in starting a company and shows how this is matched to the reader's hopes and dreams, demonstrating the link between your personal life and your business drives.

Telecommuting Success: A Practical Guide for Staying in the Loop While Working Away from the Office

Michael J. Dziak, Gil Gordon

Indianapolis, Indiana: Jist Works, 2001
256pp ISBN: 1571121099

Offering many tips, warnings, suggestions, and shortcuts, this book deals with the issues faced by telecommuters. It advocates becoming a "power telecommuter" by remaining in touch with your workplace and manager.

Understanding the Small Family Business

Denise Fletcher, ed.

New York: Routledge, 2002
224pp ISBN: 0415250536

This book offers an overview of current research in the small family business sector with the main focus on the relationship between work and family and the tensions and contradictions that can arise. The contributions are organized in three sections relating to rationality discourse, resource-based discourse, and critical discourse.

Unlocking the Value of Your Business: How to Increase It, Measure It, and Negotiate an Actual Sale Price—In Easy Step-by-Step Terms

Thomas W. Horn

Fort Collins, Colorado: Charter Oak Press, 1999
273pp ISBN: 0875210163

This easy-to-follow book explains the factors that establish business value, and how they fit together. It provides insights into the route your business should be taking in order to increase in value. The book also includes a glossary of terms which may be unfamiliar to some readers.

What No One Ever Tells You about Starting Your Own Business: Real Life Start-up Advice from 101 Successful Entrepreneurs

Jan Norman

Chicago, Illinois: Upstart Publishing, 1999
224pp ISBN: 1574101129

Drawing on the experience of, and mistakes made by, 101 businesspeople, this book contains helpful and practical advice on how to start your own business without headaches.

Your First Business Plan: A Simple Question and Answer Format Designed to Help You Write Your Own Plan 4th ed.
Joseph Covello, Brian Hazelgren
Naperville, Illinois: Sourcebooks, 2002
160pp ISBN: 1402200021
This popular book contains practical advice on writing an impressive business plan, including useful information on the constituent parts of a business.

WEB SITES
Benchmark Index
www.benchmarkindex.com
Affiliated to Business Link, this Web site offers help and advice on benchmarking to businesses, advisors, and networks. It aims to help businesses understand their current position and effectively plan for the future.

bird-online
www.bird-online.co.uk
This site, based in the United Kingdom, offers a range of information, advice, and services to small businesses.

BizMove.com
www.bizmove.com
This site, based in the United States, features the Small Business Knowledge Base, a range of free information resources for small businesses.

Business.com
www.business.com
This is an extensive and helpful search engine and directory site. The home page offers over 20 topics for users to research, including small businesses, accounting, law, and computing. Search results are presented as a series of useful click-through links.

Business Owner's Toolkit
www.toolkit.cch.com
The toolkit includes model business plans and documents for downloading and information from the SOHO guidebook.

Inc.com
www.inc.com
Inc.com is the online version of the magazine *Inc*. The Web site provides information, products, services, and online tools—accumulated from a variety of sources—for many business or management tasks. This information has also been organized into categories to help the user find quickly what they need.

IRS Small Business One Stop Resource
www.irs.gov/businesses/small/ index.html
The U.S. government's Internal Revenue Service offers a broad range of tax resources for the self-employed and those running small businesses, including online workshops, forms, and publications. In addition to this, the IRS provides more general advice to those starting, operating, or closing a business, in the form of articles, checklists, tips, and extensive Web links to other sources of information and help.

SCORE
www.score.org
This site bills itself as "Counselors to America's Small Business," and is a nonprofit organization that aims to give free support and advice to entrepreneurs, both face-to-face and remotely (via e-mail). SCORE (Service Corps of Retired Executives) has a team of more than 10,000 advisors who offer guidance on a wide variety of issues.

Welcome Business USA
www.welcomebiz.com
This site is an extensive online resource for entrepreneurs and those thinking of starting their own business. It has an alliance with SCORE, who provide a team of advisors that users can contact free. The Welcome Business site offers a variety of services, including a start-up checklist, free business counseling, information on business plans, and information on tax issues for small businesses.

ORGANIZATIONS
National Business Association
Tom Sailors
P.O. Box 700728, Dallas, Texas, 75370
T: +1 800 456 0440 or +1 972 458 0900
F: +1 972 960 9149
E: *info@nationalbusiness.org*
www.nationalbusiness.org
Established in 1982, the National Business
Association (NBA) is a nonprofit
organization, designed and managed to
assist the self-employed and small business
community in achieving their professional
goals. The NBA uses its group buying power
to provide its members with support
programs, cost and time saving products
and services, and valuable small business
resource materials.

National Federation of Independent Business
53 Century Boulevard, Suite 300, Nashville,
Tennessee, 37214
T: +1 615 872 5800
F: +1 615 872 5353
www.nfib.org
The NFIB was founded by Wilson Harder in
1942. With 600,000 members it is the largest
and probably the most influential small
business lobbying group in the United
States. It represents the interests of small
business owners at national and state
government levels and provides a range of
services for its members.

Small Business Administration
200 North College Street, Suite A-2015,
Charlotte, North Carolina, 28202
T: +1 704 344 6563
F: +1 704 344 6769
E: *answerdesk@sba.gov*
www.sbaonline.sba.gov
The Small Business Administration was set
up by the U.S. government in 1953 to
provide assistance to those starting and
running their own businesses. It provides
training, financial support, and advice
through a network of offices in every state.

Small Business Institute Directors' Association
Michael Broida, Vice-President
Miami University, Department of DSC/MIS,
311 Upham Hall, Oxford, Ohio, 45056
T: +1 513 529 4826
F: +1 513 529 4841
E: *broidams@muohio.edu*
www.sbida.org
The SBIDA promotes the development and
improvement of educational programs for
small businesses and acts as a coordinating
body for Small Business Institute programs at
universities and colleges in the United States.
The latter were started in 1972 in cooperation
with the U.S. Small Business Administration,
but became independent in 1996.

SEE ALSO
Entrepreneurs (p. 450)

Accounting

BOOKS AND DIRECTORIES
Essentials of Credit, Collections and Accounts Receivable
Mary S. Schaeffer
New York: John Wiley, 2002
272pp ISBN: 0471220744
This paperback will help the reader stay
up-to-date with the latest strategies,
developments and technologies in credit,
collections and accounts receivable. With
tips, techniques, and real-world examples,
the book offers practical solutions for the
credit and collection professional.

Excel 2002 for Dummies
Greg Harvey
New York: John Wiley, 2003
384pp ISBN: 0764537563
This book gives the reader key advice and
help on how to get to grips with this useful
computer package. It covers the basics of
setting up a worksheet to creating
formulas, charts, graphs, and spreadsheets
so that all your essential business
information can be safely and effectively
stored.

The Finance Manual for Non-Financial Managers: The Power to Make Confident Financial Decisions
Paul McKoen, Leo Gough
Philadelphia, Pennsylvania: Trans-Atlantic Publications, 1999
319pp (Smarter Solutions Series)
ISBN: 0273625594
The book aims to give the non-financial manager a practical introduction to financial management and control. It explains the basics of accounting and financial reports, with separate chapters covering costing, pricing, project analysis, corporate taxation, financing, and risk management. The accounting implications of acquisitions are also discussed.

How to Collect Debts (and Still Keep Your Customers)
David Sher and Martin Sher
New York: AMACOM, 1999
173pp ISBN: 0814404871
This book provides a step-by-step and comprehensive system which should minimize difficulties with accounts receivable. Encouraging a reevaluation of current policies and procedures, it proposes a new system—ASK (Attitude, Speed, and Knowledge)—and a dignified approach which will strengthen relationships with customers.

How to Read a Financial Report 5th ed.
John A. Tracey
New York: John Wiley, 1999
176pp ISBN: 0471329355
Tracey provides guidance on interpreting company accounts (with relation to U.S. practice), with particular reference to the three essential parts of every financial report—the balance sheet, the income statement, and the cash-flow statement. His explanations are illustrated with many examples.

Intermediate Accounting
Donald E. Keiso, Jerry J. Wygandt, Terry D. Warfield
New York: John Wiley, 2001
1438pp ISBN: 0471363049
The book is used in over 70% of the intermediate accounting courses taught in post-secondary institutions in the United States. It covers the conceptual framework underlying financial accounting, financial reporting standards and statements, and more complex topics and transactions that are encountered in today's business environment. Specific guidance is provided for numerous topics including accounting for cash and receivables, inventory, intangible assets, current and long-term liabilities, income taxes, leases, shareholders' equity, and revenue recognition.

Unlocking Company Reports and Accounts
Wendy McKenzie
Upper Saddle River, New Jersey: Financial Times Pitman, 1998
484pp ISBN: 0273632507
McKenzie provides a key to understanding company reports and accounts from first principles, explaining every point through the use of worked examples. She takes extracts from published accounts, including those of overseas companies, to illustrate accounting presentation, and enables the reader to understand and analyze a company's accounts and so build a comprehensive picture of its financial state.

WEB SITES
Accountants World
www.accountantsworld.com
This is an extensive portal based in the United States with links to a wide range of Web sites of interest to accountants. It relates mainly to U.S. accounting practice.

Accounting Web
www.accountingweb.co.uk
This site is an extensive online resource based in the United Kingdom. It contains material from a number of providers intended for accountancy and finance professionals. It has received an award as the New Media Business Web Site of the Year.

American Institute of Certified Public Accountants
www.aicpa.org
With 330,000 members, this organization

and its Web site provide information, continuing education, accreditation, advocacy, and leadership to certified public accountants in the United States. The AICPA publishes Accounting Trends and Techniques, Statements of Position, Practice Bulletins, Accounting Interpretations, and other guidance for financial accounting and reporting.

Financial Accounting Standards Board
www.fasb.org
This is the Web site for the Financial Accounting Standards Board, the independent private-sector entity that establishes generally accepted accounting principles (GAAP). The Board issues formal accounting guidance on the treatment and reporting of financial transactions and performance.

Internal Revenue Service
www.irs.gov
One of the most well-known American institutions, the Internal Revenue Service (IRS) is the main body in charge of U.S. taxes. It oversees tax laws, their enforcement, and tax collection, and has numerous resources available online, from helpful agencies to forms for download.

Tax and Accounting Sites Directory
www.taxsites.com
Created by a Professor of Accounting at the University of Northern Iowa, Dennis Schmidt, this site has numerous links to additional accounting and tax information across a broad spectrum of areas. Easy to navigate and simple to make sense of, the directory helps businesses and individuals find what they need quickly.

ORGANIZATIONS
American Institute of Certified Public Accountants
1211 Avenue of the Americas, New York, 10036
T: +1 212 596 6200
F: +1 212 596 6213
www.aicpa.org
With more than 330,000 members, the AICPA is the premier national professional association for certified public accountants in the United States.

National Society of Accountants
1010 North Fairfax Street, Alexandria, Virginia, 22314
T: +1 703 549 6400
F: +1 703 549 2984
www.nsacct.org
The National Society of Accountants is a nonprofit organization of some 17,000 professionals who provide accounting, tax preparation, financial and estate planning, and management advisory services to an estimated 19 million individuals and business clients. Most of the Society's members are independent practitioners or partners in small to midsize accounting and tax firms.

SEE ALSO
Budgeting (p. 435)
Reading a Balance Sheet (p. 129)
Taxation (p. 493)

Advertising

BOOKS AND DIRECTORIES
Advertising: What It Is and How to Do It
3rd ed.
Roderick White
New York: McGraw-Hill, 1993
246pp ISBN: 0077077644
This informative and detailed introduction to all aspects of advertising is aimed at organizations new to advertising, as well as people training in the area. It discusses the necessity and cost of advertising, the use of agents, the definitions and theories of advertising, planning advertisements, the media, and international and multinational advertising. Further sources of information are also listed.

Copywriting 2nd ed.
Jonathan J. Gabay
New York: McGraw Hill, 2001
336pp (Teach Yourself Series)
ISBN: 0658012010
The author offers a step-by-step guide to writing powerful copy. All aspects of creative advertising and promotion are covered, including direct mail, the Internet, radio and TV, business-to-business, the press, PR, charities, and posters. The book is written for both the beginner and the more experienced copywriter.

The Elements of Copywriting: The Essential Guide to Creating Copy That Gets the Results You Want
Gary Blake, Robert W. Bly
New York: Longman, 1998
184pp ISBN: 0028626303
A tightly written overview of copywriting, this book concentrates on the use of words that have exceptional impact on consumers. It is an especially useful text because it addresses several direct-marketing forms that are still comparatively new—press releases, electronic messages, and Web advertising. It also deals with traditional marketing forms such as brochures, catalogs, and print ads.

The Future of Advertising: New Media, New Clients, New Consumers in the Post-Television Age
Joe Cappo
New York: McGraw-Hill, 2003
260pp ISBN: 0071403159
Using his knowledge of the international ad industry, Joe Cappo gives professionals information about today's advertising workplace and tells them how to position themselves and their businesses for success in the coming years. Along with Cappo's writing are pieces from industry leaders to help give a better picture of what the industry's status is right now.

My Life in Advertising and Scientific Advertising: Two Works
Claude C. Hopkins
New York: McGraw-Hill, 1986

336pp (Classic Reprint Edition)
ISBN: 0844231010
This book is a classic in the advertising genre. Originally published some 80 years ago, its succinct advice on reaching customers effectively has never been bettered—which accounts for its dominance in the field. *Scientific Advertising* is the more important of the two reprints here: it details methods for copywriting and test marketing, and introduces many more ideas that have come to be accepted as the building blocks of successful advertising campaigns. Hopkins coined the phrase, "Advertising is salesmanship"; these texts are the touchstone for all advertising texts that followed.

WEB SITES
AdForum
www.adforum.com
This gateway Web site offers links to advertising agencies, press releases, videos of ads in production, advocacy agencies, consultants, the trade press, and more.

Advertising Age
www.adage.com
Adage.com is the official Web site of the 73-year-old magazine, Advertising Age, from the Ad Age Group and is a wonderful resource for the industry.

ORGANIZATIONS
The Advertising Council, Inc.
261 Madison Avenue, 11th Floor, New York, 10016
T: +1 212 922 1500
F: +1 212 922 1676
E: Info@adcouncil.org
www.adcouncil.org
This is the foremost creator of public service announcements in the United States. The Advertising Council is a nonprofit organization that was created in 1942 out of the remnants of the War Advertising Council. Its work focuses on primarily quality-of-life issues, preventive health, and community issues. Some of the most influential ad campaigns in the United States originated from this organization.

Advertising Research Foundation

641 Lexington Avenue, New York, 10022
T: +1 212 751 5656
F: +1 212 319 5265
E: *info@arfsite.org*
www.arfsite.org
A nonprofit corporate membership
association which arranges conferences,
workshops, and other events, and promotes
research and development in the field of
advertising.

American Advertising Federation

1101 Vermont Avenue, NW, Suite 500,
Washington, D.C., 20005–6303
T: +1 202 898 0089
F: +1 202 898 0159
E: *aaf@aaf.org*
www.aaf.org
The Federation has a network of local
chapters and clubs. It administers a
prestigious award, the Advertising Hall of
Fame, as well as other awards, conferences,
and exhibitions.

American Association of Advertising Agencies

405 Lexington Avenue, 18th Floor,
New York, 10174
T: +1 212 682 2500
F: +1 212 682 8391
E: *donahue@aaaa.org*
www.aaaa.org
This is an industry organization for
advertising agencies. Lobbyists under
AAAA auspices work for the industry
on Capitol Hill. The Web site features
upcoming events, news, tutorials, and
the programs and publications of the
group.

American Marketing Association

311 S. Wacker Drive, Suite 5800, Chicago,
Illinois, 60606–5819
T: +1 312 542 9000
F: +1 312 542 9001
E: *info@ama.org*
www.marketingpower.com
This association is an advocacy group
providing resources to marketing
professionals. Their site gives access to a job
directory, provides courses for skill
upgrades, and permits the tracking of trends
in the industry. It also includes articles and
tutorials for registrants.

The Direct Marketing Association

1120 Avenue of the Americas, New York,
10036–6700
T: +1 212 768 7277
F: +1 212 302 6714
E: *lmastria@the-dma.org*
www.the-dma.org
This group is the largest trade organization for
companies involved in direct marketing,
database marketing, and interactive global
marketing. It is involved in lobbying efforts,
promoting direct marketing, and
disseminating trade information on Capitol
Hill, with governmental agencies, and within
all U.S. states. It is also expanding to work on
international trade issues. It is well known for
its work on telemarketing and is spearheading
the national campaign to remove disgruntled
customers from telemarketer call lists.

SEE ALSO
Direct Marketing (p. 443)
Marketing Management (p. 464)
**Market Research and Competitor
  Intelligence (p. 469)**
Product and Brand Management (p. 481)

Bankruptcy and Business Failure

BOOKS AND DIRECTORIES
Buying a Company in Trouble: A Practical Guide 2nd ed.
Ian E. Walker
Brookfield, Vermont: Gower, 1992
144pp ISBN: 0566072890

This book provides practical guidance for
those planning to buy a company that is
formally insolvent or close to insolvency.
It considers the reasons for buying such a
company and discusses how to recognize a
company in trouble, decide when to buy,

and negotiate the offer, as well as the other matters that should be taken into account.

Corporate Bankruptcy: Tools, Strategies and Alternatives

Grant A. Newton
New York: John Wiley, 2003
256pp ISBN: 0471332682
In its examination of the complexities of restructuring and bankruptcy, this book offers a working knowledge of the bankruptcy process, its benefits and challenges for both companies and their creditors. Supported by actual case-studies, it assesses the legal and practical problems facing both debtors and creditors. A useful reference tool for every bankruptcy practitioner.

Elements of Bankruptcy 3rd ed.

Douglas G. Baird
New York: Foundation Press, 2000
236pp ISBN: 1566628687
Baird's book gives an overview of current law and practice in the United States. Recent changes in the law and topical issues are discussed and placed in context.

The Executive Guide to Corporate Bankruptcy

Thomas J. Salerno, Jordan A. Kroop, Craig D. Hansen
Frederick, Maryland: Beard Group, 2001
735pp ISBN: 1587980266
This book was written to provide a comprehensive resource for managers of financially troubled companies facing Chapter 11 bankruptcy proceedings. The authors outline the history of American bankruptcy law and bankruptcy terminology for the lay person, then provide a step-by-step guide to the bankruptcy and reorganization process, including sample documents.

The Turnaround Manager's Handbook

Richard S. Sloma
Frederick, Maryland: Beard Group, 2000
244pp ISBN: 1893122409

Designed for the corporate manager, this book provides specific details on actions undertaken to achieve a turnaround in a failing business. The author addresses operational issues and provides recommendations and tools to restore a business to profitability.

WEB SITES

ABIWorld
www.abiworld.org
ABIWorld is sponsored by the American Bankruptcy Institute and is a major source of U.S. bankruptcy information. The site includes news and statistics, information and opinions on bankruptcy cases, information on international bankruptcy legislation, an interactive newsletter, and information on how to find a bankruptcy professional. Some sections are restricted to ABI members.

Business Bankruptcy Info
www.creditworthy.com/topics/ bankruptcy.html
This Web site, hosted by Creditworthy Co., provides links to business bankruptcy information covering the United States, Canada, and the United Kingdom. It includes information on, and links to, U.S. bankruptcy courts, an overview of the U.S. Bankruptcy Code, and statistics and research on bankruptcy filings.

InsolvencyAsia
www.insolvencyasia.com
This site, based in Hong Kong, provides insolvency-related news together with information on bankruptcy legislation and listings of consultants, associations, and regulatory authorities in Asian countries.

InterNet Bankruptcy Library
www.bankrupt.com
This site, sponsored by the Bankruptcy Creditors' Service and the Beard Group, is aimed particularly at creditors. It includes a news archive, a database of bankruptcy

professionals, information on legal rules in American states, and details of publications, as well as providing access to discussion groups.

United States Bankruptcy Courts
www.uscourts.gov/ bankruptcycourts.html
Since there are specialized courts that settle bankruptcy claims in America, this site offers information about the courts themselves, offers downloadable forms, has FAQs, and links to the individual courts for a particular area.

World Internet Insolvency and Bankruptcy Resources
www.insolvency.com
This site includes a listing of U.S. and U.K. mailing lists and newsgroups connected with insolvency.

ORGANIZATIONS
American Bankruptcy Institute
44 Canal Center Plaza, Suite 404, Alexandria, Virginia, 22314
T: +1 703 739 0800
F: +1 703 739 1060
E: *info@abiworld.org*
www.abiworld.org
The ABI was founded in 1982 to provide the U.S. Congress and public with unbiased information on bankruptcy issues. Its activities include research, conferences, training programs, and publications; opportunities for the exchange of information and ideas are also provided. The membership of 7,500 includes attorneys, auctioneers, bankers, judges, accountants, and other professionals.

SEE ALSO
Accounting (p. 428)

Budgeting

BOOKS AND DIRECTORIES
Budgeting Basics and Beyond: A Complete Step-by-Step Guide for Nonfinancial Managers
Jae K. Shim, Joel G. Siegel
Englewood Cliffs, New Jersey: Prentice Hall Trade, 1994
446pp ISBN: 0133122328
A guide to effective budgeting, taking the reader through every step from preparing and presenting budgets to handling budgeting difficulties. Extra features include case studies, illustrations, and checklists, together with suggestions for getting the most out of software packages such as Simplan, Excel, Lotus, and Profit Planner.

Budgeting for Non-Financial Managers: How to Master and Maintain Effective Budgets
Iain Maitland
Philadelphia, Pennsylvania: Trans-Atlantic Publications, 2000

206pp (Smarter Solutions Series)
ISBN: 0273644947
This book takes you through each stage of the budgeting process, explaining all you need to know about it. From understanding the procedures for making budgets and forecasts to developing realistic contingency plans, it shows how to turn your budgeting strategy into a valuable management tool. It also contains a wide range of model forecasts, forms, and budgets, and comes complete with checklists and case studies.

Budgeting: Technology, Trends, Software Selection and Implementation
Nils H. Rasmussen, Christopher J. Eichorn
New York: John Wiley, 2000
290pp ISBN: 0471392073
Describing itself as a guide to "essential budget planning for the 21st century corporation," this book introduces and explains new trends in budgeting and

budgeting software. With various report and contract samples, questionnaires and interviews with leading managers, this practically oriented book guides the reader through the range of considerations that are crucial to streamlining the budget planning process.

Cashflow Reengineering: How to Optimize the Cashflow Timeline and Improve Financial Efficiency

James Sagner
New York: AMACOM, 1997
256pp ISBN: 0814403611
Sagner shows how to diagnose a company's cash flow situation accurately and prescribe the correct treatment. He presents ten management principles and procedures which, he suggests, have saved many companies large amounts of money.

Cash Flows and Budgeting Made Easy: How to Set and Monitor Financial Targets in Any Organization 4th ed.

Peter Taylor
Oxford: How To Books, 2002
160pp ISBN: 1857038037
This practical guide aims to cover the whole budgeting process, and contains information on planning financial requirements, forecasting, VAT, managing cash flows, and using IT to help make your financial life easier.

Credit Risk Management: A Guide to Sound Business Decisions

H. A. Schaeffer, Jr.
New York: John Wiley, 2000
288pp ISBN: 0471350206
This book examines the steps leading to a sound business credit decision. It is divided into four main sections: analysis for creative credit management; building up essential business credit information; considering all factors that affect the business credit decision; and making a decision or recommendation. Twelve detailed case studies are provided, illustrating common problems along with their solutions.

Handbook of Budgeting 5th ed.

Robert Rachlin, ed.
New York: John Wiley, 2003
840pp ISBN: 0471268720
Without clear budgets, companies are unable to predict profits or losses or plan for the future. This handbook guides controllers and budget directors through the preparation of many types of budget, with complete coverage of preparation, presentation, analysis, and effective use of the budget. The book includes chapters on specific industries, with checklists and examples to aid understanding.

Keys to Managing Your Cash Flow

Joel G. Siegel, Jae K. Shim
Hauppauge, New York: Barrons, 1992
153pp (Barrons Educational Series)
ISBN: 0812047559
Aimed at businesspeople who want to learn more about making the company's cash work harder, this book contains practical information on liquidity, credit control, dealing with surplus cash, preparing a cash budget, and much more.

Managing Budgets

Stephen Brookson
New York: DK Publishing, 2000
72pp (Essential Managers Series)
ISBN: 0789459698
This introductory guide to managing budgets explains the technique of budgeting and examines the processes of preparing, writing, and monitoring a budget.

Managing by the Numbers

Chuck Kremer, Ron Rizzuto, John Case
Cambridge, Massachusetts: Perseus, 2000
224pp ISBN: 0738202568
This is a handy and practical guide to reading and using balance sheets, income statements, and cash flow statements to drive business growth and profitability.

Total Business Budgeting: A Step-by-Step Guide with Forms 2nd ed.

Robert Rachlin

New York: John Wiley, 1999

321pp ISBN: 0471351032

Rachlin provides an introduction to a wide range of budgetary techniques and applications and shows how to analyze outside influences, develop performance targets and budgeting segments, and administer the right budgeting processes. He includes detailed instructions, forms, examples, schedules, and formats.

WEB SITES

Accountants World
www.accountantsworld.com

This is an extensive portal based in the United States with links to a wide range of Web sites of interest to accountants. It relates mainly to U.S. accounting practice.

Accounting Web
www.accountingweb.co.uk

This site is an extensive online resource based in the United Kingdom. It contains material from a number of providers intended for accountancy and finance professionals. It has received an award as the New Media Business Web Site of the Year.

CFO.com—Tools and Resources for Financial Executives
www.cfo.com

CFO.com is a great resource for anyone in a business financial setting. With multiple articles to read, CFO.com also has a newsletter, webcasts, and a magazine, which was named Magazine of the Year by the American Society of Business Publication Editors (ASBPE).

Credit to Cash
www.credit-to-cash.com

This U.K. portal provides a wide range of financial information and advice, specifically on credit management and policy, debt recovery, cash flow control, and other issues of interest to small businesses.

ORGANIZATIONS

American Accounting Association

5717 Bessie Drive, Sarasota, Florida, 34233–2399

T: +1 941 921 7747

F: +1 941 923 4093

E: *office@aaahq.org*

www.aaa-edu.org

The AAA is a professional body with particular interest in developments in the teaching of accountancy.

American Institute of Certified Public Accountants

1211 Avenue of the Americas, New York, 10036

T: +1 212 596 6200

F: +1 212 596 6213

www.aicpa.org

With more than 330,000 members, the AICPA is the premier national professional association for certified public accountants in the United States.

National Society of Accountants

1010 North Fairfax Street, Alexandria, Virginia, 22314

T: +1 703 549 6400

F: +1 703 549 2984

E: *jhemphill@nsacct.org*

www.nsacct.org

The National Society of Accountants is a nonprofit organization of some 17,000 professionals which provides accounting, tax preparation, financial and estate planning, and management advisory services to an estimated 19 million individuals and business clients. Most of the Society's members are independent practitioners or partners in small to midsize accounting and tax firms.

SEE ALSO

Accounting (p. 428)
Controlling a Budget (p. 101)
Controlling Costs (p. 104)
Drawing Up a Budget (p. 107)

Business Plans and Planning

BOOKS AND DIRECTORIES

By the Numbers: Using Facts and Figures to Get Your Projects, Plans, and Ideas Approved
Joseph McLeary, et al.
New York: AMACOM, 2000
286pp ISBN: 0814404995
The authors demonstrate how to present a winning business case based on figures. They explain how to research a company strategy, determine whether an idea is in keeping with industry trends, build alliances and support before a formal presentation, and prepare answers to critical questions.

The Complete Book of Business Plans: Simple Steps to Writing a Powerful Business Plan
Joseph A. Covello, Brian J. Hazelgren
Naperville, Illinois: Sourcebooks, 1994
320pp ISBN: 0942061411
This classic presents the key questions to bear in mind when writing a plan for a new business, and encourages the reader to look for the answers to the kinds of questions that investors ask, to develop marketing strategies and financial presentations, and to find ways to stay ahead of the competition.

The Definitive Business Plan: The Fast Track to Intelligent Business Planning for Executives and Entrepreneurs
Richard Stutley
Upper Saddle River, New Jersey: Financial Times Prentice Hall, 2001
332pp ISBN: 0273659219
This text is written for both the newcomer and the experienced planner. It provides a concise guide to the business planning process, and focuses attention on strategic planning and strategic and operational controls. The practical aspects of constructing various types of business plan are explained in some detail.

How to Really Create a Successful Business Plan 3rd ed.
David E. Gumpert
Boston, Massachusetts: Inc. Publishing, 1996
212pp ISBN: 1880394235
This book provides a step-by-step method for completing a high-quality business plan. It also provides models of business plans from a number of highly successful U.S. companies.

How to Write a .com Business Plan: The Internet Entrepreneur's Guide to Everything You Need to Know about Business Plans and Financing Options
Joanne Eglash
New York: McGraw-Hill, 2001
191pp ISBN: 007135753X
Written for entrepreneurs, business owners, and Web site owners, this text provides a practical guide to developing a business plan for an Internet-based business. Eglash focuses on the factors which distinguish online businesses from conventional enterprises, and covers the areas of mission statements and company descriptions, competition, markets and customers, products and services, marketing and sales, operations, financial projections, and financial management. A sample business plan and an extensive directory of helpful Web sites are included.

The Mission-driven Organization: From Mission Statement to a Thriving Enterprise, Here's Your Blueprint for Building an Inspired, Cohesive, Customer-oriented Team
Bob Wall, Mark R. Sobol, Robert S. Solum
Roseville, California: Prima Publishing, 1999
256pp ISBN: 0761518819
This book examines the move toward a more streamlined, horizontal power structure, showing how a company can be remotivated by this new way of thinking. It outlines the problems and associated laws and creates a clear, concise solution to the

complications involved with managing change and making cultural improvements.

The Mission Primer: Four Steps to an Effective Mission Statement
Richard O'Halloran, David O'Halloran
Richmond, Virginia: Mission Incorporated, 2000
130pp ISBN: 0967663504
Including an easy-to-use guide, examples of model mission statements, and a glossary of useful terms, this book will enable you to analyze and create your own mission statement.

Planning to Succeed in Business
David Irwin
Philadelphia, PA: Trans-Atlantic Publications, 1995
256pp ISBN: 0273610864
Continuous planning and making your business more efficient through a cohesive framework is the focus of this book.

The Successful Business Plan: Secrets and Strategies 4th ed.
Rhonda M. Abrams
Palo Alto, California: Running R Media, 2003
409pp ISBN: 0966963563
This book is designed to help readers create a business plan that will attract the funding they need to get started. It presents insights from some 200 business owners, venture capitalists, and C.E.O.s, but, in addition, contains worksheets and sample business plans, provides tools to help in number-crunching, and offers guidance on the length of an ideal plan and the way it should be worded and formatted.

Your First Business Plan: A Simple Question and Answer Format Designed to Help You Write Your Own Plan 3rd ed.
Joseph Covello
Naperville, Illinois: Sourcebooks, 1998
149pp ISBN: 1570712190
With little or no company history, the first business plan can be the most difficult. By outlining each part of the business plan and making suggestions for what to focus on and

what to avoid, this book will facilitate your writing. Also included are a glossary and a sample business plan.

WEB SITES
Business Planet
www.bizplanet.com
BizPlanet provides a range of resources including a newsletter, a virtual business plan, and reviews of business planning software and books.

Business Plan Guide
www.business-plans.co.uk
This site, sponsored by Miller Consultancy, provides information on business planning resources. It includes books, links to Web sites, articles, and an e-mail newsletter.

Business Plans
www.bplans.com
This site, created by Palo Alto Software, offers planning advice for small businesses and a substantial range of sample plans, which subscribers to bplans' software can download and edit. It also includes a resource center with links to other Web sites, as well as an "ask the experts" section.

More Business
www.morebusiness.com
This site has a lengthy business and marketing plans section and provides some useful sample business plans.

Small Business Association
www.sba.gov
This Web site, run by the U.S. government organization dedicated to helping small business owners, provides sources for technical, managerial, and financial advice and assistance.

Strategic Planning—University of Nebraska at Omaha
www.unomaha.edu/UNO/stratplan
This site provides some interesting material for use in strategic planning, as well as giving a good overview of the process. It includes a section that defines the terms used in strategic planning.

U.S. Small Business Administration
**www.sba.gov/starting/
indexbusplans.html**
The SBA's site provides a model business plan, addresses relevant FAQs, and offers general information on startups.

Venture Capital Resource Library
www.vfinance.com
This site provides a business plan template, general articles, and texts of SEC and UCC rules and regulations, as well as leads to sources of venture capital.

ORGANIZATIONS
Chief Executive Officers' Club
457 Washington Street, New York, 10013
T: +1 212 925 7911
F: +1 212 925 7463
E: *info@ceoclubs.org*
http://main.ceoclubs.org
Established in 1978, this association serves as a management resource for entrepreneurs and their professional advisers. Membership is by invitation only. Members must be C.E.O.s of businesses that have over $2m in annual sales. The organization selects publications on developing business plans and conducts seminars on the entrepreneurial process.

United States Small Business Administration
www.sba.gov
Providing multiple resources for the small business covering a wide range of topics, such as Starting Your Business, Financing Your Business, Managing Your Business, and Business Opportunities, this link, provided by the United States government, is a handy stop for anyone interested in business planning.

SEE ALSO
Budgeting (p. 435)
Small and Growing Businesses (p. 422)

Computers, Information Technology, and E-commerce

BOOKS AND DIRECTORIES
Absolute Beginner's Guide to Computers and the Internet
Michael Miller
Indianapolis, Indiana: Que, 2001
480pp ISBN: 0789780127
This book sets out to equip readers with the knowledge they need to carry out the most popular IT and Internet-related tasks, such as sending e-mail, Web surfing, online banking, and downloading music. Readers' basic skills are developed and these can then be applied in more specialist or business-related areas.

The Beginner's Guide to Computers and the Internet
Susan Holden, Matthew Francis
Chichester: Summersdale Publishers, 2002
395pp ISBN: 184024061X
This is a guide to the basics of using computers. Avoiding technical jargon, the book explains key terms and concepts and shows a range of time-saving shortcuts for those unfamiliar with computers. E-mail and the Internet are also covered.

E-Business for the Small Business
John G. Fisher
Dover, New Hampshire: Kogan Page, 2001
162pp (Business Enterprise Guide)
ISBN: 0749434791
E-business presents many new opportunities for businesses of all sizes. This guide takes you through the necessary steps for building a successful and sustainable e-business. It deals with: finding the funds; getting the right equipment; setting up a Web site; legal issues; online marketing and advertising; business-to-business

opportunities; and developing an e-business plan.

IT Investment: Making a Business Case
Dan Remenyi
Oxford: Digital Equipment Corp., 1999
210pp (Computer Weekly Professional Series)
ISBN: 0750645040
The author presents clear arguments for preparing an IT business case and includes model questionnaires and forms that managers can use in preparing a case of their own. He stresses in particular the importance of demonstrating the improvements an IT project can make to business processes, practice, and efficiency, and introduces a five-factor model which ties the project into an organization's corporate strategy.

Learning to Succeed in Business with Information Technology
Tim Lane, David Snow, Peter Labrow
Manchester: NCC Education, 2000
192pp ISBN: 1902343328
Aimed at managers within industry, this book addresses the reasons why it is important to invest in the IT skills of the workforce. Changes within the workforce, business attitudes to IT education, IT certification and accreditation, and methods of learning are examined in detail. The authors also make recommendations regarding best practice in IT skills training in organizations and for the IT training industry.

Learning Web Design
Jennifer Niederst
Farnham: O'Reilly U.K., 2003
488pp ISBN: 0596004842
Aimed at those new to Web design, this book is a comprehensive introduction to the fundamentals. The book is accessible in both tone and lay-out and is split into four sections: an overview of the Web design process; an introduction to HTML, the coding that makes up the background of Web pages; a guide to Web graphics; and advice on design. Jargon-free and full of practical tips, this book is ideal for beginners.

Small Business Guide to the Internet: A Practical Approach to Going Online
Richard Lewis
Dublin: Oak Tree Press, 1999
308pp ISBN: 1860761461
This practical guide to electronic commerce for small businesses examines both strategic issues, for example, which businesses are most likely to succeed with electronic commerce, and practical considerations such as getting online, designing and marketing an effective Web site, and the true cost of doing business online. Listings of ISPs and online resources are included.

Small Business Websites That Work: Get Online to Grow Your Company
Sean McManus
Upper Saddle River, New Jersey: Prentice Hall, 2001
240pp ISBN: 0273654861
A guide to help you get to grips with the essentials of Web site design and management. This book will be particularly helpful if you are outsourcing your Web site and need to learn not only how to brief people effectively so that you save time and money, but also how the basic technology behind the Web.

WEB SITES
Beginners.co.uk
www.beginners.co.uk
This Web site offers advice for both absolute beginners and those with some IT knowledge. The site offers a range of free tutorials and online training courses to help those who would like to gain or expand their IT knowledge for work or personal use. The site is easy to navigate even for Internet novices.

@Brint.com
www.brint.com
This extensive portal and community network for e-business, information,

technology, and knowledge management contains news, articles, book reviews, and links to relevant Web sites in the featured areas.

CMC Information Sources
www.december.com/cmc/info
This site, which focuses on computer-mediated communications, offers a set of links to essential Web sites concerned with computer training, applications, technology, and culture.

E-commerce focus
www.ecomfocus.com/cgi-bin/library/list.asp?sector=12
This site offers useful guidance on e-commerce and its importance for businesses and also provides a list of contacts for further information.

Which? Online
www.which.net
A subscription website, *Which?* Online offers access via the Internet to the wide range of information contained in the range of *Which?* magazines, including *Computing Which?*. The site offers a tour and a 30-day free trial. Subscribers gain access to thousands of reports contained in the print versions of all *Which?* magazines, searchable guides, and interactive features.

PC Magazine online
www.pcmag.co.uk
This easily navigable site offers a range of helpful services to the user. These include an "e-shopper" facility which allows you to compare specifications and prices on IT products and a forum whereby users can pose questions to the magazine's editors. There are also a series of information centers on news, products, downloads, advice, and careers as well as subsections on e-business, communications, business hardware, business software, security, personal computing, and gaming.

ORGANIZATIONS
Association of Information Technology Professionals
315 South Northwest Highway, Suite 200, Park Ridge, Illinois, 60068
T: +1 847 825 8124 or 800 224 9371
F: +1 847 825 1693
E: *aitp_hq@aitp.org*
www.aitp.org
This association is the founder of the Certificate in Data Processing examination. The management of information resources is a vital aspect of today's business world, and the AITP provides various resource materials, such as self-study and videotape management development courses, to aid managers and support staff in developing an information resource department.

Association of the Institute for Certification of Computing Professionals
2350 East Devon Avenue, Suite 115, Des Plaines, Illinois, 60018
T: +1 847 299 4227 or 800 843 8227
F: +1 847 299 4280
E: *office@iccp.org*
www.iccp.org
Founded in 1973, this association has over 50,000 members. The prestigious Certified Computing Professional (CCP) designation from the Institute for Certification of Computing Professionals (ICCP) is the only internationally recognized certification program in the profession. Employers value CCP certification as the highest standard of computer knowledge and professional competence. ICCP certifications exhibit knowledge and understanding of stringent industry fundamentals.

Information Technology Association of America
1401 Wilson Boulevard, Suite 1100, Arlington, Virginia, 22209
T: +1 703 522 5055
F: +1 703 522 2279
E: *hwarfield@itaa.org*
www.itaa.org

This organization, founded in 1982, has over 300 members. The ITAA is the United States' leading trade association for the information technology industry. With a special focus on computers and communications, the ITAA has developed numerous resources for anyone in the information technology field, and its information is timely and relevant in this fast-paced and ever-changing area.

Contracts and Contracting

BOOKS AND DIRECTORIES
Business Contracts Kit for Dummies
Book/CD-ROM ed.
Richard D. Harroch
New York: Hungry Minds, 2000
330pp ISBN: 0764552368
This kit comprises a book and a CD-ROM providing a reference guide to business contracts, with almost 200 sample documents and contracts.

Essentials of Contract Law
Martin A. Frey, Phyllis Hurley Frey, Terry H. Bitting
Albany, New York: Delmar Publishing, 2000
303pp ISBN: 0766821455
This textbook provides a functional approach to the study of contract law. It uses a "road map" format to present the law of contracts, discussing each rule of law first conceptually, followed by an example and a concrete problem.

Outsourcing in Brief
Mike Johnson
Woburn, Massachusetts: Butterworth-Heinemann, 1997
200pp (In Brief Series)
ISBN: 0750628766
This practical guide presents an overview of outsourcing, and reviews the pros and cons of the technique. It explains how outsourcing is done, and illustrates specific issues and options by means of checklists and case studies.

WEB SITES
Contracting and Organizations Research Initiative
http://cori.missouri.edu
CORI is a research initiative at the University of Missouri. Its mission is to improve understanding of how the economic system works by facilitating empirical research on contracting and organizational structure. It has created a collection of contracts that researchers can use.

Where in Federal Contracting?
www.wifcon.com
This nonprofit site is a free resource to help individuals and businesses find information about such areas of interest as federal assistance sites, associations, grants and cooperative agreements, contracting laws, courts and boards of contract appeals, and current legislation.

ORGANIZATIONS
National Contract Management Association
1921 Woodford Road, Vienna, Virginia, 22182
T: +1 703 448 9231
F: +1 703 448 0939
E: *info@ncmahq.org*
www.ncmahq.org
Formed in 1959, the NCMA aims to foster the professional growth and educational advancement of contract managers in order to promote business excellence. It is a professional society with individual members. It incorporates the Contract Management Institute, a nonprofit foundation established in 1991 to extend NCMA's education and research activities.

SEE ALSO
Employment Law (p. 447)
Outsourcing (p. 476)

Direct Marketing

BOOKS AND DIRECTORIES

2,239 Tested Secrets for Direct Marketing Success
Denny Hatch, Don Jackson
New York: McGraw-Hill, 1999
368pp ISBN: 0844203491
Divided in topic sections for easy reference, this book is an excellent source of direct marketing advice drawn from the experience of experts.

Commonsense Direct Marketing 4th ed.
Drayton Bird
Dover, New Hampshire: Kogan Page, 2000
352pp ISBN: 0749431210
This is a practical textbook, introducing direct marketing, that is packed with international case studies and demonstrations of successful strategies. It covers the following topics: the role of the marketing department; how to acquire and keep customers; how to achieve objectives and evaluate results; what you should sell; how to position products effectively; how to choose an agency and how to do without one; and the Internet, the direct marketer's new tool.

Direct Marketing: Strategy, Planning, Execution 4th ed.
Edward L. Nash
New York: McGraw-Hill, 2000
600pp ISBN: 0071352872
This updated edition is a classic in the direct marketing industry. The author, a direct marketing company executive, presents a thorough overview of all aspects of direct marketing, including strategic planning, media-specific marketing techniques, the economics of direct marketing, and direct marketing considerations for Internet and global marketing.

Enterprise One to One: Tools for Competing in the Interactive Age
Don Peppers, Martha Rogers
New York: Currency/Doubleday, 1997
ISBN: 0385482051
Written by the champions of customer relationship marketing, this is a best-selling guide to using new technology in your quest to get ahead, and stay ahead, of the field.

Making It Personal: How to Profit from Personalization without Invading Privacy
Bruce Kasanoff, Don Peppers, Martha Rogers
Cambridge, Massachusetts: Perseus, 2001
240pp ISBN: 0738205362
This book is a study of how the forthcoming growth in the use of personal information will affect the corporate world. Using research carried out in real life, the author investigates the contradiction that can exist between increasing profits through personal interaction and not invading privacy.

Successful Direct Marketing Methods 7th ed.
Bob Stone, Ron Jacobs
New York: McGraw-Hill, 2001
608pp ISBN: 0658001450
This newly updated edition provides a classic guide to direct marketing, combining new media with traditional marketing strategies to provide effective direct marketing to consumers. The content includes identifying and meeting consumers' needs, business to business marketing, and e-commerce techniques, such as branding strategies for Internet sites.

WEB SITES

Direct
www.directmag.com
This is the site of an American-based online magazine for senior direct marketers that covers all aspects of direct marketing.

The Direct Marketing Association
www.the-dma.org
The Direct Marketing Association is a trade association serving the needs of direct

marketing users and suppliers. Its Web site provides comprehensive information on direct marketing. This includes: conferences and seminars; professional development; industry guidelines, such as ethics guidelines and online tutorials; directories of direct marketers listed by name and type of service; privacy information; research; and legislative issues.

Direct Marketing Linked Resources
www.dmlr.org/guide.htm
Many links to useful sites connected with marketing on the Internet are to be found at this address.

DM News
www.dmnews.com
DM News is an online newspaper covering the direct marketing industry. Its Web site provides the latest information on legislative, business, and postal news affecting the industry. This site includes registration for free e-mail newsletters, an online directory of direct marketing businesses, and privacy information.

Target Marketing
www.targetonline.com
This site houses an America-based online magazine with articles and information on direct marketing.

ORGANIZATIONS
The Direct Marketing Association
1120 Avenue of the Americas, New York, 10036–6700
T: +1 212 768 7277
F: +1 212 302 6714
E: *membership@the-dma.org*
www.the-dma.org
The DMA is a trade association for users and suppliers in the fields of direct, database, and interactive marketing. Founded in 1917, it now has 4,700 member organizations in the United States and 53 other countries. Membership services include events, professional development, representation to government and in public affairs, and a library. The DMA recently acquired two e-commerce trade associations, the Association for Interactive Media and the Internet Alliance.

SEE ALSO
Marketing Management (p. 464)

Employee Benefits/Compensation

BOOKS AND DIRECTORIES
The Compensation Handbook
Lance A. Berger, Dorothy R. Berger, eds.
New York: McGraw-Hill, 1999
646pp ISBN: 0071343091
This updated and expanded edition is one of the classic books covering the field of employee compensation. The authors provide authoritative information written by experts in employee benefits and compensation. Topics covered include: base, variable, and executive compensation; measuring performance and compensation; and compensation trends and surveys.

The Executive Handbook on Compensation: Linking Strategic Rewards to Business Performance
Charles H. Fay, et al.
New York: Free Press, 2001
896pp ISBN: 0684842335
This book is written for managers at all levels of experience and provides detailed information regarding employee compensation. The authors commissioned international compensation professionals to create this guide on linking employee compensation to performance. Topics include merging compensation and business goals, and designing effective and competitive compensation packages.

Flexible Benefits: A Practical Guide
Russ Watling
Philadelphia, Pennsylvania: Trans-Atlantic Publications, Inc., 1997
76pp (Financial Times Management Briefings)
ISBN: 0273631780
This publication examines the strategy that should underlie a benefits program and identifies the key issues to be considered in any feasibility study of the subject. These include the design of flexible benefits, the ways in which benefits can become flexible, and the employment benefits strategy. A case study of Mercury Communications is provided.

The Handbook of Employee Benefits
Jerry S. Rosenbloom, ed.
New York: McGraw-Hill, 2001
1322pp ISBN: 0071371834
This book is a comprehensive reference tool for creating and implementing employee benefits plans. The author compiled information written by employee benefits experts into a thorough guide for compensation professionals. Topics include current information on benefits legislation, a survey of current benefits issues, and details on creating and maintaining medical, death, flexible, and related benefits plans.

The HR Book: Human Resources Management for Small Business
Lin Grensing Prophal
Naperville, Illinois: Sourcebooks, 1999
280pp ISBN: 1551802414
This book is a "complete guide" to human resource management for the small business.

Pensions for Today
Confederation of British Industry
London: Caspian Publishing Ltd. in association with the CBI, 2001
80pp (Business Guide)
ISBN: 1901844218
This Confederation of British Industry guide explains the key issues within the changing pensions marketplace, including the introduction of stakeholder pensions, pan-European pension provision, the changing world of work, communicating the benefits, and pension provision in the future.

WEB SITES
BenefitsAlert.Com
www.benefitsalert.com
Sponsored by the Alexander Hamilton Institute, this site provides an array of information pertaining to employee compensation and benefits issues. The site includes free reports useful to employers, covering topics such as employee benefits, benefits forms, research, information on benefits laws written for the lay person, discussion areas, e-mail newsletters, and alerts.

BenefitsLink.com
www.benefitslink.com
This large U.S. site is aimed at employers and provides news, compliance information, a question and answer service, links to articles, and a database of speakers.

Employee Benefit News
www.benefitnews.com
This site provides news and analysis of benefits issues and an e-mail newsletter. Registration is required.

Employee Benefits Survey
www.bls.gov/ncs/ebs
This site provides access to data from the U.S. Bureau of Labor Statistics Employee Benefits Survey in PDF format.

National Employee Benefits Web Site
www.benefitslink.com
This site provides comprehensive information and links related to employee benefits plans and compliance issues for businesses of any size, as well as for employee benefits specialists. The resources include articles with current

information, discussion areas involving compensation experts, links to government publications and regulations, conferences, directories of service providers, and a search engine dedicated to employee compensation issues.

Smart Benefits
www.smartbenefits.com
Information and links for benefits administrators are available on this site, including advice on choosing a plan.

ORGANIZATIONS
American Benefits Council
1212 New York Avenue NW, Suite 1250, Washington, D.C., 20005
T: +1 202 289 6700
F: +1 202 289 4582
E: *info@abcstaff.org*
www.americanbenefitscouncil.org
The American Benefits Council serves as the business community's lobbying arm on employee benefits policy. Professionals in the benefits field can remain current through the organization's weekly e-mail updates on the latest legislative and regulatory developments.

Council on Employee Benefits
4910 Moorland Lane, Bethesda, Maryland, 20814
T: +1 301 664 5940
F: +1 301 664 5944
E: *vschieber@ceb.org*
www.ceb.org
CEB, founded in 1946, is an association of companies with an interest in the management of employee benefits programs. It provides opportunities for the exchange of ideas, information, and statistics, sponsors research, and runs an annual conference.

Employee Benefit Research Institute
Suite 600, 2121 K Street NW, Washington, D.C., 20037–1896
T: +1 202 659 0670
F: +1 202 775 6312
E: *info@ebri.org*
www.ebri.org
The EBRI was founded in 1978 with the aim of encouraging and contributing to the development of employee benefits programs through education and research on a nonprofit and nonpartisan basis. It conducts research on a number of related key topics, collects and disseminates information, and sponsors lectures, debates, discussions, and study groups on employee benefit plans. Publications include the *EBRI Databook on Employee Benefits*, *Fundamentals of Employee Benefit Programs*, and monthly *Notes* and *Issue Brief* studies.

Employers' Council on Flexible Compensation
927 15th Street NW, Suite 1000, Washington, D.C., 20005
T: +1 202 659 4300
F: +1 202 371 1467
E: *info@ecfc.org*
www.ecfc.org
The ECFC was founded in 1981 by a group of Fortune 500 companies to promote a favorable regulatory climate and public opinion for flexible compensation. The organization engages in lobbying activities and provides up-to-date information for members.

SEE ALSO
Employment Law (p. 447)

Employment Law

BOOKS AND DIRECTORIES

ADA Compliance Guide 2nd ed.
Charles D. Goldman, ed.
Washington, D.C.: Thompson Publishing Group
The *Americans With Disabilities Act Compliance Guide* (updated monthly) is a handy reference source for understanding the complexities of the employment provisions of the ADA. Written in plain English, the Guide explains the meaning of "disability," "reasonable accommodation," and "undue hardship." It also contains information on the nonemployment provision accessibility standards.

Covenants Not to Compete: A State-by-State Survey 2nd ed.
Brian M. Malsberger
Washington, D.C.: BNA Books, 1996 (Supp. 2001)
1275pp ISBN: 157018030X
Written for attorneys, this supplemented volume covers a growing practice area in U.S. law—the protection of an employer's trade secrets and other confidential information. Organized by state, it covers state statutes governing restrictive covenants and the extent to which a covenant may be forced against an employee.

Employment, Disability, and the Americans with Disabilities Act: Issues in Law, Public Policy, and Research
Peter Blanck, ed.
Evanston, Illinois: Northwestern University Press, 2000
488pp (Psychological Issues)
ISBN: 081011688X
This is a collection of scholarly essays on employment law, especially as it relates to the Americans with Disabilities Act (ADA). It includes bibliographical references and indexes.

Employment Discrimination 2nd ed.
Lex K. Larson
New York: Matthew Bender (Lexis), 1994 (Supp. 1999)
ISBN: 0820516260
Larson on *Employment Discrimination* is a law library standard. This is a multivolume treatise (updated with loose-leaf supplements) providing comprehensive coverage relating to employment discrimination based on race, sex, religion, national origin, age, disability, and union membership.

Employment Discrimination Law 3rd ed.
Barbara Linemann, Paul Grossmann
Washington, D.C.: BNA Books, 1996 (Supp. 2000)
2356pp ISBN: 0871797917
Employment Discrimination Law has been the long accepted standard treatise in the field. It comprises two hardcover volumes, plus the supplement, and offers a balanced, in-depth presentation of issues from legal specialists representing every practice perspective.

Employment Law: New Challenges in the Business Environment 2nd ed.
John Jude Moran
Upper Saddle River, New Jersey: Prentice Hall, 2001
594pp ISBN: 0130896071
Aimed at Human Resource managers and those in the legal profession, this book deals with the subject by taking a simple approach to employment law with a foundation of legal principles explained in language that is easy to understand. The text discusses the overall employment relationship and discrimination topics such as sex, race, age, gender, religion, and AIDS. It looks at the regulatory aspects of employment and presents several sample cases and hypothetical situations in every chapter to illustrate the employment law problems faced by small businesses.

The Fair Labor Standards Act
Ellen K. Kearns
Washington, D.C.: BNA Books, 1999 (Supp. 2000)
1750pp ISBN: 1570181058
This is a treatise covering one of the oldest U.S. employment laws, the FLSA, which covers virtually every employee and employer in the United States. This volume provides point-by-point evaluations of each FLSA exemption to determine worker status under the law, as well as possible strategies for dealing with enforcement, remedies, and litigation.

The Family and Medical Leave Act, the Americans with Disabilities Act, and Title VII of the Civil Rights Act of 1964
U.S. Equal Employment Opportunity Commission's Office of Legal Counsel
Washington, D.C.: U.S. Equal Employment Opportunity Commission, 1995
24pp
This fact sheet provides technical assistance and discusses the interrelationship of these three federal statutes. It includes bibliographical references, and is available on order from the Equal Employment Opportunity Commission's Web site (www.eeoc.gov/publications.html).

Foundations of Employment Discrimination Law
John Donohue III
New York: Foundation Press, 1997
445pp (Interdisciplinary Readers in Law)
ISBN: 1566629918
This book presents a broad collection of edited readings covering the general development of the law from a variety of perspectives including history, philosophy, economics, law, sociology, politics, and psychology. Its two sections, one on race discrimination and the other on sex discrimination, consider the theoretical and empirical foundations of the law, its operation, and its impact.

Fundamentals of Employment Law
Karen Ford, Kerry Notestine, Richard Hill, eds.
Chicago, Illinois: American Bar Association Tort and Insurance Practice, 2000
774pp ISBN: 1570738068
This guide serves as an introduction to a rapidly expanding area of litigation. The book is a reference tool written by attorneys at a major employment law firm, offering a clear, concise look at key topics in the employment law field. As well as offering practical advice, it summarizes the federal equal employment opportunity laws that apply to most employment situations, and provides an overview of relevant legislation and court decisions on a variety of topics.

Unjust Dismissal
Lex K. Larson
New York: Matthew Bender (Lexis), 1984
3 volumes (loose-leaf) ISBN: 0820517798
This three-volume binder set focuses mainly on employment law topics outside of discrimination issues, including employee handbooks and personnel manuals, free speech and privacy in the workplace, whistleblowing, and drug and alcohol screening.

WEB SITES
Alexander Hamilton Institute (AHI) Employment Law Resource Center
www.ahipubs.com
With newsletters and multiple publications, AHI aims to keep business leaders and executives on top of what's new with employment laws to prevent future legal issues.

BenefitsLink
www.benefitslink.com
BenefitsLink is one of the oldest law sites on the Web. It offers compliance information and tools about employee benefit plans sponsored by private or governmental employers in the United States. The site contains recent articles on employee

benefits, links to key government documents, and an "ask the experts" Q&A forum.

Context
www.justis.com
Context provides a vast range of legal material on CD-ROM and on the Internet. From an employment law angle, it provides the Internet version of the official employment law case reports, known as ICR, produced by the Incorporated Council of Law Reporting.

Employment Law Information Network
www.elinfonet.com
The Employment Law Information Network is an employment law portal site containing thousands of links to employment law content on the Web. This site contains links to U.S. employment law statutes and regulations, employment law articles, and example human resource policies, forms, and contracts. The site also contains a discussion forum where visitors can post their employment law questions.

Findlaw
www.findlaw.com
Findlaw, the legal media site (now owned by West Group) contains information and links to information on virtually every aspect of U.S. law, including employment law. The employment law section includes links to databases, government agencies, sample legal documents, employment law articles, and related Web sites.

Incomes Data Services
www.incomesdata.co.uk/brief/law.htm
The site offers news, reports, and guidance on a wide range of British employment law issues. There is some free information; otherwise you are directed to the extensive range of IDS published products.

U.S. Department of Labor
www.dol.gov
The U.S. Department of Labor is responsible for the administration and enforcement of over 180 federal statutes, covering areas from wages and hours to family and medical leave. The DOL's Web site was redesigned in August 2001 and contains a vast array of legal compliance information, including "elaw Advisors"—interactive tools that provide information about federal employment laws.

U.S. Equal Employment Opportunity Commission (EEOC)
www.eeoc.gov
The EEOC is the primary federal agency that enforces the U.S. employment discrimination statutes (protecting employees from discrimination on the basis of protected traits like race, sex, age, and disability status). The Commission's site includes a wide variety of primary source documents on U.S. employment laws, including statutory and regulation text, enforcement guidance, and the Commission's compliance manual. Information is available for both employees and employers, much of which is written in non-technical terms for the layman.

WorkIndex
www.workindex.com
WorkIndex.com provides a comprehensive index of workplace related Web sites (over 3,000) as well as human resource tools and information. The site is produced and maintained by the publishers of *Human Resource Executive* magazine, in cooperation with Cornell University's School of Industrial Labor Relations. It offers business book abstracts, book reviews, a salary calculator, HR news, and a place to test HR software. Users can consult a legal clinic, post and search jobs, and read best practice reports.

ORGANIZATIONS
American Management Association (AMA)
1601 Broadway, New York, 10019
T: +1 212 586 8100
F: +1 212 903 8168
E: *customerservice@amanet.org*
www.amanet.org
One of the world's leading nonprofit membership-based educational organizations, the AMA offers a range of business education and management development programs for individuals and enterprises in the Americas, Europe, and Asia. It identifies best management practices worldwide to provide assessment, design, development, self-development, and instruction services through a variety of print and electronic media and learning methodologies, including conferences and seminars, all specially designed to enhance the growth of individuals and organizations.

Society for Human Resource Management (SHRM)
1800 Duke Street, Alexandria, Virginia, 22314
T: +1 703 548 3440
F: +1 703 535 6490
www.shrm.org
Founded in 1948, the SHRM is the world's largest human resource management association. It provides a variety of comprehensive education and information services, conferences and seminars, government and media representation, online services, and publications to more than 165,000 professional and student members around the world.

SEE ALSO
Contracts and Contracting (p. 442)
Employee Benefits/Compensation (p. 445)

Entrepreneurs

BOOKS AND DIRECTORIES
Against the Odds: An Autobiography
James Dyson
New York: Texere Publishing, 2000
341pp ISBN: 1587990148
The story of man and machine, this book charts the path to the shops of James Dyson's innovative vacuum cleaner.

Boo Hoo: A Dot-com Story
Ernst Malmsten, Erik Portanger, Charles Drazin
London: Random House Business Books, 2002
416pp ISBN: 0099418371
A cautionary tale of life at the height of the dot-com boom, this book details the rise and fall of boo.com, an online fashion site. While only portraying one side of the story, this is an entertaining tale that, if nothing else, reminds the reader of the importance of backing up fantastic-sounding plans with action and funds.

Generation Entrepreneur
Stuart Crainer, Des Dearlove
Financial Times Business, 2000
266pp ISBN: 0273649205
This title looks at the future of business in the hands of "Generation X." This inspirational book suggests that entrepreneurship is now a "lifestyle choice" for young people wise in the ways of e-commerce, but there are lessons here for more traditional businesses.

The HP Way
David Packard
New York: HarperCollins, 1996
224pp ISBN: 0887308171
In this book, Packard charts the emergence of his technology business: Hewlett Packard. He attributes the company's success to the unique outlook of the firm, "The HP Way," which promotes a combination of openness, honesty, and flexibility. The book should interest both

entrepreneurs and technologists alike, in demonstrating the growth of a major contemporary technology company.

Inside Intel: Andy Grove and the Rise of the World's Most Powerful Chip Company
Tim Jackson
New York: Plume, 1998
432pp ISBN: 0452276438
Most of today's computers operate using Intel chips, and this book provides an account of how the company under C.E.O. Andrew Grove rose to such global dominance. In using both public and private documents and a number of selected interviews, *Financial Times* columnist Tim Jackson charts the story of Intel from its conception to the present day.

Marketing and Entrepreneurship in SMEs: An Innovative Approach
David Carson, Stanley Cromie, Pauric McGowan, Jimmy Hill
Upper Saddle River, New Jersey: Prentice-Hall, 1996
296pp ISBN: 0131509705
Combining entrepreneurial theory and research with marketing knowledge to give a new perspective on the small business, this book is useful as both a reference book and as a support to general business education.

Matsushita Leadership: Lessons From the 20th Century's Most Remarkable Entrepreneur
John P. Kotter
New York: Free Press, 1997
320pp ISBN: 068483460X
This book chronicles the life of Japanese entrepreneur Konosuke Matsushita, founder of the Matsushita Electric Corporation and Panasonic. It pays particular attention to his visionary management and leadership style, and highlights his views on the social responsibility of business.

The MouseDriver Chronicles
John Lusk, Kyle Harrison
Cambridge, Massachusetts: Perseus, 2002
256pp ISBN: 0738205737

Lusk and Harrison, MBA graduates, narrate their experiences of starting their own company, and the problems they encountered along the way. Their product was the MouseDriver, a computer mouse fashioned as a golf club head, which experienced mixed fortunes in a volatile technology market. Lusk and Harrison describe the events leading up to the product's conception, and how they managed to support it in a continually changing marketplace.

The Origin and Evolution of New Businesses
Amar V. Bhide
New York: Oxford University Press, 1999
432pp ISBN: 0195131444
This book develops a comprehensive framework for understanding entrepreneurship by drawing upon anecdote and folklore, intensive research, and modern theories of business and economics. It examines the concept of entrepreneurship, beginning with the improvised business startup, through the radical shifts required to compete in niche markets, to the pursuit of entrepreneurship in large organizations.

WEB SITES
Entrepreneur.com
www.entrepreneur.com
This is a magazine site sponsored by Entrepreneur Media, Inc., offering a comprehensive range of practical information for owners of small businesses. The information includes a search engine, business tools, databases, newsletters, and message boards.

Entrepreneurial Edge
www.lowe.org
The Michigan-based Edward Lowe Foundation provides information and resources for entrepreneurs: news, articles, and an e-mail newsletter.

The Entrepreneurs' Help Page
www.tannedfeet.com
Written by young professionals for other

professionals and entrepreneurs, tannedfeet.com has numerous pages of simple business information that help individuals save time and money. Instead of hiring a professional for a fee, try finding what you need at this site instead.

EntreWorld
www.entreworld.org
This is a collection of resources for entrepreneurs provided by the Kauffman Center for Entrepreneurial Leadership in Kansas City. Three sections focus on starting, growing, and finding support for a business. The site includes articles, a glossary, practical advice, an e-mail newsletter, an events calendar, and a bookstore.

eWeb
http://eweb.slu.edu/eweb.htm
This Web site is provided by St. Louis University, and provides information on entrepreneurial education programs, organizations, research centers, and assistance for entrepreneurs, including advice on business planning.

Global Entrepreneurship Institute
www.gcase.org
The site sponsored by this nonprofit, nongovernmental organization provides open source material for entrepreneurs and managers of small businesses, and includes articles and book lists.

ORGANIZATIONS
Kauffman Center for Entrepreneurial Leadership
Ewing Marion Kauffman Foundation, 4801 Rockhill Road, Kansas City, Missouri, 64110–2046
T: +1 816 932 1000
E: *info@emkf.org*
www.emkf.org
The Kauffman Center promotes entrepreneurship in the United States through education, training, research, and a program of grants. The Center is involved in a wide range of initiatives to develop the concepts and skills of entrepreneurship in young people, and to promote the contribution entrepreneurship can make to community and economic development.

National Business Incubation Association
20 E Circle Drive, Suite 90, Athens, Ohio, 45701–3571
T: +1 740 593 4331
F: +1 740 593 1996
E: *info@nbia.org*
www.nbia.org
The NBIA provides information, education, advocacy, and networking opportunities for those involved or interested in business incubation programs. The organization conducts research, produces statistics and publications on this subject, and runs a referral service. Members include directors of incubator firms, business advisers, consultants, and investors.

National Commission on Entrepreneurship
Suite 399, 444 North Capital Street, Washington, D.C., 20001
T: +1 202 434 8060
F: +1 202 434 8065
E: *ncoe@sso.org*
www.ncoe.org
The NCOE was founded in 1999 to help leaders at local, state, and national level to formulate and implement policies designed to develop and expand an entrepreneurial economy and culture. The organization has a strong focus on the role of entrepreneurship in the national economy, and conducts research in this area.

SEE ALSO
Small and Growing Businesses (p. 422)
Venture Capital (p. 495)

Exporting

BOOKS AND DIRECTORIES

Building an Import/Export Business 3rd ed.
Kenneth D. Weiss
New York: John Wiley, 2002
320pp ISBN: 0471202495
This is a user-friendly guide to starting and building a successful import or export business. It gives guidance on potential areas of concern, such as operational procedures, trade agreements, and marketing techniques. It also provides practical advice on how best to tap into the lucrative global markets. It includes bibliographical references and an index.

Dun and Bradstreet's Guide to Doing Business Around the World
Terri Morrison, et al.
Paramus, New Jersey: Prentice Hall, 2001
527pp ISBN: 0735201080
This is a guide to business success abroad. Covering 40 countries, it provides an insight into the economic, political, and cultural issues of which it is important to be aware for successful overseas trade. The book combines up-to-date export information and risk profiles with data on the cultural aspects of doing business internationally. It includes bibliographical references and an index.

Export Savvy: From Basics to Strategy
Zak Karamally
New York: International Business Press/The Haworth Press, 1998
198pp ISBN: 0789005778
This book deals with export management from the concepts of international trade to the key elements that influence and comprise its effectiveness. It relates the export experience to the commercial experience as a whole. This involves breaking down the complicated process of exporting into simple and familiar terms. It includes bibliographical references and an index.

Global Jumpstart: The Complete Resource for Expanding Small and Midsized Businesses
Ruth Stanat, Chris West
Cambridge, Massachusetts: Perseus, 2000
198pp ISBN: 073820160X
This book is a useful resource guide for companies of the size mentioned in the title who have reached any stage of the expansion process. It provides in-depth analysis of business opportunities around the world, while also giving a valuable insight into the pitfalls in international markets for small companies.

Principles of Management in Export
James Conlan
Cambridge, Massachusetts: Blackwell Business, 1994
325pp (Principles of Export Guidebooks)
ISBN: 0631191941
Using the syllabus of the Institute of Export as a basis, the author shows how all areas of export practice can be integrated. The emphasis is on profitable export management, covering the core topics of running and structuring an export business, and including all the necessary techniques, and measuring and benchmarking systems for assessing profitability, setting strategic goals, and creating quantifiable reporting and control systems.

The Ultimate Guide to Export Management
Thomas Cook
New York: AMACOM, 2001
569pp ISBN: 0814405819
This step-by-step manual advises businesspeople on how to successfully navigate the highly complicated exporting arena. It covers all the fundamental skills and knowledge needed to participate in international business. It includes bibliographical references and an index.

WEB SITES
American Countertrade Association
www.countertrade.org

The objects of the American Countertrade Association are to promote trade and commerce between companies and their foreign customers who engage in countertrade as a form of doing business.

Business Advice Online
www.businesslink.org
This is an online service provided by the Small Business Service of the U.K. Department of Trade and Industry. It provides an extensive range of general information for small businesses as well as details of the services available through the network of 150 local Business Links. The latter provide face-to-face advice on exporting and importing for small businesses.

Customs & Border Protection, U.S. Department of Homeland Security
www.customs.gov/xp/cgov/export
This site has information regarding exporting from the United States. Features include a list of export requirements and licenses, information about blocked or denied persons, fees, and links to other government sites.

Exportinfo.org
www.exportinfo.org
Produced by students at the University of Washington Business School, exportinfo.org provides basic information for anyone new to the exportation process.

Market Access Database
www.mkaccdb.eu.int
The Market Access Database is provided by the DG Trade, European Commission. Certain parts of the site are open only to people having an ISP connection located in Europe but the section on trade barriers is open to all Internet users. The site contains details about trade barriers by market sector and country, import formalities by country and import duties by product code and by country.

Thomas Global Register
www.tgrnet.com
Formerly the American Export Register, this comprehensive Web-based directory run by Thomas Publishing gives details of some 500,000 manufacturers and distributors across 22 countries, divided into 10,500 product and service classifications.

Trade Information Center
www.trade.gov/td/tic
The Trade Information Center (TIC) is a comprehensive resource for information and advice on all U.S. Federal Government export assistance programs. It is operated by the International Trade Administration of the U.S. Department of Commerce for the 20 federal agencies comprising the Trade Promotion Coordinating Committee (TPCC). These agencies are responsible for managing the U.S. Government's export promotion programs and activities.

ORGANIZATIONS
Bureau of Export Administration, U.S. Department of Commerce
Room 3895, Washington, D.C., 20230
T: +1 202 482 0097
F: +1 202 482 2421
www.bxa.doc.gov
The Bureau of Export Administration (BXA) is concerned with advancing U.S. national security, foreign policy, and economic interests. Its key activities include regulating the export of sensitive goods and technologies in an effective and efficient manner, cooperating with and assisting other countries on export control and strategic trade issues, and promoting federal initiatives and public-private partnerships across industry sectors to protect national infrastructures.

Federation of International Trade Associations
11800 Sunrise Valley Drive, Suite 210, Reston, Virginia, 20190
T: +1 800 969 3482
F: +1 703 620 4922
www.fita.org
The Federation fosters international trade by strengthening the role of local, regional, and national associations throughout the

United States, Mexico, and Canada. Its Web site includes a directory of 3,000 Trade and Import/Export Web sites.

International Trade Administration, U.S. Department of Commerce
1401 Constitution Avenue, Room 3414, Washington, D.C., 20230
T: +1 202 482 3809
F: +1 282 482 5819
www.ita.doc.gov

This organization is the lead unit for trade in the Department of Commerce. It participates in formulating and implementing U.S. foreign trade and economic policies, and monitors market access and compliance of U.S. international trade agreements.

SEE ALSO
Importing (p. 458)

Franchising

BOOKS AND DIRECTORIES
Franchise Bible: How to Buy a Franchise or Franchise Your Own Business 4th ed.
Erwin J. Keup
Central Point, Oregon: PSI Research—Oasis Press, 2000
314pp ISBN: 1555715265
This practical guide to franchising includes sample documents and checklists aimed at helping newcomers to this form of business by providing discussion of the kinds of agreements involved, the advantages and disadvantages of franchising, how to rate potential opportunities, and how to decide if this is the right road to success for them.

The Franchise Bible: How to Buy a Franchise or Franchise Your Own Business
Erwin J. Keup
Waterloo, Ontario: Entrepreneur Press, 2000
314pp ISBN: 1555715265
Aimed at both existing and prospective franchisers, this book offers practical information on what franchising entails and the benefits it can offer. Checklists and worksheets are included.

Franchise Opportunities Guide Spring/ Summer 2001 ed.
International Franchise Association
Washington, D.C.: International Franchise Association, 2001
301pp ISBN: 9991791302

This directory provides a comprehensive listing of franchise companies.

Franchising & Licensing: Two Ways to Build Your Business 2nd ed.
Andrew J. Sherman
New York: AMACOM, 1999
449pp ISBN: 0814404502
The second edition of a guide to franchising as a growth strategy for business, this book is geared to help those who decide to franchise or leverage intellectual property in order to expand their market share while avoiding pitfalls such as disputes with franchisees. It explores the legal, operational, and management issues that arise when developing partnering relationships.

Franchising for Dummies
Michael Seid, Dave Thomas
New York: Hungry Minds, 2000
378pp ISBN: 0764551604
A simple-to-follow but detailed guide to entering the world of franchises, this volume presents the basics, ranging from initial research, selecting locations, training employees, and running and growing the business. One of the authors is the late Dave Thomas, founder of the ultra-successful *Wendy's International*; the other is a consultant with more than 20 years of hands-on experience. Their book provides practical advice on the major issues facing those who decide to follow this route to self-employment.

Tips and Traps When Buying a Franchise 2nd ed.

Mary E. Tomzack

Oakland, California: Source Book Publications, 1999

236pp ISBN: 1887137122

The second, revised edition of this guide provides those new to franchising with information on the right questions to ask at the outset, how to find the right location, where to get loans, how to find and train employees, and the ins and outs of buying equipment. It contains war stories and success secrets from a wide variety of franchisees.

WEB SITES

Entrepreneur
www.entrepreneur.com

This site is a good source of information for those interested in going into business for themselves, with an informative page on franchising as well as pages covering management and marketing.

Franchise.com—The Name Says It All
www.franchise.com

Built for both franchisers and franchisees, this site has information on a broad range of topics and includes tools such as an alphabetical directory, newsletter, global search, industry events, and research.

Franchise Handbook: Online
www.franchise1.com

This online directory provides comprehensive information about franchising opportunities and franchising companies. All contact information is provided as well as a description of the operation, franchising fee, capital requirements, and financing options. The site also contains franchise industry news, trade show information, a list of franchises for sale, and links to other franchise resources.

Franchising.org
www.franchising.org

This is a useful site with links to many other franchise organizations. Articles, advice, and information are also provided.

Franinfo
www.franinfo.com

This site provides an overview of franchising as well as advice and guidance. It contains two self-tests to determine whether you are suited to being a franchisee.

International Franchising
www.franchiseintl.com

This is a guide to international franchising and offers detailed profiles of a number of franchisers.

Nolo-Law for All
www.nolo.com

This is a good source of legal information, some of which is specifically related to franchising.

Small Business Administration
www.sba.gov

This U.S. government site provides information about resources available to those who need help with their entrepreneurial efforts, including finding financing and locating workshops and training.

World Franchising—The Definitive Guide to the World of Franchising
www.worldfranchising.com

This directory has links to over 1,100 franchises in North America and is kept up-to-date with the franchise field.

ORGANIZATIONS

American Association of Franchisees and Dealers

P.O. Box 81887, San Diego, California, 92138–1887

T: +1 800 733 9858
F: +1 619 209 3777
E: benefits@aafd.org
www.aafd.org

The Association is a nonprofit trade organization representing the rights of independent dealers and franchisees in the United States. It provides guidance and advice on how to take out a franchise.

International Franchise Association
1350 New York Avenue NW, Suite 900,
Washington, D.C., 20005–4709
T: +1 202 628 8000
F: +1 202 628 0812
E: *ifa@franchise.org*
www.franchise.org
The IFA is a membership organization
with a heavy bias toward American

franchisers, franchisees, and suppliers,
although other countries are represented.
It is a useful contact for existing or
prospective franchisers and
franchisees.

SEE ALSO
Small and Growing Businesses (p. 422)

Health

BOOKS AND DIRECTORIES
Market-Driven Healthcare: Who Wins, Who Loses in the Transformation of America's Largest Service Industry
Regina E. Herzlinger
Cambridge, Massachusetts: Perseus, 1999
416pp ISBN: 0738201367
As the Nancy R. McPherson Professor of
Business Administration at Harvard
Business School and a researcher and
analyst in the healthcare industry for
twenty-five years, Herzlinger provides deep
insight into the revolution in healthcare in
America. The book examines the reasons
why some providers succeed while others
fail in this field, the largest of the U.S.
service industries.

Med Inc.: How Consolidation Is Shaping Tomorrow's Healthcare System
Sandy Lutz, et al.
San Francisco, California: Jossey-Bass, 1998
1,992pp ISBN: 0787940402
The authors outline the four factors that are
catalyzing the rapid, turbulent consolidation
affecting the entire healthcare industry and
resulting in new corporate medical giants.
The factors include managing capital,
information, risk, and government
regulation. The authors conclude that this
climate for consolidation points toward a
future in which this is the norm.

New Frontiers in Healthcare Management: MBAs Evolving in the Business of Healthcare
Deborah Shlian, Clint Patterson

Lincoln, Nebraska: iUniverse, 2001
172pp ISBN: 0595174353
Where best to learn the ropes of healthcare
management but directly from working
healthcare managers? This book features
the collective insight of fifteen healthcare
managers in a wide variety of roles and
organizations, ranging from managed care
administrators to entrepreneurs,
consultants, and healthcare IT executives.
The book discusses the value of an MBA to
healthcare management and is particularly
helpful for those considering a career in
this field.

WEB SITES
The Academy for Healthcare Management
www.academyforhealthcare.com
This commercial site offers educational
programs in healthcare management for
personnel at all levels of the healthcare
industry. The site also provides an
extensive free glossary of managed care
terms, which is a great quick reference
resource

Healthcare and Information Management Systems Society
www.himss.org/templates/index.asp
This highly targeted site offers industry
news, online courses, a conference
calendar, books and media, surveys, a
product and service marketplace, and other
resources for the healthcare IT
professional.

Importing

BOOKS AND DIRECTORIES
Building an Import/Export Business 3rd ed.
Kenneth D. Weiss
New York: John Wiley, 2002
320pp ISBN: 0471202495
This is a user-friendly guide to starting and building a successful import or export business. It gives guidance on potential areas of concern, such as operational procedures, trade agreements, and marketing techniques. It also provides practical advice on how best to tap into the lucrative global markets. It includes bibliographical references and an index.

Import/Export: How to Get Started in International Trade 3rd ed.
Carl A. Nelson
New York: McGraw-Hill, 2000
340pp ISBN: 0071358714
This book is aimed at those wanting to make a start in international trade. Fully revised and including a section on e-commerce, it sets out to guide beginners through the myriad challenges of importing and exporting.

WEB SITES
Business Advice Online
www.businesslink.org
This is an online service provided by the Small Business Service of the U.K. Department of Trade and Industry. It provides an extensive range of general information for small businesses as well as details of the services available through the network of 150 local Business Links. The latter provide face-to-face advice on exporting and importing for small businesses.

Kelly's Directory
www.kellys.co.uk
This online searchable database lists over 140,000 U.K. manufacturers and service organizations under 50,000 product headings. A print media version of the database may also be purchased.

Kompass
www.kompass.com
This online searchable database lists some 1.6 million companies in about 70 countries under approximately 50,000 product/service codes. The databases for individual countries may also be purchased in printed format.

Market Access Database
www.mkaccdb.eu.int
The Market Access Database is provided by the DG Trade, European Commission. Certain parts of the site are open only to people having an ISP connection located in Europe but the section on trade barriers is open to all Internet users. The site contains details about trade barriers by market sector and country, import formalities by country, and import duties by product code and by country.

Thomas Global Register
www.tgrnet.com
Formerly the American Export Register, this comprehensive Web-based directory run by Thomas Publishing gives details of some 500,000 manufacturers and distributors across 22 countries, divided into 10,500 product and service classifications.

Thomas Register of American Manufacturers
www.thomasregister.com
This online searchable database includes about 168,000 American and Canadian manufacturing companies whose products are classified in about 63,000 product categories and about 135,000 brand names.

ORGANIZATIONS

American Association of Exporters and Importers

7th Floor, P.O. Box 7813, Washington, D.C., 20044–7813

T: +1 202 661 2181

F: +1 202 661 2185

E: *hq@aaei.org*

www.aaei.org

The AAEI is a trade association promoting fair and open trade for the benefit of its members and has close links with all relevant U.S. government departments and regulatory bodies. It publishes a Web-based newsletter giving details of trade matters of interest to members.

Bolero International

T: +1 212 735 0002

www.bolero.net

With offices in New York, London, Hong Kong, Tokyo, Johannesburg, Santiago, Dubai, and Amman, bolero.net offers an XML Web-based electronic document transfer system. Four grades of membership are available for global, large, medium, and small exporters/importers.

SEE ALSO

Exporting (p. 453)

Intellectual Property

BOOKS AND DIRECTORIES

Copyright Theft

John Gurnsey

Burlington, Vermont: Ashgate Publishing Company, 1995

208pp ISBN: 0566076314

Gurnsey's book attempts to cover all forms of copyright theft. It reviews both commercial and domestic theft, incorporating the experiences of a wide range of organizations. Book, electronic, database, audio, video, games, and multimedia publishing are all considered, as is the question of whether existing laws can effectively serve a rapidly changing industry.

From Ideas to Assets: Investing Wisely in Intellectual Property

Bruce M. Berman, ed.

New York: John Wiley, 2001

624pp ISBN: 0471400688

Based on the experience of expert contributors, the book argues that corporations need to understand what their intellectual property assets are and how to protect their rights to them. It covers such topics as maximizing returns on intellectual property assets, valuing those assets, and discerning performance variables.

Patent It Yourself 9th ed.

David Pressman

Berkeley, California: Nolo Press, 2002

512pp ISBN: 0873378016

As an experienced patent attorney and former patent examiner of the U.S. Patent and Trademark Office (PTO), David Pressman has developed a very useful guide containing all the instructions and forms necessary to patent an invention in the United States. The book offers comprehensive and up-to-date advice for obtaining a high quality patent and presents the information in a user-friendly, jargon-free, and well-illustrated way.

Protecting Your #1 Asset: Creating Fortunes from Your Ideas: An Intellectual Property Handbook

Michael A. Lechter

New York: Warner Books, 2001

276pp ISBN: 0446678317

Placing its emphasis on protecting intellectual property (IP), this book makes the case for understanding developments in this arena. It covers topics including identifying and benefiting from IP assets, using IP assets to build barriers to competition, licensing IP assets, and using IP assets to raise capital.

Understanding Copyright in a Week
Graham Cornish
London: Hodder & Stoughton, 2000
96pp (Business in a Week Series)
ISBN: 0340782412
This introductory text will help you understand what copyright is, why it is important to respect it, and how you can make use of copyright law in business, management, and everyday life.

WEB SITES
Copyright and Fair Use: Stanford University Libraries
http://fairuse.stanford.edu
The site provides a quick search facility and overview of copyright law, with links to Internet resources, current legislation, cases, judicial opinions, regulations, treaties, and conventions.

Copyright Clearance Center
www.copyright.com
Copyright Clearance Center, Inc., the largest licenser of text reproduction rights in the world, was formed in 1978 to facilitate compliance with U.S. copyright law. It provides licensing systems for the reproduction and distribution of copyrighted materials in print and electronic formats throughout the world.

The Copyright Licensing Agency
www.cla.co.uk
The Agency is the United Kingdom's reproduction rights organization—the U.K. equivalent of the U.S. Copyright Clearance Center.

Franklin Pierce Law Center
www.fplc.edu
Sponsored by a law school, the site offers an extensive list of articles relating to intellectual property.

Intellectual Property
www.intellectual-property.gov.uk
This site gives information and advice on patents, trademarks, design, and copyright with links to the relevant government departments. It also addresses key questions on protection, permissions, and enforcing rights.

International Intellectual Property Alliance
www.iipa.com
Sponsored by a private-sector coalition formed to protect U.S. copyrighted material around the world, the site offers articles on a variety of IP topics and country-specific copyright information.

U.K. Patent Office
www.patent.gov.uk
The Web site of the U.K. government department responsible for intellectual property—copyright, patents, designs, and trademarks—has a section of links to government, academic, and general IP sites.

United States Copyright Office
www.loc.gov/copyright
The U.S. Copyright Office is located in the Library of Congress. The site has a section for FAQs and another for requests relating to the Freedom of Information Act, besides material on copyright legislation and an international section with links to the WIPO.

United States Patent and Trademark Office
www.uspto.gov
The PTO promotes industrial and technological progress in the United States and strengthens the national economy by administering the laws relating to patents and trademarks, and advising the U.S. government on patent, trademark, and copyright protection, and on trade related aspects of intellectual property.

World Intellectual Property Organization
www.wipo.org
WIPO is a Geneva-based specialized agency of the United Nations whose mandate is to promote the protection of intellectual property worldwide. It administers 21 treaties in the field of intellectual property—15 covering industrial property and six covering copyright. The first general group of treaties defines internationally agreed basic standards of intellectual property in each of the 177 member states.

ORGANIZATIONS
American Intellectual Property Law Association (AIPLA)
2001 Jefferson Davis Highway, Suite 203, Arlington, Virginia, 22202
T: +1 703 415 0780
F: +1 703 415 0786
E: *aipla@aipla.org*
www.aipla.org
Founded in 1897 and having more than 13,000 members, this association is comprised of national bar association lawyers practicing in the fields of patents, trademarks, and copyrights. AIPLA works to promote the improvement of U.S. intellectual property systems.

Intellectual Property Owners Association (IPO)
1255 23rd St. NW, Suite 200, Washington, D.C., 20037
T: +1 202 466 2396
F: +1 202 466 2893
E: *info@ipo.org*

www.ipo.org
This group is comprised of over 400 major corporations and lawyers that work with intellectual property issues and concerns. The IPO works to support and strengthen the patent, trademark, copyright, and trade secret laws of the United States. The IPO also monitors legislative activities.

National Council of Intellectual Property Law Associations (NCIPLA)
1255 23rd St. NW, Suite 200, Washington, D.C., 20037
T: +1 202 466 2396
F: +1 202 466 2893
E: *ncipla@ncipla.org*
www.ncipla.org
NCIPLA is an association representing state and local patent law associations. The Council seeks to inform member associations of the latest changes in patent, trademark, and copyright legislation.

Logistics and Distribution

BOOKS AND DIRECTORIES
Fundamentals of Logistics
Douglas M. Lambert, James R. Stock, Lisa M. Ellram
New York: McGraw-Hill, 1997
640pp ISBN: 0256141177
This book offers a unique take on the area of logistics, approaching the topic from both a marketing and customer service perspective. The text emphasizes concept and context over actual system design proposals. The book is considered noteworthy for its insistence that logistics is much more than solving transportation problems—it is a fully integrated science demanding customer service and internal organizational attention.

The Handbook of Logistics and Distribution Management 2nd ed.
Alan Rushton, John Oxley, Phil Croucher
Dover, New Hampshire: Kogan Page, 2000
582pp ISBN: 0749433655

Written to appeal to both students and experienced managers, this handbook explains the basics of modern logistics and distribution. The authors explain the fundamental concepts of logistics and include discussions of warehousing, transportation, and information and control systems.

A Practical Guide to Transportation and Logistics
Michael B. Stroh
Dumont, New Jersey: The Logistics Network, 2001
184pp ISBN: 0970811500
This book provides the logistics manager with a guide to purchasing, traffic and transportation, warehousing, and inventory control. It includes a long chapter on computers with discussion of various software packages.

WEB SITES

Digital Neighbors
www.digital-neighbors.com/news/industry/logistics.htm
This Web site is updated regularly throughout the day. It focuses on logistics industry news, cataloging logistics news from the United States as well as stories of international interest. The site is searchable by city, country, and industry, so any specific questions about logistics capacity in certain regions can generally be answered in a timely way.

The Logistics Network
www.logisticsnetwork.com
This site offers information for the logistics manager, including a discussion forum, news, employment information, and recommended readings.

Logistics World
www.logisticsworld.com
This site provides a directory of logistics resources, including subsites devoted to freight, transportation, supply chain management, warehousing, and distribution. It is also home of the WWW Virtual Library of Logistics.

Loglink
www.loglink.com
This is a gateway Web site featuring hundreds of links to providers of logistics support, from freight, air, and rail transport, to straight logistics, providers of logistical software, and warehousing and distribution services.

ORGANIZATIONS

American Purchasing Society (APS)
N. Island Center, Suite 203, 8 E. Galena Boulevard, Aurora, Illinois, 60506
T: +1 630 859 0250
F: +1 630 859 0270
E: *propurch@aol.com*
www.american-purchasing.com
This organization certifies qualified purchasing personnel. The APS conducts research and compiles business statistical data, including tracking salary surveys. APS can also provide consulting services for materials management.

National Association of Purchasing Management (NAPM)
2055 E. Centennial Cir., P.O. Box 22160, Tempe, Arizona, 85285
T: +1 480 752 6276 or 800 888 6276
F: +1 480 752 7890
E: *rlatondr@napm.org*
www.napm.org
The more than 46,000 members of this association are supply management personnel involved in industrial, commercial, and utility firms. NAPM members work to develop efficient supply management.

Procurement and Supply Chain Benchmarking Association (PASBA)
4606 FM 1960 W, Suite 250, Houston, Texas, 77069
T: +1 281 440 5044
F: +1 281 440 6677
E: *info@pasba.com*
www.pasba.com
Founded in 1998 and with over 800 members, this association targets the procurement and supply chain managers of corporations with an interest in benchmarking. PASBA promotes the use of benchmarking to improve corporate efficiency and profitability.

Management Buyouts

BOOKS AND DIRECTORIES
The Art of M&A: A Merger Acquisition Buyout Guide
Stanley Foster Reed, Alexandra Reed Lajoux

New York: McGraw-Hill, 1999
1011pp ISBN: 0070526605
Presented in a question-and-answer format, this book looks at over 1,000

aspects of mergers, acquisitions, and buyouts. Questions covered range from locating a suitable target to closing and post-merger integration. The book gives real-world insights through synopses of dozens of landmark cases and includes sample forms and checklists.

Buyout: The Insider's Guide to Buying Your Own Company

Rick Rickersten, et al.
New York: AMACOM, 2001
304pp ISBN: 0814406262
This book gives you the tools and strategies you need to lead a successful management buyout. It includes everything from how to select the company you want to buy, through due diligence issues and finding equity partners, to running the company when you succeed in your buyout.

Management Buyout: A Guide for the Prospective Entrepreneur 2nd ed.

Ian Webb
Burlington, Vermont: Ashgate Publishing Company, 1990
176pp ISBN: 0566028107
This book provides an introduction to the process of achieving a successful buyout and considers the financial and legal issues involved. It reviews the development of the buyout market in the United Kingdom and considers the relevance of an entrepreneurial mindset to buyout situations. Five case studies are included.

Management Buyouts: Directors and Buy-out Opportunities

Tom Nash, ed.
Dover, New Hampshire: Kogan Page, 1998
84pp (Directors' Guide)
ISBN: 0749428287
In this comprehensive guide to management buyouts aimed at directors and senior managers, experienced managers give their views of the complexities and pitfalls on buying out a firm. The topics covered include: choosing a venture capital partner; buyouts and the law; knowing your banker; tax issues; and aftercare.

Successful Acquisition of Unquoted Companies: A Practical Guide 4th ed.

Barrie Pearson
Brookfield, Vermont: Gower, 1999
168pp ISBN: 0566080990
This practical guide is designed to help anyone who undertakes the acquisition of an unquoted company or a subsidiary of a quoted one. It explains the process of investigating a potential acquisition, and a checklist is provided. Management buyouts and buyins and the process of selling a business to maximize shareholder value are also covered.

WEB SITES

Are You Management Buyout Material?
www.cfo.com/Article?article=2117
Management buyouts are not for everyone. It takes the right team with appropriate backing. This checklist can help you determine whether you have what it takes to be successful.

Is a Management Buyout in Your Future?
**www.imakenews.com/rcwmirus/
e_article000017429.cfm**
This article from the Mirus Online Newsletter describes management buyouts and identifies the characteristics of typical candidate companies. It outlines what each side is looking for and presents financing options that can be used.

Orchestrating a Management Buyout
**www.southflorida.bizjournals.com/
milwaukee/stories/1996/12/09/
focus1.html**
Describing the management buyout experience as a roller coaster ride, this article points out that perseverance is often a key element in completing the buyout successfully. It provides real-world examples of how obstacles can be overcome.

Survey of the Economic and Social Impact of Management Buyouts and Buyins in Europe
**www.pwcglobal.com/fr/pwc_pdf/
pwc_economic_impact_of_buyouts.pdf**
This site contains the full text of a report based on a pan-European survey conducted

by the Centre for Management Buy-Out Research (CMBOR) on behalf of the European Private Equity and Venture Capital Association.

ORGANIZATIONS
Business Valuation Research, Inc.
1800 Century Park East, Suite 665,
Los Angeles, California 90067
T: +1 310 788 9092
Toll Free: +1 888 248 9092
F: +1 310 788 9040
www.business-value.com

In operation for more than 40 years, BVRI has experience valuing a wide variety of businesses, from corporations to limited liability companies. The company matches or exceeds report requirements for the Uniform Standards of Professional Appraisal Practice, and services extend from valuations to appraisal reviews.

SEE ALSO
Venture Capital (p. 495)

Marketing Management

BOOKS AND DIRECTORIES
The 22 Immutable Laws of Marketing: Violate Them at Your Own Risk!
Al Ries, Jack Trout
New York: HarperCollins, 1993
132pp ISBN: 0887306667
Designed by marketing strategists for marketing strategists, this illustrated book contains 22 practical rules aimed at promoting the readers' success in global marketing.

101 Ways to Market Your Business
Andrew Griffiths
Crow's Nest, New South Wales: Allen & Unwin, 2001
272pp ISBN: 1865083860
This book contains more than 101 practical marketing plans for promoting any size or type of business. With suggestions of ways to attract new customers—and keep them—and how to develop a strong corporate image, the book also features quick marketing strategies that take less than 30 minutes. Managers are encouraged to put into practice one of these strategies every week, thus greatly increasing the potential for more business and higher profits.

The Anatomy of Buzz: Creating Word of Mouth Marketing
Emanuel Rosen
New York: HarperCollins, 2001
320pp ISBN: 0006531601

Rosen discusses the benefits of "word of mouth" marketing, and explores the capacity of large companies to exploit this strategy.

Auditing Markets, Products and Marketing Plans
David Parmerlee
Lincolnwood, Illinois: McGraw-Hill Trade, 2000
240pp ISBN: 0658001337
A source of information and ideas for anyone who is building an effective marketing campaign or interested in improving existing marketing activities. This book provides you with the tools you need for every critical task—checklists, document templates, forms and tables—to enable you to complete those tasks quickly and effectively. Perfect for beginning marketers, small business owners, and entrepreneurs.

The End of Marketing As We Know It
Sergio Zyman
New York: HarperCollins, 1999
272pp ISBN: 0887309860
In this title, the author argues that for marketing to be truly efficient, it must sell the product and not merely focus on advertising image. The book contains several stories concerning campaigns at Coca-Cola, where Zyman was chief marketing officer.

Getting Business to Come to You
Douglas Edwards
New York: J P Tarcher, 1998
686pp ISBN: 087477845X
A popular book aimed at helping businesses expand their customer base. Although written from a U.S. perspective, the tips and examples offered work well wherever your business is located.

Gonzo Marketing: Winning through Worst Practices
Christopher Locke
Cambridge, Massachusetts: Capstone Publishing / Perseus, 2001
256pp ISBN: 0738204080
This book is a knuckle-whitening ride to the place where social criticism, biting satire, and serious commerce meet . . . and where the outdated ideals of mass marketing and broadcast media are being left in the dust. As master of ceremonies at the wake for traditional one-size-fits-all marketing, Locke has assembled a unique guest list, from Geoffrey Chaucer to Hunter S. Thompson, to guide us through the revolution that is rocking business today, as people connect on the Web to form powerful micromarkets. These networked communities, based on candor, trust, passion, and a general disdain for anything that smacks of corporate smugness, reflect much deeper trends in our culture, which Locke illuminates with his characteristic wit.

Guerrilla Marketing for the Home-Based Business
Jay Conrad Levinson, Seth Godin
Boston, Massachusetts: Houghton Mifflin, 1995
240pp ISBN: 0395742838
From the authors of the acclaimed *Guerilla Marketing*, this book offers advice on the most productive marketing strategies and techniques for home-based businesses. Aimed at anyone thinking of starting a business or those in business already, the book focuses on the importance of customer service, direct mail, word-of-mouth marketing, and positioning.

Guerrilla Marketing with Technology: Unleashing the Full Potential of Your Small Business
Jay Conrad Levinson
Cambridge, Massachusetts: Perseus, 1997
224pp ISBN: 0201328046
A good introduction to the "guerrilla" concept for SMEs, this book takes a simple question and answer approach to implementing innovating and exciting ideas.

Inside the Tornado
Geoffrey A. Moore
New York: HarperCollins, 1999
267pp ISBN: 0887308244
This book addresses the ever-changing face of market-focused business, aiming to highlight the importance of adapting to keep up with competitors. Moore uses examples from inside the industry to discuss a range of managerial strategies, and how they can be usefully applied in today's marketing world.

It's Not About Size: Bigger Brands for Smaller Business
Paul Dickinson
London: Virgin Books, 2001
203pp (Virgin Business Guides)
ISBN: 0753505932
This book aims to address comprehensively the issue of branding and its importance for small businesses. It covers a range of key challenges, including finding out what is best for your customers, which media will get your message across best, how to use advertising to differentiate yourself from your competitors, and how to increase profits through canny branding.

Kotler on Marketing: How to Create, Win, and Dominate Markets
Philip Kotler
New York: Free Press, 1999
257pp ISBN: 0684850338
In this title, Kotler discusses his ideas on how marketing programs should be approached by executives. The book is divided into several sections addressing strategy, tactics, administrative issues, and transformational

marketing. The latter is a term that the author uses to describe the effect of new technology, such as the Internet and cable TV, on marketing practice.

Marketing Plans That Work 2nd ed.

Malcolm H.B. McDonald and Warren Keegan

Woburn, Massachusetts: Butterworth-Heinemann, 2001

264pp ISBN: 0750673079

With discussions of new product development, market extension and diversification strategies, and a step-by-step planning system, this book offers a comprehensive guide to preparing a strategic marketing program.

Marketing Warfare

Al Ries, Jack Trout

New York: McGraw-Hill, 1997

224pp ISBN: 0070527261

A "military" approach to the world of marketing—Ries and Trout aim to teach marketers tough strategies, both defensive and offensive, to deal with the competition.

The Market Planning Guide: Creating a Plan to Successfully Market Your Business, Product or Service 6th ed.

David H. Bangs

Chicago, Illinois: Dearborn Trade Publishing, 2002

256pp ISBN: 0793159717

This book provides the tools for developing an effective marketing strategy for every size of business. This is a user-friendly workbook which helps readers master the basics before applying marketing principles to the marketing plans of actual companies.

Permission Marketing: Turning Strangers into Friends, and Friends into Customers

Seth Godin, Don Peppers

New York: Simon & Schuster, 1999

255pp ISBN: 0684856360

In this title, the authors claim that traditional forms of advertising such as magazines and radio are no longer sufficient in themselves. They assert that what is most important is to find a way of luring the customer into giving some of their time, and then creating a lasting relationship with them. The book backs up this theory concerning permission marketing by discussing the techniques of some of the companies who use it.

Rand McNally 2003 Commercial Atlas and Marketing Guide

Chicago, Illinois: Rand McNally & Co., 2003

ISBN: 0528853341

Containing population, economic, and geographic data for more than 124,000 U.S. places, and large-scale maps that are detailed and thoroughly indexed for easy cross-referencing, this "big book" should be the first point of reference for up-to-date business planning data. The many raw data listings include: 2000 census information and year 2007 projections; latest estimations on population for the U.S. states, counties, cities, MSAs, and trading areas; information on income, buying power, and sales; and corporate economic profiles.

Real Time: Preparing for the Age of the Never Satisfied Customer

Regis McKenna

Boston, Massachusetts: Harvard Business School Press, 1997

224pp ISBN: 0875847943

In this book, McKenna addresses the issue of what customers expect from the modern world. In order to fulfill customer expectations, he argues, companies must be prepared to adapt to the increasingly rapid modes of global communication (e-mail, fax, etc.). McKenna aims to clarify the abstract notion of collecting and using "real time," with the view that this can lead to greater organizational success and consumer satisfaction.

Relationship Marketing: Successful Strategies for the Age of the Customer

Regis McKenna

Cambridge, Massachusetts: Perseus, 1993

242pp ISBN: 0201622408

McKenna focuses on the importance of building strong bonds in the marketing world, in order to gain success and become dominant in the marketplace. He provides industry examples to help outline ways of achieving market ownership.

Selling the Invisible
Harry Beckwith
New York: Warner Books, 1997
252pp ISBN: 0446520942
Selling the Invisible is aimed at marketers who work to promote a service ("the invisible") rather than a tangible product. The book contains a large range of practical suggestions and ideas, addressing some new developments in marketing, and discussing how an organization can use them to best effect.

Successful Direct Marketing Methods 7th ed.
Bob Stone, Ron Jacobs
New York: McGraw-Hill, 2001
608pp ISBN: 0658001450
This newly updated edition provides a classic guide to direct marketing, combining new media with traditional marketing strategies to provide effective direct marketing to consumers. The content includes identifying and meeting consumers' needs, business to business marketing, and e-commerce techniques, such as branding strategies for Internet sites.

Successful Marketing for the Small Business 5th ed.
Dave Patten
Dover, New Hampshire: Kogan Page, 2001
271pp (Business Enterprise Guides)
ISBN: 0749435240
This updated edition of Dave Patten's popular book atempts to show how organizations can benefit from tackling marketing effectively. Aimed at those thinking of starting a business or those running one already, this book is full of practical advice on a range of key issues including advertising, market research, promotion, launches, and exporting.

WEB SITES
American Marketing Association
www.marketingpower.com
The American Marketing Association (AMA) is an international professional organization for people involved in the practice, study, and teaching of marketing. As well as setting industry standards, the AMA seeks to help marketers by providing them with information, products, and services, many of which are available online, including a career center, best practice articles, a marketer's toolkit, and newsletter. Registration is free.

Guerrilla Marketing
www.gmarketing.com
This is the online home of the very successful "Guerrilla Marketing" series of books. Users may subscribe to a free weekly newsletter offering marketing tips.

ORGANIZATIONS
American Advertising Federation
1101 Vermont Avenue NW, Suite 500, Washington D.C., 20005–6306
T: +1 202 898 0089
F: +1 202 898 0159
E: aaf@aaf.org
www.aaf.org
The AAF is a network of advertisers, ad agencies, media companies, local advertising clubs, and college chapters. Membership benefits include a membership directory, networking opportunities, updates on relevant legislation, professional development, and recruitment services.

American Marketing Association
311 S. Wacker Drive, Suite 5800, Chicago, Illinois, 60606–5819
T: +1 312 542 9000
F: +1 312 542 9001
E: info@ama.org
www.marketingpower.com
The American Marketing Association (AMA) has over 40,000 members worldwide, with nearly 400 chapters throughout North America and Canada. It is an international professional organization for people involved in the practice, study, and teaching

of marketing. As well as setting standards of best practice in the industry, the AMA seeks to help marketers by providing them with products, services, information, education, and resources. It has a large, informative Web site and publishes a wide range of journals.

Association of National Advertisers
708 Third Avenue, New York, 10017–4270
T: +1 212 697 5950
F: +1 212 661 8057
E: info@ana.net
www.ana.net
ANA is a trade association dedicated to marketing and brand-building. It offers its members conferences, regional meetings, training seminars, benchmarking studies, industry analysis, research services, and publications.

The Direct Marketing Association
1120 Avenue of the Americas, New York, 10036–6700
T: +1 212 768 7277
F: +1 212 302 6714
E: customerservice@the-dma.org
www.the-dma.org
The DMA is a trade association for businesses interested in direct, database, and interactive global marketing; its members are catalog companies, direct mailers, teleservice firms, and Internet marketers from consumer and business-to-business segments, as well as companies that provide supplies and services to marketers. Its activities include industry promotion, professional development, training, research, conferences, and networking events.

Marketing Research Association
1344 Silas Deane Highway, Suite 306, Rocky Hill, Connecticut, 06067–0230
T: +1 860 257 4008
F: +1 860 257 3990
E: email@mra-net.org
www.mra-net.org

MRA is a membership organization for the marketing research industry; its members include data collectors, full service research companies, users of research, and related service providers. Membership benefits include educational programs, training, networking opportunities, publications, and conferences.

Marketing Science Institute
1000 Massachusetts Avenue, Cambridge, Massachusetts, 02138–5396
T: +1 617 491 2060
F: +1 617 491 2065
E: msi@msi.org
www.msi.org
The MSI is a nonprofit institute, established in 1961 as a bridge between business and academia. Its mission is to support and circulate studies by academic scholars that address research issues specified by member companies. MSI functions as a working sponsorship and brings executives and leading international researchers together.

Society of Competitive Intelligence Professionals
1700 Diagonal Road, Suite 600, Alexandria, Virginia, 22314
T: +1 703 739 0696
F: +1 703 739 2524
E: info@scip.org
www.scip.org
SCIP is a nonprofit membership organization for professionals in the competitive intelligence industry. In addition to advocating ethical standards for the industry, SCIP provides seminars, networking opportunities, and publications.

SEE ALSO
Advertising (p. 430)
Direct Marketing (p. 443)
Market Research and Competitor Intelligence (p. 469)
Public Relations (p. 485)
Selling and Salesmanship (p. 490)

Market Research and Competitor Intelligence

BOOKS AND DIRECTORIES

Hearing the Voice of the Market
Vincent P. Barabba, Gerald Zaltman
Boston, Massachusetts: Harvard Business School Press, 1991
250pp ISBN: 0875842410
Aimed at managers within the organization the book functions as a plan to help increase and improve their use of market information. Managers and researchers cited in the book contribute personal insights into the subject matter. Aims to teach readers how to make informed and successful decisions in the market-based environment.

Managing Frontiers in Competitive Intelligence
Craig S. Fleisher, David Blenkhorn
Westport, Connecticut: Quorum Books, 2000
328pp ISBN: 1567203841
This book is a nice balance of the theoretical and the practical aspects of Competitive Intelligence (CI). While describing the best practices in the industry, the authors present the steps necessary to counter CI. They provide information on how to improve your intelligence collection process, methods, and tools. Significantly, they tie CI back to the needs of the business and point out its interface with finance, research and development, and product development.

Marketing Research 7th ed.
David A. Aaker, V. Kumar, George S. Day
New York: John Wiley, 2000
552pp ISBN: 0471363405
This text adopts a "macro-micro-macro" approach toward marketing research and its uses within organizations. The authors initially explore the uses and place of marketing research in managerial decision making, as well as the industry itself (briefly examining both suppliers and users) at macro-level. The authors also examine the processes of marketing research in more depth, including industry examples to fulfill the micro phase of the text. Provides coverage of the most recent research techniques.

The Marketing Research Toolbox: A Concise Guide for Beginners
Edward F. McQuarrie
New York: Sage Publications, Inc., 1996
176pp ISBN: 0803958579
Aimed at giving a basic understanding of market research tools, this book looks at market research in the context of making a business decision. Beginning with an explanation of market research, the author goes on to describe how each of the six traditional market research techniques works, along with its costs, uses, and tips for success. Also examined are the nontraditional methods that have evolved in recent years.

Market Research Matters: Tools and Techniques for Aligning Your Business
Robert Duboff, Jim Spaeth
New York: John Wiley, 2000
320pp ISBN: 0471360058
The authors explain the value of market research and forecasting techniques to successful business strategies. They describe the tools and techniques that enable analysts to anticipate marketplace shifts and the methods of using them. Among other topics, they discuss customer loyalty, brand management, competition, distribution channels, employee performance and loyalty, and the Internet. Diagnostic material to allow readers to assess the progress of their business in each area is also included.

Market Research Using Forecasting in Business
Peter Clifton, Hai Hguyen, Susan Nutt
Woburn, Massachusetts: Butterworth-Heinemann, 1992
294pp ISBN: 0750601531

The book is written from the viewpoint of people who are responsible for forecasting business results in large companies on the marketing side. It indicates the resources available to in-house forecasters, such as company sales figures and collections of industry statistics, and provides a comprehensive guide to the tools of analysis and statistics. Above all, it stresses the role of the analyst as a supporter of the entrepreneur in the tasks of fostering growth in new or unfamiliar areas and effectively exploiting new opportunities when they are offered.

Measuring the Effectiveness of Competitive Intelligence
Jan P. Herring
Alexandria, Virginia: Society of Competitive Intelligence Professionals, 1996
77pp ISBN: 0962124125
Acknowledging the need for companies to measure competitive intelligence, the Society of Competitive Intelligence Professionals (SCIP) has initiated research to evaluate competitive intelligence using Measures of Effectiveness. Herring's report includes a CI Evaluation Process to help pinpoint managerial needs within an organization and advises leaders on pursuing their goals through competitive intelligence, measuring the outcomes and conveying them to the company as a whole.

Millennium Intelligence: Understanding and Conducting Competitive Intelligence in the Digital Age
Jerry P. Miller
Medford, New Jersey: Information Today, 2000
240pp ISBN: 0910965285
Miller assembled a think tank of practicing experts in Competitive Intelligence (CI). Together they lay out the reasons for conducting a planned and thought out CI program for your company. Their book details the skills required, the tools and methods available for gathering and analyzing the information, and the reasons and methods to do so in an ethical and legal manner.

Perfectly Legal Competitor Intelligence: How to Get it, Use it, and Profit from it
Douglas Bernhardt
Upper Saddle River, New Jersey: Financial Times Management, 1994
276pp ISBN: 0273601539
Bernhardt explains how and where to get hold of competitor intelligence and how to use it to your best advantage. He focuses on the range of potential sources of information and collection techniques, the ways of protecting your own company's secrets, organizational issues, competitive benchmarking, and the key role competitive intelligence plays in the strategic process. Case studies are included.

Proven Strategies in Competitive Intelligence: Lessons from the Trenches
John E. Prescott, Stephen H. Miller, eds.
New York: John Wiley, 2001
288pp ISBN: 0471401781
The editors have assembled a collection of articles that identify and explore proven practicable approaches to competitive intelligence that can be applied across a variety of business areas. Once the concept of competitive intelligence has been introduced and its legal and ethical boundaries have been explored, further contributions from leading executives and market leaders highlight the best techniques that can be used to outwit and outperform current, emerging, and potential competitors.

The WarRoom Guide to Competitive Intelligence
Steven M. Shaker, Mark P. Gembicki
New York: McGraw-Hill, 1998
240pp ISBN: 007058057X
This book is written for managers who want to use information more intelligently, with a view to improving corporate strategies. The authors advise business leaders on gathering and analyzing information in order to become more competitive within the industry. Explores ways of creating a "WarRoom" within an individual organization in which to collate information for future use.

WEB SITES
ECNext
www.ecnext.com
This is a site offering online access to a database of business and market intelligence from global publishers.

Esomar Glossary
www.esomar.nl/EGlossary.htm
This glossary of market research terms seeks to explain frequently used marketing research terms in language that someone new to the industry can easily understand.

Euromonitor International
www.euromonitor.com
In-depth strategic analysis and up-to-date market statistics and market reports are all available to purchase online from this site.

Forrester
www.forrester.com
Forrester is a leading independent research firm that conducts technology research for its clients. Its expertise is in analyzing the research results and synthesizing the critical information. Some free information is available to nonclients on its site.

Key Note Market Information Centre
www.keynote.co.uk
This site is run by suppliers of market research reports, which are available for purchase, and provides free executive summaries.

Market Research.com
www.marketresearch.com
Collecting reports from all over the world, marketresearch.com is one of the largest collectors of published research on the Web. Reports can be bought and managed with a personal account, and the site has other features, such as an e-mail update service.

@ResearchInfo.com
www.researchinfo.com
This site is a remarkable collection of information on the market research industry. It includes the Market Research

Roundtable, a directory of research companies, software reviews, and market research calculators.

ORGANIZATIONS
American Marketing Association
311 S. Wacker Drive, Suite 5800, Chicago, Illinois, 60606–5819
T: +1 312 542 9000
F: +1 312 542 9001
E: info@ama.org
www.marketingpower.com
The AMA has over 40,000 members in 82 countries and aims to serve all sectors of the marketing industry. The AMA Publishing Group produces seven journals and magazines, including the Journal of Marketing Research and Marketing Research, both issued quarterly.

Council for Marketing and Opinion Research
4147U Crossgate Drive, Cincinnati, Ohio, 45236
T: +1 513 985 0001
F: +1 513 985 0119
E: info@cmor.org
www.cmor.org
The CMOR is a nonprofit trade association formed to protect the interests of the marketing and opinion research industry. Its members are research companies and their clients.

Marketing Research Association
1344 Silas Deane Highway, Suite 306, P.O. Box 230, Rocky Hill, Connecticut, 06067–0230
T: +1 860 257 4008
F: +1 860 257 3990
E: email@mra-net.org
www.mra-net.org
The MRA, founded in 1954, is dedicated to promoting excellence in opinion and marketing research. It provides training and development opportunities for members and acts as an advocate with government bodies and the public. Its activities include two annual national conferences and the publication of an official monthly newsletter and a directory of research services.

The Society of Competitive Intelligence Professionals
1700 Diagonal Road, Suite 600, Alexandria, Virginia, 22314
T: +1 703 739 0696
F: +1 703 739 2524
E: *info@scip.org*
www.scip.org

The Society is dedicated to helping professionals develop expertise in creating, collecting, and analyzing information, in disseminating competitive intelligence, and in engaging decision makers in a productive dialogue that creates organizational competitive advantage.

Negotiation

BOOKS AND DIRECTORIES

Business Negotiation: A Practical Workbook
Paul T. Steele, Tom Beasor
Brookfield, Vermont: Gower, 1999
270pp ISBN: 0566080729
This practical textbook provides a step-by-step guide to acquiring key negotiating skills and the techniques for using them successfully as well as identifying the key topics in negotiation. Each chapter includes a checklist of the key points made and exercises for applying what has been learned.

Difficult Conversations
Douglas Stone, Bruce Patton, Sheila Heen
New York: Penguin, 2000
272pp ISBN: 014027782X
This book aims to help readers to become calm and assertive in difficult situations (such as asking for a pay rise, or experiencing problems with colleagues). In discussing the different emotions and requirements that arise from such conversations, the book aims to pinpoint ways of managing them more effectively.

Negotiating in a Week
Peter Fleming
London: Hodder & Stoughton, 2003
96pp (In a Week)
ISBN: 0340849541
A revised edition of this popular book, this aid to negotiation aims to provide a framework for successful negotiation. The book includes information on how to research, prepare an argument, summarize, and conclude.

Negotiating Skills
Tim Hindle
New York: Dorling Kindersley, 1998
72pp (Essential Managers)
ISBN: 0751305316
A helpful introduction to the art of negotiation, including information on how to prepare your argument, brief a team, maintain good relations, and close a deal. The book is full of practical advice on how to achieve the best result.

The Negotiation Toolkit: How to Get Exactly What You Want in Any Business or Personal Situation
Roger J. Volkema
New York: AMACOM, 1999
208pp ISBN: 081448008X
This book offers a guide to negations aimed at helping people build the skills and self-confidence to become good negotiators. It explores the golden rule of negotiation, explains when not to negotiate, discusses the issue of tough negotiators and how to deal with them, describes the tactics, skills, and behaviors of star negotiators, looks at cross-cultural negotiations, and provides ways to measure your own skills.

The Power of Nice: How to Negotiate So Everyone Wins—Especially You!
Ronald M. Shapiro, Mark A. Jankowski, James Dale
New York: John Wiley, 2001
304pp ISBN: 0471080721
This book is based on Shapiro's belief that negotiation works best if two negotiators can

build a common bond between them. In exploring this theory, Shapiro offers advice on various types of negotiation, and on creating effective proposals.

WEB SITES
Banta.com—The Negotiation Resource Center
www.banta.com
Created by Eric C. Gould, this site has negotiation tips and analysis, with examples that help make the points more easily understood. Areas include Powerful Tips, Communication, Difficult Negotiations, Training, and a list of the author's favorite resources.

Interneg—For and About Negotiation
http://interneg.org/interneg/links/learning.html
This site is a directory of resources for the negotiation field with links to numerous other sites covering areas from training and teaching materials to games to programs and seminars.

Mediate.com
www.mediate.com
This site provides articles and news on mediation, conflict resolution, and arbitration. It also includes information about training, events, organizations, and academic programs in this field.

The Negotiation Skills Company, Inc.
www.negotiationskills.com
This site is provided by a consulting company that specializes in negotiation training and consultancy. It offers free information and articles, and an occasional newsletter on all aspects of the negotiation process.

ORGANIZATIONS
Institute for Operations Research and the Management Sciences
901 Elkridge Landing Road, Suite 400, Linthicum, Maryland, 21090–2909
T: +1 410 850 0300
F: +1 410 684 2963
E: *informs@informs.org*
www.informs.org
The Institute represents professionals within the operations research and management sciences fields. It has a section dedicated to group decision and negotiation that provides online discussions, organizes conferences, and publishes articles through its journal, *Group Decision and Negotiation*.

National Contract Management Association (NCMA)
1912 Woodford Road, Vienna, Virginia, 22182
T: +1 703 448 9231 or 800 344 8096
F: +1 703 448 0939
E: *massidas@ncmahq.org*
www.ncmahq.org
This Association comprises professionals concerned with all aspects of contract management. Areas of special focus are acquisition, negotiation, and management of contracts. The NCMA also has developed training materials and offers certification in contract management.

SEE ALSO
Pricing (p. 480)

New Product Development

BOOKS AND DIRECTORIES
Developing New Product Concepts
Christopher Miller
Harrisburg, Pennsylvania: Pennsylvania Chamber Educational Foundation, 1999
151pp ISBN: 1929744048

This is a workbook useful for individuals or small groups in the early stages of the development process. It has more than 125 pages of exercises, checklists, fill-in pages, and sample forms to guide you through the practical steps of creative problem solving.

Managing the Design Factory: The Product Developer's Toolkit

Donald Reinertsen

New York: Free Press, 1997

256pp ISBN: 0684839911

This book applies product development principles and integrates them with management theories. In short, it shows how the two sides of the coin must work together for successful product launching. Management theories and principles are not always incorporated well in practice with a design team. Reinertsen has practical ideas about how to make sure the entire creative team is "speaking the same language" as a product launch moves from idea to reality.

Marketing the Unknown: Developing Market Strategies for Technical Innovations

Paul Millier

New York: John Wiley, 1999

248pp ISBN: 0471986216

How do you make a product successful? This is one of the basic questions that this practical book sets out to answer. It also discusses what is the best process to follow, and how you choose or transform markets so as to ensure a successful launch. It paves the way for marketing, for R and D, and for project managers in industrial organizations to launch and market innovations successfully in a very competitive field, and outlines strategies for further development.

Product Development for the Service Sector

Robert G. Cooper, Scott J. Edgett

Cambridge, Massachusetts: Perseus, 1999

288pp ISBN: 0738201057

The book acknowledges the difficulty of service-industry product development in a world where new resources (such as the Internet) are putting pressure on the capacity for original ideas. It offers an outline of major management principles, in which the authors discuss the creation and testing of development models, and their application in any service industry.

Product Juggernauts: How Companies Mobilize to Generate a Stream of Market Winners

Jean-Philippe Deschamps, P. Ranganath Nayak

Boston, Massachusetts: Harvard Business School Press, 1995

472pp ISBN: 0875843417

The authors cite stories from real companies around the world to illustrate guidelines for determining the products customers want and designing the products they want to buy. Examples used to demonstrate the importance of company-wide focus on product include (among others) Ford, Canon, and Toshiba. Using these case studies, the authors demonstrate how organizations can achieve high market performance and improve their current strategies.

Product Leadership: Creating and Launching Superior New Products

Robert G. Cooper

Cambridge, Massachusetts: Perseus, 1999

314pp ISBN: 0738201561

Over a third of new products fail at launch, and many never gain a profitable return. So how do companies like 3M, Merck, and Procter & Gamble continually lead the way with exceptional new products? Cooper reveals the winners' secrets, and offers valuable advice on implementing and overseeing new product processes and strategies, managing product portfolios, determining which products to develop, and fostering ingenuity to outperform the competition.

The Product Manager's Handbook 2nd ed.

Linda Gorchels

New York: McGraw-Hill/NTC, 2000

304pp ISBN: 0658001353

This book focuses on skills acquisition, making it suitable for new product managers or people interested in moving into that line of work. The text is written as an overview and introduction to the skill set necessary for product managers, but segments of the book are also devoted to product development and launch.

Successful Product Development: Speeding from Opportunity to Profit

Milton D. Rosenau, Jr.

New York: John Wiley, 1999

208pp ISBN: 047131532X

This book sets out the process of product development from beginning to end, starting with the formation of ideas and moving through design and engineering to the finished product. It is intended for all practitioners involved with any aspect of developing new products and services.

World-Class New Product Development: Benchmarking Best Practices of Agile Manufacturers

Dan Dimancescu, Kemp Dwenger

New York: AMACOM, 1995

276pp ISBN: 0814403115

Recounting the findings of research, benchmarking, and working with international companies, this book shows how "corporate champions" manage robust product development operations and presents a system to enable other organizations to do the same. It covers the implementation of a holistic management style, effective cross-functional teaming, rigorous product reviews, systematic capture of the demands of customers, the involvement of suppliers, and the market driven R & D continuum. All its points are illustrated by examples.

WEB SITES

American Productivity and Quality Center

www.apqc.org

This site features articles on training, conferences, case studies, presentations, executive summaries, and more. This organization makes available several white papers on product development. The APQC is essentially a group working toward corporate organizational improvement. They sponsor conferences on product development as well as providing resources online.

Experts on New Product Development

www.expertson.com/ New_Product_Development

The resources on which information is available from this site include new product development associations, new product development centers, directories, newsgroups, mailing lists, new product development publications, and new product development reference tools.

Global New Products Database

www.gnpd.com

This site can be used to access a comprehensive database that monitors worldwide product innovation in the consumer packaged goods market, offering coverage of new product activity for both competitor monitoring and product idea generation.

Product Development and Management Association

www.pdma.org

This site is everyone's first stop when trolling the Internet for information on product development. It features articles, a job bank, conference listings, a discussion board, and more. Of special interest to users may be the access this site provides to the *PDMA Toolbook of New Product Development*.

ORGANIZATIONS

Product Development and Management Association

17000 Commerce Parkway, Suite C, Mount Laurel, New Jersey, 08054

T: +1 856 439 9052

F: +1 856 439 0525

E: pdma@pdma.org

www.pdma.org

This professional nonprofit organization is dedicated to serving people with an interest in new products and services. It is a recognized provider of knowledge and tools intended to improve the effectiveness of the development and management of new products and services. It also arranges a wide variety of events including conferences, publications, awards, meetings, and workshops, and sponsors research.

SEE ALSO

Product and Brand Management

(p. 481)

Outsourcing

BOOKS AND DIRECTORIES
Inside Outsourcing: The Insider's Guide to Managing Strategic Sourcing
Charles L. Gay, James Essinger
Naperville, Illinois: Nicholas Brealey, 2000
256pp ISBN: 1857882040
The authors together offer an insider's knowledge of the realities of managing the outsourcing process. The topics they explore are: the decision making process; the different types of outsourcing (they also include a discussion of insourcing); cosourcing and partnering; planning; and selecting service providers. They also discuss various legal aspects and human resources issues. A survey of the outsourcing practices of 500 of the United Kingdom's largest organizations completes the package.

Outsourcing in Brief
Mike Johnson
Woburn, Massachusetts: Butterworth-Heinemann, 1997
200pp (In Brief Series)
ISBN: 0750628766
This practical guide presents an overview of outsourcing and reviews the pros and cons of the technique. The way to go about outsourcing is explained, and checklists and case studies illustrate specific issues and options.

WEB SITES
Network Outsourcing Association
www.noa.co.uk
This site provides access to recent articles by members and details of Association events. It also has a members-only section.

Outsourcing Center
www.outsourcing-center.com
This Web site provides comprehensive information and links regarding outsourcing. Its content includes industry-specific outsourcing information, research, outsourcing processes, and an online journal. It also provides answers to FAQs, and material on suppliers, legal issues, and jobs.

The Outsourcing Institute
www.outsourcing.com
The Outsourcing Institute is a professional association providing information and networking resources related to outsourcing. Its Web site offers information on the outsourcing process, including needs assessment and the selection of service providers. It also has information targeted at buyers and sellers of outsourcing services. Registration is required for some information; online membership is free.

The Outsourcing Management Zone
www.theoutsourcerzone.com
This site is aimed at both outsourcing professionals and those new to the concept. It provides numerous articles, a directory, information on outsourcing, and also explains how and why outsourcing can affect your business.

Outsourcing Research Center
www.cio.com/forums/outsourcing
The site provides online access to recent articles and gives details of forthcoming events.

TechWeb Business Technology Network
www.techweb.com
This site focuses on recent news and articles on IT outsourcing, plus links to events.

Virtual Corporations and Outsourcing
www.brint.com
Recent articles on outsourcing can be sourced from this site.

ORGANIZATIONS
The Outsourcing Institute
Jericho Atrium, 500 N. Broadway, Suite 141, Jericho, New York, 11753
T: +1 516 681 0066
F: +1 516 938 1839

E: *customerservice@outsourcing.com*
www.outsourcing.com
This professional body, founded in 1993, provides outsourcing professionals worldwide with access to a business-to-business marketplace and an independent advisory network as well as with information and education on outsourcing best practice. Membership is free.

Packaging

BOOKS AND DIRECTORIES
Fifty Trade Secrets of Great Design Packaging
Stafford Cliff
Gloucester, Massachusetts: Rockport, 1999
224pp ISBN: 1564965996
This international collection of 50 outstanding packaging designs covers a broad selection of products and approaches. Each of the designs is individually profiled, outlining the challenges and problems each designer faced with the particular product. The case studies document the packaging design process and include discussion of new materials and methods of construction.

The Marketer's Guide to Successful Package Design
Herbert M. Meyers, Murray J. Lubliner
New York: McGraw-Hill/NTC, 1998
320pp ISBN: 0844234389
A guide for product marketers, this book explores the elements of marketing and design that can lead to successful packaging results. The authors' approach to the subject is analytical, including discussions on the research and planning involved in launching a new design.

The Packaging Designer's Book of Patterns 2nd ed.
Laszlo Roth, George L. Wybenga
New York: John Wiley, 2000
608pp ISBN: 0471385042
This book features over 500 patterns for paper packaging. Folding cartons, trays, tubes, sleeves, wraps, folders, corrugated containers, rigid paper boxes, and point-of-purchase displays are featured and ready for application on 100% recyclable paper products. An interesting history of papermaking is included in the introduction.

Packaging in the Environment
Geoffrey Levy, ed.
New York: Aspen Publishers, 1992
288pp ISBN: 0751400912
This book appraises the key environmental issues for packaging and how they affect trends and developments within the industry. It discusses and compares the relative environmental merits of different packaging materials and systems, while reviewing the action being taken to address these issues. It also considers legislative and regulatory developments worldwide.

WEB SITES
Environmental Packaging International
www.enviro-pac.com
Sponsored by a consulting firm specializing in compliance with state and international environmental packaging and product laws, the site provides a list of services, industry news, and links to other sites.

Packaging Business
www.packagingbusiness.com
Sponsored by a private company in the packaging industry, the site offers industry news, discussions, classifieds, job fair information, and links to other sites.

Packaging Digest
www.packagingdigest.com
This site contains articles from current and past issues of *Packaging Digest*, together with other information resources including news and reports of developments in packaging materials, machinery, technology, and market trends from around the world.

Packaging Network
www.packagingnetwork.com
This site is primarily a marketplace that also provides news, access to a library, a discussion forum, trade publications, and a job search. Site visitors may buy, sell, and advertise online. A free e-newsletter is also available.

Packaging Strategies
www.packstrat.com
This site provides a newsletter, articles, news, a product guide, and a calendar of events.

Packaging World
www.packworld.com
This online packaging magazine from the United States has databases of topical articles on machinery, products, companies, design, materials, and regulations, along with information about jobs, events, associations, and schools connected with the packaging industry.

ORGANIZATIONS
Institute of Packaging Professionals
1601 North Bond Street, Suite 101, Naperville, Illinois, 60563
T: + 1 630 544 5050
F: + 1 630 544 5055
E: *info@iopp.net*
www.iopp.org
This membership organization for the packaging industry offers its members a range of benefits, including events, education, career development, and publications.

Women in Packaging, Inc.
4290 Bells Ferry Road, Suite 106–17, Kennesaw, GA 30144–1300, U.S.
F: : + 1 770 928 2338
E: *wpstaff@womeninpackaging.org*
www.womeninpackaging.org
This organization helps provide a network of support for women who are involved in the packaging industry. Membership provides access to their magazine, forums, hotline, Speakers Bureau, and news.

Presentation/Speaking

BOOKS AND DIRECTORIES
Effective Presentation Skills: A Practical Guide for Better Speaking
Steve Mandel
Menlo Park, California: Crisp Publications, 2000
94pp ISBN: 1560525266
This basic overview of presentations offers advice on topics including skill assessment, presentation planning, visual aids, teleconferencing and videoconferencing, the presentation environment, and dealing with hostile questions. It contains an especially useful section on dealing with anxiety and projecting confidence.

Knockout Presentations: How to Deliver Your Message with Power, Punch, and Pizzazz
Diane Diresta
Madison, Wisconsin: Chandler House, 1998
300pp ISBN: 1886284253
This experienced coach presents a clear and precise method of approaching public speaking. Her suggestions are easy to implement, and many readers have found this book an invaluable reference tool.

Point, Click and Wow!: A Quick Guide to Brilliant Laptop Presentations 2nd ed.
Claudyne Wilder, Jennifer Rotondo
San Francisco, California: Jossey-Bass, 2002
240pp ISBN: 0787956694
Aimed at business people of all levels, this book offers a practical guide to using technology in effective presentations. The authors explore how to balance on-screen activity and human interaction, how to deal with software and hardware issues, and how, when, and where to

practice. The book includes checklists and illustrations.

Say It with Presentations: How to Design and Deliver Successful Business Presentations

Gene Zelazny
New York: McGraw-Hill, 1999
153pp ISBN: 0071354077
Intended as a simple overview of presentations, this book is targeted mainly at beginners but could also offer some tips to experienced presenters. The topics it covers include defining the purpose of the presentation, keeping the audience in mind, designing charts, and using humor. Its main focus is on how to deliver presentations with confidence and conviction.

Speaking for Impact: Connecting with Every Audience

Shirley E. Nice, William D. Thompson (editor)
Boston, Massachusetts: Allyn and Bacon, 1998
167pp (Essence of Public Speaking Series)
ISBN: 0205270255
Whether speaking to a small or a large group, chairing a sales meeting or giving a formal presentation, this book offers tips on how to get your message across effectively. The text suggests how you can identify the similarities and differences within audiences so you can "connect" with everyone in an audience made up of a diverse range of people.

WEB SITES

Advanced Public Speaking Institute
www.public-speaking.org
This site offers free advice and articles on all aspects of public speaking, including performance and storytelling techniques, how to develop a topic, the use of props and handouts, humor, tricks, gimmicks, and stage fright.

Art of Speaking in Public
www.artofspeaking.com
This site offers a collection of over 60 rapid read tips for effective public speaking and

effective performance in classes, presentations, conferences, seminars, events, and discussions.

PowerPointers
www.powerpointers.com
This site has many articles on making and creating effective presentations. Areas of interest include communicating effectively, building and planning a presentation, and communicating in your specialty.

Presentations.com
www.presentations.com
The online counterpart to *Presentations* magazine, the site offers news, articles, information on upcoming conferences and events, technological information, and resources.

Virtual Presentation Assistant— University of Kansas
www.ku.edu/cwis/units/coms2/vpa/ vpa.htm
Created by the Communication Studies Department at the University of Kansas, this Web site uses material by Diana Carlin to give an outline of what a good presentation should incorporate and what the speaker should think about when presenting.

ORGANIZATIONS

Advanced Public Speaking Institute
Box 2630, Landover Hills, Maryland, 20784
T: +1 301 577 3166
F: +1 301 552 0225
E: cmckinney@public-speaking.org
www.public-speaking.org
This organization offers free advice and information on all aspects of public speaking and making presentations.

Toastmasters International
23182 Arroyo Vista, Rancho Santa Margarita, California, 92688
T: +1 949 858 8255
F: +1 949 858 1207
E: tmembers@toastmasters.org
www.toastmasters.org

A nonprofit, member-based organization, Toastmasters International was established in 1924 with the aim of helping people to speak more effectively in public. It provides members with manuals on effective speaking and other resources, as well as a subscription to its monthly magazine, *The Toastmaster*. All clubs offer members the opportunity to develop presentation and leadership skills through chairing meetings, presenting impromptu and prepared speeches, and offering constructive evaluation.

Pricing

BOOKS AND DIRECTORIES

Costing, Pricing and Credit Control: How to Improve Profitability and How to Get Paid Promptly
2nd ed.
Keith Kirkland, Stuart Howard
Dover, New Hampshire: Kogan Page, 1998
189pp (Simple and Practical Series)
ISBN: 0749429305
The book aims to provide a sound understanding of how to work out the cost of a product or service, fix the right price for it, work out the break-even point, handle price discounting, deal with money-losing activities, formulate a credit control strategy, control debt, and recover bad debt through the courts.

The Strategy and Tactics of Pricing: A Guide to Profitable Decision Making
3rd ed.
Thomas T. Nagle, Reed K. Holden
Upper Saddle River, New Jersey: Prentice Hall, 2002
400pp ISBN: 013026248X
This is a complete guide that integrates pricing with overall managerial goals. It utilizes mini-case studies to illustrate success stories and examples of pricing failures. The elements of strategic pricing are explained. Other topics included are competition, segmentation of buyers, pricing and marketing mix, the psychology of pricing, and the ethical and legal aspects of pricing. Step-by-step procedures for problem analysis and strategy are provided.

WEB SITES

Professional Pricing Society
www.pricing-advisor.com
Sponsored by a professional society dedicated to pricing management, the site offers articles, discussion groups, workshop information, job postings, publications, consulting services, and survey information. Members have access to additional articles and an archive search.

Strategic Pricing Group
www.strategicpricinggroup.com
Sponsored by a consulting firm that specializes in strategic pricing, this site provides articles, self-assessment, recommended reading, a calendar of events, and information on educational services and consulting.

ORGANIZATIONS

The Professional Pricing Society
3277 Roswell Road, Suite 620, Atlanta, Georgia, 30305
T: +1 770 509 9933
F: +1 770 509 1963
E: info@pricingsociety.com
www.pricing-advisor.com
PPS is an association for price decision makers and price management personnel; its members are primarily pricing and marketing executives. It offers its members conferences and workshops, monthly and quarterly publications, consulting services, and pricing workbooks.

SEE ALSO
Marketing Management (p. 464)
Packaging (p. 477)

Product and Brand Management

BOOKS AND DIRECTORIES
The 22 Immutable Laws of Branding: How to Build a Product or Service into a World-class Brand
Laura Ries, Al Ries
New York: HarperCollins, 1998
192pp ISBN: 0887309372
In this title, the authors argue that branding is the basis of a strong marketing program, and that if it is not possible to create a strong brand, then nothing a company does, including advertising campaigns and public relations events, will help. The book looks at both successful brands and those that have failed, providing coherent explanations of the various factors involved.

Brand Warfare: 10 Rules for Building the Killer Brand
David F. D'Alessandro, Michele Owens
New York: McGraw-Hill, 2001
208pp ISBN: 0071362932
This book considers ways in which companies often mishandle their brands. The authors offer advice, based on their own experience and on company examples, to those wishing to build a successful brand in any market.

Building Strong Brands
David A. Aaker
San Francisco, California: Jossey-Bass, 1994
390pp ISBN: 002900151X
Aaker discusses the varying elements of a brand, and emphasizes the need for managers to be aware of the importance of strong brands in today's marketplace. In discussing various large corporations (such as McDonald's and Kodak), Aaker demonstrates the process of managing a hugely successful brand. The author also explores ways of retaining a certain brand while under some pressure to alter it. A reference tool for anybody involved in brand management.

Differentiate or Die: Survival in Our Era of Killer Competition
Jack Trout, Steve Rivkin
New York: John Wiley, 2000
230pp ISBN: 0471357642
This title is a useful guide on how to make your products differ from those of everyone else and lists several ways to achieve this. These include being the first person to do something, being the latest person to do a version of something, and becoming the first choice of a certain type of consumer group.

Product Strategy and Management
Michael Baker, Susan Hart
Upper Saddle River, New Jersey: Prentice Hall, 1996
550pp ISBN: 0130653683
This textbook is aimed at students and provides a broad introduction to the concepts and techniques of product strategy and management. It explores the theoretical foundations, new product strategy, product management, and product elimination.

Smart Things to Know about Brands and Branding
John Mariotti
Oxford: Capstone, 2001
240pp (Smart Series)
ISBN: 1841120391
Mariotti's purpose in this book is to give managers advice on creating a brand, understanding brand values, growing a brand, becoming a smart brand manager, measuring success, and championing their organization's brand.

What Makes Winning Brands Different: The Hidden Method behind the World's Most Successful Brands
Andreas Buchholz, Wolfram Wordemann
New York: John Wiley, 2000
222pp ISBN: 0471720259
The authors analyze the results of a research study of over 1,000 winning brands in order to establish a blueprint for brand growth and development. They argue that brands can

achieve outstanding growth by adhering to specific laws or "growth codes," of which they identify 27. Putting these "codes" into effect is explored through case studies and best practice examples.

WEB SITES

Allaboutbranding.com
www.allaboutbranding.com
This site has multiple articles concerned with branding's role in the marketplace and what it takes to create and maintain a brand name. Site features include an "Analyze Your Brand" test, free e-mail updates, quotes, definitions of useful terms, and sections that accurately cover the field.

brandchannel.com
www.brandchannel.com
This site, produced by Interbrand, provides for an online exchange about branding. It contains a debate area, features, papers, and details of books, training, and jobs.

BrandingAsia.com
www.brandingasia.com
This site focuses on branding issues in Asia, and includes brand news, tips, case studies, articles, and a discussion board. A free monthly e-mail newsletter is available.

Building Brands—Unlocking Your Potential
www.buildingbrands.com/
This site contains both free content, with articles, definitions, and did-you-knows, to premium services, which include training, Web seminars, student mentoring, and executive coaching.

KnowThis.com
www.knowthis.com/other/product.htm
This section of the Marketing Virtual Library contains links to resources for product management, branding, and packaging.

The Management Roundtable
www.managementroundtable.com
This site describes itself as the leading information resource for product development professionals. It includes a subscription area giving access to a selection of product development best practice reports.

ORGANIZATIONS

Institute for Brand Leadership
1000 Potomac Street NW, Suite 122, Washington, D.C., 20007
T: +1 202 337 1106
F: +1 202 333 2659
E: *contactus@instituteforbrandleadership.org*
www.instituteforbrandleadership.org
The Institute was established in 1997 by the Brand Consultancy to facilitate, promote, and recognize the theories and practices that contribute to brand excellence. Financial support for the IBL comes from the Brand Consultancy.

Product Development and Management Association
17000 Commerce Parkway, Suite C, Mount Laurel, New Jersey, 08054
T: +1 856 439 9052
F: +1 856 439 0525
E: *pdma@pdma.org*
www.pdma.org
This professional nonprofit organization is dedicated to serving people with an interest in new products and services. It is a recognized provider of knowledge and tools intended to improve the effectiveness of the development and management of new products and services. It also arranges conferences, publications, awards, meetings, and workshops, and sponsors research.

SEE ALSO
Advertising (p. 430)
Marketing Management (p. 464)
New Product Development (p. 473)

Project Management

BOOKS AND DIRECTORIES

The Accidental Project Manager: Surviving the Transition from Techie to Manager
Patricia Ensworth
New York: John Wiley, 2001
272pp ISBN: 047141011X
When projects fail it is often because the person in charge has no idea how to manage projects. This no-nonsense guide provides basic project management information including project planning, the roles of team members, the tools of the trade, and project control metrics. It also supplies templates, checklists, and sample forms for the beginner to use.

Effective Project Management
Robert Wysocki, et al.
New York: John Wiley, 2000
359pp ISBN: 0471360287
This book and CD-ROM package provides novices with a complete introduction to the principles of project management, and offers experienced project managers an opportunity to fine-tune their skills. It describes the management tools and techniques you need to stay on schedule and within budget without compromising quality. It adheres to the Project Management Institute's curriculum outline (PMBOK), and follows the necessary course requirements for professional certification. The CD-ROM provides a simulated environment in which to apply the principles, tools, and techniques described in the book.

A Guide to the Project Management Body of Knowledge: 2000 Edition
Project Management Institute
Newtown Square, Pennsylvania: Project Management Institute, 2001
200pp ISBN: 1880410230
This book is the basic Project Management reference and the accepted standard for the profession. It details the nine knowledge areas and 39 processes essential to a project

management model that will work in any industry. By establishing a standard, the guide also provides a common language for talking about project management. It is a key resource for those seeking Project Management Professional (PMP) certification.

Project
Ros Jay
Upper Saddle River, New Jersey: Prentice Hall, 2000
96pp (Fast Thinking)
ISBN: 0273653113
This book aims to help people cut through the muddle of panic that often sets in during the working day and to become more efficient. It offers helpful advice on what to do, say, and plan for when you have a pressing deadline and an objective to meet.

Project Management for Dummies
Stanley Portny
New York: John Wiley, 2000
284pp ISBN: 076455283X
Highly recommended by professional project managers, this book explains what project management is and then goes on to offer advice on how best to do it. It includes information on scheduling, assembling teams, and assessing resources.

Project Management: The Essential Guide to Thinking and Working Smarter
Peter Hobbs
New York: AMACOM, 2000
95pp (Self-Development for Success)
ISBN: 081447067X
This book offers advice on the key skills required by the successful project manager, including effective planning, goal and objective setting, scheduling, progress monitoring, and the control of quality and output. It includes an index.

Project Management: The Managerial Process
Clifford Gray
New York: Irwin/McGraw-Hill, 2000

544pp (Irwin/McGraw-Hill Series, Operations and Decision Sciences)
ISBN: 0072501383
This book presents a balanced view of the technical and sociocultural dimensions of managing projects. It is suitable for a course in project management, and for individuals seeking a project management handbook. The text is application-oriented for managing any type of project, and includes advice on discovering the strategic role of projects in contemporary organizations, prioritizing, planning and scheduling projects, and orchestrating the complex network of relationships. It includes a CD-ROM, bibliographical references, and an index.

The Project Manager's MBA: How to Translate Project Decisions into Business Success

Dennis J. Cohen, Robert J. Graham
San Francisco, California: Jossey-Bass, 2000
336pp (Jossey-Bass Business and Management Series)
ISBN: 0787952567
This text aims to provide an introduction to the business basics that every project manager needs to understand. These include value creation, accounting and finance strategy, and marketing. These concepts are related to the decisions project managers face every day. The aim is to develop the skills of project managers so that they can meet both their technical and their business objectives.

Project Planning, Scheduling, and Control 3rd ed.

James P. Lewis
New York: McGraw-Hill, 2000
350pp ISBN: 0071360506
This book offers an applications-oriented, non-theoretical understanding of the flexibility required in day-to-day management situations, and provides guidelines that apply to every phase of steering a project to its successful conclusion. This third edition has been updated to include easy-to-follow steps for managing multiple projects, effective risk

management strategies, and an innovative blueprint for developing a workable project methodology.

Project Skills

Sam Elbeik, Mark Thomas
Woburn, Massachusetts: Butterworth-Heinemann, 1999
200pp (New Skills Portfolio Series)
ISBN: 0750639784
The authors provide a practical and accessible guide to managing projects of all sizes and across all industries. Presented as an action-focused training guide, the book explains real-world project management and introduces the key skills and techniques needed in the six stages of managing a project.

WEB SITES

AllPM.com—The Project Manager's Homepage
www.allpm.com
This free site has optional membership, but still contains plenty of information for users even if they don't pay. The site offers a forum, event calendar, articles and tips, and a project management template library.

Association for Project Management
www.apm.org.uk
The site offers visitors details of news, events, qualifications, services, and publications in the field of project management. It also has information on member benefits and links to related organizations, and provides short reading lists.

PMFORUM
www.pmforum.org
This information dissemination and exchange forum includes a portal to information, resources, and working groups associated with project manager accreditation, certification, education, research, and standards. It also contains listings of software, consulting services, and training resources, plus a calendar of

events, and offers access to the electronic journal *Project Management World Today*.

Project Management
www.projectmagazine.com
This Web site is actually a "magazine" that is free to anyone. With meaningful, cutting edge articles, recommended Site of the Month, news for the field, and even Letters to the Editor, this is an audience-oriented resource for project managers of all levels.

Project Management Institute
www.pmi.org
The Project Management Institute (PMI) has over 75,000 members worldwide and is the leading nonprofit professional association in the area of project management. The site offers an extensive selection of information on member services, including careers and awards programs, a bookshop, links to other project management organizations, and information on project management standards. It also provides opportunities for organizations to contribute to a corporate council and lists PMI seminars.

Project Management Library
www.mapnp.org/library/plan_dec/ project/project.htm
Part of the Management Assistance Program for Nonprofits, this site's resources include a project management overview, information on team building and group leadership, general resources, and on-line discussion groups.

ORGANIZATIONS
Project Management Institute
Four Campus Boulevard, Newtown Square, Pennsylvania, 19073–3299
T: +1 610 356 4600
F: +1 610 356 4647
E: *pmihq@pmi.org*
www.pmi.org
A nonprofit professional association founded in 1969, the PMI sets project management standards, offers educational programs and professional certification, and also runs a publishing program.

Public Relations

BOOKS AND DIRECTORIES
The Complete Guide to Publicity: Maximize Visibility for Your Product, Service, or Organization
Joe Marconi
New York: McGraw-Hill/NTC, 1999
239pp ISBN: 0844200913
This book provides an effective guide for any person tasked with public relations, whether for a business or nonprofit organization. The author addresses all aspects of running a successful public relations campaign, including the difference between publicity campaigns and paid advertisement, understanding different media, how to create publicity opportunities, and a detailed procedure for creating a publicity campaign.

Effective Writing Skills for Public Relations 2nd ed.
John Foster
Dover, New Hampshire: Kogan Page, 2001
160pp ISBN: 0749436328
This book is a practical guide to writing style for students and PR practitioners. It looks at grammar, developing a house style, headlines and captions, press releases, and speeches and public speaking.

Face the Media: The Complete Guide to Getting Publicity and Handling Media Opportunities 2nd ed.
Judith Byrne
Oxford: How To Books, 2002
142pp ISBN: 1857037979
This guide offers advice on how to make contacts in the media and generate and

sustain interest in your or your business. Issues covered include: securing an interview; talking to journalists; improving confidence; developing "soundbites"; and crisis management.

Free Publicity for Your Business in a Week
Guy Clapperton
London: Hodder & Stoughton, 2002
96pp (In a Week)
ISBN: 0340858273
This book is aimed at cash-strapped small business owners and managers who need to make a splash. It covers a range of issues including how to handle the press, writing effective press releases, responding to feedback, and crisis management if things do not go to plan.

Guerrilla PR Wired: Waging a Successful Publicity Campaign Online, Offline, and Everywhere in between
Michael Levine
New York: McGraw-Hill, 2001
288pp ISBN: 0071382313
This book reexamines the principles of "Guerrilla PR" (introduced in the author's book *Guerrilla PR*, HarperCollins, 1993), the technique for creating cost-effective publicity, for the age of the World Wide Web. The book explains how the key tenets have changed with developments in technology, and introduces new tactics for conveying online messages. Readers will learn how the pros use the Web for publicity, how to focus on a target to get superior results and how to avoid all the pitfalls that lie in wait for the Web PR novice. The book also features a wide variety of empirical examples.

Harvard Business Review on Corporate Responsibility
Boston, Massachusetts: Harvard Business School Press, 2003
208pp (Harvard Business School Press)
ISBN: 1591392748
This collection of articles answers questions and offers ideas concerning the strategic significance of corporate social

responsibility, considering both the needs within the business and those of the wider community.

Planning and Managing a PR Campaign 2nd ed.
Anne Gregory
Dover, New Hampshire: Kogan Page, 2001
160pp ISBN: 0749429917
Gregory presents a step-by-step guide to the stages of a PR campaign, covering all the important aspects, and including case studies and a ten-point action plan.

Public Relations Handbook
Alison Theaker
New York: Routledge, 2001
320pp ISBN: 0415213347
A detailed introduction to the theory and practice of public relations is provided by this comprehensive handbook. It looks at all aspects of the subject, including training and entry into the profession, ethical issues, the use of new technology, and contains case studies.

Public Relations Kit for Dummies
Eric Yaverbaum, Robert Bly
New York: Hungry Minds, 2000
346pp ISBN: 0764552775
Part of a series offering concise, practical information on a variety of topics, this book addresses what all business owners and managers need to know about effective public relations. Presented in an easy to understand style, this title offers specific strategies and techniques for public relations, along with information on utilizing new technologies, such as the Internet, in PR campaigns. Also included is a CD-ROM with lists of PR firms and media contacts.

Public Relations: Strategies and Tactics 6th ed.
Dennis L. Wilcox, et al.
New York: Longman, 2000
584pp ISBN: 0321055551
This book presents a comprehensive outline of the principles, concepts, and methods of

public relations. This latest edition focuses specifically on global issues, use of the Internet and other new technologies, and ethical issues in public relations. The text differs from similar texts in the field through the inclusion of a series of up-to-date case studies.

Risk Issues and Crisis Management: A Casebook of Best Practice
Michael Regester, Judy Larkin
London: Kogan Page, 1998
160pp (PR in Practice Series)
ISBN: 0749423935
This book deals with the successful handling of crisis situations so that damage and disruption are minimized. Case studies and models illustrate how complex crises have been handled in practice, both successfully and unsuccessfully.

WEB SITES
Managing Public Relations
www.workz.com/content/292.asp
This Web site serves as a resource for small business owners. It offers comprehensive information on public relations techniques, including guides for creating effective press releases, where and how to distribute press releases, promoting your business's Web site, and a directory of PR firms and associations.

PR Navigator
www.prnavigator.com
This Web site serves as a comprehensive resource on public relations for users ranging from business leaders to students. The resources include access to current research and industry reports, links to online PR journals and newsletters, directories of public relations agencies, and links to PR associations worldwide.

PR Place
www.prplace.com
This site contains a listing of Internet resources on public relations. The categories it covers include organizations in PR, publications, news sources, and databases.

PRWeb
www.prweb.com
PRWeb is a U.S. company, based in Ferndale, Washington, that offers a free service distributing press releases over the Internet.

Public Relations Resources
www.publicrelationsresources.com
The mission of this site is to provide regular informative articles on how to promote events, people, and businesses. It includes free articles, news headlines, and a list of links.

ORGANIZATIONS
Institute for Public Relations
University of Florida, P.O. Box 118400, Gainesville, Florida, 32611–8400
T: +1 352 392 0280
F: +1 352 846 1122
www.instituteforpr.com
The mission of the IPR is to improve the effectiveness of organizations by advancing the professional knowledge and practice of public relations through research and education. It provides publications, lectures, awards, and professional development forums, and conducts research projects. Within the IPR is the Commission on Public Relations Measurement and Evaluation. IPR services are aimed at students, academics, and practitioners.

Public Relations Society of America
33 Irving Place, New York, 10003–2376
T: +1 212 995 2230
F: +1 212 995 0757
E: hq@prsa.org
www.prsa.org
The PRSA is a membership body for public relations professionals. Its aim is to unify, strengthen, and advance the profession. It conducts education and research, advances members' professional development, and offers other membership services. It also produces the magazines *Public Relations Strategist* and *Public Relations Tactics*.

Women Executives in Public Relations
FDR Station, P.O. Box 7657, New York, 10150–7657

T: +1 212 750 7373
F: +1 212 750 7375
E: *info@wepr.org*
www.wepr.org
This is an organization for senior women in the public relations field. Its mission is to support the career advancement of female practitioners and to foster the use of public relations to benefit the goals of business and society. It is an individual membership body that is involved in influencing and lobbying, and provides a forum for the exchange of career, management, and practitioner issues.

Recruitment and Selection

BOOKS AND DIRECTORIES

45 Ways for Hiring Smart! How to Predict Winners and Losers in the Incredibly Expensive People-reading Game
Pierre Mornell
Berkeley, California: Ten Speed Press, 1998
226pp ISBN: 0898159725
This is a practical guide to help employers cut through the complexities of hiring, and select the best candidate for a particular job. As the title suggests, this text presents 45 techniques designed to take the measure of potential recruits, emphasizing behavior not words.

101 Hiring Mistakes Employers Make, and How to Avoid Them
Richard Fein
Waupaca, Wisconsin: Impact Publications, 2000
144pp ISBN: 157023129X
This book is an analytical study of interviewing techniques, based on material from genuine interviews. It aims to outline some of the main hiring errors that can eventually burden an organization with an unsatisfactory employee. The author aims to help minimize "hiring mistakes" and increase the employer's understanding of interview questioning.

Finding and Keeping the Right People: How to Recruit Motivated Employees
Jon Billsberry
Upper Saddle River, New Jersey: Prentice Hall, 1996
233pp (Smarter Solutions series)
ISBN: 0273616986
Aiming to give managers and recruiters a practical perspective on recruitment and selection, this book stresses the need to pay continuous attention to the business purpose of the exercise and integrate it into the process. The text also deals with attracting and assessing applicants, making decisions about terms and conditions, and retaining employees once they have been recruited.

High Impact Hiring: How to Interview and Select Outstanding Employees
Del J. Still
Dana Point, California: Management Development Systems, 2001
301pp ISBN: 0965465985
A "must-read" for anyone responsible for interviewing and hiring, this book will help you discover the pertinent information about a candidate. The author presents his 7-step interview model which will lead you to a successful hiring decision.

A Manager's Guide to Hiring the Best Person for Every Job
Deanne Rosenberg
New York: John Wiley, 2000
320pp ISBN: 0471380741
This book on recruitment and selection interviewing is written in simple language and gives detailed help with structuring the dialogue and questioning in interviews in such a way as to retain control and focus on the job requirements involved. A matrix designed by the author for identifying trade-offs among competing candidates is included.

Recruit & Retain the Best
John McCarter, Ray Schreyer
Manassas, Virginia: Impact Publications, 2000
128pp ISBN: 1570231346
The authors claim that, to remain competitive, you must create a talent-powered company. Their solution begins with recruiting new employees based on competencies from education or previous employment. They discuss innovative recruiting tools, like the Internet and employee referral programs. However, the focus of this book is on the retention of the top employees. The last third of the book addresses ways to make your company a place where the best want to stay.

Recruiting, Interviewing, Selecting, and Orienting New Employees 3rd ed.
Diane Arthur
New York: AMACOM, 1998
400pp ISBN: 0814404014
This book is designed to give comprehensive guidance through the four stages of the employment process to HR specialists and others whose work involves recruitment and selection. Besides describing methods and techniques applicable to the basic task of hiring new employees, this revised edition takes in new material dealing with areas such as additional interviewing approaches, workplace diversity, the retention of new employees, and online recruitment.

The Selection Interview
Penny Hackett
New York, New York: Beekman, 2000
96pp (Management Shapers Series)
ISBN: 0846451433
First published in 1995, this short, clear, and easily understood book gives advice to help managers recruit more effectively through focused, well-planned, and skilled selection interviewing. It includes information on drawing up job descriptions, setting up the interview, different interview strategies and styles, questioning and listening skills, the evaluation of interview results, and decision making leading to selection.

Smart Hiring: The Complete Guide to Finding and Hiring the Best Employees 2nd ed.
Robert W. Wendover
Naperville, Illinois: Sourcebooks, 1998
240pp ISBN: 1570712131
This book offers practical advice to employers on improving their employee selection skills. Examining various topics such as hiring errors, telephone interviews, and the assessment of a potential employee, Wendover's approach is pragmatic. Also included in the book are step-by-step guides to job advertising and analyzing résumés.

Writing Job Descriptions
Alan Fowler
New York, New York: Beekman, 2000
96pp (Management Shapers Series)
ISBN: 0846451840
This booklet aims to give managers and HR professionals a focused introduction to writing clear, accurate job descriptions for effective recruitment and selection. Help is included on defining essential job constituents, legal issues, defining reporting relationships, dealing with unspecified duties, and job dimensions. The use of job descriptions for job evaluation is covered, and key points are summarized.

WEB SITES
Monster.com
www.monster.com
This site is a global online careers network, aiming to connect companies and qualified individuals. It offers member-employers various services, including job postings, résumé screening, a résumé database, and résumé routing. Job seekers can use it to access vacancies, and take advantage of features and services such as résumé management, a job-search agent, and a careers network.

Recruiters Network
www.recruitersnetwork.com
Recruiters Network is a free association for HR professionals, recruiters, and hiring managers. Its goal is to provide leading resources and information on the recruiting and Internet recruiting industry. Members

receive a monthly newsletter, access to a resource directory, and an opportunity to interact with their peers in a discussion group.

Recruiters Online Network
www.recruitersonline.com/index.phtml
Recruiters Online Network is a global community of recruiters, headhunters, and staffing firms. It features separate sections for job seekers to post résumés and search for jobs, for recruiters to post jobs and search résumé databases, and for employers to find talent or a recruiting firm.

ORGANIZATIONS
American Staffing Association
277 South Washington Street, Suite 200, Alexandria, Virginia, 22314
T: +1 703 253 2020
F: +1 703 253 2053
E: *asa@staffingtoday.net*
www.staffingtoday.net
The ASA represents the U.S. recruiting industry. Among other things, it provides job-seeking and staff-seeking services. Membership benefits include access to information and research concerned with employment, payroll, employee turnover rates, industry compensation, and other associated matters.

International Association of Corporate and Professional Recruitment
20 N. Wacker Drive, #2262, Chicago, Illinois, 60606

T: +1 312 630 9881
E: *iacpr@iacpr.org*
www.iacpr.org
Formerly the National Association of Corporate and Professional Recruiters, the IACPR was founded in 1978. This association boasts a membership of over 300 individuals who focus on providing research to human resource executives and search professionals in the recruitment and retention on employees. IACPR strives to promote the latest information and problem-solving strategies found in the corporate recruiting industry.

National Association of Personnel Services
3133 Mount Vernon Avenue, Alexandria, Virginia, 22305
T: +1 703 684 0180
F: +1 703 684 0071
E: *info@napsweb.org*
http://napsweb.org
NAPS seeks to inform and represent the personnel services industry by providing education, certification, and member services. It has been educating and training those in the staffing industry since 1961, and now represents over 100,000 individuals and 30 state associations. A selection of articles from NAPS newsletters (InsideNAPS) is available from www.napsweb.org/newsletters, and news of pending legislation relevant to personnel from www.napsweb.org/napstrack.htm.

Selling and Salesmanship

BOOKS AND DIRECTORIES
Fast Forward MBA in Selling: Become a Self-motivated Profit Center and Prosper
Joy J. D. Baldridge
New York: John Wiley, 1999
216pp ISBN: 0471348546
This book is a comprehensive guide to becoming a successful salesperson. It explores a wide range of topics, including setting the standards for success, self-

motivation, time management, getting and staying connected, preparation, technology, and successful sales calls.

How to Become a Rainmaker: The Rules for Getting and Keeping Customers and Clients
Jeffrey J. Fox
New York: Hyperion, 2000
169pp ISBN: 0091876540
This book is written to assist in identifying,

attracting and keeping customers. It identifies Rainmakers (people who bring revenue into organizations), who may be C.E.O.s, owners, partners, sales representatives, or fundraisers. Jeffrey J. Fox explains how the reader can become a Rainmaker, enabling him/her to attract more customers and rise above the competition in any company.

Improving Customer Satisfaction, Loyalty and Profit: An Integrated Measurement and Management System
Michael D. Johnson, Anders Gustafsson
San Francisco: Jossey-Bass, 2000
144pp ISBN: 0787953105
By outlining in detail five key areas, this book offers ways to improve customer loyalty. By outlining key measures of customer satisfaction and giving suggestions for marketing strategy and product development, the book enables a more cohesive measurement and management system.

Key Account Management and Planning: The Comprehension Handbook for Managing Your Company's Most Important Strategic Asset
Noel Capon
New York: Free Press, 2001
480pp ISBN: 074321188X
With a greater level of competition and increased costs of selling, the nature of the selling process has changed. Using research, real-life stories of successes and failures, and clarifying figures, the author presents his four-part "congruence model" of key account management. He explains: how to select the key account portfolio; how to manage key accounts; how to recruit, select, train, reward, and retain key account managers, and how to formulate and execute key account strategies.

Knock Your Socks Off Selling
Jeffrey Gitomer, Ron Zemke
New York: AMACOM, 1999
150pp ISBN: 0814470300
An overview of sales techniques from basic

selling to developing relationships, the book is appropriate for salespeople at every level. Placing an emphasis on making a partnership out of the buyer/seller relationship, the book discusses networking, generating leads, making presentations, and following through.

Sales Management: Concepts and Cases 7th ed.
Douglas J. Dalrymple, William L. Cron, Thomas E. DeCarlo
New York: John Wiley, 2000
640pp ISBN: 0471388807
This book includes theoretical discussions and case studies covering all aspects of sales management. The topics dealt with in its various sections are: strategic planning and budgeting; personal selling; territory management; estimating potentials and forecasting sales; recruiting and selecting personnel; sales training; leadership; motivating salespeople; compensating salespeople; and evaluating performance.

The Seven Keys to Managing Strategic Accounts
Sallie Sherman, Joseph Sperry, Samuel Reese
New York: McGraw-Hill, 2003
256pp ISBN: 0071417524
Offering market-proven strategies for generating competitive advantage by identifying and looking after your best customers, this book provides decision makers with a strategy for profitably managing their largest and most critical accounts.

SPIN Selling
Neil Rackham
New York: McGraw-Hill, 1988
197pp ISBN: 0070511136
Practical, easy-to-understand information on how to make selling easier for the salesperson. Based on extensive research, its direct and helpful advice may also be helpful in all other work situations.

The SPIN Selling Fieldbook: Practical Tools, Methods, Exercises and Resources
Neil Rackham
New York: McGraw-Hill, 1996
208pp ISBN: 0070522359
Full of case studies and practical information, this book shows the reader how to put into practice the help and advice given in *SPIN Selling*.

Tough Calls: Selling Strategies to Win Over Your Most Difficult Customers
Josh Gordon
New York: AMACOM, 1997
214pp ISBN: 0814479251
Focusing on the challenges of difficult customers, the book outlines 20 different "tough sells" and strategies to counteract them. It provides advice on what to do and what not to do with customers who, for example, are incompetent, do not have buying authority, will not see you, buy elsewhere because of company politics, or like what you say but still don't buy.

The Ultimate Sales Letter: Boost Your Sales with Powerful Sales Letters, Based on Madison Avenue Techniques 2nd ed.
Dan S. Kennedy
Holbrook, Massachusetts: Adams Media Corporation, 2000
224pp ISBN: 1580622577
This text provides clear examples that assist in writing focused sales letters that target specific customer bases. Tips and features include: creating powerful headlines, improving readability, when to use bullet points, which font to use, and which demographics to target. All this is performed within 28 structured steps, and should interest sales reps, business owners, and advertising people.

WEB SITES
BestOfSales.com
www.bestofsales.com
A list of links to sales resources on the Internet is given on this site.

Just Sell
www.justsell.com
This site comprises a sales and marketing portal with areas covering sales leads, sales jobs, daily sales intelligence, an online store, and a resource for locating sales training.

The Sales Crusader
http://sales-crusader.hypermart.net
This site presents articles on all aspects of selling and salesmanship contributed by its readers. In addition to these free articles, it also offers recommended book lists and a discussion forum.

Saleslinks.com
www.saleslinks.com/links
Run by Mentor Associates, this site is aimed at anyone who is engaged in selling for a living. It includes links to sales resources on the Internet, arranged in categories.

Salesmanship
www.dmoz.org/Business/Marketing/Salesmanship
Maintained as part of the Open Directory Project, this site contains a large list of other Web sites, each with a brief description, relating to all aspects of salesmanship.

Sales Rep Central
www.salesrepcentral.com
A portal for sales professionals, the site contains news, articles, a community message board, jobs, sales leads, and travel services.

SalesVault
www.salesvault.com
This site is aimed at professional salespeople and provides innovative and up-to-date selling information. It also includes articles, news, and advice.

Selling Power
www.sellingpower.com
The online counterpart to *Selling Power* magazine, the site offers archived issues of the magazine, electronic newsletters on several sales-related topics, a weekly quiz, and books and resources.

ORGANIZATIONS
Association of Sales and Marketing Companies
1010 Wisconsin Avenue NW, Ninth Floor, Washington, D.C., 20007
T: +1 202 337 9351
F: +1 202 337 4508
E: info@asmc.org
www.asmc.org
ASMC is a member trade association formed to promote the interests of sales and marketing agencies and manufacturers. It offers its members conferences, training resources, a referral service, the opportunity to join committees that focus on industry issues, research, publications, and group insurance programs.

Direct Selling Association
1275 Pennsylvania Avenue NW, Suite 800, Washington, D.C., 20004
T: +1 202 347 8866
F: +1 202 347 0055
E: info@dsa.org
www.dsa.org
DSA is a trade association for firms that manufacture and distribute goods and services sold directly to consumers. It offers its members research services, a monthly newsletter, a resource guide, conferences, networking councils, legislative lobbying, and salesforce support.

National Association of Sales Professionals
8300 North Hayden Road, Suite 207, Scottsdale, Arizona, 85258
T: +1 480 951 4311
F: +1 480 483 2860
E: info@nasp.cpm
www.nasp.com
Founded in 1991, NASP states that its mission is to cater for the needs of salespersons, to help in their professional development in a changing field, and to upgrade the career status of those working in sales. It runs the Certified Professional SalesPerson program, and administers the International Registry of Accredited Salespersons.

SEE ALSO
Marketing Management (p. 464)

Taxation

BOOKS AND DIRECTORIES
The Encyclopedia of Taxation and Tax Policy
Joseph J. Cordes, et al.
Washington, D.C.: Urban Institute Press, 1999
468pp ISBN: 0877666822
A compilation of 200 essays on a broad array of topics including tax administration, evasion and avoidance, and the fundamentals of equity and efficiency. The primary emphasis is on issues relating to the development, administration, and evaluation of tax policy.

State Tax Handbook, 2001
CCH Tax Law Editors
Washington, D.C.: CCH Incorporated, 2000
408pp ISBN: 0808005553
This annual volume is similar to the U.S. Master Tax Guide, but gives more detailed tax information for all 50 states plus the District of Columbia. It is perhaps the most complete source for precise information on U.S. state-level tax policy.

WEB SITES
1040.com
www.1040.com
Self-billed as the "one-stop tax source", this site provides links to finding state and federal tax forms. It also has a newsroom containing the latest tax news stories.

CCH Incorporated
www.cch.com
CCH are the publishers of numerous books and journals on taxation, including the new *Journal of Taxation of Global Transactions*. Their Web site provides links to numerous CCH information sources, mostly available for a fee.

Internal Revenue Service
www.irs.com
The IRS Web site offers downloadable income tax forms, instructions on filing taxes, and information on U.S. regulations and laws. It also features an electronic filing center.

Tax Analysts
www.tax.org
Tax Analysts, publishers of *Tax Notes* and *State Tax Notes*, provide continuously updated tax news wire, a variety of interesting links, and weekly federal, state, and international feature articles on their Web site.

Tax and Accounting Sites Directory
www.taxsites.com
This site provides an international gateway to country specific tax and accounting resources on the Web. It has a U.S. bias.

Tax Resources
www.taxresources.com
This directory has links to U.S. federal and local tax departments with tax rates and forms. It also has links to sites covering tax software, world tax, and tax articles.

ORGANIZATIONS
Federation of Tax Administrators
444 N Capitol Street NW, Suite 348, Washington, D.C., 20001
T: +1 202 624 5890
F: +1 202 624 7888
E: *webmaster@taxadmin.org*
www.taxadmin.org
This is the primary organization for state-level tax policy administrators. Its Web site provides links to each state's tax department.

Institute for Professionals in Taxation
3350 Peachtree Road NE, Suite 280, Atlanta, Georgia, 30326
T: +1 404 240 2300
F: +1 404 240 2315
E: *ipt@ipt.org*
www.ipt.org
This is a business organization focusing on property taxes and sales and use taxes.

Internal Revenue Service
1111 Constitution Avenue NW, Washington, D.C., 20224
T: +1 800 829 1040
www.irs.gov
The Internal Revenue Service is the official source for information on U.S. federal taxation. It offers downloadable income tax forms, instructions on filing taxes, and information on U.S. regulations and laws. It also features an electronic filing center.

Multistate Tax Commission
444 N Capitol Street NW, Suite 425, Washington, D.C., 20001
T: +1 202 624 8699
F: +1 202 624 8819
E: *mtc@mtc.gov*
www.mtc.gov
This organization consists of an alliance of representatives from 45 states dedicated, among other things, to the adoption of uniform state tax policies toward multinational firms.

National Association of Tax Professionals
720 Association Drive, Appleton, Wisconsin, 54914–1483
T: +1 800 558 3402
F: +1 800 747 0001
E: *natp@natptax.com*
www.natptax.com
This organization provides continuing professional education for tax professionals. It consists primarily of accountants, tax agents, lawyers, and financial planners.

National Tax Association
725 15th Street NW, Suite 600, Washington, D.C., 20005–2109
T: +1 202 737 3325
F: +1 202 737 7308
E: *natltax@aol.com*
www.ntanet.org
The NTA was founded in 1907 and is the leading association of tax professionals in the United States. It aims to promote the study and discussion of tax theory, practice, and

policy. Members of the NTA come from the public, government, corporate, and academic sectors. The Association runs a national conference and a spring symposium and publishes the *National Tax Journal* and a newsletter called the *NTA Forum*.

SEE ALSO
Accounting (p. 428)
Budgeting (p. 435)
Contracts and Contracting (p. 442)

Venture Capital

BOOKS AND DIRECTORIES
2001 Financing Start-ups: How to Raise Money for Emerging Companies
Robert Brown, Alan S. Gutterman
New York: Aspen Publishers, 2000
617pp ISBN: 0156071916
This book aims to guide owners and managers of start-ups through the rigors of finding funding, from sourcing initial funds to IPOs.

Business Angels: Securing Start Up Finance
Patrick Coveney, Karl Moore
New York: John Wiley, 1998
244pp ISBN: 0471977187
This book takes the would-be entrepreneur through the process of identifying the ideal business angel and securing a deal. It covers reasons for turning to an angel, types of business angels, and the task of creating a business plan. The role of business introduction services is also considered.

Directory of Venture Capital 2nd ed.
Kate E. Lister, Thomas D. Harnish
New York: John Wiley, 1996
400pp ISBN: 0471122831
The directory lists venture capital firms by state and provides detailed information on their preferences with regard to industry, stage of funding, geography, and size of company. The authors also provide information on the returns required by private equity investors, selecting the right lawyer, and important aspects of a venture partnership. Entrepreneurs will find the directory a good resource for locating the right venture capital firm to approach for funding.

Finance for Growing Enterprises
Roger Buckland, Edward Davis, eds.
Stamford, Connecticut: International Thomson Business Press, 1995
288pp (European Financial Institutions and Markets Series)
ISBN: 0415082331
This book examines the mechanisms by which businesses with the capacity to grow acquire the cash to make growth possible. It draws together contemporary research studies and covers the issues of market failure and gaps in funding. The financing choices facing the growing firm are also investigated.

Raising Start-Up Finance
Phil Stone
Oxford: How To Books, 2001
93pp (Essentials)
ISBN: 1857037057
This practical guide covers key steps in securing finance for your business, including: preparing your case; what the banks can offer; alternatives for the purchase of assets; using business resources to gain funding; and additional sources of finance.

The VC Way: Investment Secrets from the Wizards of Venture Capital
Jeffrey Zygmont
Cambridge, Massachusetts: Perseus, 2001
224pp ISBN: 0738203874
This text offers a behind-the-scenes perspective of the venture capital market, revealing to investors how to strategize and invest in successful companies before their profits are certain. Zygmont also offers the reader a brief tutorial in creating a portfolio of holdings that may increase in value, as Apple and Yahoo did.

Venture Capital and Private Equity 2nd ed.

Josh Lerner, et al.
New York: John Wiley, 2001
500pp ISBN: 0471079820
The book explains in detail the venture capital and private equity markets. Divided into four sections, the book covers the fundraising process required to start a venture capital fund, investment selection, and the relationship between the venture capitalist and entrepreneur, the various exit strategies available, and some key issues unique to the private equity market.

Venture Capital Investing

David Gladston
Upper Saddle River, New Jersey: Prentice Hall, 1998
400pp ISBN: 0139414282
This classic serves as a primer on venture capital investing. It outlines the key considerations for investing private capital, including an analysis of management, compensation, marketing and sales, financial statements and projections, and the production process. From due diligence and deal negotiation to the exit strategy, the author suggests a logical, step-by-step process that is filled with insights and actual examples from his experience as a venture capitalist. While most books are focused on how an entrepreneur can raise venture capital, this book provides an in-depth look at what it takes to be a successful investor in small private businesses.

Where to Go When the Bank Says No: Alternatives for Financing Your Business

David R. Evanson
Princeton, New Jersey: Bloomberg, 1998
304pp (Bloomberg Small Business Series)
ISBN: 1576600173
Practical advice for small or new businesses on raising capital is provided here by an expert in the field. He discusses the pros and cons of alternative options such as equity capital, initial public offerings (IPOs), and venture capital, and gives guidance on valuing a business and drawing up business plans and financial reports. A resources guide with contact details of organizations in the field is also included.

WEB SITES

ACE-Net (Access to Capital Electronic Network)

http://ace-net.sr.unh.edu/pub
ACE-Net was set up in consultation with the Securities and Exchange Commission to act as a clearing house of information for investors and entrepreneurs following the 1995 Conference on Small Business.

National Venture Capital Association

www.nvca.org
The National Venture Capital Association is a trade association providing advocacy, education, and networking opportunities for the venture capital industry. It boasts over 400 members representing the majority of venture firms invested in U.S.-based companies. The association's affiliate organization, American Entrepreneurs for Economic Growth (AEEG), is an advocacy group for over 14,000 C.E.O.s of emerging growth companies.

PriceWaterhouseCoopers Moneytree Survey

www.pwcmoneytree.com
This survey, sponsored by the accounting firm of PriceWaterhouseCoopers, provides a comprehensive list of venture capital investing by industry, stage of funding, geography, and type of financing on a quarterly basis. The report tracks venture capital firm investments and the enterprises receiving capital by region/state and industry.

U.S. Venture Partners (USVP)

www.usvp.com
This company aims to specifically help entrepreneurial ventures. Created in 1981, USVP has put over $1.1 billion into more than 271 companies, and their clients have gone on to become leaders in their respective fields.

vcapital
www.vcapital.com
This is an exchange site for entrepreneurs, venture capitalists, and business service providers, sponsored by Batterson Venture Partners. It features an Ask the Expert section with articles giving practical advice and help.

Venture Economics
www.ventureeconomics.com
News, statistics, product information, and a glossary of terms are to be found on this site, provided by a publisher of journals and research on the venture capital industry worldwide.

VentureOne
www.ventureone.com
This site is a database of venture-backed investors and companies and includes upcoming events, publications, and information for the venture capital industry.

Venturewire
www.venturewire.com/default.asp
This Web site hosts a family of publications that are exclusively devoted to the private equity marketplace. *Venturewire Professional*, the site's flagship publication, features the latest news on fundings, acquisitions, venture capital firms, and key personnel changes in venture-backed businesses. Venturewire also publishes *Lifescience*, *Alert*, and *People* on a daily basis and provides the Research section as a source of in-depth coverage on specific industries.

ORGANIZATIONS
National Association of Investment Companies
733 15th Street NW, Suite 700, Washington, D.C., 20005
T: +1 202 289 4336
F: +1 202 289 4329
E: *NAICHQTRS@aol.com*
www.naichq.org

NAIC is an industry association for venture capital and private equity firms. Its members are privately owned equity investment firms, small business investment companies licensed by the U.S. Small Business Administration, and investment companies chartered by state and local governments.

National Association of Small Business Investment Companies
666 11th Street NW, Suite 750, Washington, D.C., 20001
T: +1 202 628 5055
F: +1 202 628 5080
E: *nasbic@nasbic.org*
www.nasbic.org
NASBIC is a nonprofit industry association which has represented and served the SBIC industry for over 40 years. It provides educational programs for investment professionals through the Venture Capital Institute and cooperates with other business associations. Its policies and priorities are established by a board of governors.

National Venture Capital Association
1655 North Fort Myer Drive, Suite 850, Arlington, Virginia, 22209
T: +1 703 524 2549
F: +1 703 524 3940
E: *lturner@nvca.org*
www.nvca.org
The NVCA is a trade association with a membership of over 400 venture capital firms. It aims to foster understanding of the industry, to stimulate the flow of equity capital to growth companies, to promote professional standards, facilitate networking, and provide research data. It publishes *NVCA Today*, a quarterly review of legislative and regulatory developments; *Venture Capital Review*, a biannual journal which provides an overview of industry trends; and *The Venture Capital Yearbook*.

SEE ALSO
Entrepreneurs (p. 450)

Index

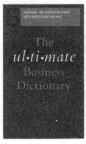